DETERRING
DEMOCRACY

SELECTED WORKS BY NOAM CHOMSKY

DETERRING
DEMOCRACY

NOAM CHOMSKY

 **HILL AND WANG**

A division of Farrar, Straus and Giroux

New York

Hill and Wang
A division of Farrar, Straus and Giroux
19 Union Square West, New York 10003

Library of Congress Cataloging-in-Publication Data
Chomsky, Noam.
Deterring democracy / Noam Chomsky. — Hill and Wang
p. cm.
1. United States—Foreign relations—1989– . I. Title.
E881.C48 1992 327.73—dc20 91-39445 CIP

SOURCES
The following chapters are based in part on articles in Zeta (Z) Magazine: Chapter 2: May
1989; Chapter 3: July 1989; Chapter 4: November 1989; Chapter 5: March, November
1990; Chapter 6: October 1990; Chapter 7: November 1990, January 1991; Chapter 8:
September, November 1988; Chapter 9: December 1989; Chapter 10: May 1990; Chapter
11: January 1989. Parts of Chapter 12 are drawn from my papers "Mental Constructions and
Social Reality," Conference on Knowledge and Language, Groningen, May 1989; "Containing
the Threat of Democracy," Glasgow Conference on Self-determination and Power, Glasgow,
January 1990; "The Culture of Terrorism: The Third World and the Global Order," Con-
ference on Parliamentary Democracy and State Terrorism after 1945, Hamburg, May 19, 1990.
All are to appear in conference proceedings. The Afterword is drawn in part from Zeta (Z)
Magazine, May, October, December 1991.

CONTENTS

... the government of the world must be entrusted to
satisfied nations, who wished nothing more for themselves
than what they had. If the world-government were in
the hands of hungry nations, there would always be
danger. But none of us had any reason to seek for anything
more. The peace would be kept by peoples who lived
in their own way and were not ambitious. Our power
placed us above the rest. We were like rich men dwelling
at peace within their habitations.

WINSTON CHURCHILL

INTRODUCTION

HISTORY does not come neatly packaged into distinct periods, but by imposing such a structure upon it, we can sometimes gain clarity without doing too much violence to the facts. One such period was initiated with the Second World War, a new phase in world affairs in which "the United States was the hegemonic power in a system of world order" (Harvard government professor and foreign policy adviser, Samuel Huntington). This phase was visibly drawing to a close in the 1970s, as the state capitalist world moved towards a tripolar structure with economic power centered in the United States, Japan, and the German-based European Community. As for the Soviet Union, the military build-up initiated after Soviet weakness was dramatically revealed during the Cuban missile crisis was beginning to level off; Moscow's capacity to influence and coerce, always far inferior to that of the hegemonic power, was continuing to decline from its late-1950s peak. Furthermore, internal pressures were mounting as the economy stagnated, unable to enter a new phase of "post-industrial" modernization, and as broader sectors of the population demonstrated their unwillingness to submit to totalitarian constraints. Plainly, Europe and Japan posed a greater potential threat to US dominance than the fading Soviet Union.

These developments were reasonably clear by the late 1970s, but a different conception was needed as a rationale for the policies then being implemented to maintain US global dominance and to provide a needed shot in the arm to high technology industry: the picture of a fearsome Soviet Union

1

marching from strength to strength and posing an awesome challenge to Western Civilization. These illusions lacked credibility at the time, and became completely unsustainable through the next decade. Meanwhile the observations of the preceding paragraph have become virtual truisms.[1]

This pattern has been standard through the postwar era—and, in fact, it illustrates far more general regularities of statecraft and the ideological structures that accompany it. As if by reflex, state managers plead "security" to justify their programs. The plea rarely survives scrutiny. We regularly find that security threats are contrived—and, once contrived for other purposes, sometimes believed—to induce a reluctant public to accept overseas adventures or costly intervention in the domestic economy. The factors that have typically driven policy in the postwar period are the need to impose or maintain a global system that will serve state power and the closely linked interests of the masters of the private economy, and to ensure its viability by means of public subsidy and a state-guaranteed market. The highly ramified Pentagon system has been the major instrument for achieving these goals at home and abroad, always on the pretext of defense against the Soviet menace. To a significant extent, the threat of the Soviet Union and other enemies has risen or declined as these ends require.[2]

Strategic theory and the policy sciences are supple instruments, rarely at a loss to provide the required argument and analysis to buttress the conclusion of the moment.

We can, then, identify a period from World War II, continuing into the 1970s, in which the US dominated much of the world, confronting a rival superpower of considerably more limited reach. We may adopt conventional usage and refer to this as the Cold War era, as long as we are careful not to carry along, without reflection, the ideological baggage devised to shape understanding in the interests of domestic power.

One of the themes of the chapters that follow is the significance and implications of these changes in the world order, but with a particular focus: with regard to US policies and those most affected by them.

There is a striking imbalance in the "post-Cold War" international system: the economic order is tripolar, but the military order is not. The United States remains the only power with the will and the capacity to exercise force on a global scale—even more freely than before, with the fading of the Soviet deterrent. But the US no longer enjoys the preponderance of economic power that had enabled it to maintain an aggressive and interventionist military posture since World War II. Military power not backed by a comparable economic base has its limits as a means of coercion and domination. It may well inspire adventurism, a tendency to lead with one's strength, possibly with catastrophic consequences.

These features of the international system have been manifest in the varying reactions of the industrial powers to the collapse of the Soviet empire, and in the early post-Cold War US military operations, the invasion of Panama and the response to Iraq's invasion of Kuwait. In the latter case, just unfolding as these words are written, the tension between economic tripolarity and military unipolarity is particularly evident. Despite the very hazardous possible consequences of military conflict, the virtually instinctive US government reaction was to direct the confrontation to the arena of force, undercutting possible diplomatic opportunities and even expressing deep concern that others might be tempted to seek to "defuse the crisis" by diplomatic means, achieving the goals sought generally by the international community but without a decisive demonstration of the effectiveness of US military power and resolve.[3]

In the evolving world order, the comparative advantage of the United States lies in military force, in which it ranks supreme. Diplomacy and international law have always been regarded as an annoying encumbrance, unless they can be used to advantage against an enemy. Every active player in world affairs professes to seek only peace and to prefer negotiations to violence and coercion—even Hitler; but when the veil is lifted, we commonly see that diplomacy is understood as a disguise for the rule of force. With the current configuration of US strengths and weaknesses, the temptation to transfer problems quickly to the arena of forceful confrontation is likely to be strong. Furthermore, though the United States cannot regain the economic supremacy of an earlier period, it is committed to maintaining its status as the sole military superpower, with no probable contestant for that role. One consequence will be exacerbation of domestic economic difficulties; another, a renewed temptation to "go it alone" in relying on the threat of force rather than diplomacy.

The Gulf conflict brought these issues to the fore. Aside from Britain, which has its own interests in Kuwait, the other major industrial powers showed little interest in military confrontation. The reaction in Washington was ambivalent. War is dangerous; defusing the crisis without a demonstration of the efficacy of force is also an unwanted outcome. As for the costs, plainly it would be advantageous for them to be shared, but not at the price of sacrificing the role of lone enforcer. These conflicting concerns led to a sharp elite split over the tactical choice between preparation for war and reliance on sanctions, with the Administration holding to the former course.

In the past, the United States and its clients have often found themselves "politically weak" (that is, lacking popular support in some region targeted for intervention) though militarily and economically strong, a formula commonly used on all sides. Under such conditions, it is natural to prefer military force, terror, and economic warfare to the peaceful means dictated by international law. With lagging economic strength, the temptation to resort to force is only heightened.

It is fitting that the first two occasions for the use of force in this (partially) new era should have been in Central America and the Gulf. Political analysts and advisers often draw a distinction between "our needs" and "our wants," the former exemplified by the Middle East, with its incomparable energy resources; the latter by Central America, of no major strategic or economic significance, but a domain in which the US rules by tradition. In the case of mere "wants," tactical preferences may vary. Our "needs" in the Middle East, it is regularly argued, legitimate extreme measures to preserve US dominance and to ensure that no independent indigenous force (or foreign power, had this been a serious possibility in the postwar era) might gain substantial influence over the production and distribution of the region's petroleum resources. To the extent feasible, these are to be dominated by the United States, its allies and regional clients, and its oil corporations—a doctrine that might virtually be regarded as "Axiom One of international affairs," I suggested in writing about this matter in the mid 1970s, at the time of the first oil crisis.[4]

These features of the international system also have their conventional expression (the United States must bear the burden of enforcing good behavior worldwide, and so on). But such ideological fetters must be removed if there is to be any hope of gaining a realistic understanding of what lies ahead.

There is, indeed, a "New World Order" taking shape, marked by the diffusion of power in US domains and the collapse of the Russian empire and the tyranny at its heart. These developments leave the US as the overwhelmingly dominant military force and offer the three economic power centers the attractive prospect of incorporating the former Soviet system into their Third World domains. These must still be controlled, sometimes by force. This has been the responsibility of the United States, but with its relative economic decline, the task becomes a harder one to shoulder.

One reaction is that the US must persist in its historic task, while turning to others to pay the bills. Testifying before Congress, Deputy Secretary of State Lawrence Eagleburger explained that the emerging New World Order will be based on "a kind of new invention in the practice of diplomacy": others will pay the costs of US intervention to keep order. A respected commentator on international economic affairs describes the Gulf crisis as a "watershed event in US international relations," which will be seen in history as having "turned the US military into an internationally financed public good," "an internationally financed police force." While "some Americans will question the morality of the US military assuming a more explicitly mercenary role than it has played in the past, ... in the 1990s there is no realistic alternative...." The tacit assumption is that the public welfare is to be identified with the welfare of the Western industrial powers, and particularly their domestic elites.[5]

The financial editor of a leading conservative daily puts the essential point less delicately: we must exploit our "virtual monopoly in the security market ... as a lever to gain funds and economic concessions" from German-led Europe and Japan. The US has "cornered the West's security market" and others lack the "political will ... to challenge the U.S." in this "market." We will therefore be "the world's rent-a-cops" and will be "able to charge handsomely" for the service; the term "rent-a-thug" would be less flattering but more appropriate. Some will call us "Hessians," the author continues, but "that's a terribly demeaning phrase for a proud, well-trained, well-financed and well-respected military"; and whatever anyone may say, "we should be able to pound our fists on a few desks" in Japan and Europe, and "extract a fair price for our considerable services," demanding that our rivals "buy our bonds at cheap rates, or keep the dollar propped up, or better yet, pay cash directly into our Treasury." "We could change this role" of enforcer, he concludes, "but with it would go much of our control over the world economic system."[6]

This conception, while rarely put so bluntly, is widely held in one or another form, and captures an essential element of the Administration reaction to the Gulf crisis. It implies that the US should continue to take on the grim task of imposing order and stability (meaning proper respect for the masters) with the acquiescence and support of the other industrial powers along with riches funneled to the US via the dependent oil-producing monarchies.

Parallel domestic developments add another dimension to the picture. Studies by the US Labor Department and others predict serious shortages of skilled labor (everything from scientists and managers to technicians and typists) as the educational system deteriorates, part of the collapse of infrastructure accelerated by Reaganite social and economic policies. The tendency may be mitigated by modification of immigration laws to encourage a brain drain, but that is not likely to prove adequate. The predicted result is that the cost of skilled labor will rise and transnational corporations will transfer research, product development and design, marketing, and other such operations elsewhere. For the growing underclass, opportunities will still be available as Hessians. It takes little imagination to picture the consequences if such expectations—not inevitable, but also not unrealistic—are indeed realized.[7]

All of these questions arise, in various ways, in the chapters that follow.

The successes of the popular movements of Eastern and Central Europe are a historic achievement in the unending struggle for freedom and democracy throughout the world. Throughout history, such successes have elicited efforts to institute order and docility and thus to contain and deter the threat to privilege. The modalities range from large-scale violence to more subtle devices of control, particularly in more democratic societies. These include the structuring of values and operative choices,[8] and measures to control thought and opinion—what we call 'propaganda' in the case of enemy states.

The concept of thought control in democratic societies—or, for that matter, the structuring of options in a democratic society by hierarchic and coercive private institutions—seems contradictory on its face. A society is democratic to the extent that its citizens play a meaningful role in managing public affairs. If their thought is controlled, or their options are narrowly restricted, then evidently they are not playing a meaningful role: only the controllers, and those they serve, are doing so. The rest is a sham, formal motions without meaning. So, a contradiction. Nevertheless, there has been a major current of intellectual opinion to the contrary, holding that thought control is essential precisely in societies that are more free and democratic, even when institutional means effectively restrict the options available in practice. Such ideas and their implementation are perhaps more advanced in the United States than anywhere else, a reflection of the fact that it is in important respects the most free society in the world.

The interplay of freedom and control is a second theme of the chapters that follow, addressed from several perspectives.

The opening and concluding chapters contain some general observations on the points just outlined. Chapters 2 through 7 survey the range of prospects and problems facing the US leadership, and active and engaged segments of the public, under the partially new conditions now taking shape. The remaining chapters consider the operative concept of democracy, and the attitude towards popular movements and independence, as revealed in concrete situations and background thinking; examples are drawn primarily from Central America and early postwar Europe, but could easily be extended to other regions, the policies being quite general, with stable institutional roots. An afterword, added in November 1991, reviews the events in the Gulf and their aftermath, placing them within the setting of the stable institutional factors that guide domestic and foreign policy.

I have discussed these topics in a number of books, to which I would like to refer as general background where specific details and documentation are not provided below.[9] The material here is based in part on articles in *Zeta (Z) Magazine* from 1988, generally excerpted from longer unpublished manuscripts; or from talks through the same period, some appearing in a different form in conference proceedings. These have been edited and revised to reduce overlap, with considerable new material added.

December 1990

Notes

The following abbreviations are used for some sources cited in the Notes:

AFP	Agence France Presse	NPR	National Public Radio
AI	Amnesty International	*NYRB*	*New York Review of Books*
AP	Associated Press	*NYT*	*New York Times*
BG	*Boston Globe*	PBS	Public Broadcasting Service
CSM	*Christian Science Monitor*	PPS	Public Papers of the Presidents
FEER	*Far Eastern Economic Review*	*TNR*	*The New Republic*
		UPI	United Press International
JP	*Jerusalem Post*	*WP*	*Washington Post*
LAT	*Los Angeles Times*	*WSJ*	*Wall Street Journal*

1. For discussion at the time, see my *Towards a New Cold War* (Pantheon, 1982), particularly the Introduction and ch. 7. This is generally presupposed in what follows, along with further comment on these matters in my *Turning the Tide* (South End, 1985), *On Power and Ideology* (South End, 1987). The quoted phrase is from a report to the Trilateral Commission in M.J. Crozier, S.P. Huntington, and J. Watanuki, *The Crisis of Democracy* (New York University, 1975).

2. See references of Note 1; also William A. Schwartz and Charles Derber, *et al.*, *The Nuclear Seduction* (University of California, 1990).

3. Thomas Friedman, "Behind Bush's Hard Line," *NYT*, August 22, 1990. See Chapter 6 for further discussion, and Chapter 1, section 5, for background.

4. "The Interim Agreement," *New Politics*, no. 3, 1976; see *Towards a New Cold War*, chs 11, 8. See the latter, and Chapter 8 below, for several examples from the foreign affairs literature making the distinction between "needs" and "wants" in essentially these terms.

5. Mary Curtius, "US asks allies to help pay for its continued leadership," *BG*, September 20; David Hale, chief economist of Kemper Financial Services, Chicago, "How to pay for the global policeman," *Financial Times* (London), November 21, 1990.

6. William Neikirk, "We are the world's guardian angels," *Chicago Tribune* business section, September 9, 1990.

7. AP, reporting a study of the Cornell University School of Industrial and Labor Relations, September 9, 1990.

8. For a lucid and penetrating discussion of these modalities within capitalist democracy, see Joshua Cohen and Joel Rogers, *On Democracy* (Penguin, 1982).

9. Among them, those cited in Note 1. Also, *Political Economy of Human Rights* (with Edward S. Herman, 2 vols) (South End, 1979), *Fateful Triangle* (South End, 1983), *Pirates and Emperors* (Claremont, Black Rose, 1986), *Culture of Terrorism* (South End, 1987), *Manufacturing Consent* (with E.S. Herman) (Pantheon, 1988), *Necessary Illusions* (South End, 1989).

ONE

Cold War: Fact and Fancy

THE great event of the current era is commonly taken to be the end of the Cold War, and the great question before us therefore is: What comes next? To answer this question, we have to begin by clarifying what the Cold War has been. There are two ways to approach this prior question. One is simply to accept the conventional interpretation; the second is to look at the historical facts. As is often the case, the two approaches yield rather different answers.

1. The Cold War as Ideological Construct

According to the conventional understanding, the Cold War has been a confrontation between two superpowers. We then find several variants. The orthodox version, which is overwhelmingly dominant, holds that the driving factor in the Cold War has been virulent Soviet aggressiveness, which the United States sought to contain. On one side of the conflict, we have a "nightmare," on the other, the "defender of freedom," to borrow the terms of the ultra-right John Birch Society, right-wing fundamentalist preachers, and liberal American intellectuals, who responded with awe and acclaim when these words were used by Václav Havel in addressing Congress in 1990.[1]

A critical variant argues that the perception of a Soviet threat was exagger-

9

ated; the dangers were less extreme than we thought. US policies, while noble in intent, were based on misunderstanding and analytic error. A still sharper critique holds that the superpower confrontation resulted from an interaction in which the United States also played a role (for some analysts, a major role) and that the contrast is not simply one of nightmare versus defense of freedom, but is more complex—in Central America and the Caribbean, for example.

According to all variants, the essential doctrines guiding US policy have been containment and deterrence, or, more ambitiously, "rollback." And the Cold War is now at an end, with the capitulation of one antagonist—the aggressor throughout, according to the orthodox version.

The orthodox version is sketched in stark and vivid terms in what is widely recognized to be the basic US Cold War document, NSC 68 in April 1950, shortly before the Korean War, announcing that "the cold war is in fact a real war in which the survival of the free world is at stake."[2] It merits attention, both as an early expression of the conventional understanding in its orthodox variant and for insights into historical realities that lie beyond these ideological constructs.

The basic structure of the argument has the childlike simplicity of a fairy tale. There are two forces in the world, at "opposite poles." In one corner we have absolute evil; in the other, sublimity. There can be no compromise between them. The diabolical force, by its very nature, must seek total domination of the world. Therefore it must be overcome, uprooted, and eliminated so that the virtuous champion of all that is good may survive to perform his exalted works.

The "fundamental design of the Kremlin," NSC 68 author Paul Nitze explains, is "the complete subversion or forcible destruction of the machinery of government and structure of society" in every corner of the world that is not yet "subservient to and controlled from the Kremlin." "The implacable purpose of the slave state [is] to eliminate the challenge of freedom" everywhere. The "compulsion" of the Kremlin "demands total power over all men" in the slave state itself, and "absolute authority over the rest of the world." The force of evil is "inescapably militant," so that no accommodation or peaceful settlement is even thinkable.

In contrast, the "fundamental purpose of the United States" is "to assure the integrity and vitality of our free society, which is founded upon the dignity and worth of the individual," and to safeguard these values throughout the world. Our free society is marked by "marvelous diversity," "deep tolerance," "lawfulness," a commitment "to create and maintain an environment in which every individual has the opportunity to realize his creative powers." It "does not fear, it welcomes, diversity" and "derives its strength from its hospitality even to antipathetic ideas." The "system of values which animates our society" includes "the principles of freedom, tolerance, the importance of the individual and the supremacy of reason over will." "The essential tolerance of our world outlook, our generous and constructive impulses, and the absence of covetousness in our international relations are assets of potentially enormous influence," particularly among those who who have been lucky enough to experience these qualities at first hand, as in Latin America, which has benefited so much from "our long continuing endeavors to create and now develop the Inter-American system."

The conflict between the forces of light and darkness is "momentous, involving the fulfillment or destruction not only of this Republic but of civilization itself." "The assault on free institutions is world-wide," and "imposes on us, in our own interests, the responsibility of world leadership." We must seek "to foster a world environment in which the American system can survive and flourish." Since "a defeat of free institutions anywhere is a defeat everywhere," no corner of the world, however tiny and insignificant, can escape our ministrations. And surely "the idea that Germany or Japan or other important areas can exist as islands of neutrality in a divided world is unreal, given the Kremlin design for world domination." Five years after the USSR was virtually annihilated by the Axis powers, they must be reconstituted within a US-dominated alliance committed to the final elimination of the Soviet system that they failed to destroy.

Given that "the integrity and vitality of our system is in greater jeopardy than ever before in our history," even in the darkest days of the War of Independence or when British troops captured Washington in 1814, it is clear that serious measures are in order; in fact, military spending nearly quadrupled shortly after, on the pretext that the invasion of South Korea was the first step in the Kremlin conquest of the world—despite the lack of compelling evidence, then or now, for Russian initiative in this phase of the complex struggle over the fate of Korea.

The memorandum calls for a huge increase in armaments, while recognizing that the slave state was far weaker than the champion of freedom by any measure. Relevant data are presented in such a way as to obscure direct comparisons and selected to exaggerate the enemy's strength, the standard pattern throughout the Cold War era.[3] Nevertheless, even the data presented show the US military budget to be double that of the USSR and its economic power four times as great, while in this early stage of rebuilding their far more powerful economies, the European allies alone already matched the Soviet Union along with its satellites.

Despite the disparity between the two opposite poles in economic level and military force, the slave state has enormous advantages. Being so backward, it "can do more with less"; its weakness is its strength, the ultimate weapon. It is both midget and superman, far behind us by every measure but with "a formidable capacity to act with the widest tactical latitude, with stealth and speed," with "extraordinary flexibility," a highly effective military machine and "great coercive power." Another problem is that the evil enemy finds a "receptive audience . . . in the free world," particularly Asia. To defend Europe and protect the freedom that has traditionally reigned in Africa, Asia, and Latin America from the "Kremlin design," we must therefore vastly increase military spending and adopt a strategy aimed at the break-up and collapse of the Soviet Union.

Our military forces are "dangerously inadequate," because our responsibility is world control; in contrast, the far weaker Soviet military forces greatly exceed their limited defensive needs. Nothing that had happened in the past years suggested that the USSR might face some security problems, in contrast to us, with our vulnerability to powerful enemies everywhere. We need vast military forces "not only for protection against disaster but also to support our foreign policy," though for public relations purposes, "emphasis should be given to the essentially defensive character" of the military build-up.

Public relations aside, our actual stance must be aggressive in "the conflict which has been imposed upon us." "Given the Kremlin design for world domination," a necessary feature of the slave state, we cannot accept the existence of the enemy but must "foster the seeds of destruction within the Soviet system" and "hasten [its] decay" by all means short of war (which is too dangerous for us). We must avoid negotiations, except as a device to placate public opinion, because any agreements "would reflect present realities and would therefore be unacceptable, if not disastrous, to the United States and the rest of the free world," though after the success of a "rollback" strategy we may "negotiate a settlement with the Soviet Union (or a successor state or states)."

To achieve these essential goals, we must overcome weaknesses in our society, such as "the excesses of a permanently open mind," "the excess of tolerance," and "dissent among us." We will have to learn to "distinguish between the necessity for tolerance and the necessity for just suppression," a crucial feature of "the democratic way." It is particularly important to

insulate our "labor unions, civic enterprises, schools, churches, and all media
for influencing opinion" from the "evil work" of the Kremlin, which seeks
to subvert them and "make them sources of confusion in our economy,
our culture and our body politic." Increased taxes are also necessary, along
with "Reduction of Federal expenditures for purposes other than defense
and foreign assistance, if necessary by the deferment of certain desirable
programs." These military Keynesian policies, it is suggested, are likely to
stimulate the domestic economy as well. Indeed, they may serve to prevent
"a decline in economic activity of serious proportions." "A large measure
of sacrifice and discipline will be demanded of the American people," and
they also must "give up some of the benefits" they enjoy as we assume
the mantle of world leadership and overcome the economic recession, already
in progress, by "positive governmental programs" to subsidize advanced
industry through the military system.

Notice that the noble purpose of the free society and the evil design
of the slave state are innate properties, which derive from their very nature.
Hence the actual historical and documentary record is not relevant to assessing the validity of these doctrines. Accordingly, it is unfair to criticize the
memorandum on the grounds that no evidence is presented to support
its conclusions, and to question such locutions as "it is apparent from the
preceding sections," or "it has been shown above," on the same grounds.
As a matter of logic, no empirical evidence is required; pure thought suffices
to establish the required truths.

In public discourse the same conceptions reigned, and still do. A characteristic expression of the conventional understanding is given by William
Hyland, editor of *Foreign Affairs*, in the lead article of the Spring 1990 issue:

> For the past fifty years American foreign policy has been formed in response
> to the threat posed by this country's opponents and enemies. In virtually every
> year since Pearl Harbor, the United States has been engaged either in war or
> in confrontation. Now, for the first time in half a century, the United States
> has the opportunity to reconstruct its foreign policy free of most of the constraints
> and pressures of the Cold War. . . . Since 1941 the United States has been fully
> entangled. Now as we move into a new era, a yearning for American nonentangle-
> ment may be returning in various guises. . . . Can America at long last come
> home? . . . The United States does in fact enjoy the luxury of some genuine
> choices for the first time since 1945. America and its allies have won the Cold
> War . . .

Thus, we had no "genuine choices" when we invaded South Vietnam, overthrew the democratic capitalist government of Guatemala in 1954 and have maintained the rule of murderous gangsters ever since, ran by far the most extensive international terror operations in history against Cuba from the early 1960s and Nicaragua through the 1980s, sought to assassinate Lumumba and installed and maintained the brutal and corrupt Mobutu dictatorship, backed Trujillo, Somoza, Marcos, Duvalier, the generals of the southern cone, Suharto, the racist rulers of southern Africa, and a whole host of other major criminals; and on, and on. We could do nothing else, given the threat to our existence. But now the enemy has retreated, so we can perhaps satisfy our "yearning for nonentanglement" in the affairs of others; though, as others add, our "yearning for democracy"[4] may yet impel us to persist in our noble endeavors in defense of freedom.

With choices available for the first time, we can turn to constructive programs for the Third World (as liberal humanists urge) or leave the undeserving poor to wallow in their misery (the conservative position). Expressing the more caring liberal view, Thomas Schoenbaum, executive director of the Dean Rusk Center of International and Comparative Law at the University of Georgia, calls for "more finely tuned and differentiated policies" in the "complex and heterogeneous areas" of the Third World. Constrained by the overwhelming imperative of resisting Soviet aggression throughout the world, we have been unable to develop such policies. But now, perhaps, we have reached "the end of the Cold War—and the good guys won." We may therefore hope that the Soviets will "mute their longstanding campaign to support communist revolutions and totalitarian regimes in the Third World," so that "the U.S. may be able to abandon its traditional posture—that priority should be given to stopping communist expansion—and adopt more positive policies."[5]

In other respects too the public record conforms to the conventions of NSC 68. In particular, it is widely recognized that the very existence of the Soviet Union constitutes aggression. Diplomatic historian John Lewis Gaddis, one of the most respected figures of liberal scholarship on the Cold War, explains that the allied intervention immediately after the Bolshevik revolution was defensive in nature, and for Woodrow Wilson, was inspired "above all else" by his fervent desire "to secure self-determination in Russia"—by forceful installation of the rulers we select. The invasion was defensive because it was "in response to a profound and potentially far-reaching intervention by the new Soviet government in the internal affairs, not just of the West, but of virtually every country in the world," namely, "the Revolution's challenge—which could hardly have been more categorical—to the very survival of the capitalist order." "The security of the United States" was "in danger" already in 1917, not just in 1950, and intervention was therefore entirely warranted in defense against the change of the social order in Russia and the announcement of revolutionary intentions.[6]

Gaddis's contemporary evaluation recapitulates the immediate Western reaction to the Bolshevik revolution. It was articulated by DeWitt C. Poole, American counselor of the Embassy in Russia, in a memorandum for Secretary of State Lansing entitled "Concerning the Purposes of the Bolsheviki: Especially with Respect to a World Revolution." Poole wrote that the "vital problem" for the United States was to steer the world "between the Scylla of reaction on the one hand and the Charybdis of Bolshevism on the other." The Charybdis of Bolshevism, however, is the more ominous threat, because "It is the essence of the Bolshevik movement that it is *international and not national in character*," aimed "directly at the subversion of all Governments."[7] In practice, the Scylla of reaction must be preferred— with regrets, among liberals—if the passage is too narrow.

Similarly, Oxford historian Norman Stone takes the position that elaborate debate over the origins of the Cold War is beside the point, because the very "character of the Soviet state" was "one of the greatest single causes of the Cold War in the 1940s." The test of Soviet intentions is its withdrawal from Eastern Europe and reduction of armaments to "defensive armaments, proper to its own economic level"; thus far below the West, which, furthermore, need not be limited to "defensive armaments" except in the expansive sense of "defense" that interprets every act of violence as defense of legitimate interests.[8] Note that the issue is not the desirability of the break-up of the Soviet internal and foreign empires or of radical reduction of armaments, but rather the conception of the Cold War and the Western "defensive" response to the very character of the Soviet state.

Much the same perception holds at the left extreme of mainstream opinion. Senior editor Hendrik Hertzberg of the *New Republic*, who is at the outer limits, writes: "revisionist quibbles aside, the basic cause of the Cold War was totalitarianism—more precisely, totalitarian ambition." Internally, Soviet totalitarianism imposed "an all-powerful, all-seeing, perfectly wise state that would answer every human need and would therefore obviate and obliterate every competing human institution." Its "external manifestation" was "a belief that all other social and political systems, judged by the standard of historical inevitability, were inferior and destined to die." In short, the basic cause of the Cold War was the internal nature of the Soviet system and its faith in its ultimate success as history unfolded, an ideological challenge that could not be tolerated.[9]

The underlying assumption is that the US system of social organization and power, and the ideology that accompanies it, must be universal. Anything short of that is unacceptable. No challenge can be tolerated, even faith in the historical inevitability of something different. That being the case, every action taken by the United States to extend its system and ideology is defensive. We may put aside revisionist quibbles about the events of history, now that their irrelevance has been demonstrated.

Journalism adopts the same stance as a matter of course. Thus, a *Washington Post* news story on "defense spending" observes that with the fading of the Soviet threat, the world has entered "a new era": "after 40 years of containing an aggressive and expansionist Soviet Union" we must now rethink the doctrine of containment that "organized our Western security strategy to protect the world from an expansionist and hostile Soviet Bloc."[10] That we have been laboring to protect the entire world from Soviet aggression is uncontroversial, a truism that requires no evidence or even comment.

The nobility of the "defender of freedom" is also standard intellectual fare. Thus, according to Michael Howard, Regius Professor of Modern History at Oxford:

> For 200 years the United States has preserved almost unsullied the original ideals of the Enlightenment: the belief in the God-given rights of the individual, the inherent rights of free assembly and free speech, the blessings of free enterprise, the perfectibility of man, and, above all, the universality of these values.

In this nearly ideal society, the influence of elites is "quite limited." But the world, he laments, does not appreciate this magnificence: "the United States does not enjoy the place in the world that it should have earned through its achievements, its generosity, and its goodwill since World War II"[11]—as illustrated in such contemporary paradises as Indochina, the Dominican Republic, the Philippines, El Salvador and Guatemala, to mention a few of the many candidates; just as belief in the "God-given rights of the individual" and the "universality" of this doctrine for two hundred years is illustrated by a century of literal human slavery and effective disenfranchisement of Blacks for another century, genocidal assaults on the native population, the slaughter of hundreds of thousands of Filipinos at the turn of the century, of millions of Indochinese, of some 200,000 Central Americans in the past decade, and a host of other examples. Again, mere fact is an irrelevance in the domain of pure thought.

To take another example from the field of scholarship, consider the study of the "Vietnam trauma" by Paul Kattenburg, one of the few early dissenters on Vietnam within the US government and now Jacobson Professor of Public Affairs at the University of South Carolina.[12] Kattenburg is concerned to identify the "salient features central to the American tradition and experience which have made the United States perform its superpower role in what we might term a particularistic way." He holds that "principles and ideals hold a cardinal place in the U.S. national ethos and crucially distinguish U.S. performance in the superpower role." These principles and ideals were "laid down by the founding fathers, those pure geniuses of detached contemplation," and were "refined by subsequent leading figures of thought and action" from John Adams to Theodore Roosevelt, Woodrow Wilson and Franklin Roosevelt. The principles were

> tested and retested in the process of settling the continent, healing the North–South breach, developing the economy from the wilderness in the spirit of free enterprise, and fighting World Wars I and II, not so much for interests as for the survival of the very principles by which most Americans were guiding their lives.

It is this unique legacy that explains the way Americans act "in the superpower role," which they approached "devoid of artifice or deception," with "the mind set of an emancipator":

> In such a mind set, one need not feel or act superior, or believe one is imposing one's ethos or values on others, since one senses naturally that others cannot doubt the emancipator's righteous cause anymore than his capacities. In this respect, the American role as superpower, particularly in the early postwar years, is very analogous to the role that can be attributed to a professor, mentor, or other type of emancipator.

Thus, "the professor is obviously capable" and

> he is clearly disinterested. ... Moreover, like the American superpower, the professor does not control the lives or destinies of his students; they remain free to come or go. ... It will help us understand America's performance and psychology as a superpower, and the whys and wherefores of its Indochina involvement, if we bear in mind this analogy of the American performance in the superpower role with that of the benevolent but clearly egocentric professor, dispensing emancipation through knowledge of both righteousness and the right way to the deprived students of the world.

This is not intended as irony or caricature, but is presented seriously, taken seriously, and is not untypical of what we find in the literature—not at the lunatic fringe, but at the respectable and moderately dissident end of the mainstream spectrum. That being the case, it is only natural that James Reston, long the leading political thinker of the *New York Times*, should say at his retirement: "I don't think there's anything in the history of the world to compare with the commitments this country has taken in defense of freedom." While at his post, Reston had performed yeoman service in the cause of freedom, as when he took pride in the US contribution to the huge slaughter in Indonesia in 1965, and explained in properly somber tones, as US military force was demolishing what was left of the South Vietnamese countryside in late 1967, that this was being done "on the principle that military power shall not compel South Vietnam to do what it does not want to do," out of our loyalty to "the deepest conviction of Western civilization"—namely, that "the individual belongs not to the state but to his Creator," and thus has rights that "no magistrate or political force may violate."[13]

The official doctrine as provided by government spokesmen, the media, political commentary, and a broad range of scholarship is illustrated, for example, in the report of the National Bipartisan (Kissinger) Commission on Central America: "The international purposes of the United States in the late twentieth century are cooperation, not hegemony or domination; partnership, not confrontation; a decent life for all, not exploitation." Walter Laqueur and Charles Krauthammer write: "Unlike the Soviet Union, the U.S. does not want to convert anyone to a specific political, social, or economic system." Samuel Huntington informs us that "The overall effect of American power on other societies was to further liberty, pluralism, and democracy.... The conflict between American power and American principles virtually disappears when it is applied to the American impact on other societies." Krauthammer, a much-respected neoliberal, assures us further that every US President from FDR to LBJ aimed at "promotion abroad of both freedom and world order," a mission revived in the Reagan Doctrine, which provided a "coherent policy" of support for those who "are risking their lives on every continent from Afghanistan to Nicaragua to defy Soviet-supported aggression" (Ronald Reagan, quoted with admiration and approval) and committed the US not only to freedom and human rights, but also to constructing American-style sociopolitical systems in the Third World—though without wanting "to convert anyone to a specific political, social, or economic system," consistency being as important as fact for the vocation of the commissar.[14]

These conventions are so widely observed that further citation is unnecessary. A notable feature throughout is the lack of any felt need to justify the flattering doctrine that in the Third World, the US has sought only to thwart the Russians and their totalitarian goals while upholding its lofty principles as best it can in these grim and trying circumstances. The reasoning is that of NSC 68: these are necessary truths, established by conceptual analysis alone. Scholars who profess a tough-minded "realistic" outlook, scorning sentimentality and emotion, are willing to concede that the facts of history hardly illustrate the commitment of the United States to, as Hans Morgenthau puts it, its "transcendent purpose"—"the establishment of equality in freedom in America," and indeed throughout the world, since "the arena within which the United States must defend and promote its purpose has become world-wide." But the facts are irrelevant, because, as Morgenthau hastens to explain, to adduce them is "to confound the abuse of reality with reality itself." Reality is the unachieved "national purpose" revealed by "the evidence of history as our minds reflect it," while the actual historical record is merely the abuse of reality, an insignificant artifact.[15] The conventional understanding is therefore self-justifying, immune to external critique.

Though the sophistication of traditional theology is lacking, the similarity of themes and style is striking. It reveals the extent to which worship of the state has become a secular religion for which the intellectuals serve as priesthood. The more primitive sectors of Western culture go further, fostering forms of idolatry in which such sacred symbols as the flag become an object of forced veneration, and the state is called upon to punish any insult to them and to compel children to pledge their devotion daily, while God and State are almost indissolubly linked in public ceremony and discourse, as in James Reston's musings on our devotion to the will of the Creator. It is perhaps not surprising that such crude fanaticism rises to such an extreme in the United States, as an antidote to the unique freedom from state coercion that has been achieved by popular struggle.[16]

2. The Cold War as Historical Process

The second approach to the Cold War era is based on the idea that logic alone does not suffice: facts also matter. If so, then to understand the Cold War era we should look at the events that constitute it. Pursuing this course,

which seems not entirely unreasonable, we find a more complex and interesting picture, which bears only a partial resemblance to the conventional
understanding. The same method of inquiry suggests several reasons why
the post-Cold War era may prove to be much like what came before,
at least for its regular victims, apart from tactics and propaganda.

Needless to say, if we *define* the Cold War as involving nothing beyond
a confrontation of two superpowers, with their allies and clients tailing
along, it follows trivially that that is precisely what it was, and that with
the withdrawal of the USSR from the conflict, it ended with a victory
for the US side. The question, however, is how to interpret the Cold
War era, and plainly that question is not answered by begging it.[17] Rather,
we want to look into the contours, character, driving forces and motives,
and major effects of the bipolar world system that emerged from World
War II. These are significant historical phenomena, worthy of study. Just
how the East–West conflict finds its place in this matrix is a matter for
discovery, not stipulation—at least, if our goal is understanding.

An understanding of the Cold War era requires an account not only
of the actual events, but also of the factors that lie behind them. The documentary record of planning becomes relevant here. We will want to know
how far policy was determined by specific features of the Cold War era,
and how far it merely adapted persistent institutional demands to new conditions. To answer these questions, we will naturally ask how the typical
events of the Cold War, and the underlying motives, compare with standard
practice and thinking before and since. It is also necessary to account for
the prevailing ideological constructions and their functions, including the
conventional understanding of the Cold War, in so far as it departs from
reality.

Approaching the Cold War era with these considerations in mind, we
find that the superpower conflict of the conventional portrayal has been
real enough, but is only a fraction of the truth. Reality protrudes when
we look at the typical events and practices of the Cold War.

On Moscow's side, the Cold War is illustrated by tanks in East Berlin,
Budapest and Prague, and other coercive measures in the regions liberated
by the Red Army from the Nazis, then held in thrall to the Kremlin; and
the invasion of Afghanistan, the one case of Soviet military intervention
well outside the historic invasion route from the West. Domestically, the
Cold War served to entrench the power of the military–bureaucratic elite
whose rule derives from the Bolshevik coup of October 1917.

For the United States, the Cold War has been a history of worldwide subversion, aggression and state terrorism, with examples too numerous to mention. The domestic counterpart has been the entrenchment of Eisenhower's "military–industrial complex"—in essence, a welfare state for the rich with a national security ideology for population control (to borrow some counterinsurgency jargon), following the prescriptions of NSC 68. The major institutional mechanism is a system of state–corporate industrial management to sustain high-technology industry, relying on the taxpayer to fund research and development and provide a guaranteed market for waste production, with the private sector taking over when there are profits to be made. This crucial gift to the corporate manager has been the domestic function of the Pentagon system (including NASA and the Department of Energy, which controls nuclear weapons production); benefits extend to the computer industry, electronics generally, and other sectors of the advanced industrial economy.[18] In such ways, the Cold War has provided a large part of the underpinnings for the system of public subsidy, private profit, that is proudly called Free Enterprise.

The call for vigorous action in NSC 68 resounded again as the Kennedy and Reagan administrations came into office, with the same dual thrust: militancy abroad to assert US power, and military spending to revive a flagging economy at home. The rhetoric was also duly revived: "the monolithic and ruthless conspiracy" on the march to destroy us (Kennedy); the "Evil Empire" that is "the focus of evil in our time," seeking to rule the world (Reagan). The decibel level predictably declines as policy shifts course—as in the mid 1980s, when it became necessary to face the costs of the fiscal mismanagement and military Keynesian excesses of the statist reactionaries of the Reagan Administration, including the huge budget and trade deficits.

Attention to the historical record reveals the realistic core enshrouded in the outlandish rhetoric of NSC 68. The Great Depression had put an end to any lingering beliefs that capitalism was a viable system. It was generally taken for granted that state intervention was necessary in order to maintain private power—as, indeed, had been the case throughout the development process.[19] It was also understood that New Deal measures had failed, and that the Depression was overcome only by the far more massive state intervention during the war. Without the benefit of Keynes, this lesson was taught directly to the corporate managers who flocked to Washington to run the quasi-totalitarian wartime command economy. The general expectation was that without state intervention, there would be a return to the Depression after pent-up consumer demand was satisfied. It appeared to be confirmed by the 1948 recession. State-subsidized agricultural production found markets in Japan and elsewhere, but it was feared that manufacturing would languish in the absence of markets—hence the concern voiced in NSC 68 over "a decline in economic activity of serious proportions" unless military Keynesian measures were adopted. These programs, it was hoped, would also contribute to the revitalization of the allies' industrial economies, helping overcome the "dollar gap" which limited the market for US manu-factured goods.

The call in NSC 68 for "sacrifice and discipline" and cutback in social programs was a natural concomitant to these perceptions. The need for "just suppression" and controls over unions, churches, schools, and other potential sources of dissidence also fell into a broader pattern. From the late 1930s, business had been deeply perturbed by the increasing politicization and organization of the general public—what was later called a "crisis of democracy" under the partially similar conditions of the post-Vietnam per-iod. The same had been true immediately after World War I. In each case, the response was the same: Wilson's Red Scare, the post-World War II repression mislabeled "McCarthyism" (actually, a campaign to undermine unions, working-class culture, and independent thought launched by business and liberal Democrats well before McCarthy appeared on the scene and made the mistake, which finally destroyed him, of attacking people with power); the programs of the national political police inaugurated by the Kennedy Administration and expanded by their successors to undermine independent political parties and popular movements by subversion and violence. Wars and other crises have a way of making people think and even organize, and private power regularly calls upon the state to contain such threats to its monopoly of the political arena and cultural hegemony.[20] The deeply anti-democratic thrust of NSC 68 reflects far more general commitments.

NSC 68 is also realistic, and conventional, in invoking the US "responsibi-lity of world leadership" and the corresponding need to dominate every corner of the world, however remote, and to exorcize the curse of neutra-lism. In these respects, it reiterates earlier planning decisions that reflect the recognition that the US had achieved a position of military and economic power with no historical parallel, and could use it to advantage.

Sophisticated sectors of the business community have been aware of the domestic factors that have driven the Cold War system, and the same is true of the better scholarship in the mainstream. In his standard work on containment, John Lewis Gaddis observes:

To a remarkable degree, containment has been the product, not so much of what the Russians have done, or of what has happened elsewhere in the world, but of internal forces operating within the United States. ... What is surprising is the *primacy* that has been accorded economic considerations [namely, state economic management] in shaping strategies of containment, *to the exclusion of other considerations* [original emphasis].

He also agrees with George Kennan's consistent view—standard among rational policymakers and analysts—that "it is not Russian military power which is threatening us, it is Russian political power" (October 1947).[21] Despite these insights, Gaddis does not depart from the conventional framework of "deterrence" and "containment of the Soviet threat," though he does recognize—on the side—that this is by no means the whole story; or, in fact, the central theme.

The major events and effects of the Cold War fall into the categories just reviewed. There were also more complex effects. Soviet support for targets of US subversion and attack gained it a degree of influence in much of the Third World, albeit of a tenuous nature. As for the United States, its intervention in the Third World, particularly in the early years, was in part impelled by the goal of securing a hinterland for the state capitalist economies that it hoped to reconstruct in Western Europe and Japan. At the same time, the Cold War conflict helped to maintain US influence over its industrial allies and to contain independent politics, labor, and other popular activism within these states—an interest shared by local elites. The US promoted the NATO alliance, one historian observes, "to corral its allies and to head off neutralism, as well as to deter the Russians."[22]

The persistence of the conventional doctrine, despite its limited relation to the actual facts of the Cold War era, is readily understandable in this light. In the West, it is commonly conceded well after the fact (the fact being some exercise of subversion or aggression in the Third World, or renewed benefits through the Pentagon system at home) that the threat of Soviet aggression was exaggerated, the problems were misconstrued, and the idealism that guided the actions was misplaced. But the requisite beliefs remained prominently displayed on the shelf. However fanciful, they could be served up to the public when needed—often with perfect sincerity, in accord with the familiar process by which useful beliefs arise from perceived interests.

Also understandable is the otherwise rather mysterious fact that security policy has been only weakly correlated with realistic security concerns.

Threats have regularly been concocted on the flimsiest evidence and with marginal credibility at best. On the other hand, potential threats of some significance have been ignored. Repeatedly, the US has sponsored the development of weapons systems that could pose serious dangers to its welfare or even survival, and has dismissed opportunities to abort such developments. The US government and the media have vociferously demanded "verification" under conditions that they expected the USSR to reject. On the other hand, Washington has been reluctant (along with its allies) to permit Soviet inspection of chemical production and other military and arms production facilities, has rejected Soviet proposals for on-site inspection of submarines to monitor a ban or limitation on sea-launched cruise missiles (SLCMs; more a threat to the US, with its long coastlines, than to the USSR), and has opposed inspection of nuclear warheads for SLCMs on ship or shore. Still more important, the political leadership has undermined possibilities for political settlement and fostered conflict in regions where such conflict could lead to a devastating nuclear war, and has sometimes come all too close—notably the Middle East. These consistent patterns make no sense on the assumption that security policy is guided by security concerns. Case by case, they fall into place on the assumption that policy is driven by the twin goals of reinforcing the private interests that largely control the state, and maintaining an international environment in which they can prosper.[23] The world is sufficiently uncertain and dangerous for alleged reasons of security to be readily devised to justify policies adopted on other grounds, then adopted as articles of faith, familiar features of statecraft and the practice of the intellectual community.

On the same grounds, we can understand why the political leadership has often failed to pursue apparent opportunities to reduce the threat of superpower confrontation, and thus to enhance national security. One early example was in 1952, when the Kremlin put forth a proposal for reunification and neutralization of Germany, with no conditions on economic policies and with guarantees for "the rights of man and basic freedoms, including freedom of speech, press, religious persuasion, political conviction, and assembly" and the free activity of democratic parties and organizations. In reply, the US and its allies objected that the West did not recognize the Oder–Neisse frontier between Germany and Poland, and insisted that a reunified Germany be free to join NATO, a demand that the Russians could hardly accept a few years after Germany alone had virtually destroyed the Soviet Union. The Western reply also referred, more plausibly, to lack of clarity about free elections; but instead of seeking further clarification, the proposal was rejected with quite unreasonable demands. Commenting at the time, James Warburg, one of the few to have argued that the opportunity should be pursued, notes that neither the text of the March 10 Kremlin proposal "nor even the fact of its arrival was disclosed by Washington until after the Western reply had been sent on March 25." He suggests that the delay may have been related to the Administration desire "to present its case for the Mutual Security Act of 1952 to the Senate Foreign Relations Committee, without having that committee's deliberations prejudiced by knowledge of the Soviet proposal"; the Act called for about $7.5 billion for Western rearmament, and was "based upon the assumption that an All-German settlement could not possibly be achieved."[24]

Had the Kremlin proposal been implemented, it would have eliminated whatever military threat the Soviet Union might have posed to Western Europe. There would probably have been no Soviet tanks in East Berlin in 1953, no Berlin Wall, no invasion of Hungary or Czechoslovakia—but crucially, no ready justification for US intervention and subversion worldwide, for state policies of economic management in the service of advanced industry, or for a system of world order in which US hegemony was founded in large part on military might. The basic reason for rejecting the proposal seems to have been the US interest in integrating a rearmed Western Germany in the NATO military alliance, whatever the security risks or the consequences for the Soviet satellites. Testifying before the Senate Foreign Relations Committee on March 28, Warburg observed that the Soviet proposal, offering a possible means for a peaceful negotiated resolution of European security issues, might be a bluff. But, he speculated, it seemed "that our Government is afraid to call the bluff for fear that it may not be a bluff at all" and might lead to "a free, neutral, democratic, and demilitarized Germany," which might be "subverted into the Soviet orbit"; and short of that, would bar the plans for rearming Germany within the NATO alliance. The rejection of these opportunities to end the Cold War followed directly from the principles of NSC 68, which ruled coexistence illegitimate.

For years, these matters were off the agenda; even to mention the facts was to risk being castigated as an apologist for Stalin. By 1989–90, however, Stalin's proposal could be cited quite freely in the press and journals. In the triumphalism of the moment, it was hoped that the USSR would be compelled to agree to incorporation of a united Germany within a US-dominated military alliance. Hence Gorbachev's proposal for neutralization of a reunified Germany must be dismissed as more "Old Thinking," the rehashing of discarded ideas, not to be taken seriously. In this context it becomes permissible, even useful, to refer to facts that were suppressed when they would serve only as a reminder of inconvenient realities.

Other Soviet proposals were also left unexplored. Raymond Garthoff, formerly a senior analyst of the CIA and an outstanding specialist on security affairs and foreign policy, observes that Gorbachev's announcement of unilateral force reduction "had an interesting precedent some thirty years ago," when, "in January 1960, Nikita Khrushchev disclosed for the first time since World War II the manpower strength of the Soviet armed forces, and dramatically announced a planned reduction by one-third over the next two years." A few months later, US intelligence verified huge cuts in active Soviet military forces. The tactical air force was cut in half, "mainly through a wholesale two-thirds reduction in light-bomber units"; and naval air fighter-interceptors, about 1500 aircraft, were removed from the navy, half of them scrapped and the rest turned over to air defense to replace dismantled planes. By 1961, nearly half the announced reduction of manpower had taken place. In 1963, Khrushchev again called for new reductions. According to military correspondent Fred Kaplan, he also withdrew more than 15,000 troops from East Germany, calling on the US to undertake similar reductions of the military budget and of military forces in Europe and generally, and to move towards further reciprocal cuts. Declassified documents reveal that President Kennedy privately discussed such possibilities with high Soviet officials, but abandoned them as the US intervention in Vietnam expanded in scale. William Kaufmann, a former top Pentagon aide and leading analyst of security issues, describes the US failure to respond to Khrushchev's initiatives as, in career terms, "the one regret I have."[25]

In the mid 1970s Soviet military spending began to level off, as later conceded, while the US lead in strategic bombs and warheads widened through the decade. President Carter proposed a substantial increase in military spending and a cutback on social programs. These proposals were implemented by the Reagan Administration, along with the standard concomitant, increased militancy abroad, and on the standard pretext: the Soviet threat —in this case a "window of vulnerability" and Soviet triumphs in the Third World. The latter were even more fraudulent than the awesome Soviet military build-up. In so far as the relics of the Portuguese and French empires fell under Russian influence in the mid 1970s, it was largely because the US refused to enter into amicable relations with them on the—always unacceptable—condition of neutralism and independence; the same was true in Latin America and elsewhere. Furthermore, these Soviet triumphs were laughable in scale, more a burden than a gain in global power—facts that were obvious at the time and conceded within a few years when the pretexts were no longer appropriate for current plans. Gorbachev's proposals in 1985–6 for a unilateral ban on nuclear weapons tests, the abolition of the Warsaw Pact and NATO, removal of the US and Soviet fleets from the Mediterranean, and other steps to reduce confrontation and tension were ignored or dismissed as an embarrassment. The virtual or sometimes complete international isolation of the United States on disarmament issues has also been regularly suppressed, even at moments of great celebration over alleged US triumphs in this cause.[26]

Turning to the superpower conflict itself, it is true enough that by its very nature, the USSR constituted an unacceptable challenge. Specifically, its autarkic command economy interfered with US plans to construct a global system based on (relatively) free trade and investment, which, under the conditions of mid century, was expected to be dominated by US corporations and highly beneficial to their interests, as indeed it was. The challenge became still more intolerable as the Soviet empire barred free Western access to other areas. The Iron Curtain deprived the capitalist industrial powers of a region that was expected to provide raw materials, investment opportunities, markets and cheap labor. These facts alone laid the basis for superpower conflict, as serious analysts were quite well aware. In an important 1955 document on the political economy of US foreign policy, a prestigious study group observed that the primary threat of Communism is the economic transformation of the Communist powers "in ways that reduce their willingness and ability to complement the industrial economies of the West," a factor that regularly motivated Third World interventions as well as hostility to the Soviet Union and its imperial system.[27]

It is, furthermore, quite true that the Soviet Union sought targets of opportunity where it could find them, entering into friendly and supportive relations with the most miserable tyrants and gangsters—Mengistu in Ethiopia and the neo-Nazi Argentine generals, to name only two examples. In this regard, the Kremlin satisfied the norms of the guardians of civilization and order. But in a criminal departure from these norms, the Soviet Union regularly offered support to targets of US subversion and attack, thus impeding the designs of the one truly global power. Material support helped these enemies to survive, and relations with the Soviet Union imposed limits on US actions, for fear of a superpower conflict from which the United States might not emerge unscathed. Such Soviet involvement is regularly condemned as intolerable interference and expansionism, even aggression—as, for example, when the Contra forces attacking Nicaragua are lauded for "risking their lives to defy ... [the] ... Soviet-supported aggression" of the Sandinistas,[28] whose incumbency is in itself an act of aggression, being counter to US demands.

Lacking an internal record from the Soviet Union, we can only speculate as to whether ominous "Kremlin designs" were indeed deterred by Western military power; the available evidence is hardly compelling. The deterrent effect of Soviet power on US designs is also largely a matter of speculation.[29] The clearest example of the success of deterrence is provided by Cuba, where the US was restricted to large-scale international terrorism instead of outright invasion after the missile crisis brought the world perilously close to nuclear war, in the judgement of the participants; understandably, this is not an example that figures prominently in the Western literature on deterrence. In both the internal and public record, new US weapons systems were justified by the need to overcome the Soviet deterrent, which might "impose greater caution in our cold war policies" because of fear of nuclear war (Paul Nitze, NSC 141, 1953). As a global power, the US often intervenes in regions in which it lacks a conventional force advantage. An intimidating military posture has therefore been necessary to protect such operations. Just before he became director of the Arms Control and Disarmament Agency in the Reagan Administration, Eugene Rostow observed that strategic nuclear forces provide a "shield" for pursuit of US "global interests" by "conventional means or theater forces"; these thereby "become meaningful instruments of military and political power," Carter Secretary of Defense Harold Brown added.[30]

Putting second-order complexities to the side, for the USSR the Cold War has been primarily a war against its satellites, and for the US a war against the Third World. For each, it has served to entrench a particular system of domestic privilege and coercion. The policies pursued within the Cold War framework have been unattractive to the general population, which accepts them only under duress. Throughout history, the standard device to mobilize a reluctant population has been the fear of an evil enemy, dedicated to its destruction. The superpower conflict served the purpose admirably—both for internal needs, as we see in the fevered rhetoric of top planning documents such as NSC 68, and in public propaganda. The Cold War had a functional utility for the superpowers: one reason why it persisted.

Now, one side has called off the game. If we have in mind the historical Cold War, not the ideological construct, then it is not true that the Cold War has ended. Rather, it has perhaps half-ended; Washington remains a player as before.

This point is not concealed. Describing the new Pentagon budget in January 1990, the press reports that "In [Defense Secretary Dick] Cheney's view, which is shared by President Bush, the United States will continue to need a large Navy [and intervention forces generally] to deal with brushfire conflicts and threats to American interests in places like Latin America and Asia." The National Security Strategy report sent to Congress two months later described the Third World as a probable locus of conflict:

> In a new era, we foresee that our military power will remain an essential under-pinning of the global balance, but less prominently and in different ways. We see that the more likely demands for the use of our military forces may not involve the Soviet Union and may be in the Third World, where new capabilities and approaches may be required

as "when President Reagan directed American naval and air forces to return to [Libya] in 1986" to bombard civilian urban targets, guided by the goal of "contributing to an international environment of peace, freedom and progress within which our democracy—and other free nations—can flourish."[31]

Furthermore, "The growing technological sophistication of Third World conflicts will place serious demands on our forces," and may "continue to threaten U.S. interests" even without "the backdrop of superpower competition." For such reasons, we must ensure the means to move forces based in the United States "to reinforce our units forward deployed or to project power into areas where we have no permanent presence," particularly in the Middle East, because of "the free world's reliance on energy supplies from this pivotal region," where the "threats to our interests" that have required direct military engagement "could not be laid at the Kremlin's door. . . . In the future, we expect that non-Soviet threats to these interests will command even greater attention." In reality, the "threat to our interests" had always been indigenous nationalism, a fact sometimes acknowledged—as when the architect of President Carter's Rapid Deployment Force (later Central Command), aimed primarily at the Middle East, testified before Congress in 1980 that its most probable use was not to resist a (highly implausible) Soviet attack, but to deal with indigenous and regional unrest, in particular the "radical nationalism" that has always been a primary concern.[32] Notice that the Bush Administration plans were presented well before Iraq's conquest of Kuwait and the ensuing crisis in August 1990—in fact, at a time when Iraq was still a favored friend.

The National Security Strategy report goes on to emphasize that the
US must be prepared for Low-Intensity Conflict, involving "lower-order
threats like terrorism, subversion, insurgency, and drug trafficking [which]
are menacing the United States, its citizenry, and its interests in new ways.
... Low-intensity conflict involves the struggle of competing principles and
ideologies below the level of conventional war," and our military forces

> must be capable of dealing effectively with the full range of threats, including
> insurgency and terrorism. ... Forces will have to accommodate to the austere
> environment, immature basing structure, and significant ranges often encountered
> in the Third World. ... Training and research and development will be better
> attuned to the needs of low-intensity conflict

—crucially, counterinsurgency in the Third World.

It will also be necessary to strengthen "the defense industrial base," creating
incentives "to invest in new facilities and equipment as well as in research
and development," a matter that "will be especially important in an era
when overall procurements are likely to decline. ... Our goal is to move
beyond containment, to seek the integration of the Soviet Union into the
international system as a constructive partner" in such areas as Central America, which "remains a disruptive factor in the U.S.–Soviet relationship"
and where "We hold the Soviet Union accountable for the behavior of
its clients" in Cuba and Nicaragua, who continue to disturb peace and
order—that is, to disobey US commands.

Military college curricula are changing accordingly. Thus the Naval War
College has announced that its curriculum and war gaming will stress urban
warfare, terrorism, and "low-intensity" crises, using such models as the
invasion of Panama. A new genre of "mid-intensity" conflicts with powerful
Third World enemies also demands special attention, given the continuing
vital need to "project power into other regions and maintain access to
distant markets and resources" (Senator William Cohen, of the Armed
Services Committee).[33]

The same questions are addressed by Marine Corps Commandant General
A.M. Gray. The end of the Cold War will only reorient our security policies,
he advises, but not change them significantly. "In fact, the majority of the
crises we have responded to since the end of World War II have not directly
involved the Soviet Union," a fact that can now not only be conceded—the
Soviet threat having lost its efficacy for domestic population control—but
must be stressed, to ensure that we may act as before when there are "threats
to our interest." The North–South conflict is the major fault line:

The underdeveloped world's growing dissatisfaction over the gap between rich and poor nations will create a fertile breeding ground for insurgencies. These insurgencies have the potential to jeopardize regional stability and our access to vital economic and military resources. This situation will become more critical as our Nation and allies, as well as potential adversaries, become more and more dependent on these strategic resources. If we are to have stability in these regions, maintain access to their resources, protect our citizens abroad, defend our vital installations, and deter conflict, we must maintain within our active force structure a credible military power projection capability with the flexibility to respond to conflict across the spectrum of violence throughout the globe.

Crucially, we must maintain our "unimpeded access" to "developing economic markets throughout the world" and "to the resources needed to support our manufacturing requirements." We therefore need "a credible forcible entry capability," forces that "must truly be expeditionary" and capable of executing a wide variety of missions from counterinsurgency and psychological warfare to the deployment of "multidivision forces." We must also bear in mind the rapidly increasing technological advances in weaponry and their availability to the new regional powers that will be springing up throughout the Third World, so that we must develop military capacities exploiting the far reaches of electronics, genetic engineering and other biotechnologies, and so on, "if our Nation is to maintain military credibility in the next century."[34]

The themes are familiar. Reviewing President Eisenhower's strategic thinking, diplomatic historian Richard Immerman observes that he "took it as an article of faith that America's strength and security depended on its maintaining access to—indeed control of—global markets and resources, particularly in the Third World." Like other rational planners, he assumed that the West was safe from any Soviet attack, and that such fears were "the product of paranoid imagination." But the periphery "was vulnerable to subversion," and the Russians, Eisenhower wrote, "are getting far closer to the [Third World] masses than we are" and are skilled at propaganda and other methods "to appeal directly to the masses."[35] These are common features of the planning record, even more clearly visible than before now that the image of the expansionist and aggressive Soviet Union has lost its credibility.

More simply, the war against the Third World will continue, and the Soviet Union will continue to be branded an aggressor if it gets in the way. Gorbachev is to be induced to proceed with his "New Thinking," which will turn the USSR into a collaborator with US plans for world order, but Washington is to persist in its "Old Thinking." There can, further-more, be no substantial "peace dividend." And since the Third World is reaching such heights of technological sophistication, we will need a high-tech military to deter and contain it. Thankfully, there will still be plenty of business for the electronics industry.

Budget changes must be geared to a capital-intensive military if it is to serve its function for advanced industry. Alternatives to military spending are theoretically possible, but—as has been understood by business from the origins of the Cold War—they tend to have undesirable effects: to interfere with managerial prerogatives, mobilize popular constituencies and thus extend the "crisis of democracy," redistribute income, and so on. The problem is not one of pure economic theory but of power and privilege, and their specific institutional structures. Advocates of conversion will be tilting at windmills unless they confront these fundamental problems.

The same is true of opponents of intervention if they keep to the frame-work of conventional understanding. Thus, it is child's play to demolish the standard justifications: promoting democracy and national security. Some of those who undertake the exercise therefore conclude that Third World intervention "never made sense, even at the height of the Cold War," and surely not now, so that we can call off the murderous wars we are sponsoring in Cambodia, Angola, Afghanistan, and El Salvador, and radically reduce our intervention forces.[36] Carrying the argument a step further, we observe that virtually the entire political class has supported intervention, except when it proves too costly to us. It follows, then, either that stupidity and incompetence have been an entry requirement for political leadership, recognized "expertise," media respectability, and the like; or that the alleged reasons are not the actual ones. Since the former conclusion is hardly credible, we move to the second, thus recognizing that the analysis is not to the point, serving to entrench illusions that we should discard. The actual reasons for intervention, whether persuasive or not in particular cases, have been far from senseless.

Current arguments for intervention forces, as in the National Security Strategy report, reveal that the ideological system is running out of pretexts for the resort to subversion and overt force in international affairs, and military Keynesian measures at home. Defense against the Stalinist hordes no longer sells. The problem of the disappearing pretext was recognized years ago, but the efforts of the 1980s to overcome it—invoking lunatic Arab terrorists or Hispanic narcotraffickers, for example—have too short a half-life to be truly effective. It therefore becomes necessary to acknowledge

COLD WAR: FACT AND FANCY

that the Third World itself is the real enemy. If the primary threat of Communism has been the economic transformation of the Communist powers "in ways that reduce their willingness and ability to complement the industrial economies of the West" (see p. 27), the same is true of "radical nationalism" generally—a fact that has not escaped planners and strategic analysts. The severity of the problem varies from region to region, with the Middle East remaining the primary Third World concern because of its incomparable energy reserves. But, in accord with the thinking of NSC 68, no corner of the world is so small and insignificant that it may be safely overlooked.

3. Before and After

In this context, we may turn to another question raised at the outset: In what ways do the typical events and practices of the Cold War differ from what came before? The bipolar system was new, and gave a different flavor to traditional practices as well as extending their scope. But the similarities undermine still further the credibility of the conventional picture.

On the Soviet side, for half a millennium, the rulers of the Grand Duchy of Moscow had extended their sway over "all the Russias," creating a huge imperial state, though one far more backward than Western Europe and not closing the gap, and by 1914 "becoming a semi-colonial possession of European capital."[37] Hardliners are quick to remind the victims of Gorbymania that "as a great power, Russia frequently deployed its armies into Europe and repeatedly crushed popular uprisings in central Europe," suppressing the Hungarian revolution in 1956 and Czech democracy in 1968 just as "Russian troops bloodily suppressed the Hungarian revolution of 1848–49 and violently put down uprisings in Poland in 1831 and again in 1863–64. ... Soviet troops occupied Berlin in 1945; Russian troops occupied and burnt Berlin in 1760." And indeed, "in pursuit of Russia's interests as a great power, Russian troops appeared many places where as yet Soviet troops have not," including Italy and Switzerland, writes Samuel Huntington.[38] One "cannot assume," he continues, that the Soviets will not "revert to the bad old ways of the past"; inclusion of the Soviet occupation of Berlin in 1945 among these "bad old ways" perhaps reflects the current tendency to lend credence to the Nazi claim to have been defending Western civilization from the Bolshevik menace.

As for the United States, scale aside, changes induced by the Cold War were in large part rhetorical. Since 1917, intervention has been in self-defense against the Soviet threat—including intervention in Russia itself immediately after the Bolshevik revolution and the clandestine support for armies established by Hitler in the Ukraine and Eastern Europe into the 1950s.[39] Before the Bolshevik revolution similar actions were taken, but in fear of other menaces. When Woodrow Wilson invaded Mexico and Hispaniola (Haiti and the Dominican Republic)—where his warriors murdered and destroyed, reestablished virtual slavery, demolished the political system, and placed the countries firmly in the hands of US investors—these actions were in self-defense against the Huns. In earlier years, conquests and interventions were undertaken in defense against Britain, Spain, the "merciless Indian savages" of the Declaration of Independence—in fact, anyone who was in the way.

· Leading thinkers have never found it difficult to identify the culprits. In the early years of the Republic, Reverend Timothy Dwight, president of Yale College and a respected author and exponent of Puritan values, devoted a poem to the savage slaughter of the Pequot Indians. The colonists viewed the Pequot Indians "with generous eye," he wrote, and strove to gain their friendship, but were thwarted by "base Canadian fiends" and thus had no choice but to massacre them, men, women and children. Thomas Jefferson attributed the failure of "the benevolent plan we were pursuing here for the happiness of the aboriginal inhabitants of our vicinities" to the English enemy; "the interested and unprincipled policy of England has defeated all our labors for the salvation of these unfortunate peoples," and "seduced" them "to take up the hatchet against us." It is the English, then, who "oblige us now to pursue them to extermination, or drive them to new seats beyond our reach." The English, not we, were thus responsible for "the confirmed brutalization, if not the extermination of this race in our America . . ." On the same grounds, he urged the conquest of Canada in a letter to John Adams, who agreed, writing: "Another Conquest of Canada will quiet the Indians forever and be as great a Blessing to them as to Us."[40]

The same theory was adopted when General Andrew Jackson rampaged through Florida, virtually annihilating much of its native population and leaving the Spanish province under US control. His murderous Seminole War campaign was defended by John Quincy Adams in a letter to Minister to Spain George Erving that "has long been recognized as one of the most important state papers in the history of American foreign relations" (William Earl Weeks). The document impressed Thomas Jefferson as being "among the ablest I have ever seen, both as to logic and style," a judgement in which modern historians have concurred. So taken was Jefferson with this racist diatribe justifying Jackson's aggression and brutality that he urged wide distribution "to maintain in Europe a correct opinion of our political morality."[41]

The actual motive for the war was expansionism and the "use of Florida as a haven by Indians and American slaves," "outrageous, from the American perspective," Weeks observes. But in this early defense of Manifest Destiny, Indian removal, slavery, violation of treaties, and the use of military force without congressional approval, Adams justified the aggression in the usual terms of self-defense. The fault lay in the machinations of England in Florida, he wrote, first during the war of 1812 when British agents encouraged "all the runaway negroes, all the savage Indians, all the pirates, and all the traitors to their country . . . to join their standards, and wage an exterminating war" against the United States; and later, when "this negro-Indian war against our borders had been rekindled" by these British criminals (two of whom were executed), so that the "peaceful inhabitants" of the United States were "visited with all the horrors of savage war" by "mingled hordes of lawless Indians and negroes." Furthermore, "from the period of our established independence to this day, all the Indian wars with which we have been afflicted have been distinctly traceable to the instigation of English traders or agents." Adams appealed to international law to justify such acts against "an inhuman enemy" as execution of prisoners. Quoting eighteenth-century sources, he observed: "The justification of these principles is found in their salutary efficacy for terror and example."[42]

Like Dean Acheson many years later, Adams recognized that in such enterprises it is a good idea to speak in a manner "clearer than truth"; in Adams's version, "it was better to err on the side of vigor than on the side of weakness." In so doing, he "articulated many of the myths which have been essential to salving the conscience of a righteous-minded nation that expanded first across a continent and then throughout the world," Weeks comments.[43]

When base foreign fiends could not readily be found, the inferiority of those in our path could be invoked. In his annual message of 1851, California Governor Peter Burnett observed "that a war of extermination will continue to be waged between the two races until the Indian race becomes extinct." While we can only anticipate this result with "painful regret, the inevitable destiny of the race is beyond the power and wisdom of man to avert." Mexican lands should be taken over for the good of mankind, Walt Whitman wrote: "What has miserable, inefficient Mexico . . . to do with the great mission of peopling the New World with a noble race?" Our conquests may "take off the shackles that prevent men the even chance of being happy and good." The Mexicans were described by travellers as "an imbecile, pusillanimous, race of men, and unfit to control the destinies of that beautiful country" of California, which by rights belonged to the Anglo-Saxons in the racist fantasies of the nineteenth century—shared, among others, by Charles Darwin, who felt that "There is apparently much truth in the belief that the wonderful progress of the United States, as well as the character of the people, are the results of natural selection."[44]

The truth of the matter, throughout, was that the real enemy has been the indigenous population of the territories from which they were driven or where they were to remain as subjects; and other powers that interfered with our right to treat these undeserving souls in accord with our wishes. The facts have sometimes been recognized, as when Wilson's Secretary of State Robert Lansing explained, with the President's acquiescence that

> In its advocacy of the Monroe Doctrine the United States considers its own interests. The integrity of other American nations is an incident, not an end. While this may seem based on selfishness alone, the author of the Doctrine had no higher or more generous motive in its declaration.

The central problem, Lansing went on, is to exclude European control over "American territory and its institutions through financial as well as other means." Wilson's practice conformed to this principle, for example, by excluding Britain from Central American oil concessions; from the early years of the century, control over oil has been recognized as a lever of great power in world affairs, not to speak of the rich profits that flow. Furthermore, the great apostle of self-determination broke no new ground.[45]

The major change after World War II was that the United States was in a position to apply these principles over a far broader range; and, of course, the Evil Empire from which it had to defend itself was no longer the Huns or the British.

To the people of the Third World, the threat posed to US security by the agents of dread foreign enemies seems difficult to appreciate. When the Kennedy Administration sought to organize collective action against Cuba in 1961, a Mexican diplomat commented: "If we publicly declare that Cuba is a threat to our security, forty million Mexicans will die laughing."[46] Sophisticated Westerners, however, respond with appropriate sobriety and concern.

With the Cold War officially ended, its practices continue as before, but in self-defense against other enemies. When the Bush Administration invaded Panama in December 1989, it was quite impossible to conjure up the Evil Empire. "Operation Just Cause" was therefore launched to defend us from narcotraffickers seeking to destroy us, among other pretexts.[47]

These continuities again reveal that the conventional understanding is more a rhetorical guise than a serious thesis.

4. Bolsheviks and Moderates

Despite the continuities, 1917 marked a critical break for policy. Earlier intervention had a somewhat *ad hoc* and opportunistic character, designed for territorial expansion or commercial advantage, or for deflecting and displacing European rivals. But the World War brought about entirely new conditions and, with them, a systematic and coherent ideological framework for intervention worldwide.

As Europe proceeded to self-destruct, the United States became for the first time a global power with decisive influence. And the Bolshevik revolution provided it with a global enemy—not because of Russian power, which was insignificant, but because of the ideological challenge "to the very survival of the capitalist order" (Gaddis). The response to a challenge of this scale and import was not in doubt. It was clearly formulated by Senator Warren Harding, soon to be elected President: "Bolshevism is a menace that must be destroyed . . . the Bolshevist beast [must be] slain."[48]

With the very survival of the existing system of privilege and domination at stake, any challenge to it, anywhere, must be regarded with utmost seriousness. Anyone who threatens the reigning order should preferably be depicted as an appendage of the beast, a Communist in disguise or a dupe of Bolshevism. And those who confront the beast or its spreading tentacles become "moderates," a label that extends to a wide range of tyrants and mass murderers, as long as they do their job. These moderates vary in their tactical choices. Some prefer to experiment with reforms to drive the beast away, turning to harsher measures if these fail. Others disdain the reformist detour and choose to aim for the heart at once. At home, the response to the challenge has ranged from harsh repression of dissidence and labor (Wilson's Red Scare and its regular successors) to a variety of more subtle means. Abroad, tactics are adapted to the specific character of the challenge, but on the principle that the beast must be slain. This general ideological framework, and the sociopolitical realities that it reflects, gave intervention a very different cast from earlier years.

The new framework was elaborated first in reaction to postwar developments in Italy, at the periphery of the Western industrial order. The pattern then established was reapplied regularly elsewhere until today. It thus deserves some scrutiny.

With rising labor militancy, Italy posed "the obvious danger of social revolution and disorganization," a high-level inquiry of the Wilson Administration determined in December 1917. "If we are not careful we will have a second Russia on our hands," a State Department official noted privately, adding: "The Italians are like children" and "must be [led] and assisted more than almost any other nation." Mussolini's Blackshirts solved the problem by violence. They carried out "a fine young revolution," the American Ambassador observed approvingly, referring to Mussolini's March on Rome in October 1922, which brought Italian democracy to an end. Fascist goons effectively ended labor agitation with government help, and the democratic deviation was terminated. The United States watched with approval. The Fascists are "perhaps the most potent factor in the suppression of Bolshevism in Italy" and have much improved the situation generally, the Embassy reported to Washington, while voicing some residual anxiety about the "enthusiastic and violent young men" who have brought about these salutary developments. The Embassy continued to report the appeal of Fascism to "all patriotic Italians," simple-minded folk who "hunger for strong leadership and enjoy . . . being dramatically governed."[49]

As Fascist darkness settled over Italy, financial support from the US government and business climbed rapidly. Italy was offered by far the best postwar debt settlement of any country, and US investment there grew far faster than in any other country as the Fascist regime established itself, eliminating labor unrest and other democratic disorders.[50]

US labor leaders viewed these developments with a generally favorable eye. The *American Federationist*, edited by AFL president Samuel Gompers, welcomed Fascism as a bulwark against Communism and a movement "capable of decisive action on a national scale," which was "rapidly reconstructing a nation of collaborating units of usefulness," Mussolini's Fascist corporations, which subordinated labor to capital and the state. The AFL journal found these corporations "a welcome replacement for the old, Bolshevik-infected industrial unions," Ronald Filippelli comments. Mussolini's activism was also attractive. "However repugnant . . . the idea of dictatorship and the man on horseback," the journal continued, "American trade unionists will at least find it possible to have some sympathy with the policies of a man whose dominating purpose is to get something done; to do rather than theorize; to build a working, producing civilization instead of a disorganized, theorizing aggregation of conflicting groups" in a society riven by class conflict.[51] Mussolini got the trains to run on time, as the standard cliché had it. The suppression of labor and democratic institutions was not too great a price to pay for this achievement, from the AFL perspective.

Mussolini was portrayed as a "moderate" with enormous popular appeal who had brought efficient administration and prosperity, slaying the beast and opening the doors to profitable investment and trade. Reflecting common attitudes in the business community, J.P. Morgan partner Thomas Lamont described himself as "something like a missionary" for Italian Fascism, expressing his admiration for Il Duce, "a very upstanding chap" who had "done a great job in Italy," and for the "sound ideas" that guided him in governing the country. Otto Kahn of Kuhn, Loeb, and Co. praised the Fascists further for ending "parliamentary wrangling and wasteful impotent bureaucracy" and bringing "a spirit of order, discipline, hard work, patriotic devotion and faith" under "the clear sighted and masterful guidance of that remarkable man, Benito Mussolini." Judge Elbert Gary of United Steel asked whether "we, too, need a man like Mussolini." The US Embassy was particularly impressed that "there has not been a single strike in the whole of Italy" since the Fascist takeover.[52]

The Embassy was well aware of Mussolini's totalitarian measures. Fascism had "effectively stifled hostile elements in restricting the right of free assembly, in abolishing freedom of the press and in having at its command a large military organization," the Embassy reported in a message of February 1925, after a major Fascist crackdown. But Mussolini remained a "moderate," manfully confronting the fearsome Bolsheviks while fending off the extremist fringe on the right. His qualifications as a moderate were implicit in the judgement expressed by Ambassador Henry Fletcher: the choice in Italy is "between Mussolini and Fascism and Giolitti and Socialism"—Giolitti being the liberal Prime Minister who had collaborated with Mussolini in the repression of labor but now found himself a target as well. The population preferred "peace and prosperity" under Fascism to "free speech, loose administration ... [and] the danger and disorganization of Bolshevism," Fletcher reported. Secretary of State Frank Kellogg joined him in labelling all opposition groups "communists, socialists, and anarchists." The chief of the State Department Western European Division, William Castle, recognized in 1926 that "the methods of the Duce are not by any means American methods," but "methods which would certainly not appeal to this country might easily appeal to a people so differently constituted as are the Italians." Il Duce and his effective methods won wide respect in the political and intellectual communities, including progressive opinion.[53]

As a Senator in 1919, Kellogg had bitterly condemned the domestic "nihilists" and "anarchists" who "try to incite the dissatisfied elements of this country to a class warfare." As Secretary of State he barred Communists from entry to the country because "this is the only way to treat these revolutionists," and lumped LaFollette's progressivism together with Socialism, Communism, and the IWW. Kellogg demanded further that the Russians "must cease their propaganda in the United States" as a condition for recognition.[54] This was an entirely natural doctrine, given the ideological nature of the threat "to the very survival of the capitalist order," and a demand that was to be reiterated regularly in one or another form in later years.

As the effects of the Great Depression hit Europe, leading to social and political unrest, Fascist Italy received mounting praise as a bastion of order and stability, free of class struggle and challenges from labor and the left. "The wops are unwopping themselves," *Fortune* magazine wrote with awe in a special issue devoted to Fascist Italy in 1934. Others agreed. State Department roving Ambassador Norman Davis praised Italy's successes in remarks before the Council on Foreign Relations in 1933, speaking after the Italian Ambassador had drawn applause from his distinguished audience for his description of how Italy had put its "own house in order. ... A class war was put down"—by means that were apparently regarded as appropriate. Roosevelt's Ambassador to Italy, Breckenridge Long, was also full of enthusiasm for the "new experiment in government" under Fascism, which "works most successfully in Italy." After World War II, Henry Stimson (Secretary of State under Hoover, Secretary of War under Roosevelt) recalled that he and Hoover had found Mussolini to be "a sound and useful leader." When Marine General Smedley Butler made some critical comments about Mussolini in 1931, Stimson had brought court-martial proceedings against him, making no effort to ascertain the facts. When Fascists won 99 percent of the vote in the March 1934 election, the State Department concluded that the results "demonstrate incontestably the popularity of the Fascist regime." Roosevelt shared many of these positive views of "that admirable Italian gentleman," as he termed Mussolini in 1933.[55]

Mussolini's invasion of Ethiopia was condemned, but did not seriously harm US relations with Fascist Italy. The essential reason was given by

Ambassador Long: if Mussolini fell and the country was left "without guidance, ... the violent manifestations of Bolshevism would be apparent in the industrial centers and in the agricultural regions where private ownership still pertains." A 1937 State Department report concluded that "Fascism is becoming the soul of Italy," having "brought order out of chaos, discipline out of license, and solvency out of bankruptcy." To "accomplish so much in a short time severe measures have been necessary," the report continued. Furthermore, like Germany under Hitler, Italy was standing in the way of Russian influence in Spain during the Civil War. Washington had adopted a form of "neutrality" that amounted to a tilt towards Spanish Fascism against the liberal democratic republic, while joining in the uniform hostility of the West and Stalin to the popular libertarian revolution.[56]

In the major academic study of the topic, David Schmitz points out that the model developed for Italy, with "moderate" Fascists holding the middle ground between the dreaded left- and right-wing extremists, was applied to Nazism as well. Here, Hitler was chosen as the representative of the moderates who promised "social order, anti-Bolshevik laws, and protection for foreign capital," Schmitz observes. The American chargé d'affaires in Berlin wrote to Washington in 1933 that the hope for Germany lay in "the more moderate section of the [Nazi] party, headed by Hitler himself . . . which appeal[s] to all civilized and reasonable people," and seems to have "the upper hand" over the violent fringe. In 1937, the State Department saw fascism as compatible with US economic interests. A report of the European Division explained its rise as the natural reaction of "the rich and middle classes, in self-defense" when the "dissatisfied masses, with the example of the Russian revolution before them, swing to the left." Fascism therefore "must succeed or the masses, this time reinforced by the disillusioned middle classes, will again turn to the left." Not until European Fascism attacked US interests directly did it become an avowed enemy. The reaction to Japanese Fascism was much the same.[57]

Though the Axis powers became enemies during World War II, the general framework of thinking never really changed. As the United States liberated southern Italy in 1943, it followed Churchill's advice that the primary consideration must be to prevent "chaos, bolshevization or civil war. ... There is nothing between the King and the patriots who have rallied round him and rampant Bolshevism," Churchill warned. The US supported the King, who had collaborated fully with the Fascist regime, and the right-wing dictatorship of Field-Marshal Badoglio, a Fascist war hero, just as Roosevelt had installed the French Fascist Admiral Darlan in

North Africa in 1942, in the first area liberated from Nazi control. Henry Stimson and the State Department sought to bring the Fascist leader Dino Grandi to power, describing this high official of the Mussolini dictatorship from its first years as a "moderate" among the Blackshirts who was "driven into [Fascism] by the excesses of the Communists"; a reconstruction of history along similar lines is familiar in contemporary right-wing and neo-Nazi circles. In Italy, as throughout the world, Fascists and collaborators were restored to power and influence by the Allied liberators. The general goal was to destroy the anti-Fascist resistance, undermine the popular forces on which it was based, and reconstruct the traditional conservative order, now under US domination.[58]

The distinction between the "moderates" led by Mussolini and the "extremists" he sought to control came "to dominate all State Department thinking on Fascism and helped to provide the ideological grounds for the continuous support of Mussolini throughout the interwar years," Schmitz comments. It was taken as the model for support of Hitler as the moderate leader of the Nazis, and "was to become a familiar and almost automatic pattern of behavior by American foreign policymakers in the name of anti-communism in the twentieth century."[59]

The pattern is particularly evident in Latin America, the traditional domain of US intervention, which took a new form, adopting the new analytical framework, immediately after World War I. Until that time, US intervention had been portrayed as a defensive reaction against European enemies: primarily Britain, France, and Germany. But with US power in the ascendant, these were less plausible antagonists, and as guardian of the capitalist order, the United States turned to the ideological challenge posed to its "very survival" by the Bolshevik revolution in 1917. The Mexican revolution, with its steps towards economic nationalism, raised the specter in a sharp form. Particularly ominous was Article 27 of the Mexican Constitution, which became a major bone of contention in 1917 because of its call for state participation in and direction of the economy (particularly development of natural resources) and for subordination of private property to the general welfare. The analogy to Bolshevism was quickly drawn in the standard dual way: these moves were a direct threat to US investors and might also encourage others, including domestic elements, to think along similar lines (the domino effect, in its realistic variant). US Ambassador to Mexico Henry Fletcher warned in 1918 that Mexico's goal was "to replace the Monroe Doctrine" so that "the hegemony of the United States on this Continent is to pass away"; Fletcher was soon to move to Italy where, as we have seen, he became a spokesman for Mussolini's Fascism as a barrier to "Bolshe-vism" (including Socialism and liberalism). Article 27, Fletcher wrote to President Wilson in 1919, would practically terminate foreign investment in Mexico.[60]

A few years later, Secretary of State Frank Kellogg declared that its pro-grams of economic nationalism had placed Mexico "on trial before the world" and "created a serious situation" for US interests. The State Depart-ment by then regarded Mexico as hardly more than an outpost of Bolshe-vism.[61]

Fletcher's warning to Wilson reflected the contempt for "miserable, in-efficient Mexico" expressed by Walt Whitman and others. The Mexicans would not be "able to keep themselves going" without foreign investment, he believed, because "they have not the genius of industrial development, nor have they had the training required." A few years later, Ambassador James Sheffield wrote of "the futility of attempting to treat with a Latin-Indian mind, filled with hatred of the United States and thirsty for vengeance, on the same basis that our government would treat with a civilized and orderly government in Europe." The Mexicans have "an Indian, not Latin, hatred of all peoples not on the reservation. There is very little white blood in the cabinet—that is it is very thin." Other officials spoke of the "low mental capacity" which renders the Mexicans—like the Italians—"utterly unfitted for self-government" and "easily dominated" by the "half-breeds" who control the government. Venezuelans too were regarded as "indolent" and suffering from "political immaturity" and "racial inferiority," along with other Latin Americans. In 1927 Elihu Root, whose long career as a statesman and peace movement leader had earned him the Nobel Prize, questioned US recognition of the independence of Latin American countries because Latin Americans are "admittedly like children and unable to maintain the obligations which go with independence." The Mexican attempt at democracy was as futile as the granting of voting rights to Blacks after the Civil War, Root commented: "a dismal step, a terrible mistake, with most serious evils following." Forty years later, his distinguished successor Dean Acheson expressed similar thoughts to the White racists of southern Africa. Root proposed to Mexico the example of Fascist Italy, enjoying a "revival of prosperity, contentment and happiness under a dictator." A US diplomat in Venezuela argued that "the Indian peon" should be given "a simple and paternalistic form of government," not formal democracy. He praised the Venezuelan dictator Juan Vicente Gómez, who, with the example of Mexico before him, had "wisely decided that a benevolent despotism was preferable to an anarchical democracy."[62]

Some found the natives less hopeless. Banker Thomas Lamont felt that "ignorant as [the Mexicans] are, unwise as they are, untrusty as they are, nevertheless, if you once take time and patience, one can handle them." Similar sentiments were privately expressed in later years as well. Secretary of State John Foster Dulles advised President Eisenhower that it should be possible to bring Latin Americans to accept US plans for their future as a source of raw materials and profits for US corporations: "you have to pat them a little bit and make them think that you are fond of them." Following the same reasoning, Ambassador to Costa Rica Robert Woodward recommended to Washington that the United Fruit Company be induced to introduce "a few relatively simple and superficial human-interest frills for the workers that may have a large psychological effect," thus eliminating problems with the peons.[63]

Given the human material with which he has to work, one can easily appreciate the trials of "the benevolent but clearly egocentric professor, dispensing emancipation through knowledge of both righteousness and the right way to the deprived students of the world" (see p. 17).

Impressed by the successful fascist model, the United States turned to dictators and tyrants to fend off the threat of social change and economic nationalism, now interpreted in the context of the worldwide Bolshevik challenge to the survival of the capitalist order. Venezuela was a striking example. The brutal despot General Gómez enjoyed reasonably good relations with the United States until the Wilson Administration, which opposed his tyranny, terror and corruption and his "preference for Germany in the present War for the Rights of Humanity," as the American Minister to Venezuela put it in 1917. But a few years later, attitudes changed (though Gómez's practices did not). Untainted by the economic nationalism and radicalism that were threatening US interests elsewhere in Latin America, the despot offered his country freely for foreign exploitation. The usual mix of racist contempt and antagonism to independent nationalism sufficed for him to be depicted as a moderate. He had saved the country from "a conflict between the privileged classes and the common people" and kept it free from "communism, or some other form of extreme radicalism," the US chargé informed the State Department in 1929. "Until the Venezuelan people could be trusted to make the right decisions concerning their political and economic direction," Michael Krenn writes, "and that time was deemed to be in the very distant future—it was best for all concerned that they be kept safe from democracy."[64]

As example after example attests, economic nationalism elicits US hostility. Where possible, the culprit is assigned to the Bolshevik conspiracy to destroy Western civilization. In any event, he must be slain. It is as close to a historical law as a complex world allows.

The essential point was captured in John F. Kennedy's celebrated remark that while we would prefer decent democratic regimes, if the choice is between a Trujillo and a Castro, we will choose the Trujillo. It is necessary only to add three points: (1) the concept of "a Castro" is very broad, extending to anyone who raises problems for the "rich men dwelling at peace within their habitations," who are to rule the world according to Churchill's aphorism, while enjoying the benefits of its human and material resources; (2) the chosen "Trujillo," however monstrous, will be a "moderate" as long as he fulfills his function; (3) the "Trujillo" will make a quick transition from favored friend to another beast to be destroyed if he shows the bad judgement of stepping on our toes. This story has been reenacted time and time again, until today. Saddam Hussein is only the most recent example.

The post–World War I pattern does constitute a departure from US intervention in an earlier period of less self-consciousness and global power. There is every reason to expect that pattern to persist, with whatever adjustments are required, after the Bolshevik challenge has lost its last shreds of credibility.

5. The Foundations of Policy

The basis for US policy in the Cold War era is outlined with considerable clarity in the internal record of planning.[65] With unprecedented economic and military preeminence, the US prepared to become the first truly global power. Not surprisingly, corporate and state managers hoped to use this power to design a world order that would serve the interests they represented.

During the war, US planners developed the concept of a "Grand Area," a region understood to be "strategically necessary for world control," subordinated to the needs of the American economy. In its early stages, the Grand Area was conceived as a US-led non-German bloc. It was to incorporate the Western hemisphere, the Far East, and the former British empire, which was to be dismantled along with other regional systems and incorporated under US control. Meanwhile the US extended its own regional systems in Latin America and the Pacific on the principle, expressed by Abe Fortas in internal discussion, that these steps were justified "as part of our obligation

to the security of the world ... what was good for us was good for the
world." British officials were unimpressed, denouncing "the economic
imperialism of American business interests, which is quite active under the
cloak of a benevolent and avuncular internationalism," and is "attempting
to elbow us out." As it became clear that Germany would be defeated,
the Grand Area concept was extended to include the Eurasian landmass
as well, as far as possible. These general plans were applied to particular
regions with much consistency.

With regard to the Soviet Union, the doves were reconciled to a form
of "containment" in which it would control most of the areas occupied
by the Red Army in the war against Hitler. The hawks had broader aspirations, as expressed in the rollback strategy of NSC 68. US policy towards
the Soviet Union has fluctuated between these positions over the years,
reflecting in part the problem of controlling the far-flung domains
"defended" by US power, in part the need for a credible enemy to ensure
that the public remains willing to support intervention and provide a subsidy
to advanced industry through the military system.

The Grand Area was to have a definite structure. The industrial societies
were to be reconstituted with much of the traditional order restored, but
within the overarching framework of US power. They were to be organized
under their "natural leaders," Germany and Japan. Early moves towards
democratization under the military occupation caused deep concern in
Washington and the business community. They were reversed by the late
1940s, with firm steps to weaken the labor movement and ensure the dominance of the traditional business sectors, linked to US capital. Britain was
later to undergo a similar process, as did the United States itself.[66]

Moves towards a European economic community, it was assumed, would
improve economic performance, reconcile all social sectors to business dominance, and create markets and investment opportunities for US corporations.
Japan was to become a regional leader within a US-dominated global system.
The thought that Japan might become a serious competitor was then too
exotic to be considered: as late as the 1960s, the Kennedy Administration
was still concerned with finding means to ensure Japan's viability. This
was finally established by the Vietnam War, which was costly to the United
States but highly beneficial to the Japanese economy, as the Korean War
had been.

There are some surprising illusions about these matters. Thus, Alan Tonelson, then editor of *Foreign Policy*, refers to the US effort to build up "industrial
centers in Western Europe and Japan in the stated hope that they would

soon rival the United States." There was neither such a hope nor such an expectation. With regard to Japan, for example, Army Undersecretary William Draper, the former vice-president of Dillon, Read & Co. who played a major role in efforts to revive the German and Japanese economies in such a way as to ensure the dominance of the business classes, "considered it doubtful that Japan would ever sell enough to the United States to earn the dollars needed to pay for American raw materials." The illusions about US hopes are on a par with the belief that the United States (or anyone else) has gone to war for "the defense of freedom," disseminated by James Reston and other ideologues.[67]

By 1947, it was perceived that European recovery was foundering and that large-scale US initiatives were required for it to proceed along the desired lines. The first major policy initiative to this end was the Marshall Plan. In his comprehensive study of this program, Michael Hogan outlines its primary motivation as the encouragement of a European economic federation much like the United States, with over $2 billion annually in US aid in the early years "to avert 'economic, social and political' chaos in Europe, contain Communism (meaning not Soviet intervention but the success of the indigenous Communist parties), prevent the collapse of America's export trade, and achieve the goal of multilateralism." Such an economic stimulus was required "to protect individual initiative and private enterprise both on the Continent and in the United States." The alternative would be "experiments with socialist enterprise and government controls," which would "jeopardize private enterprise" in the United States as well. A major concern was the "dollar gap," which prevented Europe from purchasing US manufactured goods, with grave implications for the domestic economy.[68]

The understanding that reconstruction of European (and Japanese) capitalism was essential to the health of the US economic order recapitulated the thinking of the Harding Administration after World War I. Secretary of Commerce Herbert Hoover, Secretary of State Charles Evans Hughes, and other influential planners took it for granted that European economic recovery was essential for the expansion of American exports. "The prosperity of the United States," Hughes declared in 1921, "largely depends upon economic settlements which may be made in Europe"—which required, of course, that the Bolshevist beast be slain, as the President had proclaimed.[69]

"From a strategic and geopolitical viewpoint," diplomatic historian Melvyn Leffler observes, "the impact of the Marshall Plan stretched beyond Europe." Overcoming the dollar gap, "which had originally prompted the

Marshall Plan," required a restoration of the triangular trade patterns whereby Europe earned dollars through US purchase of raw materials from its colonies. Hence European (and Japanese) access to Third World markets and raw materials was an essential component of the general strategic planning, and a necessary condition for fulfillment of the general purposes of the Marshall Plan: to "benefit the American economy," to "redress the European balance of power" in favor of US allies (state and class), and to "enhance American national security," where "national security" is understood as "control of raw materials, industrial infrastructure, skilled manpower, and military bases." The "strategic dimensions of the Marshall Plan," Leffler continues, thus required that "revolutionary nationalism had to be thwarted outside Europe, just as the fight against indigenous communism had to be sustained inside Europe." This was a difficult problem because of the prestige of the anti-Fascist resistance, often with a strong Communist element, and the discrediting of the traditional US allies in the business classes because of their association with fascism. Despite the "rhetorical commitment to self-determination," US policy demanded that the former colonies retain their dependent role; the same might be said about the commitment to democracy, which, if more than rhetoric, would have meant that popular forces to which the US was opposed—Communists, radical democrats, labor, and so on—be permitted to play more than a token role in political and social life. Marshall Plan aid was used to coerce political choices, notably in Italy in 1948, and "to force Europe to soft-pedal welfare programs, limit wages, control inflation, and create an environment conducive for capital investment—part of it financed out of labor's pocket" (Thomas McCormick).[70]

From an early stage in the Cold War, and for deep-seated reasons, the United States was set on a course against self-determination and democracy, rhetorical commitments aside. That these commitments were indeed rhetorical was acknowledged by the more cynical and intelligent planners. Dean Acheson, for example, noted that "if our present policy is to have any hope of success in Formosa [Taiwan], we must carefully conceal our wish to separate the island from mainland control," and if we intervene militarily, we should do so under a UN guise "and with the proclaimed intention of satisfying the legitimate demands of the indigenous Formosans for self-determination."[71]

William Borden observes in an important study that "few dollars changed hands internationally under the aid programs; the dollars went to American producers, and the goods were sold to the European public" in local currencies. He argues further that the failure of the aid program to overcome the dollar gap and the unwillingness of Congress to provide additional funds "led Secretary of State Acheson and his aide, Paul Nitze, to replace 'international Keynesian stimulation' of the world economy with 'international military Keynesian stimulation of the world economy'": the basic thinking behind NSC 68. Segments of the business community considered it "obvious that foreign economies as well as our own are now mainly dependent on the scope of continued arms spending in this country" (*Magazine of Wall Street*, 1951). US military expenditures provided a substantial stimulus to European industrial production, and purchase of strategic raw materials from European colonies so reduced the dollar gap that Marshall Plan aid to Britain was suspended in 1950, though longer-term effects were mixed, Hogan argues.[72] In the case of Japan, US military expenditures, particularly for the Korean War, were the primary factor in its postwar industrial recovery. South Korea benefited in a similar way from the Vietnam War, as did other US allies.

The role of the Third World within the Grand Area structure was to serve the needs of the industrial societies. In Latin America, as elsewhere, "the protection of our resources" must be a major concern, George Kennan explained. Since the main threat to our interests is indigenous, we must realize, he continued, that "the final answer might be an unpleasant one"— namely, "police repression by the local government." "Harsh government measures of repression" should cause us no qualms as long as "the results are on balance favorable to our purposes." In general, "it is better to have a strong regime in power than a liberal government if it is indulgent and relaxed and penetrated by Communists."[73] The term "Communist" is used in US discourse in a technical sense, referring to labor leaders, peasant organizers, priests organizing self-help groups, and others with the wrong priorities.

The right priorities are outlined in the highest-level Top Secret planning documents.[74] The major threat to US interests is posed by "nationalistic regimes" that are responsive to popular pressures for "immediate improvement in the low living standards of the masses" and diversification of the economies. This tendency conflicts not only with the need to "protect our resources," but also with our concern to encourage "a climate conducive to private investment" and "in the case of foreign capital to repatriate a reasonable return." The Kennedy Administration identified the roots of US interests in Latin America as in part military (the Panama Canal, strategic raw materials, and so on), but perhaps still more "the economic root whose central fiber is the $9 billion of private U.S. investment in the area" and extensive trade relations. The need "to protect and promote American investment and trade" is threatened by nationalism—that is, efforts to follow an independent course. The preference is for agroexport models serving the interests of US-based corporations (agribusiness, pesticide and fertilizer producers, and so on) and in later years, a range of such useful services as cheap labor for assembly plants.

The threat of nationalism is recognized in the public record as well. Thus, after the successful CIA-backed coup that overthrew the parliamentary regime of the conservative nationalist Mossadegh in Iran, restoring the Shah and leaving US oil companies with 40 percent of the formerly British concession, the *New York Times* commented editorially that all of this was "good news indeed"; however costly "to all concerned" (primarily Iranians), "the affair may yet be proved worthwhile if lessons are learned from it." The primary lesson is then spelled out, mincing no words:

> Underdeveloped countries with rich resources now have an object lesson in the heavy cost that must be paid by one of their number which goes berserk with fanatical nationalism. It is perhaps too much to hope that Iran's experience will prevent the rise of Mossadeghs in other countries, but that experience may at least strengthen the hands of more reasonable and more far-seeing leaders,

who will have a clear-eyed understanding of our overriding priorities.[75]

It was also recognized that the plans for the targeted countries would be unpopular there, but for their populations, no subtle measures of control are necessary. Under the cover of US government aid programs (USAID), "public safety missions" trained local police forces. The reasoning, as outlined by the State Department, is that the police "first detect discontent among people" and "should serve as one of the major means by which the government assures itself of acceptance by the majority." An effective police force can often abort unwanted developments that might otherwise require "major surgery" to "redress these threats." But police operations may not suffice. Accordingly, US planners stressed the need to gain control over the Latin American military, described as "the least anti-American of any political group." Their task, the Kennedy "action intellectuals" explained, was "to remove government leaders from office whenever, in the judgment of the military, the conduct of these leaders was injurious to the welfare of the nation"—an obligation that they should be equipped to carry out once US training has afforded them "the understanding of, and orientation toward, U.S. objectives."

Converting the mission of the military from "hemispheric defense" to "internal security," the Kennedy Administration and its successors were able to overcome the problem of nationalism (or "ultranationalism," as it is sometimes termed in the internal planning record) by establishing and backing National Security States on a neo-Nazi model, with consequences that are well known. The purpose—as explained by Lars Schoultz, the foremost US academic specialist on human rights in Latin America—was "to destroy permanently a perceived threat to the existing structure of socioeconomic privilege by eliminating the political participation of the numerical majority . . .," the "popular classes."[76] US support for these regimes follows essentially the model of the 1920s and European fascism, already discussed.

Note that this is a harsher variant of the policies designed for the industrial societies, motivated by the same world-view and social and political ideals. The harsher measures deemed appropriate for the Third World also helped to overcome the concerns expressed in the internal record over the excessive liberalism of Latin American governments, the protection of rights afforded by their legal systems, and the free flow of ideas, which undercut US efforts at indoctrination and ideological control. These stand alongside other recurrent problems, such as the "low level of intellectualism" in Guatemala deplored by the CIA in 1965, illustrated by the fact that "liberal groups . . . are overresponsive to 'Yankee imperialist' themes," perhaps because of "the long-term political and economic influence of US fruit companies in the country as well as by the US role in the Castillo Armas liberation"—the "liberation" by a CIA-backed coup that overthrew the popular democratic government and reinstated the traditional murderous rule of the military and oligarchy. Where the police and military cannot be controlled directly, as in post-Somoza Nicaragua or Panama, it is necessary to overthrow the government, install a more compliant regime, and restore a "worthy army" in the style of Somoza's National Guard, long a US favorite.[77]

These policies are givens; their basic thrust is subject to no challenge and no debate. It would be misleading to say that there is near unanimity on these matters in Congress, the media, and the intellectual community. More accurately, the basic doctrines are out of sight, out of mind, like the air we breathe, beyond the possibility of discussion.

The general framework was adapted for particular regions. Thus, Southeast Asia was to "fulfill its major function as a source of raw materials and a market for Japan and Western Europe," in the words of George Kennan's State Department Policy Planning Staff in 1949.[78] This reasoning led directly to US intervention in Indochina, at first in support of French colonialism, later alone. An independent Vietnam, it was feared, might spread the "virus" of nationalism throughout Southeast Asia, leading Japan to accommodate to a mainland Communist bloc and thus to become the industrial heartland of a "New Order" from which the US might be excluded; the Pacific War had been fought in large measure to prevent such an outcome. Japan was regarded as the "superdomino," in the appropriate phrase of Asia historian John Dower. To overcome the threat posed by Vietnamese nationalism, it was necessary to destroy the virus and inoculate the region against the disease. This result was achieved. Indochina was successfully destroyed, while the US supported killers, torturers, and tyrants in Indonesia, Thailand, the Philippines and South Korea, providing the crucial support when needed for slaughter on a massive scale, while the media, and respectable people generally, nodded in approval or chose to look the other way.

In Latin America, similar principles were applied with fair success. This region too was to fulfill its function as a source of raw materials and a market. During and after World War II, the traditional rivals of the United States in Latin America, Britain and France were largely displaced, on Henry Stimson's principle that Latin America is "our little region over here which never has bothered anybody."[79] While "stability" of the sort conducive to US elite interests has not been completely attained, nevertheless the threat of independent development was largely aborted—perhaps for ever in the Central America–Caribbean region, where US influence has been overwhelming.

Africa was to be "exploited" for the reconstruction of Europe, Kennan explained in a major State Department study on the international order. He added that the opportunity to exploit Africa should provide a psychological lift for the European powers, affording them "that tangible objective for which everyone has been rather unsuccessfully groping. . . ."[80] History might have suggested a different project: that Africa should "exploit" Europe to enable it to reconstruct from centuries of devastation at the hands of European conquerors, perhaps also improving its psychological state through this process. Needless to say, nothing of the sort was remotely thinkable, and the actual proposals have received little if any notice, apparently being regarded as uncontroversial.

In discussion of African policy particularly, the element of racism cannot be discounted. Dean Acheson warned the former Prime Minister of the White government of Rhodesia in 1971 to beware of the "American public," who "decide that the only correct decision of any issue must be one which favors the colored point of view." Echoing Nobel laureate Elihu Root, he urged that Rhodesia not "get led down the garden path by any of our constitutional clichés—equal protection of the laws, etc.—which have caused us so much trouble . . ." He was particularly disturbed by the Supreme Court's use of "vague constitutional provisions" which "hastened racial equality and have invaded the political field by the one-man-one-vote doctrine," which made "Negroes . . . impatient for still more rapid progress and led to the newly popular techniques of demonstration and violence" (September 1968). The "pall of racism . . . hovering over" African affairs under the Nixon Administration, "and over the most basic public issues foreign and domestic," has been discussed by State Department official Roger Morris, including Nixon's request to Kissinger to ensure that his first presidential message to Congress on foreign policy have "something in it for the jigs" (eliciting "the usual respectful 'Yes'"); Kissinger's disbelief that the Ibos, "more gifted and accomplished" than other Nigerians, could also be "more Negroid"; and Alexander Haig's "quietly pretend[ing] to beat drums on the table as African affairs were brought up at NSC staff meetings."[81]

In the Middle East, the major concern was (and remains) the incomparable energy reserves of the region, primarily in the Arabian peninsula. These were to be incorporated within the US-dominated system. As in Latin America, it was necessary to displace traditional French and British interests and to establish US control over what the State Department described as "a stupendous source of strategic power, and one of the greatest material prizes in world history, . . . probably the richest economic prize in the world in the field of foreign investment." Later, President Eisenhower described the Middle East as the most "strategically important area in the world."[82]

After the war, US corporations gained the leading role in Middle East oil production while dominating the Western hemisphere, which remained the major producer until 1968. The United States did not then need Middle East oil for itself. Rather, the goal was to dominate the world system, ensuring that others would not strike an independent course. Despite the general contempt for the Japanese and disparagement of their prospects, some foresaw problems even here. George Kennan proposed in 1949 that US control over Japanese oil imports would help to provide "veto power" over Japan's military and industrial policies. This advice was followed. Japan was helped to industrialize, but the US maintained control over its energy supplies and oil-refining facilities. As late as 1973, "only 10 per cent of Japan's oil supply was developed by Japanese companies," Shigeko Fukai observes. By now, Japan's diversification of energy sources and conservation measures have reduced the power of the "veto" considerably, but it is still a factor not without weight.[83]

It is, furthermore, misleading simply to assert that the US has sought to keep oil cheap, though that has generally been true. Oil prices declined (relative to other commodities) from the 1940s until the sharp rise of the early 1970s brought them back into line. This was a major boon to the Western industrial powers, though extremely harmful to the long-term interests of the Arab world; and reduction in the real cost of oil was also of critical importance for the Reaganite veneer of prosperity. But cheap oil is a policy instrument, not an end in itself. There is good reason to believe that in the early 1970s the US was by no means averse to the increase in the price of oil, harmful to its industrial rivals but beneficial to its own energy corporations and exporters. Control over energy is a lever for global dominance; the actual price and production levels gain significance within this context, and the economic effects of fluctuations are not a straightforward matter.[84]

US interest in the Philippines derives in part from similar concerns. US bases there form part of the military system surrounding the Middle East region from the Indian Ocean to Israel, Turkey, Portugal and beyond, designed to ensure that there will be no threat to control over its resources by the United States and dependable local elites. The United States is a global power, and plans accordingly.

Subsequent developments in the Middle East keep to the pattern just outlined, including the deepening relations with Israel as a "strategic asset" and mercenary state; the US rejection of a broad international consensus on a political settlement of the Arab–Israel conflict for many years;[85] and Israel's sale of US arms to Iran in the 1980s, which, as high-level Israeli sources reported in the early 1980s (long before there were any hostages), was carried out in coordination with the US government to encourage a military coup, which would restore the Israel–Iran–Saudi Arabia alliance on which US policy had been based under the Nixon Doctrine—one of many features of the Iran–Contra affair suppressed in the congressional–media damage-control operation. The same model of overthrowing an unwanted civilian government had been pursued successfully in Indonesia, Chile, and other cases.[86]

The major policy imperative is to block indigenous nationalist forces that might try to use their own resources in conflict with US interests. A large-scale counterinsurgency operation in Greece from 1947 was partially motivated by the concern that the "rot" of independent nationalism there might "infect" the Middle East, Acheson warned. Greece was regarded as an outpost of US power, protecting Middle East oil for the United States and its allies. A CIA study held that if the rebels were victorious, the US would face "the possible loss of the petroleum resources of the Middle East." A Soviet threat was concocted in the usual manner. The real threat was indigenous nationalism, with its feared demonstration effects elsewhere.

Similar factors led to the CIA coup restoring the Shah in Iran in 1953. Nasser became an enemy for similar reasons. Later, Khomeini was perceived as posing another such threat, leading the US to support Iraq in the Gulf War. The Iraqi dictator Saddam Hussein then took over the mantle, shifting status overnight from favored friend to new Hitler when he invaded Kuwait in an effort to displace US–British clients. The primary fear throughout has been that nationalist forces not under US influence and control might come to have substantial influence over the oil-producing regions of the Arabian peninsula. Saudi Arabian elites, in contrast, are considered appropriate partners, managing their resources in conformity to basic US interests, and assisting US terror and subversion throughout the Third World.

More serious analysts have been quite clear about these matters, both in Congress and in the strategic analysis literature. In May 1973, before the oil crisis erupted, the Senate's ranking oil expert, Senator Henry Jackson, emphasized "the strength and Western orientation of Israel on the Mediterranean and Iran [under the Shah] on the Persian Gulf," two "reliable friends of the United States," who, along with Saudi Arabia, "have served to inhibit and contain those irresponsible and radical elements in certain Arab States ... who, were they free to do so, would pose a grave threat indeed to our principal sources of petroleum in the Persian Gulf"—sources that the US scarcely used at the time, but sources that were needed as a reserve and as a lever for world domination. The Nixon Doctrine had established Iran under the Shah and Israel as the "cops on the beat" in the region, in the words of Defense Secretary Melvin Laird, ensuring that no "radical nationalists" would pose a danger to order. Reviewing this system in 1974, Robert Reppa, a former Middle East analyst for the Defense Intelligence Agency, wrote that Israeli power protected the regimes of Jordan and Saudi Arabia from "a militarily strong Egypt" in the 1960s, and that "the Israeli–Iranian interrelationship" continued to contribute to the stability of the region, securing US interests. As early as autumn 1958, the National Security Council concluded that a "logical corollary" of opposition to radical Arab nationalism "would be to support Israel as the only strong pro-Western power left in the Middle East." Ten years earlier, Israel's military successes had led the Joint Chiefs of Staff to describe Israel as the major regional military power after Turkey, offering the US means to "gain strategic advantage in the Middle East that would offset the effects of the decline of British power in that area." As for the Palestinians, US planners had no reason to doubt the assessment of Israeli government specialists in 1948 that the Palestinian refugees would either assimilate elsewhere or "would be crushed": "some of them would die and most of them would turn into human dust and the waste of society, and join the most impoverished classes in the Arab countries." Accordingly, there was no need to trouble oneself about them.[87]

Few issues in world affairs are so important as control of the world's energy system—or so threatening to world peace, even survival. It continues to be "Axiom One of international affairs" that any effort to tamper with the dominant role of the United States and its clients will be strenuously resisted. As long as it was possible, the "Soviet threat" was brandished to justify US actions to ensure its dominance over Middle East oil. The pretext was never credible and by 1990 had to be entirely abandoned, while policy persisted much as before. The rational conclusion about the past was not drawn, but with the propaganda veil in tatters, reality could no longer be completely concealed. When the US sent forces to Saudi Arabia in August 1990 after Iraq's invasion of Kuwait, *New York Times* chief diplomatic correspondent Thomas Friedman wrote:

> In the past, when the United States was confronting the Soviet Union and competing for influence with Moscow in the Middle East, the stake in whose allies controlled what oil reserves had a military and strategic dimension. But today, with the Soviet Union cooperating in the crisis, that argument has lost much of its urgency

—or, more accurately, the argument had lost its capacity to efface the realities, which therefore had to be stated frankly, for once: "The United States is not sending troops to the gulf simply to help Saudi Arabia resist aggression. It is sending troops to support the OPEC country that is more likely to cater to Washington's interests." In the *Washington Post*, E.J. Dionne observed that there is "something thoroughly old-fashioned" about the proceedings, quoting Tom Mann, director of governmental affairs at the Brookings Institution, who says: "This is bald self-interest we're talking about here. And in some ways, Bush's way of dealing with these Middle Eastern countries is almost colonial in character." All hasten to add that there is no hint of criticism in such characterizations.[88]

In brief, the world's major energy reserves must be in the proper hands—ours—which can be counted on to use them for the benefit of the right

people, Churchill's "satisfied nations, who wished nothing more for themselves than what they had."

Rhetoric aside, the perceived danger throughout, in the Middle East
and elsewhere, is independent nationalism, described as a "virus" that might
"infect" other countries, a "rotten apple" that might contaminate the region
and beyond, a "domino" that might topple others. The cover story is that
the dominoes will fall through conquest; Ho Chi Minh will take off to
Jakarta in a canoe and conquer the Archipelago, a launching pad for the
march to Hawaii, if not beyond; or the Russians will use their base in
Grenada for their devilish design of world conquest; and so on. Again,
we need not accept the conclusion that a form of madness is a condition
of respectability and power. The core assumption of the domino theory,
scarcely concealed, has been that the virus might spread through the demonstration effect of successful independent development. Sometimes the enemies are truly the monsters they are depicted to be. Sometimes they compare
rather favorably to the preferred "moderates." These characteristics are essentially beside the point; what counts is their accommodation to the needs
of "the rich men dwelling at peace within their habitations." Such reasoning
holds throughout the postwar period, including the extraordinary efforts
to devastate Nicaragua by terror and economic warfare, even sadistic refusal
of aid for natural catastrophe and pressure on allies to do the same. The
elite consensus on these matters reveals how deeply these imperatives are
felt, and provides no little insight into Western moral and cultural values.

The general framework of world order was to be a form of liberal internationalism guaranteeing the needs of US investors. Several factors combined
to require that the Third World specialize in export of primary products:
the needs of European and Japanese industrial recovery; the triangular trade
patterns that helped to maintain US exports at a high level in the manner
already mentioned; and ready access to resources, including raw materials
for military production, with its central role in economic management and
population control. The conflict between US policy and independent Third
World development was deeply rooted in the structure of the world system.
The persistent resort to violence to bar nationalist threats is a natural concomitant of these commitments.[89]

Though the principled opposition to independent Third World nationalism is spelled out emphatically in the internal planning record and illustrated
in practice with much consistency, it does not satisfy doctrinal requirements
and is therefore unfit to enter public discourse. One would be hard put
to find a discussion of these central features of the contemporary world

order in the popular or intellectual journals. In mainstream scholarship, the crucial facts are commonly ignored, marginalized, or flatly denied. Thus, in Gaddis's important study of the origins and evolution of the "containment" policy, we read that "all postwar chief executives" believed "that nationalism, so long as it reflected the principle of self-determination, posed no threat to American institutions" and therefore did not call forth a hostile American response—as illustrated by the "fact" that "certainly Kennedy had no objections to the Cuban revolution itself" but only to "the danger of Soviet control," and by our efforts at "deterring aggression" in South Vietnam and in "the defense of Greece" (in both cases defense against "internal aggression," as Adlai Stevenson explained at the United Nations in 1964). All of this is presented without evidence or argument (except that political figures and propagandists have claimed it to be so) and with the blithe disregard for historical fact, or even relevant documentation, typical of the genre.[90]

As noted, the basic thrust of policy is beyond challenge or even awareness. These doctrines have certain consequences. One is the striking correlation between US aid and human rights abuses that has been noted in several studies. The reason is not that US policymakers like torture. Rather, it is an irrelevance. What matters is to bar independent development and the wrong priorities. For this purpose it is often necessary (regrettably) to murder priests, torture union leaders, "disappear" peasants, and otherwise intimidate the general population. Governments with the right priorities will therefore be led to adopt such measures. Since the right priorities are associated with US aid, we find the secondary correlation between US aid and human rights violations. And since the conclusions are doctrinally unappealing, they pass into oblivion.

A second consequence is the general US opposition to social reform, unless it can be carried out in conformity to overriding US interests. While this is occasionally possible in the Third World, such circumstances are rare, and even where social reform could be pursued along with subordination to US interests (Costa Rica is a noteworthy example), Washington reacted with considerable ambivalence.[91] A third consequence is the extreme elite hostility to democracy. The reason is plain: a functioning democracy will be responsive to appeals from the masses of the population, and likely to succumb to excessive nationalism.

6. The Next Stage

As the foregoing analysis suggests, it is plausible to suppose that US policy will be "more of the same" after the Cold War has ended. One reason is that the crucial event hasn't really taken place. Viewed realistically, the Cold War has (at most) half-ended. Its apparent termination is an ideological construction more than a historical fact, based on an interpretation that masks some of its essential functions. For the United States, much of the basic framework of the Cold War remains intact, apart from the modalities for controlling the domestic population. That problem—a central one facing any state or other system of power—still remains, and will have to be addressed in new and more imaginative ways as traditional Cold War doctrine loses its efficacy.[92]

There is also a deeper reason why US policy towards the Third World is likely to pursue much the same course as before. Within a narrow range, policies express institutional needs. US policies have been consistent over a long period because the dominant institutions are stable, subject to very little internal challenge, and—in the past—relatively immune to external pressures because of the unique wealth and power of the United States. Politics and ideology are largely bounded by the consensus of the business community. On critical issues there is tactical debate within the mainstream, but questions of principle rarely arise. The changes in the global system are, indeed, momentous, but have only a limited impact upon the fundamental bases for US policies towards the Third World, though they do modify the conditions under which these policies must be executed. In particular, new pretexts must now be devised, as was illustrated in Panama and the Gulf. But this is unlikely to be more of a problem than it was for Woodrow Wilson and his predecessors before the Bolshevik revolution.

Whatever problems may be posed by the need to modify the propaganda framework, and other tactical adjustments, there is a compensating gain. The removal of the limited Soviet deterrent frees the United States in the exercise of violence. Recognition of these welcome effects has been explicit in public discourse since the early stages of the Soviet withdrawal from the international arena, and was endorsed by Elliott Abrams, expressing his pleasure over the invasion of Panama. Abrams observed that "Bush probably is going to be increasingly willing to use force." The use of force is more feasible than before, he explained, now that "developments in Moscow have lessened the prospect for a small operation to escalate into a superpower conflict."[93] Similarly, the test of Gorbachev's "New Thinking" is regularly taken to be his willingness to withdraw support from those whom the United States aims to destroy; only if he allows us to proceed without interference in whatever we choose to do will we know that he is serious about ending the Cold War.

The Russian moves have helped to dispel some conventional mystification. The official story has always been that we contain the Russians, deterring them and thwarting their malicious designs. But the reality, as has long been evident, is that the fear of potential superpower conflict has served to contain and deter the United States and its far more ambitious global designs. The frightening "Soviet intervention" in the Third World has, commonly, consisted of moves by the Kremlin to protect and sustain targets of US attack. Now that the Soviets are limiting—perhaps terminating—these efforts, the US is more free to pursue its designs by force and violence, and the rhetorical clouds begin to lift. Perhaps it will some day be possible to use the terminology of the containment doctrine in accord with its meaning and the historical facts.

Two new factors in US–Third World relations, then, are the need for tactical and doctrinal adjustments, and the greater freedom to resort to force with impunity, with the decline of the Soviet deterrent. A third factor is that forceful intervention and military dictatorships are not as necessary as before. One reason is the success of violence in devastating popular organizations. Another is the economic catastrophe in much of the Third World (see Chapter 7). In these circumstances, it becomes possible to tolerate civilian governments, sometimes even social democrats, now that hopes for a better life have been destroyed.

Yet another factor is that the US is weaker than before relative to its real rivals, Europe and Japan. This long-term tendency was enhanced by the economic mismanagement of the Reaganites, who threw a party for the rich at the expense of the poor and future generations, and severely damaged the economy in the process. In this respect, the capacity for intervention will decline. A related development is the increasing penetration of Latin America by our rivals, who do not recognize the area as "our little region over here." Japan, in particular, is expanding investment and aid in the region, primarily in the richer countries, Mexico and Brazil. An editorial in the *Japan Economic Journal* observes: "If the US is being downgraded from a leader of the Western alliance to an 'ordinary power,' Japan needs to recognize that fact and act accordingly." Japanese investment in Latin America and the Caribbean has risen to over half that of the United States—close to 20 percent of Japan's total worldwide. Japanese banks also hold about 10–15 percent of Latin American debt, compared with one-third by US banks (debt holdings are now one means to finance new investment, by trading debt for productive assets).[94]

The US views such developments with some ambivalence. On the one hand, it does not want its interests to be challenged; on the other, it would like others to pay the costs of its depredations in the region and to help maintain the viability of the sectors useful for the "satisfied nations," also underwriting at least enough development to serve as the carrot alongside the stick that blocks unwelcome popular moves towards independence, democracy, and social justice.

Still another factor is the project of Latin-Americanizing Eastern Europe. "Most American companies view the Soviet Union and the newly opening nations in Eastern Europe as potential markets for their products or as sources of low-cost manufacturing labor," a front-page New York Times story observes, adding that they are even looking forward to a version of the standard "brain drain," in which the cost of educating professionals is borne by the Third World while the benefits accrue to the industrial societies. In the present case, there is "plentiful and underused brainpower" in the "East Bloc," which offers "intellectual reserves" that are not only extremely cheap but also of high quality because "their education system is fine," a senior scientist at a major corporation observes.[95]

The goals are clear enough when we turn to practice and policy, and even its ideological cover. Consider, for example, the "Z document," which aroused much excitement in early 1990, having displaced ruminations on "the end of history" and the Hegelian Spirit, which were the previous year's fad. This document, which appears in the journal of the American Academy of Arts and Sciences under the pseudonym "Z," with excerpts pre-published in the New York Times, advises the West on the proper response to "communism's terminal crisis."[96]

We may put aside the framework, with its brooding over the immutable "essence" of Sovietism and its many insights: that Stalin was "the hero of the left," while "the liberal-to-radical mainstream of Anglo-American Sovietology" regarded Stalinism as having "a democratic cast"; that scholarship indulged in "blatant fantasies ... about democratic Stalinism," and "puerile fetishization of Lenin" and the "democratic transformation" that follows from Leninism, while simultaneously regarding Stalin as "an aberration from the Leninist main line of Sovietism" (Z sees no inconsistency in these attributions, though he is derisive about the "conceptual confusions" of the leftists who dominate academic scholarship); that Lenin "produced the world's first version of noncapitalism"; that Lenin and Trotsky regarded October 1917 as "the ultimate revolution, the revolution to end all further need of revolutions"; that "Brezhnev intervened at will throughout the Third World" and "Russia bestrode the world." And others that may help to explain why the author preferred anonymity.[97]

Stripping all this away, the document contains one general thesis and an accompanying policy recommendation. The thesis is that "there is no third way between Leninism and the market, between bolshevism and constitutional government." The recommendation is that Western aid should be limited to "the piecemeal development of parallel structures in a private sector operating on market principles . . .," with "free economic zones operating under International Monetary Fund conditions" spreading from the periphery to the interior of the USSR.

The thesis has a minor defect: its first dichotomy rules out of existence the industrial democracies (not to speak of South Korea, Taiwan, and the other "economic miracles"), all of which depart sharply from market principles; its second dichotomy also denies the existence of most of the world, neither Bolshevist nor constitutional. The recommendation, however, is straightforward enough: the Soviet empire should be converted into another region of the Third World. The rest can be dismissed as an effort to endow this basic concept with an aura of seriousness (and to lash out at hated academic enemies).

There is much concern in the United States over the fact that its rivals, particularly German-led Europe, are well ahead in the enterprise of converting the vast "East Bloc" into a new Third World, which can provide resources, markets, investment opportunities and cheap labor, and perform other useful chores. Federal Reserve Board chairman Alan Greenspan describes the "huge investment requirement" and "potential for significant rates of return" in Eastern Europe as "the most important financial issue of the [coming] decade," with "no historical precedent." But the relative decline of US economic power during the Reagan years has reduced the United States' capacity to compete for this rich prize, and the increasing dependence on foreign lenders leaves the economy vulnerable as rival powers turn to the opportunities for enrichment in the new regions opening up for exploitation. "We have lost a lot of our authority as a leader in the world," US Trust Company economic consultant James O'Leary says, echoing the sentiments of many Wall Street economists: "Ten or 15 years ago we didn't have to pay much attention to what happened elsewhere. Now we are just one of the boys."[98]

Liberal Democrats urge that aid be diverted from Central America to Eastern Europe to advance the US cause in the race to exploit these newly accessible domains; the term "aid" is a euphemism for methods by which the taxpayer funds business efforts to enhance market penetration and investment opportunities. The matter is too serious to be disguised in the usual cloak of noble intent. Thus Democratic Senator Patrick Leahy, criticizing a *New York Times* editorial calling for aid for the promising new "democracies" in Panama and Nicaragua, writes:

> The United States is left at the starting gate in Eastern Europe. You almost sound consoling in your observation that "Western Europe and Japan are already addressing Eastern Europe's needs." You can bet they are—and that is the problem. The vast trade and investment potential of Eastern Europe is rapidly being oriented toward our main trade competitors. We debate how to clean up two foreign policy debacles in Central America while the markets of 120 million people in Eastern Europe are being opened by Japan and the European community.[99]

In congressional debate, Leahy stressed that "foreign aid must do much more to strengthen American economic competitiveness abroad." Contrary to public oratory, aid is "not some international charity or welfare program. ... Properly designed, it can be an investment in new trading partners, growing export markets, and more jobs in our export industries here at home," the guiding ideas since the Marshall Plan. In the current circumstances, "our foreign assistance program must be aimed at strengthening U.S. economic involvement in the emerging democracies of Eastern Europe. We are being left behind by Western European and Japanese firms who get direct support from their governments," and our "Eastern European initiative" should be "aimed at strengthening the ability of American business to participate in the opening of this enormous new market as we enter the 21st century." Our competitors are government-backed, and the Export-Import Bank as well as our aid program should "help American businesses compete against these subsidized nations that are taking these markets away from us in Africa, Asia, and Latin America" as well. "The foreign aid bill can give American business more tools to combat predatory financing, tied aid and mixed credits. ... To compete with Japan and Western European interests, we have to back our commercial interests as effectively as the countries that are in competition for these markets"—and whose commitment to the "free market" is, in fact, on a par with ours: fine for those who expect to come out ahead in the competition; not to be taken seriously by others.[100]

Such factors as these will shape the new methods for continuing the war against the Third World, now under a different guise and with a more varied array of competing actors. Popular forces in the United States and Europe have placed certain barriers in the path of state terror, and have offered some help to those targeted for repression, but unless they gain considerably in scale and commitment, the future for the traditional victims looks grim.

Grim, but not hopeless. With amazing courage and persistence, the wretched of the earth continue to struggle for their rights. And in the industrial world, with Bolshevism disintegrating and capitalism long abandoned, there are prospects for the revival of libertarian socialist and radical democratic ideals that had languished, including popular control of the workplace and investment decisions and, correspondingly, the establishment of more meaningful political democracy as constraints imposed by private power are reduced. These and other emerging possibilities are still remote, but no more so than the possibility of parliamentary democracy and elementary rights of citizenship 250 years ago. No one knows enough to predict what human will can achieve.

We are faced with a kind of Pascal's wager: assume the worst, and it will surely arrive; commit oneself to the struggle for freedom and justice, and its cause may be advanced.

Notes

1. See Chapter 10, section 4, below.

2. *Foreign Relations of the United States (FRUS)*, 1950, vol. I, pp. 234–92, made public in 1975. National Security Council (NSC) memoranda are the highest-level government planning documents.

3. Thus, Canada is excluded and data for the USSR are targets for 1950, which are "believed to exceed in many cases the production actually achieved," while the figures for Europe are "actual data from 1948," which had already been surpassed. US data are selected to reflect the sharp decline of industrial production from 1948. Soviet figures represent the limits of what is possible; the West, it is conceded, has vast unused capacity.

4. See Chapter 8, section 7.

5. "Rethinking the Third World," *Washington Post Book World*, October 23, 1988, a dismissive review of Gabriel Kolko's *Confronting the Third World* (Pantheon, 1988), which, Schoenbaum alleges, is flawed by failure to propose better policies and by omission of facts that do not support the author's thesis (one example is given: that "American lives were in danger" when the US invaded the Dominican Republic—no justification for aggression had it been true, and long discredited).

6. Gaddis, *The Long Peace* (Oxford, 1987), p. 43. See *Necessary Illusions*, Appendix II, for further discussion.

7. Cited by Michael Krenn, *US Policy toward Economic Nationalism in Latin America, 1917–1929* (Scholarly Resources, 1990), pp. 13 f., 52 (emphasis in original). Also David Schmitz, *The United States and Fascist Italy* (University of North Carolina, 1988), p. 10.

8. Stone, "Is the Cold War Really Over?," *Sunday Telegraph* (London), November 27, 1988.

9. Hertzberg, contribution to symposium on "The 'End' of the Cold War?, The Coming Challenge for Journalism," *Deadline*, Center for War, Peace, and the News Media, Summer 1989.

10. Patrick Tyler, *WP Weekly*, August 13, 1990.

11. "The Bewildered American Raj; Reflections on a democracy's foreign policy," *Harper's*, March 1985.

12. Paul M. Kattenburg, *The Vietnam Trauma in American Foreign Policy, 1945–75* (Transaction Books, 1982), pp. 69 ff.

13. R.W. Apple, *NYT*, November 5, 1989; Reston, *NYT*, November 24, 1967. On Reston (and elite opinion generally) with regard to the Indonesian massacres, see my article in *Z Magazine*, September 1990. For further samples of his commentary, see *Towards a New Cold War, Turning the Tide*.

14. *Report of the National Bipartisan Commission on Central America*, Henry Kissinger, chairman, January 10, 1984; Laqueur and Krauthammer, *New Republic*, March 31, 1982; Huntington, *Political Science Quarterly*, Spring 1982 (see *Turning the Tide*, pp. 153 f., 161, for a review of the interesting reasoning that leads to this conclusion); Krauthammer, *New Republic*, February 17, 1986.

15. Morgenthau, *The Purpose of American Politics* (Vintage, 1964). See *Towards a New Cold War* for further discussion of this and similar examples from the record of scholarship, intellectual commentary, and journalism; and the references of the introduction for many more.

16. For some further comment, see *Necessary Illusions*, particularly Appendix II, sec. 2; Appendix V, sec. 8.

17. For an example of this fallacy, see Fred Halliday, "The Ends of Cold War," *New Left Review* 180/1990. Halliday's work on these topics, while often valuable, is marred by persistent inability to comprehend alternative conceptions and curious errors of reasoning, as in this case. See, e.g., his *Making of the Second Cold War* (Verso, 1983), p. 27, where he interprets my observation that "the real rivals" of the United States are Japan and Europe, not the USSR (obvious at the time, and by now the merest truism) as implying that the conflict with the USSR was "but a pretext used by the USA for waging conflict" with the EEC and Japan—which of course it does not.

18. On the crucial role of the Department of Defense in the computer industry, see Kenneth Flamm, *Targeting the Computer* (Brookings, 1987).

19. It is commonly recognized by economic historians that state intervention is a crucial feature of "late development," but the conclusion holds generally of successful industrial societies, including Britain, the United States, Germany, and Japan. A classic account of the state role in "delayed development" in continental Europe is Alexander Gerschenkron, *Economic Backwardness in Historical Perspective* (Harvard, 1962). On Japan, a standard work on the postwar period is Chalmers Johnson, *MITI and the Japanese Miracle* (Stanford, 1982). On Korea, see Alice Amsden's important study *Asia's Next Giant: South Korea and Late Industrialization* (Oxford University Press, 1989); and for an overview, Amsden, "East Asia's Challenge—to Standard Economics," *American Prospect*, Summer 1990. Also several articles in "Showa: the Japan of Hirohito," *Daedalus*, Summer 1990, particularly those by John Dower and Chalmers Johnson. On illusions about the effects of openness of the economy and the state role, comparing Latin America and Asia in the past several decades, see Tariq Banuri, ed., *No Panacea: the Limits of Economic Liberalization* (Oxford University Press, forthcoming) (see Chapter 7, section 7). On the crucial role of state-led economic development and social expenditures for the famed "Costa Rican exception," see Anthony Winson, *Coffee & Modern Costa Rican Democracy* (St Martin's Press, 1989). For more general discussion, including "early development," see Frederick Clairmonte, *Economic Liberalism and Underdevelopment* (Asia Publishing House, London–Bombay 1960). For a perceptive early account of the general drift towards fascist-style state capitalist systems through the 1930s, adapted to particular cultural and institutional factors, see Robert Brady, *Business as a System of Power* (Columbia, 1943). See also the classic study of the abandonment of *laissez-faire* by Karl Polanyi, *The Great Transformation* (Beacon Press, 1957).

20. See *Necessary Illusions*, pp. 29 f. and Appendix II, sec. 2, for some discussion and references, also Chapter 12 below. See Crozier, Huntington, and Watanuki, *The Crisis of Democracy*.

21. *Strategies of Containment* (Oxford University Press, 1982), pp. 356–7. Kennan quote from speech to the National War College, ibid., p. 40.

22. Frank Costigliola, in Thomas Paterson, ed., *Kennedy's Quest for Victory* (Oxford University Press, 1989).

23. For discussion, see *Turning the Tide*, Chapter 4; *On Power and Ideology*, Lecture 4; Schwartz and Derber, *Nuclear Seduction*. On the Middle East particularly, see *Towards a New Cold War, Fateful Triangle, Necessary Illusions*. Remarks on verification taken from Raymond L. Garthoff,

"Estimating Soviet Military Force Levels," *International Security* 14:4, Spring 1990. Garthoff suggests that the "main problems with verification" in the "new era" may come not from the USSR "but from our own reticence and that of some of our allies."

24. James P. Warburg, *Germany: Key to Peace* (Harvard, 1953), pp. 188 ff.

25. Garthoff; Kaplan, *BG* November 29, 1989.

26. See references Note 23, and *Towards a New Cold War*, Introduction, ch. 7. Strategic weapons during the 1970s discussed in Raymond L. Garthoff, *Détente and Confrontation* (Brookings Institution, 1985), p. 793. On US isolation at the United Nations on disarmament and other matters, and the media treatment (i.e. evasion) of these issues, see *Necessary Illusions*, pp. 82 ff. and Chapter 3, section 4, below.

27. William Yandell Elliot, ed., *The Political Economy of American Foreign Policy* (Holt, Rinehart & Winston, 1955), p. 42. For further discussion of this important and generally ignored study, see my *At War with Asia* (Pantheon, 1970), Introduction.

28. See p. 18, above.

29. For a skeptical assessment, see Schwartz and Derber, *Nuclear Delusion*.

30. See *On Power and Ideology*, p. 105. Nitze's specific proposal was for a civil defense system, which would reduce the concern over Soviet retaliation. This being completely unfeasible, the only alternative is more lethal weaponry. The "strategic" case for SDI was similar.

31. Michael Gordon, *NYT*, January 31; *National Security Strategy of the United States*, The White House, March 1990. On the attack against Libya and the media cover-up, see *Pirates and Emperors*, ch. 3; *Necessary Illusions*, pp. 272–3; William Schaap, *Covert Action Information Bulletin*, Summer 1988. Note that the question at issue is how the media dealt with the information at hand in the context of the demands of the state, and is thus quite independent of whatever the facts turn out to be, if they are ever credibly established. For relevant background, see Stephen Shalom, *Z Magazine*, April, June 1990.

32. Testimony of Robert Komer to the Senate Armed Services Committee, cited by Melvyn Leffler, "From the Truman Doctrine to the Carter Doctrine," *Diplomatic History*, vol. 7, 1983, pp. 245 f. See *Towards a New Cold War*, *Fateful Triangle*, for further discussion.

33. AP, April 3; Michael Klare, "The U.S. Military Faces South," *Nation*, June 18, 1990.

34. Gray, *Marine Corps Gazette*, May 1990.

35. Immerman, "Confessions of an Eisenhower Revisionist," *Diplomatic History*, Summer 1990.

36. Stephen Van Evera, *Atlantic Monthly*, July 1990; also *CCS Policy Report* No. 3, Institute for Peace and International Security, Cambridge, MA, June 1990.

37. See Teodor Shanin, *Russia as a 'Developing Society'* (Yale, 1985), vol. 1, pp. 103 f., 123 f., 134 f., 187 f. Quote is from D. Mirsky, *Russia, A Social History* (London 1952), p. 269, cited by Shanin.

38. *National Interest*, Fall 1989.

39. See *Turning the Tide*, p. 198, and sources cited.

40. Richard Drinnon, *Facing West: the Metaphysics of Indian-hating and Empire Building* (University of Minnesota, 1980), pp. 68, 96 f. Jefferson letters of 1812, 1813; John Adams, 1812.

41. Adams, Dispatch to Ambassador Erving, 1818. William Earl Weeks, "John Quincy Adams's 'Great Gun' and the Rhetoric of American Empire," *Diplomatic History*, Spring 1990.

42. Ibid.; Drinnon, pp. 109 ff.

43. Weeks, Drinnon. Acheson, see Chapter 3 below.

44. Reginald Horsman, *Race and Manifest Destiny* (Harvard, 1981), p. 279, 235, 210–11. Darwin, *Descent of Man* (Princeton, 1981), Part I, p. 179; I am indebted to Jan Koster for this reference.

45. For references and discussion, see *Turning the Tide*, pp. 59, 61, 146 f.

46. Quoted in Ruth Leacock, *Requiem for Revolution* (Kent State University Press, 1990), p. 33.

47. See Chapters 4 and 5 for further discussion.

48. Cited by Schmitz, *United States and Fascist Italy*, p. 40. Gaddis, see Note 6.

49. Schmitz, pp. 14, 36, 44, 52, citing Colonel House's Inquiry advising President Wilson on the Versailles negotiations; Gordon Auchincloss of the State Department, wartime diaries; Ambassador Richard Washburn Child; Embassy to Washington, 1921.

50. Schmitz, chapters 3, 4, for details.

51. Filippelli, *American Labor and Postwar Italy, 1943–1953* (Stanford, 1989), p. 15.

52. Schmitz, pp. 67 f.

53. Ibid., pp. 77 f. Kellogg, Krenn, *U.S. Policy toward Economic Nationalism*, pp. 53–4. On the favorable general response to Mussolini's Fascism in the United States, see John Diggins, *Mussolini and Fascism* (Princeton, 1972).

54. Krenn, p. 53.

55. Schmitz, ch. 6.

56. Ibid., ch. 7. On Spain, see my *American Power and the New Mandarins* (Pantheon, 1969), ch. 1, parts relevant here reprinted in James Peck, ed., *The Chomsky Reader* (Pantheon, 1987).

57. Schmitz, pp. 133, 140, 174 and ch. 9. On Japan, see my *American Power and the New Mandarins*, ch. 2.

58. Schmitz, Epilogue. See Chapter 11 below for more extensive discussion. For a review of the project, see *Turning the Tide*, ch. 4, sec. 4.4, and sources cited, particularly the groundbreaking work of Gabriel and Joyce Kolko.

59. Schmitz, pp. 60–61.

60. Krenn, pp. 40, 51 ff.

61. Ibid., p. 44. See also Walter LaFeber, *Inevitable Revolutions* (Norton, 1983).

62. Krenn, *U.S. Policy*, pp. 58 ff., 106–7. Acheson, see pp. 52–3 above.

63. Krenn, p. 62. Dulles cited by Stephen G. Rabe, *Eisenhower and Latin America* (University of North Carolina, 1988), p. 33. Woodward, see *Necessary Illusions*, Appendix V, sec. 1.

64. Krenn, ch. 6.

65. For further details, and references where not specifically cited, see sources cited in the Introduction. Also Gabriel Kolko, *Confronting the Third World* (see Note 5).

66. See Chapter 11 below.

67. Tonelson, *NYT*, April 13, 1986, reviewing *Turning the Tide*, where he finds a "theoretical problem" in my account of US foreign policy because of this alleged US effort. For similarly fallacious argument, see economic historian Charles Kindelberger, who cites Japan as a "difficult counterexample" to the theory that US foreign policy is motivated by self-interest on the grounds that Japan is not "a puppet of the United States"; by the same logic, one could prove that China and Romania disprove the theory that Soviet policy was motivated by self-interest. The argument holds only if one adds the assumption that the US and the USSR are omnipotent. In the real world, they were motivated by self-interest, but faced limits to their power. Kindelberger, *Public Policy*, Summer 1971. For further discussion, see my *For Reasons of State* (Pantheon, 1973), pp. 45–6. Draper, cited by Michael Schaller, *American Occupation of Japan* (Oxford University Press, 1985), p. 127. Reston, see above, p. 18.

68. Hogan, *The Marshall Plan* (Cambridge University Press, 1987), pp. 42–3, 45, citing a May 1947 memorandum by William Clayton; 91–2.

69. Schmitz, *United States and Fascist Italy*, pp. 37 f.

70. Leffler, "The United States and the Strategic Dimensions of the Marshall Plan," *Diplomatic History*, Summer 1988; McCormick, "'Every System Needs a Center Sometimes'," in Lloyd Gardner, ed., *Redefining the Past: Essays in Diplomatic History in Honor of William Appleman Williams* (Oregon State, 1986). We return to these matters in Chapter 11.

71. Cited by Bruce Cumings, "Power and Plenty in Northeast Asia," *World Policy Journal*, Winter 1987–8.

72. Borden, *The Pacific Alliance* (Wisconsin, 1984), pp. 27, 12, 245; Hogan, pp. 337, 393.

73. For references, see LaFeber, Kolko; and *Turning the Tide*.

74. See *On Power and Ideology*, pp. 19–23, for some particularly clear examples, drawn from NSC 5432, "U.S. Policy Toward Latin America," August 18, 1954, immediately after the successful destruction of Guatemalan democracy. These principles are reiterated elsewhere, often verbatim (e.g., NSC 5613/1, September 25, 1956).

75. Editorial, *NYT*, August 6, 1954. On media treatment of the Iranian "affair" and its aftermath, see *Necessary Illusions*, Appendix V, sec. 3, and sources cited.

76. Schoultz, *Human Rights and United States Policy toward Latin America* (Princeton, 1981), p. 7.

77. CIA, Office of Current Intelligence, "The Role of Public Opinion in Latin American Political Stability," May 13, 1965, OCI No. 1803/65. On the support for Somoza and the National Guard under the Carter Administration, see Chapter 10 below. For more on the "low level of intellectualism" in Guatemala, see Chapter 12, pp. 393–4; Chapter 8, pp. 262–3 f.

78. Minutes summarizing PPS 51, April 1949, cited by Michael Schaller, "Securing the Great

Crescent: Occupied Japan and the Origins of Containment in Southeast Asia," *Journal of American History*, September 1982. See also Schaller, *American Occupation of Japan*, p. 160. On planning for Southeast Asia, see also *For Reasons of State*, pp. 31 ff., and several essays in Chomsky and Howard Zinn, eds, *Critical Essays, The Pentagon Papers*, Senator Gravel Edition, vol. 5 (Beacon, 1972), particularly those by John Dower and Richard Du Boff. See also Chapter 11, section 3, below.

79. Stimson, explaining in May 1945 why all regional systems must be dismantled in the interests of liberal internationalism, apart from our own, which are to be extended. See *Turning the Tide*, pp. 63 f. See *On Power and Ideology*, pp. 21 f., on the plans to displace the influence of our traditional European enemies over the military.

80. PPS 23, February 24, 1948; see *FRUS*, vol. I, 1948, p. 511.

81. Douglas Brinkley and G. E. Thomas, "Dean Acheson's Opposition to African Liberation," *Transafrica Forum* (Summer 1988); Morris, *'Uncertain Greatness'* (Harper & Row, 1977).

82. The specific reference is to Saudi Arabian oil. For references and further discussion, see *Towards a New Cold War*. Also Aaron David Miller, *Search for Security* (University of North Carolina, 1980); Irvine Anderson, *Aramco, the United States and Saudi Arabia* (Princeton, 1981); Michael Stoff, *Oil, War and American Security* (Yale, 1980); David Painter, *Oil and the American Century* (Johns Hopkins University, 1986). Eisenhower cited in Steven Spiegel, *The Other Arab–Israeli Conflict* (University of Chicago, 1985), p. 51.

83. Cumings; Fukai, "Japan's Energy Policy," *Current History*, April 1988. See also *Towards a New Cold War*, pp. 97–8.

84. See *Towards a New Cold War*, ch. 11.

85. On the diplomacy of the Arab–Israel conflict as it evolved in the post-1967 period, see *Towards a New Cold War, Fateful Triangle*; and on the current phase of US efforts to block a comprehensive settlement, see *Necessary Illusions* and my article in *Z Magazine*, January 1990.

86. For details, see *Fateful Triangle*, pp. 457 f.; *Culture of Terrorism*, ch. 8. Also John Marshall, Peter Dale Scott, and Jane Hunter, *The Iran Contra Connection* (South End, 1987), chs 7, 8; Samuel Segev, *The Iranian Triangle* (Free Press, 1988).

87. Avi Shlaim, *Collusion Across the Jordan* (Columbia, 1988), p. 388, paraphrasing 1948 JCS records; 491, citing the Israeli state archives. For references and further details, see *Towards a New Cold War* (ch. 7) and *Fateful Triangle* (ch. 2).

88. Friedman, "U.S. Gulf Policy: Vague 'Vital Interests'," *NYT*, August 12; Dionne, "Drawing Lessons From History," *WP Weekly*, August 13, 1990. On the Iraqi invasion of Kuwait, see Chapter 6 below.

89. For an informative examination of these topics, see Borden, *Pacific Alliance*.

90. Gaddis, *Strategies of Containment*, pp. 201, 231, 240, 286.

91. See *Necessary Illusions*, pp. 111 f. and Appendix V, sec. 1, for a review of the declassified record and other relevant material.

92. See Chapter 4 below for further discussion.

93. Stephen Kurkjian and Adam Pertman, *BG*, January 5, 1990; latter quote is the reporter's paraphrase. See Chapter 3 below for earlier expression of the same perception, and Chapter 5 for the Panama context.

94. Doug Henwood, *Left Business Observer*, May 15, 1989.

95. John Holusha, "Business Taps the East Bloc's Intellectual Reserves," *NYT*, February 20, 1990.

96. *Daedalus*, Winter 1990; *NYT*, January 4, 1990.

97. The author was later identified as University of California professor Martin Malia, who then alleged that anonymity was necessary to protect his friends in Moscow (*NYT*, August 31, 1990).

98. David Francis, "US Edgy as Money Flows to Europe," *CSM*, February 26, 1990.

99. Letter, *NYT*, April 10, 1990.

100. Senator Patrick Leahy, "New Directions in U.S. Foreign Aid Policy," *Congressional Record*, S 7672, June 11, 1990.

TWO

The Home Front

THE Reagan era was widely heralded as virtually revolutionary in its import. Reality was considerably less dramatic, but the impact on the domestic social order and the world was not slight. Some reflections follow on what was bequeathed to the new Administration in early 1989. The focus in this chapter is at home, and in the next, on broader international issues and policy implications.

1. The "Unimportant People"

These matters have large-scale human consequences, and should therefore be faced dispassionately. That is not an easy matter. It is first necessary to dispel the most vivid images conjured up by the words "Reagan," "Shultz," and "Bush"—images of tortured and mutilated bodies by the tens of thousands in El Salvador and Guatemala and of dying infants in Nicaragua, succumbing once again to disease and malnutrition thanks to the successes in reversing the early achievements of the Sandinistas. And others like them in Mozambique, Gaza, and other corners of the world from which we prefer to avert our eyes—by "we" I mean a larger community for which we all share responsibility. These images we must somehow manage to put aside.

We should not move on, however, without at least a word on how easily we refrain from seeing piles of bones and rivers of blood when we are the agents of misery and despair. To truly appreciate these accomplishments one must turn to the liberal doves, who are regularly condemned for their excessive sensitivity to the plight of our victims. To *New Republic* editor Hendrik Hertzberg, who writes of the "things about the Reagan era that haven't been so attractive," like sleaze, Rambo movies, and Lebanon—referring, presumably, to dead Marines, not dead Lebanese and Palestinians—but without a word on Central America, where nothing has happened that even rises to the level of "unattractive," apparently. Or even to Mary McGrory, in a very different category, who nevertheless tells us that "the real argument, of course, is what is more important in Nicaragua: peace, as the Democrats cry; or freedom, as the Republicans demand." The shred of truth in these words is that the Democrats are as committed to peace as the Republicans are to freedom.[1]

Or we can turn to the journal *Indochina Issues*, of the Center for International Policy, which has compiled a very laudable record in its work for peace and justice. Here, a senior associate of the Carnegie Foundation for International Peace calls for reconciliation with Vietnam, urging that we put aside "the agony of the Vietnam experience" and "the injuries of the past," and overcome the "hatred, anger and frustration" caused us by the Vietnamese, though without forgetting "the humanitarian issues left over from the war": those missing in action, those qualified to emigrate to the United States, and the remaining inmates of reeducation camps. These are the only humanitarian issues that we see, apparently, when we cast our eye on three countries littered with corpses, broken bodies, hideously deformed fetuses and hundreds of thousands of other victims of chemical warfare in South Vietnam, destruction on a colossal scale—all caused by some unknown hand, unmentioned here. Meanwhile we contemplate what they have done to us, the agony and injury they have forced us to endure.[2]

On such assumptions, we can perhaps even read without cringing that James Fallows "is now fully aware after a recent visit to Vietnam that the war 'will be important in history mostly for what it did, internally, to the United States, not what difference it made in Indochina'" (*Dissent* editor Dennis Wrong, quoting Fallows with approval). The slaughter of millions of Indochinese and the destruction of their countries is far too slight a matter to attract the attention of the muse of history while she ponders the domestic problems caused for the important people, those who really count. Perhaps, some day, a thoughtful German commentator will explain that the Holocaust will be important in history mostly for what it did, internally, to Germany, not for what difference it made for the Jews.[3]

A leading authority on Native Americans, Francis Jennings, once observed: "In history, the man in the ruffled shirt and gold-laced waistcoat somehow levitates above the blood he has ordered to be spilled by dirty-handed underlings." We will not be able to face the problems that lie ahead realistically unless we come to grips with these striking and pervasive features of our moral and intellectual culture.

Central America has been a foreign policy obsession throughout the eighties, and the effects are evident. Before this grim and shameful decade, Central America had been one of the most miserable corners of the world. That its fate might teach us some lessons about the great power that has long dominated the region and repeatedly intervened in its affairs is a thought foreign to the minds of the important people, and it is understood that they are not to be troubled by such discordant notes. Thus in the *New York Times Magazine*, James LeMoyne ruminates on the deep-seated problems of Central America, recalling the role of Cuba, the Soviet Union, North Korea, the PLO, Vietnam, and other disruptive foreign forces. One actor is missing, apart from the phrase that in El Salvador, "the United States bolstered the Salvadoran Army, insisted on elections and called for some reforms." In another *Times Magazine* story, Tad Szulc gives a similar treatment to the Caribbean, observing that "the roots of the Caribbean problems are not entirely Cuban"; the "Soviet offensive" is also to blame, along with the consequences of "colonial greed and mismanagement" by European powers. The US is charged only with "indifference" to the brewing problems.[4]

In a later *Times Magazine* story, Stephen Kinzer concedes that in Guatemala—which he had offered as a model for the errant Sandinistas—the progress of "democracy" leaves something to be desired. To be sure, there are some encouraging signs; thus murders by the security forces we bolster have declined to perhaps two a day: definitely an improvement over the period when Reagan and his cohorts were enthusiastically hailing Lucas García and Ríos Montt, whom Kinzer now describes as "two of the most ruthless military presidents" (in fact, mass murderers). But Kinzer, who knows the role of the US in Guatemala well, also knows the rules of decorum: in his version, Guatemala's democratic interlude of 1944–54 ended for some unstated reason, and the subsequent US role, until today, receives no mention whatsoever. We find again only an oblique reference to general indifference: "rich countries—notably the United States—welcomed, and in some cases helped to force the transitions to civilian rule in Latin America," but without sufficient commitment or recognition of "longer-term challenges." If in Guatemala "more people are unemployed, and more people now eat out of garbage dumps, than ever in memory," if the army maintains its vicious and murderous regime, if the military and super-rich who rule behind a thin civilian façade persist in what the Catholic bishops call the "inhuman and merciless" abuse of the impoverished peasants, then it must be a reflection of their inherent worthlessness. Surely no respectable person could imagine that the United States might share some responsibility for instituting and maintaining this charnel house.[5]

The practice is virtually a literary convention. Reporting the Bosch–Balaguer 1990 election campaign in the Dominican Republic, Howard French tells us that Juan Bosch, "a lifelong Marxist," "was removed from office in a military coup shortly after winning the country's first free elections, in 1963," and that his rival, Joaquín Balaguer, defeated Bosch in the 1966 presidential election. Omitted are a few pertinent facts, among them: that there had been no prior free elections because of repeated US interventions, including long support for the murderer and torturer Trujillo until he began to interfere with US interests; that the "lifelong Marxist" advocated policies similar to those of the Kennedy Democrats; that the US was instrumental in undermining him and quickly backed the new military regime; that when the populace arose to restore constitutional rule in 1965, the US sent 23,000 troops on utterly fraudulent pretexts to avert the threat of democracy, establishing the standard regime of death squads, torture, repression, slave labor conditions, increase in poverty and malnutrition, vast emigration, and wonderful opportunities for its own investors, and tolerating the "free election" of 1966 only when the playing field had been leveled by ample terror.[6]

Even such major atrocities as the slaughter in Cambodia that the US conducted and presided over in the early 1970s have faded quietly away. As a matter of routine, when the *New York Times* reviews the horror story of Cambodia, it begins in April 1975, under the heading "The Cambodia Ordeal: A Country Bleeds for 15 Years." No one bled, apparently, from the time of the first sustained US bombings in March 1969 through April 1975, when 600,000 people were killed, according to CIA estimates.[7]

The moral cowardice would be stunning, if it were not such a routine feature of intellectual life.

Returning to Central America, a decade ago there were glimmerings of hope for constructive change. In Guatemala, peasants and workers were organizing to challenge one of the most primitive oligarchies on the face of the earth. In El Salvador, Church-based self-help groups, unions, peasant associations and other popular organizations were offering a way for the general population to escape grinding poverty and repression and to begin to take some control of their lives and fate. In Nicaragua, the tyranny that had served as the base for US power in the region for decades was overthrown in 1979, leaving the country in ruins, littered with 40,000 corpses, the treasury robbed, the economy devastated. But the National Guard was driven out and new popular forces were mobilized. Here too there was hope for a better future, and it was realized to a surprising degree, despite extreme adversity, in the early years.

The Reagan Administration and its liberal Democrat and media accomplices can take credit for having reduced these hopes to ashes. That is a rare accomplishment, for which history will assign them their proper place, if there is ever an honest accounting.

2. Political Successes

But let us put aside such disquieting thoughts—as we all too easily do—and try to assess the impact of these years where it matters to history by the lights of the sophisticated: internally, for the domestic society of the United States, and in particular for those who hold its reins.

To face these questions sensibly, we have to try to understand our own societies. It is not a simple picture. In the United States we see, for example, the tiny Jesuit center Quest for Peace which, with no resources, was able to raise millions of dollars for hurricane relief in Nicaragua from people who have been able, somehow, to keep their independence of thought and their hold on simple moral values. On the other hand, we see the rigid fanaticism, willful ignorance, and intellectual and moral corruption of the elite culture. We see a political system in which formal mechanisms function with little substance, while at the same time dissidence, activism, turbulence and informal politics have been on the rise and impose constraints on state violence that are by no means negligible.

With regard to the political system, the Reagan era represents a significant advance in capitalist democracy. For eight years, the US government functioned virtually without a chief executive. That is an important fact. It is quite unfair to assign to Ronald Reagan, the person, much responsibility for the policies enacted in his name. Despite the efforts of the educated classes to invest the proceedings with the required dignity, it was hardly a secret that Reagan had only the vaguest conception of the policies of his Administration and, if not properly programmed by his staff, regularly produced statements that would have been an embarrassment, were anyone to have taken them seriously. The question that dominated the Iran–Contra hearings—did Reagan know, or remember, what the policy of his Administration had been?—was hardly a serious one. The pretense to the contrary was simply part of the cover-up operation; and the lack of public interest over revelations that Reagan was engaged in illegal aid to the Contras during a period when—he later informed Congress—he knew nothing about it, betrays a certain realism.

Reagan's duty was to smile, to read from the teleprompter in a pleasant voice, tell a few jokes, and keep the audience properly bemused. His only qualification for the presidency was that he knew how to read the lines written for him by the rich folk, who pay well for the service. Reagan had been doing that for years. He seemed to perform to the satisfaction of the paymasters, and to enjoy the experience. By all accounts, he spent many pleasant days enjoying the pomp and trappings of power and should have a fine time in the retirement quarters that his grateful benefactors have prepared for him. It is not really his business if the bosses left mounds of mutilated corpses in death squad dumping grounds in El Salvador or hundreds of thousands of homeless in the streets. One does not blame an actor for the content of the words that come from his mouth. When we speak of the policies of the Reagan Administration, then, we are not referring to the figure set up to front for them by an Administration whose major strength was in public relations.

The construction of a symbolic figure by the public relations industry is a contribution to solving one of the critical problems that must be faced in any society that combines concentrated power with formal mechanisms that in theory allow the general public to take part in running their own affairs, thus posing a threat to privilege. Not only in the subject domains but at home as well, there are unimportant people who must be taught to submit with due humility, and the crafting of a figure larger than life is a classic device to achieve this end. As far back as Herodotus we can read how people who had struggled to gain their freedom "became once more subject to autocratic government" through the acts of able and ambitious leaders who "introduced for the first time the ceremonial of royalty," distancing the leader from the public while creating a legend that "he was a being of a different order from mere men" who must be shrouded in mystery, and leaving the secrets of government, which are not the affair of the vulgar, to those entitled to manage them. In the early years of the Republic, an absurd George Washington cult was contrived as part of the effort "to cultivate the ideological loyalties of the citizenry" and thus create a sense of "viable nationhood," historian Lawrence Friedman comments. Washington was a "perfect man" of "unparalleled perfection," who was raised "above the level of mankind," and so on. To this day, the Founding Fathers remain "those pure geniuses of detached contemplation," far surpassing ordinary mortals (see p. 17). Such reverence persists, notably in elite intellectual circles, the comedy of Camelot being an example. Sometimes a foreign leader ascends to the same semi-divinity among loyal worshippers, and may be described as "a Promethean figure" with "colossal external strength" and "colossal powers," as in the more ludicrous moments of the Stalin era, or in the accolade to Israeli Prime Minister Golda Meir by *New Republic* owner-editor Martin Peretz, from which these quotes are taken.[8]

Franklin Delano Roosevelt attained similar heights among large sectors of the population, including many of the poor and working class, who placed their trust in him. The aura of sanctity remains among intellectuals who worship at the shrine. Reviewing a laudatory book on FDR by Joseph Alsop in the *New York Review of Books*, left-liberal social critic Murray Kempton describes the "majesty" of Roosevelt's smile as "he beamed from those great heights that lie beyond the taking of offense.... Those of us who were born to circumstances less assured tend to think of, indeed revere, this demeanor as the aristocratic style.... [We are] as homesick as Alsop for a time when America was ruled by gentlemen and ladies." Roosevelt and Lucy Mercer "were persons even grander on the domestic stage than they would end up being on the cosmic one," and met the great crisis in their lives, a secret love affair, "in the grandest style." "That Roosevelt was the democrat that great gentlemen always are in no way abated his grandeur.... [His blend of elegance with compassion] adds up to true majesty." He left us with "nostalgia" that is "aching." His "enormous bulk" stands between us "and all prior history ... endearingly exalted ... splendidly eternal for romance," etc., etc. Roosevelt took such complete command that he "left social inquiry ... a wasteland"—so much so that "ten years went by before a Commerce Department economist grew curious about the distribution of income and was surprised to discover that its inequality had persisted almost unchanged from Hoover, through Roosevelt and Truman ..." But that is only the carping of trivial minds. The important fact is that Roosevelt brought us "comfort ... owing to his engraving upon the public consciousness the sense that men were indeed equal," whatever the record of economic reform and civil rights may show. There was one published reaction, by Noel Annan, who praised "the encomium that Murray Kempton justly bestowed on Roosevelt."[9] Try as they might, the spinners of fantasy could not even approach such heights in the Reagan era.

The political and social history of Western democracies records all sorts of efforts to ensure that the formal mechanisms are little more than wheels spinning idly. The goal is to eliminate public meddling in policy formation. That has been largely achieved in the United States, where there is little in the way of political organizations, functioning unions, media independent of the corporate oligopoly, or other popular structures that might offer people means to gain information, clarify and develop their ideas, put them forth in the political arena, and work to realize them. As long as each individual is facing the television tube alone, formal freedom poses no threat to privilege.

One major step towards barring the annoying public from serious affairs is to reduce elections to the choice of symbolic figures, like the flag, or the Queen of England—who, after all, opens Parliament by reading the government's political program, though no one asks whether she believes it, or even understands it.[10] If elections become a matter of selecting the Queen for the next four years, then we will have come a long way towards resolving the tension inherent in a free society in which power over investment and other crucial decisions—hence the political and ideological systems as well—is highly concentrated in private hands.

For such measures of deterring democracy to succeed, the indoctrination system must perform its tasks properly, investing the leader with majesty and authority and manufacturing the illusions necessary to keep the public in thrall—or at least, otherwise occupied. In the modern era, one way to approach this task is to rhapsodize (or wail) over the astonishing popularity of the august figure selected to preside from afar. From the early days of the Reagan period it was repeatedly demonstrated that the tales of Reagan's unprecedented popularity, endlessly retailed by the media, were fraudulent. His popularity scarcely deviated from the norm, ranging from about one-third to two-thirds, never reaching the levels of Kennedy or Eisenhower and largely predictable, as is standard, from perceptions of the direction of the economy. George Bush was one of the most unpopular candidates ever to assume the presidency, to judge by polls during the campaign; after three weeks in office his personal approval rating was 76 percent, well above the highest rating that Reagan ever achieved.[11] Eighteen months after taking office, Bush's personal popularity remained above the highest point that

Reagan achieved. Reagan's quick disappearance once his job was done should surprise no one who attended to the role he was assigned.

It is, none the less, important to bear in mind that while the substance of democracy was successfully reduced during the Reagan era, still the public remained substantially out of control, raising serious problems for the exercise of power.

The Reagan Administration faced these problems with a dual strategy. First, it developed the most elaborate Agitprop apparatus in American history, its Office of Public Diplomacy, one major goal being to "demonize the Sandinistas" and organize support for the terror states of Central America. This mobilization of state power to control the public mind was illegal, as a congressional review irrelevantly observed, but entirely in keeping with the advocacy of a powerful and intrusive state that is a fundamental doctrine of what is called "conservatism." The second device was to turn to clandestine operations, at an unprecedented level. The scale of such operations is a good measure of popular dissidence.

Clandestine operations are typically a secret only from the general population at home, not even from the media and Congress, pretense aside. For example, as the Reagan Administration turned to the task of dismantling the Central American peace accords immediately after they were signed in August 1987, the media and Congress chose not to know that illegal supply flights to the Contras almost tripled from the already phenomenal level of one a day as Washington sought desperately to keep its proxy forces in the field in violation of the accords, so as to maximize violence and disruption, and to bring the people of Nicaragua to understand that removal of the Sandinistas was a prerequisite to any hope for decent survival. A year later, the media and Congress chose not to know that CIA supply flights from the Ilopango air base near San Salvador to Contras within Nicaragua were being reported by the same sources that had been ignored in the past, then proven accurate, as finally conceded; the "Hasenfus route," publicized at last when an American mercenary was shot down in October 1986 and the long-known facts could no longer be suppressed—for a few weeks.[12]

Similarly, the media (like Congress) pretended not to understand the absurdity of the historic agreement between the Bush Administration and congressional liberals "committing the Administration and Congress to aid for the Nicaraguan rebels and support for the Central American peace efforts" (Bernard Weinraub, New York Times); a flat and transparent self-contradiction, since the "peace efforts" explicitly bar the aid. A Times editorial solemnly explained that US goals are now "consistent with the regional pact" that was flagrantly violated by the agreement that the editors hailed. The historic agreement "reaffirms the policy that the strong may do whatever they wish, regardless of the will of others," exactly as Daniel Ortega was reported to have said on the same day as the *Times* editorial.[13]

The practice was uniform as the media followed their marching orders, quite oblivious to the fact that explicitly, and without ambiguity, "the Central America peace efforts" ruled out any form of aid for the US-run forces except for resettlement, and that the aid provided did not qualify as "humanitarian" by any standards, as was unequivocally determined by the World Court in a ruling that displeased US elite opinion and therefore was never mentioned in the long and vigorous debate—or what passed for such—over "humanitarian aid." The blatant self-contradiction in the (quite typical) statement quoted from the *Times* is evident and transparent, whether we consider the terms of the Esquipulas II Accord of August 1987 that was successfully demolished by Washington and the media within a few months, the Sapoà cease-fire agreement of March 1988 which Congress and the Administration immediately violated with the support of the media, or the February 1989 agreement of the Central American presidents, at once undermined by the Administration and Congress with the usual support of the media, which exhibit a tolerance for fabrication, even direct self-contradiction, that would have impressed Orwell mightily.

The facts are clear and unambiguous. The February 1989 declaration of the Central American presidents (Esquipulas IV) was for the most part a reflection of the triumph of the US government and the media in demolishing the August 1987 accords. Thus the crucial "symmetry" provisions were eliminated so that the US terror states were exempt, and Nicaraguan efforts to restore the international monitoring of Esquipulas II, eliminated under US pressure in the session of January 1988, were once again rejected, allowing the US and its clients full freedom to violate any agreement as they liked—confident, and rightly so, that the press would play along. But despite this capitulation to US power, the agreement

> firmly repeated the request contained in Numeral 5 of the Esquipulas II Accord that regional and extra-regional governments, which either openly or secretly supply aid to irregular forces [the Contras] or insurrectional movements [indigenous guerrillas] in the area, immediately halt such aid, with the exception of humanitarian aid that contributes to the goals of this document,

which are stipulated to be "the voluntary demobilization, repatriation or relocation in Nicaragua and in third countries" of Contras and their families.

The article of Esquipulas II to which reference is made specified one "indispensable element" for peace: namely, a termination of open or covert aid of any form ("military, logistical, financial, propagandistic") to the Contras or to indigenous guerrillas. The Sapoà cease-fire agreement of March 1988 reaffirmed the same principles, designating the Secretary-General of the Organization of American States as the official in charge of monitoring compliance; his letter of protest to George Shultz as Congress at once voted to violate the agreement (while explicitly pledging to observe it) was excluded by the media as improper. It would hardly have been helpful to their task of uniting in applause for the congressional decision to advance the cause of peace by undermining the cease-fire agreement and contradicting the terms of Congress's own legislation.[14]

Throughout, the media, and the Western intellectual community generally, successfully concealed what was happening before their eyes, operating much in the style of a totalitarian state, though without the excuse of fear. As regularly in the past, the cost is paid in blood and misery by the unimportant people.

The basic principle, rarely violated, is that what conflicts with the requirements of power and privilege does not exist. Therefore it is possible simultaneously to violate and to support the Esquipulas II Accords, the March 1988 cease-fire, and "the Central American peace efforts" narrowed to satisfy Washington's demands in February 1989.

The purpose of the government–media campaign to undermine the peace process is not obscure. It was important to ensure that Nicaragua would remain under at least a low level of terrorist attack within and military threat at the borders, so that it could not devote its pitiful resources to the awesome and probably hopeless task of reconstruction from US violence, and so that internal controls would allow US commentators to bemoan the lack of freedom in the country targeted for attack. The same logic lay behind the Pentagon directives to the proxy forces (explicitly authorized by the State Department, and considered reasonable by liberal doves) to attack undefended "soft targets." The reasoning was explained by a Contra defector who was so important that he had to be as rigorously avoided by the independent media as the Secretary-General of the OAS: Horacio Arce, chief of Contra (FDN) intelligence, whose *nom de guerre* was *Mercenario* ("mercenary")—talk about "freedom fighters" and "democrats" is for the educated classes at home. Contras were accorded ample media attention, more than the Nicaraguan government, but Arce received different treatment.

Arce had a good deal to say when he was interviewed in Mexico in late 1988 after his defection. In particular, he described his illegal training in an air force base in the southern United States, identified by name the CIA agents who provided support for the Contras under an AID (Agency for International Development) cover in the US Embassy in Tegucigalpa, outlined how the Honduran army provided intelligence and support for Contra military activities, and reported the sale of CIA-supplied Soviet-style arms to the FMLN guerrillas in El Salvador (later offered as "proof" of Cuban and Nicaraguan arms shipments). Arce then explained: "We attack a lot of schools, health centers, and those sort of things. We have tried to make it so that the Nicaraguan government cannot provide social services for the peasants, cannot develop its project ... that's the idea." Evidently, the careful US training was successful in getting the basic idea across.

It was never seriously in doubt that congressional liberals and media doves would support measures of economic strangulation and low-level terror guided by these principles until Nicaragua achieved "democracy"—that is, until political power passed to business and landowning elites linked to the United States, who are "democrats" for this reason alone, no further questions asked.[15] They can also be expected to lend at least tacit support to further Washington efforts to undermine and subvert any government that fails to place the security forces under effective US control or to meet proper standards of subservience to domestic and foreign business interests.

A government turns to clandestine terror and subversion, relatively in-efficient modes of coercion, when it is driven underground by its domestic enemy: the population at home. As for the Reaganite propaganda exercises, they achieved the anticipated success among educated elites. It was scarcely possible to imagine any deviation from the basic principles of the Party Line, however absurd they might be: for example, that El Salvador and Guatemala are (perhaps flawed) democracies with elected presidents, while Nicaragua under the Sandinistas is a totalitarian dictatorship that never con-ducted an election approaching the impressive standards of the US terror states (the 1984 elections did not exist by Washington edict, faithfully honored in respectable sectors). But the propaganda was less effective, it appears, among the general population. There is reason to believe that the substantial improvement in the general cultural and moral levels set in motion in the 1960s continued to expand, imposing conditions that any system of concentrated power must meet.

3. The Achievements of Economic Management

The Reagan era largely extended the political program of a broad elite consensus. There was a general commitment in the 1970s to restore corporate profitability and impose some discipline on an increasingly turbulent world. In the US variety of state capitalism, that means recourse to military Keynesian devices at home, now adapted to the decline in US power and therefore with a right-wing rather than liberal slant, the "great society" programs being incompatible with the prior claims of the important people. Abroad, the counterpart is large-scale subversion and international terrorism (whatever term is chosen to disguise the reality). The natural domestic policies were transfer of resources to the rich, partial dismantling of the limited welfare system, an attack on unions and real wages, and expansion of the public subsidy for high-technology industry through the Pentagon system, which has long been the engine for economic growth and preserving the technological edge.

Plans reflecting these general elite perceptions of the 1970s were proposed by Carter and implemented by the Reaganites—including military spending, which, overall, largely followed Carter projections. The method adopted was to sink the country into a deep recession to reduce inflation, weaken unions, and lower wages; then to lift it out through deficit spending while organizing the subsidy to high-tech industry and shaking a fist at the world, policy choices that commonly go hand in hand. It should be recognized that while talk about free trade is fine for editorials and after-dinner speeches, those with a stake in policy decisions do not take it too seriously. The historical evidence shows that the economies that developed and industrialized, including the United States, adopted protectionist measures when these were advantageous. The most successful economies are those with substantial state coordination, including Japan and its periphery, and Germany—where, to mention only one feature, the IMF estimates that industrial incentives are the equivalent of a 30 percent tariff. In the United States, the two major components of the economy that are competitive internationally—capital-intensive agriculture and high-technology industry—are both heavily subsidized by the state, which also provides them a guaranteed market. These two sectors are also, not surprisingly, the "villains" behind the federal deficit, the *Wall Street Journal* observes. The other "villain" is the untouchable entitlements; correcting for statistical chicanery, if the Social Security surplus were removed from the budget, as it would be if properly devoted to capital formation for future needs, the deficit would rise by $50 billion,

Franco Modigliani and Robert Solow estimate.[16]

The right-wing military Keynesians were also highly protectionist, quite apart from the expansion of the protected state market for high-tech production under the euphemism of "defense." The Reaganites initiated a Pentagon-based consortium for semiconductor research and development, and increasingly gave the Pentagon the task of functioning in the manner of Japan's state–corporate planners, organizing R&D in chip and computer design, superconductivity, high-definition television, and other areas of advanced technology. Star Wars fantasies constituted only one of the methods concocted to induce the public to provide a subsidy to high-technology industry, which will reap the profits if there are commercial applications in accord with the doctrines of "free enterprise." Reagan also introduced more import restrictions than the past six presidents combined; the percentage of total imports subjected to quota and restraint agreements doubled from 12 to 24 percent under Reaganite "conservatism."[17]

The results of these policies were apparent by the mid 1980s, and became increasingly so as the presidential transition approached. Expressing a fairly general consensus among economists and business elites, David Hale, chief economist of Kemper Financial Services, observed: "seldom has a new American administration taken office against such a pervasive backdrop of economic gloom as that which now confronts President George Bush," with "the country seemingly awash in a sea of red ink as the Reagan era ends."[18] There was a rapid increase in the federal deficit, and a seventy-year climb to the status of the world's leading creditor nation was quickly reversed as the US became the world's leading debtor. Hale estimates that "by 1991 the United States will probably have a $1 trillion external debt," a transfer of well over a trillion dollars in a decade—no mean feat on the part of those who regularly deride "Sandinista mismanagement." The investment balance also swung radically in favor of foreign investors. Private and corporate savings deteriorated to a historic low, relative to GNP. Private wealth rose more slowly than in the late 1970s, and real wages stagnated. Income was sharply redistributed upwards; the rich gained, the poor suffered, as intended. Government economic management led to consumption by the rich, speculation and financial manipulation, but little in the way of productive investment. "Investment is a smaller fraction of the GNP today than it was in the late 1970s, when we were not borrowing abroad," Lester Thurow observes, adding: "our current international borrowing is going into either public or private consumption and will therefore eventually extract a reduction in the future American standard of living." US net investment, relative to GNP, is now the lowest of the big seven industrial countries. Even that low level of investment was maintained only by the large increase in capital imports, Modigliani and Solow note. Military R&D rose from 46 to 67 percent of federal spending from fiscal years 1980 to 1988, another development that in the long run will severely harm the US economy. These and other factors also contributed to the trade deficit, which may be ineradicable if US investors shift their operations abroad.[19]

For the first time in its history, the General Accounting Office issued a study on the perilous state of the economy left by an outgoing Administration.[20] The report by the head of the GAO, the chief federal auditor and a Reagan appointee, outlined the "staggering" costs to be paid as a result of Reaganite economic mismanagement and environmental destruction. The GAO also noted the rapid rise in homelessness, the deterioration of the limited welfare net for the poor and the middle class, the lowered safety standards for workers, and numerous other consequences of the blind pursuit of short-term gain. There was an aura of prosperity thanks to the willingness of foreign investors to throw a party for the rich—not, of course, out of charity; they can call in their chips. The same is true of the wealthy at home. Tax reductions induced lending to government by the beneficiaries, who will gain the further benefits. In this way too, fiscal policy constitutes a long-term shift of resources to the wealthy. The "staggering" costs discussed by the federal auditors will be paid by the poor and the working class who have been left out of the consumption binge that economists now blame for the clouds on the horizon, just as the taxpayer is called upon to bail out speculators hoping to profit from deregulation of the Savings and Loan institutions, and probably, before too long, the banks that reaped enormous profits by lending to the wealthy classes and neo-Nazi military rulers who took over much of Latin America with US backing from the early 1960s.

The state managers were selective in the forms of state intervention in the economy that they adopted. Where deregulation could yield short-term profits, it was considered a worthy goal. The Savings and Loan fiasco is one dramatic consequence. The wild abandon of these years has had its effects more broadly in the deterioration of infrastructure, health and education standards, the conditions of the environment, and the general state of the economy. Regulatory programs to encourage energy conservation went the way of plans to develop renewable energy resources, on the pretext that the price of oil would be lowered by the miracle of the free market (the price in practice has generally been administered by the US client

regime of Saudi Arabia and the major oil corporations, who maintain production at a level that will ensure prices high enough for rich profits but low
enough not to encourage a search for alternatives, with US government
pressures in the 1980s to lower the price so as to sustain the recovery from
the deep recession of 1982). This form of foolishness has ample precedent
and, as in the past, is bound to have grave repercussions.[21]

Reaganite foot-dragging on environmental protection is likely to have
other long-term effects. The issues are addressed in a scientific study submit-
ted at an October 1990 UN conference. The international panel reached
virtual unanimity on the conclusion that global warming had occurred over
the past century and that the risk of further warming is serious, ranging
from significant to near-catastrophic, largely a result of fossil fuel combustion.
"The US press has focused on the outlying views [that question the consen-
sus] without pressing hard on justifying them," one American scientist on
the panel told *Science* magazine. A British scientist who is an author of
the section on observed climate change added: "In America, a few extreme
viewpoints have taken center stage. There are none like that elsewhere."
Not a single member of the panel of two hundred people agreed with
the skeptical views that have received wide attention in the United States,
gaining such headlines as "U.S. Data Fail to Show Warming Trend" (*New
York Times*) and "The Global Warming Panic: a Classic Case of Over-
reaction" (cover of *Forbes*), and with television coverage structured to leave
the impression that scientific opinion is uncertain and divided.[22]

The British press reported that the scientists' consensus was overridden
by the UN political committees, under the pressure of the US and Japan.
Even Thatcher's England finally abandoned free-market fantasies, leaving
Washington and its media in the forefront of the effort to delay a constructive
response to what might prove to be a major catastrophe. The guiding principle, again, is that government policy should be designed for the short-term
gain of the privileged, the basic doctrine of Reaganite conservatism.[23]

A congressional study released in March 1989 shows that the average
family income of the poorest fifth of the population declined by over 6
percent from 1979 through 1987, meanwhile rising by over 11 percent
for the richest fifth; these statistics are corrected for inflation and include
welfare benefits. For the poorest fifth, personal income declined by 9.8
percent while rising by 15.6 percent for the richest fifth of the population.
One reason is that "more jobs now pay poverty level wages or below,"
the chief economist of the House Ways and Means Committee commented.
The National Association of Children's Hospitals and Related Institutions

released a study showing that health care for children in the US had declined to its lowest point in ten years, with appalling statistics. For example, the proportion of low birth weights (which contribute to the unusually high infant mortality rates) is 1.7 times as high as in Western Europe; for Black children the proportion is far worse.[24]

The consequences for one wealthy city are outlined by columnist Derrick Jackson of the *Boston Globe*. He notes that UNICEF ranks the US second to Switzerland in *per capita* GNP and twenty-second in infant mortality, with a worse record than Ireland or Spain—a decline from its 1960 position of tenth. For African-Americans, the rate is almost double the US average. In the Roxbury section of Boston, populated largely by ethnic minorities, the rate is almost triple the US average, which "would rank Roxbury, supposedly part of the world's second-richest nation, 42nd in infant mortality." Though Boston is one of the world's great medical centers, Roxbury's infant mortality rate is worse than that of Greece, Portugal, the Soviet Union and all of Eastern Europe, and much of the Third World. A Harvard medical school expert on infant mortality, Paul Wise, commented: "The only place where you see social disparities like you see in the US infant-mortality rate is South Africa," the only other industrialized nation without guaranteed health care. Jackson continues:

> Long before pregnancy, women are outside the loop on nutrition and health education. ... While the leaders in Washington are puffing their chests this week over the tearing down of walls in Europe, vast and growing numbers of African-Americans, Latinos, Cambodians, Haitians and Vietnamese are blocked from hospitals and clinics by lack of money, health insurance or language.[25]

Facts such as these, which can be duplicated throughout the country, provide a most remarkable commentary on the variety of state capitalism practiced in what should be by far the richest country in the world, with incomparable advantages, frittered away during the Reagan years even beyond the disgraceful norm.

The spirit of these years is captured by Tom Wolfe, who depicts them as "one of the great golden moments that humanity has ever experienced." So they doubtless were for the important people for whom he speaks.[26] The intended goals of domestic economic management were to a large extent achieved, just as the bipartisan Washington consensus achieved its intended goal of deflecting the threat of democracy and social reform in Central America.

4. Restoring the Faith

Reagan's greatest accomplishment is supposed to be that he made us "feel good about ourselves," restoring the faith in authority, which had sadly flagged. As the editors of the *Wall Street Journal* put it, "he restored the efficiency and morale of the armed services [and] demonstrated the will to use force in Grenada and Libya"—two military fiascos, but no matter. We were able to kill a sufficient number of people and are once again "standing tall," towering over the upstarts who had sought to overcome us but succumbed to the cool courage and "the strength of the Cowboy"— the words of British journalist Paul Johnson, while swooning over the manliness of his idol Ronald Reagan, who had in reality shown the courage of a Mafia don who sends a goon squad to break the bones of children in a kindergarten. With these achievements, Reagan overcame our "sickly inhibitions against the use of military force," Norman Podhoretz intoned.[27]

Actually, all of this is sham. Frightened little men may strut about in awe of their cowboy hero, but the general public seems more opposed to violent intervention than before and—I hope, though I do not know— more committed to acting to block it.

5. Public Vices

Sponsorship of state-guided international terrorism and economic management designed for short-term gain for the wealthy are the most notable features of the Reagan era, but there are others. In this brief review, I have not even mentioned what may be the most dangerous legacy of Reagan, Thatcher, and the rest. Coming generations are going to face problems that are quite different in scale and complexity from any that have arisen before. The possible destruction of a physical environment that can sustain human life in anything like its present mode is one of the most dramatic of these, along with the proliferating threat of weapons of mass destruction and continuing conflicts among adversaries with increasing capacity to cause terrible damage. That these problems have a solution is not so obvious. That exaltation of greed to the highest human value is *not* the answer is quite obvious. Tales about private vices yielding public benefits could be tolerated in a world living less close to the margin, but surely can no longer. By celebrating the ugliest elements of human nature and social life, the

Reaganites have set back, by some uncertain measure, the prospects for coming to terms with grave dilemmas and possible catastrophes.

Coming generations will pay the costs. That is the legacy of these years, even if we permit ourselves not to see the misery and torture of our victims throughout much of the world.

Notes

1. Hertzberg, *TNR*, February 6, 1989; McGrory, *Boston Globe*, February 6, 1989.

2. Frederick Z. Brown, *Indochina Issues*, November 1988. For further reflections on the suffering imposed upon us by the Vietnamese, see *Manufacturing Consent*, pp. 238 f.; *Necessary Illusions*, pp. 33 ff.

3. Wrong, review of Fallows, *More Like Us, NYT Book Review*, March 26, 1989.

4. LeMoyne, *NYT Magazine*, April 6, 1986; Szulc, *NYT Magazine*, May 25, 1980.

5. Kinzer, *NYT Magazine*, March 26, 1989.

6. French, *NYT*, May 8, 1990. See *Turning the Tide*, pp. 150 f. The elections was in 1962, not 1963.

7. *NYT*, July 19, 1990. See *Manufacturing Consent* for many similar cases, and details on Cambodia.

8. Friedman, *Inventors of the Promised Land* (Knopf, 1975), ch. 2; *New Republic*, August 10, 1987.

9. Kempton, *NYRB*, April 15, 1982; Annan, letters, *NYRB*, June 10, 1982.

10. On the effects of the institution of royalty on British culture, see Tom Nairn, *The Enchanted Glass* (Hutchinson, 1988).

11. *BG*, February 17, 1989, reporting on ABC/*Washington Post* poll. See references of Chapter 12, Note 39 on fact versus fraud concerning Reagan's popularity.

12. AP, December 15; *Barricada Internacional* (Managua, San Francisco), December 22, 1988. Since the reports were on the wires, the suppression was conscious. On the sharp escalation of supply flights from October 1987 and media complicity in suppressing the facts, see my articles in *Z Magazine*, January, March, 1988; and for a review, *Necessary Illusions*.

13. Weinraub, *NYT*, March 25; editorial, March 28, 1989; Mark Uhlig, *NYT*, same day.

14. For details, see *Necessary Illusions*, and on the February 1989 agreements, the Managua Jesuit journal *Envío*, March 1989 (published at Loyola University, New Orleans).

15. See *Necessary Illusions* for further details. Needless to say, this prediction in March 1989 proved accurate.

16. James Perry, *WSJ*, January 5; Modigliani and Solow (both Nobel laureates in economics), letter, *NYT*, March 12, 1989. Germany; Amsden, "East Asia's Challenge."

17. Andrew Pollack, "America's Answer to Japan's MITI," *NYT*, business section, March 5; David Hale, "Just Say No: The GOP Abandons Free Markets," *International Economy*, January/February 1989, and "Picking up Reagan's Tab," *Foreign Policy*, Spring 1989.

18. Ibid.

19. Robert Cowen, "R&D Spending Under Reagan," *CSM*, January 20, 1989; Benjamin Friedman, "The Campaign's Hidden Issue," *New York Review of Books*, October 13, 1988; John Berry, "The Legacy of Reaganomics," *WP Weekly*, December 19, 1988. Arthur MacEwan, *Dollars & Sense*, January/February 1989; Thurow, "Winners and Losers," *BG*, March 7, 1989; *Economist*, March 25, 1989; Modigliani and Solow.

20. Robert Pear, "Reagan Leaving Many Costly Domestic Problems, G.A.O. Tells Bush," *NYT*, November 22, 1988.

21. On earlier phases, see *Towards a New Cold War*, especially chs 2, 11. With the Middle East crisis of mid 1990, the problems finally began to receive public attention.

22. "Research News," *Science*, August 3, 1990.

23. Geoffrey Lean, "UN setback for global warming action plan," *Observer*, May 20, 1990.

See also Craig Whitney, "Scientists Warn of Danger in a Warming Earth," *NYT*, May 26, 1990, noting US isolation, attributed to "the uncertainties in scientific research on climate change" that have "exasperated" policymakers, according to President Bush. It was reported at the same time that the US was the only country at an international conference on rainforest destruction to oppose setting a year 2000 goal for protection of the world's tropical forests. In April, the US was the only country at a Geneva conference to oppose a fund to help developing countries stop using ozone-depleting chemicals. Participants in an April White House-sponsored conference on global warming allege that the government manipulated the agenda to prevent consideration of mandatory restrictions in greenhouse gases. Jeff Nesmith, *NYT* news service, May 23, 1990.

24. Martin Tolchin, *NYT*, March 23; Alexander Reid, *BG*, March 2, 1989.

25. Jackson, *BG*, December 24, 1989.

26. *BG*, February 18, 1990.

27. Editorial, *WSJ*, January 19, 1989; Johnson, *Sunday Telegraph*, June 1, 1986. Johnson and Podhoretz are exulting over Libya and Grenada, respectively. A notorious apologist for terrorism and atrocities, Johnson also applauded Israel for "having the moral and physical courage to violate a so-called sovereign frontier" by invading Lebanon in 1982 to excise "the terrorist cancer"—with an estimated 20,000 or more killed, mostly Lebanese and Palestinian civilians (quoted by Wolf Blitzer, *Jerusalem Post*, June 29, 1984). In the real world, the invasion had nothing whatsoever to do with "the terrorist cancer," except in so far as Israel hoped that the attack might return the PLO to the terrorist policies Israel preferred by undermining its self-restraint in the face of repeated and murderous Israeli cross-border attacks, and terminating PLO efforts to move towards a peaceful political settlement, intolerable to both major Israeli political coalitions. There was ample evidence on these matters from Israeli sources at the time Johnson produced these typically inane comments. See *Fateful Triangle*, *Pirates and Emperors*, and *Necessary Illusions*.

THREE

The Global System

1. Separation Anxieties

A POLITICAL cartoon depicts a snowman with a helmet and a rifle, melting under a bright sun while an anxious George Bush holds an umbrella over him to deflect its rays. The snowman is labeled "Cold War," and the caption reads: "Not permanent? What'll We Dooo?"[1] The dilemma is real.

As discussed in Chapter 1, the Cold War has served important functions for state managers. When a government stimulus was needed for a faltering economy or to foster new and costly technologies, state managers could conjure up Russian hordes on the march to induce the public to expand the subsidy to advanced industry via the Pentagon. Forceful intervention and subversion to bar independent nationalism in the Third World could be justified in the same terms, and there were ancillary benefits in maintaining US influence over its allies. Quite generally, the Evil Empire has been invoked when needed for domestic economic management and for controlling the world system. A replacement will not be easy to find.

These are serious concerns. Intervention carries material and moral costs that the population may not be willing to bear. With an obedient population and quite different cultural patterns, such economic powerhouses as Japan can conduct state–corporate economic planning on the assumption that people will follow orders. In a less disciplined society, it is necessary to manufacture consent. To a nontrivial extent, current US economic problems derive from the relatively free and open character of the society, which precludes the more efficient fascist-style methods that are now hailed as a triumph of free enterprise and democracy. Thus, to cite typical cases, the *New York Times* proclaims that "as an economic mechanism, democracy demonstrably works," as illustrated in the "newly industrializing countries" (NICs) South Korea, Taiwan, Singapore and Hong Kong. And sociologist Dennis Wrong, writing in the democratic socialist journal *Dissent*, describes the "striking capitalist successes" of these four countries "under capitalist economies free from control by rickety authoritarian governments" as compared to the "economic failures of Cuba, North Korea, Vietnam, and, more recently Nicaragua," all attributable solely to Marxist–Leninist dogma; what is valid in the comparison is that the authoritarian governments were efficient, not "rickety," in organizing economic growth.[2] Short of a real counter-revolution, reversing many social and political gains of the past and imposing novel repressive patterns, the United States cannot adopt these forms of authoritarian state–corporate rule.[3]

Faced with such problems, the traditional method of any state is to inspire fear. Dean Acheson warned early on that it would be necessary "to bludgeon the mass mind of 'top government'" with the Communist threat in order to gain approval for the planned programs of rearmament and intervention. The Korean War, shortly after, provided "an excellent opportunity . . . to disrupt the Soviet peace offensive, which . . . is assuming serious proportions and having a certain effect on public opinion," he explained further. In secret discussion of Truman's proposal for intervention in Greece and Turkey (the Truman Doctrine), Senator Walter George observed that Truman had "put this nation squarely on the line against certain ideologies," a stance that would not be easy to sell to the public. Senator Arthur Vandenberg added that "unless we dramatize this thing in every possible way," the public would never understand. It would be necessary to "scare hell out of the American people," he advised. The public was fed tales much like those used to bludgeon the mass mind of recalcitrant officials, in a style that was "clearer than truth," as Dean Acheson later said approvingly. As a new crusade was being launched in 1981, Samuel Huntington explained: "You may have to sell [intervention or other military action] in such a way as to create the misimpression that it is the Soviet Union that you are fighting. That is what the United States has done ever since the Truman Doctrine." An important insight into the Cold War system, which applies to the second-ranked superpower as well. By the same logic, it follows that "Gorbachev's public relations can be as much a threat to American interests in Europe as were Brezhnev's tanks," Huntington warned eight years later.[4]

One persistent problem is that the enemy is hard to take seriously. It takes some talent to portray Greece, Guatemala, Laos, Nicaragua, or Grenada as a threat to our survival. This problem has typically been overcome by designating the intended victim as an agent of the Soviet Union, so that we attack in self-defense. The Soviet threat itself has also required some labors, ever since the first major call for postwar rearmament, and "rollback" and break-up of the Soviet Union, in NSC 68.

The basic problems are institutional, and will not fade away.

2. The Changing Tasks

In the early post-World War II period, US planners hoped to organize most, if not all, of the world in accord with the perceived needs of the United States economy. With 50 percent of the world's wealth and a position of power and security without historical parallel, the "real task" for the US was "to maintain this position of disparity," by force if necessary, State Department Policy Planning chief George Kennan explained. The vision was partially achieved, but over time the US position of dominance was bound to erode. The Kennedy Administration attempted a "Grand Design" to remedy the growing problem, expecting that Britain would "act as our lieutenant (the fashionable word is partner)," in the words of one senior Kennedy adviser who carelessly let slip the true meaning of the lofty phrases about partnership.[5] By that time it was becoming difficult to manage and control Europe, the major potential rival. The problems mounted as US allies enriched themselves through their participation in the destruction of Indochina, which proved costly to the US economy.

Both superpowers have been declining in their power to coerce since the late 1950s. Now Washington's "real task" is to maintain a position of dominance that is seriously challenged. These long-term developments in the international system continued during the 1980s, accelerated by Reaganite social and economic mismanagement with its deleterious effects, which some regard as a "crippling blow" to a "decaying America" (Senator Ernest Hollings).[6] For years, the world has been drifting towards three major economic blocs: a dollar bloc; a yen bloc based on Japan and its periphery; and a German-centered European bloc, moving towards further unity in

1992. The incorporation of Canada within a US-dominated free trade system in 1988 is a step towards consolidation of the dollar bloc, which is also intended to incorporate northern Mexico with its supply of cheap labor for assembly plants and parts production, and whatever else may be viable economically in Latin America. The Caribbean Basin Initiative is a halting step in the same direction. Europe and Japan have different ideas, however, not to speak of the region itself. These tendencies towards the formation of conflicting power blocs may be heightened by Washington's efforts to induce Europe and Japan to bail the US out of its trade deficit and other economic problems, and by the impact on Third World exporters if the US abandons the role as consumer of last resort for the countries that adopted an export-oriented development model under US pressure.[7]

The Kennedy Grand Design was an effort to ward off the growing danger of an independent European bloc with its own global designs. In Henry Kissinger's "Year of Europe" speech in 1973, he admonished the Europeans to keep to regional interests within an "overall framework of order" managed by the United States, and refrain from developing a larger trading bloc to which the US would be denied privileged access. The conflicts with Japan are by now front-page news. In earlier eras such developments have led to serious conflict, even major wars. Presumably, the interpenetration of the global economies and the awesome nature of means of destruction will avert direct confrontation, but the seeds are there.

What role will the Soviet Union play in this world system? The Cold War had a regular rhythm of confrontation and détente, influenced heavily by domestic factors within each superpower and its need to exert force within its own international system; for us, most of the world. The Soviet Union made a number of efforts to extricate itself from a confrontation that it lacked the economic power to sustain; since they were rebuffed, we cannot know how serious they were (see Chapter 1, pp. 24 f.). The present case, however, is qualitatively different.

Gorbachev's moves towards détente had little to do with US table-pounding, militarization of the economy, or the expansion of international terrorism under the Reagan Doctrine. They were undertaken in an effort to drive the cruel and inefficient centralized state constructed by Lenin and his successors towards economic and social change, an effort at reform from above that has given rise to a wide range of popular responses and initiatives with exciting but uncertain prospects, and to much uglier features as well, from deterioriation of the economy to chauvinist, racist, and anti-Semitic excesses.

Fortuitously, these moves towards détente and internal reform coincided with the natural flow of American politics. By the mid 1980s, the task for the US political leadership was not to terrify the public into paying for military programs it did not want, but rather to deal with the costs of the Reaganite welfare state measures for the wealthy. As early as 1982, 83 percent of top corporate executives surveyed in a *Wall Street Journal/* Gallup poll favored a reduction in military spending in order to reduce the rapidly mounting federal deficit,[8] and within a few years it was clear that under the conditions of the 1980s, with the United States having lost its position of overwhelming dominance over its industrial rivals, the old devices of state intervention in the economy were no longer feasible. For purely domestic reasons, then, the international environment came to be portrayed as less threatening. With the imaginary "window of vulnerability" no longer needed and therefore closed, the Evil Empire was not quite on the verge of swallowing us up after all; and international terrorists were no longer lurking behind every corner. The world had become a safer place—not so much because the world itself had changed, but because new problems were arising at home. A statesmanlike pose became mandatory. Reagan even revealed himself to be a closet Leninist. In this context, it was possible to be at least somewhat receptive to Gorbachev's moves, undertaken for independent reasons.

Nevertheless, the decline of the Soviet threat is a dark cloud on the horizon for the reasons already mentioned. Long before the Cold War, H.L. Mencken commented: "The whole aim of practical politics is to keep the populace alarmed (and hence clamorous to be led to safety) by menacing it with an endless series of hobgoblins, all of them imaginary." The Soviet hobgoblin has served admirably for the domestic and international designs of US elites, who are far from overjoyed to see it fade from view. The question of the Soviet role in the emerging international system is also casting a shadow over planning. On the surface, disputes with the allies concerned technical issues, such as the US demand that Lance missiles be upgraded to just below the level of those dismantled by the Russians under the INF Treaty—in Soviet eyes, a tacit abandonment of the Treaty. But these matters were of little moment,[9] serving as a cover for the more serious issue of relaxation of East–West tensions. The real problem is that the United States' major rivals are exploring closer relations with the Soviet Union, which is eager to obtain capital and technology and to forge closer economic links with the West, reestablishing something like the quasi-colonial relations of earlier years. Germany and Japan particularly have capital and technology that the USSR and its satellites badly need; in turn, they offer resources to be developed and exploited, markets for excess production, and perhaps cheap labor and opportunities for export of pollution and waste, as expected of well-behaved semi-developed dependencies. Germany and other European countries are eagerly exploring these prospects. Before too long, there may even be a free trade zone for Japan in Vladivostok and Japanese exploitation of oil and other resources in Siberia—developments which, if realized, could materially alter the structure of the world order.

A drift towards closer links between the industrial rivals of the United States and the Soviet bloc would awaken the worst nightmares of US geopolitical thinking, which sees the United States as an island power standing off the Eurasian landmass, just as committed to prevent its unification as England was with regard to continental Europe in the era of its more limited hegemony. For such reasons, Washington has been distinctly uneasy about the growing ties with the Soviet Union. Throughout the 1980s, it sought to block expanding economic relations that would have eased Cold War tensions and furthered the integration of the Soviet economy into the Western zone. In late 1989, the US was isolated in opposing high-technology exports to the USSR, alleging security concerns, though these were hardly even a joke by that time. In an October 1989 meeting of COCOM, the committee of fifteen NATO nations, Japan, and Australia which regulates trade with the Soviet bloc, the United States stood alone in seeking to prevent high-technology sales. COCOM partners accused the US of trying "to stifle foreign competitors of American manufacturers," who could profit from these trade relations, AP reported.[10] The US has since continued to try to erect impediments to aid to the USSR—"aid" being understood as an export promotion device that the US is now ill-equipped to employ, in comparison with its rivals, particularly after the Reaganite blows to the domestic economy.

3. Containing "Gorby Fever"

In this context, one can appreciate the concerns aroused in the late 1980s by Gorbachev's moves, which require a new form of containment: a cure for "Gorby Fever" in Western Europe, or at least confinement of the disease. A headline in the *Wall Street Journal* reads: "Anti-Nuclear Fever Presents a Dilemma for Bush as Soviets Ease Confrontation." The article goes on to outline one of Bush's "most thankless but important jobs": to defend "the virtue of nuclear weapons in the face of a relentless and sometimes brilliant Soviet crusade to rid Europe of them." This new "Soviet strategy" has "deprived Western hardliners of their best weapon," and "appears to be working" among the disobedient Europeans, though European elites are also concerned that relaxation of tension might free their own populations from the controls of Cold War confrontation. Dan Rather reported from Germany that Helmut Kohl might be about to make the same mistake that Chamberlain made in 1939, believing Gorbachev just as Chamberlain believed Hitler and succumbing to fantasy about "peace in our time"; Americans can help keep Germany from making that mistake, he advises. Liberal Sovietologist Jerry Hough of the Brookings Institution warned that the US had given in too readily to "the complacent optimism that Gorbachev cannot possibly succeed." "Perhaps this optimism will be justified," he writes, but we cannot be sure, and must be more cognizant of the "looming difficulties and challenges."[11]

One problem has been Europe's failure to see the moves towards détente in the proper terms: as a victory for capitalist democracy achieved by the courage of Ronald Reagan, then his skills as a peacemaker after his firm resolve compelled the enemy to throw in the towel. The London *Financial Times* welcomed "the rosy glow of the new détente," adding, however, that "everybody knows that the architect of that détente is not Ronald Reagan but Mikhail Gorbachev." As for Reagan, his

> contribution to the gaiety of nations includes the Evil Empire, Star Wars, the invasion of Grenada, the bombing of Libya, the 1986 Reykjavik summit at which he almost agreed to give away America's nuclear arsenal, and Irangate. Plus, of course, the steady piling up of the budget and trade deficits; and when they are eventually paid for, the price to the American people will be very high.

Public opinion polls showed Gorbachev to be more popular than Reagan; Gorbachev's initiatives are playing havoc with West European politics, the *New York Times* reports, and his "charm has so captivated European public opinion that it could inhibit NATO's room for maneuver," a senior US government official laments.[12]

A more comforting view of the matter was crafted by former *Times* executive editor A.M. Rosenthal. "Nobody is telling the truth," he writes— not implausibly, for once. The "truth," he proceeds, is that Western Europe is terrified by West Germany's unwillingness to upgrade NATO missiles as the US demands. Germany's intransigence on this critical matter and its moves towards accommodation with the USSR arouse European fears of "a mighty Germany working in tandem with a rejuvenated Soviet Union," with echoes of the Hitler–Stalin pact.

But the Europeans, again, refused to see matters as they were told they did—which is not to deny that there are fears of a mighty Germany and its ambitions. As Rosenthal was expounding European concerns over Germany's intransigence, public support for Germany's position mounted through most of Europe, while polls showed little fear of the USSR. Such results are not new; to cite one of many prior cases, classified US Information Agency (USIA) opinion polls leaked in Europe (but apparently unpublished in the US media) revealed that Europeans blamed Reagan by wide margins for the breakdown of the 1986 Reykjavik summit. In the conflict over missiles, the London *Guardian* observed, the US and Britain—the two "island powers"—are "isolated in Nato, and not the Germans," who are supported by most of the alliance. The *Guardian* adds correctly that the issue is not missiles, but Germany's "ambition to lead Western Europe into a rapprochement with the Soviet Union—one out of which could flow much mutual economic and political benefit"; exactly the concern of American planners and, for the present, their British lieutenant with its enduring illusions of partnership.[13]

4. The Community of Nations

Putting a bold face on the matter, George Bush, arriving in Europe for NATO consultations, said that the US is "prepared to move beyond containment toward a policy that works to bring the Soviet Union into the community of nations."[14] A worthy objective, doubtless, but some queries remain.

There is a "community of nations," with an organized forum in which the world community has expressed some opinions on the matters of disarmament and détente, about which Bush now offers his kind tutelage to the errant Soviet Union. Thus, while Reagan was being extolled (in the United States) for leading the world towards peace at the December 1987 Washington summit, where the INF Treaty was signed, the United Nations General Assembly, speaking for "the community of nations," voted a series of disarmament resolutions. It voted 154–1, with no abstentions, opposing the build-up of weapons in outer space (Reagan's Star Wars) and 135–1 against developing new weapons of mass destruction. The Assembly voted 143–2 for a comprehensive test ban, and 137–3 for a halt to all nuclear test explosions. The US voted against each resolution, joined in two cases by France and one by Britain. None of this was reported in the Free Press, the "community of nations" being irrelevant when it fails to perceive the Truth.[15]

The US alone boycotted a UN disarmament conference in New York in 1987 to consider how reduction of armaments might release funds for economic development, particularly in the Third World. Shortly before, the US was alone at the General Assembly in opposing a South Atlantic "zone of peace" (voted 124–1). By that time, Gorbachev's proposal that the US join the unilateral test ban (largely suppressed in the US), his call for steps towards dismantling the pacts, removal of US and Soviet fleets from the Mediterranean, outlawing sea-launched cruise missiles, and other annoying actions had become an acute embarrassment—so much so that George Shultz was compelled to call upon him to "end public diplomacy," drawing sober approval from media pundits. The White House complained that Gorbachev was behaving like a "drugstore cowboy" with his depressingly popular scattershot proposals. On numerous other issues (among them: observance of international law, terrorism, South Africa, a Middle East political settlement) the US has been alone or in a small minority, and it is far in the lead in recent years in Security Council vetoes. The deviant behavior of the world community has elicited some anxious commentary in the media, which are naturally concerned over the failure of the community of nations to comprehend truths that are simple and uncontroversial—as is demonstrated, conclusively, by the fact that they are put forth by US power. This thoughtful concern over the deficiencies of the world community coexists, somewhat uneasily perhaps, with our earnest efforts to uplift and civilize the Evil Empire and bring it into the community of nations.[16]

5. The Silver Lining

In its final think piece for 1988 on the Cold War, the *New York Times* features Dimitri Simes, senior associate at the Carnegie Endowment for International Peace. He begins with conventional doctrine: "For more than 40 years, America's international strategy has been subordinated to one overriding concern—deterring Soviet global designs against the West." But if Gorbachev really is reducing these threats, "there may be sizable advantages to exploring the Kremlin's opening, uncertain as it may be, in order to liberate American foreign policy from the straitjacket imposed by superpower hostility."[17]

Simes identifies three "national security challenges" that can be addressed if Gorbachev's words are followed by appropriate deeds. First, the US can shift NATO costs to its European competitors, one element of the larger problem of competing blocs already discussed. Second, we can end "the manipulation of America by third world nations." The US will be able to "resist unwarranted third world demands for assistance" and will be "in a stronger bargaining position vis-a-vis defiant third world debtors." The problem of the manipulation of America by the undeserving poor is particularly acute with regard to Latin America, which transferred some $150 billion to the industrial West from 1982 to 1987 in addition to $100 billion of capital flight; the capital transfer amounts to twenty-five times the total value of the Alliance for Progress and fifteen times the Marshall Plan, Robert Pastor writes. The Bank for International Settlements in Switzerland estimates that between 1978 and 1987, some $170 billion in flight capital left Latin America, not including money hidden by falsified trade transactions. The *New York Times* cites another estimate that anonymous capital flows, including drug money and flight capital, total $600 billion to $800 billion. This huge hemorrhage is part of a complicated system whereby Western banks and Latin American elites enrich themselves at the expense of the general population of Latin America, saddled with the "debt crisis" that results from these manipulations, and taxpayers in the Western countries who are ultimately called upon to foot part of the bill. And now we can tighten the screws further on the poor majority—the second advantage accruing to us from Gorbachev's capitulation, according to Simes's analysis.[18]

The third and most significant opportunity afforded us, Simes continues, is that the "apparent decline in the Soviet threat . . . makes military power more useful as a United States foreign policy instrument . . . against those who contemplate challenging important American interests," considering them "easy prey." The US need no longer be inhibited by fear of "triggering counterintervention" if it resorts to violence to suppress such challenges. Had it not been for these inhibitions, the US could have used force to prevent the 1973 oil embargo (in reality, the US found the price rise not unwelcome as a weapon against Europe and Japan); and "the Sandinistas and their Cuban sponsors" will be "a little nervous" that Gorbachev may not react "if America finally lost patience with their mischief." America's hands will be "untied" if concerns over "Soviet counteraction" decline. This will permit Washington "greater reliance on military force in a crisis."

Things may be looking up, then, despite Gorbachev's maneuvers and the "erosion in clarity" they have caused. The clouds have a silver lining, and we may yet benefit from the Gorbachev maneuvers, if we handle them properly.

As this analysis reveals, Gorbachev's initiatives have had the salutary effect of clearing the air and sharpening the distinction between rhetoric and policy. At the rhetorical level, the US "contains" the Soviet Union and "deters its global designs." But in practice, as more acute analysts have long understood, fear of "Soviet counteraction" has deterred the pursuit of US global designs. Since these designs require periodic resort to force and subversion in far-flung areas where the US lacks conventional force advantage, Washington has been compelled to maintain an intimidating military posture—one reason why a policy of Third World intervention has led to the demand for continual expansion of strategic weapons capacities. As all recognize, a major Soviet crime has been Moscow's assistance to Third World countries or movements that the United States intends to subvert or crush. The hopeful element in Gorbachev's initiatives is that now the Soviet Union may remove the barriers to Washington's resort to violence to achieve its global designs and punish the mischief of those who do not properly understand their subordinate role.[19]

For the ideologist, there is indeed an "erosion in clarity" as it becomes more difficult to manipulate the Soviet threat in a manner "clearer than truth." But for people who want to escape the bludgeoning of the mass mind, there is an increase in clarity. It is helpful to read in the pages of the *Times* that the problem all along has been Soviet deterrence of US designs, though admittedly the insight is still masked. It is also useful to read in *Foreign Affairs* that the détente of the 1970s "foundered on the Soviet role in the Arab–Israeli war of 1973, Soviet assistance to the Vietnamese communists in their war of conquest in Indochina, and Soviet sponsorship of Cuban intervention in Angola and Ethiopia" (Michael Mandelbaum). Those familiar with the facts will be able to interpret these charges properly: the Soviet Union supported indigenous elements resisting the forceful imposition of US designs—a criminal endeavor, as any right-thinking intellectual comprehends. It is even useful to watch the tone of hysteria mounting among the more accomplished comic artists—for example Charles Krauthammer, who welcomes our victory in turning back the Soviet program of "unilaterally outflanking the West ... economically or geopolitically" by establishing "new outposts of the Soviet empire" in the 1970s: "Afghanistan, Nicaragua, Cambodia, and, just for spite, Grenada." Putting aside the actual

facts, it is doubtless a vast relief to have liberated ourselves from these awesome threats to the very survival of the West.[20]

6. The Soviet Threat

Deceit and manipulation aside, the Soviet Union has always been considered
a major threat to the US and its allies, and for good reason. In part this
follows from its very existence as a great power controlling an imperial
system that could not be incorporated within the Grand Area; in part from
its occasional efforts to expand the domains of its power, as in Afghanistan,
and the alleged threat of invasion of Western Europe, if not world conquest.
But it is necessary to understand how broadly the concept of "defense"
is construed if we wish to evaluate the assessment of Soviet crimes.

As we have seen, leading scholars consider the Western invasion of the
Soviet Union to have been justified on defensive grounds because of the
Bolsheviks' revolutionary intentions (see p. 14). Thus an appeal for social
change justifies aggression in self-defense, though the intellectual community
does not draw the further consequence that the Soviet Union and many
other states would always have been entirely justified in carrying out attacks
against the United States, given its declared intention to change their social
order.

Since 1917—and particularly after World War II—intervention abroad
and repression at home have been cloaked in the guise of defense against
the "Kremlin design for world domination" (NSC 68), a concept broad
enough to include aggression by allies, once the US decides to support
it. John Lewis Gaddis refers blandly to "the Eisenhower administration's
strategy of deterring aggression by threatening the use of nuclear weapons"
in Indochina in 1954, "where French forces found themselves facing defeat"
at Dien Bien Phu "at the hands of the Communist Viet Minh," the aggressors
who attacked our French ally defending Indochina. In his history of nuclear
weapons, McGeorge Bundy notes that "the first operational test of the
Eisenhower administration's new policy on the use of nuclear weapons
came in the climactic months of the French effort to defend against Communist insurgency in Vietnam"—at Dien Bien Phu, where France was defending Indochina from its population; in Western parlance, from the Russians
and their minions.[21]

We need not suppose that the appeal to alleged security threats is mere
deceit. The authors of NSC 68 may have believed their hysterical flights

of rhetoric, though some understood that the picture they were painting was "clearer than truth." In a study of policymakers' attitudes, Lars Schoultz concludes that they were sincere in their beliefs, however outlandish: for example, that Grenada—with its population of 100,000 and influence over the world nutmeg trade—posed such a threat to the United States that "an invasion was essential to US security."[22] The same may be true of those who, recalling our failure to stop Hitler in time, warned that we must not make the same mistake with Daniel Ortega, poised for world conquest. And Lyndon Johnson may have been sincere in his lament that without overwhelming force at its command, the United States would be "easy prey to any yellow dwarf with a pocket knife," defenseless against the billions of people of the world who "would sweep over the United States and take what we have." Eisenhower and Dulles may have believed that the "self-defense and self-preservation" of the United States were at stake in the face of the terrible threat posed by Guatemala in 1954—though it is interesting that in the secret planning record the only example cited to justify their desperate anxiety is "a strike situation" in Honduras that might "have had inspiration and support from the Guatemalan side of the Honduran border."[23] The same may even be true of those who instituted and maintained a national emergency from 1985 to defend us from the "unusual and extraordinary threat" to our national security posed by Nicaragua under the Sandinistas.

In such cases, we need not conclude that we are sampling the productions of psychotics; that is most unlikely, if only because these delusional systems have an oddly systematic character and are highly functional, satisfying the requirements stipulated in the secret documentary record. Nor need we assume conscious deceit. Rather, it is necessary only to recall the ease with which people can come to believe whatever is convenient to believe, however ludicrous it may be, and the filtering process that excludes those lacking these talents from positions of state and cultural management.

In passing, we may note that while such matters may be of interest to those entranced by the personalities of leaders, for people concerned to understand the world, and perhaps to change it, they are of marginal concern at best, on a par with the importance for economists of the private fantasies of the CEO while he (or rarely she) acts to maximize profits and market share. Preoccupation with these matters of tenth-order significance is one of the many devices that serve to divert attention from the structural and institutional roots of policy, and thus to contribute to deterring the threat of democracy, which might be aroused by popular understanding of how the world works.

In so far as one chooses to dwell on these insignificant questions, answers are highly uncertain. Thus, Schoultz may be right in supposing that policy-makers were quaking in their boots in fear of Grenada. But a different conclusion is surely suggested by his discussion of the background: the immediate hostility aroused by the "progressive social programs" of the Bishop government in 1979 (meanwhile continuing the "repressive politics" that aroused great outrage in the U.S., unlike vastly worse repression by client states) and the harsh measures taken by the Carter Administration, escalated by the Reaganites, to punish the criminals. Such doubts can only be enhanced by a look at the tales spun by the White House, then retailed by a new cadre of "Latin America experts" constructed by the media when the professional scholars refused to play the game: for example, that "the Cubans surely appreciate that Grenada is strategically located by the route over which about one-half of U.S. imported oil passes" (Robert Leiken), doubtless a threat before which the US could only quiver in helplessness. Schoultz himself concludes that the claims of General Vernon Walters and other Administration officials about the need to protect (nonexistent) south-ern sea lanes were nothing more than a device to justify close relations with Pinochet and the Argentine generals, "prime examples of how a national security consideration can be employed to manipulate U.S. foreign policy debates." The same conclusion is no less plausible in a wide range of other cases, if one chooses to explore the (basically uninteresting) question of whether the doctrines that serve interest are, or are not, sincerely believed once constructed for that end.[24]

Throughout, we find that more intelligent elements are aware of the fraud used to beguile others and to defend oneself from unpleasant reality. As it prepared to overcome the danger of independent capitalist democracy in Guatemala, the US cut off military aid and threatened attack, so that Guatemala turned to the Soviet bloc for arms, other sources having been barred by US power. Guatemala City Embassy officer John Hill advised that the US could now take steps to bar "movement of arms and agents to Guatemala," stopping ships in international waters "to such an extent that it will disrupt Guatemala's economy." This would in turn "encourage the Army or some other non-Communist elements to seize power," or else "the Communists will exploit the situation to extend their control," which would "justify the American community, or if they won't go along, the U.S. to take strong measures."[25] We thus compel Guatemala to defend itself from our threatened attack, thereby creating a threat to our security which we exploit by destroying the Guatemalan economy so as to provoke a military coup or an actual Communist takeover which will justify our violent response—in self-defense. Here we see the real meaning of the phrase "security threat," spelled out with some insight.

The Soviet Union has been a threat to world order when it supported anyone opposing US designs: South Vietnamese engaged in "internal aggression" against their selfless American defenders; Guatemalan democrats committed to independent nationalism; or Nicaraguans illegitimately defending themselves against US-run terrorist forces. Such support proves that Soviet leaders are not serious about détente and cannot be trusted, commentators soberly observe. "Nicaragua will be a prime place to test the sanguine forecast that [Gorbachev] is now turning down the heat in the Third World," the *Washington Post* editors proposed in 1987, placing the onus for the US attack against Nicaragua on the Russians while warning of the threat of this Soviet outpost to "overwhelm and terrorize" its neighbors while the US stands helplessly by.[26] The US has "won the Cold War," from this point of view, when it is free to exercise its will in the rest of the world without Soviet interference.

The *Post* test of Gorbachev's seriousness was standard fare. A front-page story by *Times* chief diplomatic correspondent Thomas Friedman reported that the Bush Administration was urging Gorbachev "to cut Soviet assistance to Nicaragua or to condition future aid on steps by Managua to make democratic reforms"—unnecessary in neighboring countries where US clients maintain power by violence. Buried at the end of his report is Washington's rejection of the Soviet offer to cut aid "if Washington cut its military assistance to its allies in the region"—an utter absurdity, as outlandish as a (hypothetical) Soviet request that the US condition its military aid to Turkey on "democratic reforms" or reduce its offensive military forces there, with missiles on alert status aimed at the Russian heartland. As *Post* columnist Stephen Rosenfeld helpfully explained, Gorbachev "fails to distinguish between foreign interference [on the US model] intended to bestow the opportunity for choice" and, on the other hand, Soviet-style foreign interference, "undertaken to make or sustain ... a minority regime that could exist only by armed power." In predictable accord with White House dictates, he cites Nicaragua under the Sandinistas as an example of the latter, since it never permitted "a free vote" (for example in the 1984 elections, which did not occur in state-sanctioned history), while El Salvador, Guatemala, and other beneficiaries of US intervention illustrate our fervent commitment to bestow the opportunity for choice without any resort to "armed power." Friedman later reported Secretary of State Baker's "test" of Gorbachev's "New Thinking": if the USSR will "eliminate military aid to Nicaragua and press the Sandinista Government on Central American peace, Washington will promise not to plan any military attacks against Managua and hold out the prospect of economic aid"; surely a fair and forthcoming offer, at once lauded as such by the *Post* editors and others.[27]

Jonathan Swift, where are you when we need you?

To satisfy the demands of respectable thought, Gorbachev's "New Thinking" must permit free rein for the US resort to violence. The point is obvious enough. Hugh O'Shaughnessy writes in the British press that as Gorbachev has "moved closer to the Washington viewpoint" with regard to Central America, "he gave the impression that the guilty party" is Nicaragua, not "the Governments of El Salvador and Guatemala, whose political and human rights records are sickening, or the Government of Honduras, the base for the offensive against Nicaragua," all of which Gorbachev failed to criticize when visiting Cuba to exhibit his New Thinking. Similarly, "as Moscow tries to minimise causes of friction with Washington, Soviet aid to the South African liberation movements and to the front-line States appears to be faltering," and more generally, "the time when a Third World government could often benefit itself handsomely by playing off East and West against each other appears to be over."[28]

Such Soviet moves might be beneficial if accompanied by comparable steps in Washington or, better yet, by support for democracy and social reform and constructive aid programs geared to the real needs of the people of the Third World. These are idle dreams, however. Scarcely concealed behind a thin rhetorical cover is the fact that US elites want to see the Third World turned over to Washington's whims, not liberated to pursue independent goals.

Notes

1. Auth cartoon, *Philadelphia Inquirer*, April 28, 1989.

2. James Markham, *New York Times Week in Review*, lead story, September 25, 1988; Dennis Wrong, *Dissent*, Spring 1989.

3. There is, by now, a virtual industry on "what makes Japan tick," varying in quality. Not without interest, despite racist undertones and illusions about the West, is Karel van Wolferen, *The Enigma of Japanese Power* (Knopf, 1989). On South Korea, see Alice Amsden, *Asia's Next Giant*.

4. Acheson, *Present at the Creation* (Norton, 1969), pp. 374–5. William Borden, *Pacific Alliance*, p. 144. Lloyd Gardner, *Diplomatic History*, Winter 1989. Huntington, *International Security*, Summer 1981; *National Interest*, Fall 1989.

5. Costigliola, in Paterson, ed., *Kennedy's Quest for Victory*.

6. *WP Weekly*, May 8, 1989.

7. For some recent discussion of these matters, see Walter Russell Mead, "The United States and the World Economy," *World Policy Journal*, Winter 1988–9. A year later, a free trade zone with Mexico was under active discussion, and a vague plan to extend it to all of Latin America was floated by President Bush.

8. See Brad Knickerbocker, "Defense spending no longer off limits to budget-cutters," *CSM*, April 21, 1982.

9. Within a year, these meaningless diversions had collapsed, along with the Berlin Wall and the remaining shreds of the Soviet imperial system in Eastern Europe.

10. Mort Rosenblum, AP, October 25, 1989.

11. John Walcott, *WSJ*, February 6, 1989. Dan Rather, CBS radio news, 4:40 p.m., WEEI, Boston, January 30, 1989. Hough, *International Economist*, January/February 1989.

12. Ian Davidson, *Financial Times*, reprinted in *World Press Review*, December 1988; Thomas Friedman, *NYT*, February 14, 1989.

13. Rosenthal, *NYT*, May 2, 1989; USIA polls, see *Culture of Terrorism*, 197; *Manchester Guardian Weekly*, May 7, 1989. For the polls and related discussion of the mood in Europe, see Diana Johnstone, who has long been the most informative commentator on European affairs, *In These Times*, May 17, 1989.

14. John Mashek, *BG*, May 27, 1989.

15. Votes critical of the Soviet Union were prominently reported at exactly that time. The disarmament votes were obviously timely, given the outpouring of praise for Reagan the Peacemaker. I found nothing. See *Culture of Terrorism*, p. 195, and *Necessary Illusions*, pp. 82 f., 218 ff., for details on these matters. On US isolation on environmental issues, see below: Chapter 2, section 3 and Note 23. See also Chapters 5, 6.

16. Serge Schmemann, *NYT*, March 27, 30; *BG*, October 28; AP, Berlin, April 21, 1986. Joseph Nye, *Foreign Affairs*, Fall 1986. Shultz, Bernard Gwertzman, *NYT*, March 31, 1986. Bernard Weinraub, *NYT*, May 17, 1989. On US commentary on the world community and its inadequacies, see *Necessary Illusions*, Appendix IV, sec. 4. I apologize to the ghost of President McKinley for borrowing his rhetoric, as he launched his liberation of the Philippines.

17. Dimitri K. Simes, "If the Cold War Is Over, Then What?," *NYT*, December 27, 1988.

18. Robert Pastor, "Securing a Democratic Hemisphere," *Foreign Policy*, Winter 1988–9; Pastor was Director of Latin American and Caribbean Affairs for the National Security Council under the Carter Administration. Jeff Gerth, *NYT*, February 12, 1990.

19. See Chapter 1, p. 59, for a similar insight a year later by Elliott Abrams.

20. Mandelbaum, "Ending the Cold War," *Foreign Affairs*, Spring 1989; Krauthammer, "Beyond the Cold War," *New Republic*, December 19, 1988.

21. Gaddis, *Long Peace*, p. 129. Bundy, *Danger and Survival* (Random House, 1988), p. 260.

22. Schoultz, *National Security and United States Policy toward Latin America* (Princeton, 1987), pp. 239 ff.

23. Johnson, *Congressional Record*, March 15, 1948, House, 2883; *Public Papers of the Presidents*, 1966, Book II (Washington, 1967), p. 563, speech of November 1. Eisenhower–Dulles, *FRUS*, 1952–4, vol. IV, c. 1132. Invocation of "self-defense and self-preservation" was proposed by Attorney General Herbert Brownell as providing legal justification for violating international law by intercepting ships in international waters. Memorandum of NSC discussion, May 27, 1954.

24. Schoultz, pp. 239 f., 185–6; Leiken, cited from *Foreign Policy*, Spring 1981. On the defection of Latin American scholarship from the cause, see pp. 22 f. Schoultz concludes that the stance of independent scholarship allowed critics "to dominate the intellectual debate over what is actually happening in Latin America," but he fails to take account of the fact that the media, including intellectual journals of opinion, compensated for the defection by creating new "experts" to replace them, so that the *New York Times* could present the spectrum of opinion as bounded by Mark Falcoff of the American Enterprise Institute on the right, and Contra lobbyist Robert Leiken, a hitherto unknown Maoist, on the "left." See *Culture of Terrorism*, pp. 205 and Note 8; and that book, *Manufacturing Consent*, and *Necessary Illusions* on the success of this strategy in controlling the spectrum of articulate opinion and news reporting in the mainstream.

25. Bryce Wood, *The Dismantling of the Good Neighbour Policy* (University of Texas, 1985), p. 177.

26. *WP Weekly*, December 28, 1987.

27. Friedman, *NYT*, March 30, May 9; Rosenfeld, *WP*, April 7; editorial, *WP*, May 2, 1989.

28. London *Observer*, April 23, 1989.

FOUR

Problems of Population Control

THE last two chapters were concerned with the political, economic, and cultural effects of the so-called Reagan revolution, and the global system taking shape with the decline of the two superpowers and the erosion of the Cold War confrontation that had proven so useful for mobilizing the domestic population in support of intervention abroad and privilege at home. Since these remain core policy objectives, some new thinking is required.

For US elites the easing of Cold War tensions was a mixed blessing. True, the decline of the Soviet deterrent facilitates US resort to violence and coercion in the Third World, and the collapse of the Soviet system paves the way to integration of much of East and Central Europe into the domains that are to "complement the industrial economies of the West." But problems arise in controlling the ever-threatening public at home and maintaining influence over the allies, now credible rivals in terms of economic power and ahead in the project of adapting the new Third World to their needs. Here lie many problems, of a potentially serious nature. It was therefore hardly surprising that Gorbachev's initiatives should have elicited such ambivalent reactions, tinged with visible annoyance and thoughts as to how they could be exploited to Washington's advantage; or that his unilateral concessions and offers were so commonly interpreted as moves in a game of PR one-upmanship, in which our side unfortunately lacked the talent to compete.

1. "The Unsettling Specter of Peace"

The "Unsettling Specter of Peace" raises "knotty 'peace' questions," the *Wall Street Journal* observes.[1] Crucially, it threatens the regular resort to the military Keynesian programs that have served as the major device of state economic management through the postwar years. The *Journal* quotes former army chief of staff General Edward Meyer, who thinks that a more capital-intensive and high-tech military will ensure "a big business out there for industry": robot tanks, unmanned aircraft, sophisticated electronics—all of dubious use for any defensive (or probably any) military purpose, but that is not the point. It is, however, a rather lame hope; how will the public be bludgeoned into paying the costs, without a plausible Red Menace on the horizon?

Concerns deepened as the shadow of the specter lengthened. "Doom and gloom pervaded one of the first congressional forums for the Economic Stabilization, Adjustment and Defense Industry Conversion Act of 1990," the press reported from Washington, under the headline "House mulls ways to soften the blow as peace breaks out." Appearing before a House Armed Services subcommittee a few days earlier, Matthew Coffey, president of the National Tooling and Machining Association, testified: "We've got a serious, wrenching experience that we're going to go through" if the military budget declines. There is broad agreement that the state will have to provide export credits and other benefits to industry: "Unless there's a fall-back position, it will be impossible to cut weapons systems," New York liberal Democrat Ted Weiss commented. Ohio Republican John Kasich agreed, while grumbling about "corporate welfare," an unusual concession to the real world.[2]

The problem is not new, though it is arising in a more severe form than heretofore. "Peace scares" have given rise to uneasiness and anxiety from the early days of the Cold War. Business circles have long taken for granted that the state must play a major role in maintaining the system of private profit. They may welcome talk about free enterprise and *laissez-faire*, but only as a weapon to prevent diversion of public resources to the population at large, or to facilitate the exploitation of the dependencies. The assumption has been that a probable alternative to the Pentagon system is investment for social needs. While perhaps technically feasible by the abstract standards of the economist, this option interferes with the prerogatives of owners and managers and is therefore ruled out as a policy option. But unless driven by fear, the public will neither choose the path that best serves corporate interests nor support foreign adventures undertaken to subordinate the Third World to the same demands.

Problems of social control mount in so far as the state is limited in its capacity to coerce. It is, after all, hardly a law of nature that a few should command while the multitude obey, that the economy should be geared to ensuring luxuries for some instead of necessities for all, or that the fate— even the survival—of future generations be dismissed as irrelevant to planning. If ordinary folk are free to reflect on the causes of human misery (in Barrington Moore's phrase), they may well draw all the wrong conclusions. Therefore, they must be indoctrinated or diverted, a task that requires unremitting efforts. The means are many; engendering fear of a threatening enemy has always been a powerful tool in the kit.

The Vietnam years awakened many minds. To counter the threat, it was necessary to restore the image of American benevolence and to rebuild the structure of fear. Both challenges were addressed with the dedication they demand.

The congressional human rights campaign, itself a reflection of the improvement in the moral and intellectual climate, was skillfully exploited for the former end. In the featured article of the *Foreign Affairs* annual review of the world, Robert Tucker comments, cynically but accurately, that since the mid 1970s "human rights have served to legitimize a part of the nation's post-Vietnam foreign policy and to give policy a sense of purpose that apparently has been needed to elicit public support." He adds "the simple truth that human rights is little more than a refurbished version of America's historic purpose of advancing the cause of freedom in the world," as in Vietnam, a noble effort "undertaken in defense of a free people resisting communist aggression."[3] Such State Department handouts are all that one can expect about Vietnam in respectable circles; the plain truth is far too threatening to be thinkable. But the comments on "America's historic purpose"—also conventional—do merit some notice. Such rhetoric would elicit only ridicule outside of remnants of pre-Enlightenment fanaticism— perhaps among the mullahs in Qom, or in disciplined Western intellectual circles.[4]

In the Reagan years, a "yearning for democracy" was added to the battery of population control measures. As Tucker puts it, under the Reagan Doctrine "the legitimacy of governments will no longer rest simply on their effectiveness, but on conformity with the democratic process," and "there is a right of intervention" against illegitimate governments—a goal too ambitious, he feels, but otherwise unproblematic. The naive might ask why we failed to exercise this right of intervention in South Korea, Indonesia,

South Africa, or El Salvador, among other candidates. There is no inconsistency, however. These countries are committed to "democracy" in the operative meaning of the term: unchallenged rule by elite elements (business, oligarchy, military) that generally respect the interests of US investors, with appropriate forms for occasional ratification by segments of the public. When these conditions are not satisfied, intervention is legitimate to "restore democracy."

To take the fashionable case of the 1980s, Nicaragua under the Sandinistas was a "totalitarian society" (Secretary of State James Baker) and a "Communist dictatorship" (the media generally), where we must intervene massively to assure that elites responsive to US interests prevail as elsewhere in the region.[5] Colombia, in contrast, is a democracy with a "level playing field," in current jargon, since these elements rule with no political challenge.

A closer look at Colombia is directly relevant to what follows, and provides further insight into what counts as "democracy." In Colombia, the *New York Times* informs us, courageous people threatened by "violence from cocaine gangs" are struggling "to preserve democratic normalcy" and "to keep democratic institutions alive." The reference is not to peasants, union leaders, or advocates of social justice and human rights who face the violence of the military and the oligarchy. And crucially, democratic normalcy has never been threatened by the fact that the two parties that share political power are "two horses [with] the same owner" (former President Alfonso Lopez Michaelsen)—not exactly a circumstance unfamiliar to us. Nor does a problem arise from the actual conditions of this "democratic normalcy." To mention a few, death squads have killed about 1000 members of the one party not owned by the oligarchy (the Patriotic Union, UP) since its founding in 1985,[6] leaving the unions and popular organizations with no meaningful political representation. Disappearance and execution of labor, Indian and community leaders is a regular part of daily life while "many Colombians insist that army troops often act as though they were an occupation force in enemy territory" (Americas Watch). These death squads dedicated to extermination of "subversives" are in league with the security forces (Amnesty International). An official government inquiry made public in 1983 found that over a third of members of paramilitary groups engaged in political killings and other terror were active-duty officers, a pattern that continues to the present, along with alliances with drug dealers, according to human rights inquiries (Alfredo Vásquez Carrizosa, president of the Colombian Permanent Committee for Human Rights and former Minister of Foreign Affairs). The death squads sow "an atmosphere of terror, uncertainty and despair," and "all families in which even one member is somehow involved in activities directed towards social justice" are under constant threat of disappearance and torture, conducted with "impunity" by the military and their allies (Pax Christi Netherlands), including "cocaine gangs" and the owner of the two horses. Political killings in 1988 and 1989 averaged eleven a day (Andean Commission of Jurists, Bogotá office).[7]

All of this leaves the playing field level and poses no threat to "democratic institutions," no challenge to "America's historic purpose."

Similarly, the growth of the drug cartels in Guatemala "has sparked sharp concern for the survival of the country's nascent democracy," Lindsey Gruson warns in the *New York Times*. "Guatemala's emergence as a major player in the international drug bazaar"—along with Honduras and Costa Rica, now "routinely" used for drug transshipment—"has sparked concern among United States diplomats that it will lead to a bitter Congressional debate over aid to this country, which is just emerging from international isolation after years of military rule."[8]

But events a few days earlier, routine for many years and too insignificant to reach the *Times*, aroused no qualms about the "nascent democracy" and did not threaten the flow of US military and other aid. Wire services reported that "terrified by a new wave of political violence, the family of an abducted human rights activist fled this country [on September 23] after spending nearly six weeks holed up in a room at the Red Cross." The deputy federal attorney general for human rights says "It is incredible how this family has been persecuted" because of the human rights activities of Maria Rumalda Camey, a member of the Mutual Support Group of relatives of the disappeared. She was kidnapped by armed men in August, the fourth person in her family to disappear in ten months; "the others eventually turned up—all shot dead and dumped on roadsides." The family fled to the Mutual Support Group office in Guatemala City, but were evacuated by the Red Cross when a grenade was lobbed through the window half an hour after their arrival. "In the last two months," the report continues, "there has been a surge of killings and bombings," with mutilated bodies left by roadsides as warnings; this "surge" is beyond the normal level of atrocities by security forces and their unofficial wings and associates. Thus, on September 15, the Guatemalan press reported fifteen bodies bearing signs of torture found in one twenty-four-hour period in one southwestern province; before the men were abducted they had been followed by an army vehicle from a nearby military base, according to a survivor. A few days later, the body of a student was found, the seventh of twelve recently "disappeared" in the classic style of the security forces of the US client states. Other bodies were found with parts cut off and signs of torture. Thousands of peasants who returned from Mexico after promises of land and security are planning to flee to Mexican refugee camps as a result of the violence and the government's failure to honor its promises, the local press reports.[9]

The targets are peasants, activists and organizers. Hence the "nascent democracy" suffers at most minor flaws, and is secure from international isolation or funding cutoff—at least, as long as it does not offend the master's interests.[10]

By such means as skillful manipulation of human rights concerns and a finely tuned "yearning for democracy," the ideological institutions labored to reconstruct the image of benevolence; and among articulate elites at least, their success has been remarkable. The complementary task was to reconstruct the climate of fear. To this end, it was necessary to bewail the triumphs of the Soviet enemy, marching from strength to strength, conquering the world, building a huge military system to overwhelm us. The effort achieved a brief success, though by the mid 1980s it had to be abandoned as the costs of "defense" against these fearsome challenges became intolerable. We may therefore concede that "it is now clear that the gravity of developments in 1980 was exaggerated" (Robert Tucker): the threat to our existence posed by Soviet influence in South Yemen, Laos, Grenada, and other such powerhouses was not quite so grave as he and other sober analysts had thought. By 1983, the CIA conceded that since 1976 the growth rate of Soviet defense spending had dropped from 4–5 percent to 2 percent and the growth rate of weapons procurement had flattened—exactly contrary to the claims advanced to justify the Carter program of rearmament that was implemented in essentials in the Reagan years. In a careful reanalysis of the data, economist Franklyn Holzman concludes that the ratio of Soviet military expenditures to GNP scarcely changed after 1970 and the total appears to be "considerably less" than US expenditures (not to speak of the fact that US NATO allies outspend Soviet Warsaw Pact allies by more than five to one, that 15–20 percent of Soviet expenditures are devoted to the China front, and that its allies have hardly been reliable). "The Soviet military spending gap," he concludes, "like the 'bomber gap' of the 1950s and the 'missile gap' of the 1960s, turns out to be a myth."[11]

From the early years of the Cold War, the real menace has been "Soviet political aggression" (Eisenhower) and what Adlai Stevenson and others called "internal aggression." A powerful NATO military alliance, Eisenhower held, should "convey a feeling of confidence which will make [its members] sturdier, politically, in their opposition to Communist inroads"— that is, to "political aggression" from within by "Communists," a term understood broadly to include labor, radical democrats, and similar threats to "democracy." Citing these remarks in his history of nuclear weapons, McGeorge Bundy adds that Eisenhower "did not believe the Russians either wanted or planned any large-scale military aggression."[12]

This understanding was common among rational planners, which is not to deny that they readily convinced themselves that Soviet hordes were on the march when such doctrines were useful for other ends. Part of the concern over the fading of the Soviet threat is that the appropriate images can no longer be conjured up when we must again rush to the defense of privileged sectors against internal aggression.

In the early Reagan years, the Soviet threat was manipulated for the twin goals of Third World intervention and entrenching the welfare state for the privileged. Transmitting Washington's rhetoric, the media helped to create a brief period of public support for the arms build-up while constructing a useful myth of the immense popularity of the charismatic "great communicator" to justify the state-organized party for the rich. Other devices were also used. Thanks to the government–media campaign, 60 percent of the public came to perceive Nicaragua as a "vital interest" of the United States by 1986, well above France, Brazil, or India. By the mid 1980s, international terrorism, particularly in the Middle East, assumed center stage. To appreciate the brilliance of this propaganda feat, one must bear in mind that even in the peak years of concern, 1985–6, the US and its Israeli ally were responsible for the most serious acts of international terrorism in this region, not to speak of the leading role of the United States in international terrorism elsewhere in the world, and in earlier years. The worst single terrorist act in the region in 1985 was a car-bombing in Beirut that killed eighty people and wounded 250. It was graphically described, but did not enter the canon, having been initiated by the CIA. To cite another striking example, in 1987 it was revealed that one of the many terrorist operations mounted against Cuba took place at a particularly tense moment of the missile crisis; a CIA-dispatched terrorist team blew up a Cuban industrial facility with a reported death toll of four hundred workers, an incident that might have set off a nuclear war. I found not a single reference in the media in the midst of the continuing fury over the "plague of international terrorism" spread by crazed Arabs backed by the KGB in the effort to undermine the West. Respected scholarly work also keeps strictly to the official canon.[13]

Such menaces as Nicaragua and international terrorists have the advantage that they are weak and defenseless. Unlike the Soviet enemy, Grenada and Libya can be attacked with impunity, eliciting much manly posturing and at least a few moments of rallying round the flag. In contrast, we could rail against the Soviet enemy, but no more. But for the same reason, the menace is difficult to sustain. To enhance credibility, the selected targets have regularly been linked to the Evil Empire, evidence having its usual irrelevance. But these charges too have lost their force, and new monsters are badly needed to keep the population on course.

Enter the Medellín cartel.

2. The Drug War

To fit the part, a menace must be grave, or at least portrayable as such. Defense against the menace must engender a suitable martial spirit among the population, which must accord its rulers free rein to pursue policies motivated on other grounds and must tolerate the erosion of civil liberties, a side benefit of particular importance for the statist reactionaries who masquerade as conservatives. Furthermore, since the purpose is to divert attention away from power and its operations—from federal offices, corporate boardrooms, and the like—a menace for today should be remote: "the other," very different from "us," or at least what we are trained to aspire to be. The designated targets should also be weak enough to be attacked without cost; the wrong color helps as well. In short, the menace should be situated in the Third World, whether abroad or in the inner city at home. The war against the menace should also be designed to be winnable, a precedent for future operations. A crucial requirement for the entire effort is that the media launch a properly structured propaganda campaign, never a problem.

A war on drugs was a natural choice for the next crusade. There is, first of all, no question about the seriousness of the problem; we turn to the dimensions directly. But to serve the purpose, the war must be narrowly bounded and shaped, focused on the proper targets and crucially avoiding the primary agents; that too was readily accomplished. The war is also structured so that in retrospect, it will have achieved some of its goals. One major objective of the Bush–Bennett strategy was a slow regular reduction in reported drug use. The test is to be the Federal Household Survey on

Drug Abuse, which, a few weeks before the plan was released, showed a decline of 37 percent from 1985 to 1988.[14] The stated objective thus seemed a rather safe bet.

The war was declared with proper fanfare by President Bush in early September 1989—or rather, re-declared, following the convention established twenty years earlier by President Nixon when he issued the first such dramatic declaration. To lay the ground properly for the current phase, Drug Czar William Bennett announced that there had been a remarkable doubling in frequent use of cocaine since 1985—"terrible proof that our current drug epidemic has far from run its course"—and that we are faced with "intensifying drug-related chaos" and an "appalling, deepening crisis"; a few months later, the White House called a news conference to hail a new study "as evidence that their national drug strategy was succeeding and that narcotics use was becoming unfashionable among young Americans," Richard Berke reported in the *New York Times*. So the drug warriors, in the truest American tradition, were stalwartly confronting the enemy and overcoming him.

There are, however, a few problems. The decline in 1989 simply continues a trend that began in 1985–6 for cocaine and in 1979 for other illicit drugs, accompanied by a decline in alcohol consumption among the elderly, though there was no "war on alcohol." Cocaine use declined sharply in 1989, with a drop of 24 percent in the third quarter, prior to the declaration of war, according to government figures. Bennett's "doubling" is a bit hard to reconcile with the figures on decline of cocaine use, but a few months after the shocking news was announced with proper fanfare and impact, the paradox was revealed to be mere statistical fakery. On the back pages, we read further that a study by the State Department Bureau of International Narcotics Matters contradicted Bennett's claims that "the scourge is beginning to pass," thanks to his efforts.[15]

As required, the war is aimed at "them," not "us." Seventy percent of the Bush–Bennett drug budget was for law enforcement; if the underclass cannot be cooped up in urban reservations and limited to preying on itself, then it can be imprisoned outright. Countering criticism from soft-hearted liberals, Bennett supported "tough policy" over "drug education programs": "If I have the choice of only one, I will take policy every time because I know children. And you might say this is not a very romantic view of children, not a very rosy view of children. And I would say, 'You're right'." Bennett is somewhat understating his position when he says that punishment is to be preferred if only one choice is available. In his previous post as

Secretary of Education, he sought to cut drug education funds and has expressed skepticism about their value.[16]

The flashiest proposal was military aid to Colombia after the murder of presidential candidate Luis Carlos Galán. However, as his brother Alberto pointed out, "the drug dealers' core military power lies in paramilitary groups they have organized with the support of large landowners and military officers." Apart from strengthening "repressive and anti-democratic forces," Galán continued, Washington's strategy avoids "the core of the problem"— that is, "the economic ties between the legal and illegal worlds," the "large financial corporations" that handle the drug money. "It would make more sense to attack and prosecute the few at the top of the drug business rather than fill prisons with thousands of small fish without the powerful financial structure that gives life to the drug market."[17]

It would indeed make more sense, if the goal were a war on drugs. But it makes no sense for the goal of population control, and it is in any event unthinkable, because of the requirement that state policy protect power and privilege, a natural concomitant of the "level playing field" at home.

As Drug Czar under the Reagan Administration, George Bush was instrumental in terminating the main thrust of the real "war on drugs." Officials in the enforcement section of the Treasury Department monitored the sharp increase in cash inflow to Florida (later Los Angeles) banks as the cocaine trade boomed in the 1970s, and "connected it to the large-scale laundering of drug receipts" (Treasury Department brief). They brought detailed information about these matters to the Drug Enforcement Agency (DEA) and the Justice Department. After some public exposés, the government launched Operation Greenback in 1979 to prosecute money-launderers. It soon foundered; the banking industry is not a proper target for the drug war. The Reagan Administration reduced the limited monitoring, and Bush "wasn't really too interested in financial prosecution," the chief prosecutor in Operation Greenback recalls. The program was soon defunct, and Bush's new war on drugs aims at more acceptable targets. Reviewing this record, Jefferson Morley comments that the priorities are illustrated by the actions of Bush's successor in the "war against drugs." When an $8 billion surplus was announced for Miami and Los Angeles banks, William Bennett raised no questions about the morality of their practices and initiated no inquiries, though he did expedite eviction notices for low-income, mostly Black residents of public housing in Washington where drug use had been reported.[18]

There may also be some fine-tuning. A small Panamanian bank was pressured into pleading guilty on a money-laundering charge after a sting operation. But the US government dropped criminal charges against its parent bank, one of Latin America's major financial institutions, based in one of the centers of the Colombian drug cartel.[19] There also appear to have been no serious efforts to pursue the public allegations by cartel money-launderers about their contacts with major US banks.

The announced war on drugs has a few other gaps that are difficult to reconcile with the announced intentions, though quite reasonable on the principles that guide social policy. Drug processing requires ether and ace-tone, which are imported into Latin America. Rafael Perl, drug-policy adviser at the Congressional Research Service, estimates that more than 90 percent of the chemicals used to produce cocaine comes from the United States. In the nine months before the announcement of the drug war, Colombian police say they seized 1.5 million gallons of such chemicals, many found in drums displaying US corporate logos. A CIA study concluded that US exports of these chemicals to Latin America far exceed amounts used for any legal commercial purpose, concluding that enormous amounts are being siphoned off to produce heroin and cocaine. Nevertheless, chemical com-panies are off limits. "Most DEA offices have only one agent working on chemical diversions," a US official reports, so monitoring is impossible. And there have been no reported raids by Delta Force on the corporate headquarters in Manhattan.[20]

Reference to the CIA brings to mind another interesting gap in the pro-gram. The CIA and other US government agencies have been instrumental in establishing and maintaining the drug racket since World War II, when Mafia connections were used to split and undermine the French labor unions and the Communist Party, laying the groundwork for the "French connec-tion" based in Marseilles. The Golden Triangle (Laos, Burma, Thailand) became a major narcotics center as Chinese Nationalist troops fled to the region after their defeat in China and, not long after, as the CIA helped implement the drug flow as part of its effort to recruit a mercenary "clan-destine army" of highland tribesmen for its counterinsurgency operations in Laos. Over the years, the drug traffic came to involve other US clients as well. In 1989 General Ramón Montano, chief of the Philippine constabu-lary, testified in a public hearing in Manila that drug syndicates operating in the Golden Triangle use the Philippines as a transshipment point to other parts of Asia and the West, and conceded that military officers are involved, as a Senate investigation had reported. The Philippines are on their way to "becoming like Colombia," one Senator observed.[21]

The effect was the same as the CIA shifted its attention to the terrorist war against Nicaragua and the Afghan resistance against Soviet occupation. The complicity of the Reagan–Bush administrations in the drug rackets in Central America as part of their Contra support operations is by now well known. Pakistan is reported to have become one of the major international centers of the heroin trade when Afghan manufacturers and dealers "found their operations restricted after the Soviet invasion in 1979," and moved the enterprise across the borders (*South*). "The U.S. government has for several years received, but declined to investigate, reports of heroin trafficking by some Afghan guerrillas and Pakistani military officers with whom it cooperates," the *Washington Post* reported well after the drug war was charging full steam ahead. United States officials have received first-hand accounts of "extensive heroin smuggling" by the leading Afghan recipients of US aid and the Pakistani military establishment, who gave detailed information to the press in Pakistan and Washington. "Nevertheless, according to U.S. officials, the United States has failed to investigate or take action against some [read "any"] of those suspected." US favorite Gulbuddin Hekmatyar, the terrorist leader of the fundamentalist Hizbe-Islami Party, is reported to be deeply implicated in drug trafficking. Other reports indicate that the Aghan rebels are being "debilitated by increasingly fierce local battles for the lucrative heroin trade."[22]

As in Asia, US allies in Central America are also caught up in the drug traffic. Only Costa Rica has a civilian government (despite pretenses), and its Legislative Assembly's Drug Commission has provided information about these matters. Former president Daniel Oduber was cited for accepting a campaign contribution from James Lionel Casey, a US citizen in prison in Costa Rica on charges of drug trafficking. The Commission recommended that Oliver North, Admiral John Poindexter, former Ambassador Lewis Tambs, former CIA station chief Joe Fernandez, and General Richard Secord "never again be allowed to enter Costa Rica," the Costa Rican press reported in July 1989, blaming them for "opening a gate" for arms and drug traffickers as they illegally organized a "southern front" for the Contras in Costa Rica. A rural guard Colonel was charged with offering security for drug traffickers using airstrips—probably including those used for supplying Contras in Nicaragua, the Commission President told reporters. Oliver North was charged with setting up a supply line with General Noriega that brought arms to Costa Rica and drugs to the US. The Commission also implicated US rancher John Hull. Most serious, the Commission reported, was "the obvious infiltration of international gangs into Costa Rica that made use of the [Contra] organization," on requests "initiated by Colonel North to General Noriega," which opened Costa Rica "for trafficking in arms and drugs" by "this mafia," in part as an "excuse to help the contras."[23]

There are good reasons why the CIA and drugs are so closely linked. Clandestine terror requires hidden funds, and the criminal elements to whom the intelligence agencies naturally turn expect a quid pro quo. Drugs are the obvious answer. Washington's long-term involvement in the drug racket is part and parcel of its international operations, notably during the Reagan–Bush administrations. One prime target for an authentic drug war would therefore be close at hand.

These facts are too salient to have been ignored completely, but one has to look well beyond the media to become aware of the scale and significance of the "Washington connection" over many years. The public image conveyed is very different. A typical illustration is a story by *New York Times* Asia correspondent Steven Erlanger, headed "Southeast Asia Is Now No. 1 Source of U.S. Heroin." The story opens with the statement that "The Golden Triangle of Southeast Asia, whose flow of drugs the United States has been trying to control for 25 years, is once again the single-largest source of heroin coming into America ..." Why has the Golden Triangle been such a problem to US officials since 1965—a year that carries some associations, after all? The question is not raised, and there is no mention of the role of the United States government and its clandestine terror agencies in creating and maintaining the problem that "the United States has been trying to control." The US figures merely as a victim and guardian of virtue. Discussion about drugs between US and Thai officials is becoming more "forthright" and "even, at times angry," Western diplomats say, Thailand having become the main smuggling and shipment center for the Golden Triangle. Not coincidentally—though no hint appears here—Thailand was also designated as the focal point for US military, terror, and subversion operations in the secret planning to undermine the 1954 Geneva Accords a few weeks after they were adopted over US objections, and after that, served as the major base for US bombing operations and clandestine war, as well as a source of mercenary forces for Indochina. "We're trying to get across to the Thais that drugs are an international problem and that Thailand is a target too," a diplomat said. That, however, is the limit of the US role in Thailand generally or the Golden Triangle drug operations specifically, as far as the *Times* is concerned.[24]

The media rallied to the narrowly conceived drug war with their usual efficiency and dispatch. The President's decision to send military aid to Colombia and the September 5 declaration of war against "the toughest domestic challenge we've faced in decades" set off a major media blitz, closely tailored to White House needs, though the absurdities of the program were so manifest that there was some defection at the margins. Several (unscientific) samples of wire service reports through September showed drug-related stories surpassing Asia, Africa, Latin America, and the Middle East combined. Media obedience reached such comical proportions as to elicit sarcastic commentary in the *Wall Street Journal*, where Hodding Carter observed that the President proceeded on the basis of "one lead-pipe cinch": that the media would march in step. "The mass media in America," he went on, "have an overwhelming tendency to jump up and down and bark in concert whenever the White House—any White House—snaps its fingers."[25]

The short-term impact was impressive. Shortly after the November 1988 elections, 34 percent of the public had selected the budget deficit as "George Bush's No. 1 priority once he takes office." Three percent selected drugs as top priority, down from previous months. After the media blitz of September 1989, "a remarkable 43% say that drugs are the nation's single most important issue," the *Wall Street Journal* reports, with the budget deficit a distant second at 6 percent. In a June 1987 poll of registered voters in New York, taxes were selected as the number 1 issue facing the state (15 percent), with drugs far down the list (5 percent). A repeat in September 1989 gave dramatically different results: taxes were selected by 8 percent while the drug problem ranked far above any other, at a phenomenal 46 percent. The real world had hardly changed; its image had, as transmitted through the ideological institutions, reflecting the current needs of power.[26]

A martial tone has broader benefits for those who advocate state violence and repression to secure privilege. The government–media campaign helped create the required atmosphere among the general public and Congress. In a typical flourish, Senator Mark Hatfield, often a critic of reliance on force, said that in every congressional district "the troops are out there. All they're waiting for is the orders, a plan of attack, and they're ready to march." The bill approved by Congress widens the application of the death penalty, limits appeals by prisoners, and allows police broader latitude in obtaining evidence, among other measures. The entire repressive apparatus of the state is looking forward to benefits from this new "war," including the intelligence system and the Pentagon (which, however, is reluctant to be drawn into direct military actions that will quickly lose popular support). Military industry, troubled by the unsettling specter of peace, scents new markets here, and is "pushing swords as weapons in the drug war," Frank

Greve reports from Washington. "Analysts say sales for drug-war work could spell relief for some sectors, such as commando operations, defense intelligence and counterterrorism," and Federal military laboratories may also find a new role. Army Colonel John Waghelstein, a leading counter-insurgency specialist, suggested that the narco–guerrilla connection could be exploited to mobilize public support for counterinsurgency programs and to discredit critics:

> A melding in the American public's mind and in Congress of this connection would lead to the necessary support to counter the guerrilla/narcotics terrorists in this hemisphere. Generating that support would be relatively easy once the connection was proven and an all-out war was declared by the National Command Authority. Congress would find it difficult to stand in the way of supporting our allies with the training, advice and security assistance necessary to do the job. Those church and academic groups that have slavishly supported insurgency in Latin America would find themselves on the wrong side of the moral issue. Above all, we would have the unassailable moral position from which to launch a concerted offensive effort using Department of Defense (DOD) and non-DOD assets.[27]

In short, all proceeded on course.

3. The Contours of the Crisis

A closer look at the drug crisis is instructive. There can be no doubt that the problem is serious. "Substance abuse," to use the technical term, takes a terrible toll. The grim facts are reviewed by Ethan Nadelmann in *Science* magazine.[28] Deaths attributable to consumption of tobacco are estimated at over 300,000 a year, while alcohol use adds an additional 50,000 to 200,000 annual deaths. Among fifteen-to-twenty-four-year-olds, alcohol is the leading cause of death, also serving as a "gateway" drug that leads to use of others, according to the National Council on Alcoholism.[29] In addition, a few thousand deaths from illegal drugs are recorded: 3562 deaths were reported in 1985, from all illegal drugs combined. According to these estimates, over 99 percent of deaths from substance abuse are attributable to tobacco and alcohol.

There are also enormous health costs, again primarily from alcohol and tobacco use: "the health costs of marijuana, cocaine, and heroin combined amount to only a small fraction of those caused by either of the two licit substances," Nadelmann continues. Also to be considered is the distribution of victims. Illicit drugs primarily affect the user, but their legal cousins seriously affect others, including passive smokers and victims of drunken driving and alcohol-induced violence; "no illicit drug . . . is as strongly associated with violent behavior as is alcohol," Nadelmann observes, and alcohol abuse is a factor in some 40 percent of roughly 50,000 annual traffic deaths.

The Environmental Protection Agency estimates that 3800 nonsmokers die every year from lung cancer caused by breathing other people's tobacco smoke, and that the toll of passive smoking may be as many as 46,000 annually if heart disease and respiratory ailments are included. Officials say that if confirmed, these conclusions would require that tobacco smoke be listed as a very hazardous carcinogen (class A), along with such chemicals as benzene and radon. University of California statistician Stanton Glantz describes passive smoking as "the third leading cause of preventable death, behind smoking and alcohol."[30]

Illegal drugs are far from uniform in their effects. Thus, "among the roughly 60 million Americans who have smoked marijuana, not one has died from a marijuana overdose," Nadelmann reports. As he and others have observed, federal interdiction efforts have helped to shift drug use from relatively harmless marijuana to far more dangerous drugs.

One might ask why tobacco is legal and marijuana not. A possible answer is suggested by the nature of the crop. Marijuana can be grown almost anywhere, with little difficulty. It might not be easily marketable by major corporations. Tobacco is quite another story.

Questions can be raised about the accuracy of the figures. One would have to look into the procedures for determining cause of death, the scope of these inquiries, and other questions, such as the effects on children of users. But even if the official figures are far from the mark, there is little doubt that William Bennett is right in speaking of "drug-related chaos" and an "appalling, deepening crisis"—largely attributable to alcohol and tobacco, so it appears.

Further human and social costs include the victims of drug-related crimes and the enormous growth of organized crime, which is believed to derive more than half of its revenues from the drug trade. In this case, the costs are associated with the illicit drugs, but because they are illicit, not because they are drugs. The same was true of alcohol during the Prohibition era. We are dealing here with questions of social policy, which is subject to decision and choice. Nadelmann advocates legalization and regulation. Similar proposals have been advanced by a wide range of conservative opinion (the London *Economist*, Milton Friedman, and so on), and by some others.

Responding to Friedman, William Bennett argues that after repeal of Prohibition, alcohol use soared. Hence legalization cannot be considered. Whatever the merits of the argument, it is clear that Bennett doesn't take it seriously, since he does not propose reinstituting Prohibition or banning tobacco—or even assault rifles. His own argument is simply that "drug use is wrong" and therefore must be barred. The implicit assumption is that use of tobacco, alcohol, or assault rifles is not "wrong," on grounds that remain unspoken, and that the state must prohibit and punish what is "wrong." Deceit, perhaps?[31]

Radical statists of the Bennett variety like to portray themselves as humanists taking a moral stance, insisting on "the difference between right and wrong." Transparently, it is sheer fraud.

4. The Narcotraffickers

Social policies implemented in Washington contribute to the toll of victims in other ways, a fact illustrated dramatically just as the vast media campaign orchestrated by the White House peaked in September 1989. On September 19, the US Trade Representative (USTR) panel held a hearing in Washington to consider a tobacco industry request that the US impose sanctions on Thailand if it does not agree to drop restrictions on import of US tobacco. Such US government actions had already rammed tobacco down the throats of consumers in Japan, South Korea, and Taiwan, with human costs of the kind already sketched.

This huge narcotrafficking operation had its critics. A statement by the American Heart Association, American Cancer Society and American Lung Association condemned the cigarette advertising in "countries that have already succumbed to the USTR crowbar of trade threats," a campaign "patently designed to increase smoking by . . . young Asian men and women who see young U.S. men and women as role models." US Surgeon General Everett Koop testified at the USTR panel that "when we are pleading with foreign governments to stop the flow of cocaine, it is the height of hypocrisy for the United States to export tobacco." Denouncing the trade policy "to push addicting substances into foreign markets" regardless of health hazards, he said: "Years from now, our nation will look back on this application of free trade policy and find it scandalous." Koop told reporters that he had not cleared his testimony with the White House because it would not have been approved, and said he also opposed actions under the Reagan Administration to force Asian countries to import US tobacco. During his eight years in office, ending a few days after his testimony, Koop backed reports branding tobacco a lethal addictive drug responsible for some 300,000 deaths a year.

Thai witnesses also protested, predicting that the consequence would be to reverse a decline in smoking achieved by a fifteen-year campaign against tobacco use. They also noted that US drug trafficking would interfere with Washington's efforts to induce Asian governments to halt the flow of illegal drugs. Responding to the claim of US tobacco companies that their product is the best in the world, a Thai witness said, "Certainly in the Golden Triangle we have some of the best products, but we never ask the principle of free trade to govern such products. In fact we suppressed [them]."

Critics invoked the analogy of the Opium War 150 years ago, when the British government compelled China to open its doors to opium from British India, sanctimoniously pleading the virtues of free trade as they forcefully imposed large-scale drug addiction on China. As in the case of the US today, Britain had little that it could sell to China, apart from drugs. The US sought for itself whatever privileges the British were extracting from China by violence, also extolling free trade and even the "great design of Providence to make the wickedness of men subserve his purposes of mercy toward China, in breaking through her wall of exclusion, and bringing the empire into more immediate contact with western and christian nations" (American Board of Commissioners for Foreign Missions). John Quincy Adams denounced China's refusal to accept British opium as a violation of the Christian principle of "love thy neighbor" and "an enormous outrage upon the rights of human nature, and upon the first principles of the rights of nations." The tobacco industry and its protectors in government invoke similar arguments today as they seek to relive this triumph of Western civilization and its "historic purpose."[32]

Here we have the biggest drug story of the day, breaking right at the peak moment of the government–media campaign: the US government is perhaps the world's leading drug peddler, even if we put aside the US role in establishing the hard drug racket after World War II and maintaining it since. How did this major story fare in the media blitz? It passed virtually unnoticed— and, needless to say, without a hint of the obvious conclusion.[33]

The drug traffic is no trivial matter for the US economy. Tobacco exports doubled in annual value in the 1980s, contributing nearly $25 billion to the trade ledger over the decade according to a report of the Tobacco Merchants Association, rising from $2.5 billion in 1980 to $5 billion in 1989. Tobacco provided a $4.2 billion contribution to the trade balance for 1989, when the deficit for the year was $109 billion. Senator Mitch McConnell of Kentucky took due note of these figures while testifying in support of the tobacco companies at a Senate hearing. The president of the American Farm Bureau Federation, commenting on the benefits to the US economy from tobacco exports, "cited the removal of overseas trade barriers, primarily in Japan, Taiwan and South Korea" as a contributory factor.[34]

We see that it is unfair to blame the huge trade deficit on the policies of the Reagan–Bush administrations without giving them credit for their efforts to overcome it by state intervention to increase the sale of lethal addictive drugs.

As the drug war proceeded, opposition to tobacco exports began to receive some attention. In April 1990 Dr James Mason, Assistant Secretary for Health, declared that it was "unconscionable for the mighty transnational tobacco companies—and three of them are in the United States—to be peddling their poison abroad, particularly because their main targets are less-developed countries." A few weeks later, however, he cancelled a scheduled appearance before a congressional hearing on the matter, while the Department of Health and Human Services "backed away from its past criticism of efforts to open new markets for American cigarettes around the world." The Department said that "the issue was one of trade, not health," Philip Hilts reported in the *New York Times*. A Department spokesman explained that Dr Mason's appearance was cancelled for that reason. Citing the trade figures, another official described Mason's criticism of tobacco exports as "an unwelcome intrusion on the Administration's efforts to open new cigarette markets"—particularly in Thailand, Hilts reported further. Meanwhile US Trade Representative Carla Hills dismissed Thai protests about US imperialists thrusting cancer sticks upon them, saying, "I don't see how health concerns can enter the picture if the people are smoking their own cigarettes."[35]

Or, by the same logic, smoking their own crack. In our passion for free trade, then, we should surely allow the Medellín cartel to export cocaine freely to the United States, to advertise it to young people without constraint, and to market it aggressively.

Others continued to voice objections. In an open letter to Colombian president Virgilio Barco, Peter Bourne, who was Director of the Office of Drug Abuse Policy in the Carter Administration, wrote:

perhaps nothing so reflects on Washington's fundamental hypocrisy on [the drug] issue as the fact that while it rails against the adverse effects of cocaine in the United States, the number of Colombians dying each year from subsidized North American tobacco products is significantly larger than the number of North Americans felled by Colombian cocaine.

The *Straits Times* in Singapore found it "hard to reconcile the fact that the Americans are threatening trade sanctions against countries that try to keep out U.S. tobacco products" with US efforts to reduce cigarette smoking at home (let alone its efforts to bar import of illicit drugs)—a surprising failure to perceive the clear difference between significant and insignificant nations, to borrow some neoconservative rhetoric.[36]

The American Medical Association also condemned trade policies that ignore health problems, estimating that some 2.5 million excessive or premature deaths per year are attributable to tobacco—about 5 percent of all deaths. At a World Conference on Lung Health in May 1990, former Surgeon General Koop, noting that US tobacco exports had risen 20 percent the preceding year while smoking dropped 5 percent in the US, again called the export of tobacco "a moral outrage" and denounced it as "the height of hypocrisy" to call on other governments to stop the export of cocaine "while at the same time we export nicotine, a drug just as addictive as cocaine, to the rest of the world." In Taiwan, Koop said, the government had been able to cut smoking drastically by an antismoking campaign, until Washington threatened trade sanctions in 1987, leading to a 10 percent rise in smoking. "America better stop being a drug pusher if we expect to have any credibility in our war on drugs," Congressman Chester Atkins said at a news conference. Public health experts warned of a "global epidemic" from tobacco-related deaths as a result of the surge in overseas sales, now one-sixth of US production, predicting that the death toll will rise to twelve million annually by mid twenty-first century. Speaking for the government, the USTR spokesman repeated that the matter is simply one of free trade: "Our question is basically one of fairness." Coverage was again slight.[37]

Thatcher's England was not far behind. The alternative press reported a London *Sunday Times* exposé of a multimillion dollar marketing drive by British American Tobacco (BAT) to sell cheap and highly addictive cigarettes in Africa—an easy, regulation-free market—with levels of tar and nicotine far above those permitted in the West. A corporation letter to the country's head of medical services stated that "BAT Uganda does not believe that cigarette smoking is harmful to health ... [and] we should not wish to endanger our potential to export to these countries which do not have a health warning on our packs." A British cancer specialist described the situation in the Third World as similar to that in England in the early years of the century, when one in ten men was dying of lung cancer. He estimated that in China alone fifty million of today's children will die through tobacco-related diseases.[38]

If such estimates are anywhere near accurate, the reference to the Opium Wars is not far from the mark, and it might be fair to warn of the blurring of the boundary between narcotrafficking and genocide.

5. Social Policy and the Drug Crisis

Serious concern over the drug crisis would quickly lead to inquiry into a much wider range of government policies. US farmers can easily be encouraged to produce crops other than tobacco. Not so Latin American peasants, who, with far fewer options, turned to cocaine production for survival as subsistence agriculture and profits from traditional exports declined. In the case of Colombia, for example, suspension of the international coffee agreement in July 1988, initiated by US actions based on alleged fair trade violations, led to a fall of prices of more than 40 percent within two months for Colombia's leading legal export.[39]

Furthermore, US pressures over the years—including the "Food for Peace" program—have undermined production of crops for domestic use, which cannot compete with subsidized US agricultural exports. US policy is to encourage Latin America to consume the US surplus while producing specialized crops for export: flowers, vegetables for yuppie markets—or coca leaves, the optimal choice on grounds of capitalist rationality. The Council on Hemispheric Affairs comments that "only economic growth in Latin America, the promotion of financing of alternate legal crops and a decrease in U.S. demand will provide a viable alternative" to cocaine production.[40]

As for US demand for illegal drugs, middle-class use has been decreasing. But the inner city is a different matter. Here again, if we are serious, we will turn to deep-seated social policy. The cocaine boom correlates with major social and economic processes, including a historically unprecedented stagnation of real wages since 1973,[41] an effective attack against labor to restore corporate profits in a period of declining US global dominance, a shift in employment either to highly skilled labor or to service jobs, many of them dead-end and low-paying, and other moves towards a two-tiered society with a large and growing underclass mired in hopelessness and despair. Illegal drugs offer profits to ghetto entrepreneurs with few alternative options, and to others, temporary relief from an intolerable existence. These crucial factors receive occasional notice in the mainstream. Thus, a specialist quoted in the *Wall Street Journal* comments that "what is new is large numbers of inner-city people—blacks and Hispanics—sufficiently disillusioned, a real level of hopelessness. Most northern European countries have nothing remotely comparable."[42]

In a British television film on drugs, a political figure draws the obvious conclusion: "We cannot police the world. We cannot stop [heroin] supplies. We can only limit the demand for it by producing a decent society that people want to live in, not escape from."[43]

With their contributions to the growth and punishment of the underclass, the Reagan–Bush administrations helped to create the current drug crisis, yet another fact that merits headlines. And the current "war" may well exacerbate the crisis. Meeting with congressional leaders, Bush outlined his proposals for paying the costs of the drug plan, including elimination of almost $100 million from public housing subsidies and a juvenile justice program. The National Center on Budget priorities estimated that the Bush program would remove $400 million from social programs.[44] The misery of the poor is likely to increase, along with the demand for drugs and the construction of prisons for the superfluous population.

6. The Usual Victims

The Colombian operation illustrates other facets of the drug war. The military aid program for Colombia finances murderous and repressive elements of the military with ties to the drug business and landowners. As commonly in the past, the current US drug programs are likely to contribute to counterinsurgency operations and destruction of popular organizations that might challenge elite conceptions of "democracy." These prospects were illustrated at the very moment when the President made his grand declaration of an all-out war on the drug merchants, featuring aid to the Colombian military, in September 1989. As the media blitz peaked, the Andean Commission of Jurists in Lima published a report on the Colombian military entitled "Excesses in the Anti-Drug Effort." "Waving as pretext the measures adopted against drug trafficking," the report begins, "the military have ransacked the headquarters of grass roots organizations and the homes of political leaders, and ordered many arrests." A series of illustrations follow from the first two weeks of September 1989. On September 3, two days before President Bush's dramatic call to battle, the army and the Department of Security Administration (DAS) ransacked homes of peasants in one region, arresting forty laborers; the patrols are led by hooded individuals who identify targets for arrest, townspeople report. In a nearby area house searches were aimed principally against members of the Patriotic Union (whose leaders and activists are regularly assassinated) and the Communist Party, some alleged to have "subversive propaganda" in their possession. In Medellín, seventy activists and civic leaders were arrested in poor neighborhoods. Elsewhere at the same time, two union leaders, one an attorney for the union, were assassinated and another disappeared. Other leaders received death threats. Hired assassins murdered three members of the National Organization of Indigenous People, injuring others, while unidentified persons destroyed a regional office.[45]

These are examples of the regular behavior of the forces to whom President Bush pledged US aid and assistance, published just at the moment of the domestic applause for his announcement —but not available to the cheering section that pays the bills.

Ample publicity was, however, given to the capture in mid September of twenty-eight people charged with being leftist guerrillas working with the drug cartel, and to claims by the Colombian military that guerrilla organizations had formed an alliance with the Medellín drug traffickers and carried out bombings for them. The Colombian military in Medellín charged that staff members of the Popular Education Institute (IPC), arrested in a raid by security forces, were members of a guerrilla organization hired as terrorists by the cartel. Unreported, however, was the conclusion of the Andean Commission of Jurists that the charges are "clearly a set-up by the military forces which are looking to discredit the popular work [of] the IPC," a community-based organization working in popular education, training and human rights. The staff workers arrested—all those present at the time, including the director—were held incommunicado and tortured, according to the Colombian section of the Andean Commission. The Colombian Human Rights Committee in Washington reported increasing harassment of popular organizations as new aid flowed to the military in the name of "the war on drugs." Other human rights monitors have also warned of the near inevitability of these consequences as the US consolidates its links with the Colombian and Peruvian military, both of whom have appalling records of human rights violations.[46]

The *New York Times* reports that senior Peruvian military officers say that they will use the new US money "to intensify their campaign against the guerrillas and to try to prevent the smuggling of chemicals" (mainly from US corporations, which suggests another strategy that remains unmentioned). US officials concur with the strategy, though they profess to be uneasy that it "is steering clear of the growers and traffickers." In Bolivia, also a recipient of US military aid and hailed as a great success story, the military does not match its Peruvian and Colombian colleagues in the scale of state terror, but there was no US reaction to the declaration of a state of emergency by the President of Bolivia, followed by the jailing of "hundreds of union leaders and teachers who he said threatened his Government's anti-inflation policies with their wage demands."[47] This is not, after all, Nicaragua under the Sandinistas, so passionate concern over human rights issues would have no purpose.

It should be borne in mind that human rights have only an instrumental function in the political culture, serving as a weapon against adversaries and a device to mobilize the domestic public behind the banner of our nobility, as we courageously denounce the real or alleged abuses of official enemies.

In this regard, human rights concerns are very much like the facts of past and present history: instruments to serve the needs of power, not to enlighten the citizenry. Thus, one would be unlikely to find a discussion in the media of the background for the state terrorism in Colombia that the Bush Administration intends to abet. The topic is addressed in a discussion of human rights in Colombia by Alfredo Vásquez Carrizosa, president of the Colombian Permanent Committee for Human Rights. "Behind the façade of a constitutional regime," he observes, "we have a militarized society under the state of siege provided" by the 1886 Constitution. The Constitution grants a wide range of rights, but they have no relation to reality. "In this context poverty and insufficient land reform have made Colombia one of the most tragic countries of Latin America." Land reform, which "has practically been a myth," was legislated in 1961, but "has yet to be implemented, as it is opposed by landowners, who have had the power to stop it"—again, no defect of "democracy," by Western standards. The result of the prevailing misery has been violence, including *la Violencia* of the 1940s and 1950s, which took hundreds of thousands of lives. "This violence has been caused not by any mass indoctrination, but by the dual structure of a prosperous minority and an impoverished, excluded majority, with great differences in wealth, income, and access to political participation."

The story has another familiar thread. "But in addition to internal factors," Vásquez Carrizosa continues, "violence has been exacerbated by external factors. In the 1960s the United States, during the Kennedy administration, took great pains to transform our regular armies into counterinsurgency brigades, accepting the new strategy of the death squads." These Kennedy initiatives

> ushered in what is known in Latin America as the National Security Doctrine, . . . not defense against an external enemy, but a way to make the military establishment the masters of the game . . . [with] the right to combat the internal enemy, as set forth in the Brazilian doctrine, the Argentine doctrine, the Uruguayan doctrine, and the Colombian doctrine: it is the right to fight and to exterminate social workers, trade unionists, men and women who are not supportive of the establishment, and who are assumed to be communist extremists. And this could mean anyone, including human rights activists such as myself.[48]

The president of the Colombian Human Rights Commission is reviewing facts familiar throughout Latin America. Military-controlled National Security states dedicated to "internal security" by assassination, torture, disappearance, and sometimes mass murder, constituted one of the two major legacies of the Kennedy Administration to Latin America; the other was the Alliance for Progress, a statistical success and social catastrophe. The basic thrust of policy was established long before, and has been pursued since as well, with a crescendo of support for murderous state terror under the Reagan Administration. The "drug war" simply provides another modality for pursuit of these long-term commitments. One will search far for any hint of these fundamental truths in the drum-beating for a war of self-defense against the terrible crimes perpetrated against us by Latin American monsters.

As the first anniversary of the drug war approached, the House Government Operations Committee released a study concluding that US antidrug efforts had made virtually no headway in disrupting the cocaine trade in Peru and Bolivia, largely because of "corruption" in the armed forces of both countries. This "corruption" is illustrated by the stoning of DEA agents and Peruvian police by local peasants led by Peruvian military personnel, and the firing by Peruvian military officers on State Department helicopters when they approached drug-trafficker facilities—in short, by the well-known fact that "the drug dealers' core military power lies in paramilitary groups they have organized with the support of large landowners and military officers," the beneficiaries of US aid, exactly as Alberto Galán pointed out at the moment when his brother's murder provided the pretext to set the latest "drug war" into high gear.[49]

The domestic enemy is likely to be subjected to the same kind of treatment as the poor abroad. In keeping with the general commitments of neoconservatism, the drug war seeks to undermine civil liberties with a broad range of measures, such as random searches based on police suspicion, aimed primarily at young Blacks and Hispanics. The attack on civil rights has aroused some concern, though not because of the increased abuse of the underclass. Rather, it is "the threat to individual rights from the drug war" as it shifts to "middle-class whites who are casual drug users" (John Dillin, reporting on the threat to civil liberties in the lead story of the *Christian Science Monitor*). "As middle America comes under scrutiny," Dillin continues, "critics expect a growing outcry about violations of civil liberties."[50]

Power can defend itself. In practice, the capitalist ethic treats freedom as a commodity: a lot is available in principle, and you have what you can buy.

The links between the drug war and US intervention sometimes reach a remarkable level of cynicism. Thus, Colombia requested that the US install a radar system near its southern border to monitor flights from its neighbors to the south, which provide the bulk of the cocaine for processing by Colombian drug merchants. The US responded by installing a radar system, but as far removed from drug flights to Colombia as is possible on Colombian territory: on San Andrés Island in the Caribbean, 500 miles from mainland Colombia and remote from the drug routes, but only 200 miles off the coast of Nicaragua. The Colombian government accused the Pentagon of using the fight against drugs as a ruse to monitor Nicaragua, a charge confirmed by Senator John Kerry's foreign affairs aide. He added that Costa Rica had "requested radar assistance against small flights moving cocaine through the country and was given a proposal" by the Pentagon. Lacking technical experts, Costa Rican officials asked for an evaluation from the British Embassy, which informed them that the US proposal had no relevance to the drug traffic but was designed to monitor the Sandinistas. In its study of the drug cartel, Kerry's Senate Subcommittee on Terrorism, Narcotics and International Operations had reported that foreign policy concerns, including the war against Nicaragua, "interfered with the U.S.'s ability to fight the war on drugs," delaying, halting and hampering law enforcement efforts to keep narcotics out of the United States—a polite way of saying that the Reagan Administration was facilitating the drug racket in pursuit of its international terrorist project in Nicaragua and other imperatives, a standard feature of policy for decades. The current drug war adds another chapter to the sordid story.[51]

This too escapes the front pages and prime-time television. In general, the central features of the drug crisis received scant notice in the media campaign. It is doubtful that the core issues reach beyond a fraction of 1 percent of media coverage, which is tailored to other needs.

The counterinsurgency connection may also lie behind the training of Colombian narcotraffickers by Western military officers, which received some notice in August 1989 when, a few days after the Galán assassination, retired British and Israeli officers were found to be training Colombian cocaine traffickers, including teams of assassins for the drug cartel and their right-wing allies. A year earlier, a July 1988 Colombian intelligence report (Department of Security Administration: DAS) entitled "Organization of Hired Assassins and Drug Traffickers in the Magdalena Medio" noted that "At the training camps, the presence of Israeli, German and North American instructors has been detected." Trainees at the camp, who are supported by cattle ranchers and farmers involved in coca production and by the Medellín cartel, "apparently participated in peasant massacres" in a banana region, the report continues. After the discovery of British and Israeli trainers a year later, the *Washington Post*, citing another DAS document, reported that "the men taught in the training centers [where British and Israeli nationals were identified] are believed responsible for massacres in rural villages and assassination of left-leaning politicians." The same document states that one Israeli-run course was abbreviated when the instructors went "to Honduras and Costa Rica to give training to the Nicaraguan contras." The allegation that US instructors were also present has not been pursued, or to my knowledge reported in the press. [52]

Israel claimed that Colonel Yair Klein and his associates in the Spearhead security operation, who were identified as trainers in an NBC film clip, were acting on their own. But Andrew Cockburn points out that Klein's company publicly insisted that they always worked "with the complete approval and authorization of our Ministry of Defense." They also trained Contras in Honduras and Guatemalan officers; one associate of Klein's, an Israeli colonel, claims that they trained every Guatemalan officer above the rank of captain, working on a contract arranged by the state-owned Israel Military Industries. "The Americans have the problem of public opinion, international image," the marketing director of Spearhead explained. "We don't have this problem." Therefore, the dirty work of training assassins and mass murderers can be farmed out to our Israeli mercenaries. In the London *Observer*, Hugh O'Shaughnessy reported that in a letter of March 31, 1986 signed by Israeli Defense Minister Yitzhak Rabin of the Labor Party, in the journal's possession, Rabin gave Spearhead official authorization for "the export of military know-how and defense equipment," stipulating further that "It is necessary to receive a formal authorization for every negotiation."[53]

The Israeli press reports that Colonel Klein and his associates used a network of ultra-orthodox American Jews to launder the money they received for their services in Colombia. It claims further that Klein held a position of high responsibility and sensitivity as Commander of the War Room of the Israeli General Staff. An Israeli reserve general reported to be involved in the Israel–Colombia affair attributed the flurry of publicity to US government revenge for the Pollard spy caper and "an American trick contrived in order to remove Israel from Colombia," so that the US can run the arms supply there without interference.[54]

Jerusalem Post columnist Menachem Shalev raised the question: "Why the moral outrage" over this affair? "Is it worse to train loyal troops of drug barons than it is to teach racist killers of Indians, Blacks, Communists, democrats, et cetera?" A good question. The answer lies in the US propaganda system. Current orders are to express moral outrage over the Colombian cartel, the latest menace to our survival. But Israel's role as a US mercenary state is legitimate, part of the service as a "strategic asset" that earns it the status of "the symbol of human decency" in *New York Times* editorials.[55]

7. The Best-laid Plans . . .

When the Bush plan was announced, the American Civil Liberties Union at once branded it a "hoax," a strategy that is "not simply unworkable" but "counterproductive and cynical."[56] If the rhetorical ends were the real ones, that would be true enough. But for the objective of population control and pursuit of traditional policy goals, the strategy has considerable logic, though its short-term successes are unlikely to persist.

Part of the difficulty is that even the most efficient propaganda system is unable to maintain the proper attitudes among the population for long. The currently available devices have none of the lasting impact of appeal to the Soviet threat. Another reason is that fundamental social and economic problems cannot be swept under the rug for ever. The temporarily convenient program of punishing the underclass carries serious potential costs for interests that really count. Some corporate circles are awakening to the fact that "a third world within our own country" will harm business interests (Brad Butler, former chairman of Procter & Gamble). According to Labor Department projections, over half the new jobs created between 1986 and the year 2000 must be filled by children of minorities, who are expected to constitute one-third of the workforce before too long. These jobs require skills—including computer literacy and other technical knowledge—that will not be gained in the streets and prisons and deteriorating schools.[57]

As in South Africa, business will sooner or later come to realize that its interests are not well served under Apartheid, whether legal or *de facto*. But a reversal of longstanding policies that reached the level of serious social pathology during the Reagan–Bush years will be no simple matter.

Notes

1. John Fialka, *WSJ*, August 31, 1989.
2. Nancy Walser, *BG*, July 22, 1990.
3. Tucker, "Reagan's Foreign Policy," *Foreign Affairs, America and the World*. 1988–89.
4. See Chapter 1, section 1 above.
5. Baker, *WP*, September 22, 1989; Richard C. Hottelet, long-time CBS correspondent, an example selected virtually at random. He adds that the "communist dictatorship ... built military supremacy in the region," which is nonsense, apart from the fact that there were some (unmentioned) reasons for the military build-up. Such mindless parroting of government propaganda is so standard that citation of an individual case is misleading and unfair.
6. As of mid 1990, the most recent case is the assassination of presidential candidate Bernardo Jaramillo at the Bogotá airport in March. Ten months earlier, the party president was assassinated at the same airport. The previous president was murdered in October 1987. The Party had "lost some ground," Douglas Farah reports, "in part because so many of its local and regional leaders were killed"—about a thousand since its founding in 1985, including at least eighty in the first three months of 1990. There were reports implicating the drug cartel, but that seems questionable, since Jaramillo was an outspoken advocate of dialogue and opponent of extradition. The Party has blamed military-backed death squads throughout, and human rights groups generally concur. Reuters, *NYT*, March 23; Douglas Farah, *BG*, March 23, 1990.
7. James Brooke, *NYT*, September 24, 1989; Tina Rosenberg, *TNR*, September 18, 1989; Americas Watch, *Human Rights in Colombia as President Barco Begins*, September 1986; AI analyst Robin Kirk, *Extra!* (FAIR), Summer 1989; Vásquez Carrizosa, in *Colombia Update*, Colombian Human Rights Committee, December 1989, citing Attorney General's study of 1983, Americas Watch report of April 1989, and other sources; *Impunity*, Pax Christi Netherlands and the Dutch Commission Justitia et Pax, report of an October–November 1988 investigative mission. For extensive details, see the report of the Permanent Peoples' Tribunal of the International League for the Rights of Peoples, Bogotá, November 4–6, 1989, and International League, *El Camino de la Niebla* (Bogotá, 1990); also Chapter 7, pp. 226 f. below.
8. Gruson, *NYT*, October 1, 1989.
9. AP, September 23; Human Rights Update, Guatemala Human Rights Commission, September 25, 1989.
10. Some months later, the US government turned against the Christian Democratic government,

hoping to install more reactionary clients in the forthcoming elections. Predictably, the press ran a few articles on Guatemalan atrocities as part of the effort. See Chapter 12, pp. 383 f. below.

11. Holzman, "Politics and Guesswork: CIA and DIA estimates of Soviet Military Spending," *International Security*, Fall 1989.

12. Bundy, *Danger and Survival*, pp. 237–8.

13. John E. Rielly, *American Public Opinion and U.S. Foreign Policy, 1987* (Chicago Council on Foreign Relations, 1987). On terrorism and terrorology, see references of Chapter 12, Note 45.

14. Richard Berke, *NYT*, September 24, 1988.

15. Berke, *NYT*, February 14; Philip Shenon, *NYT*, September 2; Franklin E. Zimring, director, and Gordon Hawkins, senior fellow, at the Earl Warren Legal Institute at the University of California at Berkeley, "Bennett's Sham Epidemic," Op-Ed, *NYT*, January 25, 1990. Berke, "Drug Study Faults Role of State Dept.," *NYT*, February 6, 1990, section D, p. 24.

16. Richard Berke, "Bennett Asserts Drug Education Isn't Key," *NYT*, February 3, 1990.

17. Galán, *BG*, September 26, 1989.

18. Morley, *Nation*, October 2, 1989.

19. COHA's *Washington Report on the Hemisphere*, September 27, 1989.

20. Brook Larmer, "US, Mexico Try to Halt Chemical Flow to Cartels," *CSM*, October 23, 1989, reporting on the *lack* of any serious efforts and blaming Mexico.

21. See Alfred W. McCoy, Cathleen B. Reach, and Leonard D. Adams, *The Politics of Heroin in Southeast Asia* (Harper & Row, 1972); Peter Dale Scott, *The War Conspiracy* (Bobbs-Merrill, 1972); Henrik Krueger, *The Great Heroin Coup* (South End, 1980); Leslie Cockburn, *Out of Control* (Atlantic Monthly, 1987). Carlo Cortes, AP, Manila, October 25, 1989.

22. *South*, "the business magazine of the developing world," October 1989; James Rupert and Steve Colt, "Guerrillas for God, Heroin Dealers for Man," *WP Weekly*, May 21, 1990; Ahmed Rashid, *FEER*, September 14, 1990. On Central America, see Leslie Cockburn, *Out of Control*.

23. Peter Brennan, *Tico Times*, July 28, 1989, reviewing earlier reports. Costa Rica subsequently attempted to extradite Hull from the US on charge of participating in the 1984 La Penca bombing of a news conference in which four people were killed; Lindsey Gruson, *NYT*, February 27, 1990. See Nina Wax and Michael Hardesty, "Drug Trade," *Z Magazine*, April 1990.

24. Erlanger, *NYT*, February 11, 1990.

25. *NYT*, September 6; Carter, *WSJ*, September 14, 1989.

26. AP, *WSJ*, November 28, 1988; *WSJ*, September 22, 1989; AP, September 27, 1989, reporting polls of the Marist College Institute for Public Opinion.

27. AP, September 27, 1989; Greve, *Philadelphia Inquirer*, January 21, 1990; Waghelstein, *Military Review*, February 1987.

28. Nadelmann, "Drug Prohibition in the United States: Costs, Consequences, and Alternatives," *Science*, September 1, 1989. See also letters, *Science*, December 1.

29. Catherine Foster, *CSM*, September 18, 1989.

30. Philip Hilts, *NYT*, May 10; Reuters, *BG*, June 26; AP, *NYT*, May 21, 1990.

31. Friedman, *WSJ*, September 7; Bennett, *WSJ*, September 19, 1989. See also Anthony Lewis, *NYT*, September 24, 1989, noting the absurdity of Bennett's argument.

32. Richard van Alstyne, *The Rising American Empire* (Oxford University Press, 1960), pp. 170 f.

33. AP, September 19, 20. The *Wall Street Journal* and *Christian Science Monitor* took note of the hearings, omitting the major points, however. See the sharp editorial in the *Boston Globe*, September 24, 1989; and Alexander Cockburn, *Nation*, October 30, 1989.

34. AP, April 17, May 4, 1990.

35. Hilts, *NYT*, May 18, 1990; Mary Kay Magistad, *BG*, May 31, 1990.

36. Bourne, *COHA (Council on Hemispheric Affairs) News and Analysis*, June 5, 1990. *Straits Times*, in *International Herald Tribune*, April 9, 1990. On the relative significance of nations, see Chapter 12, p. 365, below.

37. AP, *NYT*, June 27, also briefly noting the World Conference on Lung Health a month earlier; AP, May 21; Ron Scherer, *CSM*, May 23; Betsy Lehman, *BG*, May 22,1990.

38. Ben Lowe, "Third World is butt of deadly trade ploy," *Guardian* (New York), May 30, 1990.

39. Joseph Treaster, "Coffee Impasse Imperils Colombia's Drug Fight," September 24, 1988.

40. *Washington Report on the Hemisphere*, September 13, 1989. On the Food for Peace program and others like it, see *Necessary Illusions*, p. 363, and sources cited.

41. See David Gordon, "Real Wages Are on a Steady Decline," *Los Angeles Times*, July 16, 1989.

42. Alan Otten, *WSJ*, September 6, 1989.

43. John O'Connor, *New York Times News Service*, April 17, 1990, reviewing the TV film "Traffik" shown over PBS.

44. Michael Kranish, *BG*, September 5; James Ridgway, *Village Voice*, September 19, 1989.

45. *Andean Newsletter*, Andean Commission of Jurists, Lima, September 1989.

46. *New York Times*, September 16, 17, 18. Ursula Marquez, *Guardian* (New York), October 11, 1989; Colombian Human Rights Committee, POB 3130, Washington DC 20010.

47. Joseph Treaster, *NYT*, December 6, 1989.

48. *Colombia Update* 1.4, December 1989.

49. See p. 116. House study, *WP–BG*, August 21, 1990, p. 76. Apparently missed by the *New York Times*.

50. Dillin, "Nation's Liberties at Risk?", *CSM*, February 2, 1990. See also Seth Mydans, "Powerful Arms of Drug War Arousing Concern for Rights," *NYT*, October 16, 1989.

51. Michael Frisby, "Colombians rap US plan on radar base," *BG*, April 5, 1989, citing Richard McCall. For review of the Kerry Commission report, see *Washington Spectator*, August 15, 1989; Jay Hatheway, *Z Magazine*, October 1989.

52. NBC Nightly News, August 25, 1989; DAS report, Bogotá, July 20, 1988, reproduced in Pax Christi, *Impunity*; Eugene Robinson, *WP*, August 9, 1989. A comment by Tina Rosenberg (*TNR*, September 18, 1986) may be a reference to the July 1988 DAS report on the alleged presence of US instructors.

53. Andrew Cockburn, *NYT*, Op-Ed, September 8; O'Shaughnessy, *Observer*, October 1, 1989. See also Jane Hunter, *The Israeli Connection: Israeli Involvement in Paramilitary Training in Colombia*, Arab American Institute, September 1989.

54. Ron Ben-Yishai, *Yediot Ahronot*, August 30; Uriel Ben-Ami, Al Hamishmar, August 31; military correspondent Danny Sadeh, *Yediot Ahronot*, August 29, 1989.

55. *JP*, August 29, 1989; editorial, *NYT*, February 19, 1988.

56. AP, *BG*, September 7, 1989.

57. Edward Fiske, "Impending U.S. Jobs 'Disaster': Work Force Unqualified to Work," *NYT*, September 25, 1989. See Introduction.

FIVE

The Post-Cold War Era

THE reactionary statist tendencies of the post-Vietnam period arose in response to a dual challenge: the decline of US dominance of the international order and the popular activism of the 1960s, which challenged the dominance of the same privileged sectors at home. Neither Kennedy's "Grand Design" nor the efforts of the Nixon Administration succeeded in restricting Europe to its "regional interests" within the "overall framework of order" managed by the United States, as Kissinger urged. There was no alternative to the trilateralism embraced by the Carter neoliberals, who, like their predecessors, were no less troubled by the popular democratic thrust at home—their "crisis of democracy" that threatened to bring the general population into the political arena in a meaningful way.

As already discussed, these challenges inspired a campaign to restore the population to apathy and obedience and thus overcome the "crisis of democracy," and to enhance business power generally. By 1978, UAW President Doug Fraser had seen the handwriting on the wall. Resigning from the Labor–Management Group, he denounced the "leaders of the business community" for having "chosen to wage a one-sided class war in this country—a war against working people, the unemployed, the poor, the minorities, the very young and the very old, and even many in the middle class of our society," and having "broken and discarded the fragile, unwritten compact previously existing during a period of growth and progress." A year later, in another recognition of reality, Cleveland's populist mayor Dennis

Kucinich told a UAW meeting that there is only one political party in the United States, the pro-business "Demipublicans."[1]

The period of steady economic progress was over. The challenge of rival powers was real for the first time since World War II, and the fragile social compact could not be sustained. Programs designed through the 1970s were implemented, with an extra touch of crudity, during the Reagan years, with the general support of the other faction of the business party and the ideological apparatus.

The historical and planning record and underlying institutional factors provide good reason to expect the post-Cold War era to be much like the past as far as relations between the United States and the Third World are concerned, apart from tactics and propaganda. "Radical nationalism" and experiments with independent development geared to domestic needs will raise the danger flags and call forth a reaction, varying with circumstances and the functions of the region. The same continuity is to be expected with regard to the concomitants of these policy goals, including the persistent support for human rights violations, the general hostility to social reform, and the principled antagonism to democracy.

Democratic forms can be tolerated, even admired, if only for propaganda purposes. But this stance can be adopted only when the distribution of effective power ensures that meaningful participation of the "popular classes" has been barred. When they organize and threaten the control of the political system by the business–landowner elite and the military, strong measures must be taken, with tactical variations depending on the ranking of the target population on the scale of importance. At the lowest rank, in the Third World, virtually no holds are barred.

If the security forces are under control, the death squads can be unleashed while we wring our hands over our painful inability to instill our passion for human rights in the hearts of our unworthy allies. Other means are required when control of the security forces has been lost. Nicaragua, the obsession of the 1980s, was one such case, a particularly dangerous one because it was feared that the government in power was one "that cares for its people," in the words of José Figueres, referring to the Sandinistas, who, he said, brought Nicaragua the first such government in its history, popularly elected in a free and fair election that he observed in 1984. It was for expressing such improper sentiments as these that the leading figure of Central American democracy had to be rigorously excluded from the US media throughout the 1980s.[2]

It is therefore not at all surprising that hostility to the Sandinistas was

virtually uniform in media commentary and other elite circles.[3] The official
reasons (human rights, democracy, the Soviet threat, and so on) are too
far-fetched to take seriously, and were, in any event, thoroughly refuted
so many times, with no effect, as to reveal the pointlessness of the exercise.
The real issue is the one Figueres identified. Throughout, the only debatable
question has been tactical: how to restore Nicaragua to "the Central American mode" and impose "regional standards"—those of the US client states.
Such matters as freedom of the press and human rights aroused profound
libertarian and moral passions in Nicaragua, as distinct from the death squad
democracies next door, or other states with vastly worse records but with
the compensating merit that they too were properly respectful of US priorities.[4] Similarly, elections in the terror states revealed heartening progress
towards democracy, but not in Nicaragua, where radically different standards
were applied. The 1984 elections were intolerable to the United States
because they could not be controlled. Therefore Washington did what it
could to disrupt them, and they were dismissed and eliminated from history
by the media, as required. In the case of the long-scheduled 1990 elections,
the US interfered massively from the outset to gain victory for its candidates,
not only by the enormous financial aid that received some publicity, but—far
more significant and considered quite uncontroversial—by White House
announcements that only a victory by the US candidate would bring an
end to the illegal US economic sanctions and restoration of aid.

In brief, Nicaraguan voters were informed that they had a free choice:
Vote for our candidate, or watch your children starve.[5]

These efforts to subvert the 1990 election in Nicaragua are highlighted
by a comparison to the reaction at exactly the same time to elections in
neighboring Honduras. Its November 1989 elections received scanty but
generally favorable coverage in the US media, which described them as
"a milestone for the United States, which has used Honduras as evidence
that the democratically elected governments it supports in Central America
are taking hold." President Bush, meeting with Honduran President Rafael
Callejas after his election, called the Honduran government "an inspiring
example of the democratic promise that today is spreading throughout the
Americas."[6]

A closer look helps us to understand what is meant by "democracy"
in the political culture. The November elections were effectively restricted
to the two traditional parties. One candidate was from a family of wealthy
industrialists, the other from a family of large landowners. Their top advisers
"acknowledge that there is little substantive difference between the two

and the policies they would follow as president," we learn from the press report that hails this milestone in the progress of democracy. Both parties represent large landowners and industrialists and have close ties with the military, the effective rulers, who are independent of civilian authority under the Constitution but heavily dependent on the United States, as is the economy. The Guatemalan *Central America Report* adds: "in the absence of substantial debate, both candidates rely on insults and accusations to entertain the crowds at campaign rallies and political functions"—if that sounds familiar to a US audience, it is not mere coincidence. Popular participation was limited to ritual voting. The legal opposition parties (Christian Democratic and Social Democratic) charged massive electoral fraud.

Human rights abuses by the security forces escalated as the election approached. In the preceding weeks there were attacks with bombs and rifle fire against independent political figures, journalists, and union leaders, condemned as a plan to repress popular organizations by the head of the Coordinating Committee of Popular Organizations, ex-rector of the National University Juan Almendares. In preceding months the armed forces conducted a campaign of political violence, including assassination of union leaders and other extrajudicial executions, leaving tortured and mutilated bodies by roadsides for the first time. The human rights organization CODEH reported at least seventy-eight people killed by the security forces between January and July, while reported cases of torture and beatings more than tripled over the preceding year. But state terror remained at levels low enough not to disturb US elite opinion.

Starvation and general misery are rampant, the extreme concentration of wealth increased during the decade of "democracy," and 70 percent of the population are malnourished. Despite substantial US aid and no guerrilla conflict, the economy is collapsing, with capital flight and a sharp drop in foreign investment, and almost half of export earnings devoted to debt service. But there is no major threat to order, and profits flow.[7]

In short, Honduras, like Colombia, is a praiseworthy democracy, and there is no concern over the "level playing field" for its elections, unlike those in Nicaragua.

Even El Salvador and Guatemala, murderous gangster states run by the US-backed military, are considered democracies. Elite opinion expresses considerable pride in having established and maintained these charnel houses, with "free elections" permitted after a wave of slaughter, torture, disappearance, mutilation, and other effective devices of control. Physical destruction of the independent media and murder of editors and journalists by the security forces passes virtually without comment—often literally without report—among their US colleagues, among many other atrocities.

Occasionally, one hears an honest comment. Joachim Maitre of Boston University, one of the leading academic supporters of Reagan Administration policies in Central America, observes that the US has "installed democracies of the style of Hitler Germany" in El Salvador and Guatemala.[8] But such candor is far from the norm.

Nicaragua, however, was different, because of the threat of independent nationalism and social reform, heightened by the loss of US control of the security forces—a problem that has arisen elsewhere as well, and a serious one, because the standard device for repressing and eliminating undesirable tendencies is then no longer available. In the case of Guatemala and Chile it was necessary to resort to economic strangulation, subversion, and military force to overthrow the democratic regimes and establish the preferred regional standards. In the case of the Dominican Republic in 1965, direct invasion was required to bar the restoration of a constitutional regime. The response to the Cuban problem was direct aggression at the Bay of Pigs, and when Soviet deterrence made further such attempts unfeasible, an unprecedented campaign of international terrorism along with unremitting economic and ideological warfare—again, surely not motivated by the reasons advanced in the official government–media line, which are hardly credible. Other cases require different measures, including Panama, another long-term target of US intervention, to which we turn directly.

1. Creeping Colonialism

We may continue to think of the Third World in the terms used in early post-World War II planning: as the region that is to "fulfill its major function as a source of raw materials and a market" for the Western industrial societies.[9] One longstanding source of international conflict was the Soviet empire's failure to fulfill its function in the required way. This problem, it is hoped, will now be remedied as Eastern Europe advances towards the conditions of Mexico, Brazil, and the Philippines. The fear of "creeping Communism" can then be put to rest, as the modern forms of colonialism expand towards their natural borders.

The three major power groupings are eagerly swooping down upon the collapsing Soviet empire (as on China, a few years earlier) in search of markets, resources, opportunities for investment and export of pollution, cheap labor, tax havens, and other familiar Third World amenities. These efforts to impose the preferred model of two-tiered societies open to exploitation and under business rule are accompanied by appropriate flourishes about the triumph of political pluralism and democracy. We can readily determine the seriousness of intent by a look at the reaction to popular movements that might actually implement democracy and pluralism in the traditional Third World countries, and to the "crisis of democracy" within the industrial societies themselves. The rhetoric need not detain us.

We may also take note of the broad—if tacit—understanding that the capitalist model has limited application; business leaders have long recognized that it is not for them. The successful industrial societies depart significantly from this model, as in the past—one reason why they are successful industrial societies. In the United States, the sectors of the economy that remain competitive are those that feed from the public trough: high-tech industry and capital-intensive agriculture, along with pharmaceuticals and others. Departures are still more radical in most of the other state capitalist systems, where planning is coordinated by state institutions and financial-industrial conglomerates, sometimes with democratic processes and a social contract of varying sorts, sometimes not. The glories of Free Enterprise provide a useful weapon against government policies that might benefit the general population, and of course, capitalism will do just fine for the former colonies and the Soviet empire. For those who are to "fulfill their functions" in service to the masters of the world order, the model is highly recommended; it facilitates their exploitation. But the rich and powerful at home have long appreciated the need to protect themselves from the destructive forces of free-market capitalism, which may provide suitable themes for rousing oratory, but only so long as the public handout and the regulatory and protectionist apparatus are secure, and state power is on call when needed.

2. Bush's "New Thinking"

What, then, is the probable evolution of US policy towards the Third World in the post-Cold War era? The answer to this question, implicit in the earlier discussion, was announced loud and clear by the Bush Administration on December 20, 1989: More of the same.

But not precisely the same. One problem is that some adjustments are needed in the propaganda framework. The US invasion of Panama is a historic event in one respect. In a departure from the routine, it was not justified as a response to an imminent Soviet threat. When the US invaded Grenada six years earlier, it was still possible to portray the act as a defensive reaction to the machinations of the Russian bear, seeking to strangle us in pursuit of its global designs. The chairman of the Joint Chiefs of Staff could solemnly intone that in the event of a Soviet attack on Western Europe, Grenada might interdict the Caribbean sea lanes and prevent the US from providing oil to its beleaguered allies, with the endorsement of a new category of scholars created for the purpose.[10] Through the 1980s, the attack against Nicaragua was justified by the danger that if we don't stop the Commies there, they'll be pouring across the border at Harlingen, Texas, two days' drive away. There are more sophisticated (and equally weighty) variants for the educated classes. But in the case of Panama, not even the imagination of the State Department and the editorial writers extended that far.

Fortunately, the problem had been foreseen. When the White House decided that its friend Noriega was getting too big for his britches and had to go, the media took their cue and launched a campaign to convert him into the most nefarious demon since Attila the Hun, a repeat of the Qaddafi project a few years earlier. The effort was enhanced by the "drug war," the government–media hoax launched in an effort to mobilize the population in fear now that it is becoming impossible to invoke the Kremlin design—though for completeness, we should also take note of the official version, dutifully reported as fact in the *New York Times*: "the campaign against drugs has increasingly become a priority for the Administration as well as Congress as a diminishing Soviet threat has given Washington an opportunity to turn to domestic issues."[11]

The propaganda operation was a smashing success. "Manuel Noriega belongs to that special fraternity of international villains, men like Qaddafi, Idi Amin, and the Ayatollah Khomeini, whom Americans just love to hate," Ted Koppel orated, so "strong public support for a reprisal [*sic*] was all but guaranteed."[12] Why did Americans hate Noriega in 1989, but not in 1985? Why is it necessary to overthrow him now, but not then? The questions that immediately come to mind were systematically evaded. With a fringe of exceptions—mostly well after the tasks had been accomplished— the media rallied around the flag with due piety and enthusiasm, funnelling the most absurd White House tales to the public[13] while scrupulously refraining from asking the obvious questions, or seeing the most obvious facts.

There were some who found all this a bit too much. Commenting on the Panama coverage, David Nyhan of the *Boston Globe* described the media as "a docile, not to say boot-licking, lot, subsisting largely on occasional bones of access tossed into the press kennel," happy to respond to lies with "worshipful prose." The *Wall Street Journal* noted that the four television networks gave "the home team's version of the story." There was a scattering of skepticism in reporting and commentary, but most toed the line in their enthusiasm for what George Will called an exercise of the "good-neighbor policy," an act of "hemispheric hygiene" expressing our "rights and responsibilities" in the hemisphere—whatever the delinquents beyond our borders may think, as revealed by their near-universal condemnation.[14]

The Bush Administration was, naturally, overjoyed. A State Department official observed that "the Republican conservatives are happy because we were willing to show some muscle, and the Democratic liberals can't criticize because it's being so widely seen as a success";[15] the State Department follows standard conventions, contrasting "conservatives," who advocate a powerful and violent state, with "liberals," who sometimes disagree with the "conservatives" on tactical grounds, fearing that the cost to us may be too high. These salutary developments "can't help but give us more clout," the same official continued.

As for the general population, many doubtless were also enthusiastic about the opportunity to "kick a little ass" in Panama—to borrow some of the rhetoric designed by George Bush's handlers in their comical effort to shape an effete New England aristocrat into a Texas redneck. But it is interesting to read the letters to the editor in major newspapers, which tended to express hostility to the aggression, along with much shame and distress, and often provided information, analysis and insights that the professionals were careful to avoid.

A more professional reaction was given by the respected *Washington Post* correspondent David Broder. He notes that there has been some carping at "the prudence of Bush's action" from "the left" (meaning, presumably, the National Council of Churches and some centrist liberals, anything else being far beyond his horizons, as is the idea that there might be criticism on grounds other than prudence). But he dismisses "this static on the left" with scorn: "what nonsense." Rather, the invasion of Panama helped to clarify "the circumstances in which military intervention makes sense." The "best single definition" of the "new national consensus," he goes on to explain, was given by Reagan's Defense Secretary, Caspar Weinberger, who outlined six "well-considered and well-phrased" criteria. Four of them state that intervention should be designed to succeed. The other two add that the action should be deemed "vital to our national interest" and a "last resort" to achieve it.[16]

Oddly, Broder neglected to add the obvious remark about these impressive criteria: they could readily have been invoked by Hitler.

Broder believes that "Democratic nominee Michael Dukakis, after floundering around on the question of military interventions, came up with a set of standards strikingly similar to Weinberger's" during the 1988 presidential campaign. These standards, as outlined by his senior foreign policy adviser, were that US force could be used "to deter aggression against its territory, to protect American citizens, to honor our treaty obligations and take action against terrorists," after peaceful means had failed. "The Panama invasion met all of those tests," Broder concludes with satisfaction.

One can appreciate the joyful mood among State Department propagandists. Even they did not dare to claim to be deterring Panamanian aggression or taking action against terrorists. And while they did act out the usual routine about protecting American lives, it is unlikely that they anticipated more than polite smiles.

There was also the ritual gesture towards international law, but it too was hardly intended seriously. The nature of the endeavor was indicated by UN Ambassador Thomas Pickering, who informed the United Nations that Article 51 of the UN Charter (which restricts the use of force to self-defense against armed attack until the Security Council acts) "provides for the use of armed force to defend a country, to *defend our interests* and our people." It was clarified further by the Justice Department theory that the same provision of the Charter entitles the US to invade Panama to prevent "its territory from being used as a base for smuggling drugs into the United States"—so that, a fortiori, Nicaragua would be entitled to invade and occupy Washington.[17]

In fact, it is transparently impossible to reconcile the invasion with the supreme law of the land as codified in the UN Charter, the OAS Charter, or the Panama Canal treaty. Even the pre-invasion efforts to topple Noriega are manifestly in conflict with our solemn obligations as a law-abiding nation—including the economic warfare that destroyed the economy, "about as clear-cut an instance of direct or indirect intervention and 'coercive measures of an economic character' as can be imagined," Charles Maechling observes, citing Articles 18 and 19 of the OAS Charter which explicitly bar such measures "for any reason whatever," and other equally clear proscriptions. The same obligations, of course, rule out the economic warfare against Nicaragua that was condemned by the World Court and the GATT Council, and supported across the US political spectrum. US measures against

Panama were also condemned by the Latin American countries, routinely and irrelevantly. Thus, on July 1, 1987 the OAS condemned US intervention in Panama by a vote of 17–1 (the US alone in opposition, and several client states abstaining or absent). Commenting on this (typically ignored) event, Adolfo Aguilar Zinser, Mexican political commentator and senior associate at the Carnegie Endowment for International Peace, observes: "We Latins believe that altruistic causes such as 'democracy' and 'freedom' and even economic assistance are often mere pretexts to hide illegitimate purposes," which is also why US policies towards Nicaragua received no support in Latin America, even among "Latins who do not like the Sandinistas and would prefer to see them turned out of power."[18]

Broder is pleased that "we have achieved a good deal of clarity in the nation on this question [of the right of intervention], which divided us so badly during and after the Vietnam war." And this "important achievement ... should not be obscured by a few dissident voices on the left," with their qualms about the prudence of the action. His evaluation recalls a comment by one of the more significant figures in twentieth-century America, the radical pacifist A.J. Muste: "The problem after a war is with the victor. He thinks he has just proved that war and violence pay. Who will now teach him a lesson?"

Ever since the latter days of the Indochina wars, elite groups have been concerned over the erosion of popular support for force and subversion ("the Vietnam syndrome"). Intensive efforts have been made to cure the malady, but in vain. The Reaganites assumed that it had been overcome by the propaganda triumphs over the suffering and tragedies of the societies ravaged by US terror in Indochina, the Iran hostage crisis, and the Soviet invasion of Afghanistan. They learned differently when they tried to return to the traditional pattern of intervention in Central America but were driven underground by the public reaction, forced to retreat to clandestine and indirect measures of terror and intimidation. Throughout the 1980s, hopes were voiced that we had finally overcome "the sickly inhibitions against the use of military force" (Norman Podhoretz, referring to the grand triumph in Grenada). In the more nuanced tones of the liberal commentator, Broder too is expressing the hope that finally the population has been restored to health and will end its childish obsession with the rule of law and human rights.

His "new consensus," however, is largely illusory, restricted to those who have always recognized that US global designs require the resort to state violence, terror, and subversion. The new consensus is more properly described as a heightened self-confidence on the part of those who shared the old consensus on the legitimacy of violence and the "salutary efficacy" of terror.

The elite reaction to the invasion did not pass unnoticed abroad. An editorial in Canada's leading journal condemned "the shallow, boosterish U.S. media" with their "chilling indifference to the fate of innocent Panamanians who have been victimized by this successful little military deployment." A columnist commented on "the mood of jingoism" fostered by the media, the "peculiar jingoism so evident to foreigners but almost invisible for most Americans. . . . Reporters seeking alternative comments on the invasion typically have to go to the fringe of U.S. society merely to gather opinions on the invasion that would be common in other countries," and the foreign consensus in opposition to this use of force was "given short shrift in the U.S. media." A typical example is the (null) reaction to the US veto of a UN Security Council resolution condemning the ransacking of the residence of Nicaragua's ambassador to Panama by US troops, voted 13–1 with only Britain abstaining.[19]

As always, if the world is out of step, it's their problem, not ours.

3. Operation Just Cause: the Pretexts

In this context, we may turn to the Panama invasion, inaugurating the "post-Cold War era." After floating various trial balloons, the White House settled on the need to "protect American lives" as the reason for the invasion. There had been "literally hundreds of cases of harassment and abuse of Americans" in recent months by Noriega's forces, the White House announced—though, curiously, no warning to American travellers to stay away from Panama. A US soldier was killed after his car had driven "through a military roadblock near a sensitive military area" (New York Times). Panamanian officials alleged that the US officers had fired at a military headquarters, wounding a soldier and two civilians, including a one-year-old girl; a wounded Panamanian soldier in a military hospital confirmed this account to US reporters.[20]

But what tipped the scales was the threat to the wife of an officer who had been arrested and beaten. Bush "often has difficulty in emotionally charged situations," the New York Times reported, "but his deep feelings clearly came through" when he spoke of this incident, proclaiming in his best Ollie North rendition that "this President" is not going to stand by while American womanhood is threatened.[21]

The press did not explain why "this President" refused even to issue a protest when, a few weeks earlier, an American nun, Diana Ortiz, had been kidnapped, tortured, and sexually abused by the Guatemalan police—or why the media did not find the story worth reporting when it appeared on the wires on November 6, and have ignored repeated calls for an investigation by religious leaders and congressional representatives. Nor were Bush's "deep feelings" contrasted with the response of "this President" to the treatment of American women and other religious and humanitarian workers in El Salvador a few weeks later, a small footnote to the brutal government actions praised by James Baker at a November 29 press conference as "absolutely appropriate"—a comment given little notice, perhaps regarded as not too useful right after the assassination of the Jesuit priests.[22]

The murder of Sisters Maureen Courtney (from Milwaukee) and Teresa Rosales by US-organized terrorists in Nicaragua on January 1, a few days after Bush had impressed the media with his "deep feelings," also passed quietly, and with no call for action to protect American womanhood. The same had been true when Sister Mary McKay was severely wounded by gunmen firing from a pickup truck in San Salvador four days after inflammatory condemnations of the political opposition by the US Embassy. The murder of Ben Linder by Contras in 1987 also aroused no call for the protection of American lives, even after the head of operations for the Contras, Fermin Cardenas, stated in a deposition that Contra commander Enrique Bermúdez had ordered Linder killed to sabotage a small dam project on which he was working in a remote village—another fact that somehow escaped notice.[23]

Another pretext offered was our commitment to democracy, deeply offended when Noriega stole the 1989 election that had been won by the US-backed candidate, Guillermo Endara, now placed in office by the invasion. An obvious test comes to mind: what happened in the preceding election in 1984, when Noriega was still *our* thug? The answer is that Noriega stole the election with considerably more violence than in 1989, with two killed and forty wounded when troops fired at a protest demonstration. These actions successfully barred the victory of Arnulfo Arias in favor of Nicolas Ardito Barletta, since known as "fraudito" in Panama. Washington opposed Arias, who it feared "would bring an undesirable ultranationalist brand of politics to power" (State Department official), preferring Barletta, a former student of Secretary of State George Shultz, whose campaign received US government funds, according to US Ambassador Everett Briggs.

Shultz was sent down to legitimate the fraud, praising the election as "initiating the process of democracy"; US approval was symbolized by President Reagan's congratulatory message to Barletta, seven hours before his victory had been certified.[24]

The media looked the other way, uninterested in the report of fraud by ex-Congressman Father Robert Drinan, speaking for foreign observers monitoring the election. There was no criticism of the election in leading journals (*New York Times*, *Washington Post*, *Los Angeles Times*, *Miami Herald*, and others), though they changed tune quickly and began to publish editorial attacks on Noriega's failure to meet our lofty democratic standards as soon as the Reagan Administration gave the signal by turning against him.[25]

The US-backed candidate of 1989, Guillermo Endara, was close to Arias and remained his spokesman in Panama until his death in 1988 in self-imposed exile. Endara had served as Arias's Minister of Planning in 1968, and "used to speak, almost dreamily, of the day when Arias would return 'as a sign of providence' to lead the country" (AP). The *Washington Post* now comments that Endara was chosen to run in 1989 "largely because of his close ties to the late legendary Panamanian politician Arnulfo Arias, who was ousted from the presidency by the military three times since the 1940s"—accurate, but a bit selective. The media once again politely looked the other way when, during the invasion, Endara denounced the "fraud of 1984." And they do not ask why our "yearning for democracy" was awakened only after Noriega had become a nuisance to Washington rather than an asset.[26]

Perhaps the reason for Noriega's fall from grace was his gangsterism and corruption. We can quickly dismiss this idea. Noriega was known to be a thug when he was a US ally, and remained so with no relevant change as the government (hence the media) turned against him. Furthermore, he does not approach the criminality of people the US cheerfully supports. The 1988 Americas Watch report on Human Rights in Panama details abuses, but nothing remotely comparable to the record of US clients in the region, or elsewhere, even the lesser criminals such as Honduras. But facts did not disfigure the media crusade. Ted Koppel's version, quoted above, was standard fare. His ABC colleague Peter Jennings denounced Noriega as "one of the more odious creatures with whom the United States has had a relationship," while CBS's Dan Rather placed him "at the top of the list of the world's drug thieves and scums." Others followed suit.[27]

The Bush Administration, in fact, took pains to make it clear that Noriega's crimes were not a factor in the invasion, with little notice. Just as the troops attacked Panama, the White House announced new high-technology sales to China, noting that $300 million in business for US firms was at stake and that contacts had secretly resumed a few weeks after the Tiananmen Square massacre. Washington also barred entry to two Chinese scholars invited by US universities, in deference to the Chinese authorities. New subsidized agricultural sales to China were announced; a few weeks later, the Export–Import Bank announced a grant to China for the purchase of equipment for a Shanghai subway from US companies. The White House also took the occasion of the invasion of Panama to announce plans to lift a ban on loans to Iraq.[28]

The plans to expedite loans for Iraq were implemented shortly after—to achieve the "goal of increasing U.S. exports and put us in a better position to deal with Iraq regarding its human rights record . . .," the State Department explained with a straight face. The first goal is the familiar one. According to the chairman of the House Banking Committee, Representative Henry Gonzalez—here, as often, a lone voice—the scale of these US credits was not insignificant, nor was their impact: a matter to which we return.[29]

US plans to resume bank credits to Iraq had been reported on network television by ABC Middle East correspondent Charles Glass a few days before the Panama invasion. He reported further that "the U.S. has become Iraq's largest trading partner."[30] For some time, Glass had been waging a lonely campaign in the mainstream media to expose Iraqi atrocities and the critically important US backing for the regime, eliciting evasion or denials from Washington. The media generally were not interested until several months later, when the Iraqi threat was "discovered" in the context of the search for new enemies to justify the Pentagon budget, and in August, with Iraq's conquest of Kuwait.

Senate minority leader Robert Dole proclaimed that the capture of Noriega "proves America won't give up or cave in to anyone, no matter how powerful or corrupt."[31] In comparison to Bush's friends in Beijing and Baghdad, Noriega could pass for a choirboy.

Some sensed a "lack of political and moral consistency" in the action against Noriega just as Washington "kisses the hands of the Chinese dictators" (A.M. Rosenthal).[32] The apparent inconsistency vanishes as soon as doctrinal constraints are put aside. In all cases, the actions serve the needs of US power and privilege; it was good for business, as White House spokesman Marlin Fitzwater and the State Department explained in the case of Iraq and China. The media succeeded in overlooking these not-too-subtle points—and even most of the facts.

Another refrain was that the Panamanian Assembly had declared war against the United States on December 15. In fact, international law professor Alfred Rubin pointed out, the Assembly had declared what amounts to a state of emergency "for the duration of the aggression unleashed" by the US government, in the official wording.[33]

Still another pretext, regularly invoked, was that Noriega was involved in the drug racket—as was known long before, while he was on the CIA payroll. John Dinges, author of a book on Noriega, reports that "in 1984, as Panama's de facto ruler and eager to become a major political player in Central America, General Noriega began to clean up his act." His criminal indictment after the US government turned against him lists only one charge of alleged trafficking after 1984. DEA and narcotics agents describe his cooperation with US authorities in drug interdiction activities as genuine. In a letter of May 1986, DEA administrator John Lawn expressed his "deep appreciation" to Noriega "for the vigorous anti-drug trafficking policy that you have adopted," and Attorney General Edwin Meese added his praise in May 1987.[34]

As the whitewash proceeded in subsequent months, the official fairy tales took on the status of established fact. The convention in news reporting and commentary is to select one of the many pretexts floated by the Administration, and present it with unwavering confidence—but without even a token gesture towards possible evidence. Correspondent Pamela Constable selected human rights as the motive for the US disaffection with Noriega: "Domestic opponents were repressed with increasing harshness after 1987, leading the Reagan administration to sever the long US alliance with Noriega." In the New York Review, Michael Massing chose the drug racket, writing that "Washington was willing to accept Noriega's political usurpations, including the stealing of an election in 1984, but once his drug-trafficking involvement became widely known, American tolerance came to an end."[35]

In fact, internal affairs of Panama aside, it is hardly possible to suggest seriously that Noriega's repression offended the enthusiastic backers of the Salvadoran and Guatemalan military next door; the stealing of the 1984 election was not reluctantly "accepted," but greeted with open enthusiasm by the United States; Noriega's drug trafficking was well known long before, but was widely publicized by the media only when government policy shifted, providing the signal. As hypotheses, these would be quickly dismissed. As confident assertions, they tell us only about the conventions of intellectual life. As a service to power, their merits are obvious.

As for the drug connection, whatever Noriega's role may have been, he was surely not alone. Shortly after he stole the 1984 election by fraud and violence, to US applause, the Federal district attorney in Miami identified Panamanian banks as a major conduit for drug money. A year earlier, a Senate report on banking had described Panama as a center of criminal capital, and a key link in drug transshipment and drug-money-laundering. These practices largely ended when the US sanctions in 1987 virtually closed the banks, the press reported after the invasion.[36]

The bankers were returned to power in Panama with the invasion, as the media finally deigned to notice. The Attorney General and the Treasury Minister installed by the US invasion (also, reportedly, the new president of the Supreme Court) are former directors of the First Interamericas Bank, owned by one of the leading Colombian drug bosses and used by the Colombian cocaine cartel to launder profits; it was shut down by Noriega in 1985 in a move considered by the DEA to be an important blow to the cartel. President Endara, a corporate lawyer, had for years been a director of one of the Panamanian banks discovered by the FBI to be involved in money-laundering. The *Miami Herald* reports that Guillermo Ford, Vice-President under Endara and president of the banking commission, along with his brother Henry, had close business ties to Ramón Milián Rodríguez, the cartel money-launderer who is serving a thirty-five-year prison sentence. They were co-directors of companies that were used to launder money, Milián Rodríguez testified. Another link to the Endara government was exposed in April 1989, when Carlos Eleta, a leading businessman and Noriega opponent, was arrested on charges of importing cocaine and money-laundering. According to a high-ranking US source, Eleta had been recruited by the CIA to help distribute $10 million in covert US aid for Endara's election to the presidency a month later.[37]

Queried on a report that banking practices would be modified to deter drug-money-laundering, President Endara said that any changes would be "not that profound" and that "the bankers want changes that are reasonable and will not duly change the banking environment." A month later, US negotiators had "given up efforts to change Panama's bank-secrecy laws, which have made that nation the most notorious center for drug-money laundering in the hemisphere," Frank Greve reports, adding that at least ten major Panamanian banks are "willingly involved" in drug-money-laundering according to US authorities,

and experts believe billions of dollars in drug money have flowed through Panamanian banks in general in the last decade. ... Asked why the United States yielded
on bank secrecy, a State Department official replied, "We don't want to alienate
the Panamanians just as we're sitting down to negotiate with them. ... Rather
than tell them whether their laws are sufficient, we'll let them decide."

They decided in the predictable way, with a few cosmetic changes: "I can't
say now there's less money-laundering," the Banking Association of Panama
President Edgardo Lasso says, "But it may be happening without our knowledge."[38] The artificial Panamanian economy relies heavily on this "banking
environment," and Washington is unlikely to interfere very seriously.

It all makes good sense. Milián Rodríguez himself had been invited to
the Reagan inaugural, Leslie Cockburn reports, "in recognition of the
$180,000 in campaign contributions from his clients" (the cocaine cartel,
who regarded Reagan as "our kind of candidate," he said).[39] As Drug Czar
in the early 1980s, George Bush cancelled the small Federal program aimed
at banks engaged in laundering drug money, and this critical link in the
trade was put to the side in the new phase of the "drug war." Ghetto
kids who sell crack arouse our ire, but not the civilized folk in the plush
offices.

After the US government had determined to rid itself of Noriega, it
continued to support the Panama Defense Force that he headed, though
it was well known that the PDF was involved in the rackets at every level.
When George Shultz produced an accolade to the PDF in March 1988,
describing it as "a strong and honorable force that has a significant and
proper role to play," the New York Times commented: "it is odd to hear
Administration officials sing the military's praises when it is layered with
General Noriega's cronies who have shared in the profits from drug-trafficking and other criminal activities." With the successful completion of Operation Just Cause, the PDF was reconstituted under essentially the same
leadership—who, it is expected, will be more loyal to their US commanders
than the unpredictable Noriega. Noriega's successor was Colonel Eduardo
Herrera Hassan, whose troops "most energetically shot, gassed, beat and
tortured civilian protesters during the wave of demonstrations against General
Noriega that erupted here in the summer of 1987," the New York Times
observed while reporting that the Colonel, "a favorite of the American
and diplomatic establishment here," is to be placed in command of the
military with their new human rights" orientation. In its May 1990 report
on the Panama invasion, Americas Watch expressed considerable shock over

the appointment of Colonel Hassan, who "directed the most brutal repression of peaceful demonstrations in Panamanian history, on July 10, 1987, which Noriega's opponents called 'Black Friday'. . . . By any reasonable standard, he himself should be on trial"—as should George Bush, one might add.[40]

Government–media doctrine holds that Bush "had few alternatives" to invasion, having failed to oust Noriega by other means (R.W. Apple). "Mr. Bush may have seen no alternative to invasion," Tom Wicker added, though as a dove, he regards Bush's arguments as not "conclusive."[41] The underlying assumption is that the US has every right to achieve its aims, so that violence is legitimate if peaceful means fail. This principle has broad application. It could readily be invoked by the terrorists who destroyed Pan Am 103, an act bitterly denounced on its first anniversary just as the US invaded Panama. They too could plead that they had exhausted peaceful means. But the doctrine has another crucial feature: the right to violence is reserved to the United States and its clients.

The fundamental doctrine is further clarified by the treatment of international law. That its precepts were violated by the invasion was sometimes noted, but dismissed, on the grounds that the "legalities are murky" (*Wall Street Journal*),[42] or simply an irrelevance. Exactly ten years earlier, Vietnam invaded Cambodia after murderous attacks against Vietnamese villages with thousands of casualties, overthrowing the Pol Pot regime. By any standards, the justification for this invasion is far more plausible than anything that Washington could offer. But in that case, the legalities were neither murky nor irrelevant. Rather, Vietnam's violation of international law deeply offended our sensibilities, establishing the Vietnamese as "the Prussians of Southeast Asia" (*New York Times*) whom we must punish, along with the people of Cambodia, by economic warfare and tacit support for the Khmer Rouge. The radically different reactions are readily explained by the doctrine that only the US and its clients enjoy the right of lawless violence. But the obvious questions remain unasked, and understanding of the real world is effectively suppressed.

Largely keeping to the government agenda, the press scarcely investigated such matters as civilian casualties. Some blamed the failure on Pentagon interference, but that excuse is hard to credit. Nothing prevented the press from visiting hospitals and interviewing their directors, who reported overflowing morgues from the first days and appealed to Latin America and Europe to send medical equipment because "the United States is only giving us bullets," or publishing the wire service stories reporting these facts. Linda

Hossie of the *Toronto Globe & Mail* reported "open skepticism" about the official figures, quoting slum-dwellers, Church workers, and others who tell of many civilians "buried because there were no transports to take them to a morgue." "Virtually all the Panamanians interviewed," she writes, "agreed that the vast majority of the dead are civilians." The Argentine press was able to find government spokesmen who said "they have taken the necessary legal steps for the cremation of great quantities of dead bodies piled in the morgues of the central hospitals now overflowing with cadavers." One of the few to make the effort, J.D. Gannon, reported that hospitals, morgues and funeral homes recorded about six hundred civilian deaths in Panama City, while diplomats and relief workers estimated four hundred more in rural areas.[43]

The media were much impressed with a CBS poll showing over 90 percent approval for the invasion, but did not ponder the fact that 10 percent of the population of 2.4 million said they had a good friend or relative killed (23 percent, killed or wounded). A few calculations on reasonable assumptions indicate that either the poll is totally meaningless, or that the numbers killed run to thousands on conservative estimates. The question did not arise.[44]

The lack of interest in the civilian toll was shared by Congress. On February 1, the House passed a resolution, 389–26, "commending Bush for his handling of the invasion and expressing sadness over the loss of 23 American lives," AP reported. A possible omission comes to mind, but seems to have passed unnoticed.[45]

This is a mere sample, but enough to illustrate "the kind of hard-hitting, no holds barred reporting that makes the press such an essential component of this country's democratic system," as Sanford Ungar writes, overcome with awe at the magnificence of his profession.[46]

Only a step away, the veil lifts and elementary truths are easily perceived. Israel's leading military analyst, Ze'ev Schiff, comments that there is nothing remarkable about the US invasion, "neither from a military standpoint—in that the American forces are killing innocent Panamanian civilians ... nor from a political standpoint, when a great power employs its military forces against a small neighbor, with pretexts that Washington would dismiss at once if they were offered by other states." Like the bombing of Libya and other military operations, this one reveals "that Washington permits itself what other powers, including the USSR, do not permit themselves, though they plainly have no less justification."

In another client state, the mainstream Honduran press took a harsher tone. An editorial in *El Tiempo* bitterly denounced the "international totali-tarianism" of George Bush "in the guise of 'democracy'"; Bush has "declared plainly to Latin America that for the North American government, there is no law—only its will—when imposing its designs on the hemisphere." A columnist calls "Just Cause" a

> coarse grotesque euphemism, neither more nor less than an imperialist invasion of Panama. ... We live in a climate of aggression and disrespect ... hurt by our poverty, our weakness, our naked dependence, the absolute submission of our feeble nations to the service of an implacable superpower. Latin America is in pain

—while Congress gives George Bush a rousing ovation for his triumph.[47]

4. Operation Just Cause: the Reasons

The reasons for the invasion were not difficult to discern. Manuel Noriega had been working happily with US intelligence since the 1950s, right through the tenure of George Bush as CIA director and later Drug Czar for the Reagan Administration. His relations with US intelligence began when he reported on leftist tendencies among fellow students, officers, and instructors, at the Military Academy. These services became contractual in 1966 or 1967, according to US intelligence officials. The spy network he organized "would serve two clients," Frederick Kempe reports: "the Panamanian government, by monitoring political opponents in the region, and the U.S., by tracking the growing Communist influence in the unions organized at United Fruit Co.'s banana plantations ..." (an appropriate concern for the US government, it is assumed without comment). After various vicissitudes, he was recognized as a kindred spirit by the Reagan Administration, and was put back on the US payroll with payments from the CIA and DIA averaging nearly $200,000 a year.[48] His assistance in stealing the 1984 election has already been noted. He also played a supportive role in the US war against Nicaragua and was considered by the DEA to be a valuable asset in the war against drugs.

By 1985–6, however, the US was beginning to reassess his role and finally decided to remove him. A largely upper- and middle-class "civic opposition" developed, leading to street protests that were brutally suppressed by the Panamanian military under the command of the US favorite, Colonel Herrera Hassan. A program of economic warfare was undertaken, designed to minimize the impact on the US business community, a GAO official testified before Congress.[49]

One black mark against Noriega was his support for the Contadora peace process for Central America, to which the US was strongly opposed. His commitment to the war against Nicaragua was in question, and when the Iran–Contra affair broke, his usefulness was at an end. On New Year's Day 1990, administration of the Panama Canal was to pass largely into Panamanian hands, and a few years later the rest was to follow, according to the Canal Treaty. A major oil pipeline is 60 percent owned by Panama. Clearly, traditional US clients had to be restored to power, and there was not much time to spare. With January 1 approaching, the London *Economist* noted, "the timing was vital" and a new government had to be installed.[50]

Further gains from the invasion were to tighten the stranglehold on Nicaragua and Cuba, which, the government and media complain, had been making use of the free and open Panamanian economy to evade the illegal US trade sanctions and embargo (yet another condemnation of the embargo by the UN while the US invaded Panama, with only the US and Israel voting against, was too insignificant a matter even to merit report). These intentions were signalled symbolically by the contemptuous violations of diplomatic immunity, including the break-in at the Nicaraguan Embassy and repeated detention of Cuban Embassy personnel—all grossly illegal, but that arouses no concern in a lawless state apart from the danger of a precedent from which the US might suffer; one never knows when the next Somoza or Marcos might seek shelter in a US Embassy. Even the vulgar display by the US military outside the Vatican Embassy, with rock music blaring and other childish antics, was generally considered good clean fun—and by the military, "a very imaginative use of psychological operations" (Colonel Ted Sahlin of the Kennedy Special Warfare Center). White House spokesman Fitzwater was "certainly glad to see the American sense of whimsy come forward in this situation"—which, as conceded on all sides, was part of a pattern of gross violation of Federal and international law on diplomatic privilege. The press adhered to its fabled canons of objectivity—for example, when television crews in a hotel overlooking the Vatican Embassy displayed a pineapple cut in half outside their room, or when National Public Radio amused its elite intellectual audience with an interview with a fruit and vegetable dealer who was asked whether Noriega's pockmarked face really did look like a pineapple.[51]

Seven months later, Iraqi troops surrounded the US and other embassies in an effort to compel the countries participating in the blockade against Iraq to withdraw their missions. "They have not made any moves against the embassy or intruded in any fashion, but they are none the less present," the White House spokesman announced. The media were outraged. The *Times* editors wrote: "Saddam Hussein now lashes out against diplomacy itself." The editors proclaimed further, for the first time, that the Iraqi leaders are now "becoming war criminals in the classic Nuremberg sense," and should be tried under the Nuremberg Principles, which hold that "a crime against world law is liable to punishment," including heads of states and those who obey their orders. It would be too much to expect the editors to recall that the state they hail as "the symbol of human decency," on invading West Beirut in September 1982 in violation of a cease-fire and a unanimous UN Security Council resolution, at once broke into the Soviet Embassy grounds, seizing the consulate building and holding it for two days, a gratuitous provocation (the Embassy had also been repeatedly shelled during Israel's bombardment of civilian targets in Beirut).[52] But they might, perhaps, have been able to dredge out of memory some events in Panama City a few months earlier.

The invasion restored to power the traditional White European elite that had been displaced by General Torrijos in his 1968 coup. Under the heading "Quayle Gets Warm Welcome in Panama," *Times* correspondent Robert Pear notes at the end of an upbeat report that "pro-American sentiment is expressed more forcefully by affluent and middle-class Panamanians than by those with lower income," the Black and Mestizo majority. He reports further that the Vice-President did not visit the poor neighborhoods. Rita Beamish reports for AP, however, that "before leaving Panama City, Quayle took a driving tour of the impoverished Chorillo neighborhood. . . . As his motorcade slowly drove by the area, onlookers gathered in groups and peered out windows, watching in stony silence. Their reaction was in stark contrast to the enthusiastic cheering Sunday from a well-dressed congregation at a Roman Catholic church Quayle attended in another neighborhood," prominently featured on television.[53]

The "stark contrast" remained unnoticed. *Times* reporter Larry Rohter and others found general support and approval for the US ventures among those who had suffered from the economic warfare and were ruined by the invasion.

The few reporters who strayed from the beaten track discovered the expected pattern. Diego Ribadeneira reports a demonstration protesting the arrest of two leaders of the telecommunications union by US soldiers. "Most political activists and labor leaders" are "on a list of several hundred people whom the Endara government seeks to detain," he continues. A senior official in the US Embassy professed to have no knowledge of the reasons: "We weren't given any details, just that the Endara government wanted us to get them. They're bad guys of some sort, I guess."[54]

So they are, like political activists and labor leaders throughout the region, and elsewhere, if they fail to toe the line.

Leaving nothing to chance, the US military sent hundreds of psywar specialists into Panama to "spread pro-American propaganda messages throughout the country" in a campaign to "bolster the image of the United States" and "to stamp American influence on almost every phase of the new government," the press reports. "These guys are ... very sophisticated in the psychological aspects of war," an army official said. "They are engaged in propaganda." [55]

Noriega's career fits a standard pattern. Typically, the thugs and gangsters whom the US backs reach a point in their careers when they become too independent and too grasping, outliving their usefulness. Instead of just robbing the poor and safeguarding the business climate, they begin to interfere with Washington's natural allies, the local business elite and oligarchy, or even US interests directly. At that point, Washington begins to vacillate; we hear of human rights violations that were cheerfully ignored in the past, and sometimes the US government acts to remove them—even to attempt to assassinate them, as in the case of Trujillo. By 1986–7, the only question was when and how Noriega should be removed, though there were holdouts. As late as August 1987, Elliott Abrams, obsessed as always by the attraction of violence in Nicaragua, opposed a Senate resolution condemning Noriega.[56]

Another indication of possible ambivalence in high places is the curious Israel–Panama relation. Apparently, as in the case of Somoza, Israel was not compelled to cancel arms shipments and other assistance to Noriega until virtually the end. According to the Israeli press, when Noriega stopped being Washington's "bosom friend" in 1986, "Israel was ordered to behave—it was permitted to continue to sell weapons, but required to keep a lower profile in its relations with Noriega." About 20 percent of the half-billion dollars of Israeli weapons sales to Panama in the past decade were from the last three years, in addition to other military equipment, Efraim Davidi reports in the Labor Party press. He believes that the Americans were following the usual plan of providing weapons to military elements which, they hoped, would eliminate their specific target—much the same scenario as in Israel's sale of US weapons to Iran from the early 1980s.[57]

All in all, a successful operation. The US can now proceed to foster democracy and successful economic development, as it has done with such success in the region for many years. The prospect is seriously put forth, in blissful disregard of the relevant history and the reasons for its regular course. The cheery reports on these prospects did not raise even the most obvious questions: What were the consequences of the most recent invasions, conducted with the same promises?

It took real dedication to miss the point. On the day of the Panama invasion, the back pages carried obituary notices for Herbert Blaize, who presided over the triumph of democracy and reconstruction after the liberation of Grenada to much acclaim—a perfect occasion for an analysis of the realization of the promise. Initially, the US poured $110 million into the tiny island to stimulate US investment and tourism, to little effect. The country is saddled with a foreign debt of close to $50 million and a trade deficit of $60 million. In early December 1989, a strike of virtually all public employees demanded payment of wage increases promised from 1987; funds are unavailable, despite heavy borrowing to curb a growing budget deficit. The official unemployment figure is 20 percent, estimated at 40 percent among young workers. Alcoholism and drug addiction are said to have reached record levels, along with homicides and other signs of social dissolution. The health care system instituted under Maurice Bishop was dismantled after Blaize expelled the Cuban personnel who staffed it. Two percent of the population are estimated to have emigrated in 1986. In June 1987, President Blaize pushed through an Emergency Powers Act that gave the security forces extensive powers, including detention without trial, house arrest, deportation, and the right to declare a curfew, also establishing a board to censor "politically sensitive songs." There are no more appeals to "Reagan the Provider," who will build us homes, give us food and jobs, and lead us to the pot of gold at the end of the rainbow, as he promised. Instead, graffiti on walls read "Yankees Out" and "Yankees Go Home." "Recent wall scrawlings are more likely to say things like 'Reagan is the world terrorist No. 1'," Gary Krist reports with incomprehension, and "the most flattering description of George Bush" that he heard on the island was that "he's just another Ronald Reagan, only not as aggressive"; that was before the rerun of the script in Panama.[58]

Or we could look to the Dominican Republic, liberated by a US invasion in 1965 and set on the road to democracy—though only after years of death squad killings and torture, and the takeover by US corporations of most of what they had not acquired during earlier occupations. This too is regarded as a triumph of democracy, with civilians elected and the military not taking power—in fact, happy to leave the job of policing to the civilians and the IMF. But "on an island blessed like few others with varied mineral resources, fertile soils, lush forests, and plentiful fish and fowl," Latin America scholar Jan Knippers Black observes, "an ingenious and industrious people continues to struggle with little relief or progress against the ravages of hunger and disease," and the country remains a "virtual appendage of the United States," lacking even minimal independence, with no escape from misery for the general population.[59]

While US troops were "restoring order" in Panama in January, a boat filled with Dominican refugees fleeing to the US sank, with dozens drowned; another had caught fire a few days earlier, with no survivors. As usual, these incidents were not reported. Unknown numbers of these illegal boat people sail on rickety boats to Puerto Rico each year, with many drowned and thousands arrested and deported. The US Immigration and Naturalization Service expected to capture more than 10,000 of them in 1990, some 10–20 percent of those attempting illegal entry, double the number for 1989. Relative to population, a comparable flight from Vietnam would be in the range of half a million to a million, a figure that would arouse vast international protest about the horrors of Communism. The Dominican Republic was not devastated by foreign invaders and economic warfare. But unlike the Vietnamese boat people, there is no political capital to be made from anguishing over the fate of those fleeing its shores, so they remain hidden from view, much like the thousands of boat people fleeing Haiti, some 20,000 returned forcefully during the Reagan years, while others escape to the neighboring Dominican Republic—or are captured and brought there by force—to work as virtual slaves on the sugar plantations.[60]

No such thoughts interrupted the praise of Operation Just Cause and its rich promise—which is not entirely empty. Bush's announcement of $1 billion in aid to reconstruct the society destroyed by US economic warfare and military attack included $400 million to finance sales of US products to Panama, another $150 million to pay off bank loans, and $65 million in private-sector loans and guarantees for US investors—all gifts to the rich at home by the US taxpayer.[61]

5. Good Intentions Gone Awry

In the months following the Panama invasion, the successful affair largely disappeared from view.[62] US goals had been achieved, the triumph had been properly celebrated, and there was little more to say except to record subsequent progress towards freedom, democracy, and good fortune—or, if that strains credulity, to produce occasional musings on how the best of intentions go awry when we have such poor human material to work with.

Central American sources continued to give considerable attention to the impact of the invasion on civilians, but they were ignored in the occasional reviews of the matter here. *New York Times* correspondent Larry Rohter devoted a column to casualty estimates on April 1, citing figures as high as 673 killed, and adding that higher figures, which he attributes only to Ramsey Clark, are "widely rejected" in Panama. He found Panamanian witnesses who described US military actions as restrained, but none with less happy tales.[63]

Among the many readily accessible sources deemed unworthy of mention we find such examples as the following.

The Mexican press reported that two Catholic bishops estimated deaths at perhaps 3000. Hospitals and nongovernmental human rights groups estimated deaths at over 2000.[64]

A joint delegation of the Costa Rica-based Central American Human Rights Commission (CODEHUCA) and the Panamanian Human Rights Commission (CONADEHUPA) published the report of its January 20–30 inquiry, based on numerous interviews. It concluded that "the human costs of the invasion are substantially higher than the official U.S. figures" of 202 civilians killed, reaching 2–3000 according to "conservative estimates." Eyewitnesses interviewed in the urban slums report that US helicopters aimed their fire at buildings with only civilian occupants, that a US tank destroyed a public bus, killing twenty-six passengers, that civilian residences were burned to the ground with many apartments destroyed and many killed, that US troops shot at ambulances and killed wounded, some with bayonets, and denied access to the Red Cross. The Catholic and Episcopal Churches gave estimates of 3000 dead as "conservative." Civilians were illegally detained, particularly union leaders and those considered "in opposition to the invasion or nationalistic. . . . All the residences and offices of the political sectors that oppose the invasion have been searched and much of them have been destroyed and their valuables stolen." The US imposed severe censorship. Human rights violations under Noriega had been "unacceptably high," the report continues, though of course "mild compared with the record of U.S.-supported regimes in Guatemala and El Salvador." But the US invasion "caused an unprecedented level of deaths, suffering, and human rights abuses in Panama." The title of the report is: "Panama: More than an invasion, . . . a massacre."[65]

Physicians for Human Rights, with the concurrence of Americas Watch, reached tentative casualty figures higher than those given by the Pentagon but well below those of CODEHUCA and others in Panama. Their estimate is about 300 civilians killed. Americas Watch also gives a "conservative estimate" of at least 3000 wounded, concluding further that civilian deaths were four times as great as military deaths in Panama, and over ten times as high as US casualties (officially given as twenty-three). They ask: "How does a 'surgical operation' result in almost ten civilians killed (by official US count) for every American military casualty?" By September, the count of bodies exhumed from several of the mass graves had passed 600.[66]

The CODEHUCA report emphasizes that a great deal is uncertain, because of the violent circumstances, the incineration of bodies, and the lack of records for persons buried in common graves without having reached morgues or hospitals, according to eyewitnesses.[67] Its reports—and the many others of which a few have been cited here—may or may not be accurate. A media decision to ignore them, however, reflects not professional standards but a commitment to power.

While Larry Rohter's visits to the slums destroyed by US bombardment located only celebrants, or critics of US "insensitivity" at worst, others found a rather different picture. Mexico's leading newspaper reported in April that Rafael Olivardia, refugee spokesman for the 15,000 refugees of the devastated El Chorillo neighborhood, "said that the El Chorillo refugees were victims of a 'bloodbath' during and after the invasion." "He said that those victims 'saw North American tanks roll over the dead' during the invasion that left a total of more than 2000 dead and thousands injured, according to unofficial figures." "You only live once," Olivardia said, "and if you must die fighting for an adequate home, then the U.S. soldiers should complete the task they began" on December 20.

The Spanish-language press in the United States was less celebratory than its colleagues. Vicky Pelaez reports from Panama that "the entire world continues in ignorance about how the thousands of victims of the North-american invasion of Panama died and what kinds of weapons were used, because the Attorney-General of the country refuses to permit investigation of the bodies buried in the common graves." An accompanying photo shows workmen exhuming corpses from a grave containing "almost 200 victims of the invasion." Quoting a woman who found the body of her murdered father, Pelaez reports that "just like the woman at the cemetery, it is 'vox populi' in Panama that the Northamericans used completely unknown armaments during the 20 December invasion." The head of a Panamanian human rights group informed the journal that:

> They converted Panama into a laboratory of horror. Here, they first experimented with methods of economic strangulation; then they successfully used a campaign of disinformation at the international level. But it was in the application of the most modern war technology that they demonstrated infernal mastery.

The CODEHUCA report also alleges that "the U.S. Army used highly sophisticated weapons—some for the first time in combat—against unarmed civilian populations," and "in many cases no distinction was made between civilian and military targets."[68]

One case of "highly sophisticated weapons" did receive some attention. F-117A stealth fighters were used in combat for the first time, dropping 2000-lb bombs with time-delay mechanisms in a large open field near an airstrip and barracks that housed an elite PDF battalion. The Air Force had kept this plane under close wraps, refusing to release cost or performance data about it. "There were conflicting reports as to the rationale for employing the sophisticated aircraft, which cost nearly $50 million apiece, to conduct what appeared to be a simple operation," *Aviation Week & Space Technology* reported. The Panamanian air force has no fighters, and no military aircraft were stationed permanently at the base that was attacked. Its only known air defenses "were a pair of aging small caliber antiaircraft guns." An American aeronautical engineering consultant and charter operator in Panama said he was "astonished" to learn of the use of the F-117A, pointing out that the target attacked did not even have radar: "They could have bombed it with any other aircraft and not been noticed." The aerospace journal cites Defense Secretary Dick Cheney's claim that the aircraft was used "because of its great accuracy," then suggesting its own answer to the puzzle: "By demonstrating the F-117A's capability to operate in low-intensity conflicts, as well as its intended mission to attack heavily defended Soviet targets, the operation can be used by the Air Force to justify the huge investment made in stealth technology" to "an increasingly skeptical Congress."[69]

A similar conclusion was reached, more broadly, by Colonel (Retired) David Hackworth, a former combat commander who is one of the nation's most decorated soldiers. He described the Panama operation as technically efficient, though in his judgement "100 Special Forces guys" would have sufficed to capture Noriega, and "this big operation was a Pentagon attempt to impress Congress just when they're starting to cut back on the military."

The National Security Strategy report of March 1990 lends credibility to these suggestions.[70]

If these were indeed among the motives for the exercise, they may have suffered a slight setback when it turned out that one of the stealth fighter-bombers had missed its undefended target by more than 300 yards, despite its "great accuracy." Defense Secretary Cheney ordered an inquiry.[71]

The nature of the US victory became clearer, along familiar lines, in the following months. Its character is described by Andres Oppenheimer in the *Miami Herald* in June, under the heading "Panama Flirts with Economic Recovery"—that is, recovery from the depths to which it was plunged by illegal US economic warfare, then invasion and occupation. But there is a qualification: "Six months after the U.S. invasion, Panama is showing signs of growing prosperity—at least for the largely white-skinned business class that has regained its influence after more than two decades of military rule." The luxury shops are again full of goods, and "Panama's nightlife is also perking up" as "foreign tourists, mostly U.S. businessmen, can be seen most evenings sipping martinis in the lobbies of the biggest hotels," which are sometimes "booked solid—a contrast to the moribund atmosphere there before the invasion." Newspapers are filled with advertisements from department stores, banks, and insurance firms. "The upper class and the middle classes are doing great," a Western European diplomat observes: "They had the money in U.S. bank accounts and are bringing it back to the country. But the poor are in bad shape, because the government is bankrupt and can't help them." "The Catholic Church has begun to denounce what it sees as a lack of government concern for the poor," Oppenheimer continues. An editorial in a Church weekly "lashed out at authorities for devoting their energies to helping the private sector while breaking their original promises not to fire low-income public workers."[72] In short, the important people are doing just fine.

On August 2, the Catholic bishops of Panama issued a pastoral letter condemning US "interference in the country's internal affairs" and denouncing the December invasion as "a veritable tragedy in the annals of the country's history." The statement also condemned Washington's failure to provide aid to the people who continue to suffer from the invasion, and criticized the government for ignoring their plight. Their protest appears in the Guatemala City *Central America Report* under the heading "Church Raises Its Voice"—though not loudly enough to be heard in Washington and New York.[73]

In August, a presidential commission proposed a plan for reconstructing the devastated economy. It called for an end to the "occupation of the State and its territory by U.S. troops" and the reestablishment of Panamanian sovereignty. Again, its voice did not reach the aggressors.[74]

The white-skinned sector, which owns most of the land and resources, is estimated at about 8 percent of the population. The "two decades of military rule" to which the *Miami Herald* refers had some other characteristics as well. The Torrijos dictatorship had a populist character, which largely ended after his death in 1981 in an airplane accident (with various charges about the cause) and the subsequent Noriega takeover. During this period, Black, Mestizo, and Indigenous Panamanians gained their first share of power, and economic and land reforms were undertaken. In these two decades, infant mortality declined from 40 percent to less than 20 percent and life expectancy increased by nine years. New hospitals, health centers, houses, schools and universities were built, and more doctors, nurses and teachers were trained. Indigenous communities were granted autonomy and protection for their traditional lands, to an extent unmatched in the hemisphere. For the first time, Panama moved to an independent foreign policy—still alive in the 1980s to an extent, as Panama participated in the Contadora peace efforts. The Canal Treaty was signed in 1977, theoretically awarding control over the canal to Panama by the year 2000, though the prospects are doubtful. The Reagan Administration took the position that "when the Carter–Torrijos treaties are being renegotiated"—an eventuality taken for granted—"the prolongation of the US military presence in the Panama Canal area till well after the year 2000 should be brought up for discussion" (State Department).[75]

The post-invasion moves to place Panamanian military forces under US control may be motivated by more than just the normal doctrine. It will probably be argued that Panama is not in a position to defend the Canal as the Treaty requires, so that US bases must be retained.

Pamela Constable reports that "bankers and business owners" find that things are looking up, though "a mood of anger and desperation permeates the underclass" in "the blighted shantytowns." Vice-President Guillermo Ford says: "The stores have reopened 100 percent, and the private sector is very enthusiastic. I think we're on the road to a very solid future." Under his "proposed recovery program," public enterprises would be sold off, "the labor code would be revised to allow easier dismissal of workers and tax-free export factories would be set up to lure foreign capital."

Business leaders "are bullish on Ford's ideas," Constable continues. In contrast, "Labor unions are understandably wary of these proposals," but "their power has become almost negligible" with "massive dismissals of public workers who supported Noriega and the unprecedented jobless rate." The US emergency aid package approved by Congress is intended largely "to make back payments on Panama's foreign debt and shore up its credit-worthiness with foreign lending institutions"; in translation: it is a taxpayer subsidy to international banks, foreign investors, and the important people in Panama. The thousands of refugees from El Chorillo, now living in what some of them call "a concentration camp," will not be returning to the devastated slum. The original owners, who had long wanted "to transform this prime piece of real estate into a posher district," may now be able to do so. Noriega had stood in the way of these plans, allowing the poor to occupy housing there rent-free. But by bombing the neighborhood into rubble and then levelling the charred ruins with bulldozers, US forces overcame "that ticklish legal and human obstacle" to these intentions, Constable reports.[76]

With unemployment skyrocketing, nearly half the population cannot meet essential food needs. Crime has quadrupled. Aid is designated for businesses and foreign banks (debt repayment). It could be called the "Central Americanization" of Panama, correspondent Brook Larmer aptly observes.[77]

The US occupying forces continued to leave little to chance. The Mexican journal *Excelsior* reports that US forces established direct control over ministries and public institutions. According to an organization chart leaked to the journal by political and diplomatic sources, US controls extend to all provinces, the Indian community, the Town Halls of the ten major cities, and the regional police offices: "Washington's objective is to have a strategic network in this country to permanently control all the actions and decisions of the government." With the establishment of this "parallel government" closely controlling all decision-making, "things have returned to the way they were before 1968 in Panama." The journal scheduled an interview with President Endara to discuss the matter, but it was cancelled without explanation.[78]

The report provides extensive details, including names of US officials and the tasks assigned them in the organization chart. All of this could easily be checked by US reporters, if home offices were interested. They are not. "The information that we reveal here," *Excelsior* reports, "is supposed to be known only to very restricted groups"—not including the US public.

The occupying forces also moved to limit such irritants as freedom of expression. *Excelsior* reports that "United States intelligence services exercise control not only over local information media but also over international news agencies," according to the president of the Journalist Union of Panama. An opposition activist alleges that the first Panamanian publishing company, ERSA, with three daily papers, was occupied by US tanks and security forces "in order to turn it over to a businessman who had lost it in a lawsuit," a member of an oligarchical family that "favors the interventionist line of the United States." According to Ramsey Clark's Independent Commission of Inquiry, the offices of the daily *La Republica* were "ransacked and looted by US troops the day after the newspaper reported on the large number of deaths caused by the U.S. invasion." Its editor was arrested and held for six weeks by US troops, then sent to a Panamanian prison without charges. The publisher of one of the few opposition voices was arrested in March on charges of alleged misconduct when he was a government minister, and the government closed a radio station for broadcasting editorials critical of the US invasion and the government it established.[79]

Miguel Antonio Bernal, a leading Panamanian intellectual and anti-Noriega activist, writes that "freedom of press is again under siege in Panama." Vice-President Ricardo Arias Calderón proposed a new law to restrict press criticism of the government, saying: "We will not tolerate criticism." He also urged stockholders of Panama's largest newspaper, *La Prensa*, to fire its editor and founder Roberto Eisenman because of the journal's criticism of the government, and called on members of his Christian Democratic Party to work for Eisenman's ouster. Describing such acts, the increasing terror, and the reconstruction of the military with Noriega associates who were implicated in drug running and corruption, Bernal asks why the US is "turning the same blind eye" as in the past to these developments.[80]

Bernal's question is surely rhetorical. Latin Americans know the answer very well.

Those not restricted to the US quality press could learn that President Endara's government received "one of its worst diplomatic setbacks" on March 30, when it was formally ousted from the Group of Eight—what are considered the major Latin American democracies. Panama had been suspended from the group in 1988 in reaction to Noriega's repression, and with the further deterioration of the political climate under foreign occupation Panama was ousted permanently at the March meeting of Foreign Ministers. The Group issued a resolution stating that "the process of democratic legitimation in Panama requires popular consideration without foreign interference, that guarantees the full right of the people to freely choose their governments." The resolution also indicated that the operations of the US military are affecting Panama's sovereignty and independence as well as the legality of the Endara government. This decision extends the pattern of strong Latin American opposition to the earlier US measures against Panama and the invasion. As the media here barely noted, President Endara's inaugural address four weeks after the invasion was boycotted by virtually all Latin American ambassadors.[81]

The Washington–media position is that the Endara government is legitimate, having won the 1989 elections that were stolen by Noriega. Latin American opinion commonly takes a different view. In 1989 Endara was running against Noriega, with extensive US backing, open and covert. Furthermore, the elections were conducted under conditions caused by the illegal US economic warfare that was demolishing the economy. The United States was therefore holding a whip over the electorate. For that reason alone the elections were far from free and uncoerced, by any sensible standards. Today, the political scene is quite different. On these grounds, there would be every reason to organize a new election, contrary to the wishes of Endara and his US sponsors.

The official position is offered by Michael Massing in the *New York Review*. Reporting from Panama, he writes that Endara's willingness to "go along" with the US request that he assume the presidency "has caused the leaders of some Latin American countries, such as Peru, to question his legitimacy. ... The Panamanians themselves, however, have few such qualms," because his "clear victory" in the 1989 election "provided Endara with all the credentials he needs." Citation of Peru for dragging its feet is a deft move, since President García was an official enemy of the US who had been recalcitrant about Nicaragua, had restricted debt payment, and in general failed to observe proper standards; best to overlook the rest of the Group of Eight, however, among "some Latin American countries." As for the views of the "Panamanians themselves," no further indication is given as to how this information was obtained.[82]

Massing reports on the police raids in poor neighborhoods, the protests of homeless and hungry people demanding jobs and housing, the reconstruction of Noriega's PDF, the restoration of the oligarchy with a "successful corporate lawyer" at the head of a government "largely made up of businessmen," who receive US corporate visitors sponsored by OPIC (which ensures US investments abroad) "as if they were visiting heads of state." The business climate is again "attractive" in this "land ruled by merchants, marketers, and moneylenders. ... The government is drafting plans to revive Panama's banking industry, relax its labor laws, expand the free trade zone, and attract foreign investors," and to privatize state enterprises and "radically cut public spending."

Drawn from the "tiny white elite," the government has been accused of "wanting to turn the clock back to 1968, when a small rich group ruled the country"—namely, exactly the group now restored to power. But "the charge is unfair," Massing comments. The proof is that when employees from Air Panama fearful of losing their jobs held a vigil outside his office, President Endara "sent them coffee and made a point of talking with them." What is more, while fasting in the Cathedral in an effort to expedite US aid (or to lose weight, some unkind locals quipped), "he invited striking sanitation workers in for a chat and eventually negotiated a settlement." Furthermore, Vice-President Arias Calderón has said that he favors a "social market economy" in which the government seeks to correct disparities created by the market. True, no projects that might illustrate these plans "are in the works" and the Endara government "opposes the idea" of using US aid for such purposes, "determined to leave virtually everything to the private sector." But that proves nothing, in the face of the powerful evidence showing that "the charge is unfair," just reviewed in its entirety.

Massing is not pleased with the outcome, particularly the restoration of Noriega's PDF, "despite all the good intentions" of the United States (taken as given, in accordance with the norms of the intellectual culture) and its efforts "to atone for its past misbehavior." The problem does not lie in the US military aid programs, which have trained security forces that "have been guilty of horrible excesses" in El Salvador, Guatemala, Honduras, and Noriega's Panama (and other cases unmentioned). Rather, the problem lies in what the US "had to work with." It's those folks who are bad, not us, please.

The consistent effects of our military training, the policies of which it is a part, the documentary record explaining the reasons—in fact, all of history is irrelevant. We are always willing to admit that there were aberrations in the past. But at every moment of time, we have changed course and put the errors of the past behind us.

We are Good, our intentions are Good. Period.

6. The War Goes On

In its essentials, the invasion of Panama is so familiar an exercise of US power as to be no more than a footnote to history. Rhetoric aside, it remains a high priority to block independent nationalism. Arguably, it is more important than before as the US seeks to shore up its own domains in the developing conflict with the other two major world power centers.

The capacity for intervention, however, is undergoing changes. In one significant respect, it is increasing. The decline of the Soviet deterrent and of Soviet willingness to sustain targets of US attack grants Washington greater freedom to crush anything in its path, as Elliott Abrams and others perceive. But in other respects the intervention capacity is declining. The major factor is the tenacity and courage of indigenous resistance. A second impediment is the diversification of the world scene. Though Europe and Japan are now entranced by the opportunities for exploitation of the new Third World in the East, they may not readily allow the US to have its way in its traditional domains. The world is out of control, as well as out of step.

For the countries of the region, this possibility offers some advantages. Doug Henwood observes that the Japanese (and Europe as well) "are well aware that the state is the friend of economic growth, not its enemy," which is "good news for Latin elites interested in more national sovereignty," and their involvement "offers an alternative to dependency on the U.S."[83] It is not that the intentions of Europe and Japan are any more benign. But, arguably, it is better to have three robbers with their hands in your pocket than only one, since they may fall out over how to divide up the loot and thereby offer some room for maneuver. And constructive initiatives are not unthinkable, particularly under the influence of domestic solidarity movements.

Another factor is dissidence within the United States. The popular movements have had significant success in education and raising consciousness, and in imposing constraints on state violence, thus enlarging the scope for freedom and justice. It is that factor, whatever its weight, that will be the primary concern for people who regard themselves as moral agents.

Notes

1. Kim Moody, *An Injury to All* (Verso, 1988), pp. 147–50.
2. See references of Chapter 12, Note 58.
3. See *Necessary Illusions* for extensive evidence.
4. Editorial *WP Weekly*, March 1, 1986.
5. On the reaction to the success of this strategy, see Chapter 10. For a comparative study of media treatment of the 1984 elections in Nicaragua and those in El Salvador, see *Manufacturing Consent*, ch. 3. The same model was used by Lex Rietman in a very careful study of the European press. The range was much wider than in the US media. Thus, the London *Guardian*, keeping to professional standards, applied the same criteria in both cases, unlike the US media, which

shaped their criteria to the requirements of the state. At the other extreme, the allegedly independent leftist *Libération* in Paris dutifully marched to Reaganite commands. The study is revealing with regard to the cultural colonization of Europe in the past decades, particularly France. Rietman, *Over objectiviteit, betonrot en de pijlers van de democratie: De Westeuropese pers en het nieuws over Midden-Amerika*, Instituut voor massacommunicatie, Universiteit Nijmegen, 1988. On the comparative treatment of the 1989–90 Salvadoran and Nicaraguan elections in the *New York Times*, see Patricia Goudvis, "Making Propaganda and Mobilizing Support" (Institute of Latin American Studies, University of Texas), demonstrating the same pattern of subordination to shifting US government agendas rather than any concern for democratic values or professional standards. Thus, in the case of El Salvador, there was no mention of freedom of speech, assembly, or the press, and scarcely a comment on army harassment and death threats against opposition candidates, or the general climate of terror and fear. In the case of Nicaragua, where conditions were far more benign, the agenda was reversed. No mention was made of Contra disruption of elections, which was severe, while FMLN rebels in El Salvador were regularly discussed in these terms. And so on, in the well-documented pattern.

6. Wilson Ring, *BG*, November 24, 1989. Also *NYT*, November 27. Bush, AP, April 17, 1990.

7. *Central America Bulletin* (CARIN), August 1989; Council on Hemispheric Affairs, *News and Analysis*, November 24; *Washington Report on the Hemisphere*, November 22; *Central America Report* [*CAR*] (Guatemala), November 17, 24; *Latinamerica Press* (Peru), August 24, 1989.

8. Discussion after "Chronicle," ABC TV, Boston, December 20, 1989; quoted with his authorization.

9. See Chapter 1, p. 5.

10. See Chapter 3, p. 102, and Note 24.

11. Andrew Rosenthal, *NYT*, January 26, 1990.

12. Quoted from ABC TV in *The Progressive*, February 1990.

13. An example is the tale of Noriega's stores of cocaine, which turned out to be tamales, as noted a few weeks after the proper effect had been obtained. Susanne Schafer, *BG*, January 24, 1990.

14. *BG*, January 4, 1990. José de Cordoba, *WSJ*, December 22; Will, *WP Weekly*, December 25, 1989.

15. Stephen Kurkjian and Adam Pertman, *BG*, January 5, 1990.

16. Broder, "When US intervention makes sense," *WP Weekly*, January 22, 1990. National Council of Churches condemnation, James Franklin, *BG*, December 21, 1989.

17. AP, December 20, 1989, my emphasis; Richard Cole, AP, *BG*, February 3, 1990.

18. Maechling, a former senior State Department official and professor of international law, "Washington's Illegal Invasion," *Foreign Policy*, Summer 1990. Aguilar Zinser, "In Latin America, 'Good' U.S. Intervention Is Still No Intervention," *WP*, August 5, 1987. See also Alfred P. Rubin, professor of international law at the Fletcher School of Law and Diplomacy, Tufts University, "Is Noriega Worth Subverting US Law?," *CSM*, March 19, 1990, discussing the blatantly illegal actions against Noriega personally.

19. Editorial, *Toronto Globe & Mail*, January 3, 1990; Martin Mittelstaedt, *G&M*, December 22, 1989. *NYT*, January 18, 1990.

20. Marlin Fitzwater, cited by John Mashek, *BG*, December 20, 1989; Elaine Sciolino, *NYT*, January 4, 1990; Ian Ball, *Daily Telegraph* (London), December 21; Eloy Aguilar, AP, December 18; Lindsey Gruson, *NYT*, December 20, 1989.

21. Andrew Rosenthal, *NYT*, December 22, 1989.

22. AP, November 6, December 2, 1989; January 6, 1980. AP, *Miami Herald*, November 7, 1989. Patti McSherry, *In These Times*, December 20, 1989. Rita Beamish, AP, November 29, 1989.

23. AP, *NYT*, January 3; Mark Uhlig, *NYT*, January 4, Oswaldo Bonilla, *BG*, January 4. AP, January 3, 4, and *Miami Herald*, January 6, citing the testimony of two peasants who had been kidnapped by the Contras and witnessed the ambush. Reuters, *BG*, January 24; Don Podesta, *WP Weekly*, January 22; Mark Uhlig, *NYT*, January 28, 1990. The last three finally report the evidence that had been available at once about the witnesses, along with other information implicating

the Contras. *Links*, Fall, 1989. AP, February 1, 1990, reporting the Linder family's court suit in Miami.

24. *CAA*, 1984, vol. XI, no. 33; Seymour Hersh, *NYT*, June 22, 1986; Alfonso Chardy, *Miami Herald*, February 29, March 3, 1988; Edward Cody, *WP Weekly*, January 8, 1990. John Weeks, "Panama: The roots of current political instability," *Third World Quarterly*, July 1987; COHA "News and Analysis," April 5, 1988.

25. Ken Silverstein, *Colombia Journalism Review*, May/June 1988.

26. Julia Preston, *WP Weekly*, December 25; AP, December 20, *BG*, December 21, 1989.

27. Cited in "Talk of the Town," *New Yorker*, January 8, 1990.

28. Andrew Rosenthal, "Bush Eliminates Some Restrictions on Beijing Trade," *NYT*, December 20; Maureen Dowd, "2 U.S. Officials Went to Beijing Secretly in July," *NYT*, December 19; Anthony Flint, "US blocks 2 Chinese scholars," *BG*, December 21, 1989. AP, December 20, 1989, February 9, 1990. Iraq, AP, December 22, 1989.

29. Official State Department response to an inquiry from Senator Daniel Inouye, January 26, 1990. Gonzalez, AP, *BG*, August 5, 1990.

30. Glass, ABC World News Tonight, December 15, 1989.

31. David Shribman and James Perry, *WSJ*, January 5, 1990.

32. *NYT*, December 22, 1989.

33. Letter, *NYT*, January 2, 1990, reviewing the alleged legal basis for the aggression. Quote is from the official declaration.

34. Dinges, *NYT*, Op-Ed, January 12, 1990; Lawn, US Department of Justice, letter, May 8, 1986; John Weeks and Andrew Zimbalist, "The failure of intervention in Panama," *Third World Quarterly*, January 1989.

35. Constable *BG*, July 9, 1990; Massing, *NYRB*, May 17, 1990.

36. *CAR*, vol XI, no. 31, 1984, citing *Miami Herald*. Staff Study, "Crime and Secrecy: The Use of Offshore Banks and Companies," Permanent Subcommittee on Investigations of the Committee on Governmental Affairs, US Senate, 1983. Michael Kranish, *BG*, January 1, 1990.

37. Philip Bennett, *BG*, February 5; Stephen Labaton, *NYT*, February 6, 1990.

38. AP, January 20; Greve, *Philadelphia Inquirer*, February 22; Lasso, *CSM*, August 15, 1990, an upbeat report on Panamanian recovery—for the rich.

39. Cockburn, *Out of Control*, p. 154.

40. *NYT*, March 22, 27, 1988, cited by Weeks and Zimbalist; Larry Rohter, *NYT*, January 2, 1990; Americas Watch, *The Laws of War and the Conduct of the Panama Invasion*, May 1990. Constable, *BG*, July 10, 1990; Massing, op.cit. In August, Herrara was replaced as head of the national police force by Colonel Fernando Quezada; AP, *BG*, August, 23, 1990.

41. *NYT*, December 21, 22, 1989.

42. Headline, *WSJ*, December 26.

43. Walter Robinson, "Journalists constrained by Pentagon," December 25; Eloy Aguilar, AP, December 22, 1989, citing Dr Elmer Miranda, deputy director of San Tomás Hospital in Panama City. Hossie, *G&M*, January 8; *La Nación* (Buenos Aires), cited by historian Thomas Boylston Adams, *BG*, February 3, 1990. Gannon, *CSM*, December 29, 1989.

44. Michael Kagay, "Panamanians Strongly Back U.S. Move," *NYT*, January 6; Gary Langer, AP, January 6, 1990. Alexander Cockburn cites a statistician's analysis showing that if Panamanians average 100 relatives or close friends, the death toll would have been over 2500; considerably more, on realistic assumptions. *Nation*, February 26, 1990.

45. Joan Mower, AP, *BG*, February 2, 1990.

46. *Foreign Policy*, Winter 89/90.

47. *Ha'aretz*, December 21, 1989; *El Tiempo*, January 5, 1990.

48. Frederick Kempe, *WSJ*, October 18, 1989.

49. Paul Blustein and Steven Mufson, *WP Weekly*, December 25, 1989. Also Steve Ropp, *Current History*, January 1990.

50. Martha Hamilton, *WP Weekly*, December 25; Economist, December 23, 1989.

51. Mark Uhlig, "Managua Economy Hinges on Panama," *NYT*, December 28, 1989; Gerald Seib and John Fialka, *WSJ*, January 4, 1990; *NYT*, December 30; Diego Ribadeneira, *BG*, December 30, 1989; NPR, reported by Blase Bonpane, referring to Linda Wertheimer on "All Things Con-

sidered," UN vote condemning the trade embargo, passed 82–2 (US and Israel), December 22, 1989, not reported in the *New York Times*; noted in *Mesoamerica* (Costa Rica), January 1990.

52. See *Fateful Triangle*, pp. 362, 450.

53. Robert Pear, *NYT*, January 29; Rita Beamish, AP, January 29, 1990.

54. "Resentment of US spreads in Panama City," *BG*, January 1, 1990.

55. *WP–BG*, December 30, 1989.

56. Elaine Sciolino, *NYT*, August 14, 1987.

57. Davidi, *Davar*, December 22, 1990, translated by Israel Shahak. The figures on weapons sales are attributed to "foreign publications," but, Shahak notes, this is probably a device to pass censorship with information from reliable Israeli sources. On the arms sales to Iran, see reference of Chapter 1, Note 26.

58. Glenn Fowler, *NYT*, December 20; Reuters, *BG*, December 20; Caribbean Development Bank, cited in AP, December 9; Robert Glass, AP, December 22; Grenadan intellectual Gus John, personal communication; Alexander Cockburn, *In These Times*, December 21, 1989; William Steif, *Progressive*, January 1990; Krist, *New Republic*, April 24, 1989. See NACLA's *Report on the Americas*, February 1990, for more details on Grenada's decline, including discussion of the harmful effects of the US AID program.

59. Black, "The Dominican Military's Conditional Retreat," in Constantine Danopoulos, ed., *Military Intervention and Withdrawal* (Routledge, 1990). See also Chapter 8 below.

60. AP, January 7, 1990. *Economist*, December 23, 1989; August 25, 1990. Haiti, AP, November 4, 1989, citing Americas Watch. On the selective concern for refugees, see *Political Economy of Human Rights*, vol. II, ch. 3.

61. Robert Pear, *NYT*, January 26; AP, January 25, 1990.

62. In the mainstream, that is. See, however, Alexander Cockburn, *Nation*, January 29, 1990, and subsequent articles of his.

63. Rohter, "Panama and U.S. Strive to Settle on Death Toll," *NYT*, April 1, 1990.

64. *Excelsior*–AFP, January 27, cited in *Latin America News Update (LANU)*, March 1990; *Mesoamerica* (Costa Rica), May 1990; *CAR*, March 2, 1990.

65. *Brecha*, CODEHUCA, "Report of Joint CODEHUCA–CONADEHUPA delegation," January–February 1990, San José.

66. See Physicians for Human Rights, " 'Operation Just Cause': The Medical Cost of Military Action in Panama," Boston, March 15, 1990; Americas Watch, *Laws of War and the Conduct of the Panama Invasion. CAR*, September 7, 1990.

67. See CODEHUCA letter to Americas Watch, June 5, 1990, commenting on the Americas Watch report.

68. *Excelsior* (Mexico City), April 14, 1990; *Central America NewsPak*, Austin, Texas. Pelaez, *El Diario–La Prensa*, May 7, 1990.

69. *Aviation Week & Space Technology*, January 1, 1990.

70. John Morrocco, ibid.; Hackworth, interview with Bill Baskervill, AP, February 25, 1990. March 1990 report, see Chapter 1, section 2.

71. Michael Gordon, *NYT*, April 11, 1990.

72. Oppenheimer, *Miami Herald*, June 20, 1990.

73. *CAR*, August 17, 1990.

74. *Latinamerica Press* (Lima), August 30, 1990.

75. Joy James, "US policy in Panama," *Race & Class*, July–September 1990; State Department letter to Jesse Helms, stating that the Department "shares your view" on the matter in question, March 26, 1987, cited by James. On these and other matters discussed here, see also Daphne Wysham, *Labor Action*, April–May 1990; Martha Gellhorn, "The Invasion of Panama," *Granta*, Spring 1990.

76. Constable, *BG*, July 11, 1990.

77. *CSM*, April 9, 1990.

78. *Excelsior*, February 28, 1990; *LANU*.

79. Felicitas Pliego, *Excelsior*, April 29, 1990; Commission of Inquiry release, February 17; COHA *News and Analysis*, May 1, 1990.

80. Bernal, "Panama's fight for free expression," *Chicago Tribune*, May 29, 1990.
81. *CAR*, April 6; Andres Oppenheimer, *MH*, January 19, 1990.
82. Massing, op. cit.
83. See Chapter 1, Note 94.

SIX

Nefarious Aggression

THE second act of aggression of the post–Cold War era took place on August 2, 1990, when Iraq invaded Kuwait, later annexing it outright after international sanctions were imposed. Any Middle East crisis at once assumes ominous proportions because of the incomparable energy reserves of the region. The events of August were no exception.

The reaction to Saddam Hussein's aggression followed two distinct paths, uneasily related. The UN Security Council at once condemned the invasion and called for economic sanctions; implicit in this approach is a diplomatic track to arrange a negotiated withdrawal. This option offered unusually high prospects for success; for one reason, because the regular violators of sanctions (the US, Britain, France, and their allies) strongly supported them in this particular case. The US and Britain followed a different course, preparing for a military strike against Iraq and its occupying forces in Kuwait. The divergence is understandable, in the light of history and the distribution of power in the contemporary world.[1]

Middle East oil was initially in the hands of England and France, joined later by the United States, an arrangement formalized in the Red Line agreement of 1928. After World War II, France was excluded by legal chicanery and the US took over the dominant role.[2] As discussed earlier, it has always been a guiding policy that Middle East oil should be under the control of the United States, its allies and clients, and its oil corporations, and that independent "radical nationalist" influences are not to be tolerated. This doctrine is a corollary of the general hostility to independent Third World nationalism, but one of unusual significance.

The US and its British ally reacted vigorously to Iraq's challenge to their traditional privilege. The political leadership and ideological managers professed great indignation that a powerful country would dare to invade a defenseless neighbor. The matter was raised to cosmic significance, with eloquent rhetoric about a New World Order based on peace, justice, and the sanctity of international law, at last within our grasp now that the Cold War has ended with the triumph of those who have always upheld these values with such dedication. Secretary of State James Baker explained:

> We live in one of those rare transforming moments in history. The Cold War is over, and an era full of promise has begun. ... And after a long period of stagnation, the United Nations is becoming a more effective organization. The ideals of the United Nations Charter are becoming realities. ... Saddam Hussein's aggression shatters the vision of a better world in the aftermath of the Cold War. ... In the 1930s, the aggressors were appeased. In 1990, the President has made our position plain: This aggression will not be appeased.[3]

The analogy to Hitler and Munich became a virtual cliché. Though unable to defeat Iran even with the backing of the US, USSR, Europe, and virtually the entire Arab world, Iraq was now poised to take over the Middle East and control the world. The stakes were high; the course of history would be determined by our willingness to avenge Saddam Hussein's invasion of a weak and defenseless country—an unprecedented atrocity—and to destroy the new Hitler before it is too late.

The US at once dispatched a huge expeditionary force, which virtually doubled after the November elections. While a deterrent force could be kept in the desert and offshore, hundreds of thousands of troops could not be maintained in place for long. The predictable effect of this decision was to undercut the reliance on sanctions, which would have their impact over an extended period. The US also made it clear and explicit that diplomacy would not be tolerated; contacts with Iraq would be limited to delivery of an ultimatum. This flat rejection of diplomacy is what the President called "going the extra mile" to explore all peaceful diplomatic means; with the rarest of exceptions, articulate opinion followed the leader. To justify this unprecedented rejection of diplomacy, the US claimed to be upholding immutable high principles, a rhetorical stance that successfully undercut any form of diplomacy (sometimes called "linkage") and also barred withdrawal of the expeditionary force without Iraqi capitulation. The rhetorical stance cannot survive a moment's scrutiny, but that caused no problem, because it was subjected to none within the mainstream. Debate continued, but on narrow tactical issues, a framework in which the Administration was sure to prevail. From almost the first moment, then, the options were successfully narrowed to the threat or use of force.

1. Our Traditional Values

The fundamental issue was clearly articulated by a distinguished Cambridge University professor of political theory:

> Our traditions, fortunately, prove to have at their core universal values, while theirs are sometimes hard to distinguish with the naked eye from rampant (and heavily armed) nihilism. In the Persian Gulf today, President Bush could hardly put it more bluntly . . .[4]

One who fails to grasp this principle might find it hard to distinguish Saddam Hussein's invasion of Kuwait from many other crimes, some far worse than his, that the West has readily tolerated, or supported, or perpetrated directly, including one case only a few months before, with its lessons about the New World Order.

Our traditions and the values at their core had long been evident in the Gulf. Keeping just to Iraq, they were illustrated during the insurrection of 1920 against British rule, one episode of "a contagion of unrest afflicting the British Empire from Egypt to India."[5] British sensibilities were deeply offended by this rampant nihilism, a stab in the back at a time when the empire had been weakened by the World War. Sir Arnold Wilson fumed: "To kick a man when he is down is the most popular pastime in the East, sanctioned by centuries of precept and practice." The India office traced the Iraqi revolt to local "ultra-extremists," who desired the "abolition of European control of all sorts throughout the East." Winston Churchill agreed, calling the revolt "only part of a general agitation against the British empire and all it stands for."

Plainly, the situation called for strong measures. In India a year before, British troops had fired on a peaceful political assembly at Amritsar, leaving nearly four hundred dead. Lacking ground forces in Iraq, Britain turned to air power to bomb native villages, but as part of a larger strategy. Churchill, then Colonial Secretary, observed that "sheer force" would not suffice for "holding Mesopotamia." What was needed was a government and ruler

who would be "freely accepted" by the people of Iraq and—just to assure
that none would stray from that free acquiescence—"supported by the
[British] Air Force, and by British organised levies, and by 4 Imperial batta-
lions." The tactic had its problems. Commenting on "the means now in
fact used"—namely, "the bombing of the women and children of the villages"—the Secretary of State for War warned: "If the Arab population
realize that the peaceful control of Mesopotamia ultimately depends on
our intention of bombing women and children, I am very doubtful if we
shall gain that acquiescence" for which Churchill hoped. Britain proceeded
to establish a puppet regime while the RAF conducted terror bombing
to overcome "tribal insubordination" (as explained by the Colonial Secretary
of the Ramsay MacDonald Labour Cabinet in 1924) and to collect taxes
from tribesmen who were too poor to pay.

As Secretary of State at the War Office in 1919, Churchill had already
had opportunities to articulate our traditional values. He was approached
by the RAF Middle East Command for permission to use chemical weapons
"against recalcitrant Arabs as experiment." Churchill authorized the experiment, dismissing objections by the India office as "unreasonable":

> I do not understand this squeamishness about the use of gas. . . . I am strongly
> in favour of using poisoned gas against uncivilised tribes. . . . It is not necessary
> to use only the most deadly gasses; gasses can be used which cause great incon-
> venience and would spread a lively terror and yet would leave no serious perma-
> nent effects on most of those affected.

Churchill added: "we cannot in any circumstances acquiesce in the non-
utilisation of any weapons which are available to procure a speedy termination of the disorder which prevails on the frontier." Chemical weapons
were merely "the application of Western science to modern warfare." They
had in fact already been used by the British air force in North Russia against
the Bolsheviks, with great success, according to the British command. The
common belief that "the taboo against the use of chemical weapons which
has held sway since the First World War has now lost much of its force"
because of Iraqi actions and threats is hardly accurate, even if we put aside
the massive resort to chemical warfare by the US in South Vietnam with its
terrible human toll, of no interest to the guardians of our traditional values.[6]

In the aftermath of World War I, chemical weapons were regarded much
as nuclear weapons were after Hiroshima and Nagasaki. It thus comes as
no real surprise that even before the 1948 Berlin blockade, Churchill privately

urged the US government to threaten the Soviet Union with nuclear attack unless the Russians withdrew from East Germany.[7]

In July 1958, a military coup by nationalist officers in Iraq threatened US–British control of the oil-producing regions for the first time (a threat by the conservative nationalist government of Iran had been aborted by the US–British intervention to restore the Shah five years earlier). The coup set off a wide range of reactions, including a US Marine landing in Lebanon. In an analysis of the crisis based on the public record, William Quandt concludes that the US "apparently agreed to help look after British oil interests, especially in Kuwait," while determining that an Iraqi move against Kuwait, infringing upon British interests, would not be tolerated, though it seemed unlikely. Quandt takes President Eisenhower to have been referring to nuclear weapons when, in his own words, he ordered Joint Chiefs Chairman General Twining to "be prepared to employ, subject to [Eisenhower's] approval, *whatever* means might become necessary to prevent any unfriendly forces from moving into Kuwait." The issue was "discussed several times during the crisis," Quandt adds. The major concern at the time was Egypt's Gamal Abdel Nasser—the Hitler of the day—and his Arab nationalism.[8]

Recently declassified documents add more information, though the US record is defective because of heavy censorship, presumably reflecting the Reagan-era commitment to protect state power from the public. After discussions in Washington immediately after the Iraqi coup, British Foreign Secretary Selwyn Lloyd sent a secret telegram to the Prime Minister in which he considered two options with regard to Kuwait: "immediate British occupation" of this semi-dependency, or moves towards nominal independence. He advised against the harsher choice. Though "The advantage of this action would be that we would get our hands firmly on the Kuwait oil," it might arouse nationalist feelings in Kuwait and "The effect upon international opinion and the rest of the Arab world would not be good." A better policy would be to set up "a kind of Kuwaiti Switzerland where the British do not exercise physical control." But "If this alternative is accepted, we must also accept the need, if things go wrong, ruthlessly to intervene, whoever it is has caused the trouble." He stressed "the complete United States solidarity with us over the Gulf," including the need to "take firm action to maintain our position in Kuwait" and the "similar resolution" of the US "in relations to the Aramco oilfields" in Saudi Arabia; the Americans "agree that at all costs these oilfields [in Kuwait, Saudi Arabia, Bahrain and Qatar] must be kept in Western hands." Six months before the Iraqi coup, Lloyd had noted that "Minor changes in the direction of greater independence are inevitable" for Kuwait, such as taking over postal services. He also summarized "The major British and indeed Western interests in the Persian Gulf" as:

(a) to ensure free access for Britain and other Western countries to oil produced in States bordering the Gulf; (b) to ensure the continued availability of that oil on favourable terms and for sterling; and to maintain suitable arrangements for the investment of the surplus revenues of Kuwait; (c) to bar the spread of Communism and pseudo-Communism in the area and subsequently beyond; and, as a pre-condition of this, to defend the area against the brand of Arab nationalism under cover of which the Soviet Government at present prefers to advance.[9]

US documents of the same period outline British goals in similar terms: "the U.K. asserts that its financial stability would be seriously threatened if the petroleum from Kuwait and the Persian Gulf area were not available to the U.K. on reasonable terms, if the U.K. were deprived of the large investments made by that area in the U.K. and if sterling were deprived of the support provided by Persian Gulf oil." These British needs, and the fact that "An assured source of oil is essential to the continued economic viability of Western Europe," provide an argument for the US "to support, or if necessary assist, the British in using force to retain control of Kuwait and the Persian Gulf." The counterargument is that force will lead to confrontation with "radical Pan-Arab nationalism" and "U.S. relations with neutral countries elsewhere would be adversely affected." In November 1958, the National Security Council recommended that the US "Be prepared to use force, but only as a last resort, either alone or in support of the United Kingdom," to insure access to Arab oil. The National Security Council also advised that Israel might provide a barrier to Arab nationalism, laying the basis for one element of the system of control over the Middle East (called "security" or "stability").[10]

The concern that Gulf oil and riches be available to support the ailing British economy was extended by the early 1970s to the US economy, which was visibly declining relative to Japan and German-led Europe. Furthermore, control over oil serves as a means to influence these rivals/allies. Capital flow from Saudi Arabia, Kuwait, and the other Gulf principalities to the US and Britain has provided significant support for their economies, corporations, and financial institutions. These are among the reasons why the US and Britain have often not been averse to increases in oil price.

The issues are too intricate to explore here, but these factors surely remain operative.[11] It comes as no great surprise that the two states that established the imperial settlement and have been its main beneficiaries and guarantors were girding for war in the Gulf, while others kept their distance.

2. Framing the Issues

While the first two acts of aggression of the post-Cold War era are similar by the criteria of principle and of law, inevitably there are also differences. The most significant disparity is that the US invasion of Panama was carried out by our side, and was therefore benign, whereas the Iraqi invasion of Kuwait ran counter to critical US interests, and was therefore nefarious, in violation of the most august principles of international law and morality.

This array of events posed several ideological challenges. The first task was to portray Iraqi dictator Saddam Hussein as a vicious tyrant and international gangster. That was straightforward enough, since it is plainly true.

The second task was to gaze in awe at the invader of Panama and manager of "the unlawful use of force" against Nicaragua as he denounced the unlawful use of force against Kuwait and proclaimed his undying devotion to the United Nations Charter, declaring that "America stands where it always has, against aggression, against those who would use force to replace the rule of law" and "If history teaches us anything, it is that we must resist aggression or it will destroy our freedoms" (August 20, 7, 1990).

It might seem that this task would prove a shade more difficult than the first. Not so, however. The President's steely-eyed visage graced the front pages along with his inspiring words on the need to resist aggression, highlighted so that all would honor his valor and dedication to the ideals we cherish. Even his invocation of the "vivid memories" of Vietnam as a lesson in the need to resist aggression and uphold the rule of law passed without a clamor—even a whisper—of condemnation, a mark of true discipline. The press solemnly observed: "Bush has demonstrated that the United States is the only superpower ... [able] to enforce international law against the will of a powerful aggressor," and otherwise reiterated our unwavering commitment to the rule of law and the sanctity of borders.[12]

Across the spectrum, there was acclaim for this renewed demonstration of our historic advocacy of the ways of peace—though a number of old-fashioned right-wingers asked why we should do the dirty work.[13] At the outer limits of dissidence, Mary McGrory wrote that while Hussein "may

have a following among have-not Arabs," Americans "are emotionally
involved in getting rid of the beast" by one means or another. She considered
bombing Baghdad, though it might be unwise because of possible retaliation
against Americans. The *Washington Post* leaked a White House plan to eliminate the beast, approved by the President when he was informed by CIA
director William Webster "that Hussein represented a threat to the long-term
economic interests of the United States."[14]

That these economic interests were driving policy decisions was acknowledged by the White House and political commentators generally. The US
sent major military forces to Saudi Arabia and helped to organize an international embargo and virtual blockade, with the notably tepid support of
most of its allies, who doubtless would prefer the US and its clients to
Saddam Hussein as a dominant influence over the administration of oil
production and price, but appeared reluctant to risk or spend much to
achieve this end. And, needless to say, they share with Washington the
high principle that Might does not make Right—except when we want
it to.

US aggression was not entirely overlooked. "This isn't Panama or Grenada
here," former chairman of the Joint Chiefs of Staff William Crowe somberly
declared, warning of the hazards of our current mission. "The costs and
risks are momentous," the *New York Times* editors added in agreement,
"going well beyond U.S. military operations in Lebanon, Grenada and
Panama." Former *Times* military correspondent Bernard Trainor, now director of the national security program at Harvard's Kennedy School of Government, described Saddam Hussein as "the Noriega of the Middle East. Like
his Panamanian counterpart, he has to go." In reality, the comparison
between Noriega and Hussein extends about that far.[15]

The parallels, then, did not pass unnoticed: in all cases, the US was acting
in self-defense, in the service of world order and high principle—another
of those truths of logic that floats blissfully over the world of fact.

The editors of the liberal *Boston Globe* praised Bush for standing up for
our fundamental values and drawing a line in the sand before the raging
beast. "The line is clearer than that drawn in Korea, Vietnam and Lebanon,"
they observed. Others too made reference to such past proofs of our willingness to face any burden to discipline those who resort to force, or otherwise
depart from our traditions of nonviolence and commitment to the rule
of law.[16]

Letters to the editor, in contrast, made frequent reference to the hypocrisy
of the pose, asking "what is the difference between our invasion of Panama

and Iraq's invasion of Kuwait?," among many other cases of benign aggression. The dramatic difference between letters and professional commentary
again illustrates the failure of the ideological offensive of the past years to
reach beyond educated elites to all sectors of the general public. Overseas,
simple truths could be perceived outside of the major power centers, where
deviation from established truths is too dangerous. A lead editorial in the
Dublin *Sunday Tribune*, headlined "Moral Indignation is Pure Hypocrisy,"
recalls the Western reaction to Iraq's invasion of Iran, the US invasion
of Grenada and Panama, Israel's invasion of Lebanon, and "the injustice
done to the Palestinians [which] is a continuing cause of justifiable anger
in the Middle East" and will lead to "continued turmoil." *Irish Times* Washington correspondent Sean Cronin, noting the impassioned words of UN
Ambassador Thomas Pickering in support of the Security Council resolution
condemning Iraq, recalled some events just eight months before: the
December 23 US veto of a Security Council resolution condemning the
invasion of Panama (with British and French assistance, in this case); and
the December 29 General Assembly resolution demanding the withdrawal
of the "US armed invasion forces from Panama" and calling the invasion
a "flagrant violation of international law and of the independence, sovereignty and territorial integrity of states."[17]

But respectable commentators at home never flinched. The parallels to
the Panama invasion were ignored with near unanimity, while the more
audacious, recognizing that attack is the best defense, went so far as to
compare George Bush's actions in Panama with his dispatch of troops to
Saudi Arabia, not to Saddam Hussein's invasion of Kuwait. Grenada, Vietnam, and Lebanon were also regularly invoked as precedents for our defense
of the principle of nonintervention.[18]

With comparable unanimity, responsible commentators failed to recall
Israel's invasion of Lebanon in 1982, with the goal of establishing a puppet
regime in a "New Order" subordinated to Israel's interests and bringing
to a halt the increasingly irritating PLO initiatives for a peaceful diplomatic
settlement—all of this frankly discussed within Israel from the first moments,
though kept from the American audience. That act of aggression, conducted
by a client state, qualifies as benign. It therefore benefited from the active
support of the Reagan Administration, which was condemned by Democratic
liberals and others farther to the left for not exhibiting proper enthusiasm
for this merciless assault, which left over 20,000 dead, overwhelmingly civilians. Also notably lacking was a comparison to Israel's continued occupation
of territories conquered in 1967 and annexation of East Jerusalem and the

Syrian Golan Heights, and the US reaction. Syria's bloody intervention in Lebanon (with US backing in the early stages, when it was aimed at the Palestinians and their Lebanese allies) was also overlooked. Also forgotten was Turkey's conquest of northern Cyprus, with thousands of casualties and hundreds of thousands of refugees after an orgy of killing, torture, rape and pillage to extirpate the last remnants of Greek culture back to classical antiquity; George Bush praised Turkey for serving "as a protector of peace" as it joined those who "stand up for civilized values around the world." Few could recall the US-backed Moroccan invasion of the Western Sahara in 1976, justified by Moroccan authorities on the grounds that "one Kuwait in the Arab world is enough"; it is unjust for such vast resources to be in the hands of a tiny population.[19] Outside the region, the decisive US (also French, British, Dutch, and so on) support for Indonesia's near-genocidal invasion of East Timor, still under way, was also easily overlooked, among many other obvious parallels.

The missing comparisons were drawn by Arabs and other Third World observers sampled in the press. But the matter was left at that, without further analysis, or they were chided for their visceral anti-Americanism, emotionalism, or simple naiveté. In a *New York Times* report on Arab–American reactions, Felicity Barringer reminds the Arab spokesmen she interviews that the comparison they draw with Israel's 1982 invasion of Lebanon "does not take into account a crucial difference: that Kuwait had not attacked Iraq, while southern Lebanon was home to Palestinian bases that had repeatedly shelled Israeli territory."

Barringer's gentle admonition suffers from only one flaw: the facts. In brief, Israel had subjected southern Lebanon to violent and murderous attacks since the early 1970s, often without even a pretense of provocation, killing thousands of people and driving hundreds of thousands from their homes. The purpose, as formulated by Israeli diplomat Abba Eban, was to hold the whole population hostage under the threat of terror, with the "rational prospect, ultimately fulfilled" that "affected populations" would bend to Israel's demands. After its 1978 invasion of Lebanon, which left the southern sector under Israeli control, Israel carried out extensive bombardment of civilian targets. A rash of unprovoked Israeli attacks in 1981 led to an exchange in which six Israelis and hundreds of Palestinians and Lebanese were killed when Israel bombed densely populated areas. A US-initiated cease-fire was observed by the PLO, but repeatedly violated with many civilian casualties by Israel, desperately seeking to provoke some PLO action that could serve as a pretext for the long-planned invasion. After the 1982 invasion, Israel returned to the traditional practice of bombing Lebanon at its pleasure, with ample terror in its southern "security zone."

It would be unfair, however, to fault Barringer for turning the facts on their head. The fairy tales she recounts are the standard version offered in the *New York Times* and elsewhere, and few would think to question established dogma. Inversion of the facts in this case is, in any event, only a minor triumph when compared to really significant achievements of the propaganda system, such as the conversion of the US attack against South Vietnam into a noble effort to defend it from aggression.[20]

We may say the same about other irate commentators who bitterly denounce Arabs for drawing a parallel to the 1967 war, condemning as well the "gullibility and ignorance" of television anchormen and journalists who allow them to speak such nonsense (Henry Siegman, Executive Director, American Jewish Congress); in both cases, Siegman explains to these gullible fools, "Arab countries invaded a peaceful neighbor without provocation," though "the primary aggressors" in 1967 "were Egypt, Syria and Jordan," not Iraq. The *Times* editors added their endorsement, denouncing Moscow and other miscreants for trying to "legitimize Baghdad's argument that its takeover of Kuwait is in any way comparable to Israel's occupation of the West Bank," a gambit that is "absurdly wrong and diversionary" because the occupation of the West Bank "began only after Arab armies attacked Israel." It is not even controversial that in 1967 Israel attacked Egypt. Jordan and Syria entered the conflict much as England and France went to war when Germany attacked their ally Poland in 1939. One might argue that the Israeli attack was legitimate, but to convert it into an Arab invasion is rather audacious—or would be, if the practice were not routine.[21]

The *Times* editorial is carefully crafted. It refers to the West Bank, not Gaza and the Golan Heights. Gaza is best overlooked because, uncontroversially, Israel attacked Egypt, taking over Gaza. The case of the Golan Heights is also difficult, not only because Israel annexed this Syrian territory (and was unanimously condemned by the UN Security Council for doing so, though a US veto blocked sanctions) but because Israel attacked and conquered it in violation of the cease-fire. In the case of the West Bank, the editors could claim in their defense that Israeli troops took it over after Jordan had entered the war—honoring its alliance with Egypt, already attacked by Israel.

Throughout, we see how important it is to take possession of history and to shape it to the purposes required by the powerful, and how valuable is the contribution of the loyal servants who do their bidding.

3. Paths away from Disaster

There was a brief threat that the Israeli connection might come to the fore when, on August 12, Saddam Hussein proposed a settlement linking Iraqi withdrawal from Kuwait to withdrawal from other occupied Arab lands: Syria from Lebanon, and Israel from the territories it conquered in 1967. The London *Financial Times* felt that although his offer did not reduce the imminent dangers, it "may yet serve some useful purpose," offering "a path away from disaster . . . through negotiation." Furthermore, he "may well have a point" in "citing Israel's refusal to relinquish its control of occupied territories as a source of conflict in the region." In linking Iraqi withdrawal from Kuwait to Israeli "withdrawal from Palestinian and Syrian territory, Mr Saddam has said something with which no Arab leader or citizen, no matter how pro-American, can disagree," and the refusal to consider the matter might "bring closer the risk of an all out Middle East war involving the Jewish state." The "immediate issue" is for "Iraq to get out of Kuwait"; but in the light of Iraq's proposal, however unsatisfactory it may be as it stands,

> The onus is now on everyone involved, including Middle Eastern and western powers, to seize the initiative and harness diplomacy to the show of political, military and economic force now on display in the Gulf.[22]

The US reaction was different. In official response and general commentary, there was no thought that the proposal might be explored to find a peaceful resolution for a very serious crisis. There was not even a ritual bow to the possibility that there might be a valid point buried somewhere in the suggestion. Rather, the proposal was dismissed with utter derision. Television news that day featured George Bush the dynamo, racing his power boat, jogging furiously, playing tennis and golf, and otherwise expending his formidable energies on important pursuits, far too busy "recreating" (as he put it) to waste much time on the occasional fly in Arab garb that he might have to swat. As the television news clips were careful to stress, the President's disdain for this irritant was so great that he scarcely even broke his golf stroke to express his contempt for what the anchorman termed Hussein's "so-called offer," not to be regarded as "serious." The proposal merited one dismissive sentence in a news story on the blockade in the next day's *New York Times*.[23]

The danger that the issues might be addressed was quickly extinguished. The media also quietly passed over the fact that, two days before, the Israeli

Ministry of Agriculture had published full-page statements in newspapers saying: "It is difficult to conceive of any political solution consistent with Israel's survival that does not involve complete, continued Israeli control of the water and sewerage systems [of the occupied territories], and of the associated infrastructure, including the power supply and road network, essential to their operation, maintenance and accessibility." A grant of meaningful self-determination to the Palestinians would "gravely endanger ... Israel's vital interests," the statement emphasized. The "continued existence" of Israel is at stake in ensuring Israeli control over the West Bank.[24]

In short, no meaningful withdrawal from the conquered territories or recognition of Palestinian national rights is conceivable, the consistent position of US–Israeli rejectionism, which, for twenty years, has posed the primary barrier to any diplomatic resolution of the Arab–Israel conflict. The facts have been rigorously excluded from US commentary, including the current US position: support for the Shamir–Peres plan which declares Jordan to be the Palestinian state; bars any change in the status of the Israeli-occupied territories except in accord with the guidelines of the Israeli government, which preclude any meaningful self-determination; rejects negotiations with the PLO, thus denying Palestinians the right to choose their own political representation; and calls for "free elections" under harsh Israeli military control with much of the Palestinian leadership rotting in Israeli jails. Small wonder that the terms of the US position, while designated "the peace process" and "the only game in town," do not seem ever to have been published in the mainstream media.[25]

Another possible problem arose when Saddam Hussein proposed on August 19 that the matter of Kuwait be left an "Arab issue," to be dealt with by the Arab states alone, without external interference, in the manner of the Syrian occupation of Lebanon and Morocco's attempt to take over the Western Sahara.[26] The proposal was dismissed on the reasonable grounds that, in this arena, Hussein could hope to gain his ends by the threat and use of force. One relevant fact was overlooked: the Iraqi dictator was again stealing a leaf from Washington's book. The traditional US position with regard to the Western hemisphere is that "outsiders" have no right to intrude. If the US intervenes in Latin America or the Caribbean, it is a hemispheric issue, to be resolved here, without external interference. The message is: Strangers, keep out; we can handle our own affairs—in an arena in which the regional hegemon can expect to prevail.

To mention only one example, clearly pertinent here: on April 2, 1982, the US set a precedent by vetoing two Security Council resolutions on two different topics the same day. The first called for Israel to reinstate three elected mayors who were recent targets of Jewish terrorist attacks. The second called upon the Secretary-General to keep the Security Council informed about the Central America crisis, naming no names and making no charges, but implicitly directed against US intervention in Nicaragua. The US delegation objected to the resolution on the grounds that it "breeds cynicism," "mocks the search for peace," and "undermines the Inter-American system" which should deal with these matters without UN interference; a more extreme variant of Saddam Hussein's position today.[27]

On August 23, a former high-ranking US official delivered another Iraqi offer to National Security Adviser Brent Scowcroft. The proposal, confirmed by the emissary who relayed it, and by memoranda, was made public by Knut Royce in Newsday, on August 29. According to sources involved and documents, Iraq offered to withdraw from Kuwait and allow foreigners to leave in return for the lifting of sanctions, guaranteed access to the Gulf, and full control of the Rumailah oilfield "that extends slightly into Kuwaiti territory from Iraq" (Royce), about two miles over a disputed border. Other terms of the proposal, according to memoranda that Royce quotes, were that Iraq and the US negotiate an oil agreement "satisfactory to both nations' national security interests," "jointly work on the stability of the gulf," and develop a joint plan "to alleviate Iraq's economical and financial problems." There was no mention of US withdrawal from Saudi Arabia, or other preconditions. An Administration official who specializes in Mideast affairs described the proposal as "serious" and "negotiable."[28]

The reaction was, again, illuminating. Government spokesmen ridiculed the whole affair. The New York Times noted the Newsday report briefly on page 14, the continuation page of an article on another topic, citing government spokespersons who dismissed it as "baloney." After framing the matter properly, the Times concedes that the story was accurate, quoting White House sources who said the proposal "had not been taken seriously because Mr. Bush demands the unconditional withdrawal of Iraq from Kuwait." The Times also noted quietly that "a well-connected Middle Eastern diplomat told the New York Times a week ago [that is, August 23] of a similar offer, but it, too, was dismissed by the Administration." That news had not been published, though it could not be ignored entirely once it was leaked a week later to the suburban journal Newsday, which is prominently displayed on New York City newsstands—suggesting a certain hypothesis about what happened.[29] Others disposed of the problem in a similar manner.

Several features of the media system are illustrated here. Deviations from the propaganda line can occur—more readily, as in this case, out of the national spotlight. That raises the problem of damage control. A standard journalistic device to suppress unwanted facts that have unfortunately come to light is to report them only in the context of government denials. More generally, to satisfy the conditions of objectivity, a news story must be framed in accordance with the priorities of power. In this case, the *Times* news report—the one that enters History—takes its lead from government authorities. The unwanted facts are first dismissed as "baloney," then conceded to be accurate—but irrelevant, because Washington isn't interested. We also learn that the journal has suppressed earlier offers that are "baloney" for the same reason. That ends the matter. We can breathe easily, the threat that there might be "a path away from disaster through negotiation" having been averted.

4. Steady on Course

Some problems arose in dealing with the fact that US allies are not a particularly attractive lot; there is, after all, little to distinguish Saddam Hussein from Hafez el-Assad apart from current services to US needs. An inconvenient Amnesty International release of November 2 reported that Saudi security forces tortured and abused hundreds of Yemeni "guest workers," also expelling 750,000 of them, "for no apparent reason other than their nationality or their suspected opposition to the Saudi Arabian government's position in the gulf crisis." The press looked the other way, though in the case of Arab states, there is no shortage of commentators to denounce their evil nature.[30]

The alliance with Turkey—the "protector of peace" in Cyprus (see p. 188)—also required some careful handling, in particular because of the question of the Kurds in northern Iraq. It was difficult not to notice that Iraqi forces facing US troops would be severely weakened if the US were to support a Kurdish rebellion. Washington rejected this option, presumably out of concern that a Kurdish rebellion in Iraq might spread to Eastern Turkey, where the huge Kurdish population (not recognized as such by the Turks) suffer brutal oppression. In a rare notice of the issue in the press, the *Wall Street Journal* observed: "the West fears that pressing the 'Kurdish question' with Turkey, Syria and Iran ... could weaken the anti-Iraq alliance." The report adds that "the U.S. administration pointedly refused to meet with an Iraqi Kurdish leader who visited Washington in August" to ask for support, and that "Kurds say Ankara is using the Gulf crisis and Turkey's resulting popularity in the West as cover for a crackdown."[31]

Even on this dramatic issue, discipline was maintained. Hardly a word was to be found (perhaps none at all) on the willingness of the Bush Administration to sacrifice many thousands of American lives—even putting aside the plight of the Kurds, who have been exploited with the most extraordinary cynicism by the government and the media.[32]

It was also necessary to deal somehow with the fact that prior to Hussein's attack on Kuwait the Bush Administration and its predecessors treated this murderous thug as an amiable friend, encouraging trade with his regime and credits to enable it to purchase US goods. Before that, Washington had supported his invasion of Iran, and then tilted so far towards Iraq in the Gulf War that military forces were sent to "protect shipping" from Iran (the main threat to shipping having been Iraqi), persisting in this course even after the USS *Stark* was attacked in 1987 by Iraqi aircraft. As the nation rallied to destroy the beast, Texas Congressman Henry Gonzalez, chairman of the House Banking Committee, charged that one Atlanta-based bank alone extended $3 billion in letters of credit to Iraq, $800 million of it guaranteed by the Department of Agriculture's Commodity Credit Corporation, which underwrites bank loans to finance exports of US farm products. Gonzalez charged further that there is clear evidence that armaments, possibly including chemical weapons, were obtained by Iraq under the deal. "There is no question but those $3 billion are actually financing the invasion of Kuwait," he said. "There is no question that the greater portion of that was dealing with armaments."[33] The Bush Administration's new initiatives to bolster Saddam Hussein that were announced as Operation Just Cause was launched to defend the world from Manuel Noriega's iniquity, and the lack of notice or reaction, have already been discussed.

This unpleasant matter was difficult to evade entirely. On August 13, the *New York Times* finally acknowledged that Iraq had reached its heights of power "with American acquiescence and sometimes its help," including "a thriving grain trade with American farmers, cooperation with United States intelligence agencies, oil sales to American refiners that helped finance its military and muted White House criticism of its human rights and war atrocities." From 1982, Iraq became one of the biggest buyers of US rice and wheat, "purchasing some $5.5 billion in crops and livestock with federally guaranteed loans and agricultural subsidies and its own hard cash." It also

received about $270 million in government-guaranteed credit to buy other
US goods, despite loan defaults. According to 1987 data, the latest available,
over 40 percent of Iraq's food was imported from the United States, and
in 1989 Iraq received $1 billion in loan assurances, second only to Mexico.
The US became the main market for Iraqi oil, Charles Glass reports, "while
the US–Iraqi Business Forum, headed by prominent American businessmen
and former diplomats, were praising Saddam's moderation and his progress
towards democracy." The Reagan and Bush administrations scarcely reacted
when Iraq purchased US helicopters and transferred them to military use
in violation of promises, used poison gas against Iranian troops and its own
Kurdish citizens, and relocated half a million Kurds and Syrians by force,
among other atrocities.[34]

Just a mistake in judgement, one of those ironies of history, according
to the official story. Nothing is said about why the *Times* is reporting this
now, after Washington had turned against Iraq, not before—for example,
at the moment of the Panama invasion—when the evidence was readily
available and might have helped to fend off what has now taken place.

Another assignment was to suppress the fact that Iraq's excuses for its
flagrant violation of international law bear comparison to those accepted—
even lauded—by the media in the case of benign aggression by the US
and its clients. Iraq alleged that its economic health was severely threatened
by Kuwait's violation of the OPEC agreement on oil production quotas,
harming Iraq's attempt to recover from the war with Iran. That these violations were extremely harmful to Iraq is not disputed. Iraq's complaints on
this score were largely ignored, along with its charge, prior to its attack,
that Kuwait's drawing oil from fields at the border, allegedly draining Iraq's
own fields, constituted "theft tantamount to military aggression." This seems
not to have been reported at the time, though a month later there was
a belated recognition that "whether [Saddam Hussein] is Hitler or not,
he has some reason on his side" and from Iraq's viewpoint, the Kuwait
government was "acting aggressively—it was economic warfare."[35]

These Iraqi protestations surely have a familiar ring. The right to "defend
our interests" by force is conferred upon the United States by the UN
Charter, according to the official view presented in justification of the
invasion of Panama (see p. 147). Israel's attack on Egypt in 1967 was in
large measure motivated by the economic problems caused by the mobilization of the reserves during a period of crisis and tension. A potential threat
to US economic interests was invoked by the United States to justify
its steps to counter Iraqi aggression, as in many cases of intervention and

subversion. The threat posed by Kuwait's actions to Iraq's interests was not potential.

More broadly, the Iraqi dictator justified his aggression as a noble act "in defense of the Arab nation," charging that Kuwait was an artificial entity, part of the legacy of European colonialists who carved up the Arab world for their own selfish interests. These machinations ensured that the vast oil wealth of the Arab world would benefit not the Arab masses, but the Western industrial powers and a tiny domestic elite linked to them. Despite the utter cynicism of Saddam Hussein's posturing, the charges themselves are not without merit and have considerable popular appeal, not least among the 60 percent non-Kuwaiti population that did the work that enriched the native minority, though not their "Arab brothers."

Hatred for the United States in the Arab world was noted, but without any serious analysis of why it should exist. The standard reflex is to attribute the antagonism to the emotional problems of people who have been bypassed by the march of history because of their own inadequacies. It would have been next to impossible to offer a rational account of such central matters as the US–Israel–Palestine interactions, since the long and very successful US efforts to bar a peaceful political settlement have been excised from history with such admirable efficiency.[36] The deep strain of anti-Arab racism in the dominant culture facilitates the familiar gambit of attributing antagonism to the United States to the faults of others.

The undercurrent is that the Arabs basically have no right to the oil that geological accident happened to place under their feet. As Walter Laqueur put the matter in 1973, Middle East oil "could be internationalized, not on behalf of a few oil companies but for the benefit of the rest of mankind." This could be done only by force, but that raises no moral problem because "all that is at stake is the fate of some desert sheikdoms." It is necessary only to decode slightly. For "internationalization," read: "control by the US and its clients" (as long as they remain firm supporters of Israel). For "few oil companies," read: "undeserving Arabs." The logic is that of the Moroccans conquering the Sahara: "one Kuwait is enough"; it is unfair for rich resources to be in the hands of the unimportant people when the rich men who run the world need them. The vision of the West, of course, is much vaster than that of Morocco, covering the whole region and its resources—in fact, the resources of the entire world.

Correspondingly, the uplifting concern "for the benefit of mankind" expressed by Laqueur and others does not lead them to suggest that North American and Middle East oil should have been internationalized during the postwar years when the West (with the US well ahead) had effective control over energy resources, nor does it lead them to draw the same conclusion for the industrial, agricultural, and mineral resources of the West, happily exploited by and for the rich and satisfied nations. The distinction, as always, rests on the scale of "significance."[37]

It is worth recalling how little is new in any of this. Recall the earlier explanations of why the "miserable, inefficient" Mexicans have no right "to control the destinies" of their rich lands. At the turn of the century, the influential strategist and historian Admiral Alfred T. Mahan, known for his devotion to Christian values and the doctrine of natural rights, argued that these rights had to be modified in the case of "inefficient" countries such as China, which must be administered "in such a manner as to insure the natural right of the world at large that resources should not be left idle," or misused. The rights of humanity transcend those of the Chinese, who are "sheep without a shepherd" and must be led, their country partitioned, taught Christian truths, and otherwise controlled by Western policies of "just self-assertion"—not for selfish motive, but "for the welfare of humanity." Great thoughts have a way of reappearing in every age.[38]

5. The UN Learns to Behave

The United Nations came in for some unaccustomed praise. Under the headline "The UN's coming of age," the editors of the Boston Globe hailed "a signal change in the history of the organization," a new mood of responsibility and seriousness as it backed US initiatives to punish the aggressor.[39] Many others also lauded this welcome departure from the shameful pattern of the past.

The salutary change in UN practices was attributed to the improved behavior of the Soviet enemy and the US victory in the Cold War. A Globe news report states that "Moscow's quick condemnation of the [Iraqi] invasion freed the UN Security Council, long paralyzed by superpower rivalry, to play a critical role" in responding to the aggression. Times correspondent R.W. Apple writes that Washington is "leaning harder in its policy-making on the United Nations, now more functional than in decades because of the passing of the cold war." A Times editorial hailed the "wondrous sea change" as the UN finally gets serious, silencing "most of its detractors" and allowing President Bush to pursue his noble effort to create a "new world order to resolve conflicts by multilateral diplomacy and collective security." In the *Washington Post*, John Goshko reviewed the background for this "rare moment for the United Nations," which "is suddenly working the way it was designed to," "transformed" into an agency for world peace "after years of being dismissed as a failure and a forum for Third World demagoguery" during "the long Cold War rivalry between the United States and the Soviet Union and their allies." The original conception of the UN as guardian of a peaceful world "was thwarted from the outset by the bitter Cold War between the United States and the Soviet Union. In those early years, the images of the United Nations that became engraved on the world's consciousness were of grim-faced Soviet ambassadors casting vetoes or storming out of Security Council meetings," while the new Third World members "turned the [General] Assembly into a forum for frequently shrill, anti-Western rhetoric. . . . Then, about two years ago, a change began to set in as the result of the détente-oriented changes in Soviet foreign policy." The *Post*'s leading political commentator, David Broder, added his imprimatur:

> During the long Cold War years, the Soviet veto and the hostility of many Third World nations made the United Nations an object of scorn to many American politicians and citizens. But in today's altered environment, it has proved to be an effective instrument of world leadership, and, potentially, an agency that can effect both peace and the rule of law in troubled regions.

A critical analysis of Administration policy in the *New York Review* by George Ball opens: "With the end of the cold war and the onset of the Gulf crisis, the United States can now test the validity of the Wilsonian concept of collective security—a test which an automatic Soviet veto in the Security Council has precluded for the past forty years." In a BBC report on the UN, editor Mark Urban says: "Time and again during the Cold War, the Kremlin used its veto to protect its interests from the threat of UN intervention. As long as the answer was 'Nyet,' Council debates remained adversarial." But now "the Soviet attitude is quite different," with the economy facing collapse and "with a leader who believes in cooperation."[40]

We are to understand, then, that superpower rivalry, Russian obstructionism and the persistent Soviet veto, and the psychic disorders of the Third World, had prevented the UN from meeting its responsibilities in the past.

These themes were sounded in dozens of enthusiastic articles, all with one notable feature: no evidence was adduced to support what are, apparently, to be understood as self-evident truths. There are ways to determine why the UN had not been able to function in its peacekeeping role. It is necessary only to review the record of Security Council vetoes and isolated negative votes in the General Assembly. A look at the facts explains quickly why the question was shelved in favor of self-serving political theology.

The US is far in the lead since 1970 in vetoing Security Council resolutions and rejecting General Assembly resolutions on all relevant issues. In second place, well behind, is Britain, primarily in connection with its support for the racist regimes of southern Africa. The grim-faced ambassadors casting vetoes had good English accents, while the USSR was regularly voting with the overwhelming majority.[41] The US isolation would, in truth, have been more severe, were it not for the fact that its enormous power kept major issues from the UN agenda. The Soviet invasion of Afghanistan was bitterly and repeatedly censured, but the UN was never willing to take on the US war against Indochina.

The UN session just preceding the "wondrous sea change" (winter 1989–90) can serve to illustrate. Three Security Council resolutions were vetoed: a condemnation of the US attack on the Nicaraguan Embassy in Panama (US veto, Britain abstained); of the US invasion of Panama (US, UK, France against); of Israeli abuses in the occupied territories (US veto). There were two General Assembly resolutions calling on all states to observe international law—one condemning the US support for the Contra army, the other the illegal embargo against Nicaragua. Each passed with two negative votes: the US and Israel. A resolution opposing acquisition of territory by force passed 151–3 (US, Israel, Dominica). The resolution once again called for a diplomatic settlement of the Arab–Israeli conflict with recognized borders and security guarantees, incorporating the wording of UN Resolution 242, with self-determination for the Palestinians, implicitly calling for a two-state settlement. The US has been barring such a settlement—virtually alone, as the most recent vote indicates—since its January 1976 veto of this proposal, advanced by Syria, Jordan, and Egypt with the backing of the PLO. The US has repeatedly vetoed Security Council resolutions and blocked General Assembly resolutions and other UN initiatives on a whole range of issues, including aggression, annexation, human rights abuses, disarmament, adherence to international law, terrorism, and others.[42]

In its new-found zeal for international law and the United Nations, the *New York Times* repeatedly turned to one heroic figure: Daniel Patrick Moynihan. He was brought forth as an expert witness on "the new spirit of unanimity at the United Nations," explaining that there were "some pretty egregious violations of international law in the past," but now "the major powers have convergent interests and the mechanism of the U.N. is there

waiting to be used." His "firm espousal of international law" was lauded
in a review of his study *The Law of Nations*. The reviewer took note of
his "sardonic, righteous anger," which recalls "the impassioned professor
who suspects no one's listening" while he is "clearly fuming that an idea
as morally impeccable as international law is routinely disregarded as dispos-
able and naive." In a *Times Magazine* story, we learn further that Moynihan
is "taking particular delight" in being proven right in his long struggle
to promote international law and the United Nations system, "abstractions"
that "matter dearly" to him. At last, everybody is "riding Moynihan's hobby-
horse" instead of ignoring the principles he has upheld with such conviction
for so many years. No longer need Moynihan "revel in his martyrdom."
Now "history has caught up with him."[43]

Omitted from these accolades was a review of Moynihan's record as
UN Ambassador, when he had the opportunity to put his principles into
practice. In a cablegram to Henry Kissinger on January 23, 1976, he reported
the "considerable progress" that had been made by his arm-twisting tactics
at the UN "toward a basic foreign policy goal, that of breaking up the
massive blocs of nations, mostly new nations, which for so long have been
arrayed against us in international forums and in diplomatic encounters generally." Moynihan cited two relevant cases: his success in undermining a UN
reaction to the Indonesian invasion of East Timor and to Moroccan aggression in the Sahara, both supported by the US, the former with particular
vigor. He had more to say about these matters in his memoir of his years
at the United Nations, where he describes frankly his role as Indonesia
invaded East Timor in December 1975:

> The United States wished things to turn out as they did, and worked to bring
> this about. The Department of State desired that the United Nations prove utterly
> ineffective in whatever measures it undertook. This task was given to me, and
> I carried it forward with no inconsiderable success.

He adds that within a few weeks some 60,000 people had been killed,
"10 percent of the population, almost the proportion of casualties experienced by the Soviet Union during the Second World War."[44]

The UN episode, briefly sampled here, gives no little insight into the
intellectual culture. The UN is "functional" today because it is (more or
less) doing what Washington wants, a fact that has virtually nothing to do
with the end of the Cold War, the Russians, or Third World maladies.
The "shrill, anti-Western rhetoric" of the Third World has, very often,
been a call for observance of international law. For once, the US and its
allies happened to be opposed to acts of aggression, annexation, and human

rights violations. Therefore the UN was free from the regular US–UK veto. These truths being unacceptable, they do not exist. They belong to the domain of "abuse of reality" (actual history), not reality itself (what we prefer to believe).[45]

These are basic elements of our traditional intellectual values. Our traditional moral values were also illustrated throughout, notably as elite opposition to the US war plans began to crystallize. An early sign was an interview with the commander of the US forces, General Norman Schwarzkopf, featured in a front-page story in the *New York Times* that opened as follows:

> The commander of the American forces facing Iraq said today that his troops could obliterate Iraq, but cautioned that total destruction of that country might not be "in the interest of the long-term balance of power in this region."

His warning was elaborated by others. In a typical example, *Times* Middle East specialist Judith Miller, under the heading "Political Cost of Victory Questioned," wrote:

> There are few who doubt that if there is a war in the Persian Gulf, the United States and its allies can "turn Baghdad into a parking lot," as an American diplomat in the Middle East recently put it. But many analysts are increasingly concerned about the probable effect of such a victory on longer-term American interests in the region. William Crowe, a former Chairman of the Joint Chiefs of Staff, warned last week that "many Arabs would deeply resent a campaign that would necessarily kill large numbers of their Muslim brothers . . ."

In short, we could slaughter seventeen million people and wipe a country off the face of the earth, but mass extermination might be tactically unwise, harmful to our interests. The issues were thoughtfully discussed in many articles, which were notable for the lack of any signs of the "squeamishness" exhibited by the India office in 1919 over the use of poison gas against "uncivilised tribes." Those who have expressed concern over the decline of our traditional values may rest assured.[46]

6. Moderates and Nationalists

Largely missing from the story was the usual reflex, the Soviet threat, now lost beyond redemption. The President's inability to articulate exalted goals received much criticism, but the reasons for his floundering were left un-

examined. The criticism was surely unfair. One could hardly expect the
truth, any more than in the past, and the standard pretexts were not available.
One try followed another, tracking the public opinion polls with the information they provided about what might sell. Occasionally, some voices
even conceded the usually inexpressible reality: that Third World intervention is motivated by US "strategic" and economic concerns, in this case,
"to support the OPEC country that is more likely to cater to Washington's
interests."[47]

Iraqi influence over the world's cheapest and most abundant source of
energy is seen, correctly, as extremely threatening. US influence over the
resources of the Arab world is, in contrast, taken to be benign—to be
sure, not for the majority of the people living in Kuwait or the region
generally, or others like them elsewhere,[48] but rather for the important
people. Always we see the same fundamental principle: the resources and
government of the world must be in the hands of the "rich men dwelling
at peace within their habitations." The hungry and oppressed must be kept
in their place.

On the same Churchillian assumptions, the rich men who do our bidding
in the Arab world are "moderates," joining the ranks of Mussolini, Suharto,
the Guatemalan generals, and others like them. Expounding the consequences of the Iraqi invasion, the *New York Times* reports that "the Middle
East has now split into a clearly moderate pro-Western camp" and "a fiercely
nationalistic anti-Western constellation," which includes "the Arab man
in the street," a major Tunisian daily observes, commenting on the "growing
pro-Iraqi stand among Arabs in poorer countries." If Saddam Hussein were
to fulfill "his threat to scorch" Israel, Bernard Trainor adds, "it would gener-
ate further support from millions of disfranchised Arabs who lionize him
and who could ignite civil disorder in the conservative and moderate Arab
states"—those ruled and managed by princes and business school graduates
who, in the eyes of these millions of Arabs, are Western businessmen who
happen to pray to Allah, while worshipping Mammon.[49]

Note that Trainor follows convention in denouncing Hussein as a Hitler-
ian maniac on grounds of his threat to scorch Israel—in retaliation for Israeli
aggression, a fact completely overlooked, as in this case, or simply dismissed
as irrelevant. In contrast, a murderous Israeli reaction to Iraqi aggression,
were it to be authorized, would be regarded as a righteous act of self-defense.
Note also that the phrases "moderate pro-Western" and "fiercely nationalistic anti-Western" are redundant. "Pro-Western" implies "moderate"; "anti-
Western" implies "fiercely nationalistic"—that is, evil and fanatical.

7. The Diplomatic Track

By mid August, it was clear that the US was not exactly leading a rousing chorus at the United Nations as it attempted to mobilize support for the use of force in the Gulf. Despite threats, pleas, and cajolery, US travelling diplomats were unable to rally more than token participation in anything beyond sanctions of the kind that the UN has attempted to impose in other cases of aggression, often to be blocked by the US. The isolation of the United States in the Saudi deserts (apart from Britain) could hardly be overlooked, but there was little questioning of the official line that when the world is in trouble, it calls for the sheriff, and we are the only ones honorable and tough enough to shoulder the burden.

Germany announced that it would not help to finance US military operations because the arrangement between the US and Saudi Arabia was bilateral, not authorized by the UN. The European Community took the same position. Commenting on the EC decision not to support US operations in the Gulf, while contributing some $2 billion for 1990–91 (15 percent of the estimated cost) to countries suffering from the embargo, the Italian Foreign Minister stated: "The military action of the United States was taken autonomously. Don't forget the principle of no taxation without representation." Japan politely agreed to do very little, while South Korea pleaded poverty. The Third World reaction was muted, with little enthusiasm for the US effort and often much popular antagonism. The Arab states generally kept their distance. In pro-Western Tunisia, a poll showed 90 percent support for Iraq, with many condemning the "double standard" revealed by the US attitude towards Israeli aggression, annexation, and human rights abuses. Commentators occasionally noted that support for the US military initiative was least in the governments that had "nascent democratic movements": Jordan, Algeria, Yemen, and Tunisia (Judith Miller). Administration analysts expressed concern that if US troops were kept in place too long, the "Islamic religious periods" (the Hajj and Ramadan) would allow more expression of popular feelings and "could set off protests and perhaps coups" that "could topple western-oriented governments in the region and cut the diplomatic ground out from under US-led troops facing Iraq" (Peter Gosselin, who also reported accurately that no congressional critic questions Bush's "first principles: that the Persian Gulf is crucial to the United States and that the United States therefore must defend its interests with military force"—a "first principle" that Saddam Hussein could easily appreciate). Brookings Institution Middle East specialist Judith Kipper said: "To me, the gut issue is the regimes versus the people, because none of the Arab regimes represent their people, and this is why there is such cheering in the streets" for Saddam Hussein, seen to be defending the interests of the Arab masses against the ruling clique that used the oil wealth of the Arab nations to enrich themselves and the Western world. There was little comment on the significance of the fact that in so far as elements of pluralism exist in the Arab world, the governments cannot line up in the US cause.[50]

The press tried to put a bold face on all of this, stressing the amazing unanimity of world opinion in support of the US stand and finessing the details as best possible. The kinds of problems faced were captured in an AP summary of the top stories of the day: "Treasury Secretary Nicholas Brady is declaring his global fund-raising effort a success even though he received no specific pledges of new assistance to help pay." Columnists and editors, however, denounced Japan (and occasionally Germany) as "fair-weather allies" who are refusing "to contribute their full and fair share to the common effort to contain Iraq." There was little effort, however, to explore the odd refusal to "get on board" on the part of those who were, in theory, the main beneficiaries of the US actions.[51]

Such problems led to a noteworthy account (and endorsement) of the militant US stance in the *New York Times*, in a front-page article by Thomas Friedman. He attributed the Administration's refusal even to consider "a diplomatic track" to its concern that negotiations might "defuse the crisis" and restore the previous status quo at the cost of "a few token gains in Kuwait" for the Iraqi dictator (perhaps "a Kuwaiti island or minor border adjustments," all matters long under dispute). Thus, anything short of a total victory for US force is unacceptable, even if it means a catastrophic war, with unpredictable consequences. As for the possibility that diplomacy might defuse the crisis, leaving such fateful and long-neglected questions as proliferation of lethal weaponry in the region (not just in Iraq) to be approached calmly through diplomatic means—that is a disaster to be avoided, not an option to be explored.[52]

The *Times* chief diplomatic correspondent went on to attribute the pressure for negotiations to Jordan and the ever-slimy PLO, whose effort to mediate is their "only way to justify their support for President Hussein's invasion." Jordan had not supported the invasion, though it also did not support the US response to it; as British correspondent Martin Woollacott reports more accurately from Amman, the King's "efforts since the crisis began have been aimed at putting the genie back in the bottle, bringing about a withdrawal from Kuwait, and in general restoring the status quo." And even though the *Times* judged the fact unfit to print it is hard to believe that its leading Middle East specialist was unaware that, a few days before he wrote, the PLO had issued its first official declaration on the crisis, which called for a solution that would "safeguard the integrity and security of Iraq, *Kuwait*, Saudi Arabia, of the Gulf and the whole Arab region" (my emphasis; carried by wire services). Placing the blame on "the Palestinian interpretation of events" and on the bad behavior of Jordan is another notable contribution to establishing the US–Israel propaganda line.[53]

Little solid information was available on the Jordanian and PLO positions. The Israeli press quoted a PLO plan read by Palestinian activist Faisal Husseini in Jerusalem, calling for immediate withdrawal of Iraqi forces from Kuwait, peace talks between Iraq and Kuwait on borders and oil policy, and the right of the Kuwaiti people "to choose the central government in their land, with no foreign influence, either Arab or other." According to PLO sources, Jordan and the PLO advanced a plan under which the UN would introduce a peacekeeping force and coordinate talks on the future government of Kuwait, possibly calling for a plebiscite in Kuwait. Like other proposals for a diplomatic track, these were ignored or quickly dismissed by the White House, Congress, and the media.[54]

While warning against the temptations of the diplomatic track, the *Times* also called for diplomacy in preference to the immediate resort to force. But, as already noted, "diplomacy" meant delivery of an ultimatum: capitulate or die. In reality, diplomatic possibilities were undercut from the outset, along with the sanctions option.

One should bear in mind that the US government, like any actor in world affairs, will always be publicly advocating diplomacy, not force. That was the US stance while seeking to bar negotiations and political settlement in Vietnam and Central America, and has always been the public posture with regard to the Israel–Arab conflict, even as the US has been leading the rejectionist camp. Whatever the US position may be, the media depict it as a yearning for diplomacy and peaceful means. Thus we read of "the American effort to keep attention focused on diplomacy and sanctions, not the drums of war"[55]—when in fact the effort is to block the diplomatic track, reject negotiations, and keep to force and coercion—under an international cover if possible, otherwise alone. As in other cases, it is a point of logic, immune to fact, that Washington is seeking to resolve the problem peacefully, without the use of force.

Several early openings for a "diplomatic track" have been mentioned: the August 12 Iraqi proposal concerning withdrawal from all occupied Arab lands; the August 19 proposal that the status of Kuwait be settled by the Arab states alone; the August 23 offer published by *Newsday*, and a "similar offer" (or perhaps this same one) that the *Times* kept under wraps at the same time; and the reported Jordanian and PLO proposals. Others continued to surface, receiving similar treatment. The business pages of the *New York Times* and *Wall Street Journal* reported a "near-panic of stock buying late in the day" on December 4, after a British television report of an Iraqi offer to withdraw from Kuwait apart from the Rumailah oilfields, with no other conditions except Kuwaiti agreement to discuss a lease of the two Gulf islands after the withdrawal. Wire services carried the story, but not the news sections. News reports did, however, express uneasiness that proposed discussions with Iraq (actually, delivery of an ultimatum, according to the White House) "might encourage some European partners to launch unhelpful peace feelers ..."[56]

In late December, Iraq made another proposal, disclosed by US officials on January 2: an offer "to withdraw from Kuwait if the United States pledges not to attack as soldiers are pulled out, if foreign troops leave the region, and if there is an agreement on the Palestinian problem and on the banning of all weapons of mass destruction in the region."[57] Officials described the offer as "interesting" because it dropped the border issues, and "signals Iraqi interest in a negotiated settlement." A State Department Mideast expert described the proposal as a "serious prenegotiation position." The US "immediately dismissed the proposal," the report notes. It passed without mention in the national press, and was barely noted elsewhere.

The *New York Times* did, however, report on the same day that Yasser Arafat, after consultations with Saddam Hussein, indicated that neither of them "insisted that the Palestinian problem be solved before Iraqi troops get out of Kuwait."[58] According to Arafat, the report continues, "Mr Hussein's statement Aug. 12, linking an Iraqi withdrawal to an Israeli withdrawal from the West Bank and Gaza Strip, was no longer operative as a negotiating demand." All that is necessary is "a strong link to be guaranteed by the five permanent members of the Security Council that we have to solve all the problems in the Gulf, in the Middle East and especially the Palestinian cause."

Two weeks before the deadline for Iraqi withdrawal, then, it seemed that war might be avoided on these terms: Iraq would withdraw completely from Kuwait with a US pledge not to attack withdrawing forces; foreign troops leave the region; the Security Council indicates a serious commitment to settle other major regional problems. Disputed border issues would be left for later consideration. The possibility was flatly rejected by Washington, and scarcely entered the media or public awareness. The US and Britain maintained their commitment to force alone.

The strength of that commitment was again exhibited when France made a last-minute effort to avoid war on January 14, proposing that the Security Council call for "a rapid and massive withdrawal" from Kuwait along with a statement that Council members would bring their "active contribution" to a settlement of other problems of the region, "in particular, of the Arab–Israeli conflict and in particular to the Palestinian problem by convening, at an appropriate moment, an international conference" to assure "the security, stability and development of this region of the world." The French proposal was supported by Belgium (a Council member), and Germany, Spain, Italy, Algeria, Morocco, Tunisia, and several non-aligned nations. The US and Britain rejected it (along with the Soviet Union, irrelevantly). UN Ambassador Thomas Pickering stated that the proposal was unacceptable, because it went beyond previous UN resolutions on the Iraqi invasion.[59]

The Ambassador's statement was technically correct. The wording of the proposal is drawn from a different source, namely, a Security Council decision of December 20, adjoined to Resolution 681, which calls on Israel to observe the Geneva Conventions in the occupied territories. In that statement, the members of the Security Council called for "an international conference, at an appropriate time, properly structured," to help "achieve a negotiated settlement and lasting peace in the Arab–Israeli conflict." The statement was excluded from the Resolution itself to prevent a US veto, and left as a codicil. Note that there was no "linkage" to the Iraqi invasion, which was unmentioned.

We cannot know whether the French initiative might have succeeded in averting war. The US feared that it might, and therefore blocked it, in accord with its zealous opposition to any form of diplomacy, and, in this case, its equally strong opposition to an international conference. In this rejectionism, George Bush was joined by Saddam Hussein, who gave no public indication of any interest in the French proposal, though doing so might possibly have averted war.

The unwavering US position was expressed with great clarity by President Bush in the letter that he wrote to Saddam Hussein on January 5, which was rejected by Iraqi foreign minister Tariq Aziz when it was presented to him by Secretary of State James Baker, on the grounds that its language was inappropriate for correspondence between heads of state. In this letter, Bush stated: "There can be no reward for aggression. Nor will there be any negotiation. Principle cannot be compromised." He merely "informed" Saddam Hussein that his choice was to capitulate without negotiation, or be crushed by force.[60] Diplomacy is not an option.

One might fairly question how serious or promising these options were. To ignore them or dismiss them as "baloney" is to demand a resolution through the threat or use of military force, whatever the consequences, which could be horrendous. The significance and longer-term import of these facts should not be obscured.

Given the current US concern to ensure that Iraq's nonconventional weapons capacity be destroyed, it is worth recalling another rejected Iraqi offer. On April 12, 1990, Saddam Hussein, then still a friend and ally, offered to destroy his arsenal of chemical and other nonconventional weapons if Israel agreed to eliminate its chemical and nuclear weapons. Again in December, the Iraqi Ambassador to France stated: "Iraq would scrap chemical and mass destruction weapons if Israel was also prepared to do so," Reuters reported. Responding to the April offer, transmitted by a group of US Senators, the State Department said that it welcomed Iraq's willingness to destroy its arsenals but opposed the link "to other issues or weapons systems" (State Department spokesman Richard Boucher).[61] Note that the other weapons systems are left unmentioned; the phrase "Israeli nuclear weapons" cannot be pronounced by any US official, because acknowledgement of their existence would raise the question why all US aid to Israel is not illegal under amendments to the Foreign Aid Act from the 1970s barring aid to any country engaged in clandestine nuclear weapons development.

It is not the threat of mass destruction and the capacity to coerce that disturbs us; rather, it is important that it be wielded by the proper hands: ours or our client's.

The general contours of a possible diplomatic settlement were evident by August, involving arrangements concerning Iraqi access to the Gulf, perhaps by lease of two uninhabited islands; a settlement of the dispute over the Rumailah oilfields; the opening of steps towards a regional security settlement; perhaps some mode for determination of public opinion within Kuwait. The US adamantly opposed all such steps from the first moment, arguing that "aggression cannot be rewarded," that "linkage" is in conflict with our high moral stand, and that we cannot enter into lengthy negotiations. Rather, Iraq must at once capitulate to the US show of force, after which maybe—*maybe*—Washington will permit discussion of other issues. The rejection of "linkage" derives from the unspeakable truth that the US is opposed to a diplomatic settlement of all of the "linked" issues. In particular, it has long been opposed to an international conference on the Arab–Israel conflict, because such efforts could only lead to pressures to achieve the kind of peaceful diplomatic settlement that the US has success-fully barred by means of what is called "the peace process" in conventional ideology.

In numerous similar cases, the US has been quite happy to reward aggres-sion, conduct lengthy negotiations, and pursue "linkage" (even putting aside those cases in which the criminal acts are approved). In the case of Namibia, for example, the UN condemned South Africa's occupation of the territory in the 1960s, followed by a World Court judgement calling for South Africa's exit. The US pursued "quiet diplomacy" and "constructive engagement" while South Africa looted and terrorized Namibia and used it as a base for its murderous attacks against its neighbors (on the estimated human and material cost, see p. 239 below). Secretary of State George Shultz's "peace plan" for Lebanon in 1983 cheerfully "rewarded the aggressors." The plan in effect established a "Greater Israel," as the passionately pro-Israel *New York Times* conceded, while Syria was simply ordered to conform to the US–Israeli dictates (as, predictably, it refused to do); an extreme form of linkage.[62] Israel was also "rewarded" for its invasion of Egypt in 1956. US clients or the master himself are not expected to slink away from aggres-sion and terror without satisfaction of their "needs" and "wants." The pattern is general, as Third World commentators commonly observe, with little effect on the well-disciplined Western political culture.

It is entirely reasonable to take the position that Iraq should withdraw forthwith, unconditionally, with no "linkage" to anything, and that it should pay reparations and even be subjected to war crimes trials; that is a tenable position for people who uphold the principles that yield these conclusions. But as a point of logic, principles cannot be selectively upheld. As a point of fact, among those who publicly espouse the standard position, very few can claim to do so on grounds of principle, as the most elementary inquiry will quickly show.

The rejection of "linkage," accepted with striking unanimity by elite opinion, is particularly noteworthy in this case because it is combined with the demand that the security problems of the region must be settled as part of the Iraqi withdrawal. Now that Iraq has shown itself to be an enemy, not a reliable client as was supposed, it cannot be left with its ominous military capacities intact. But the "long-term balance of power in the region" requires that it remain as a barrier to Iran, as General Schwarz-kopf indicated. And it is hardly realistic to expect the Arab world to observe passively while the major US client in the region not only occupies Arab territory and subjects the population to harsh repression, but also expands its nuclear arsenals and other military advantages. Clearly, the questions of "security" and "stability" require consideration of regional issues, the dread "linkage." Being opposed to diplomatic settlements generally, for reasons of its political weakness, the US (and educated opinion) must, however, oppose "linkage" on the grand principle that "aggressors cannot be rewarded"—in this case.

Three days after reporting and justifying US fears that others might be tempted by the "diplomatic track," the *Times* editors, outraged that Saddam Hussein had surrounded foreign embassies with troops, denounced him for "lash[ing] out at diplomacy itself."[63] As noted earlier, this extreme defiance of international law impelled the *Times* editors to demand that Hussein be treated as a war criminal under the Nuremberg Principles.

The editors charged Hussein with such crimes as "initiating a war of aggression in violation of international treaties," citing the invasion of Iran in 1980; "the ill treatment of civilian populations in occupied territories"; stripping people of their citizenship and abusing innocent civilians; and this new outrage against "diplomats whose special status is protected by the Vienna Conventions." The charges are all accurate, and the Nuremberg Principles do indeed apply. The worst crimes, by far, are from the period when the editors pretended not to see US government support for its Iraqi friends. And one can think of some other countries that have recently been engaged in similar crimes, including one regularly hailed by the *Times* as the noble guardian of world order and human rights, and another that it praises as the very "symbol of human decency," "a society in which moral sensitivity is a principle of political life."[64] But the editors did not see fit to lead their readers through the byways of historical irrelevance.

8. Safeguarding our Needs

By any standards, Saddam Hussein is a monstrous figure, surely in comparison to the minor criminal Manuel Noriega. But his villainy is not the reason for his assumption of the role of Great Satan in August 1990. It was apparent long before, and did not impede Washington's efforts to lend him aid and support. And few words need be wasted on our traditional commitment to resist aggression and uphold the rule of law. Hussein became a demon in the usual fashion: when it was finally understood, beyond any doubt, that his independent nationalism threatened US interests. His record of hideous atrocities then became available for propaganda needs, but beyond that, it had essentially nothing to do with his sudden transition in August 1990 from cherished friend to new incarnation of Genghis Khan and Hitler.

The military occupation of Kuwait—which, if successfully maintained, would make the Iraqi dictator a major player on the world scene—does not raise the threat of superpower confrontation and nuclear war, as did earlier conflicts in the region. That not insignificant fact reflects, of course, the collapse of the Soviet system, which leaves the US unchallenged in military force and under strong temptation to demonstrate the efficacy of the instrument that it alone wields. That strategic conception is by no means unchallenged, even in elite circles, where a conflict began to emerge within several months, along familiar lines.[65] The global strategy of world control through the threat or use of force runs into conflict with the goals of maintaining economic health and international business interests—by now very serious problems, and hard to address without significant changes in social policy at home. The shape of the New World Order will depend, to no small degree, on which of these conceptions prevails.

Notes

1. On the latter, see the Introduction.

2. See Chapter 1, pp. 53 f., and sources cited.

3. "Why America is in the Gulf," Address by James Baker to the Los Angeles World Affairs Council, October 29, 1990; US Department of State.

4. John Dunn, "Our insecure tradition," *Times Literary Supplement*, October 5, 1990.

5. William Stivers, *Supremacy and Oil* (Cornell University, 1982), from which the following is drawn (pp. 34 ff.; 74 ff.)

6. Andy Thomas, *Effects of Chemical Warfare* (Stockholm International Peace Research Institute [SIPRI], Taylor & Francis, 1985), ch. 2; taboo, Victor Mallet, *Financial Times* (London), December 18, 1990. On the effects of US chemical warfare, years after the war ended, see *Necessary Illusions*, pp. 38 f. and sources cited.

7. Marc Trachtenberg, *International Security*, Winter 1988/9.

8. Quandt, "Lebanon, 1958, and Jordan, 1970," in Barry Blechman and Stephen Kaplan, eds, *Force without War* (Brookings Institution, 1978), pp. 247, 238. Emphasis Eisenhower's.

9. Telegram no. 1979, July 19, 1958, to Prime Minister from Secretary of State, from Washington; File FO 371/132 779. "Future Policy in the Persian Gulf," January 15, 1958, FO 371/132 778.

10. Undated sections of NSC 5801/1, "Current Policy Issues," "Issues Arising Out of the Situation in the Near East," mid to late 1958; NSC 5820/1, November 4, 1958. See Chapter 1, pp. 53 ff.;

see *Fateful Triangle*, ch. 2. I am indebted to Kirsten Cale and Irene Gendzier for British and US documents, respectively. For excerpts and discussion, see Cale, "Ruthlessly to intervene," *Living Marxism* (London), November 1990; Gendzier,"The Way They Saw It Then," ms., November 1990.

11. For some discussion in the 1970s, see *Towards a New Cold War*, chs 2, 11; Christopher Rand, *Making Democracy Safe for Oil* (Little, Brown and Co., 1975).

12. *BG*, August 8, 1990, and the media generally. Pamela Constable *et al.*, *BG*, August 20, 1990.

13. For a few exceptions, well outside the mainstream, see Alexander Cockburn's columns in the *Los Angeles Times* and *Nation*, September 10; Erwin Knoll, *Chicago Tribune*, August 17, 1990.

14. McGrory, *BG*, August 8; Mary Curtius and Stephen Kurkjian, *BG*, August 6, 1990, citing the *Washington Post*.

15. Crowe, Peter Gosselin and Stephen Kurkjian, *BG*, August 8; Trainor, "Saddam Hussein, Mideast's Noriega, Has to Go," *NYT* Op-Ed, August 12, 1990.

16. Editorials, *BG*, *NYT*, August 9, 1990.

17. Michael Carlin, letter, *BG*, August 9, and many others; editorial, *Dublin Sunday Tribune*, August 12; Cronin, *Irish Times*, August 11, 1990.

18. By November, a division among elites began to develop with much clarity. Discussion broadened in the usual manner to include this spectrum of tactical judgement.

19. Christopher Hitchens, *Cyprus* (Quartet, 1984); Bush, Reuters, September 26, 1990; for a rare exception to the general evasion of the Turkish invasion, see Walter Robinson, *BG*, October 7, 1990. Thomas Franck, "The Stealing of the Sahara," *American Journal of International Law*, vol. 70, 1976, pp. 694 f.

20. Barringer, *NYT*, August 16, 1990. On the facts, and the version of them crafted by the propaganda system, see *Fateful Triangle*, ch. 5, secs 3, 4; *Pirates and Emperors*, ch. 2; *Necessary Illusions*, pp. 275–7 and Appendix III. For a recent update on Israeli terror in Lebanon, see my "Letter from Lexington," *Lies of Our Times*, August 1990. For a knowledgeable though apologetic Israeli perspective, see Ze'ev Schiff and Ehud Ya'ari, *Israel's Lebanon War* (Simon & Schuster, 1984).

21. Siegman, letter, *NYT*, August 26, 1990; editorial, *NYT*, September 7, 1990. On the 1967 war, see, among others, Donald Neff, *Warriors for Jerusalem* (Simon & Schuster, 1984).

22. Editorial, *Financial Times*, August 13, 1990.

23. Tom Brokaw, NBC News, 6:30 p.m., August 12; Michael Gordon, *NYT*, August 13, 1990. Excerpts from the Iraqi statement appear on an inside page without comment.

24. *JP*, *Yediot Ahronot*, August 10, 1990. Reuters, *BG*, August 11, 1990, p. 40, 90 words; zero in the *Times*. On the undermining of any diplomatic resolution as the process unfolded, and the refraction of the facts through the ideological prism, see the essays collected in *Towards a New Cold War* and *Fateful Triangle*. See *Necessary Illusions*, and my article in *Z Magazine*, January 1990, on the impressive success in suppressing and distorting the record in the current period.

25. Ibid. for the unpublishable facts, and references of preceding note for earlier background.

26. "Proposal by Iraq's President Demanding U.S. Withdrawal," *NYT*, August 20, 1990.

27. See *Fateful Triangle*, p. 114.

28. Royce, *Newsday*, August 29, 1990.

29. R.W. Apple, *NYT*, August 30, 1990.

30. AI, AP, November 2, 1990.

31. Tony Horwitz, "Gulf Crisis Finds Kurds in Middle Again," *WSJ*, December 3, 1990.

32. See *Necessary Illusions*, pp. 286 f.

33. AP, *BG*, August 5, 1990.

34. Michael Wines, "U.S. Aid Helped Hussein's Climb," *NYT*, August 13; 1987 data, Larry Tye, "Food embargo may be an effective weapon," *BG*, August 22; Glass, *Spectator*, August 25, 1990.

35. Liesi Graz, *Middle East International*, August 3; Thomas Hayes, *NYT*, September 3, 1990, quoting energy specialist Henry Schuler. See also Laurent Belsie, *CSM*, August 9, noting that "Kuwait was one of the most flagrant violators of the quota system, oil analysts say." Iraq also condemned Kuwait for insisting that Iraq pay the huge costs of defending the Arab world, including the Kuwaiti elite, from Iran.

36. See references of Note 21.

37. Laqueur, *NYT Magazine*, December 16, 1973. For further comment, see my *Peace in the Middle East* (Pantheon, 1974), Introduction.

38. See Chapter 1, pp. 35 f.; Marilyn B. Young, *Rhetoric of Empire: American China Policy, 1985–1901* (Harvard, 1968).

39. Editorial, *BG*, August 8, 1990.

40. Pamela Constable *et al.*, *BG*, August 20; Apple, *NYT*, August 21; editorial, *NYT*, September 24; Goshko, Broder, *WP Weekly*, September 3; Ball, *NYRB*, December 6; BBC "Newsnight," November 29, 1990, circulated by MTS (Defence Information), Newton-le-Willows, Merseyside.

41. From 1970 through 1989, the US vetoed 45 Security Council resolutions alone, 7 others with the UK, 4 with the UK and France. Britain had 26 negative votes (7 with the US, 4 with the US and France). France had 11 (7 alone) and the USSR 8 (one with China). Records obtained by Norman Finkelstein. In 1990, the US added two more vetoes: on Panama (see Chapter 5, Note 19) and on Israeli abuses in the occupied territories (May 31). Thus 58 "Noes" from 1970 through 1990.

42. See Chapter 3, section 4; Chapters 2, 5; my article in *Z Magazine*, January 1990. For further discussion, see *Necessary Illusions*, pp. 82 ff. and Appendix IV, sec. 4; Norman Finkelstein, *Z Magazine*, November 1990; Cheryl Rubenberg, *Arab Studies Quarterly*, Fall 1989; Nabeel Abraham, *American–Arab Affairs*, Winter 1989–90.

43. Elaine Sciolino, "Peacekeeping in a New Era: The Superpowers Act in Harmony," *NYT*, August 28; Roger Rosenblatt, "Give Law a Chance," lead review, *NYT Book Review*, August 26; James Traub, *NYT Magazine*, September 16, 1990.

44. *NYT*, January 28, 1976; Moynihan, *A Dangerous Place* (Little, Brown, 1978).

45. See p. 19.

46. Youssef Ibrahim, *NYT*, November 2; Judith Miller, *NYT*, December 6, 1990. General Schwarzkopf did inform the "Iraqi people" that "our argument is not with" them, and that we would prefer to avoid the "thousands and thousands of innocent casualties."

47. Thomas Friedman, *NYT*, August 12, 1990.

48. Merely to note one issue, a case can be made that for the longer-term interests of the people of the region, oil should be held back from the market, keeping prices higher now and preserving the resources for the future, instead of leaving hundreds of millions of people with no future but death and starvation in several generations, when their only resource is exhausted, wasted for the benefit of the West and local elites.

49. Youssef Ibrahim, "The Split Among Arabs Unleashes a People's Anger," *NYT*, August 12, 1990; Trainor. The facts are more complex; it is the interpretation and its doctrinal significance that we consider here.

50. "Bonn says it won't fund US buildup," *WP–BG*, September 6; Serge Schmemann, "Bonn's Iraq-Embargo Aid," *NYT*, September 7; Alan Riding, Thomas Friedman, *NYT*, September 8; James Sterngold, "Brady finishes Tour," *NYT*, September 8; James Clad, Ted Morello, *Far Eastern Economic Review*, September 6; Friedman, Reuters, *NYT*, September 7; Edward Schumacher, "Tunis, Long Friendly to West, Bristles With Hostility to U.S. Gulf Moves," *NYT*, September 6; AP, September 7; Michael Gordon, "Combined Force in Saudi Arabia Is Light on Arabs," *NYT*, September 5; Miller, *NYT*, December 6; Gosselin, *BG*, November 26, 27; Kipper, John Kifner, *NYT*, August 12, 1990. The real picture is again more complex; it is the interpretation that is relevant here.

51. AP, September 7; Tom Wicker, Editorial, *NYT*, September 6, 1990.

52. Friedman, "Behind Bush's Hard Line," *NYT*, August 22, 1990.

53. Ibid.; Woollacott, *Manchester Guardian Weekly*, August 26; "PLO says it favors integrity of Kuwait," Reuters, *BG*, August 20, 1990.

54. Yehuda Litani, *Hadashot*, August 17 (*The Other Front*, Jerusalem, August 23). UPI, *BG*, August 26; compare the proposals in the *Times* editorial the same day. See also Paul Lalor, *Middle East International*, August 31, 1990.

55. Andrew Rosenthal, *NYT*, September 3, 1990.

56. AP, December 4; *WSJ*, sec. C, p. 2. December 5; *NYT*, business section, December 5; Gerald Seib, *WSJ*, December 3, 1990.

57. Knut Royce, *Newsday*, January 3, 1991.

58. Patrick Tyler, *NYT*, January 3.

59. Trevor Rowe, *BG*, January 15; Paul Lewis, *NYT*, January 15; AP, January 15, 1991.

60. AP, January 14, 1990.

61. AP, April 13, 1990. Reuters, *BG*, April 14; *Financial Times*, December 18, 1990.

62. See *Fateful Triangle*, pp. 425 f.

63. Editorial, *NYT*, August 25, 1990. See above, p. 160.

64. *NYT*, August 25, 1990. For these and numerous other examples of *Times* gushing over Israel, see *Towards a New Cold War*, *Fateful Triangle*, and *Necessary Illusions*.

65. For some other examples, see Chapter 12, section 5; also Introduction.

SEVEN

The Victors

ACCORDING to the conventional picture, the US has won the Cold War. Righteousness has triumphed over evil with the victory of democracy, free-market capitalism, justice and human rights. As standard-bearer of the cause, the United States now leads the way to a New World Order of peace, economic development, and cooperation among those who have seen the light—virtually everyone except for some holdouts like Cuba which still complains that the Third World isn't getting its due, and Saddam Hussein, despite our dedicated efforts to improve his behavior by the carrot rather than the stick; an error of judgement to be rectified by the sword of the righteous avenger.

We have inquired into the validity of this picture from several points of view. Another natural approach is to have a look at the traditional domains of Western power and ask how their people fare at this historic moment, as they contemplate their side's victory in the Cold War conflict. We may ask how they are celebrating the triumph of liberal capitalism and democracy, as they evidently should be, if the standard version is to be taken seriously.

1. The Fruits of Victory: Central America

Few regions of the world have been so dominated by a great power as Central America, which emerged from its usual oblivion in the 1980s, moving to center stage as the traditional order faced an unexpected challenge with the growth of popular movements, inspired in part by the Church's new orientation towards "a preferential option for the poor." After decades of brutal repression and the destructive impact of the US aid programs of the 1960s, the ground was prepared for meaningful social change. The mood in Washington darkened further with the overthrow of the Somoza dictatorship.

The reaction was vigorous and swift: violent repression, which decimated popular organizations. The ranks of the small guerrilla organizations swelled as state terror mounted. "The guerrilla groups, the revolutionary groups, almost without exception began as associations of teachers, associations of labor unions, campesino unions, or parish organizations ..." with practical and reformist goals, ex-Ambassador Robert White testified before Congress in 1982. The same point was made by the assassinated Salvadoran Jesuit intellectual Father Ignacio Martín-Baró, among many others.[1]

A decade later, the United States and its local allies could claim substantial success. The challenge to the traditional order was effectively contained. The misery of the vast majority had deepened, while the power of the military and the privileged sectors was enhanced behind a façade of democratic forms. Some 200,000 people had been killed. Countless others were maimed, tortured, "disappeared," driven from their homes. The people, the communities, the environment were devastated, possibly beyond repair. It was truly a grand victory.

Elite reaction is one of gratification and relief. "For the first time, all five of the countries are led by presidents who were elected in contests widely considered free and fair," *Washington Post* Central America correspondent Lee Hockstader reports from Guatemala City, expressing the general satisfaction over the victory of "conservative politicians" in elections which, we are to understand, took place on a level playing field with no use of force and no foreign influence. It is true, he continues, that "conservative politicians in Central America traditionally represented the established order," defending the wealthy "despite their countries' grossly distorted income patterns. ... But the wave of democracy that has swept the region in recent years appears to be shifting politicians' priorities," so the bad old days are gone for ever.[2]

The student of American history and culture will recognize the familiar moves. Once again, we witness the miraculous change of course that occurs whenever some particularly brutal state excesses have been exposed. Hence all of history, and the reasons for its persistent character, may be dismissed as irrelevant, while we march forward, leading our flock to a new and better world.

The *Post* news report does not merely assert that the new conservatives are dedicated populists, unlike those whom the US used to support in the days of its naiveté and inadvertent error, now thankfully behind us. It goes on to provide evidence for this central claim. The shift of priorities to a welcome populism is demonstrated by the outcome of the conference of the five presidents in Antigua, Guatemala, just completed. The presidents, all "committed to free-market economics," have abandoned worthless goals of social reform, Hockstader explains. "Neither in the plan nor in the lengthier and more general 'Declaration of Antigua' was there any mention of land reform or suggestion of new government social welfare programs to help the poor." Rather, they are adopting "a trickle-down approach to aid the poor." "The idea is to help the poor without threatening the basic power structure," a regional economist observes, contemplating these imaginative new ideas on how to pursue our vocation of serving the suffering masses.

The headline reads: "Central Americans to use Trickle-down Strategy in War on Poverty," capturing the basic thrust of the news story and the assumptions that frame it: aiding the poor is the highest priority of this new breed of populist conservatives, as it always has been for Washington and the political culture generally. What is newsworthy, and so promising, is the populism of the conservatives we support, and their ingenious and startlingly innovative approach to our traditional commitment to help the poor and suffering, a trickle-down strategy of enriching the wealthy—a "preferential option for the rich," overcoming the errors of the Latin American bishops.

One participant in the meeting is quoted as saying: "These past ten years have been gruesome for poor people, they've taken a beating." Putting aside the conventions, one might observe that the political outcomes hailed as a triumph of democracy are in no small measure a tribute to the salutary efficacy of US terror, and that the presidents who hold formal power, and their sponsors, might have had something other than a war on poverty in mind. There is also a history of trickle-down approaches to relieving poverty that might be explored. Such an inquiry might lead us to expect that the next ten years will be no less gruesome for the poor. But that path is not pursued, here or elsewhere in the mainstream.

While the three-day conference of populist conservatives was taking place in Antigua, thirty-three tortured, bullet-riddled bodies were discovered in

Guatemala. They did not disturb the celebration over the triumph of freedom and democracy, or even make the news. Nor did the rest of the 125 bodies, half with signs of torture, found throughout the country that month, according to the Guatemalan Human Rights Commission. The Commission identified seventy-nine as victims of "extrajudicial execution" by the security forces. Another twenty-nine were kidnapped and forty-nine injured in kidnap attempts. The report comes to us from Mexico, where the Commission is based, so that human rights workers can survive now that the US has succeeded in establishing democracy in their homeland. [3]

The UN Economic Commission for Latin America and the Caribbean (CEPAL) reports that the percentage of the Guatemalan population living in extreme poverty increased rapidly after the establishment of democracy in 1985: from 45 percent in that year to 76 percent in 1988. A study by the Nutritional Institute of Central America and Panama (INCAP) estimates that half the population live under conditions of extreme poverty, and that in rural areas, where the situation is worse, thirteen out of every hundred children under five die of illnesses related to malnutrition. Other studies estimate that 20,000 Guatemalans die of hunger every year, that more than 1000 children died of measles alone in the first four months of 1990, and that "the majority of Guatemala's four million children receive no protection at all, not even for the most elemental rights." The Communiqué of the January 1990 Conference of Guatemalan Bishops reviews the steady deterioration of the critical situation of the mass of the population, as "the economic crisis has degenerated into a social crisis" and human rights, even "the right to dignity, . . . do not exist."[4]

Throughout the region, the desperate situation of the poor majority has become still more grave with the grand triumph of our values. Three weeks before the Antigua conference, in his homily marking the completion of President Alfredo Cristiani's first year in office, Archbishop Rivera y Damas of San Salvador deplored the policies of his administration, which have worsened the already desperate plight of the poor; the new conservative populist so admired in Washington and New York "is working to maintain the system," the Archbishop said, "favoring a market economy which is making the poor yet poorer."[5]

In the neighboring countries, the situation is much the same. A few days after the encouraging *Washington Post* report on the Antigua meeting, an editorial in a leading Honduran journal appeared under the headline "Misery is increasing in Honduras because of the economic adjustment," referring to the new trickle-down strategy that the *Post* found so promising—

actually the traditional strategy, its lethal features now more firmly entrenched. The main victims are "the usual neglected groups: children, women, and the aged," according to the conclusions of an academic seminar on "Social Policy in the Context of Crisis," confirmed by "the Catholic Church, the unions, several political parties, and noted economists and statisticians of the country." Two-thirds of the population live below the poverty line, over half of these below the level of "dire need." Unemployment, undernourishment, and severe malnutrition are increasing.[6]

The Pan American Health Organization estimates that of 850,000 children born every year in Central America, 100,000 will die before the age of five and two-thirds of those who survive will suffer from malnutrition, with attendant physical or mental development problems. The Inter-American Development Bank reports that *per capita* income has fallen to the level of 1971 in Guatemala, 1961 in El Salvador, 1973 in Honduras, 1960 in Nicaragua, 1974 in Costa Rica, and 1982 in Panama.[7]

Nicaragua was an exception to this trend of increasing misery, but the US terrorist attack and economic warfare succeeded in reversing earlier gains. Nevertheless, infant mortality halved over the decade, from 128 to 62 deaths per thousand births: "Such a reduction is exceptional on the international level," a UNICEF official said, "especially when the country's war-ravaged economy is taken into account."[8]

Studies by CEPAL, the World Health Organization, and others "cast dramatic light on the situation," Mexico's leading daily reports. They reveal that fifteen million Central Americans, almost 60 per cent of the population, live in poverty, of whom 9.7 million live in "extreme poverty." Severe malnutrition is rampant among children. Seventy-five percent of the peasants in Guatemala, 60 percent in El Salvador, 40 percent in Nicaragua, and 35 percent in Honduras lack health care. To make matters worse, Washington has applied "stunning quotas on sugar, beef, cocoa, cheese, textiles, and limestone, as well as compensation laws and 'antidumping' policies in cement, flowers, and operations of cellulose and glass." The European Community and Japan have followed suit, also imposing harmful protectionist measures.[9]

The environment shares the fate of those who people it. Deforestation, soil erosion, pesticide poisoning, and other forms of environmental destruction, increasing through the victorious 1980s, are traceable in large measure to the development model imposed upon the region and US militarization of it in recent years. Intense exploitation of resources by agribusiness and export-oriented production have enriched wealthy sectors and their foreign sponsors, and led to statistical growth, with a devastating impact on the land and the people. In El Salvador, large areas have become virtual wastelands as the military has sought to undermine the guerrillas' peasant base by extensive bombardment, and by forest and crop destruction. There have been occasional efforts to stem the ongoing catastrophe. Like the Arbenz government overthrown in the CIA-run coup that restored the military regime in Guatemala, the Sandinistas initiated environmental reforms and protections. These were desperately needed, both in the countryside and near Managua, where industrial plants had been permitted to dump waste freely. The most notorious case was the US Penwalt Corporation, which poured mercury into Lake Managua until 1981.[10]

The foreign-imposed development model has emphasized "nontraditional exports" in recent years. Under the free-market conditions approved for defenseless Third World countries, the search for survival and gain will naturally lead to products that maximize profit, whatever the consequences. Coca production has soared in the Andes and elsewhere for this reason, but there are other examples as well. After the discovery of clandestine "human farms" and "fattening houses" for children in Honduras and Guatemala, Dr Luís Genaro Morales, president of the Guatemalan Pediatric Association, said that child trafficking "is becoming one of the principal nontraditional export products," generating $20 million of business a year. The International Human Rights Federation, after an inquiry in Guatemala, gave a more conservative estimate, reporting that about three hundred children are kidnapped every year, taken to secret nurseries, then sold for adoption at about $10,000 per child.

The IHRF investigators could not confirm reports that babies' organs were being sold to foreign buyers. This macabre belief is widely held in the region, however; indicative of the general mood, though hardly credible. The Honduran journal *El Tiempo* reported that the Paraguayan police rescued seven Brazilian babies from a gang that "intended to sacrifice them to organ banks in the United States, according to a charge in the courts." Brazil's Justice Ministry ordered federal police to investigate allegations that adopted children are being used for organ transplants in Europe, a practice "known to exist in Mexico and Thailand," the London *Guardian* reports, adding that "handicapped children are said to be preferred for transplant operations" and reviewing the process by which children are allegedly kidnapped, "disappeared," or given up by impoverished mothers, then adopted or used for transplants. *Tiempo* reported shortly after that an Appeals Judge in Honduras ordered "a meticulous investigation into the sale of Honduran children for the purpose of using their organs for transplant operations." A year earlier, the Secretary-General of the National Council of Social Services, which is in charge of adoptions, had reported that Honduran children "were being sold to the body traffic industry" for organ transplant.[11]

A Resolution of the European Parliament on the Trafficking of Central American Children alleged that near a "human farm" in San Pedro Sula, Honduras, infant corpses were found that "had been stripped of one or a number of organs." At another "human farm" in Guatemala, babies ranging from eleven days old to four months old had been found. The director of the farm, at the time of his arrest, declared that the children "were sold to American or Israeli families whose children needed organ transplants at the cost of $75,000 per child," the Resolution continues, expressing "its horror in the light of the facts" and calling for investigation and preventive measures.[12]

As the region sinks into further misery, these reports continue to appear. In July 1990, a right-wing Honduran daily, under the headline "Loathsome Sale of Human Flesh," reported that police in El Salvador had discovered a group, headed by a lawyer, that was buying children to resell in the United States. An estimated 20,000 children disappear every year in Mexico, the report continues, destined for this end or for use in criminal activities such as transport of drugs "inside their bodies." "The most gory fact, however, is that many little ones are used for transplant of organs to children in the U.S.," which, it is suggested, may account for the fact that the highest rate of kidnapping of children from infants to eighteen-year-olds is in the Mexican regions bordering on the United States.[13]

The one exception to the Central America horror story has been Costa Rica, set on a course of state-guided development by the José Figueres coup of 1948, with social-democratic welfare measures combined with harsh repression of labor, and virtual elimination of the armed forces. The US has always kept a wary eye on this deviation from the regional standards, despite the suppression of labor and the favorable conditions for foreign investors. In the 1980s, US pressures to dismantle the social-democratic features and restore the army elicited bitter complaints from Figueres and others who shared his commitments. While Costa Rica continues to stand apart from the region in political and economic development, the signs of what the Guatemalan *Central America Report* calls "The 'Central American-ization' of Costa Rica" are unmistakable.[14]

Under the pressure of a huge debt, Costa Rica has been compelled to follow the IMF model of free-market capitalism designed for the Third

World, with austerity for the poor, cutback in social programs, and benefits for domestic and foreign investors. The results are coming in. By statistical measures, the economy is relatively strong. But more than 25 per cent of the population—715,000 people—live in poverty, 100,000 in extreme poverty, according to a study published by the ultra-right journal *La Nación* (one feature of Costa Rican democracy being a monopoly of the Spanish-language media by extreme-right sectors of the business community). A study by the Gallup office in Costa Rica published in *Prensa Libre* gives even higher figures, concluding: "approximately one million people cannot afford a minimum diet, nor pay for clothing, education or health care."[15]

The neoliberal economic policies of the 1980s increased social discontent and labor tensions, *Excelsior* reports, evoking an "intense attack by unionists, popular organizations," and others against the Arias Administration, which implemented these measures in conformity with US demands and the priorities of privileged sectors. Church sources report that "the belt-tightening measures of the 1980s, which included the elimination of subsidies, low interest credit, price supports and government assistance programs, have driven many campesinos and small farmers off their land," leading to many protests. The Bishop of Limón issued a pastoral letter deploring the social deterioration and "worsening of the problems" to which "banana workers, in great majority immigrants from rural settings where they were property owners, have been subject." He also deplored the harsh labor code and government policies that enabled the growers to purge union leaders and otherwise undermine workers' rights, and the deforestation and pollution the companies have caused, with government support.[16]

Environmental degradation is serious here as well, including rapid deforestation and sedimentation that has severely affected virtually every major hydroelectric project. Environmental studies reveal that 42 percent of Costa Rica's soil shows signs of severe erosion. "Topsoil is Costa Rica's largest export," the Vice-Minister of Natural Resources commented. Expanding production for export and logging has destroyed forests, particularly the cattle boom of the 1960s and 1970s promoted by the government, international banks and corporations, and the US aid program, which also undermined food production for domestic needs, as elsewhere in Central America. Environmentalists blame government and business for "ecological illiteracy"—more accurately, pursuit of profit without regard for externalities, as prescribed in the capitalist model.[17]

Submissiveness to these demands has yet to meet the exacting standards of the international guardians of business rights. The IMF suspended assistance to Costa Rica in February 1990, cancelling credits. US aid is also falling, now that there is no longer any need to buy Costa Rica's cooperation in the anti-Sandinista *jihad*.[18]

Economic constraints and foreign pressures have narrowed the political system in the approved manner. In the 1990 elections, the two candidates had virtually identical (pro-business) programs, and were highly supportive of US policies in the region. The Central Americanization of Costa Rica is also revealed by the increasing repression through the 1980s. From 1985, the Costa Rican Human Rights Commission (CODEHU) reported torture, arbitrary arrest, harassment of campesinos and workers, and other abuses by the security forces, including a dramatic rise in illegal detentions and arrests. It links the growing wave of abuses to the militarization of the police and security forces, some of whom have been trained in US and Taiwanese military schools. These charges were supported further when an underground torture chamber was found in the building of the Costa Rican Special Police (OIJ), where prisoners were beaten and subjected to electric shock treatment, including torture of a pregnant woman who aborted and electric shock administered to a thirteen-year-old child to elicit a false confession. CODEHU alleges that thirteen people have died in similar incidents since 1988. "Battered by charges of corruption and drug trafficking, the Arias administration receives another blow to its diminishing reputation as a bulwark of democracy" from these revelations, the *Central America Report* observed.[19]

Arias's image "is about to be tarnished" further, according to reports from San José that investigators of the Legislative Drug Commission discovered that he had received a check for $50,000 for his campaign fund from Ocean Hunter Seafood, but had put it in his personal bank account. This Miami-based company and its Costa Rican affiliate, Frigarificos de Puntarenas, were identified by US Congressional investigators as a drug-trafficking operation.[20] I leave it to the reader to imagine the sardonic story in the *New York Times* if something similar were hinted about a minor Sandinista official, however flimsy the evidence.

According to official government figures, the security budget increased 15 percent in 1988 and 13 percent in 1989. The press has reported training of security officers in Fort Benning, Georgia, in US bases in Panama, and in a Taiwanese military academy, as well as by Israeli secret police, the army of El Salvador, the Guatemalan army special forces, and others. Fifteen private paramilitary, vigilante, and security organizations have been identified, with extreme nationalist and right-wing agendas. A member of the special commission of the legislature set up to investigate these matters described the police as an "army in disguise ... out of control." The executive secretary of Costa Rica's Human Rights Commission, Sylvia Porras, noted that "the psychological profile of the police has changed as a result of military training," adding: "we cannot talk any longer of a civilian police force. What we have now is a hidden army."[21]

Annual US military aid in the 1980s shot up to about eighteen times what it had been from 1946 through 1979. US pressures to rebuild the security forces, reversing the Figueres reforms, have been widely regarded as a factor in the drift towards the Central American mode. The role of Oscar Arias has evoked a good deal of annoyance south of the border. After an Arias article in the *New York Times* piously calling on Panama to follow the Costa Rican model and abolish the army, the well-known Mexican writer Gregorio Selser published a review of some Costa Rican realities, beginning with the violent repression of a peaceful demonstration of landless campesinos in September 1986 by Arias's Civil Guard, with many serious injuries. The absence of an army in Costa Rica, he alleges, has become largely a matter of semantics: different words for the same things. He cites an Arias decree of August 5, 1987—just at the moment of the signing of the Esquipulas Accords that brought Arias a Nobel Peace Prize—establishing a professional army in all but name, with the full array of ranks and structure; and a 1989 CODEHU report on the training of hundreds of men in military academies of the US and its client states.[22]

Little of this has ever reached the United States, except far from the mainstream. In the context of the drug war, however, some notice has been taken. An editorial in the *Miami Herald* on "Costa Rica's anguish" cites the comments by Sylvia Porras quoted above on the effects of US military training, which has changed the "psychological profile" of the civilian police, turning them into "a camouflaged army." The judgement is not "hyperbole," the editorial concludes, attributing the rapid growth of the army and the recent killing of civilians by the security forces to the Nicaraguan conflict and the drug war—but with no mention of US pressures, following the norms of the Free Press.[23]

2. The Fruits of Victory: Latin America

Turning to the rest of "our little region over here which has never bothered anybody" (see p. 52), a World Bank study in 1982 estimated that

40 percent of households in Latin America live in poverty, meaning that they cannot purchase the minimum basket of goods required for the satisfaction of their basic needs, and ... 20 percent of all households live in destitution, meaning that they lack the means of buying even the food that would provide them with a minimally adequate diet.

The situation worsened in the 1980s, largely because of the huge export of capital to the West (see Chapter 3, p. 98). Speaking in Washington in preparation for the 1989 General Assembly of the OAS, Secretary General Soares described the 1980s as a "lost decade" for Latin America, with falling personal income and general economic stagnation or decline. He said that in the past year (1988), in the worst crisis since the Depression of the 1930s, average income had fallen to the level of 1978. In 1989, average *per capita* product declined again, and the export of capital continued in a flood, CEPAL reported. According to World Bank figures, average *per capita* income in Argentina fell from $1990 in 1980 to $1630 in 1988. Mexico's GNP declined for seven straight years. Real wages in Venezuela fell by a third from 1981, to the 1964 level. Argentina allotted 20 percent of its budget to education in 1972, 6 percent in 1986. David Felix, a specialist on Latin American economics, writes that *per capita* output for the region declined almost 10 percent from 1980; real investment per worker, which declined sharply in the 1980s, fell to below 1970 levels in most of the heavily indebted countries, where urban real wages are in many cases 20–40 percent below 1980 levels, even below 1970 levels; the brain drain quickened and physical and human capital per head shrank because of the decline of public and private investment and collapse of infrastructure. Much of the sharp deterioration of the 1980s, Felix and others conclude, can be traced to the free-market restructuring imposed by the industrial powers, a matter to which we return.[24]

Mexicans continue to flee to the United States for survival, and here too macabre tales abound. The Mexican press reports drownings, disappearances, and "the disappearance or theft of women for the extraction of organs for use in transplants in the U.S." (quoting a regional Human Rights Committee representative). Others report torture, high rates of cancer from chemicals used in the maquiladora industries (assembly plants near the border, for shipment to US factories), secret prisons, kidnapping, and other horror stories. *Excelsior* reports a study by environmental groups, presented to President Salinas, claiming that 100,000 children die every year as a result of pollution in the Mexico City area, along with millions suffering from pollution-induced disease, which has reduced life expectancy by an estimated ten years. The "main culprit" is the emissions of lead and sulfur from operations of the national petrochemical company Pemex, which is free from the controls imposed elsewhere—one of the advantages of Third World production that is not lost on investors.[25]

The Mexican Secretariat of Urban Development and the Environment described the situation as "truly catastrophic," *Excelsior* reports further, estimating that less than 10 percent of Mexican territory is able to support "minimally productive agriculture" because of environmental degradation, while water resources are hazardously low. Many areas are turning into "a real museum of horrors" from pollution because of the blind pursuit of profits. The Secretariat estimates further that more than 90 percent of industry in the Valley of Mexico, where there are more than 30,000 plants, violate global standards; and in the chemical industry, more than half the labor force suffers irreversible damage to the respiratory system.[26]

Maude Barlow, chairperson of a Canadian study group, reports the results of their inquiry into maquiladoras "built by Fortune 500 to take advantage of a desperate people," for profits hard to match elsewhere. They found factories full of teenage girls, some fourteen years old, "working at eye-damaging, numbingly repetitive work" for wages "well below what is required for even a minimum standard of living." Corporations commonly send the most dangerous jobs here because standards on chemicals are "lax or nonexistent." "In one plant," she writes, "we all experienced headaches and nausea from spending an hour on the assembly line," and "we saw young girls working beside open vats of toxic waste, with no protective face covering." Unions are barred, and there is no lack of desperate people to take the place of any who "are not happy, or fall behind in quotas, or become ill or pregnant." The delegation "took pictures of a lagoon of black, bubbling toxic waste dumped by plants in an industrial park," following it to "where it met untreated raw sewage and turned into a small river running past squatters' camps (where children covered in sores drank Pepsi Cola from baby bottles) to empty into the Tijuana River."[27]

We have already noted the economic and political conditions in Colombia, another success story of capitalist democracy flawed only by the drug cartels. A study by Evan Vallianatos of the US government Office of Technology Assessment amplifies the dimensions of the victory here. "Colombia's twentieth century history is above all stained in the blood of the peasant poor," he writes, reviewing the gruesome record of atrocities and massacre to keep the mass of the population in its place. The US Aid program, the Ford

Foundation, and others have sought to deal with the plight of the rural population "by refining the largely discredited trickle-down technology and knowledge transfer process," investing in the elite and trusting in "competition, private property, and the mechanism of the free market"—a system in which "the big fish eats the small one," as one poor farmer observes. These policies have made the dreadful conditions still worse, creating "the most gross inequalities that the beast in man has made possible." It is not only the rural poor who have suffered beyond endurance. To illustrate the kind of development fostered by the transnational corporations and the technocrats, Vallianatos offers the example of the small industrial city of Yumbo, "rapidly becoming unfit for human habitation" because of uncontrolled pollution, decay, and "corrosive slums" in which "the town's spent humanity has all but given up."[28]

Brazil is another country with rich resources and potential, long subject to European influence, then US intervention primarily since the Kennedy years. We cannot, however, simply speak of "Brazil." There are two very different Brazils. In a scholarly study of the Brazilian economy, Peter Evans writes that "the fundamental conflict in Brazil is between the 1, or perhaps 5, percent of the population that comprises the elite and the 80 percent that has been left out of the 'Brazilian model' of development." The Brazilian journal *Veja* reports on these two Brazils—the first modern and Westernized, the second sunk in the deepest misery. Seventy percent of the population consume fewer calories than Iranians, Mexicans, or Paraguayans. Over half the population have family incomes below the minimum wage. For 40 percent of the population the median annual salary is $287, while inflation skyrockets and even minimal necessities are beyond reach. A World Bank report on the Brazilian educational system compares it unfavorably to those of Ethiopia and Pakistan, with a dropout rate of 80 percent in primary school, growing illiteracy, and falling budgets. The Ministry of Education reports that the government spends over a third of the education budget on school meals, because most of the students will either eat at school or not at all.[29]

The journal *South*, which describes itself as "The Business Magazine of the Developing World," reports on Brazil under the heading "The Underside of Paradise." A country with enormous wealth, no security concerns, a relatively homogeneous population, and a favorable climate, Brazil nevertheless has problems:

The problem is that this cornucopia is inhabited by a population enduring social conditions among the worst in the world. Two-thirds do not get enough to eat. Brazil has a higher infant mortality rate than Sri Lanka, a higher illiteracy rate than Paraguay, and worse social indicators than many far poorer African countries. Fewer children finish first-grade school than in Ethiopia, fewer are vaccinated than in Tanzania and Botswana. Thirty-two percent of the population lives below the poverty line. Seven million abandoned children beg, steal and sniff glue on the streets. For scores of millions, home is a shack in a slum, a room in the inner city, or increasingly, a patch of ground under a bridge.

The share of the poorer classes in the national income is "steadily falling, giving Brazil probably the highest concentration of income in the world." It has no progressive income tax or capital gains tax, but it does have galloping inflation and a huge foreign debt, while participating in a "Marshall Plan in reverse," in the words of former President José Sarney, referring to debt payments.

It would only be fair to add that the authorities are concerned with the mounting problem of homeless and starving children, and are trying to reduce their numbers. Amnesty International reports that death squads, often run by the police, are killing street children at a rate of about one a day, while "many more children, forced onto the streets to support their families, are being beaten and tortured by the police" (Reuters, citing AI). "Poor children in Brazil are treated with contempt by the authorities, risking their lives simply by being on the streets," AI alleged. Most of the torture takes place under police custody or in state institutions. There are few complaints by victims or witnesses because of fear of the police, and the few cases that are investigated judicially result in light sentences.[30]

For three-quarters of the population of this cornucopia, the conditions of Eastern Europe are dreams beyond reach, another triumph of the Free World. A UN "Report on Human Development" ranks Brazil, with the world's eighth largest economy, in eightieth place in general welfare (as measured by education, health, hygiene)—near Albania, Paraguay and Thailand. The UN Food and Agriculture Organization (FAO) announced on October 18 that more than 40 percent of the population (almost fifty-three million people) are hungry. The Brazilian Health Ministry estimates that hundreds of thousands of children die of hunger every year.[31]

Recall that these are the conditions that hold on the twenty-fifth anniversary of "the single most decisive victory of freedom in the mid-twentieth century" (Lincoln Gordon, US Ambassador to Brazil at the time)—that is, the overthrow of parliamentary democracy by Brazilian generals backed by the United States, which then praised the "economic miracle" produced by the neo-Nazi National Security State they established. In the months before the generals' coup, Washington assured its traditional military allies of its support and provided them with aid, because the military was essential to "the strategy for restraining left-wing excesses" of the elected Goulart government, Ambassador Gordon cabled the State Department. The US actively supported the coup, preparing to intervene directly if its help was needed for what Gordon described as the "democratic rebellion" of the generals. This "de facto ouster" of the elected president was "a great victory for the free world," Gordon reported, adding that it should "create a greatly improved climate for private investment." US labor leaders demanded their proper share of the credit for the overthrow of the parliamentary regime, while the new government proceeded to crush the labor movement and subordinate poor and working people to the overriding needs of business interests, primarily foreign. Secretary of State Dean Rusk justified US recognition for the regime on the grounds that "the succession there occurred as foreseen by the Constitution," which had just been blatantly violated. The US proceeded to provide ample aid as torture and repression mounted, the relics of constitutional government faded away, and the climate for investors improved under the rule of what Washington hailed as the "democratic forces."[32]

The circumstances of the poor in Brazil continue to regress as austerity measures are imposed on the standard IMF formula in an effort to deal somehow with this catastrophe of capitalism. The same is true in Argentina, where the Christian Democratic Party called on its members to resign from the Cabinet in March 1990 "in order not to validate, by their presence in the government, the anti-popular [economic] measures of the regime." In a further protest over these measures, the Party expelled the current Minister of the Economy. Experts say that the socioeconomic situation has become "unbearable," and that a third of the population lives in extreme poverty.[33]

The fate of Argentina is addressed in a report in the *Washington Post* by Eugene Robinson. One of the ten richest countries in the world at the turn of the century, with abundant resources and great advantages, Argentina is becoming a Third World country, Robinson observes. About one-third of its thirty-one million inhabitants live below the poverty line. Eighteen thousand children die each year before their first birthday, most from malnutrition and preventable disease. The capital, once considered "the most elegant and European city this side of the Atlantic," is "ringed by a widening belt of shantytowns, called *villas miserias,* or 'miseryvilles,' where the homes are cobbled-together huts and the sewers are open ditches." Here too the IMF-style reforms "have made life even more precarious for the poor."

Robinson's article is paired with another entitled "A Glimpse Into the Lower Depths," devoted to a mining town in the Soviet Union. Subtitled "A mining town on the steppes reveals 'the whole sick system'," the article stresses the comparison to capitalist success. The article on Argentina, however, says nothing about any "sick system." The catastrophe in Argentina and the general "economic malaise" in Latin America are attributed vaguely to "economic mismanagement." Again the usual pattern: *their* crimes reveal their evil nature, *ours* are the result of personal failings and the poor human material with which we are forced to work.[34]

David Felix concludes that Argentina's decline results from "political factors such as prolonged class warfare and a lack of national commitment on the part of Argentina's elite," which took advantage of the free-market policies of the murderous military dictatorship. These led to massive redistribution of income towards the wealthy and a sharp fall in *per capita* income, along with a huge increase in debt as a result of capital flight, tax evasion, and consumption by the rich beneficiaries of the system; Reaganomics, in essence.[35]

In oil-rich Venezuela, over 40 percent live in extreme poverty according to official figures, and the food situation is considered "hyper-critical," the Chamber of Food Industries reported in 1989. Malnutrition is so common that it is often not noted in medical histories, according to hospital officials, who warn that "the future is horrible." Prostitution has also increased, reaching the level of about 170,000 women or more, according to the Ministry of Health. The Ministry also reports an innovation, beyond the classic prostitution of women of low income. Many "executive secretaries and housewives and college students accompany tourists and executives during a weekend, earning at times up to [about $150] per contact." Child prostitution is also increasing and is now "extremely widespread," along with child abuse.[36]

Brutal exploitation of women is a standard feature of the "economic miracles" in the realms of capitalist democracy. The huge flow of women from impoverished rural areas in Thailand to service the prostitution industry—one of the success stories of the economic takeoff sparked by the Indochina wars—is one of the many features of the Free World triumph that escape notice.[37] The savage working conditions for young women largely from the rural areas are notorious; *young* women, because few others are capable of enduring these conditions of labor, or survive to continue with it.

Chile under the Pinochet dictatorship is another famous success story. Antonio Garza Morales reports in *Excelsior* that "the social cost which has been paid by the Chilean people is the highest in Latin America," with the number of poor rising from one million after Allende to seven million today, while the population has remained stable at twelve million. Christian Democratic Party leader Senator Anselmo Sule, returned from exile, says that economic growth that benefits 10 percent of the population has been achieved (Pinochet's official institutions agree), but development has not. Unless the economic disaster for the majority is remedied, "we are finished," he adds. According to David Felix, "Chile, hit especially hard in the 1982–84 period, is now growing faster than during the preceding decade of the Chicago Boys," enthralled by the free-market ideology that is, indeed, highly beneficial for some: the wealthy, crucially including foreign investors. Chile's recovery, Felix argues, can be traced to "a combination of severe wage repression by the Pinochet regime, an astutely managed bailout of the bankrupt private sector by the economic team that replaced the discredited Chicago Boys, and access to unusually generous lending by the international financial institutions," much impressed by the favorable climate for business operations.[38]

Environmental degradation is also a severe problem in Chile. The Chilean journal *Apsi* devoted a recent issue to the environmental crisis accelerated by the "radical neoliberalism" of the period following the US-backed coup that overthrew the parliamentary democracy. Recent studies show that about half the country is becoming a desert, a problem that "seems much farther away than the daily poisoning of those who live in Santiago," the capital city, which competes with São Paolo (Brazil) and Mexico City for the pollution prize for the hemisphere (for the world, the journal alleges). "The liquid that emerges from the millions of faucets in the homes and alleys of Santiago have levels of copper, iron, magnesium and lead which exceed by many times the maximum tolerable norms." The lands that "supply the fruits and vegetables of the Metropolitan Region are irrigated with waters that exceed by 1000 times the maximum quantity of coliforms acceptable," which is why Santiago "has levels of hepatitis, typhoid, and parasites which are not seen in any other part of the continent" (one of every three children in the capital has parasites). Economists and environmentalists attribute the problem to the "development model," crucially, its "transnational style," "in which the most important decisions tend to be adopted outside the ambit of the countries themselves," consistent with the assigned "function" of the Third World: to serve the needs of the industrial West.[39]

The fashion is to attribute the problems of Eastern Europe to the "sick system" (quite accurately), while ignoring the catastrophes of capitalism or, on the rare occasions when some problem is noticed, attributing them to any cause *other* than the system that consistently brings them about. Latin American economists are generally ignored, but some of them have been useful for ideological warfare and therefore have attained respectability in the US political culture. One example is Francisco Mayorga, a Yale PhD in economics and the leading economist of the US-backed UNO coalition, who became one of the most respected commentators on Nicaragua because he could be quoted on the economic debacle caused by Sandinista misman-agement. He remained a favorite as he became the economic Czar after the UNO victory in the February 1990 election, though he disappeared when he was removed after the failure of his highly touted recovery policies (which failed, in large part, because of US foot-dragging, the UNO govern-ment being nowhere near harsh and brutal enough for Washington's tastes).

But Mayorga was never quoted on what he actually wrote about the Nicaraguan economy, which is not without interest. His 1986 Yale doctoral dissertation is a study of the consequences of the development model of the US-backed Somoza regime, and the likely consequences of alternative policy choices for the 1980s. He concludes that "by 1978 the economy was on the verge of collapse" because of the "*exhaustion* of the agroindustrial model" and the "monetarist paradigm" that the US favored. This model had led to huge debt and insolvency, and "the drastic downturn of the terms of trade that was around the corner was clearly going to deal a crucial blow to the agroindustrial model developed in the previous three decades," leading "inexorably" to an "economic slump in the 1980s." The immense costs of the US-backed Somoza repression of 1978–9 and the Contra war made the "inexorable" even more destructive. Mayorga estimates capital flight from 1977 to 1979 at $.5 billion, and calculates the "direct economic burden" of war from 1978 to 1984 at more than $3.3 billion. That figure, he points out, is one and a half times the "record GDP level of the country in 1977," a year of "exceptional affluence" because of the destruction of the Brazilian coffee crop, hence regularly used by US propagandists (includ-ing some who masquerade as scholars) as a baseline to prove Sandinista failures. The course of the economy from 1980, Mayorga concludes, was the result of the collapse of the agroindustrial export model, the severe downturn in the terms of trade, and the unbearable burden of the 1978–9 war and then the Contra war (his study ends before the US embargo exacerbated the crisis further). Sandinista policies, he concludes, were ineffective in dealing with the "inexorable" collapse: they "had a favorable impact on output and a negative effect on rural wages and farming profits," favoring industrial profits and redistributing income "from the rural to the urban sector." Had there been "no war and no change in economic regime," his studies show, "the Nicaraguan economy would have entered a sharp slump."[40]

These conclusions being useless or worse, Mayorga's work on the Nicaraguan economy passes into the same oblivion as all other inquiries into the catastrophes of capitalism. The example is noteworthy because of Mayorga's prominence at the very same time, in so far as he could serve a propaganda function.

3. The Fruits of Victory: the Caribbean

Brazil and Chile are not the only countries to have basked in praise for their achievements after US intervention set them on the right course. Another is the Dominican Republic. After the latest US invasion under Lyndon Johnson in 1965, and a dose of death squads and torture, democratic forms were established, and Western commentators have expressed much pride in the peaceful transfer of power—or better, governmental authority, power lying elsewhere. The economy is stagnant and near bankrupt, public services function only intermittently, poverty is endemic, malnutrition is increasing and the standard of living of the poor continues its downward slide. In the capital city, electricity supply is down to four hours a day; water is available for only an hour a day in many areas. Unemployment is rising, the foreign debt has reached $4 billion, the 1989 trade deficit was $1 billion—up from $700 million the year before. Estimates of the number who have fled illegally to the US range up to a million. Without the remittances of Dominicans working in Puerto Rico and on the US mainland—illegally for the most part—"the country could not survive," the London *Economist* reports. US investors, assisted by Woodrow Wilson's invasion and later Johnson's, had long controlled most of the economy. Now foreign investment in seventeen free-trade zones is attracted by fifteen-year tax holidays and average wages of 65 cents an hour. Some "remain upbeat about the Dominican Republic's situation," *South* reports, citing US Ambassador Paul Taylor and offering some objective grounds for his cheerful view of the prospects:

> Optimists point to the political and labour harmony in the Dominican Republic, the substantial pool of cheap workers and the transport, banking and communications services as continuing strong incentives to investors. Indeed, as a Dominican factory manager notes: "Anyone who gets involved in unions here knows that they'll lose their job and won't work in the free trade zone any more."

As in Brazil and elsewhere, the American Institute for Free Labor Development (AIFLD), the AFL–CIO foreign affairs arm supported by the government and major corporations, "has been instrumental in discouraging hostile [sic] union activity in order to help US companies maximise their profits," *South* reports.[41]

Elsewhere in the Caribbean basin we find much the same picture—including Grenada, also liberated by US benevolence, then restored to its proper status (see Chapter 5, p. 162). The US pursued a somewhat different path to ensure virtuous behavior in Jamaica. Upstarts led by the social democrat Michael Manley and his People's National Party (PNP) sought to explore the forbidden path of independent development and social reform in the 1970s, eliciting the usual hostility from the United States and sufficient pressures to achieve an electoral victory for US favorite Edward Seaga, who had pledged to put an end to such nonsense. Seaga's pursuit of free-market principles was lauded by the Reagan Administration, which announced grandly that it would use this opportunity to create a showcase for democracy and capitalism in the Caribbean.[42] Massive aid flowed. USAID spent more on Jamaica than on any other Caribbean program. The World Bank also joined in to oversee and expedite this estimable project. Seaga followed all the rules of the much-admired (and not so new) "trickle-down approach to aid the poor," introducing austerity measures, establishing Free Trade Zones where non-union labor, mostly women, work in sweatshops for miserable wages in foreign-run plants subsidized by the Jamaican government, and generally keeping to the IMF prescriptions.

There was some economic growth, "mainly as a result of laundered 'ganja' dollars from the marijuana trade, increased tourism earnings, lower fuel import costs, and higher prices for bauxite and alumina," NACLA reports. The rest was the usual catastrophe of capitalism, including one of the highest *per capita* foreign debts in the world, collapse of infrastructure, and general impoverishment. According to USAID, by March 1988, along with its "crippling debt burden," Jamaica was a country where economic output was "far below the production level of 1972," "distribution of wealth and income is highly unequal," "shortages of key medical and technical personnel plague the health system," "physical decay and social violence deter investment," and there are "severe deficits in infrastructure and housing." This assessment was made before hurricane Gilbert dealt a further blow.

At this point, Michael Manley, now properly tamed, was granted the right to return to power to administer the ruins, all hope for constructive change having been lost. Manley "is making all the right noises" to reassure the Bank and foreign investors, Roger Robinson, World Bank senior economist for Jamaica, said in a June 1988 pre-election interview. He explained further:

> Five years ago, people were still thinking about "meeting local needs," but not any more. Now the lawyers and others with access to resources are interested in external export investment. Once you have that ingrained in a population, you can't go back easily, even if the PNP and Michael Manley come in again. Now there's an understanding among individuals who save, invest, and develop their careers that capital will start leaving again if the PNP, or even [Seaga's] JLP, intervenes too much.

Returned to office, Manley recognized the handwriting on the wall, outdoing Seaga as an enthusiast for free-market capitalism. The journal of the Private Sector of Jamaica was much impressed with the new signs of maturity. "The old gospel that government should be operated in the interests of the poor is being modified, even if not expressly rejected, by the dawning realization that the only way to help the poor is to operate the government in the interest of the productive!," the journal exulted—here the term "productive" refers not to the people who produce, but to those who manage, control investment, and reap profits. The public sector is "on the verge of collapse," the Private Sector report continues, with schools, health care and other services rapidly declining. But with the "nonsensical rhetoric of the recent past" abandoned, and privatization of everything in sight on the way, there is hope—for "the productive," in the special intended sense.

Manley has won new respect from the important people now that he has learned to play the role of "violin president," in Latin American terminology: "put up by the left but played by the right."[43] The conditions of capital flight and foreign pressures—state, private, international economic institutions—have regularly sufficed to bar any other course.

4. The Fruits of Victory: Asia

Turning elsewhere in the domains of freedom, capitalism, and democracy, we naturally begin with the Philippines, which have been lucky enough to be under the wing of the leader of the Free World for almost a century. The desperate state of Filipinos in the post-Marcos democracy is reviewed in the *Far Eastern Economic Review*, firmly dedicated to economic liberalism and the priorities of the business community, under the heading "Power to the plutocrats." Its reports conclude: "Much of the country's problems now ... seem to be rooted in the fact that the country has had in its entire history no form of social revolution." The consequences of this failure include "the jinxed land reform programme," a failure that "profoundly affects the prognosis for the incidence of poverty" among the 67 percent of poor Filipino families living in rural areas, condemning them to permanent misery, huge foreign debt, "massive capital flight," an increase in severe malnutrition among pre-school children since the Aquino government took power, widespread underemployment, and survival for many on incomes far below government-defined poverty thresholds, "the growth of a virtual society of beggars and criminals," and the rest of the familiar story. Government and academic experts expect things to get considerably worse. For the "rapidly expanding disadvantaged," the only way out is to seek work abroad: "legal and illegal workers from the Philippines now comprise the greatest annual labour exodus in Asia." With social programs abandoned, the only hope is if "the big-business elite, in a situation of little government interference, forego the Philippine elite traditional proclivity towards conspicuous consumption, and instead use profits both for their employees' welfare and to accumulate capital for industrial development."[44]

These conditions can be traced in no small measure to the US invasion at the turn of the century with its vast slaughter and destruction, the long colonial occupation, and the subsequent policies including the postwar counterinsurgency campaign and support for the Marcos dictatorship as long as it was viable. But the Philippines did gain the (intermittent) gift of democracy. In the same business journal, a columnist for the Manila *Daily Globe*, Conrado de Quiros, reflects on this matter under the heading "The wisdom of democracy." He compares the disaster of the Philippines to the economic success story of Singapore under Lee Kuan Yew, whose harsh tyranny is another of those famous triumphs of democracy and capitalism. De Quiros quotes the Singapore Minister of Trade and Industry, Lee's son, who condemns the US model imposed on the Philippines for many flaws, the "worst crime" being that it granted the Filipinos a free press; in his own words, "An American-style free-wheeling press purveyed junk in the marketplace of ideas, which led to confusion and bewilderment, not to enlightenment and truth." With a better appreciation of the merits of fascism, his Singapore government is too wise to fall into this error.[45]

The Americans did introduce a form of democracy, de Quiros continues. However, it "was not designed to make Filipinos free but to make them comfortable with their new chains." It may have given the Filipinos more newspapers, but "it has given them less money with which to buy them. It has made the rich richer," with "one of the world's worst cases of inequity in the distribution of wealth," according to the World Bank. Democracy "was an instrument of colonisation," and was not intended to have substantive content:

> For most Filipinos, American-style democracy meant little more than elections every few years. Beyond this, the colonial authorities made sure that only the candidates who represented colonial interests first and last won. This practice did not die with colonialism. The ensuing political order, which persisted long after independence, was one where a handful of families effectively and ruthlessly ruled a society riven by inequality. It was democratic in form, borrowing as many American practices as it could, but autocratic in practice.

Under Philippine democracy, most of the population is not represented. The politicians are lawyers, wealthy businessmen, or landowners. As the political structure bequeathed to the Philippines by the American occupation was reconstituted after the overthrow of the US-backed dictator by "people power," Gary Hawes writes, "it is only those with money and muscle who can be elected." Candidates are mainly "former elected officials, relatives of powerful political families and/or members of the economic elite," unrepresentative of the rural majority or even "the citizens who had demonstrated to bring down Marcos and who had risked their lives to protect their ballots for Corazon Aquino." There did exist a party (PnB) based on the popular organizations that arose against the dictatorship, with broad support from the peasantry, the labor force, and large reformist sections of the middle class, but it was to have no political role. In the elections, PnB was outspent by the traditional conservative parties by a ratio of up to 20 to 1. Its supporters were subjected to intimidation and threats of loss of jobs, housing, and city licenses. The military presence also served to inhibit PnB campaigning. Interviews with poor farmers and workers revealed a preference for PnB candidates, but a recognition that since the military and the rural elite opposed them, "the next best choice was to take the money or the rewards and vote for the candidates endorsed by the Aquino government."[46]

Under the reconstituted elite democracy, Hawes continues, "the voices of the rural dwellers"—almost two-thirds of the population—"have seldom been heard," and the same is true of the urban poor. The cure for agitation in the countryside is militarization and the rise of vigilantes, leading to a record of human rights violations "as bad as, if not worse than, during the time of Marcos," a 1988 human rights mission reported, with torture, summary executions, and forced evacuations. There is economic growth, but its fruits "have seldom trickled down to the most needy." Peasants continue to starve while paying 70 percent of their crop to the landlord. Agrarian reform is barely a joke. Support for the National Democratic Front (NDF) and its guerrillas is mounting after years of rural organizing.

De Quiros suggests that there has been "substantive democracy in the Philippines—despite colonialism and elite politics. ... This is so because democracy took a life of its own, expressing itself in peasant revolts and popular demand for reforms." It is just this substantive democracy that the United States and its allies are dedicated to repress and contain. Hence the absence of any social revolution of the kind that he and several other commentators in this most respectable business journal see as sorely lacking in the Philippines—though if it can join the club of "capitalist democracies" of the Singapore variety, the tune will probably change.

Meanwhile, Survival International reports that tribal peoples in the Philippines are being attacked by the private army of a logging company, which, in a six-month campaign of terror, has killed and tortured villagers, burned down houses, destroyed rice stores, and driven thousands from their homes. They are also among the many victims of bombing of villages and other practices of the government counterinsurgency campaigns. Appeals to the Aquino government have been ignored. An appeal to the US government, or Western circles generally, cannot be seriously proposed. The same is true in Thailand, where the government announced a plan to expel six million people from forests where it wants to establish softwood plantations.[47]

Miracles of capitalism are also to be found elsewhere in Asia. Charles Gray, executive director of the AFL–CIO's Asian-American Free Labor Institute (noted for its pro-business stance), observes in the *Far Eastern Economic Review* that transnational corporations "generally insist the host government suppress the right of workers to organise and join unions, even when that right is guaranteed in the country's own constitution and laws." The organization that coordinates trade in the Free World (GATT) does not have a single rule that "covers the subsidies that transnational corporations get through pressures on Third World governments to permit 19th century-type exploitation of labour." In Malaysia, "US and other foreign corporations forced the Labour Ministry in 1988 to continue the government's long-standing prohibition of unions in the electronics industry by threatening to shift their jobs and investments to another country." In Bangladesh, con-tractors for the transnationals "discriminate against women and girls by paying them starvation wages as low as 9 US cents an hour." In China's Guangdong province, hailed as one of the miracles of capitalist success in a generally bleak Chinese scene, when the government found that

> the factory of a leading toy manufacturer was engaged in labour law violations—
> such as 14-hour workdays and seven-day workweeks—it approached the managers
> to ask them to respect the law. The managers refused, and said that if they
> were unable to operate the way they wanted they would close their Chinese
> factories and move to Thailand

—where there are no such unreasonable demands.[48]

5. The Fruits of Victory: Africa

The scene in Africa is more awful still. To mention only one small element of a growing catastrophe: a study by the UN Economic Commission for Africa estimates that "South Africa's military aggression and destabilization of its neighbors cost the region $10 billion in 1988 and over $60 billion and *1.5 million lives in the first nine years of this decade*."[49] Meanwhile, unlike the case of Iraq, the US cautiously undertook "quiet diplomacy," recognizing the concerns of the racist regime and the domestic and foreign business interests it fostered. Congress imposed sanctions on South Africa in 1986 over Reagan's veto, but their impact has been limited. The American Com-mittee on Africa reports that only 25 percent of US–South African trade has been affected, and that iron, steel, and (until late 1989) half-finished uranium continued to be imported. After the sanctions were put in place, US exports to South Africa increased from $1.28 billion in 1987 to $1.71 billion in 1989, according to the US Commerce Department. This was an improvement over the reaction to the UN sanctions on Rhodesia, which impelled Congress to pass the Byrd amendment authorizing the import of Rhodesian chrome (in force from 1971 to 1977); "Many nations had covertly been violating the sanctions," Stephen Shalom observes, "but the U.S. became one of only three UN members—the others were [fascist] Portugal and South Africa—to officially violate the sanctions."[50]

The disasters of much of Africa are commonly attributed to "socialism," a term used freely to apply to anything we don't like. But there is an exception, "an island of freewheeling capitalism in a sea of one-party socialist states," Africa correspondent Howard Witt of the conservative *Chicago Tribune* writes. He is referring to Liberia, which, like the Philippines, can attribute its happy state to the fact that it was "America's only toehold on the African continent"—for a century and a half, in this case. Liberia took on special significance during the Cold War years, Witt continues, particularly after President Samuel Doe, a "brutish, nearly illiterate army sergeant . . . seized power in 1980 after disemboweling the previous president in his bed" and proceeded to elevate his fellow tribesmen—4 percent of the population—to a new ruling elite, and to persecute and savagely oppress the rest of the population. The Reagan Administration, much impressed, determined to turn Liberia, like Jamaica, into a showcase of capitalism and democracy. In the first six years of Doe's regime, the US poured military and economic aid into "the backward country," "even as evidence mounted that Doe and his ministers were stealing much of the money," and after he "brazenly stole" the 1985 election, with Washington's approval, in a replay of the Noriega story a year earlier. A "respected expatriate Liberian dissident and former government minister," Ellen Johnson-Sirleaf, says: "At the time, an American official told me bluntly, 'Our strategic interests are more important than democracy'."[51]

The results of the aid are evident, Witt writes: "The soldiers of President Samuel Doe's army wear the uniforms of American GIs as they go about their business murdering Liberian civilians on the streets of the capital, Monrovia," named after President Monroe, and "the bodies of many of the civilian victims are dumped in the morgue at the American-built John F. Kennedy Hospital," where "combat-hardened doctors" say "they have never witnessed such brutality." Monrovia is a death trap, he writes. Those who are not struck down by starvation, cholera, or typhoid try to escape the army or the rebel forces under Charles Taylor, a former Doe aide—or later, those under the command of a breakaway unit led by Prince Johnson.

The results of the US aid became even clearer when reporters entered Monrovia with the African peacekeeping force after Doe was tortured and murdered by Johnson's guerrillas. They found "a bloody legacy" of the "10 years in power" of the US favorite, UPI reporter Mark Huband writes:

piles of bleached bones and skulls, many smashed; "half-clothed, decomposed heaps of flesh ... littered with millions of maggots"; "contorted bodies ... huddled beneath church pews" and "piled up in a dark corner beside the altar"; bodies "rotting into their mattresses"; "a large meeting hall for women and children [where] clothes clung to the skeletons of female and underaged victims."[52]

Not everyone, of course, has suffered in this "island of freewheeling capitalism." For a century and a half, the oligarchy of freed American slaves and their descendants "oppressed and exploited the indigenous population" while "the U.S. looked the other way." And lately, the Reagan favorites did quite well for themselves until their turn came to be dispatched. Others merely benefited, escaping any such unpleasant fate: "U.S. corporations like Firestone and B.F. Goodrich made healthy profits from the expansive Liberian operations," proving that freewheeling capitalism has its virtues.[53] The US built a huge Voice of America transmitter in Liberia, perhaps to broadcast the happy message.

6. The "Unrelenting Nightmare"

The World Health Organization estimates that eleven million children die every year in the world of the Cold War victors ("the developing world") because of the unwillingness of the rich to help them. The catastrophe could be brought to a quick end, the WHO study concludes, because the diseases from which the children suffer and die are easily treated. Four million die from diarrhea; about two-thirds of them could be saved from the lethal dehydration it causes by sugar and salt tablets that cost a few pennies. Three million die each year from infectious diseases that could be overcome by vaccination, at a cost of about $10 a head. Reporting in the London *Observer* on this "virtually unnoticed" study, Annabel Ferriman quotes WHO director-general Hiroshi Nakajima, who observes that this "silent genocide" is "a preventable tragedy because the developed world has the resources and technology to end common diseases worldwide," but lacks "the will to help the developing countries."[54]

The basic story was summarized succinctly by President Yoweri Museveni of Uganda, chairman of the Organization of African Unity. Speaking at the UN conference of the world's forty-one least-developed countries, he called the 1980s "an unrelenting nightmare" for the poorest countries. There was a plea to the industrial powers to more than double their aid to a munificent 0.2 percent of their GNP, but no agreement was reached, the *New York Times* reports, "principally because of opposition from the United States"—as always, proudly defending the "universal values" at the core of "our traditions," which stand in such contrast to "theirs" (see p. 181).[55] The decade was scarcely less of a nightmare elsewhere in the traditional domains of the Free World, apart from "the rich men dwelling at peace within their habitations."

As capitalism and freedom won their Grand Victory, the World Bank reports, the share of the world's wealth controlled by poor and medium-income countries declined from 23 to 18 percent (1980 to 1988). The Bank's 1990 report adds that in 1989, resources transferred from the "developing countries" to the industrialized world reached a new record. Debt-service payments are estimated to have exceeded new flows of funds by $42.9 billion, an increase of $5 billion from 1988; and new funds from the wealthy fell to the lowest level in the decade:[56] in short, Reaganomics and Thatcherism writ large.

These are some of the joys of capitalism that are somehow missing in the flood of self-praise and the encomia to the wonders of our system—of which all of this is a noteworthy component—as we celebrate its triumph. The media and journals are inundated with laments (with an admixture of barely concealed glee) over the sad state of the Soviet Union and its domains, where even a salary of $100 a month enjoyed by the luckier workers is "scandalously high by the niggardly standards of Communism."[57] One will search far, however, for derisive commentary on "the niggardly standards of capitalism" and the suffering endured by the huge mass of humanity who have been cast aside by the dominant powers, long the richest and most favored societies of the world, and not without a share of responsibility for the circumstances of most of the others.

The missing view also unveils a possible future that may await much of Eastern Europe, which has endured many horrors but is still regarded with envy in large parts of the Third World domains of the West that had comparable levels of development in the past, and are no less endowed with resources and the material conditions for satisfying human needs. "Why have the leaders, the media, the citizens of the Great Western Democracies cared long and ardently for the people of Central Europe, but cared nothing for the people of Central America?," correspondent Martha Gellhorn asks:

> Most of them are bone poor, and most of them do not have white skin. Their lives and their deaths have not touched the conscience of the world. I can testify

that it was far better and safer to be a peasant in communist Poland than it is to be a peasant in capitalist El Salvador.

Her question is, unfortunately, all too easy to answer. It has been demonstrated beyond any lingering doubt that what sears the sensitive soul is the crimes of the enemy, not our own, for reasons that are all too obvious and much too uncomfortable to face. The comparison that Gellhorn draws is scarcely to be found in Western commentary, let alone the reasons for it.[58]

As in Latin America, some sectors of Eastern European society should come to share the economic and cultural standards of privileged classes in the rich industrial world that they see across their borders, much of the former Communist Party bureaucracy quite possibly among them. Many others might look to the second Brazil, and its counterparts elsewhere, for a glimpse of a different future, which may come to pass if matters proceed on their present course.

7. Comparisons and their Pitfalls

The chorus of acclaim for the triumph of capitalism delights in comparison of Western and Eastern Europe, deploring the deprivation, suffering, and environmental damage in the regions that have been subjected to Soviet rule. But many in the Third World seem reluctant to join the celebration of victory, even regarding the victims of Soviet tyranny as luckier than they in respects that are far from trivial (see chapter 12, section 1). One reason offered by priests, journalists and others is that the state terror faced on a daily basis by Latin Americans who dare to raise their heads has been qualitatively different from the repression in Eastern Europe in the post-Stalin period, terrible as that was in its own ways; and they do not share our reluctance to see the powerful and systematic influence of the states and corporations of the state capitalist world in establishing and maintaining the grim conditions of their lives. It takes some discipline to avoid seeing these facts.

Another comparison that might be addressed is suggested by the huge flow of capital from Latin America to the United States and the West generally (see pp. 98, 242). Again, the situation in the Soviet satellites was different. One commentator on their affairs, Lawrence Weschler, observes:

Poles, like most Eastern Europeans, have long lived under the delusion that the Soviets were simply bleeding them dry; in fact, the situation has been considerably more complex than that. (The Soviet dominion was in fact that unique historical perversity, an empire in which the center bled *itself* for the sake of its colonies, or rather, for the sake of tranquility in those colonies. Muscovites always lived poorer lives than Varsovians.)

Throughout the region, journalists and others report, shops are better stocked than in the Soviet Union and material conditions are often better. It is widely agreed that "Eastern Europe has a higher standard of living than the USSR," and that while "Latin-Americans claim mainly economic exploitation," "Soviet exploitation of Eastern Europe is principally political and security-oriented" (Jan Triska, summarizing the conclusions of a Stanford University symposium on the USSR in Eastern Europe and the US in Latin America).[59]

In the 1970s, according to US government sources, the Soviet Union provided an $80 billion subsidy to its Eastern European satellites (while their indebtedness to the West increased from $9.3 billion in 1971 to $68.7 billion in 1979). A study at the Institute of International Studies of the University of California (Berkeley) estimated the subsidy at $106 billion from 1974 to 1984. Using different criteria, another academic study reaches the estimate of $40 billion for the same period—omitting factors that might add several billion, they note. When Lithuania was faced with Soviet economic retaliation after its declaration of independence, the *Wall Street Journal* reported that the Soviet subsidy to that country alone might approach $6 billion annually.[60]

Such comparisons cannot simply be taken at face value; complex issues arise, and they have never been properly addressed. The only extensive recent effort to compare the US impact on Latin America with that of the USSR on Eastern Europe, to my knowledge, is the Stanford symposium just cited, but it does not reach very far. Among many striking gaps, the contributors entirely disregard repression and state terror in Latin America and the US role in implementing it. Writing in May 1986, the editor states that "some left-wing forces in Latin America and all dissidents in Eastern Europe have little hope of bringing about substantive changes, either peacefully or through violence." One contributor even takes seriously (though rejecting) the astonishing statement by Mexican writer Octavio Paz in 1985 that it is "monstrous" even to raise the question of comparing US policies with those of the Soviet Union. Most take it as obvious—hence needing no real evidence—that US influence has been disinterested and benign. In fact, this 470-page study contains very little information altogether.[61]

Many questions would arise if such comparisons were to be undertaken in a meaningful way. Contrary to standard conventions (generally followed in the Stanford symposium) it is hardly plausible to regard US security concerns in Latin America as comparable to those of the Soviet Union in Eastern Europe, or even to take seriously the conventional doctrine that security concerns are "probably the greatest factor in shaping US policy toward Latin America" (Robert Wesson, presenting the "historical overview and analysis" for the Stanford symposium). In recent memory, the United States has not been repeatedly invaded and virtually destroyed by powerful enemies marching through Central America. In fact, its authentic security concerns are virtually nil, by international and historical standards. As one participant in the symposium finally concedes, "U.S. national security interests in the Caribbean [as elsewhere in the hemisphere, we may add] have rested on powerful economic investments" (Jiri Valenta)—which is to say that they are termed "security interests" only for purposes of the delusional system. Furthermore, it makes little sense to attribute to the United States greater tolerance for "political-ideological deviations" on the grounds that it does not insist on "the U.S. brand of democracy" and tolerates "authoritarian dictatorships," while the USSR insists on Leninist regimes (Valenta). What the US demands is an economic order geared to its interests; the political form it takes is largely an irrelevance, and it is surely not in question that the US often regards murderous terrorist states quite favorably if they satisfy the operative criteria.[62]

The matter of capital flow is also complex. In the first place, the regional hegemons are not remotely comparable in wealth and economic level, and never have been, so that their role in economic transactions will differ greatly. For another, investment has intricate effects. It can lead to economic growth, benefit certain sectors of the population while severely harming others, lay the basis for independent development or undermine such prospects. The numbers in themselves tell only a small part of the story, and must be complemented by the kind of analysis that has yet to be undertaken in comparing Eastern Europe and Latin America.

It should be evident without further comment that the standard comparison of Eastern to Western Europe, or the Soviet Union to the United States, is virtually meaningless, designed for propaganda, not enlightenment.

Other subordinate and dependent systems have yet a different character. Discussing the rapid economic growth of South Korea and Taiwan after the powerful stimulus given by Vietnam War spending, Bruce Cumings observes that it resumes a process of development begun under Japanese colonialism. Unlike the West, he notes, Japan brought industry to the labor and raw materials rather than vice versa, leading to industrial development under state—corporate guidance, now renewed. Japan's colonial policies were extremely brutal, but they laid a basis for economic development. These economic successes, like those of Singapore and Hong Kong, are no tribute either to democracy or to the wonders of the market; rather, to harsh labor conditions, efficient quasi-fascist political systems, and, much as in Japan, high levels of protectionism and planning by financial-industrial conglomerates in a state-coordinated economy.[63]

Comparison of the former Japanese colonies to the regions under US influence is not common here, but right-wing Japanese are not reluctant to pursue it. Shintaro Ishihara, a powerful figure in the ruling Liberal Democratic Party, which holds a virtual monopoly of political power, contrasts the domains of Japanese influence and control with the Philippines. The countries that were once under Japanese administration are "success stories" from the economic point of view, he writes, while the Philippines are an economic disaster and the "showcase of democracy" is largely an empty form. "Philippine landowners have accumulated incredible power and wealth, siphoning everything from the ordinary people," while "tradition is dismantled" in favor of a shallow and superficial veneer of American culture, "an atrocity—a barbaric act."[64]

This spokesman for right-wing nationalism is plainly not a trustworthy independent source, but there is more than a little truth to what he says.

Comparison of the Latin American economies with those of East Asia is another topic that has rarely been undertaken seriously. Editorials, news reporting, and other commentary commonly allege that the comparison reveals the superiority of economic liberalism, but without providing the basis for that conclusion. It is not easy to sustain, if only because of the radical departures from liberal capitalism in the success stories of Asia. The topic was addressed at a conference on global macroeconomics in Helsinki in 1986.[65] Several contributors observed that the situation is complex, and concluded that the disparities that developed in the 1980s (though not before) are attributable to a variety of other factors—among them the deleterious effects of greater openness to international capital markets in large parts of Latin America, which permitted vast capital flight, as in the Philippines, but not in the East Asian economies, with more rigid controls by government and central banks; and in the free-market miracle of South Korea, by punishment up to the death penalty.[66]

The complexity of the issues that arise is shown in a revealing study of Indian development, in comparison to China and others, by Harvard economist Amartya Sen. He observes that "a comparative study of the experiences of different countries in the world shows quite clearly that countries tend to reap as they sow in the field of investment in health and quality of life." India followed very different policies from China in this regard. Beginning at a comparable level in the late 1940s, India has added about fifteen years to life expectancy, while China added ten or fifteen years beyond that increase, approaching the standards of Europe. The reasons lie in social policy—primarily, the much greater focus on improving nutrition and health conditions for the general population in China, and providing widespread medical coverage. The same was true, Sen argues, in Sri Lanka and probably Vietnam, and in earlier years in Europe as well—where, for example, life expectancy rose rapidly in England and Wales after large-scale public intervention in the distribution of food and health care and expansion of public employment.

But this is not the whole story. In the late 1950s, life expectancy in China plunged for several years to far below that of India because of a huge famine, which took an estimated thirty million lives. Sen attributes the famine to the nature of the Chinese regime, which did not react for three years and may not even have been aware of the scale of the famine because totalitarian conditions blocked information flow. Nothing similar has happened in India, with its pluralist democracy. Nevertheless, Sen calculates, if China's lower mortality rates prevailed in India, there would have been close to four million fewer deaths a year in the mid 1980s. "This indicates that every eight years or so more people in addition die in India—in comparison with Chinese mortality rates—than the total number that died in the gigantic Chinese famine," the worst in the world in this century.

In further confirmation of his thesis, Sen observes that life expectancy in China has suffered a slow decline since 1979, when the new market-oriented reforms were undertaken. Another relevant example is the Indian state of Kerala, long under leftist rule and with "a long history of extensive public support in education, health care, and food distribution." Here, improvement in life expectancy is comparable to China's, though it is one of India's poorer states.[67]

These are all serious and difficult questions, with far-reaching human consequences. The development strategies imposed upon the Third World by Western power, implemented by the international economic institutions or the states and corporations themselves, have enormous effects on the lives of the targeted populations. The record shows plainly enough that the policies that are advocated or enforced by the Western powers, and the confident rhetoric that accompanies them, are guided by the self-interest of those who hold the reins, not by any solid understanding of the economics of development or any serious concern for the human impact of these decisions. Benefits that may accrue to others are largely incidental, as are the catastrophes that commonly ensue.

As the collapsing Soviet system resumes traditional quasi-colonial relations with the West, it is coming to be subjected to the same prescriptions—in part by choice, given the intellectual vacuity that is one of the consequences of decades of totalitarian rule. One Polish critic writes that if the words of the popular Chicago School

> become flesh, this government would be the first in the history of the world to adhere firmly to this doctrine. All developed countries, including those (such as the Federal Republic of Germany) whose governments pay obeisance to the liberal doctrine, apply a wide spectrum of government interventions, such as in resource allocation, in investments, in developing technology, income distribution, pricing, export and import.[68]

If the result is Third World norms, popular resistance is likely to follow. And it is also likely to elicit the classic response by those who uphold our traditional values.

On a visit to Europe a few days before he was assassinated by elite government forces in San Salvador in November 1989, Father Ignacio Ellacuría, rector of the University of Central America, addressed the West on the underlying issues. You "have organized your lives around inhuman values," he said. These values

> are inhuman because they cannot be universalized. The system rests on a few using the majority of the resources, while the majority can't even cover their basic necessities. It is crucial to define a system of values and a norm of living that takes into account every human being.[69]

In our dependencies, such thoughts are subversive and can call forth the death squads. At home, they are sometimes piously voiced, then relegated to the ashcan in practice. Perhaps the last words of the murdered priest deserve a better fate.

Notes

1. White, cited in Schoultz, *National Security and United States Policy*, p. 91. Martín-Baró, see Chapter 12, pp. 386 f.

2. Hockstader, *WP*, June 20, 1990.

3. *Mesoamerica* (Costa Rica), July 1990. Detailed updates are circulated regularly from the Washington office of the Commission, 1359 Monroe Street NE, Washington DC 20017.

4. *Central America Report (CAR)*, Guatemala, November 10, 1989; July 27; April 6; March 2, 1990.

5. AP, *BG*, June 4, 1990, a seventy-five word item, which is more than elsewhere.

6. Editorial, *Tiempo*, July 2, 1990.

7. César Chelala, "Central America's Health Plight," *CSM*, March 22; *CAR*, March 2, 1990.

8. *Latinamerica Press (LP)* (Peru), November 16, 1989.

9. *Excelsior*, October 18, 1989 (*Latin America News Update [LANU]*, December 1989).

10. For a review, see Joshua Karliner, "Central America's Other War," *World Policy Journal*, Fall 1989.

11. Anne Chemin, *Le Monde*, September 21, 1988; *Guardian Weekly*, October 2. Ibid., September 30, 1990. *Tiempo*, August 10, 17, September 19, 1988. Dr Morales, cited by Robert Smith, *Report on Guatemala*, July/August/September 1989 (Guatemala News and Information Bureau, POB 28594, Oakland CA 94604).

12. Ibid.

13. *La Prensa Dominical*, Honduras, July 22, 1990.

14. *CAR*, April 28, 1989. For discussion of these matters, see references of Chapter 12, Note 58.

15. *CAR*, December 1, 1989

16. *Excelsior*, March 24; *LP*, February 15, 1990.

17. Karliner; *CAR*, March 16, 1990. See Douglas R. Shane, *Hoofprints on the Forest: Cattle Ranching and the Destruction of Latin America's Tropical Forests* (ISHI, 1986); Tom Barry and Deb Preusch, *The Soft War* (Grove, 1988); and for background, William H. Durham, *Scarcity and Survival in Central America* (Stanford, 1979).

18. *CAR*, March 16; *Mesoamerica*, March 1990.

19. Elections, *CAR*, January 26, 1990. *LP*, December 7; *CAR*, April 28, July 27; *Excelsior*, April 30; COHA *Washington Report on the Hemisphere*, September 27, 1989. For several examples of repression in the late 1980s of the kind that aroused great fury when reported in Nicaragua, see *Necessary Illusions*, pp. 249, 268; for a much worse case, see *Culture of Terrorism*, p. 243.

20. *Mesoamerica*, September 1990.

21. "Costa Rica: Arming the country of peace," *CAR*, July 27, 1990.

22. Ibid.; COHA, "News and Analysis," August 18, 1988; *Washington Report on the Hemisphere*, September 27, 1989. Selser, *La Jornada* (Mexico), January 23, 1990, citing Arias's *NYT* Op-Ed on January 9.

23. Editorial, *Miami Herald*, July 31, 1990.

24. Oscar Altimir, World Bank Staff Working Paper No. 522 (World Bank 1982), cited by Schoultz, *National Security and United States Policy*, p. 75. Soares, Carl Hartman, AP, November 7, 1989. CEPAL, *Excelsior* (Mexico), December 27, 1989; *LANU*, February 1990. World Bank, Ed McCullough, AP, December 11, 1989. Felix, "Latin America's Debt Crisis," *World Policy Journal*, Fall 1990.

25. *Excelsior*, March 3, 1990; November 11, 1989 (*LANU*, May, January, 1990).

26. *Excelsior*, August 19, July 1, 1990; *LANU*, October, September 1990.

27. Maude Barlow, chairperson of Council of Canadians, *Toronto Globe & Mail*, November 5, 1990.

28. E.G. Vallianatos, *Fear in the Countryside* (Ballinger, 1976).

29. Evans, *Dependent Development* (Princeton, 1979) p. 4. *Veja*, November 1; *Excelsior*, November 3, 1989 (*LANU*, December 1989).

30. *South*, November 1989. Reuters, *NYT*, September 6, 1990.

31. Mario de Carvalho Garnero, chairman of Brasilinvest Informations and Telecommunications,

O Estado de São Paulo, August 8 (*LANU*, September 1990); *Latin America Commentary*, October 1990.

32. Phyllis R. Parker, *Brazil and the Quiet Intervention, 1964* (University of Texas, 1979), pp. 58 ff., 80 ff., 103 ff. See also Jan Knippers Black, *United States Penetration of Brazil*; and Leacock, *Requiem for Revolution*. See Black, ch. 6, on the role of US labor leaders in the demolition of the Brazilian labor movement, and their pride in bringing about "the revolution."

33. *Excelsior*, March 7 (*LANU*, May 1990).

34. *WP Weekly*, October 28, 1990. For a very similar example, see Avi Chomsky, *Lies of Our Times*, November 1990, commenting on a *New York Times* analogue: paired articles, one deploring the failures of the sick Communist system in Romania and heralding the new hopes with the transition to a free market, the other describing the plight of a middle-class Argentinian family, with no reasons given apart from alleged *failure* to follow free-market policies.

35. Felix; Guido Di Tella and Rudiger Dornbusch, *The Political Economy of Argentina, 1946–1983* (Pittsburgh, 1989), cited by A. Chomsky.

36. *Excelsior*, March 7; AFP, *Excelsior*, February 26, 1990 (*LANU*, May 1990).

37. See Pasuk Phongpaichit, *From Peasant Girls to Bangkok Masseuses*, International Labor Office (ILO), Geneva, 1982.

38. *Excelsior*, December 17, 1989; *LANU*, February 1990; Felix.

39. *Apsi*, Chile, July 1990 (*LANU*, September 1990).

40. Mayorga, *The Nicaraguan Economic Experience, 1950–1984: Development and exhaustion of an agroindustrial model*, Yale University PhD thesis, 1986. See *Barricada Internacional*, April 29, 1990, for relevant discussion.

41. John Craney, *The Times of the Americas*, March 7; *Economist*, August 25; Terry McCoy, *CSM*, May 15; *South*, April 1990. See Chapter 5, pp. 162 f. For more on the aftermath of Johnson's invasion, see *Political Economy of Human Rights*, vol. I, ch. 4, sec. 4.

42. See "Jamaica: Leveraged Sellout," NACLA *Report on the Americas*, February 1990, from which the material that follows is drawn.

43. Martin Needler, *The Problem of Democracy in Latin America* (Lexington 1987), p. 136.

44. Rigoberto Tiglao, Margot Cohen, *FEER*, July 12, 1990.

45. De Quiros, *FEER*, November 2, 1989.

46. Hawes, "Aquino and Her Administration: A View from the Countryside," *Pacific Affairs*, Spring 1989.

47. Survival International Urgent Action Bulletin, May 1990; *News*, February 1990.

48. Charles Gray, executive director of the Asian-American Free Labor Institute, *FEER*, September 13, 1990. See "The Guangdong Dynamo," *South*, November 1990, reviewing Ezra Vogel, *One Step Ahead in China: Guangdong under Reform* (Harvard, 1989).

49. UPI, *BG*, October 14, 1989 (my emphasis).

50. Hans Schattle, "Loopholes cut impact of US sanctions law," *BG*, January 26, 1990. On Reaganite support for South Africa under the guise of "constructive engagement," see Bernard Magubane, "Reagan and South Africa," *Transafrica Forum*, Spring–Summer 1989. Shalom, *Z Magazine*, October 1990.

51. Witt, "U.S. fingerprints—not heart—are all over Liberia," *Chicago Tribune*, August 22, 1990.

52. *BG*, October 11, 1990.

53. On the US government role in Firestone's Liberian investments, motivated in part by concern over Britain's dominance of rubber production and restrictive practices, see Stephen Krasner, *Defending the National Interest* (Princeton, 1978), pp. 98 f.

54. Ferriman, *Observer*, October 1, 1989. Merle Bowen, *Fletcher Forum*, Winter 1991.

55. Reuters, *BG*, September 5; Steven Greenhouse, *NYT*, 1990.

56. *CAR*, October 5; *Financial Times*, September 17, 1990.

57. Francis X. Clines, *NYT*, July 30, 1990.

58. Gellhorn, "Invasion of Panama." For extensive evidence on the reaction to comparable crimes of our enemies and our own, see *Political Economy of Human Rights, Manufacturing Consent, Necessary Illusions*; Edward Herman, *The Real Terror Network* (South End, 1982).

59. Weschler, "Poland," *Dissent*, Spring 1990; Triska, "Introduction," in Triska, ed., *Dominant Powers and Subordinate States: The United States in Latin America and the Soviet Union in Eastern Europe* (Duke, 1986).

60. Raymond Garthoff, *Détente and Confrontation*, p. 499. M. Marrese and J. Vanous, *Soviet Subsidization of Trade with Eastern Europe* (California, 1983); P. Marer and K. Poznanski, "Costs of Domination, Benefits of Subordination," in Triska; Peter Gumbel, "Gorbachev Threat Would Cut Both Ways," *WSJ*, April 17, 1990.

61. Triska, p. 11; Paz, cited by Jeffrey Hughes, p. 29.

62. Wesson, Valenta, in Triska, pp. 63, 282.

63. On these matters, see particularly Amsden, *Asia's Next Giant*; and for some recent reflections on Taiwan and Japan, Carl Goldstein, Bob Johnstone, *FEER*, May 3, May 31, 1990. Cumings, "The origins and development of the Northeast Asian political economy," *International Organization* 38.1, Winter 1984.

64. Akio Morita and Shintaro Ishihara, *The Japan That Can Say No* (Konbusha, Tokyo), translation distributed privately, taken from *Congressional Record*, November 14, 1989, E3783-98.

65. Banuri, *No Panacea* (see Chapter 1, Note 19).

66. Amsden, "East Asia's Challenge" (Chapter 1, Note 19).

67. Sen, "Indian Development: Lessons and Non-Lessons," *Daedalus*, vol. 118 of the *Proceedings of the American Academy of Arts and Sciences*, 1989. For further details on the Kerala exception, see Richard Franke and Barbara Chasin, *Kerala: Radical Reform As Development in an Indian State* (Institute for Food & Development Policy, Food First Development Report No. 6, October 1989).

68. Mieczyslaw Mieszczanowski, *Polityka*, December 16, 1989, cited by Abraham Brumberg, *Foreign Affairs*, "America and the World," 1989–90.

69. *Envío* (Managua), May 1990.

EIGHT

The Agenda of the Doves: 1988

THE basic contours of domestic and foreign policy are determined by institutional structures of power and domination. Since these are stable over long periods, policies vary little, reflecting the perceived interests and shared understanding of those whose domestic privilege confers power. There is a range of tactical choices falling within these narrow bounds. This consensus is articulated by "experts" in the sense candidly defined by Henry Kissinger, a master in the art: one qualifies as an "expert," he explains, by "elaborating and defining" the consensus of one's constituency "at a high level." In practice, the "expert" is the loyal and useful servant of those who hold the reins of power.[1]

As for public opinion, it is considered a threat to order and good government. The reason lies in the "ignorance and superstition of the masses" and "the stupidity of the average man," with the result that "the common interests very largely elude public opinion entirely, and can be managed only by a specialized class whose personal interests reach beyond the locality" (Harold Lasswell, Reinhold Niebuhr, and Walter Lippmann, respectively). The "specialized class" include the "experts" in the Kissingerian sense, articulating the "common interests"—otherwise known as "the national interest."

Presidential transitions commonly elicit commentary on the agenda for the future, thus revealing the bounds of elite consensus. We focus here on the liberal-dove extreme as it was articulated at the end of the Reagan

era in 1988, a picture that offers the best case for those who look forward
to a "kindler, gentler" New World Order.

1. The Common Interests: 1980

In the aftermath of the Vietnam War, the common interests were to overcome the "crisis of democracy" that arose at home with the awakening
of the ignorant masses, to reverse the declining fortunes of US business
in the face of international competition and lowered profitability, and to
overcome the threat of Third World "ultranationalism" that responds to
domestic concerns and popular pressures rather than the transcendent needs
of the rich industrial societies. The common interests therefore required
an attack on labor and the welfare system, expansion of the public subsidy
to high-technology industry through the standard Pentagon funnel and other
measures to enrich the wealthy, a more aggressive foreign policy, and domestic propaganda to whip the ignorant masses into line in fear for their
lives. Such policy proposals were advanced by the Carter Administration,
then implemented under Reagan; military spending, for example, was in
general accord with Carter Administration projections apart from the shape
of the curve, a brief propaganda success at the outset having been exploited
to accelerate spending, which then leveled off. Throughout the period,
the public continued its long-term drift towards support for New Deal-style
welfare state measures, while in articulate opinion the "L word" ("liberal")
followed the "S word" ("socialist") into disgrace and oblivion, and government policy, with general bipartisan support, implemented the agenda of
the powerful.

The common interests were outlined by the experts as state management
shifted from Carter to the Reaganites, committed to the use of state power
as an instrument of privilege. In the domain of international policy, a perceptive analysis by Robert Tucker in *Foreign Affairs* gave a foretaste of what
was to come on the eve of the inauguration.[2] The costs of the Vietnam
War had compelled a temporary abandonment of the postwar policy of
containment in favor of détente, he observed, but now a more activist
foreign policy was required for a "resurgent America."

Tucker distinguished between "needs" and "wants." Domination of the
oil-producing regions of the Middle East is a "need"; therefore we should
be prepared to use force to bar threats arising "from developments indigenous
to the Gulf" that might endanger our "right of access" or our "economic

well-being and the integrity of [the nation's] basic institutions." Turning
from "the realm of necessity," Tucker identified a second major area where
forceful intervention was in order: Central America, where we have only
"wants," not "needs." Our right to satisfy our "wants" in this region is
conferred by history: "We have regularly played a determining role in making
and unmaking governments, and we have defined what we have considered
to be the acceptable behavior of governments." Thus "reasons of pride
and historical tradition" confer upon us the authority to ensure that "radical
movements or radical regimes must be defeated" while "right-wing governments will have to be given steady outside support, even, if necessary, by
sending in American forces." Such intervention should be relatively costless
for us, so the liberal counterargument is voided, he argued.

Tucker feared that "the prevailing public mood" might permit only the
halfway measures of "moderate containment" and impede the proper pursuit
of our "wants." He therefore recommended the conventional appeal to
"security interests" to manufacture consent to these imperatives; as events
were to show, the refractory public was less malleable than he had anticipated.
Meanwhile Jeane Kirkpatrick derided the idea that "forceful intervention
in the affairs of another nation is impractical and immoral," while the editors
of the *New Republic* deplored Carter's "failure to defend the capitalist democratic idea" and his "moralistic excesses," urging military intervention if
necessary to rescue the ruling killers in El Salvador, and preference for
a Somoza over the Sandinistas if these are the only realistic alternatives.[3]
The bloody onslaught on Central America ensued.

2. The Common Interests: 1988

As the Reagan term drew to an end, the common interests were perceived
somewhat differently. It was clearly necessary to face the costs of Reaganite
military Keynesianism and refrain from writing "hot checks for $200 billion
a year" to create the illusion of prosperity, as vice-presidential candidate
Lloyd Bentsen phrased the perception of conservative business elements
in his acceptance speech at the Democratic convention. State-directed international terrorism (the celebrated "Reagan Doctrine") is also perceived as
too costly to us, hence dubious practice. Correspondingly, there was a tendency in the later Reagan years to favor détente over confrontation, economic
and ideological warfare over outright terror. Inflammatory rhetoric also,
predictably, gave way to more statesmanlike tones.

Still, it is understood that we must keep up our guard. Editor H.D.S. Greenway of the liberal *Boston Globe* cites a Cavafy poem portraying "a classical kingdom incapacitated by the imminent arrival of barbarians who, of course, threaten civilization itself."[4] We are in the same position: "For more than 40 years, the United States has braced its walls to keep barbarians at bay." A critic of Reaganite excesses, Greenway warns that we should beware "lest the buttresses become a substitute for strategy. . . . The perceived necessity of standing up to communism in Indochina did more damage to our domestic tranquility than anything since World War II"—also harming the "tranquility" of others, as the former Saigon bureau chief of *Time-Life* is well aware, but does not remind us. "The deficit we incurred in order to build our defenses in the 1980s may have similar repercussions in the 1990s"; repercussions of this defensive stance in Central America and elsewhere likewise pass unnoticed. Today, thanks to Gorbachev's initiatives and the success of the Reagan Administration in "keeping up the pressure and making it hot for Soviet adventurism," new opportunities are open to us. While "the Soviet Union under Mikhail Gorbachev may not be exactly suing for peace," nevertheless the INF Treaty was signed, "the Soviet fleet is assuming a more defensive and less aggressive posture than before," and Gorbachev is "now talking about reducing Soviet troops in Eastern Europe." But "letting down our guard is not the answer and might tempt the Soviets into seeking advantages instead of accommodations with us." Greenway noted approvingly that Democratic presidential candidate Michael Dukakis was "moving right" on these issues, taking the position that these new opportunities "require a tough, pragmatic step-by-step effort" to test the possibility that the barbarians at the walls might at last agree to limit their onslaught against civilization itself, thanks to our steadfast defense of virtue.

That is the liberal view. The conservative stance is expressed in an accompanying report by columnist David Wilson from South Africa under the headline "Despite the odds, South Africa survives." The South African White community, he writes,

> have built a society of authentic grandeur in a country of great comfort and physical beauty and long-term potential for the creation of even more wealth. They know this and are proud of it. And they cannot see why they should commit cultural and economic suicide and bring all this down just to appease the fantasies of drug-drenched American undergraduates and mendacious politicians.

Across the spectrum, it is agreed that the task of keeping the barbarians at bay falls on our shoulders. The world economy may be tripolar, but there is only one tough guy on the street to keep order when trouble brews, a stance only reinforced by the later Gulf crisis, with its more explicit call for the US to be "the world's cop"—or, more accurately, the gunman who makes sure that people know their place—while others pay for the service.

Within the foreign domains defended by American power, the common interests also regularly "elude public opinion entirely," so that disciplinary action is required, as in Central America in the past decade. But in 1988 the measures employed seemed only partially successful. Though tens of thousands were slaughtered and this traditional domain of US influence was plunged still more deeply into misery and suffering, deluded natives persist in their resistance, leading to fears that US efforts may have failed. In the case of Nicaragua, the hawks feared that we might abandon the cause, while doves responded that our efforts "to force the Sandinista revolution into the American democratic mold" may not be worth "the risk" (John Oakes) and that Nicaragua may be "beyond the reach of our good intentions" (Jefferson Morley).[5] And in El Salvador, the "moderate center," marching towards reform and democracy under our tutelage while seeking to stem the terrorism of the left and ultra-right, was facing collapse, though ARENA, the party of the death squads, still offers prospects for our benevolence, as do the "fledgling democracies" of Guatemala and Honduras. These too are doctrinal truths.

Throughout the Reagan years, the general public at home also proved unmanageable, sufficiently so to drive the government underground to clandestine terror. Although the specialized class performed their function, the ignorant masses were never adequately tamed.

3. The Freedom to Act Responsibly

As in 1980, it is worthwhile attending carefully to the words of the experts as the new Administration took charge in 1988, particularly the liberal doves who set the limits of permissible dissent, in effect announcing: "Thus far, and no further." As amply documented elsewhere,[6] throughout the Reagan years the media allowed virtually no challenge to the project of "establishing democracy" in the US-backed terror states of Central America and "restoring democracy" in Nicaragua, a "noble cause" even if the means were flawed in the latter case because the proxy forces attacking Nicaragua proved to be an "imperfect instrument." Later assessments rarely depart from these doctrinal conditions.

An enlightening perspective is provided by political scientist Robert Pastor, director of Latin American and Caribbean Affairs on the National Security Council through the Carter years, in a valuable study of US policy towards Nicaragua.[7] The basic "question of substance" that he raises is whether it is "possible for a powerful, idealistic nation like the United States and small, poor nations on its periphery to establish fair and respectful relationships." His policy proposals have to do with "ways in which future succession crises and revolutions could be managed more effectively by the United States"; the role of "manager" is assumed, along with the principle that "U.S. interventionism" had been "almost always undertaken with good intentions."

There has hardly been a figure in the political or ideological system more committed to liberal values and avoidance of forceful means, so Pastor's perceptions gain particular interest in assessing the prospects for a New World Order. Pastor is highly critical of the Reaganite effort to "promote democracy in Nicaragua" by supporting the Contras. He rejects the common belief that the Sandinistas alone are to blame for the tensions and conflict. Rather, he sees the problem as one of "mutual obsessions" on the part of Managua and Washington: "both governments were insecure and distrusted each other so completely that they were unable to consider any way to influence the other except by force."

By recognizing "mutual obsessions" and "insecurity" on both sides, Pastor stakes out a position at the far-left extreme of the admissible spectrum, opposed to the dominant view that the Sandinistas alone bear responsibility for the violence and suffering of these years. On similar grounds, President Carter held that we owe the Vietnamese no debt because "the destruction was mutual." In contrast, those who are not given to his "moralistic excesses" (p. 255) assign sole responsibility to Hanoi and its Vietcong minions (or their masters in the Kremlin and Beijing) for the "mutual destruction."

Despite the sharing of responsibility, the blame for the reliance on force by Nicaragua and the United States "to influence the other" falls primarily on the Sandinistas, Pastor holds. Because of Sandinista "preconceptions of imperialism, the United States was limited in its ability to influence them positively"—for example, to influence them to accept negotiations, which they "viewed . . . as a sign of weakness" (and in reality regularly advocated, while the US consistently ruled out these and other peaceful means, unattractive to a contestant who is politically weak though militarily and economically strong),

Sandinista responsibility goes still deeper, Pastor continues:

> By calling their opponents class enemies and mercenaries, the Sandinistas have precluded a dialogue that could permit them to negotiate an exit from their war and their national predicament. Instead, the harder they fight, the further they move from their original aims. The Sandinistas sought independence, but they have been forced to become more dependent on the Soviet Union. They sought to build a new nation, but they have turned their nation into an army. They sought to improve the quality of life for the poor, but it is the poor who are fighting and dying. The important advances made at the beginning of the revolution in health care and literacy and their commendable efforts at land reform have been jeopardized by the militarization of the country and the diversion of scarce resources to the war.

Thus, while the Reaganites overreacted to Sandinista provocations, nevertheless the responsibility for the virtual demolition of Nicaragua falls primarily on the Sandinistas, because of their verbal denunciation of the domestic opposition. Such harsh treatment of dissidents is deeply offensive to the United States. To measure the depth of this concern, we need only reflect upon the reaction of the Carter and Reagan administrations to what was happening in El Salvador and Guatemala during the same years, or the treatment of dissident opinion in the United States itself during the first and second World Wars.[8]

A second cause for the conflict, Pastor continues, was the support of the Sandinistas for those driven to the hills by US-backed terror in El Salvador. Reacting with excessive zeal to this crime, the US produced "the Reagan Doctrine on national liberation [which] came to resemble the Sandinistas' 'revolution without borders'." This last reference is a tribute to one of the great achievements of Reaganite Agitprop ("public diplomacy"): a speech by Tomás Borge, in which he emphasized that Nicaragua would *not* try to export its revolution but rather hoped to be a model for others, was brilliantly converted by US commissars into a threat to conquer the hemisphere ("a revolution without borders")—a propaganda coup so useful that it remained quite immune to the exposures from the first days of these conscious State Department lies, and has by now been established as virtual official history.[9]

In short, plainly it is their fault, however improper the obsessive Reaganite response after the forthcoming Carter years. In those better days, Somoza's

Nicaragua was a friend, and remained one of the highest *per capita* recipients of US aid in Latin America—including military aid, because, as the AID mission explained in 1977, Somoza was a valued ally and "U.S. investment is welcomed in Nicaragua's developing free enterprise economy." "As late as May 1979," Walter LaFeber observes, "two months before Somoza fled, the United States supported his request for a $66 million loan from the IMF," and shortly after, the White House "declared the Guard had to be kept to 'preserve order'" while "at that moment Somoza's troops were dive-bombing slums, murdering unarmed people in the streets, and looting the cities, . . . killing thousands of women and children."[10]

Reviewing the Carter years, Pastor makes it clear that no thought was given to displacing Somoza until the tyrant had become "indefensible" in the face of internal opposition so broad as to include the conservative business community, the natural US allies. "Somoza's decision to strike at the moderate opposition" in September 1978, including the arrest of the far-right corporate manager Adolfo Calero and other business leaders, "was one of the major factors motivating the United States to review its previous policy of strict noninterference in internal affairs." The fate of the poor at his hands had elicited no such review.

The US then sought to ease Somoza out—but, as Pastor makes clear, always on the condition that his National Guard, which had been attacking the population "with the brutality a nation usually reserves for its enemy," remain intact. In November 1978, the Policy Review Committee of the National Security Council "emphasized again that the unity of the Guard was an important objective for U.S. policy. . . . There was no disagreement on this latter point," he writes, "as everyone recognized that a post-Somoza government that lacked a firm military base would be overrun by the [Sandinista] FSLN."[11]

As the policy of sustaining "Somocismo without Somoza" collapsed, the objective remained to support the "democrats" against the Sandinistas. A meeting of June 29, three weeks before the end, "was the first time in a year of NSC meetings that anyone had suggested the central U.S. objective was something other than preventing a Sandinista victory"; efforts to maintain the National Guard and exclude the Sandinistas from power had by then collapsed after the refusal of the "moderates," including the business association COSEP, to go along with the US plan. Carter doves then sought "to moderate the FSLN" through military training and economic aid, classic means of control. When the US-backed regime collapsed, Carter offered economic aid, mostly to the private sector, with the enthusiastic support of business lobbyists, "including the Council of the Americas, which represented 80 percent of U.S. businesses with investments in Latin America."[12]

Meanwhile policymakers weighed such "tough questions" as whether to support an October 1980 coup attempt by "a group of moderate civilians" led by "the young and dynamic president of the Union of Nicaraguan Agricultural Producers," Jorge Salazar—a question put to rest when Salazar was killed in a confrontation with security forces. And the Administration remained "unaware" when National Guard officers including Enrique Bermúdez (later Contra commander) met with Somoza lobbyist congressman John Murphy and held a press conference in Washington in August 1979, warning of the threat of Communism and meeting to prepare plans to overthrow the Sandinistas. Presumably, it also remained "unaware" when the Argentine military regime sent advisers to train ex-Guardsmen in Honduras for the attack against Nicaragua a year later. Sandinista transgressions then set the mutual reliance on force on its inevitable course, according to Pastor's account.

Pastor calls for an end to "the resulting relationship of counterproductive policies and strident name-calling." He endorses the position of the "moderates" who are "interested in democracy," specifically Ramiro Gurdián, the leader of the pro-US business opposition (other qualifications as a "moderate democrat" are not offered), who calls for "reality" in place of "mutual obsession."

Pastor holds that the United States has never been motivated primarily by "a desire to extract resources or to implant a political philosophy, although the history of U.S. policy in Central America is replete with examples of both"; rather, by fear. This is perhaps "an unseemly fear," but nevertheless one that is quite real: "the fear that a hostile group could come to power and ally with a rival of the United States"—what we bitterly denounce as the "Brezhnev Doctrine" when advanced by the enemy, which, perhaps, has security concerns in Eastern Europe approaching ours in Central America, in the light of history.

Pastor's basic thesis is straightforward, and a clear expression of political opinion at the left-dove dissident extreme:

> The United States did not want to control Nicaragua or the other nations in the region, but it also did not want to allow developments to get out of control. It wanted Nicaraguans to act independently, *except* when doing so would affect U.S. interests adversely. [Original emphasis]

In short, Nicaragua and other countries should be free—free to do what we want them to do; they should choose their own course independently, as long as their choice conforms to US interests. If they use the freedom we accord them unwisely, we have every right to respond in self-defense, though opinions vary as to the proper tactical choices.

Note that the conception of freedom and independence corresponds closely to liberal doctrine concerning the domestic population, who must also be free to ratify the decisions of their betters, but not to choose unwisely out of failure to comprehend the common interests that lie beyond their limited grasp. One should appreciate the intensity of the concern that the ignorant masses might choose a path that is not laid out for them by their betters.

Another example, pertinent here, is provided by a declassified National Intelligence Estimate of July 26, 1955, on "probable developments in Guatemala" after the successful CIA coup of 1954 that terminated Guatemala's ten-year experiment in capitalist democracy—or, as the intelligence analysts prefer to put it, after "the Arbenz regime collapsed in June 1954" when army leaders, "concerned at his tolerance of Communists in the government," forced Arbenz to resign.[13] US intelligence detected an impressive commitment of the US-imposed Castillo Armas regime to "democratic forms and practices, to land reform, to the development of a modern economy, and to the protection of a free labor movement and social gains"; the evidence is that democratic forms were dismantled by violence and most of the population was disenfranchised, land reform was reversed, "the Guatemalan economy weakened considerably following the fall of Arbenz," the labor movement was "virtually destroyed" and "rural groups are having even more difficulty in obtaining favorable government action" with the destruction of peasant organizations and the denial of "the right to organize," while the social gains of the democratic decade were abolished. Equally impressive was the fact, explained by Assistant Secretary Holland, that Castillo Armas "led the first liberation movement ever to free a nation which had fallen captive to international Communism" (in a country where "there were almost certainly no more than 4,000, and perhaps substantially fewer, Communists . . . at the height of Arbenz's power").

Nevertheless, despite these favorable developments, some problems still remained. One problem was that "Most politically conscious Guatemalans believe that the US planned and underwrote the 1954 revolution," an unacceptable insight into the reality that must be concealed even in an internal intelligence analysis. "A keen sense of nationalism, at times verging on the irrational, colors Guatemalan politics. There is a strong tendency to attribute

Guatemala's backwardness to foreign investors, especially those from the US"—who had been prime movers in the unmentionable CIA operation. "Even the most pro-US elements in the area are not immune to this type of extreme nationalism"—the "low level of intellectualism" of the people of Guatemala constantly deplored by the CIA, for which no cure has yet been found.[14]

No less serious was "the heritage of the revolution of 1944." "Many Guatemalans are passionately attached to the democratic-nationalist ideals of the 1944 revolution," particularly to "the social and economic programs initiated by the Arévalo and Arbenz regimes." During these years of excessive democracy, "the social and economic needs of labor and the peasantry were articulated and exploited by the small Communist leadership" who "were able to promote measures which appeared to meet some of the aspirations of these groups," including "considerable progress in the organization of urban and rural unions" and "inducing the government to expropriate large tracts of land for distribution among the landless" in a successful agrarian reform.

Though these strange delusions are held by "many Guatemalans," including workers and peasants and even the political class and pro-US elements, nevertheless "there are probably not over 200,000 Guatemalans who are more than marginally politically conscious." And of this tiny minority, "few understand the processes and responsibilities of democracy," so that "responsible democratic government is therefore difficult to achieve."

Once again, the benevolence of the US government is thwarted by the "stupidity of the average man." And subsequent history reveals how Guatemala too remained "beyond the reach of our good intentions." It is not easy to manage democracy in the dependencies when the ignorant masses fail to comprehend their responsibilities and fall "out of control." These problems have bedeviled us for generations. They are not likely to disappear.

This National Intelligence Estimate is typical of the genre in the scrupulous evasion of unwanted fact, the easy tolerance of self-contradiction, and the parroting of ideological pieties in a manner that we would regard as comical in the case of some official enemy. The editors of the government publication (*Foreign Relations of the United States*) in which it appears introduce it with the observation that "National Intelligence Estimates (NIEs) were high-level interdepartmental reports presenting authoritative appraisals of vital foreign policy problems," carefully drafted, discussed and revised by the CIA and other agencies represented on the Intelligence Advisory Committee, and "circulated under the aegis of the CIA to the President, appropriate officers of cabinet level, and the National Security Council." An important function of intelligence, as of the specialized class generally, is to construct a framework of illusion that protects decision-makers and other influential elite sectors from awareness of the meaning of what they are doing, so that they can carry out their necessary tasks—articulated with brutal clarity when necessary—with no compunction and a sense of rectitude. It is not easy to man the ramparts in defense against the barbarians on all sides, and those who bear the burden need all the help they can get.

In addressing the ignorant masses, in contrast, the illusions suffice, and the parallel articulation of actual policy goals must be carefully suppressed. We thus find a characteristic difference between the "public diplomacy" conducted by the media and much of scholarship, on the one hand, and the internal record, on the other. Both spin the required web of illusion, but the parallel analysis of actual policy concerns and goals is restricted to the internal record in a properly functioning ideological system.

4. Containment without Rollback

During the Carter years, the policy-planning spectrum ran from the hawkish National Security Adviser Zbigniew Brzezinski to the liberal doves: Pastor at the National Security Council and Viron Vaky, Assistant Secretary of State for Inter-American Affairs. Brzezinski's principle was: "we have to demonstrate that we are still the decisive force in determining the political outcomes in Central America and that we will not permit others to intervene."[15] In the liberal journal *Foreign Policy,* Vaky offered his assessment of the Reagan years and his proposals for "positive containment in Nicaragua," avoiding the Reaganite fallacies.[16] Let us consider the alternative promoted by the doves.

Vaky sees two "realistic" policy choices: "containment" or "rollback." The violent "rollback" option of the Reaganites has failed, so we must seek "alternatives for containing the Sandinista revolution." "The principal arguments" for supporting the Contras

> have been that a longer war of attrition will so weaken the regime, provoke such a radical hardening of repression, and win sufficient support from Nicaragua's discontented population that sooner or later the regime will be overthrown by popular revolt, self-destruct by means of internal coups or leadership splits, or simply capitulate to salvage what it can.

Vaky suggests no qualms concerning these aims, but he does see a problem.

The Contras "have been unable to elicit significant political support within Nicaragua even with declining Sandinista popularity" and have not "registered any significant military successes"—a most remarkable fact, incidentally, given the historically unprecedented advantages afforded them by their superpower sponsor.[17] It is, furthermore, a fact that can neither be acknowledged nor discussed within the US ideological institutions. The media and assorted commentary cannot, for example, ask why it is unnecessary for the KGB to fly daily supply flights with arms, food and equipment to keep the Salvadoran rebels in the field, while the Contras break for their Honduran sanctuaries when deprived of a regular flow of equipment and supplies on a scale, and of a quality, that no authentic guerrillas in history could have even imagined, and would have quickly been dispersed, all agree, had the US not introduced military force and threatened further retaliation to protect them in their sanctuaries at the border.

To the extent that the Administration had a diplomatic objective, Vaky continues, it has been "a negotiation on the terms and schedule under which the Sandinistas would turn over power." But "however reasonable or idealistic these demands may seem," they are not realistic, and alternatives must be considered. Note that it is "reasonable and idealistic" to demand that the elected government should "turn over power" to US proxy forces that "have been unable to elicit significant political support." Again we see clearly displayed the true meaning of "democracy" in the political culture.

The preferred alternative must rest on the recognition that "none of the contending forces in Central America, including the United States, can impose a negotiated settlement entirely satisfactory to itself"; that the U.S. should be one of the "contending forces in Central America"—indeed, the decisive one—remains the unquestionable premiss of analysis. If indeed "allowing the Sandinistas to survive would by itself be devastating to U.S. security and the global balance of power," then we must fault the Administration strategy in that the means were inadequate to the "logically inevitable ... conclusion that the regime must be ousted." But the premiss is dubious; perhaps the US might survive as a viable society even if Nicaragua is out of control. Assuming so, we must move "toward a realistic form of containment," meeting

the same objectives that rightly concern the administration: preventing Nicaragua from posing a military threat to the United States by becoming a platform for Soviet or Cuban power; keeping the Sandinista regime from subverting its neighbors; and promoting the evolution of Nicaragua's internal system into a more open, less virulent one

—perhaps even one as benign as those we have sponsored in El Salvador, Guatemala and Honduras. To this end, we should provide economic aid for these "Central American democracies" while "draw[ing] a line for the Sandinista regime." We should demand that Nicaragua refrain from accepting Cuban and Soviet "bases, missiles, and high-performance aircraft," an imminent threat to our security in the past years, apparently.

In our magnanimity, we should permit Nicaragua "to participate in a multilateral development program to the degree it moves toward a more open, pluralistic society" like its neighbors, which are "pluralistic" in that the efficient use of violence has eliminated any challenge to the "democrats": the security forces in effective control, the oligarchy, business interests, and rising professional classes—all "moderate" in that they recognize the need to satisfy the common interests of the master of the region. And we must take steps "to deal with the threat of Nicaraguan aggression or subversion against its neighbors" by means of a peace treaty calling for "no aggression, no cross-border subversion, no terrorism, no foreign bases, specified armed force levels, observance of human rights, and amnesty for combatants"; the events of the past decade do not, evidently, suggest that such conditions need be imposed on some actors in the Central American drama apart from the treacherous Sandinistas. The advantage of this approach is that "it would catch the Sandinistas in a web of international commitments" and "make it more difficult for the Soviet Union and Cuba to challenge or sabotage a settlement." This too is a most natural proposal, in the light of the firm United States commitment to such instruments of international order as the United Nations and the World Court, and its scrupulous observance of the legal obligation to refrain from the threat or use of force in international affairs. The US should further insist on "border inspection teams" and other measures of verification—of a sort that Nicaragua has requested since 1981, requests rejected consistently by the United States and generally unreported.

In the light of the readily established facts, these policy proposals from a knowledgeable Central American specialist at the liberal extreme of the spectrum provide considerable insight into the prevailing political culture. We might ask ourselves, again, how we would react to a similar performance on the part of some enemy commissar. Whatever the answer, at home it is regarded as the height of judicious assessment and responsible analysis.

Vaky observes that there is a "larger problem": to ensure compliance with any agreement. "The United States frankly will have to bear the major share of enforcement, and that means being prepared to use force if necessary—for example, to repel an invasion, to patrol borders or sea and airspace, or to remove bases or installations established in violation of the treaty." Not falling under this injunction are US bases in Honduras, or in Panama and Puerto Rico, or the sole foreign military installation in Cuba, the US naval base at Guantanamo.

We should not suppose, Vaky continues, "that Americans do not have the will or staying power to support the use of force abroad and therefore will back down from enforcing any settlement or any security line drawn." We have "maintained a strategic containment line around Cuba for 25 years," and Americans will show the same fortitude in the case of the Nicaraguan threat, he assures us. Thus if the liberal model prevails, Nicaraguans might look forward to economic strangulation; terrorist attacks to destroy industrial installations, blow up civilian aircraft, sink fishing boats, and bombard hotels; the spreading of epidemics to destroy livestock; and the other concomitants of our "strategic containment" of Cuba for twenty-five years, all happily forgotten here—and, incidentally, eliminated from the new "scholarly discipline" of terrorology.

Finally, Vaky turns to "the most difficult" objective to achieve: "the objective of promoting Nicaraguan self-determination," which motivated our "reasonable and idealistic" effort to transfer power, by force, into the hands of terrorist elements unable to gain political support. But we will have to pursue "the objective of a more open Nicaraguan political system," and the "self-determination" to which we have been dedicated, "by other strategies": those just outlined.

Writing in the *Washington Post*, the liberal editor of *Foreign Policy*, Charles Maynes, sees the main problem in Central America in a similar light:[18] "The issue is no longer whether Nicaragua can be regained as an American pawn on the geopolitical chessboard but whether it can be tamed and contained. ... There remains at least an outside chance that Nicaragua's relative isolation both economically and politically will persuade its leaders that the main hope for the country lies in cooperation with its neighbors," who should "set as a price for cooperation a relative democratization of life inside Nicaragua. ... For Nicaragua to be contained, the administration would have to end its opposition to direct U.S. negotiations with Managua." We should at least attempt the diplomatic path to determine whether Nicaragua will be willing "to meet U.S. security concerns" and provide us with "relevant commitments." Nicaraguan security concerns, and "a relative democratization of life" in the US death squad democracies, are not a problem.

The editors of the *Washington Post*, ruminating on "the Central American mess" under the proud slogan "An Independent Newspaper," ask "what went wrong" during the Reagan years. "Each country is different," they observe, "but the common aggravation of their difficulties can be traced to the onset of leftist revolutions—built of local tinder, blown to fire by Soviet-bloc support—in Guatemala, El Salvador and Nicaragua," with "spillovers ... in Honduras, which in fear of Nicaragua lent itself to an anti-Sandinista insurgency sponsored by the United States, and in Panama, whose strong man's usefulness to the anti-Sandinista cause long blinded Washington to his corruption and unreliability." The strong man's defects are now happily recognized—crucially, his unreliability, which compelled a reassessment of policy and a somewhat belated discovery of his corruption by the Independent Newspapers.

"Inevitably," the editors continue, "the revolutions evoked an American response." Finally, "the policy broke down," and now "American frailties compound Central America's"—particularly, the failure to address properly "the lingering and unresolved post-Vietnam issue of intervention in the cause of anticommunism." The "formula for enlightened engagement" that the editors have recommended "has its own flaw": "It does not adequately address the change brought about by Soviet power in making Moscow-oriented revolution possible in Central America and the Caribbean." We should try to engage Latin Americans in our quest for democracy and self-determination, and thus "to spare the United States the political loneliness that comes from being an activist and interventionist in the region." But this is difficult, because "the cast built into democratic Latin politics by leftism and resentment of American intervention has hindered Latins in dealing with these revolutions themselves and in delegating the task to Washington."

The editors are deeply sensitive to "the wounds American policy has suffered in Central America," so "fresh" as to impede a constructive course; no other "wounds" are identified. We should somehow steer a path between two extremes: "an engagement that in its carelessness took policy beyond the reach of feasibility in the field and support at home"; and "detachment in frustration and disgust." Such detachment on our part would threaten the very survival of Central America, the editors warn.[19]

Strikingly absent from these ruminations is any consideration of what Central Americans might think about the course the US should follow. Evidence on the matter is not too hard to find. For El Salvador one might, for example, turn to the published records of the National Debate for Peace, bringing together under Church auspices virtually all organized groups in the country. These records, readily available not far from the editorial offices, provide some useful insights into Salvadoran attitudes towards the issues addressed by the *Post* editors. On the danger that US "detachment" might threaten the survival of Central America, there was near-unanimous condemnation of "the enormous interference of the US in El Salvador's national affairs," of US military aid, of military interference in state and society "in support of the oligarchy and dominant sectors, and thus in support of North American interests" as the country is "subjugated to the interests of international capital," and so on. Since such conclusions are unacceptable to US elite opinion, the entire enterprise has been expunged from the record, ignored by the media and other commentary, a clear sign of how important the opinions of Salvadorans are to their benefactors. If our little brown brothers reveal their stupidity in such ways, it is hardly to be expected that we will humor them by paying attention.[20]

The return to forceful intervention during the Reagan years, and the Iran–Contra affair, prompted reassessment of the resort to covert action more generally. Reviewing books by Gregory Treverton on covert action and Trumbull Higgins on the Bay of Pigs affair, Stanley Hoffmann of Harvard University, who stretches critical dissent to its outer limits within mainstream scholarship, considers the "risks and costs" of these ventures.[21] He notes that "both men show how much euphoria about covert action was created by two early successes of the CIA": restoring the Shah to power in Iran in 1953 and overthrowing the Arbenz government in Guatemala a year later. But the lessons of history "are stark. ... As the targets of United States action became more formidable (Castro learned from Arbenz's fate), the chances of success decreased." Furthermore, "the fine-tuning of covert actions is difficult," and more generally, "covert action raises formidable issues in an open society." Taking the position of "the idealists," Treverton "recognizes that covert operations may be necessary at times" but "he doubts they'll remain secret, warns about their unintended effects and long-term costs" (to us, that is), and urges better procedures. His study is "enlightening, thoughtful and wise"—particularly his conclusion that "most covert-action successes have been small, ambiguous and transitory (Iran and Guatemala in the 1950s, for example)."

These are the only words of evaluation; further thoughts that might be suggested by the fate of Iran, Guatemala, Laos, and other targets of our initiatives remain unmentioned, apart from the limits and "ambiguity" of these successes. Only an irresponsible fanatic would recall the hundreds of thousands of corpses, the disappeared, the countless victims of torture, starvation, disease and semi-slave labor. The victims of official enemies do warrant such concern in an enlightened society, but not the dregs of the world that we have to kick out of our way, in self-defense.

Further insights into the foreign policy agenda are provided in a study of "bipartisan objectives for foreign policy" in *Foreign Affairs* by the Secretaries of State of the 1970s, Henry Kissinger and Cyrus Vance, who span the spectrum of thinking among the specialized class.[22] They are concerned that many Americans appear less willing than before to accept "the global responsibilities thrust on the United States," in a national mood of "frustration" over the failure of other nations to "assume greater risks, responsibilities and financial burdens for the maintenance of world order and international prosperity" and for "the cause of freedom" to which we have been dedicated. But the United States must continue "to play a major and often vital role," and can do so because of its economic and military strength, and because it is "a model democracy and a society that provides exceptionally well for the needs of its citizens"; no comparative statistics on such matters as infant mortality, homelessness, and other quality-of-life indices are provided to buttress this judgement.

Keeping just to Central America, Vance and Kissinger see one essential problem: Nicaragua. We must "obtain the withdrawal of Cuban and Soviet military advisers from Nicaragua, significant reductions in the armies and armaments in the region (especially in Nicaragua), a total ban on Sandinista help to guerrillas elsewhere, and the internal democratization of Nicaragua." "The situation in Central America," they observe, "can be one measure of U.S.–Soviet relations: whether the Soviet Union is willing to suspend arms shipments into this area of our most traditional relationships." Nothing is said about the consequences for Nicaragua, deprived of any other support by U.S. edict. The US must also "continue to support democracy within Nicaragua," providing "diplomatic and material aid to those who work for pluralistic economy and representative political process." No problems are perceived in the terror states, already within the reach of our benevolence.

5. Laying Down the Law

Another alternative to the flawed Reagan policies is presented by Alan Tonelson, a respected liberal policy analyst, in the *New Republic*.[23] He urges that we transcend the sterile debate between defenders of the Contras and their critics—the latter being those who note "correctly that the *contras* cannot

possibly achieve military victory." As usual, those who object in principle
to terror and "the unlawful use of force" (to borrow the terms of the
World Court ruling) are off the spectrum entirely. A new policy, "more
palatable to both the hawks and doves,"

> involves handling the Sandinistas and other threats in Central America the way
> that great powers have always dealt with pesty, puny neighbors: by laying down
> the law unilaterally and enforcing our will through intimidation and direct uses
> of military force. If the intimidation is successful—as it easily could be—the
> actual use of force would be unnecessary.

This "back-to-basics approach would satisfy America's needs in Central
America, if not all of our wants"; unlike Robert Tucker, the liberal critic
is willing to sacrifice some of "our wants"—reluctantly, to be sure. Peace
treaties, such as the Arias plan, are faulty because they "would prohibit
Washington from responding to foreign Communist presences unless local
states agreed," and one could hardly expect a Mexican politician in an election year "to endorse an American retaliatory strike against Nicaragua."
Besides, "legal constructs like treaties raise the prospect of lengthy deliberations to document and prove charges, protracted appeal processes, the filing
of countercharges, and other complicated procedures that all conflict with
the security need to respond to violations quickly, before they become
dangerous."

Legal instruments being too unwieldy and unreliable for the liberal mentality, and proxy terror having failed, the United States should turn to "frankly
intimidating and pushing Nicaragua around with our own military power."
After all, "the U.S. Navy still rules the waters off Central America" and
"Nicaragua is defenseless against American air and sea power" if intimidation
does not suffice. "If Ortega and Company have a healthy sense of self-
preservation, Americans should be able to bring Nicaragua to heel without
slogging through its jungles—especially if it is clear that good behavior will
bring a postponement of the regime's rendezvous with the ash heap of
history." Latin Americans may object to the show of force, but "it is unreasonable to expect the United States to await a favorable consensus to develop
among its politically fragile neighbors before acting to protect itself," and
"the hemispheric bargain proposed here would permit a modicum of mutual
respect but would also reflect power realities."

We should announce "general guidelines" for Central America, but
should not be too specific in our demands: "Vagueness in Washington can
keep Central Americans looking over their shoulders—and to the skies—and

more likely to err on the side of caution." Thinking along similar lines, the Reagan White House announced that it had formulated a list of demands for Nicaragua going well beyond the August 1987 peace agreements, but "the list has not been published or formally given to the Nicaraguans or to Congress," the *New York Times* reported in a front-page story. The subsequent sabotaging of the despised cease-fire talks follows the same script, with the constant invention of new and often outlandish demands when Nicaragua, always "pesty" in these matters, accepts the previous list.[24]

We should avoid "paralyzing debates," Tonelson continues; "the verdict must be left up to the president." The doves need not fear that some president will "order air strikes just for the fun of it, without genuine provocation"; the American people will ensure that in this case, he "will pay politically," which should satisfy any hapless victims—or at least, any surviving friends and relatives. With a properly orchestrated campaign of intimidation and with adequate force at the ready, Washington can "return Central America to the obscurity it so richly deserves."

Both the tone and the substance provide further understanding of the prevailing political culture in its more moderate and liberal range, as does the absence of any reaction to such thoughts in the left-liberal community they address.

These samples are, to my knowledge, representative. There are differences between the hawks and the doves. Given the scale of American power, even small differences translate into large effects for the victims. Illusions about the political culture generally will impede the one mechanism available to deter the resort to intimidation and violence and other means available to a superpower faced with "pesty, puny" adversaries that stand in the way of its "needs" and "wants": an unmanageable public at home. That lesson has been taught over and over again, and should not be forgotten by those concerned with their fate.

6. Foreign Agents

At home, the spectrum ranges from doves to hawks, though there are also some odd creatures who express skepticism about the very doctrines of the faith, those who McGeorge Bundy once called "wild men in the wings," succinctly capturing the common view.[25] Abroad, there are moderates and extremists. The moderates are those who accept the basic norms—crucially, the need to maintain a favorable climate for business operations, investment, and resource extraction. They hold the middle ground, confronting the extremists on all sides. The extremists are a motley crew, including advocates of social reforms that challenge privilege, excessive nationalism, or other such disorders. Another category of extremists are the perpetrators of atrocities that we find embarrassing and therefore choose not to attribute to our moderate friends, who, in reality, are often directing them or fronting for them in the service of our cause. The moderates range from such figures as Mussolini, Suharto, Saddam Hussein, assorted Latin American and Caribbean mass murderers and dictators, and so on, to figureheads of the Duarte variety who are constructed to salve the liberal conscience while arms flow to the killers. Moderates become villains if they attack US interests.

Let us turn now to the extreme doves among the Central American moderates. This quest carries us to Costa Rica, the one Western-style democracy. As noted earlier, the US always regarded this experiment with some ambivalence, despite the political leadership's commitment to safeguarding the needs of investors and serving US interests generally. Its leading figure, José Figueres, was always most sensitive to the needs of business and particularly foreign investors, and supportive of US policies (see Chapter 12, pp. 385–6). In the Kennedy period, he advocated secret funding from the CIA for projects of the "Democratic Left," and dismissed later revelations of CIA funding as "silly and adolescent" while praising the CIA for the "delicate political and cultural tasks" it was performing "thanks to the devotion of the liberals in the organization." He particularly valued the contributions of Jay Lovestone and other US labor bureaucrats, who had worked effectively to undermine the labor movement in Latin America and elsewhere for many years. Figueres supported the Bay of Pigs invasion, anticipating "a quick victory by the democratic forces which have gone into Cuba" and later expressing his regrets at their "lamentable" defeat. He suggested that the Dominican Republic be used as a base for intervention in Cuba, though only after his enemy Trujillo was deposed. When the Johnson Administration invaded the Dominican Republic to prevent the reestablishment of the constitutional government under the democratic capitalist reformer Juan Bosch, Figueres pleaded for understanding of Johnson's actions which, he held, were necessary to avoid his impeachment.[26]

As the US geared up for its attack on popular organizations and social reform in Central America in the 1980s, Costa Rica continued to cooperate, though with insufficient enthusiasm by Reaganite standards. Figueres became a nonperson in the media—apart from ritual invocation of his name in the course of denunciations of Nicaragua—because of his completely unacceptable reactions to the Sandinista revolution, the US attack against Nicaragua, and Reagan Administration efforts to reverse Costa Rican exceptionalism. Other leading figures of Costa Rican democracy also remained beyond the pale, among them, former president Daniel Oduber, who had the poor taste to observe that the "thugs" who threaten "the lives of Central Americans and their families ... are not the Leninist commissars but the armed sergeants trained in the United States." Ex-president Rodrigo Carazo, who had assisted the Sandinistas in overthrowing Somoza (a long-time enemy of Costa Rica), was described by Assistant Secretary for Inter-American Affairs Thomas Enders as "a thieving crook." The Monge government of the early 1980s was better-mannered, joining in the Contra war and acceding to US pressure to rebuff Sandinista efforts to create a demilitarized zone along the border, but it too had its faults. Thus the media could hardly be expected to report the observations of Monge's Vice-Foreign Affairs Minister Gerardo Trejos Salas on how the US "strongly pressured" Costa Rica and its client states as "Washington tried by all means available to block the signing of the Contadora Peace Act."[27]

President Oscar Arias was at first profoundly disliked by the Reagan Administration, but by 1988 he was tolerated, and in liberal circles always regarded with great respect. His credentials as an authentic dove were made official by the Nobel Peace Prize he won for his initiatives leading to the Esquipulas Accords of August 1987. His record is therefore instructive with regard to the agenda of the doves.

Internally in Costa Rica, Arias promoted a neoliberal economic model, participating in the dismantling of the social-democratic institutions. He also presided over the Reagan-backed restoration of the police to a "camouflaged army" and the increase in human rights violations by the security forces,[28] though these remained far below the level of his Central American colleagues. Arias supported the system of obligatory press licensing condemned by the Inter-American Human Rights Court, rejecting its ruling that state licensing limits freedom of expression and refusing to comply with it. Unlike Figueres, he did not—at least in commentary in the United States—condemn the media structure of Costa Rica, where, though the media are free from censorship or state terror, in practice "Costa Ricans often can obtain only one side of the story, since wealthy ultraconservatives control the major daily newspapers and broadcasting stations," the Council on Hemispheric Affairs and the Newspaper Guild observed. Figueres complained bitterly that "the oligarchy owns the newspapers and the radio stations, by which it has heavily influenced public opinion in Costa Rica" in support of US policies for the country and the region.[29] In these respects, Costa Rica was always in violation of the Esquipulas Accords (often misleadingly called "the Arias plan"), which require free access to the media for "all ideological groups."

Shortly after his inauguration in early 1986, Arias joined newly elected president Vinicio Cerezo of Guatemala in opposing overt US violence against Nicaragua. These moves brought Costa Rica into line with general Latin American opinion and elite opinion in the United States, which by then was overwhelmingly critical of the Contra effort as unsuccessful and too costly. Both presidents pressed for a political settlement, to the dismay of the Reaganites though with the general support of the political class and the business community in the United States.

Arias always accepted the basic norms, describing Washington's client states as "democracies" and condemning the Sandinistas for failing to observe the regional standards to which the terror states conform. At a meeting of Central American presidents in May 1986, he objected to Daniel Ortega's inclusion among the leaders "freely elected by the majority wills of their respective countries." By his standards, the US clients were democratic leaders, elected under conditions of freedom and the rule of law. In taking this stand, Arias again lined up with hawk–dove doctrine in the United States, in opposition to a broad range of other opinion, including Amnesty International, Americas Watch, and all *bona fide* human rights organizations, none of which exhibits his tolerance for the death squad democracies and their practices; and with regard to Nicaragua, including Costa Rica's leading democratic figure, José Figueres, and virtually all of the large number of election observers from Western governments, human rights groups, the professional association of Latin American scholars, and others. Arias also repeatedly called upon the USSR and Cuba to halt arms shipments to Nicaragua, so that it would be left defenseless against US terror, the US having successfully pressured its allies to refrain from providing Nicaragua with means of self-defense. But he is not on record with objections to military support for Washington's terror states and the "thugs" who run them.[30]

Arias's tolerance for terror and repression in the US-backed "fledgling democracies" made him particularly welcome to US elite opinion. His probity was further demonstrated as he cooperated fully with the US government in undermining the Esquipulas Accords. He kept silent about the rapid escalation of US supplies to the Contras immediately after the Accords, in violation of what the Accords termed the one "indispensable condition" for peace in the region. He also backed US initiatives to revise the Accords so that they would apply to Nicaragua alone, and to eliminate international supervision that would stand in the way of Washington's efforts to disrupt them. Thus, he fully accepted the blatant violations of the Accords in the states where he recognizes "freely elected governments," agreeing that mounting atrocities there are of no real significance. Arias naturally continued to insist upon the provisions of the Accords that call for "the fully guaranteed participation of the people in truly democratic political processes based on justice, freedom and democracy," guarantees for "the inviolability of all forms of life and liberty, ... social justice, respect for human rights," and so on—but only as these apply to Nicaragua. His tolerance for the practices of his "democratic" colleagues, who provide a fig leaf for state terror as he knows, has served effectively to legitimate, and thus enhance, the continuing atrocities and US participation in them, another reason for his immense popularity and prestige in the West.

Observing these principles, Arias informed the press in August 1988: "I told Mr. Shultz that the Sandinistas today are bad guys, and you are good guys, that they have unmasked themselves." The Sandinistas had "unmasked themselves" when police used tear gas and violence after they had been attacked at a protest march at Nandaime in July 1988, arresting several dozen participants. The Council on Hemispheric Affairs commented that this

> mob assault on police followed exactly instructions in the notorious August 1984 CIA psychological warfare manual issued to the contras. U.S. embassy officials were present, and videotapes and accounts of eyewitnesses support Nicaraguan government charges that they directed the affair.

That the US had been actively engaged in fomenting opposition to the government with the goal of evoking a repressive response had long been known, including Embassy activities of a sort that few countries would tolerate for a moment, surely not the United States.[31]

The Nicaraguan reaction was a "major sin" against the peace accords, Arias announced, singling out Nicaragua for criticism and urging that "it is time to rally some support to put pressure on those who fail to comply"— that is, Nicaragua alone. During these July transgressions, the Sandinistas had behaved much in the manner of the Costa Rican security forces at the same time, approaching some of the lesser abuses of the "democratic" states—which were not only continuing to break up demonstrations with tear gas and violence, but also conducting their "pedagogy of terror" in the bloodier manner that Arias found acceptable, escalating since the 1987 accords were signed. The Sandinista-style abuses in these other countries evoked not a whisper of protest, and in fact hardly a mention in news reports.[32]

At a meeting with the presidents of El Salvador, Guatemala, and Honduras, and Secretary of State George Shultz, Arias said: "Nicaragua has unfortunately failed us." He expressed "my disappointment, my pain, my sadness," as he discussed abuses in Nicaragua with his colleagues from the "democratic" states; about their murderous repression he expressed no disappointment, pain or sadness, at least so far as the media report. "Mr. Shultz and the Foreign Ministers of Honduras, Guatemala, El Salvador and Costa Rica expressed 'their respect for the principles of peace, democracy, security, social justice and economic development'," Stephen Kinzer reported without comment.[33]

For Oscar Arias, Mr Shultz is a "good guy" despite his enthusiastic sponsorship of extreme and continuing terror in the "fledgling democracies," where he sees "the results [as] something all Americans can be proud of" (see p. 388). Evidently, Arias agrees. Accordingly, he is granted the role of arbiter of adherence to the provisions of the peace accords and of democratic practice, though he is a shade too independent for the hardliners who demand still higher standards of obedience.

Arias lent his support to the demolition of the peace Accords in other ways as well. The *New York Times* reported him as saying that "Honduras could not be expected to close contra camps and ban clandestine supply flights if the Sandinistas do not negotiate a cease-fire with the contras and issue a broad amnesty."[34] The Accords set no such condition on cessation of Contra aid, and Arias did not announce that foreign aid to the indigenous guerrillas in El Salvador and Guatemala is legitimate until the governments begin to live up to the terms of the Accords and accept guerrilla offers to negotiate. The continued refusal of these governments to negotiate despite appeals from the Church, from Arias, and others, while Nicaragua did reach a cease-fire agreement in March 1988, also did not affect Arias's judgement that Nicaragua alone stands in the way of a peace settlement.

In subsequent months, the process of tightening the screws on Nicaragua through the device of demand escalation by the Contras continued, no doubt following the script of Arias's "good guys" in the State Department. Each new government agreement, going far beyond the terms of the Accords, simply led to new demands. Sandinista proposals to renew negotiations were repeatedly rejected by the US and its clients. Arias backed the project all the way, expressing his pain and sadness over Sandinista iniquity as the

US and its forces continually pressed for further advantage, and atrocities continued to mount in the terror states under the cover of legitimation provided by Arias and his fellow democrats, and in violation of the long-forgotten peace accords. In August 1988, Senate doves implemented legislation providing renewed aid to the Contras—in violation of international law and the Accords—and warning Nicaragua that military aid would follow if they continued to stand alone in the way of peace and democracy or attack the Contra forces, who, at that time, were refusing to enter into negotiations and continuing to carry out terrorist atrocities in Nicaragua.[35] Across the political spectrum, it was taken to be illegitimate, a further proof of Communist totalitarianism, for Nicaragua to defend itself against US attack or to protect the population from US-run terrorists.

If Arias had any objections to what his "good guys" were up to, I have been unable to discover it. He also apparently kept silent about the delivery of "humanitarian" aid to the Contras—which does not qualify as humanitarian under international law, as the World Court determined unequivocally. The aid was also in blatant violation of the terms of the March 1988 cease-fire agreement and the congressional aid legislation, and elicited a strong protest from OAS Secretary-General Soares, who was assigned responsibility for monitoring the agreement, to which the congressional legislation was explicitly subordinated. Arias remained untroubled. Doubtless aware of the character of these aid deliveries, he banned them in Costa Rica; government spokesman Guido Fernández stated that to permit supplies to pass through Costa Rica to the Contras would be a form of "aggression against a government of the region" and "contrary to the peace accords," the Honduran press reported. But I have found no statement available to the American public.[36]

7. Yearning for Democracy

While domestic hawks and doves differ on tactical choices, they are in accord in preferring democratic forms, where this is feasible. Some see this preference as an absolute passion. Thus, *New York Times* diplomatic correspondent Neil Lewis writes: "The yearning to see American-style democracy duplicated throughout the world has been a persistent theme in American foreign policy." Lewis was reflecting on the situation in Haiti, where the US-backed military government had suppressed the scheduled elections by violence, the widely predicted consequence of US support for the junta.

These events, Lewis observed, are "the latest reminder of the difficulty American policy-makers face in trying to work their will, no matter how benevolent, on other nations." Our righteous endeavors had succeeded in the Philippines, with the overthrow of Marcos by "people power," but were coming to grief in Haiti.[37]

The sentiments are conventional. At the rhetorical level, the yearning for democracy has indeed been a persistent theme, coexisting easily with the regular resort to violence and subversion to undermine democracy.

Given the conventions of ideological warfare, it is quite possible to describe even the most brutal regimes as "democracies," as long as they serve the goals of the policymakers. The example of the "fledgling democracies" of Central America is notorious. Another familiar case is the doctrine that "democracy is on the ideological march" because the experience of the last several decades shows that it leads to prosperity and development: "As an economic mechanism, democracy demonstrably works," James Markham writes in the lead article in the *Times Week in Review*.[38] We are to understand, then, that the economic miracles of South Korea, Taiwan, Hong Kong and Singapore took place under democracy. The conventional thesis that Markham expresses reveals, once again, the prevailing contempt for democracy.

The countries that inspired Neil Lewis's thoughts about our unfulfilled yearnings are, in fact, instructive examples of the attitude towards democracy. In the case of the Philippines, few seem to find it jarring to read an upbeat report on "the return of full democracy" to the country under the headline "Aquino's decree bans Communist Party," with a lead paragraph explaining that a presidential decree stipulated penalties of imprisonment for membership in the Party, which had been legalized under the Marcos dictatorship. Not long before, Marcos himself had been a model democrat, a man "pledged to democracy" (Ronald Reagan); "we love your adherence to democratic principle and to the democratic processes" and your "service to freedom," Vice-President George Bush proclaimed in Manila. That, however, was before Marcos had lost control and, with it, his credentials as a freedom-loving democrat. The nature of Philippine democracy before and after the Marcos dictatorship also evokes little self-reflection—or even comment.[39]

The reference to Haiti is also instructive. After many earlier interventions, Woodrow Wilson launched murderous counterinsurgency wars in Haiti and the Dominican Republic (Hispaniola), leaving the countries shattered and demoralized, the constitutional structure reduced to mere farce, and American corporations able to "work their will" without local impediments.

In subsequent years, the US supported savage tyrants, turning against them only when they began to infringe upon US interests or lose their effectiveness, with direct intervention when necessary to ensure that events proceeded on their proper course.[40]

The Reagan Administration continued to certify the progress of "democratic development" in Haiti as President-for-Life Jean-Claude Duvalier invoked still more repressive legislation in 1985, described as "an encouraging step forward" by the US Ambassador at a July 4th celebration. But not long after, it became clear that the dictator's days were numbered. As the *Wall Street Journal* observed perceptively, when "U.S. analysts learned that Haiti's ruling circle had lost faith" in Duvalier, "U.S. officials, including Secretary of State George Shultz, began openly calling for a 'democratic process' in Haiti."[41] At the same time, the US favorite Marcos lost his usefulness, with similar consequences. Since then, we sing our praises for these renewed demonstrations of our yearning for democracy.

Throughout the period, the independent media and other right-thinking people have been much impressed with our benevolence. A survey of *New York Times* editorials from 1916 through 1928 illustrates the prevailing conception, which persists to this day. As Wilson set forth on his crusades in Hispaniola, the editors wrote that the long record of US intervention "clearly shows that the attitude of the United States has been unselfish and helpful." We had acted "in a fatherly way" and were now doing so again as Haiti "sought help here," provided by the Marines. This "unselfish intervention" over the years "has been moved almost exclusively by a desire to give the benefits of peace to people tormented by repeated revolutions," without any thought for "preferential advantages, commercial or otherwise. The people of the island should realize that [the US government] is their best friend" while Wilson's troops rampage. "The good-will and unselfish purposes of our own government" are demonstrated by the consequences, the editors wrote six years later, when they were all too apparent. Two years before, they had explained that it was necessary for us to see to it that "the people were cured of the habit of insurrection and taught how to work and live"; they "would have to be reformed, guided and educated," and this "duty was undertaken by the United States." "To wean these peoples away from their shot-gun habit of government is to safeguard them against our own exasperation," with the righteous resort to force that it elicits.[42]

Similarly in Nicaragua, as the Marines pursued the "elusive bandit chief" Sandino, it was plain that we were continuing to act, as we always had, with "the best motives in the world," the *Times* editors assured the reader. And surely no serious person could accept "the mistaken assumption that the presence of the marines is distasteful" to the Nicaraguans, or could heed the attacks on our policy "by professional 'liberals' in this country." The editors did, however, regard it as unfortunate that the clash "comes just at a time when the Department of State is breathing grace, mercy and peace for the whole world." No less admirable is our record in Cuba, where we were able "to save the Cubans from themselves and instruct them in self-government," granting them "independence qualified only by the protective Platt amendment"—which "protected" US corporations and their local allies who turned the country into a US plantation, averting the threat of democracy and independent development. In the preferred version, "Cuba is very near at hand to refute" the charge of "the menace of American imperialism." We were "summoned" three times until the Cuban people, under our tutelage, "mastered the secret of stability." And while it is true that "our commercial interests have not suffered in the island," "we have prospered together with a free Cuban people," so "no one speaks of American imperialism in Cuba."[43]

The years pass, the inspiring thoughts remain.

Notes

1. *American Foreign Policy* (Norton, 1969), p. 28.
2. Tucker, "The Purposes of American Power," *Foreign Policy*, Winter 1980/1. For more extensive discussion, see *Towards a New Cold War*, ch. 8.
3. *Commentary*, January 1981; *TNR*, November 29, 1980.
4. *BG*, July 24, 1988.
5. Oakes, "The Wrong Risk in Nicaragua," *NYT*, February 10, 1987; Morley "Beyond the Reach of our Good Intentions," *NYT Book Review*, April 12, 1987.
6. See *Culture of Terrorism, Necessary Illusions*.
7. Pastor, *Condemned to Repetition* (Princeton, 1987).
8. For comparison of the record in Nicaragua with that of the United States and its most favored client (Israel; comparison with the US terror states is an absurdity, of course), see *Necessary Illusions*, Appendix II, sec. 2, and Appendix V, secs 6–8. Also Michael Linfield, *Freedom Under Fire* (South End, 1990).
9. See *Turning the Tide*, p. 270; *Culture of Terrorism*, pp. 219 f.; *Necessary Illusions*, pp. 71 f.
10. Tom Barry and Deb Preusch, *The Soft War*; LaFeber, *Inevitable Revolutions*.
11. On the support for the Guard by Carter doves, see Chapter 10.
12. See Chapter 10, section 3, for more on these efforts and the reasons for them.
13. *FRUS*, 1955–7, vol. VII, pp. 88 f., NIE 82–85.
14. See Chapter 1, p. 51; Chapter 12, section 5.
15. Pastor, citing Brzezinski's diaries.
16. *Foreign Policy*, Fall 1987.
17. See *Culture of Terrorism*, pp. 90 f.
18. *WP–Manchester Guardian Weekly*, November 29, 1987.

19. Editorial, *WP*, June 20, 1988.

20. See *Necessary Illusions*, pp. 243–4.

21. *NYT Book Review*, November 29, 1987.

22. *Foreign Affairs*, Summer 1988.

23. *TNR*, October 5, 1987.

24. Joel Brinkley, *NYT*, October 4, 1987. On the strategy of demand escalation to prevent a political settlement, see "Cease-Fire Primer," *International Policy Report*, July 1988. For a review of the demolition of the accords through 1988, see *Necessary Illusions*. On subsequent steps, see Chapters 2, 9.

25. Bundy's reference was to those who questioned the basic assumptions of the "first team" that was directing US policy in Vietnam; *Foreign Affairs*, January 1967. See *Manufacturing Consent*, pp. 175 f.

26. See Charles Ameringer, *Don Pepe* (University of New Mexico, 1978); *Necessary Illusions*, pp. 111 f., and Appendix V, sec. 1.

27. Oduber, cited in Kenneth M. Coleman and George C. Herring, eds, *The Central American Crisis* (Scholarly Resources Inc., 1985). Carazo, Monge, see Roy Gutman, *Banana Diplomacy* (Simon & Schuster, 1988), pp. 67, 302n. The charge against Carazo, possibly accurate, was that he had profited from gun-running, Oduber's record may also be none too savory (see p. 118), but that has never been a problem here. Trejos Salas, see *Culture of Terrorism*, p. 135.

28. See Chapter 7, pp. 223 f.

29. COHA–Newspaper Guild, *Survey of Press Freedom in Latin America*, 1986. On Figueres's attitudes, see *Necessary Illusions*, and sources cited.

30. Gutman, *Banana Diplomacy*, pp. 327 ff., 359.

31. Arias, Richard Boudreaux, *Los Angeles Times*, August 5, 1988; COHA, "News and Analysis," September 23, 1988. For more on this US propaganda triumph, see next chapter, p. 287.

32. See *Necessary Illusions*, pp. 247 ff.

33. Boudreaux, *LAT*, August 5; Kinzer, *NYT*, August 2, 1988.

34. Stephen Kinzer, *NYT*, October 15, 1987.

35. For one serious example, three days earlier, see Chapter 9, p. 289.

36. See *Necessary Illusions*, pp. 94 f.; Fernández, *El Tiempo* (Honduras), August 22, 1988. See next chapter, p. 297.

37. Lewis, *NYT*, December 6, 1987.

38. *NYT*, September 25, 1988. See Chapter 3, p. 90, for another example.

39. UPI, *BG*, July 27, 1987. Reagan, *NYT*, February 12, 1985; Bush, *State Department Bulletin* 81, August 1981, p. 30. On democracy under Aquino, see Chapter 7, sec. 4.

40. For details, see *Turning the Tide* and *On Power and Ideology*.

41. *WSJ*, February 10, 1986.

42. Editorials, *NYT*, September 2, December 5, 1916; July 13, 1922; October 5, 1920; May 12, 1928.

43. Editorials, *NYT*, January 4, 14, May 3, 1928; May 3, 1922; January 8, 1928.

NINE

The Mortal Sin of Self-Defense

THROUGHOUT the US war against Nicaragua, periodic White House–Congress–media campaigns were organized to demonstrate the perfidy of the victim: arms to the FMLN guerrillas in El Salvador; MiGs to threaten the hemisphere; unprovoked invasions of innocent Honduras; internal repression too horrifying for us to bear; and so on. Each exercise served its temporary purpose. When each tale unraveled, it was shelved as new candidates were found. These episodes tell us little about Central America, but a good deal about the United States and its intriguing political and intellectual culture. One remarkable and revealing example was the propaganda triumph orchestrated at the October 1989 summit of presidents in Costa Rica, at the early stages of the February 1990 election campaign, to which we turn in the final section and the next chapter.

1. The Skunk at the Garden Party

On November 1, 1989 President Daniel Ortega announced the suspension of the Nicaraguan government's unilateral cease-fire. The official Nicaraguan communiqué condemned the infiltration of armed Contra forces from their Honduran bases and the "dramatic escalation over the last few weeks of attacks against civilian economic and military targets with the ensuing loss of civilian life among the Nicaraguan population," intended to "put obstacles in the path of the electoral process." The communiqué reaffirmed the government's commitment to the scheduled February 25, 1990 elections and called for a meeting of the parties concerned at UN headquarters in New York "to approve the logistical and technical matters that can promote repatriation and the integration into the political process of all those persons linked to counterrevolutionary activities or their resettlement in third countries, as stipulated in the Tela accords" of the Central American Presidents on August 7, 1989.[1]

Nicaragua alleged that during its nineteen-month cease-fire, over 730 soldiers and civilians had been killed in Contra attacks, with the pace increasing through October 1989. The essence of these allegations was confirmed in the occasional remarks in the US media. It was casually reported in mid October that "since August, the contras are believed to have deployed nearly 2,000 more troops inside Nicaragua, and reports of clashes between Contra and Sandinista forces have risen sharply in recent weeks"; and two weeks later, that Contra soldiers who had been ordered back to Nicaragua "were being told by their commanders to prepare for combat." On October 21, nineteen reservists were reported killed in a Contra attack on trucks bringing them to register to vote. "As Ortega deliberated his next move" about the cease-fire on October 30, Brook Larmer observed in the *Christian Science Monitor*, "the contras raided a cooperative 60 miles southeast of Managua, killing five civilians."[2]

Witness for Peace (WFP), which issued regular reports based on eyewitness testimony, gave figures of forty-nine civilians killed, wounded, or kidnapped in fourteen Contra attacks in October. This partial record registered an increase over previous months, though the character of the Contra attacks persisted unchanged. Thus the WFP Hotline of October 3 (ignored by the media, as was generally the case) reported a Contra ambush of a political brigade on their way to inform villagers of the location of voter registration tables and the dates for registration, leaving one dead (the body mutilated), one in critical condition, and two wounded. In the same region northeast of Matagalpa, five men were reported kidnapped by Contra marauders, another near Wiwili. Near Rio Blanco, a Catholic lay worker driving a truckload of pigs for a Church project assisting campesinos resettled because of the war (and a frequent target of Contra attacks) was killed in an ambush on November 1. A delegation of Hemisphere Initiatives, which was monitoring the election, reported that Contras "are engaging in intensified offensive military actions" according to witnesses and townspeople in Rio Blanco, including a former Contra who accepted amnesty in October and seven top local leaders of the US-backed opposition alliance UNO. An eighty-year-old peasant woman described to the press how Contra attackers dragged her three adult sons out of their isolated home on October 28, slashing their throats and killing them. The Sandinista press published a photocopy of an alleged Contra communiqué, signed by Commander Enrique Bermúdez, ordering his forces to remain armed and mobilized "to guarantee the triumph of the UNO." Contras who had recently accepted amnesty said that they "had orders to coerce Nicaraguans to vote for the opposition in elections next February," wire services reported.[3]

Little of this found its way into print—not a word to the Newspaper of Record. The occasional references elsewhere are themselves instructive. Thus a Reuters report on the Contra orders to disrupt the elections by violence made it to the bottom of a column on another topic on page 83 of the *Boston Globe*, where the source is identified as "deserters"—meaning, men who "deserted" the US-run forces, accepting amnesty as required by the Tela Accords that the US is committed to disrupt. In contrast, real or fabricated threats by FMLN guerrillas to disrupt elections in El Salvador are major news stories, constantly reiterated as the media extol our yearning for democracy and the barriers we must overcome to satisfy it.[4]

After the October 21 ambush, Nicaragua announced that such "criminal actions" might compel it to resort to force in self-defense. Ortega's announcement that the government would indeed pursue this course provoked a "universal storm of outrage," the *New York Times* commented approvingly. President Bush denounced this "little man" as "an unwanted animal at a garden party," concurring with a television reporter who described Ortega as "a skunk at a picnic." The "picnic" was the presidential summit meeting at which Ortega announced that the cease-fire might be rescinded. The summit was reduced to the level of a garden party by Washington's flat refusal to permit any substantive issue to be discussed. The infantile excuse was that President Bush's name could not be permitted to appear on any statement signed by Ortega; the probable reason was fear of US isolation if serious questions were permitted to arise, a regular embarrassment in international forums.[5]

The US sabotage of the summit merited little comment. The approved focus was that Ortega's announcement "ran head-on against the themes of peace and democracy," as Mark Uhlig put it in the *New York Times*. The escalating attacks by the US-run proxy forces, in contrast, do not run "head-on" against these noble themes, nor does the vastly greater terror conducted with utter impunity by the military forces that effectively rule the "democracies" of El Salvador and Guatemala (or the more subdued terror of the Honduran military), all with firm US support. US officials and others offered grim speculations that the Sandinistas had fabricated the alleged Contra attacks or even carried them out themselves, dressed as Contras, seeking an excuse to cancel the elections. Profound concern was expressed that Nicaragua's resort to force to defend the country from Contra violence would seriously undermine the possibility of conducting the elections fairly.[6]

Congress and media responded in the expected manner. Ortega "united Congress and the Administration against him," the *Times* accurately reported. Both houses of Congress voted overwhelmingly to condemn Ortega in bitter terms (the Senate, 95–0). The Sandinistas must "end their aggression in the region" and "their tyranny over their own people," the resolution read. Congressional doves trembled with indignation. Senator John Kerry of Massachusetts described Ortega as without a doubt "Nicaragua's worst enemy," whatever Nicaraguans might think. Representative David Obey said, "Daniel Ortega is a damned fool and he's always been a damned fool." Senator Patrick Leahy added that he had again demonstrated his "remarkable ability of snatching defeat from the jaws of victory." Television news, again displaying the objectivity and professionalism for which the media are renowned, referred to Ortega and General Noriega as "the bad boys in the backyard." The respected liberal commentator Daniel Schorr asked sarcastically whether Ortega was a double agent working for the CIA. The *Times* editors denounced him as "foolish and thuggish"; his "stunning misstep" had "confounded hopes for free elections and an end to his nation's interminable war," thrown "a grenade into a promising, arduously wrought regional peace plan," and "undermines Secretary of State Baker" and his carefully crafted efforts for peace and democracy. The theme that Ortega had again struck a blow at the liberals who had sacrificed so much for his cause was sounded with much dismay and anger. With the notable exception of Anthony Lewis, who asked whether we would "suffer in silence" in the face of unremitting military and economic warfare by some unimaginable superpower, the chorus of denunciation was marred by scarcely a discordant note.[7]

Commentators aghast at Sandinista perfidy trotted out the familiar litany of complaints. Daniel Schorr informed his readers that "Mr. Ortega kept the pot boiling with such things as joining Fidel Castro in endorsing the massacre of pro-democracy students in Beijing in 1989." This was one of the fables concocted by the propaganda system as it sought to exploit the tragedy in Tiananmen Square to defame its various foreign and domestic enemies, immediately exposed as a lie in the mainstream press by Randolph Ryan and Alexander Cockburn, and long ago conceded to have been a pure invention. Another "outrageous" act, Schorr continues, took place in 1985, when "virtually singlehandedly, Mr. Ortega made Congress reverse itself and vote for more aid for the contras." Ortega forced a reluctant Congress to abandon its efforts on his behalf by following Russian orders to show up in Moscow and embrace Gorbachev, Schorr explains. He is referring to what historian Thomas Walker describes as Ortega's "carefully balanced trip to Europe in May 1985" in an effort to obtain aid, with "stops in both Eastern Bloc *and* Western European countries," which "the Reagan administration, the media, and a surprisingly large number of liberals in the U.S. Congress characterized simply as 'Ortega's trip to Moscow'." For Schorr, as for an unsurprisingly large number of other liberals, Nicaragua's attempt to obtain aid when the US is trying to destroy its economy is a shameful act.[8]

The *Times* news columns presented the same picture of Ortega's skill at snatching defeat from the jaws of victory, offering as proof two examples: his "trip to Moscow," "outraging American opponents and supporters alike"; and the "crackdown on internal dissent" which provoked "sharp, astonished international condemnation" in July 1988, when the Sandinistas again confounded their friends and "shot themselves in the temple," a "foreign expert" noted. The latter charge refers to another great triumph of the US propaganda system. It is indeed true that there was sharp, astonished condemnation after the police broke up a rally at Nandaime, using tear gas for the first time ever (after having been "pelted ... with sticks and rocks," the *Times* reported in paragraph 13, a fact that quickly disappeared), leading to an impassioned condemnation of this "brutal suppression of human rights" by Congress (91–4 in the Senate, 358–18 in the House) and indignant front-page stories and commentary on Sandinista barbarity that persisted for months. At the very same time, security forces used tear gas and force to break up rallies and protests in Costa Rica, El Salvador, Honduras, and Guatemala, eliciting no indignation—and virtually no news coverage. A reasonable judgement in the case of the US terror states, where actions comparable to Nandaime are hardly noteworthy in the context of the regular atrocities continuing right through that period—also with little notice and virtually no public condemnation.[9]

Just as the *Times* was recalling the famous case when the Sandinistas approached the regular lesser abuses of the US clients, Israeli paratroopers used force to disperse a prayer service and sit-in by a hundred Americans and local inhabitants at Beit Sahour who were protesting the brutal Israeli reaction to nonviolent disobedience in this West Bank town (Israeli peace activists and journalists were kept away by the army); and Cory Aquino's forces used water cannons and tear gas to drive off thousands of demonstrators protesting her refusal to allow Ferdinand Marcos's body to be brought home for burial. These are just two of the regular occurrences in US client states that the *Times* considered unworthy of mention; again with reason, since they pale into insignificance in the face of far more severe abuses by these and other US clients that pass with little or no report or comment, and no show of annoyance.[10]

The *Times* editors were particularly incensed that Ortega should respond with force to "the pinpricks of contras," thus revealing that his "new spirit of conciliation" is a fraud. Surely the US would not resort to force if thousands of Cuban-run marauders were killing and kidnapping in the hills of Kentucky (hundreds of thousands, to make the analogy more accurate). Imagine how the editors would thunder in righteous anger if Israel were to call upon its army in response to the pinpricks of PLO infiltrators murdering and kidnapping Kibbutz members or reserve soldiers on their way to register.

At the presidential summit, "the pinpricks of the contras" were regarded somewhat more seriously than in the *Times* Manhattan offices. Brook Larmer reported that the Latin American presidents said "they sympathized with the ruling Sandinistas' frustration over the stalled plan to dismantle the contra camps in Honduras, . . . understood [Ortega's] anger at the escalating contra attacks within Nicaragua," and recognized that he "has legitimate gripes," while questioning whether suspension of the cease-fire was the right move. Larmer quoted a foreign diplomat in Managua who added: "There are so many Latin countries with insurgencies that a lot of countries would be hypocritical to criticize the Sandinistas for doing exactly what they are doing themselves—carrying out an aggressive counterinsurgency effort."[11]

But hypocrisy is the name of the game, and anyone who knows the rules will understand the "universal storm of outrage" in Congress and the media.

Perhaps the kindest comment was that Ortega had again shown himself to be a bad politician.[12] The conclusion has merit. In the same sense, a therapist who tries to persuade psychotics by rational argument that the world is not as they see it might be criticized as a "bad psychologist." Like many others in the Third World, Ortega probably does not comprehend the psychotic streak in the dominant intellectual culture, in particular the doctrine that no one has a right to defend themselves from US attack. This doctrine has deep roots in American history. It explains why the US can regularly be depicted as the victim of the evil deeds of Vietnam—and why for two-hundred years few shuddered, or even noticed, when reading with due reverence the words of the Founding Fathers in the Declaration of Independence condemning King George III for having unleashed "the merciless Indian savages" against the innocent colonists. There is no shortage of illustrations.

This fundamental doctrine was operative throughout the war against Nicaragua. In August 1988, with passionate supporting speeches by leading doves, the Senate passed the Byrd amendment calling for military aid to the Contras if the Sandinistas carried out any "hostile action" against them. Three days before, Contras had attacked the crowded passenger vessel *Mission of Peace*, killing two and wounding twenty-seven, including a Baptist minister from New Jersey heading a US religious delegation. Senators Byrd, Dodd, and others made no mention of this event, but their logic is clear: if the treacherous Sandinistas resort to "hostile action" to prevent such "pin-pricks," plainly we have the right to punish them for the crime by sending arms to our proxy forces terrorizing Nicaragua. Since this position is considered righteous and principled, it evoked no comment whatsoever.[13]

The same reasoning was displayed during the periodic MiG scares concocted by Reaganite Agitprop. When the Reagan Administration floated the story in 1984 as part of its successful campaign to eliminate the Nicaraguan elections from history, the doves responded that if the charge were accurate, the US would have to bomb Nicaragua because these vintage 1950s jets are "also capable against the United States," hence a threat to our security (Senator Paul Tsongas of Massachusetts, with the support of other leading doves).[14] When the disinformation was exposed after it had served its purpose, there was some criticism of the media for uncritically swallowing government propaganda, but the really significant fact was ignored: the general agreement that such behavior on the part of Nicaragua would be entirely unacceptable. The reason for this oversight is simple: by the norms of the political culture, it would be an unspeakable scandal for Nicaragua to attempt to defend itself from US-run terrorist operations.

Nicaragua, of course, had no special interest in MiGs. The Sandinista leadership was happy to tell anyone who asked that they would have been pleased to obtain jet planes from France. But their efforts to obtain arms from France were blocked by pressure from Washington, which insisted that Nicaragua be armed solely by the Russians, so that commentators could refer in suitably ominous tones to "the Soviet-supplied Sandinistas" as the farce was replayed week after week; "French-supplied" just doesn't have the same ring. All of this was well known but, running counter to doctrinal requirements, it remained unreported and undiscussed.

It was also understood throughout that the aging MiGs that Nicaragua was accused of trying to sneak into its territory could have only one purpose: to protect Nicaraguan airspace from the CIA supply flights that were required to keep the US proxy forces in the field and the regular surveillance flights that provided them with up-to-the-minute information on the disposition of Nicaraguan troops, so that they could safely attack civilian targets in accordance with their instructions and training. Understood, but scarcely mentioned. A search of the liberal *Boston Globe*, perhaps the least antagonistic to the Sandinistas among major US journals, revealed *one* editorial reference to the fact that Nicaragua needs air power "to repel attacks by the CIA-run contras, and to stop or deter supply flights" (November 9, 1986). Again, the conclusion is clear and unmistakable: no one has the right of self-defense against US attack.

Failure to comprehend these facets of US political culture is common. In late December 1987, Nicaraguan Foreign Minister Miguel d'Escoto privately expressed great hopes for the scheduled presidential meeting in January at which the International Verification and Control Commission was to present its report on the compliance of the Central American countries with the August 1987 Central American Accords. He was convinced that the report would be favorable to Nicaragua, and that the impact would advance the process of achieving the goals of the Accords. His expectations with regard to the report were confirmed; on the impact, he was quite wrong. He failed to understand some elementary facts about Western democracy. The US government was committed to demolition of the Accords; the Free Press would therefore loyally perform its duty, and the distribution of power would render the facts null and void. These are, again, the rules of the game.

The rules apply quite generally; the present case is no aberration. Thus in March 1964, when *Times* Executive Editor Max Frankel was learning his trade as a war correspondent in Indochina, Saigon army forces accompanied by US advisers attacked a Cambodian village, leaving many villagers killed and wounded. Since a US army pilot was captured, the incident could not be ignored or denied in the usual manner. Frankel reported it with great indignation—against Prince Sihanouk, who was "stomping on

U.S. toes," "leading the pack in big-power baiting," and borrowing "a page from Fidel Castro's book" by daring to request reparations for this US atrocity. We were the injured innocents.[15]

As in this case, our clients regularly inherit the same rights. *Times* chief diplomatic correspondent Thomas Friedman writes that in 1982 the Israeli army "arrived in Beirut like innocents abroad and they left three years later like angry tourists who had been mugged, cheated, and had all their luggage stolen with their travelers' checks inside." As he knows well, the invading innocents murdered, destroyed, brutally mistreated prisoners and civilians, and generally laid waste whatever stood in their path; and they left Lebanon, apart from the 10 percent they virtually annexed, because unanticipated resistance caused them more casualties than they were willing to accept. This statement is selected as the prime example of Friedman's "sharp perceptions" by Roger Rosenblatt in a laudatory front-page review in the *Times Book Review*.[16]

2. The Guests so Sorely Troubled

Bush was not the only guest at the garden party to be appalled by the unwanted animal's misbehavior. The *Times* account of Ortega's crimes quotes President Alfredo Cristiani of El Salvador, who lamented that Ortega's decision to abrogate the government's unilateral cease-fire "has destroyed everything that has been accomplished so far" and "will complicate the situation a great deal."[17]

El Salvador, of course, declared no cease-fire. On the contrary, when the FMLN declared a unilateral cease-fire as a gesture of good faith during the peace talks they had initiated a few weeks earlier, the Salvadoran military responded by launching operations into most of the guerrilla base areas and stepping up arrests of union activists and other repression. During the period before the March 1989 election the armed forces had also escalated their operations—actions widely hailed in the US as demonstrating their dedication to the electoral process. To judge by the reaction here, we must assume that another contribution was the presence of troops at the polling booths, where they could observe the transparent receptacles in which voters place their numbered ballots made of paper so thin that the voter's "X" is visible even through the back—all of this clearly shown in photographs by independent US observers, if not the media.[18]

While Cristiani was bemoaning Ortega's vulgar disruption of the picnic, a bomb exploded at the headquarters of a leading anti-government union (FENASTRAS), killing ten people including union leader and outspoken government critic Febe Elizabeth Velásquez. Amnesty International appealed to the government to investigate the bombing, noting that after an FMLN attack on the Defense Ministry compound the day before, Defense Minister General Larios had issued a statement that the labor movement would suffer the consequences. A few hours earlier, another bomb badly damaged the headquarters of the Committee of the Mothers of the Disappeared, injuring four persons, including a three-month-old baby. Neighbors reported seeing uniformed soldiers running from the offices just before the explosion. "The attacks came as monitoring groups and Western diplomats noted a sharp surge in human rights violations and repression," Lindsey Gruson reported in the *Times*, including "a steep increase in the use of physical and psychological torture by the armed forces and in the number of peasants, union members and students arrested." María Julia Hernández, the Director of the Church Human Rights Office Tutela Legal, observed that "arrests, disappearances and torture have all increased recently," adding: "The problem is structural. The military have more power than the president" in this celebrated "democracy." Archbishop Rivera y Damas, in his Sunday homily, said that Tutela Legal believed the "ominous death squads" were responsible for the bombing and called for an "in-depth investigation to put an end once and for all to these massacres."[19]

In accord with the usual convention, the escalating violence was attributed to "extremists of the left and right," with the reform-minded government standing by in helpless impotence. This is the standard technique by which editors, commentators, and congressional doves mask their tacit support for death squads and other methods "used to shield the government from accountability for the torture, disappearances and extrajudicial executions committed in their name" (Amnesty International, corroborating other independent analyses). The source of the terror is adequately demonstrated by the impunity with which it is conducted, not to speak of ample direct evidence implicating the security forces—truisms that human rights monitors have regularly emphasized, to no avail. During the funeral for six of the victims of the bombing, soldiers lobbed tear gas canisters into "the demonstration," Gruson reports, referring to the funeral march.[20]

While the guests at the garden party were compelled to suffer Ortega's presence in San José, Salvadoran army deserter César Vielman Joya Martínez was informing reporters and congressional aides in Washington about his participation in torture and murder operations conducted by the special forces group GC-2 of the Salvadoran army's First Brigade, with the certain knowledge of its US advisers, who "had control of the department"—unless, for tactical reasons, they chose not to know. Joya Martínez claimed that his orders were issued by the Salvadoran Joint Chiefs of Staff and sent to the commanders of the Brigade, that he had seen orders for seventy-two executions from April through July, and that he had taken part in eight of these death squad murders. The victims were first almost beaten to death during interrogation, then their throats were usually slit and their bodies were thrown over a cliff into the Pacific Ocean or buried in secret cemeteries, he said, giving a detailed account, many parts of which were independently confirmed. Among the First Brigade officers he implicated were its former commander, who is now the Vice-Minister of Defense, and the current commander of the elite Belloso battalion. They and others cited are "leaders and operators of the so-called death squadrons ...," he charged. The Bush Administration denied the charges, while recognizing that they were "very serious" and claiming that an investigation was in process.[21]

In the days immediately before the meeting of the presidents, Cristiani's ARENA government denounced the FMLN peace proposal because it called for the removal of military officers involved in the massive atrocities of the 1980s. The entire military command met with journalists and termed this demand "absurd, ridiculous and impossible," as did the notorious killer Roberto d'Aubuisson, Honorary ARENA President-for-Life. Cristiani also publicly denounced this proposal as "ridiculous"; doubtless it is ridiculous to expect the country's effective rulers to purge themselves. The *New York Times* evidently agreed. Lindsey Gruson reported that neither the government nor the FMLN was attempting to "advance the nascent peace process." Both intended only to score debating points. The proof is that the government demanded complete surrender by the FMLN but "offered almost no concessions to the rebels and did not address the underlying social and economic issues that led the guerrillas to take up arms," while the rebels called for the dismissal of senior commanders who were linked to human rights abuses—two equally outlandish proposals.[22]

The coordinator of the Permanent Committee of the Church-initiated National Debate for Peace did not agree, however. Rather, he said, the "self-cleansing and transformation" of the armed forces is necessary to put an end to abuses and contribute to the achievement of peace.[23] The problem of controlling the military is the familiar one that arises in all the Latin American terror states that the US has established or supported for many years. It is irresoluble as long as their institutional structures remain unchanged, as Washington demands, with the general concurrence of domestic elites.

On October 26, as Cristiani was on his way to San José, a fragmentation grenade was hurled into a crowd of students at the public University of El Salvador (UES) preparing for a march to commemorate the assassination of human rights activist Herbert Anaya. It wounded fifteen students, five seriously. The perpetrators departed through a university gate guarded by First Infantry Brigade troops. The same day, three UES students were abducted by security forces. The UES rector stated that the government, which had attacked and partially destroyed the university in 1980 with many killed and kept it closed for four years, now intends "to eliminate the university . . . through terror tactics." Other atrocities were reported in the following days. The director of the human rights office of the Jesuit university UCA attributed the continuing atrocities against civilians to "an entire strategy of war and repression." In the weeks before, there had been a rash of abductions, rapes, torture, and other abuses aimed at the unions and other popular organizations. Human rights activists described the wave of repression as "an Army campaign to instill terror in the populace."[24]

UES was under the control of the First Brigade, which conducted regular atrocities there with the usual impunity. Thus on July 17, troops guarding the university entrances fired on students, leaving ten wounded. They were protesting the military presence and pressing for the release of fourteen students and professors who had been detained by the security forces in recent weeks. President Cristiani claimed that the soldiers opened fire only after they were attacked by students, but the university chancellor denied this charge, calling the army attack an "act of aggression" against the university and pointing out that soldiers suffered no injuries. Five days later, the print shop at UCA, which publishes several journals that analyze and criticize government policies, was dynamited. UCA authorities blamed the military, observing that the attackers had broken through the university walls when the city was under "strict military vigil" and movement was difficult, and that the bombing was "part of a series of attacks and accusations against the Jesuits." There was no interest here.[25]

In late September, Senator Christopher Dodd, the leader of the congressional doves, lauded the ARENA government's new respect for human rights as he co-sponsored a resolution with Jesse Helms to increase military aid to El Salvador. Two days before, the army had attacked a church to which protestors had fled from riot police, flushing them out with tear gas and beating and arresting sixty-one labor activists, thirty-nine of whom appeared in court bruised and beaten, some barely able to walk, several charging rape. Congress approved the Dodd–Helms military aid increase, rejecting any human rights conditions. Archbishop Rivera y Damas condemned the decision, urging that aid "go toward rehabilitating the thousands of Salvadorans maimed in the war and not for weapons."[26] The Newspaper of Record again ignored all of this, choosing instead to remind its readers of the events at Nandaime in July 1988, with appropriate dismay and horror over the atrocious acts of the animal who was now disturbing the garden party.

One will search in vain for a suggestion that El Salvador—or Guatemala, where the situation is even worse—should rein in its military to enhance the prospects for democracy and the peace process. Their leadership are not skunks at picnics, but estimable (if somewhat ineffectual) democrats, and the military rulers are "reforming" and overcoming past harsh practices under benign US influence—a permanent process, untroubled by annoying fact.

3. From Illusion to Reality

Let us depart now from the world of ideological constructions and turn to the events that were unfolding. As noted, Nicaragua called for a meeting at UN headquarters to implement the August 1989 Tela Accords of the Central American presidents, now restricted to Nicaragua in accordance with US dictates. The participants were to be the Nicaraguan and Honduran governments, representatives of the Contras, and the International Verification and Support Commission.

Honduras immediately rejected the invitation to participate, stating that it had no responsibility for the US-run forces based in its territory and no intention of carrying out its commitment under the Tela Accords to implement the demobilization of the Contras by December. If the Contras maintain armed camps in sectors of Honduras that they have taken over after having expelled local residents, and launch attacks into Nicaragua from their Honduran bases, that is not the affair of sovereign Honduras. The purpose of these maneuvers was to ensure that the UN meeting, rather than providing a mechanism to implement the peace process (which the White House and Congress had long been committed to disrupt), could be portrayed as a victory for US force; that is, as a reluctant Sandinista recognition of the legitimacy of the Contras in a face-to-face meeting of the sort that "we have called for for a long time" (White House Spokesman Marlin Fitzwater).[27] By removing Honduras from the discussions, the US could also protect its policy of sustaining the Contras in violation of the Tela Accords.

Washington's tactics were perfectly understandable and in accord with long-term strategic goals. Preference for force over diplomacy is traditional, reflecting comparative advantage. But by 1986, US elite opinion was overwhelmingly opposed to reliance on the Contras (80 percent of "leaders," according to polls). Rational observers understood that economic and ideological warfare provide more cost-effective means to strangle and destroy a weak impoverished country dependent on its relations with the United States, and do not have the negative side-effect of arousing domestic and international opinion. At the same time, the elite consensus is that the US terror states must be maintained, and their leadership—defined as "democrats"—protected from any challenge as they fulfill their function of serving privilege and wealth, while murdering and torturing anyone who gets in the way. The Reaganites, with their insistence on violence for its own sake, were increasingly isolated.

By 1988, it had become clear that Contra forces could no longer be sustained as a major military power within Nicaragua. But it was also clear that a mercenary army in Honduras and a low level of regular terrorism would prevent demobilization in Nicaragua, guarantee further suffering among its people, and in general advance the primary goal of strangling the country and bringing its recalcitrant population to comprehend that survival requires submission to the will of the master of the hemisphere. In May 1988, a Defense Department official explained:

> Those 2000 hard-core guys [maintained by the US within Nicaragua] could keep some pressure on the Nicaraguan government, force them to use their economic resources for the military, and prevent them from solving their economic problems—and that's a plus. . . . Anything that puts pressure on the Sandinista regime, calls attention to the lack of democracy, and prevents the Sandinistas from solving their economic problems is a plus.

Contra commander Israel Galeano, in an August 1989 interview, said: "we're sure we'll be able to make sure the Sandinistas can't live in peace." By then the Contras were recognized to be solely a military force, all pretenses about their democratic credentials having been abandoned. An American official frankly remarks: "we knew all along that [the military] were in charge," exactly as in "the fledgling democracies"; the "political apparatus" was "grafted on" by the US. In reality, the primary purpose of the failed graft was to offer grist for the propagandists' mill, now no longer necessary.[28]

These US policies merely recapitulate the basic terms of the program that the Administration adopted in 1981, outlined by ex-CIA analyst David MacMichael in his World Court testimony: to use the proxy army (as its backers termed it in internal documents) to "provoke cross-border attacks by Nicaraguan forces and thus serve to demonstrate Nicaragua's aggressive nature"; to pressure the government to "clamp down on civil liberties within Nicaragua itself, arresting its opposition, demonstrating its allegedly inherent totalitarian nature"; and to undermine its shattered economy.[29]

As already discussed, the US from the first moment dismissed with contempt the August 1987 (Esquipulas II) agreement of the Central American presidents. The US at once rapidly escalated the illegal supply flights to the Contras that the Accords expressly prohibited, while the press cooperated by virtually suppressing these crucial facts, diverting attention from the client states and their massive violation of the Accords, and feigning vast indignation over far lesser abuses in Nicaragua. By January 1988 the US and its ideological system had completed the demolition of the unwanted Accords. In March 1988, Nicaragua and the Contras reached a temporary cease-fire, agreeing that further US aid to the Contras should be delivered only by "neutral organizations" and restricted to repatriation and resettlement. OAS Secretary-General Soares was assigned the responsibility of monitoring compliance with the agreement. Congressional doves at once joined the White House in support of legislation to violate these conditions. Contra aid, Congress decreed, was to be administered by the State Department through USAID for the purpose of maintaining the Contras as a military force in Honduras. Secretary-General Soares wrote to Secretary of State George Shultz to protest this flagrant violation of the agreement, eliciting the usual silence. A year later, the story was repeated. On February 14, 1989, the Central American presidents reiterated their agreement that US aid to the Contras should be restricted to "the voluntary demobilization, repatriation or relocation in Nicaragua and in third countries" of Contras and their families. Congress proceeded at once to violate this request by providing direct aid to maintain the Contras in Honduras, in a "historic agreement" with the White House that was hailed by the press as "consistent with the regional pact" that it flagrantly violated.[30]

The official media tale then and since is that the US was faithfully complying with the agreements. When President Ortega wrote in the *New York*

Times that US aid was being sent to the Contras in violation of the Central American agreements, few could understand what he meant.[31] His remarks could therefore be dismissed as more thuggish Commie twaddle. To the rules of the game we must add yet another: truth is an utter irrelevance when it does not serve power.

4. The 1990 Elections

The 1990 elections in Nicaragua were an event of considerable significance. For understanding US policy, and the operative concept of democracy in the dominant political culture, it is important to pay close attention to what was known about them in the preceding months, and the way they were later interpreted. The first of these questions is addressed in this section, published before the elections; the second in the next chapter, written afterwards. To distinguish clearly between these two topics—what was evident before and hindsight—I leave this section in its original form.[32]

In 1984, Nicaragua ran elections that were superior by any rational standards to those conducted in the US terror states. They were observed as closely as any in history by the professional association of Latin American scholars, Western governments and parliaments, and others. The general conclusion was that they were fair and equitable, surely by the standards of the region, more so than the elections in El Salvador celebrated by the US government and media as a triumph of democracy. The US labored effectively to disrupt the elections, as is now quietly conceded. By the rules of the game, these facts are irrelevant. The elections did not take place. Alone in the region, Nicaragua had no elected president, but only a dictator.[33]

The next election was scheduled for 1990. The official fable here is that the totalitarian Sandinistas agreed to a 1990 election only because of the steadfastness of the US and the Contras. In the real world, the only detectable effect of US pressure was to advance the scheduled elections by a few months. The US intervened massively in an effort to disrupt the elections. The embargo and other economic warfare were a clear message to Nicaraguan voters: If you want your children to eat, vote the way we order you to.

By its rejection of the Tela Accords and insistence on blocking Contra demobilization, *Globe* editor Randolph Ryan observed, Washington was sending "an implicit message ... to the Nicaraguan electorate: If you want a secure peace, vote for the opposition." In a backhanded way, even the *New York Times* conceded this subversion of the electoral process. Reporting with much pleasure how the collapse of the economy had "alienated" the working class and turned them against the Sandinistas, the *Times* observed that Managua workers understood that restoration of relations with the US was the key to overcoming the economic crisis and that "the opposition is better suited to the job" than the Sandinistas: "well-publicized foreign donations to the opposition parties here have been interpreted by many Nicaraguans as proof that the opposition, not the Sandinistas, has better access to the foreign money necessary to relieve Nicaragua's crisis."[34]

In early November 1989, the Bush Administration brought the US candidate Violeta Chamorro to Washington for some publicity. President Bush issued a promise "to lift the trade embargo and assist in Nicaragua's reconstruction" if Chamorro won the election, the White House announced.[35]

It took no great genius to perceive that the US would continue to torture Nicaragua, with elite support across the spectrum, until it restored US clients to power. This renewed display of the traditional fear and contempt for democracy among US elites, which reached new peaks in the 1980s, could hardly be understood in respectable circles here, however. There was much discussion over proposals to send aid to the opposition or to involve the CIA in covert operations. In comparison with the actual and virtually unchallenged US actions designed to subvert free elections in Nicaragua, these questions are trivialities.

In relative terms, that is; in absolute scale, US financial intervention in support of its clients amounted to over half the monthly wage per person in Nicaragua. The Council on Hemispheric Affairs observes that the equivalent here would be a flow of $2 billion into a US election campaign by a foreign power (a vastly greater sum if we consider comparative wage scales)—though the US, as distinct from totalitarian Nicaragua, does not permit a penny to flow from abroad for such purposes.[36]

There is nothing subtle about any of this. A Canadian observer mission sponsored by unions and development agencies, along with Church, human rights, and academic groups, completed a four-week investigation of the election preparations in Nicaragua just as the garden party celebrating "democracy" opened with much fanfare in Costa Rica. Its conclusion, as reported by wire services (but apparently unpublished here), was that the US "is doing everything it can to disrupt the elections set for next year. ... American intervention is the main obstacle to the attainment of free and fair elections in Nicaragua," the report of the mission stated. It added further that the Contras were attempting to sabotage the elections. They were "waging a campaign of intimidation with the clear message, 'if you support the [Sandinista government], we will be back to kill you'." The Canadian mission estimated that the Contras killed forty-two people in "election violence" in October.[37]

One may debate whether it was right or wrong for Nicaragua to rescind its unilateral cease-fire. But it requires considerable naiveté for liberal doves to criticize this action on the grounds that it would undermine the prospect for "a full restoration of US–Nicaraguan relations," which "will not come until Bush can point to an election that he considers fair" (*Boston Globe*).[38] Bush will "consider an election fair" when his candidates win, even if their victory is based on wholesale terror and intimidation, as in El Salvador; otherwise, it is illegitimate. Furthermore, "Bush" can stand as a metaphor for elite opinion generally. The record of the past decade makes this a fairly safe conclusion, and it is only buttressed by a broader inquiry into historical practice.

It would be unrealistic to expect the United States to tolerate a political system that is not dominated by business, oligarchy, and military elements that subordinate themselves to US elite interests. Still less will the US willingly tolerate a government that diverts resources to the poor majority, thus demonstrating its utter failure to recognize the right priorities, and embarking on a course that may have dangerous demonstration effects if the experiment is permitted to succeed. Accordingly, US policy has not veered from the principle that the client terror states must be maintained and the Sandinistas eliminated in favor of elements with a proper understanding of the needs of the privileged in Nicaragua and, crucially, the United States.

Notes

1. AP, November 1, 1989.

2. *WP*, October 14; Philip Bennett, *BG*, October 30. Ambush, Lindsey Gruson, October 28, *NYT*; also briefly noted in an AP report, *NYT*, October 23. Larmer, *CSM*, November 3, 1989.

3. WFP, "All Things Considered," NPR, November 2; HOTLINE, Washington DC, October 3; wire services, November 5; Ralph Fine, Op-Ed, *BG*, November 6; *Barricada*, November 3; Reuters, *BG*, November 7, 1989.

4. See references of Chapter 5, Note 5.

5. AP, October 23; editorial, *NYT*, October 31; Lindsey Gruson, *NYT*, October 29, 1989.

6. Uhlig, *NYT*, October 30; Adam Pertman, *BG*, October 30, November 2; Dan Rather, CBS evening news, October 27, 1989.

7. Robert Pear, *NYT*, November 2; *BG*, November 3. Kerry, CBS radio, 8:30 a.m., November 3; Adam Pertman, *BG*, November 2; Brit Hume, ABC TV Evening News, November 7; Editorials, *NYT*, October 31, November 1; Uhlig, *NYT*, October 30; Schorr, Lewis, *NYT*, November 5,

1989. See also Mary McGrory, *WP Weekly*, November 13, 1989, dismissing Ortega as "obnoxious" but not without justification in announcing that "he intended to defend his people and fire when fired upon."

8. Ryan, *BG*, June 9; Cockburn, *WSJ*, June 15, *Nation*, July 10; Walker, *Nicaragua* (Westview Press, 1986), p. 133; original emphasis.

9. See Chapter 8, p. 276, and for many details, *Necessary Illusions*, pp. 247 ff.

10. AP, November 5; AP, November 3; UPI, *BG*, November 4, 1989.

11. Editorial, *NYT*, October 31; Larmer, *CSM*, November 3, 1989.

12. Pertman, *BG*, November 2, quoting peace activist Jim Morrell.

13. See *Necessary Illusions*, pp. 57 f., 251.

14. *BG*, November 9, 1984, citing also similar comments by Democratic dove Christopher Dodd.

15. For more details, see *Manufacturing Consent*, pp. 269–70.

16. Friedman, *From Beirut to Jerusalem* (Farrar Straus Giroux, 1989), p. 128; Rosenblatt, *NYT Book Review*, July 9, 1989.

17. Lindsey Gruson, *NYT*, October 29, 1989.

18. Chris Norton, *CSM*, September 22, 1989. See photographs and reports by freelance journalist Terry Allen, Richmond, Vermont, transmitted to Congress (with no reaction).

19. Douglas Farah, *BG*, November 1; Lindsey Gruson, *NYT*, November 1. AI, AP, November 6; Chris Norton, *CSM*, November 6, on the report of soldiers fleeing. Tutela Legal, quoted by National Labor Committee in Support of Democracy and Human Rights in El Salvador, October 31. Rivera y Damas, *BG*, November 6, brief notice on p. 35; editorial, November, 1989.

20. *NYT*, November 3, 1989.

21. AP, October 26, 27, 28; *WP*, October 27; *BG*, October 29, p. 26; *El Salvador On Line (ESOL)*, October 30, 1989. The actual story, as it predictably unfolded, was that the Bush Administration sought in every way to silence Joya Martínez and ship him to El Salvador before his information could do too much damage. See Chapter 12, p. 389 f.

22. AP, October 20; *ESOL*, October 30; Gruson, *NYT*, October 18, 1989.

23. *ESOL*, October 30, 1989. On the National Debate, see pp. 268 f., above.

24. *ESOL*, October 30; Frank Smyth, *Austin American-Statesman*, September 28, 1989.

25. *Central American Report*, Guatemala, July 28, 1989. The press and Congress remained uninterested until six leading Jesuit intellectuals had their brains blown out a few weeks later, after this article went to press.

26. COHA's *Washington Report on the Hemisphere*, October 10; *BG*, September 20; El Rescate *Human Rights Chronology*, September 1989.

27. Mark Uhlig, *NYT*, November 3; Adam Pertman, *BG*, November 4, 1989. Honduras later agreed to observe the talks, though not to take part; *BG*, November 7.

28. Doyle McManus, *LAT*, May 28, 1988. Galeano, AP, October 28; Mark Uhlig, *NYT*, November 5, 1989.

29. See *Culture of Terrorism*, p. 121.

30. For details, see *Necessary Illusions*, and Chapter 2 above. On the subversion of the Accords generally and the crucial media role in facilitating the process, and the earlier record of barring diplomatic settlement, see *Culture of Terrorism*, ch. 7; *Necessary Illusions*, particularly ch. 4, Appendix IV, sec. 5. This record is almost completely suppressed in the media and is destined to be eliminated from history, along with earlier similar successes in undermining diplomacy. For examples from Indochina, see *Towards a New Cold War*, chs 3, 4; *Manufacturing Consent*, ch. 5, sec. 5.3.

31. Ortega, Op-Ed, *NYT*, November 2, 1989.

32. *Z Magazine*, December 1990; there are slight and irrelevant editing changes, particularly changes of tense to avoid confusion. See also Chapter 5.

33. See references of Chapter 5, Note 5.

34. *BG*, October 26; Mark Uhlig, *NYT*, November 7, 1989.

35. AP, November 8, 1989.

36. COHA's *Washington Report on the Hemisphere*, November 8, 1989, reporting estimates by Hemisphere Initiatives.

37. AP, October 26, 1989; *Miami Herald*, October 27, 1989, brief notice.

38. Editorial, *BG*, November 2, 1989.

TEN

The Decline of the Democratic Ideal

ONE fundamental goal of any well-crafted indoctrination program is to direct attention elsewhere, away from effective power, its roots, and the disguises it assumes. Thus to enter into debate over Vietnam, or the Middle East, or Central America, one is required to gain special knowledge of these areas, not of the United States. Rational standards are permitted for the study of Soviet intervention, which focuses on Moscow, not Kabul and Prague; for us, however, the problems lie elsewhere. Respectable commentators can even speak of "the tragic self-destruction of Central America," with the two superpowers playing a (symmetrical) background role (Theodore Sorenson). A similar comment about Eastern Europe would merely evoke ridicule.[1]

The serviceability of the doctrine is apparent. Those who hope to understand world affairs will naturally resist it. The February 1990 elections in Nicaragua are a case in point. The forces at work within Nicaragua are surely worth understanding,[2] the reactions to the elections here no less so—far more so, in fact, given the scale and character of US power. These reactions provide quite illuminating insight into the topics addressed in these chapters. They provide further and quite dramatic evidence that in the dominant political culture, the concept of democracy is disappearing even as an abstract ideal.

1. The Winner: George Bush

As a point of departure, consider a few reactions beyond the borders. In Mexico City, the liberal *La Jornada* wrote:

> After 10 years, Washington examines with satisfaction the balance of an investment made with fire and blood . . ., an undeclared war of aggression. . . . The elections were certainly cleanly prepared and conducted, but a decade of horror was behind them.

While welcoming the electoral outcome, the right-wing daily *El Universal* acknowledged that

> The defeated Sandinista Front does not have all of the responsibility for the disasters that have fallen upon Nicaraguans. Its lead role in the construction of Nicaragua in recent years cannot be denied, either. But the voters have made an objective use of the essential prerogative of democracy: to vote for who they believe can better their situation

—surely George Bush's candidate, in the light of unchanging US policies that are as familiar to Latin Americans as the rising of the sun.

The familiar background was recalled in the commentary on the elections by León García Soler, one of the leading political analysts of the daily *Excelsior*. Taking note of the fraudulent democracy of Mexico itself, he discussed the elections conducted under US threat in Nicaragua in the context of "the expansionism that led [the US] to embrace the continent from ocean to ocean; of the Manifest Destiny which led it to the imperial wars, to the protectorates and colonies, to the endless invasions of the nations of our America. . . . The Nicaraguan people voted for peace," he wrote, "with the clear threat by the interventionists that they would never recognize the legitimacy of the elections if the Sandinistas won," and would simply continue the terrorist war and economic strangulation if the electoral outcome were not satisfactory to Washington.

In the Mexican weekly *Punto*, liberation theologist Miguel Concha wrote:

> the elections in Nicaragua were won in the first place by the inhuman and criminal Low Intensity War of the imperialist government. The objective and subjective elements behind the winning coalition [are . . .] without any doubt the policy of the U.S. administrations, call them Reagan or Bush, . . . based on unrestricted and evident contempt for all norms of international law, with military aggression and economic blockade as the most important spearheads during the

last decade. This heavily influenced the choice of the majority of Nicaraguans . . ., people desperately looking for peace, [a vital question] for a people so severely beaten by this whip, for a people which for ten years have seen their children die, after a revolutionary triumph which was seen as the solution to its problems, for a people that has been confronted by a fratricidal war, arranged by the blind, stubborn will of the "enemies of humanity" who, insisting on their power, seek to be immortal.

"The UNO triumph was legal," he concluded, "but not just."

For the independent *El Tiempo* in Colombia, passionately opposed to "frightening communism" and the Sandinistas who represent it on the continent, "The U.S. and President Bush scored a clear victory."[3]

In Guatemala, the independent *Central America Report* observed that the 1990 elections "were mandated in the Nicaraguan Constitution, adopted in January 1987, before the Arias Peace Plan"—in fact, at a time when the US was pulling out every stop to block the threat of peace. Though "the concessions granted by the Sandinistas were the result of the regional peace accords," the elections were not brought about by the diplomacy of the Central American presidents, still less by the "armed pressure of the contras" as Washington claims. Regarding the diplomatic process itself, the journal notes that Nicaragua alone lived up to the Accords, which were defied by the United States and its proxy forces, and its three client states. "Reforms aimed at internal democratization" were blocked in El Salvador, Honduras and Guatemala, where human rights abuses are on the rise and no progress has been made in realizing any aspect of the agreements. The journal continues:

> The exemplary elections conducted by the Sandinistas appear to be the only relevant "success" of the diplomatic process begun in 1987. Given that the contras have remained in place despite repeated agreements to disband—the last being the December 8, 1989 deadline of the August 1989 Tela Accords—editorials question the Sandinistas' political wisdom in holding up their side of the bargain.

With regard to the "exemplary elections," "Most analysts agree that the UNO victory marks the consummation of the US government's military, economic and political efforts to overthrow the Sandinistas." Under the heading *The Winners*, the journal added:

> US President George Bush emerged as a clear victor in the Nicaraguan elections. The decade-long Reagan/Bush war against Nicaragua employed a myriad of

methods—both covert and open—aimed at overthrowing the Sandinistas. Bush's continuation of the two-pronged Reagan policy of economic strangulation and military aggression finally reaped tangible results. Following the elections, Ortega said that the outcome was not in retrospect surprising since the voters went to the polls "with a pistol pointed at their heads" ...

—a conclusion that the journal accepts without comment. "The consensus attributes the population's defection ... to the critical economic crisis in Nicaragua," the report continues, citing an editorial in the Guatemala City press that "pointed out that more than ten years of economic and military aggressions waged by a government with unlimited resources created the setting for an election determined by economic exhaustion." "It was a vote in search of peace by a people that, inevitably, were fed up with violence," the Guatemala City editorial concluded: "It is a vote from a hungry people that, more than any idea, need to eat."[4]

The analysis ends with this comment:

> While many observers today are remarking that never before has a leftist revolutionary regime handed over power in elections, the opposite is also true. Never has a popular elected leftist government in Latin America been allowed to undertake its reforms without being cut short by a coup, an invasion or an assassination.

Or, we may add, subversion, terror, or economic strangulation. Readers in Guatemala, or elsewhere in Latin America, need no further reminders of these truisms. One will search far for any hint of such a thought, let alone a discussion of what it implies, in US commentary. Even the fact that Nicaragua had a popular elected government is inexpressible in the US propaganda system, with its standards of discipline that few respectable intellectuals would dare to flout.

In London, the editors of the *Financial Times* observe: "The war against the Contras has eroded the early achievements in health and education of the Sandinista revolution and brought the country close to bankruptcy." The victors, they add, are the Contras—which is to say, the White House, Congress, and the support team who set up, maintained, and justified what was conceded to be a "proxy army" by Contra lobbyists, who hoped that Washington might somehow convert its proxies into a political force (Bruce Cameron and Penn Kemble). Managua correspondent Tim Coone concludes that "Nicaraguans appeared to believe that a UNO victory offered the best prospect of securing US funds to end the country's economic misery"— correctly, of course.[5]

The English-language Costa Rican monthly *Mesoamerica* added this comment: "The Sandinistas fell for a scam perpetrated by Costa Rican President Oscar Arias and the other Central American Presidents," which "cost them the 25 Feb. elections." Nicaragua had agreed to loosen wartime constraints and advance the scheduled elections by a few months "in exchange for having the *contras* demobilized and the war brought to an end." The White House and Congress broke the deal at once, maintaining the Contras as a military force in violation of the agreements and compelling them to be modified to focus on Nicaragua alone. With the deal effectively broken, the US candidate could promise to end the war, while Ortega could not. Faced with this choice, "war weary Nicaraguans voted for peace."[6]

Summarizing the basic thrust, the winner of the elections was George Bush and the Democrat–Republican coalition that waged ten years of economic and military aggression, leaving a hungry and distraught people who voted for relief from terror and misery. Democracy has been dealt a serious blow, with a "popular elected leftist government" replaced by one elected under duress, by violent foreign intervention that proved decisive.

2. United in Joy

Returning home, we find a different picture. The basic lessons were drawn by correspondent Hugh Sidey of *Time* magazine, a respected commentator on the presidency. Under the heading "Credit Where Credit Is Due," he calls for "a little fairness" to Ronald Reagan: "The end result of the Nicaraguan episode seems to be what the U.S. has vainly sought all over the globe in its support of freedom; few American lives were committed or lost, with a cost of only $300 million in U.S. aid to the contras," and a mere $1.3 million for the economic warfare. "Compare Viet Nam," Sidey continues: "58,000 Americans killed, $150 billion spent, the nation rent in bitterness, a bitter defeat."[7]

In short, Reagan deserves credit for good management: his cohorts ran a cost-effective operation, expending only trivial sums to cause Nicaragua some $15 billion in damages and 30,000 killed outright, along with unknown numbers of others who died from disease and hunger. Note, however, that Sidey is a bit unfair to Reagan's predecessors, who did, after all, succeed in murdering millions in Indochina and leaving three countries in total ruin—no small achievement, despite the excessive cost to us.

Time proceeded to laud the methods that were used to bring about the latest of the "happy series of democratic surprises" as "democracy burst forth" in Nicaragua. The method was to "wreck the economy and prosecute a long and deadly proxy war until the exhausted natives overthrow the unwanted government themselves," with a cost to us that is "minimal," leaving the victim "with wrecked bridges, sabotaged power stations, and ruined farms," and thus providing the US candidate with "a winning issue": ending the "impoverishment of the people of Nicaragua." The only issue dividing conservatives and liberals, *Time* correctly concludes, is "who should claim credit" for this triumph of democracy, in a free and fair election without coercion.

Time might be assigned to the "conservative" end of the spectrum, so let us turn to the leading journal of mainstream liberalism, the *New Republic*. Its editorial is entitled "Who Won Nicaragua?" The answer is: "Why, the Nicaraguans, of course"—not George Bush and US aggression. "Those who supported aid to the Contras . . ., as did this magazine, can find considerable vindication in the outcome," which "made nonsense of both the left-wing myth that anti-Yankeeism is the centerpiece of all Latin America's political identity and the right-wing myth that Leninists can never be induced to change." Adding what remains unsaid, the former "myth" succumbed to the successful use of terror and economic strangulation, and the latter is based on the loyal denial of familiar and well-attested facts about "the Sandinistas, who had won free and fair elections in 1984" (London *Observer*, March 4, 1990). "Gratifying as the election results are," the editorial continues, "democracy is not yet quite safe in Nicaragua," and "having served as an inspiration for the triumph of democracy in our time, the United States now has an opportunity to see to it that democracy prevails"— "democracy," *New Republic*-style: the kind that "prevails" in the Central American domains where the US has had ample opportunity to entrench it, to take the obvious example.[8]

Perhaps it is unfair to illustrate the liberal alternative by editorials in a journal that gave "Reagan & Co. good marks" for their support for state terror in El Salvador as it peaked in 1981, and then, surveying the carnage three years later, advised Reagan & Co. that we must send military aid to "Latin-style fascists . . . regardless of how many are murdered," because "there are higher American priorities than Salvadoran human rights." In assessing US political culture let us, then, put aside the more passionate advocates of state terror—though not without noting that these values, familiar from the Nazi era, in no way diminish the reputation of the journal, or even merit a word of comment in left-liberal circles. Let us turn, rather, to less bloodthirsty sectors of what is called the "establishment left" by editor Charles William Maynes of *Foreign Policy*. He is referring specifically to the *New York Times*, but doubtless would include also the *Washington Post*, the major television news bureaus, the *Boston Globe* (which perhaps qualifies as "ultra-left"), and his own journal, the more liberal of the two major foreign affairs quarterlies.[9]

To seek out the establishment left, we might begin with public debates. Public Broadcasting (PBS), generally regarded as dangerously left-wing, ran a debate between Elliott Abrams and Hendrick Hertzberg the day before the election, moderated by the pro-Contra columnist Morton Kondracke. Representing the left (and indeed, at the far left of expressible opinion), Hertzberg said that he would support a continuation of the embargo against Nicaragua if the Sandinistas won the election and observer reports were less than totally favorable. He has never advocated that an embargo be imposed upon the US client states nearby, where elections were held in an "atmosphere of terror and despair, of macabre rumor and grisly reality," in the words of the spokesman for the British Parliamentary Human Rights Group, Lord Chitnis, observing the 1984 election in El Salvador. He has also not suggested that the hideous atrocities of these US clients merit such a response. We conclude, then, that by the standards of the establishment left, the crimes of the Sandinistas far exceed those of the death squad states. A comparison of these crimes tells us a great deal about the values upheld at the left extreme of the establishment spectrum.[10]

Turning to the establishment left press, we begin with the *New York Times*, where Elaine Sciolino reviewed the US reaction to the elections. The headline reads: "Americans United in Joy, But Divided Over Policy." The policy division turns out to be over who deserves credit for the joyous outcome, so we are left with "Americans United in Joy."[11]

Such phrases as "United in Joy" are not entirely unknown. One might find them, perhaps, in the North Korean or Albanian press. Obviously the issue was contentious, certainly to Nicaraguans, to others in Latin America as well. But not to educated US elites, who are quite eager to depict themselves as dedicated totalitarians.

The review of opinion opens by noting that "the left and the right and those in between [have] a fresh opportunity to debate one of the United States' most divisive foreign policy issues of the last decade." The left–right debate now reduces to who can justly claim credit. Sciolino begins with eleven paragraphs reviewing the position of the right, followed by five devoted to the left. In the former category she cites Elliott Abrams, Jeane

Kirkpatrick, Fred Iklé of the Pentagon, Oliver North, Robert Leiken of the Harvard University Center for International Affairs, and Ronald Reagan. They portray the outcome as "spectacular," "great, wonderful, stunning," a tribute to the Contras who, "when history is written, ... will be the folk heroes," a victory "for the cause of democracy" in a "free and fair election."

Sciolino then turns to the left: "On the other side, Lawrence A. Pezzullo, who was appointed Ambassador to Nicaragua by President Carter, called the election results 'fantastic'." We will return to Pezzullo's left-wing credentials shortly. The second representative of "the other side" is Sol Linowitz, who, as Carter Administration Ambassador to the Organization of American States (OAS), sought in vain to mobilize Latin America in support of Carter's program of "*Somocismo sin Somoza*" ("Somozism without Somoza") after the murderous tyrant could no longer be maintained in power, and later urged pressures to make Nicaragua more democratic—like El Salvador and Guatemala, both just fine and hence needing no such pressures. The final representative of the left is Francis McNeil, whose credentials as a leftist lie in the fact that he quit the State Department in 1987 when his pessimism about Contra military prospects aroused the ire of Elliott Abrams.[12]

The last paragraph of Sciolino's report observes that some "were not entirely comfortable with the results" of the election, citing Lawrence Birns of the Council on Hemispheric Affairs, who "seemed to side with the Sandinistas," expressing his "inner rage that the corner bully won over the little guy."

Sciolino remarks incidentally that "Sandinista supporters expressed sadness, and said that the defeat was a product of Nicaragua's economic troubles—a result of the American trade embargo and other outside pressures"—thus lining up with much of Latin America. But recall that Americans were United in Joy. By simple logic, it follows that these miscreants are not Americans, or perhaps not people.

In summary, there are "two sides," the right and the left, which differed on the tactical question of how to eliminate the Sandinistas in favor of US clients and are now "United in Joy." There is one person who *seems* to side with the Sandinistas, but couldn't *really* be that far out of step, we are to understand. And there are some non-Americans who share the exotic opinions of Latin Americans as to what happened and why. Having failed to obey state orders, these strange creatures are off the left–right spectrum entirely, and do not participate in the great debate over the sole issue still unresolved: Who deserves the credit for the happy outcome?

The *Times* conception of the spectrum of opinion is, then, very much like that of *Time* magazine and *Foreign Policy* editor Charles Maynes. Or former Undersecretary of State David Newsom, now director of the Institute for the Study of Diplomacy at Georgetown University, who urges "the ideological extremes of the nation's political spectrum" to abandon the fruitless debate over the credits for our victories. Or Jimmy Carter, who explained to the press that his observer commission was "carefully balanced—half Democrat and half Republican," thus carefully balanced between two groups that satisfy the prior condition of objectivity: passionate opposition to the Sandinistas and support for Washington's candidates.[13]

Throughout, we see with great clarity the image of a highly disciplined political culture, deeply imbued with totalitarian values.

3. The Case for the Doves

In the new phase of the debate, the right attributes the defeat of the Sandinistas to the Contras, while the establishment left claims that the Contras impeded their effort to overthrow the Sandinistas by other means. But the doves have failed to present their case as strongly as they might. Let us therefore give them a little assistance, meanwhile recalling some crucial facts that are destined for oblivion because they are far too inconvenient to preserve.

We begin with Lawrence Pezzullo, the leading representative of the left in the *Times* survey of opinion. Pezzullo was appointed Ambassador in early 1979, at a time when Carter's support for the Somoza tyranny was becoming problematic. Of course no one contemplated any modification in the basic system of power, surely no significant role for the Sandinistas (FSLN). As we have seen, there was complete agreement that Somoza's National Guard must be kept intact, and it was not until June 29, shortly before the fall of the Somoza regime, that any participant in an NSC meeting "suggested the central U.S. objective was something other than preventing a Sandinista victory." By then it was finally realized that means must be sought "to moderate the FSLN," who could not be marginalized or excluded, as hoped.[14]

As in US political democracy generally, the Carter Administration had its left–right spectrum, with National Security Adviser Zbigniew Brzezinski on the right, warning of apocalyptic outcomes if the US did not intervene, and on the left, Secretary of State Cyrus Vance and Assistant Secretary of State for Inter-American Affairs Viron Vaky, pursuing a more nuanced approach. Pezzullo's task was to implement the policy of the left—that is, to bar the FSLN from power through the "preservation of existing institutions, especially the National Guard" (Vaky, June 15, 1979). This plan was proposed to the OAS, but rejected by the Latin American governments—all ultra-left extremists, by US standards. Pezzullo was then compelled to inform Somoza that his usefulness was at an end. On June 30, he noted in a cable to Washington that "with careful orchestration we have a better than even chance of preserving enough of the [National Guard] to maintain order and hold the FSLN in check after Somoza resigns," even though this plan would "smack somewhat of *Somocismo sin Somoza*," he added a few days later. For the "successor government," the Carter Administration approached Archbishop Obando y Bravo (in contrast, our religious sensibilities are deeply offended by political engagement of priests committed to the preferential option for the poor) and the right-wing businessman Adolfo Calero (later civilian director of the main Contra force); and for head of the National Guard, it considered Colonel Enrique Bermúdez, who later became Contra commander.[15]

At the time, the National Guard was carrying out murderous attacks against civilians, leaving tens of thousands killed. Pezzullo recommended that the bloodbath be continued: "I believe it ill-advised," he cabled Washington on July 6, "to go to Somoza and ask for a bombing halt." On July 13, Pezzullo informed Washington that the "survivability" of the Guard was doubtful unless Somoza left—as he did, four days later, fleeing to Miami with what remained of the national treasury. On July 19, the game was over—that phase, at least.[16]

As the FSLN entered Managua on July 19, the Carter Administration "began setting the stage for a counterrevolution," Peter Kornbluh observes, mounting a clandestine operation to evacuate Guard commanders on US planes disguised with Red Cross markings. This is a war crime punishable under the Geneva conventions, the London *Economist* observed years later, when the same device was used to supply Contras within Nicaragua (pictures of CIA supply planes disguised with Red Cross markings appeared without comment in *Newsweek*, while the vigorous denunciation of this violation of international law by the Red Cross passed without notice generally). Within six months after the overthrow of Somoza, the Carter Administration had initiated the CIA destabilization campaign, inherited and expanded by the Reaganites. The Carter doves did not give direct support to the National Guard forces that they helped to reconstitute. Rather, training and direction were in the hands of neo-Nazi Argentine generals serving "as a proxy for the United States" (Rand Corporation terrorism expert Brian Jenkins). The US took over directly with the Reagan presidency.[17]

Pezzullo's next task was to "moderate the FSLN." The Carter doves proposed economic aid as "the main source of U.S. influence" (Pastor). The US business community supported this plan, particularly the banks, which, as noted in the *Financial Times*, were pressuring Carter to provide funds to Nicaragua so that their loans to Somoza would be repaid (courtesy of the US taxpayer). The banks were particularly concerned that if Nicaragua, reduced to utter ruin and bankruptcy by Somoza, were to default on the debt he had accumulated, it would serve as a bad example for other US clients. It was also recognized that aid directed to anti-Sandinista elements in the ruling coalition was the last remaining device to block the FSLN and its programs.[18]

After Nicaragua reached a settlement with the banks, $75 million in aid was offered, about 60 percent for the private business sector, with $5 million a grant for private organizations and $70 million a loan (partly credits to buy US goods, another taxpayer subsidy to corporations). One of the conditions was that no funds be used for projects with Cuban personnel—a way of ensuring that nothing would go to schools, the literacy campaign, health programs, or other reform measures for which Nicaragua was likely to turn to those with experience in such projects and willingness to serve. Nicaragua had no choice but to agree, since, as the *Wall Street Journal* noted, without this "signal of U.S. confidence in the stability of the country" there would be no bank loans, which were desperately needed. Nicaragua's request for US military aid and training was rejected, and efforts to obtain such aid from the West were blocked by US pressure, compelling reliance on East bloc aid as the external threat mounted.[19]

As these events pass through the US doctrinal system, they undergo a subtle alchemy and emerge in a different form: the Sandinistas

enjoyed American encouragement at first; having helped get rid of Somoza, the Carter administration also gave them $75 million in aid. But when the Sandinistas brought in Cuban and East German military advisers to help build their Army into the region's largest fighting force, conflict with Washington was sure to follow .... [20]

Nicaragua also attempted to maintain its trade links with the US and the West, and succeeded in doing so throughout the mid 1980s despite US efforts. But Washington naturally preferred that they rely on the East bloc, to ensure maximal inefficiency and to justify our defensive attack on these "Soviet clients." The US also blocked aid from international development organizations and, after failing to displace the FSLN, sought to destroy private business in Nicaragua to increase domestic discontent and undermine the mixed economy (a major and predicted effect of the Reagan embargo, and the reason why it was bitterly opposed by the Nicaraguan opposition that the US claimed to support).[21]

So enormous was the devastation left as Somoza's final legacy that a World Bank Mission concluded in October 1981 that "per capita income levels of 1977 will not be attained, in the best of circumstances, until the late 1980s" and that "any untoward event could lead to a financial trauma." There were, of course, "untoward events," but such facts do not trouble the ideologues who deduce Sandinista responsibility for the subsequent debacle from the doctrinal necessity of this conclusion. A standard rhetorical trick, pioneered by the Kissinger Commission, is to demonstrate Sandinista economic mismanagement by comparing living standards of the eighties to *1977*, thus attributing the effects of the US-backed Somoza terror to the Marxist–Leninist totalitarians. 1977 is a particularly useful choice because it was a year of "exceptional affluence" (UNO economist Francisco Mayorga).[22]

Despite the horrendous circumstances, Nicaragua's economic progress through the early 1980s was surprisingly good, with the highest growth rate in Central America by a large margin, an improvement in standard of living in contrast to a substantial fall for the rest of Central America and a somewhat lesser fall for Latin America as a whole, and significant redistribution of income and expansion of social services. In 1983, the Inter-American Development Bank reported that Nicaragua's "noteworthy progress in the social sector" was "laying a solid foundation for long-term socio-economic development." The World Bank and other international development organizations lauded the "remarkable" Nicaraguan record and outstanding success, in some respects "better than anywhere in the world" (World Bank).[23]

But US pressures succeeded in terminating these dangerous developments. By early 1987, business leader Enrique Bolaños, well to the right of the UNO directorate, attributed the economic crisis in Nicaragua to the war (60 percent, presumably including the economic war), the international economic crisis (10 percent), the contraction of the Central American Common Market (10 percent), and decapitalization by the business sector and government errors (20 percent). The *Financial Times* estimates the costs

of the Contra war at $12 billion; Mayorga adds $3 billion as the costs of
the embargo. Actual totals are uncertain, but plainly fall within the range
of the "untoward events" which, the World Bank predicted, would lead
to catastrophe.[24] The idea that the US might pay reparations for what it
has done can be relegated to the same category as the notion that it might
observe international law generally. The press blandly reports that the Bush
Administration is "exerting sharp pressure" on the Chamorro government,
informing it that "future United States aid to Nicaragua will depend on"
Nicaragua's abandonment of "the judgment of as much as $17 billion that
Nicaragua won against the United States at the International Court of Justice
during the contra war."[25] The US holds Nicaragua hostage while eloquent
oratory flows in abundance about the sanctity of international law and the
solemn duty of punishing those who violate it. There is no perceptible
sense of incongruity.

In Chapter 8, we reviewed the thoughts of the Carter doves (Pastor,
Vaky, Vance). With a sufficiently powerful microscope one can distinguish
this left-wing perspective from that of the right—for example, the Pentagon
official who informed the press in 1988 that a small number of US-backed
terrorists could "keep some pressure on the Nicaraguan government, force
them to use their economic resources for the military, and prevent them
from solving their economic problems." Or the State Department insider
who is reported to have observed in 1981 that Nicaragua must be reduced
to "the Albania of Central America." Or the government official who
informed the press in 1986 that the US did not expect a Contra victory,
but was "content to see the contras debilitate the Sandinistas by forcing
them to divert scarce resources toward the war and away from social programs"; the consequences could then be adduced as proof of "Sandinista
mismanagement." Since this understanding is common to hawks and doves,
it is not surprising that there was no reaction when it was reported in
the *Boston Globe*, just as no reaction was to be expected to David Mac-
Michael's World Court testimony on the goals of the Contra program cited
earlier—crucially, the effort to pressure Nicaragua to "clamp down on civil
liberties" so as to demonstrate "its allegedly inherent totalitarian nature and
thus increase domestic dissent within the country." We need not comment
further on the enthusiasm with which the educated classes undertook the
tasks assigned to them.[26]

It thus made perfect sense for the US command to direct its proxy forces
to attack "soft targets"—that is, undefended civilian targets—as SOUTH-
COM commander General John Galvin explained; to train the Contra forces

to attack schools and health centers so that "the Nicaraguan government cannot provide social services for the peasants, cannot develop its project," as Contra leader Horacio Arce informed the press (in Mexico).[27]

The Maynes–Sciolino left did not object to these policies in principle. They had no fundamental disagreement with the conclusion of George Shultz's State Department that "Nicaragua is the cancer and [is] metastasizing" and that "the Sandinista cancer" must be removed, "by radical surgery if necessary."[28] Furthermore, the Carter doves effectively set these policies in motion. They can therefore claim to have succeeded in their aims, as the election showed. Their only fault was excessive pessimism over the prospects for terror and economic strangulation; in this respect the judgement of the right was correct, and it is unreasonable for the left to deny that their right-wing opponents had a sounder appreciation of what violence can achieve. We should give "Credit Where Credit Is Due," as *Time* admonished, recognizing that terror and economic warfare have again proven their salutary efficacy. Thus left and right have every reason to be United in Joy at the triumph of democracy, as they jointly conceive it: Free choice, with a pistol to your head.

4. "Rallying to Chamorro"

The Kim Il Sung-style unanimity considered so natural and appropriate by the *Times* has, in fact, been characteristic of the "divisive foreign policy issue" that is said to have rent the United States in the past decade. As has been extensively documented, both reporting and permissible opinion in the media were virtually restricted to the question of the choice of means for returning Nicaragua to "the Central American mode." There was indeed a "division": Should this result be achieved by Contra terror, or, if violence proved ineffective, by arrangements enforced by the death squad democracies that already observe the approved "regional standards," as advocated by Tom Wicker and other doves? This spectrum of thought was safeguarded at a level approaching 100 percent in the national press, a most impressive achievement.[29]

Pre-election coverage maintained the same high standards of conformism. It was uniformly anti-Sandinista. The UNO coalition were the democrats, on the sole grounds that the coalition had been forged in Washington and included the major business interests, sufficient proof of democratic credentials by the conventions of US political discourse. On similar assumptions,

Bob Woodward describes the CIA operations launched by Carter as a "program to boost the democratic alternative to the Sandinistas"; no evidence of any concern for democracy is provided, or needed, on the conventional understanding of the concept of democracy.

Commentary and reporting on the Sandinistas was harsh and derisive. Some did break ranks. The *Boston Globe* ran an Op-Ed by Daniel Ortega a few days before the election, but the editors were careful to add an accompanying caricature of an ominous thug in a Soviet Field-Marshal's uniform wearing designer glasses, just to ensure that readers would not be misled.[30] Media monitors have yet to come up with a single phrase suggesting that an FSLN victory might be the best thing for Nicaragua. Even journalists who privately felt that way did not say it, perhaps because they thought the idea would be unintelligible, on a par with "the U.S. is a leading terrorist state," or "Washington is blocking the peace process," or "maybe we should tell the truth about Cambodia and Timor," or other departures from dogma. Such statements lack cognitive meaning. They are imprecations, like shouting "Fuck You" in public; they can elicit only a stream of abuse, not a rational response. We see here the ultimate achievement of thought control, well beyond what Orwell imagined. Large parts of the language are simply determined to be devoid of meaning. It all makes good sense: In a Free Society, *all* must goose-step on command, or keep silent. Anything else is just too dangerous.

On television, Peter Jennings, also regarded as prone to left-wing deviation, opened the international news by announcing that Nicaragua was going to have its "first free election in a decade."[31] Three crucial doctrines are presupposed: first, the elections under Somoza were free; second, there was no free election in 1984; third, the 1990 election was free and uncoerced. A standard footnote is that Ortega was driven to accept the 1990 elections by US pressure; here opinion divides, with the right and the left each claiming credit for the achievement.

We may disregard the first point, though not without noting that it has been a staple of the "establishment left," with its frequent reference to "restoring democracy" in Nicaragua. The second expresses a fundamental dogma, which brooks no deviation and is immune to fact; I need not review this matter, familiar outside of the reigning doctrinal system. The footnote ignores the unacceptable (hence unreportable) fact that the next election had been scheduled for 1990, and that the total effect of US machinations was to advance it by a few months.

The most interesting point, however, is the third. Suppose that the USSR were to follow the US model as the Baltic states declare independence, organizing a proxy army to attack them from foreign bases, training its terrorist forces to hit "soft targets" (health centers, schools, and so on) so that the governments cannot provide social services, reducing the economies to ruin through embargo and other sanctions, and so on, in the familiar routine. Suppose further that when elections come, the Kremlin informs the population, loud and clear, that they can vote for the CP or starve. Perhaps some unreconstructed Stalinist might call this a "free and fair election." Surely no one else would.

Or suppose that the Arab states were to reduce Israel to the level of Ethiopia, then issuing a credible threat that they would drive it the rest of the way unless it "cried uncle" and voted for their candidate. Someone who called this a "democratic election," "free and fair," would rightly be condemned as an outright Nazi.

The pertinence of the analogies is obvious. Simple logic suffices to show that anyone who called the 1990 Nicaraguan elections "free and fair," a welcome step towards democracy, was not merely a totalitarian, but one of a rather special variety. Fact: that practice was virtually exceptionless. I have found exactly *one* mainstream journalist who was able to recognize—or at least state—the elementary truth.[32] Surely other examples must exist, but the conclusion, which we need not spell out, tells us a great deal about the reigning intellectual culture.

It was apparent from the outset that the US would never tolerate free and fair elections.[33] The point was underscored by repeated White House statements that the terror and economic war would continue unless a "free choice" met the conditions of the Enforcer. It was made official in early November when the White House announced that the embargo would be lifted if the population followed US orders.[34]

To be sure, the kinds of "divisions" that the *Times* perceives were to be found on this matter as well. There were a few who simply denied that the military and economic wars had any notable impact; what could a mere $15 billion and 30,000 dead mean to a society as rich and flourishing as Nicaragua after Somoza?[35] Turning to those who tried to be serious, we find the usual two categories. The right didn't mention these crucial factors, and hailed the stunning triumph of democracy. The establishment left did mention them, and *then* hailed the stunning triumph of democracy.[36] Keeping to that sector of opinion, let us consider a few examples to illustrate the pattern.

Michael Kinsley, who represents the left on the *New Republic* editorial staff and in CNN television debate, presented his analysis of the election in the journal he edits (reprinted in the *Washington Post*). He recalled an earlier article of his, omitting its crucial content, to which we return. Kinsley then observes that "impoverishing the people of Nicaragua was precisely the point of the contra war and the parallel policy of economic embargo and veto of international development loans," and it is "Orwellian" to blame the Sandinistas "for wrecking the economy while devoting our best efforts to doing precisely that. ... The economic disaster was probably the victorious opposition's best election issue," he continues, and "it was also Orwellian for the United States, having created the disaster, to be posturing as the exhorter and arbiter of free elections."[37]

Kinsley then proceeds to posture, Orwellian-style, as the arbiter of free elections, hailing the "free election" and "triumph of democracy," which "turned out to be pleasanter than anyone would have dared to predict."

At the extreme of the establishment left, Anthony Lewis of the *New York Times* writes that "the Reagan policy did not work. It produced only misery, death and shame." Why it did not work, he does not explain; it appears to have worked very well. Lewis then proceeds to hail "the experiment in peace and democracy," which "did work." This triumph of democracy, he writes, gives "fresh testimony to the power of Jefferson's idea: government with the consent of the governed, as Václav Havel reminded us the other day. To say so seems romantic, but then we live in a romantic age."[38]

We are "dizzy with success," as Stalin used to say, observing the triumph of our ideals in Central America and the Caribbean, the Philippines, the Israeli-occupied territories, and other regions where our influence reaches so that we can take credit for the conditions of life and the state of freedom.

The reference to Havel merits some reflection. Havel's address to Congress had a remarkable impact on the political and intellectual communities. "Consciousness precedes Being, and not the other way around, as the Marxists claim," Havel informed Congress to thunderous applause; in a Woody Allen rendition, he would have said "Being precedes Consciousness," eliciting exactly the same reaction. But what really enthralled elite opinion was his statement that the United States has "understood the responsibility that flowed" from its great power, that there have been "two enormous forces—one, a defender of freedom, the other, a source of nightmares." We must put "morality ahead of politics," he went on. The backbone of our actions must be "responsibility—responsibility to something higher than my family, my country, my company, my success"; responsibility to suffering people in the Dominican Republic, Guatemala, Timor, Indochina, Mozambique, the Gaza Strip, and others like them who can offer direct testimony on the great works of the "defender of freedom."[39]

These thoughts struck the liberal community as a revelation from heaven. Lewis was not alone in being entranced. The *Washington Post* described them as "stunning evidence" that Havel's country is "a prime source" of "the European intellectual tradition," a "voice of conscience" that speaks "compellingly of the responsibilities that large and small powers owe each other." The *Boston Globe* hailed Havel for having "no use for clichés" as he gave us his "wise counsel" in a manner so "lucid and logical." Mary McGrory revelled in "his idealism, his irony, his humanity," as he "preached a difficult doctrine of individual responsibility" while Congress "obviously ached with respect" for his genius and integrity. Columnists Jack Germond and Jules Witcover asked why America lacks intellectuals so profound, who "elevate morality over self-interest" in this way. A front-page story in the *Globe* described how "American politicians and pundits are gushing over" Havel, and interviewed locals on why American intellectuals do not approach these lofty heights.[40]

This reaction too provides a useful mirror for the elite culture. Putting aside the relation of Being to Consciousness, the thoughts that so entranced the intellectual community are, after all, not entirely unfamiliar. One finds them regularly in the pontifications of fundamentalist preachers, Fourth of July speeches, American Legion publications, and the journals and scholarly literature generally. Indeed, everywhere. Who can have been so remote from American life as not to have heard that we are "the defender of freedom" and that we magnificently satisfy the moral imperative to be responsible not just to ourselves, but to the Welfare of Mankind? There is only one rational interpretation: liberal intellectuals secretly cherish the pronouncements of TV evangelist Pat Robertson and the John Birch society, and can therefore gush in awe when these very same words are produced by Václav Havel.

Havel's "voice of conscience" has another familiar counterpart. In the Third World, one sometimes hears people say that the Soviet Union defends their freedom while the US government is a nightmare. Journalist T.D. Allman, who wrote one of the few serious reports on El Salvador as the terror was peaking in 1980–81, described a visit to a Christian base community, subjected to the standard practices of the US-backed security forces. An old man told him that he had heard of a country called Cuba across the seas that might have concern for their plight, and asked Allman to "tell us, please, sir, how we might contact these Cubans, to inform them of our need, so that they might help us."[41]

Let us now try another thought experiment. Suppose that Allman's Salvadoran peasant or a Vietnamese villager had reached the Supreme Soviet to orate about moral responsibility and the confrontation between two powers, one a nightmare and the other a defender of freedom. There would doubtless have been a rousing ovation, while every party hack in *Pravda* would have gushed with enthusiasm. I do not, incidentally, mean to draw a comparison to what actually took place here. It is easy to understand that the world might look this way to someone whose experience is limited to US bombs and US-trained death squads on the one hand, and, on the other, Soviet tractors and anti-aircraft guns, and dreams of rescue by Cubans from unbearable torment. For victims of the West, the circumstances of existence make the conclusion plausible while barring knowledge of a broader reality. Havel and those who swoon over his familiar pieties can offer no such excuse.

We once again learn something about ourselves, if we choose.

The other *Times* spokesman for the left, Tom Wicker, followed the same script. He concludes that the Sandinistas lost "because the Nicaraguan people were tired of war and sick of economic deprivation." But the elections were "free and fair," untainted by coercion.[42]

Still at the dissident extreme, Latin America scholar William LeoGrande also hailed the promise of the "democratic elections in Nicaragua," while noting that "In the name of democracy, Washington put excruciating military and economic pressure on Nicaragua in order to force the Sandinistas out of power." Now, he continues, "the United States must show that its commitment to democracy in Central America extends to pressuring friendly conservative governments as well." Thus, having demonstrated its "commitment to democracy" by terror and economic warfare, the US should "extend" this libertarian fervor to pressure on its friends.[43]

Turning to the shining light of American liberalism, the lead editorial in the *Boston Globe* was headlined "Rallying to Chamorro." All those who truly "love Nicaraguans," editorial page editor Martin Nolan declared, "must now rally to Chamorro." Suppose that in 1964 someone had said that all Goldwater supporters "must now rally to Johnson." Such a person would have been regarded as a throwback to the days when the Gauleiters and Commissars recognized that everyone must rally behind the Leader. In Nicaragua, which has not yet risen to our heights, no one issued such a pronouncement. We learn more about the prevailing conception of democracy.[44]

Nolan goes on to explain: "Ortega was not an adept politician. His beloved masses could not eat slogans and voted with their stomachs, not their hearts." If Ortega had been more adept, he could have provided them with food—by following Nolan's advice and capitulating to the master. Now, in this "blessing of democracy, ... at long last, Nicaragua itself has spoken"—freely and without duress.

Times correspondent David Shipler contributed his thoughts under the headline "Nicaragua, Victory for U.S. Fair Play." Following the liberal model, Shipler observes that "it is true that partly because of the confrontation with the U.S., Nicaragua's economy suffered terribly, setting the stage for the widespread public discontent with the Sandinistas reflected in Sunday's balloting." Conclusion? "The Nicaraguan election has proved that open, honorable support for a democratic process is one of the most powerful foreign policy tools at Washington's disposal"—to be sure, after imposing "terrible suffering" to ensure the proper outcome in a "Victory for U.S. Fair Play." Shipler adds that now Nicaragua "needs help in building democratic institutions"—which he and his colleagues are qualified to offer, given their understanding of true democracy.[45]

In *Newsweek*, Charles Lane recognized that US efforts to "democratize Nicaragua" through the Contra war and "devastating economic sanctions" carried "a terrible cost," including 30,000 dead and another half million "uprooted from their homes," "routine" resort to "kidnapping and assassination," and other unpleasantness. So severe were the effects that "by the end of 1988, it was pride alone that kept the Sandinistas from meeting Reagan's demand that they 'cry uncle'!" But the population finally voted for "a chance to put behind them the misery brought on by 10 years of revolution and war. ... In the end, it was the Nicaraguans who won Nicaragua." We must "celebrate the moment" while reflecting "on the peculiar mix of good intentions and national insecurities that led us to become so passionately involved in a place we so dimly understood."[46]

Editorials in the national press hailed "the good news from Nicaragua," "a devastating rebuke to Sandinistas," which "will strengthen democracy elsewhere in Central America as well" (*New York Times*). The editors do recognize that one question is "debatable"—namely, "whether U.S. pressure and the contra war hastened or delayed the wonderful breakthrough." But "No matter; democracy was the winner," in elections free and fair. The *Washington Post* editors hoped that these elections would launch "Nicaragua on a conclusive change from a totalitarian to a democratic state," but are not sure. "The Masses Speak in Nicaragua," a headline reads, employing a term that is taboo apart from such special occasions. The *Christian Science Monitor* exulted over "another stunning assertion of democracy."[47]

For completeness, it is only fair to point out that at the outer limits of respectable dissidence some qualms were indeed expressed. In the *New Yorker*, often virtually alone in the mainstream in its departures from official theology, the editors observe that "As both Nicaragua and Panama have recently shown, it's one thing to drive a tyrant from power, another to take on the burden of bankrolling his country out of the resulting shambles." The cost to us of repairing the wreckage caused by Noriega and Ortega before we succeeded finally in driving the tyrants from power should, therefore, lead us to think twice about such meritorious exercises.[48]

Perhaps that is enough. I have sampled only the less egregious cases, keeping to the left–liberal spectrum. It would be hard to find an exception to the pattern.

Several features of the election coverage are particularly striking. First, the extraordinary uniformity. Second, the hatred and contempt for democracy revealed with such stark clarity across the political spectrum. And third, the utter incapacity to perceive these simple facts. Exceptions are rare indeed.

5. Within Nicaragua

I have kept to the circumstances and the US reaction, saying nothing about why Nicaraguans voted as they did—an important question, but a different one. The Nicaraguan reaction also has something to tell us about US political culture.

Within the United States, the standard reaction was joyous acclaim for the Nicaraguan "masses" who had triumphed over their oppressors in fair elections. In Nicaragua, the reaction seems to have been rather different. After informing us that the winners were "the Nicaraguans, of course," the *New Republic* turns to its Managua correspondent, Tom Gjelten, who writes: "UNO victory rallies were small, mostly private affairs, and there was no mass outpouring into the streets. Most people stayed home." Almost a month after the elections, AP reported that "UNO supporters still have not held a public celebration." Many other reports from around Nicaragua confirm the somber mood, which contrasts strikingly to the Unity in Joy here. The comparison may suggest something about who won and who lost, but the thought was not pursued—in the US, that is; in Latin America, the meaning was taken to be clear enough.[49]

Subsequently, there was a celebration of the victory, an inaugural ball for President Chamorro at a former country club. "Gentility is back in style," AP correspondent Doralisa Pilarte reported, describing the "dressed-to-kill crowd of upper-crust Nicaraguans" with their "straw hats, cocktail dresses and manicured nails, ... fine gowns and designer shoes, ... refined manners and a glittering atmosphere that left some people gaping, ... something not seen in leftist Nicaragua for more than a decade." "It's like 'The Great Gatsby'," a South American diplomat said the next morning. Pilarte, whose reporting has been extremely critical of the Sandinistas, comments on the change from the past decade: "Even in diplomatic circles, a relaxed, down-home attitude had been encouraged by the Sandinistas, themselves generally more at ease in nicely pressed combat uniforms and in working-class barrios than in glitzy halls."[50]

I found nothing about this in the press, a noteworthy omission after years of Sandinista-bashing highlighted by much sarcasm about Ortega's designer glasses and other examples of Sandinista self-indulgence while the poor were suffering—commentary that would have been fair enough, had it been something more than just another service to the state propaganda system.

Yet another Nicaraguan reaction is described by *Times* reporter Larry Rohter, in a typically bitter and scornful condemnation of the "internationalists," who carry out such despicable activities as fixing bicycles and distributing grain "to child care centers and maternity clinics," and who intend to continue "serving the vast majority of workers and peasants whose needs have not diminished," an activist in the Casa Benjamin Linder says. Rohter quotes Vice President-elect Virgilio Godoy, who says that the new government will keep a close eye on these intruders: "we are not going to permit any foreigner to interfere in our domestic political problems."[51]

In a well-disciplined culture, no one laughs when such statements are reported. Under the totalitarian Sandinistas, foreigners were permitted to forge a political coalition based upon the terrorist force they created to attack the country; and they were allowed to pour millions of dollars into supporting it in the elections. Foreigners engaged in what the World Court condemned as "the unlawful use of force" against Nicaragua were allowed to fund a major newspaper that called for the overthrow of the government and openly identified with the terrorist forces pursuing these ends, proxies of the foreign power funding the journal. Under these totalitarians, such foreigners as Jeane Kirkpatrick and US Congressmen were permitted to enter the country to present public speeches and news conferences calling for the overthrow of the government by violence and supporting the foreign-run terrorist forces. "Human Rights" investigators accompanied by Contra lobbyists posing as "experts" were permitted free access, as were journalists who were scarcely more than agents of the foreign power attacking the country. Nothing remotely resembling this record can be found in Western democracies; in the United States, Israel, England, and other democracies, such freedoms would be inconceivable, even under far less threat, as the historical record demonstrates with utter clarity.

But now, at last, totalitarianism is yielding to freedom, so Nicaragua will no longer tolerate "interference" from foreigners who have the wrong ideas about how to contribute to reform and development, foreigners who are not working for the violent overthrow of the government but rather are supporting the only mass-based political force in the country. We learn more about what is meant by "freedom" and "democracy" in the reigning political culture.

A word might be added about the disgust aroused by the internationalists, which the *Times* correspondent can barely suppress. This has been a standard feature of media commentary for years; it has been quite remarkable to see what revulsion and ridicule these volunteers inspire. But for complete-ness, we should add that the reaction is not completely uniform. One radical exception is a column by *Washington Post* correspondent David Broder, who writes with immense admiration of a project in Mobile, Alabama, "nurtured by love and incredible dedication," which is sending "volunteer English teachers" abroad. "The remarkable thing," Broder continues, "is that all this is being done with volunteered funds and energy. Each teacher pays his or her own travel expenses (at discounted rates, negotiated by a Mobile travel agency) and carries his own instructional materials."[52]

The volunteers who inspire his awe, however, are not Ben Linders heading for remote villages in Nicaragua, or young people volunteering to work in schools and universities there (without "discounted rates"). Rather, volun-teer English teachers going off to suffer in the miserable conditions of Prague. The distinction will be obvious to any fair-minded observer.

6. Looking Ahead

Let us depart now from the factual record and turn to a few speculations.

A fundamental goal of US policy towards Latin America (and elsewhere), longstanding and well documented, is to take control of the police and military so as to assure that the population will not act upon unacceptable ideas. One goal, then, will be eventually to restore something like the Somozist National Guard, following the prescriptions of the Carter doves.

A secondary goal is to destroy any independent press. Sometimes this requires murderous violence, as in El Salvador and Guatemala. The broad elite approval of the practice is evident from the reaction when it is carried out: typically, silence, coupled with praise for the advances towards democracy. Sometimes market forces suffice, as in Costa Rica, where the Spanish-language press is a monopoly of the ultra-right.

More generally, there are two legitimate forces in Latin America: first and foremost, the United States; secondarily, the local oligarchy, military, and business groups that associate themselves with the interests of US economic and political elites. If these forces hold power without challenge, all is well. The playing field is level, and if formal elections are held, it will be called "democracy." If there is any challenge from the general population, a firm response is necessary. The establishment, left and right, will tolerate some range of opinion over appropriate levels of savagery, repression, and general misery.

In Nicaragua, it will not be so simple to attain the traditional objectives. Any resistance to them will be condemned as "Sandinista totalitarianism." One can write the editorials in advance.

Perhaps the political coalition constructed by Washington will be unable to meet the demands imposed upon it by the master. If so, new managers will be needed. One option is a turn to the right, a virtual reflex. Vice-President Virgilio Godoy may qualify as an adequate hardline autocrat, and ex-Contras should be available to use the terrorist skills imparted to them by their trainers from the US and its mercenary states. Or others may be found to do the job, as circumstances allow. Another option is to follow a different and also well-traveled road. There is one mass-based political organization in Nicaragua. It may disintegrate under repression, or social and economic deterioration, or simply the inevitable pressures under monopoly of resources by the right-wing and its imperial associate. Or it may regain the vitality it has at least partially lost. If it remains, and if it can be brought to heel, perhaps its leadership can be assigned the task of social management under US command. The point was made obliquely by the *Wall Street Journal*, in its triumphal editorial on the elections. "In time," the editors wrote, "Daniel Ortega may discover the moderating influences of democratic elections, as did Jamaica's Michael Manley, himself formerly a committed Marxist."[53]

Translating from Newspeak, the US may have to fall back on the Jamaican model, first working to undermine and destroy a popular movement, then lavishly supporting the preferred capitalist alternative that proved to be a miserable failure, then turning to the populist Manley to manage the resulting disaster—but *for us*.[54]

The point is widely understood, though generally left tacit in polite commentary. As if by instinct, when the election returns were announced Ortega was instantaneously transformed from a villain into a statesman, with real promise. He can be kept in the wings, to be called upon if needed to follow our directions, if only he can learn his manners.

The policy is routine. Once the rabble have been tamed, once the dream of a better future is abandoned and "the masses" understand that their only hope is to shine shoes for Whitey, then it makes good sense to allow a "democratic process" that may even bring former enemies to power. They can then administer the ruins—for us. A side benefit is that populist forces are thereby discredited. Thus the US was quite willing to permit Manley to take over after the dismal failure of the Reaganite free-market experiment, and would have observed with equanimity (indeed, much pride in our tolerance of diversity) if Juan Bosch had won the 1990 elections in the Dominican Republic. There is no longer any need to send the Marines to bar him from office as in 1965, when the population arose, defeating the army and restoring the populist constitutional regime that had been overthrown by a US-backed coup. After years of death squads, starvation, mass flight of desperate boat people, and takeover of the rest of the economy by US corporations, we need not be troubled by democratic forms. On the same reasoning, it is sometimes a good idea to encourage Black mayors— if possible, civil rights leaders—to preside over the decline of what is left of the inner cities of the domestic Third World. Once demoralization is thorough and complete, they can run the wreckage and control the population. Perhaps Ortega and the Sandinistas, having come to their senses after a dose of reality administered by the guardian of order, will be prepared to take on this task if the chosen US proxies fail.

Years ago, a Jesuit priest working in Nicaragua, who had been active in Chile prior to the Pinochet coup, commented: "In Chile, the Americans made a mistake," killing the revolution there "too abruptly" and thus failing to "kill the dream." "In Nicaragua they're trying to kill the dream," he suggested.[55] That is surely a more rational policy, because if the dream is not killed, trouble might erupt again. But once the hope of a more free and just society is lost, and the proper habits are "ingrained" (as in

Manley's Jamaica, according to the World Bank official whose satisfied evaluation was quoted earlier), then things should settle down to the traditional
endurance of suffering and privation, without disturbing noises from the
servants' quarters.

If all works well, Maynes's establishment left will once again be able
to celebrate what he calls the US campaign "to spread the cause of democracy." It is true, he observes, that sometimes things don't quite work out.
Thus "specialists may point out that the cause of democracy suffered some
long-run setbacks in such places as Guatemala and Iran because of earlier
CIA 'successes' in overthrowing governments there." But ordinary folk
should not be troubled by the human consequences of these setbacks. More
successful is the case of Grenada, where the cause of democracy triumphed
at not too great a cost to us, Maynes observes, "and the island has not
been heard from since." There has been no need to report the recent meaningless elections, the social dissolution and decay, the state of siege instituted
by the official democrats, the decline of living conditions, and other standard
concomitants of "the defense of freedom." Perhaps, with luck, Nicaragua
will prove to be a success of which we can be equally proud. Panama
is already well along the familiar road.

With proper management, then, we should be able to leave the Sandinistas,
at least in anything like their earlier incarnation, down somewhere in "the
ash heap of history" where they belong, and "return Central America to
the obscurity it so richly deserves" in accord with the prescriptions of the
establishment left (Alan Tonelson, Maynes's predecessor at *Foreign Policy*).[56]

Outside of the official left–right spectrum, the nonpeople have other
values and commitments, and a quite different understanding of responsibility
to something other than themselves and of the cause of democracy and
freedom. They should also understand that solidarity work is now becoming
even more critically important than before. Every effort will be made to
de-educate the general population so that they sink to the intellectual and
moral level of the cultural and social managers. Those who do not succumb
have a historic mission, and should not forget that.

Notes

1. Sorenson, Op-Ed, *NYT*, November 13, 1987.
2. For illuminating discussion, see the articles by Carlos Vilas and George Vickers in NACLA
Report on the Americas, June 1990.
3. *Jornada, Universal, Tiempo*, cited in *World Press Review*, April 1990. Soler, *Excelsior*, March
4; Concha, *Punto*, February 27, in *Latin America News Update*, May, April 1990.

4. *Central America Report*, March 9, 2, 1990.

5. *Financial Times*, February 27, 1990. After noting that the Contra war brought the country close to bankruptcy, with $12 billion in damages in addition to the vast costs of the economic sanctions, they attribute primary responsibility to Sandinista "economic mismanagement" and their "totalitarian system." I leave the logic to others to decipher. Cameron and Kemble, *From a Proxy Force to a National Liberation Movement*, MS., February 1986, circulated privately in the White House.

6. Tony Avirgan, *Mesoamerica*, March 1990.

7. *Time*, March 12, 1990. AP, May 1, 1990, reporting the President's accounting to Congress on "what it cost to wage economic war."

8. *TNR*, March 19, 1990.

9. Maynes. *Foreign Policy*, Spring 1990. *TNR*, editorials, May 2, 1981; April 2, 1984. For further details, see *Turning the Tide*, pp. 117, 167 f.

10. Hertzberg, cited in *Extra!* (FAIR), March/April 1990. Lord Chitnis, "Observing El Salvador: the 1984 elections," *Third World Quarterly*, October 1984.

11. Sciolino, *NYT*, February 27, 1990.

12. On Linowitz, see below and *Culture of Terrorism*, p. 119. McNeil, *War and Peace in Central America* (Scribner's, 1988), p. 33.

13. Newsom, *CSM*, March 22; Mike Christensen, *NYT* news service, February 7, 1990.

14. Robert Pastor, *Condemned to Repetition*, pp. 107, 157; see Chapter 8 on his account from the inside.

15. Ibid., p. 161; Peter Kornbluh, *Nicaragua* (Center for Policy Studies, Washington, 1987), pp. 15 f. For general discussion, see Holly Sklar, *Washington's War on Nicaragua* (South End, 1988). Brzezinski, Vaky, and Vance, see Chapter 8, section 4.

16. Kornbluh.

17. Ibid., p. 19; see *Culture of Terrorism*, p. 86; Bob Woodward, *Veil* (Simon & Schuster, 1987), p. 113; Jenkins, *New Modes of Conflict* (Rand Corporation, June 1983).

18. Pastor, pp. 157, 208–9; Susanne Jonas, in Stanford Central America Action Network, *Revolution in Central America* (Westview, 1983), pp. 90 f.

19. Ibid.; Theodore Schwab and Harold Sims, in Thomas Walker, ed., *Nicaragua: the First Five Years* (Westview, 1988), p. 461.

20. Charles Lane, another spokesman for the establishment left, *Newsweek*, March 12, 1990.

21. Walker, *Nicaragua*, pp. 67 f.; Michael Conroy, in Walker, ed.; *La Prensa* (Managua), April 20, 1988, and Stephen Kinzer, "Anti-Sandinistas Say U.S. Should End Embargo," *NYT*, January 12, 1989.

22. Conroy; Mayorga, Chapter 7, p. 232.

23. Conroy, pp. 232–3, 223, 239; Diana Melrose, *Nicaragua: the Threat of a Good Example?* (Oxfam, 1985); Sylvia Maxfield and Richard Stahler-Short, in Walker, ed.; Kornbluh, pp. 105 f.

24. *Culture of Terrorism*, p. 52; Andrew Marshall, *Financial Times*, February 27; Christopher Marquis, *Miami Herald*, February 21, 1990.

25. Mark Uhlig, "U.S. Urges Nicaragua to Forgive Legal Claim," *NYT*, September 30, 1990.

26. Chapter 8, p. 296; State Department official cited by Thomas Walker in Coleman and Herring, *Central American Crisis*. Government official cited by Julia Preston, *BG*, February 9, 1986. MacMichael, see p. 297 above.

27. *Necessary Illusions*, pp. 204 f., 71–2; *Culture of Terrorism*, pp. 43, 219–22; Chapter 2, pp. 79 f.

28. Bill Gertz, *Washington Times*, December 5, 1988, citing a leaked classified State Department report.

29. See *Necessary Illusions*, particularly pp. 61–6; *Manufacturing Consent*.

30. *BG*, February 22, 1990.

31. ABC World News Tonight, February 20, 1990.

32. Randolph Ryan, *BG*, February 28. Also, outside the mainstream, Alexander Cockburn, *Wall Street Journal*, March 1. See also *New Yorker*, "Talk of the Town," March 12, 1990.

33. See my articles in *Z Magazine*, December 1989, March 1990; Chapters 9, 5 here.

34. See Chapter 9, p. 299.

35. See, e.g., Robert Leiken, *BG*, March 4, 1990, reprinted from the *Los Angeles Times*. On

Leiken's intriguing method of merging his Maoist convictions with Reaganism, and the appreciative reception for this useful amalgam, see *Culture of Terrorism*, pp. 213, 205–6.

36. We note, however, that the distinction is not crystal clear. Thus *Time* magazine, as we have seen, did take ample note of the murder and destruction that had paved the way to the great triumph of democracy, though presumably it should be listed on the conservative side. The spectrum of articulate opinion is so narrow that the alleged distinctions are often hard to follow.

37. Kinsley, *TNR*, March 19; *WP*, March 1, 1990. On his earlier article, see Chapter 12, p. 377.

38. Lewis, *NYT*, March 2, 1990.

39. See Excerpts, *NYT*, February 22; *WP Weekly*, March 5, 1990.

40. Editorial, *WP*, February 26; *BG*, February 23, February 26, February 24, March 1, 1990.

41. *Harper's*, March 1981.

42. Wicker, *NYT*, March 1, 1990.

43. LeoGrande, *NYT*, March 17, 1990.

44. Nolan, *BG*, February 27, 1990. Nolan identified himself to the *Nation* as the author of these fine words.

45. Shipler, Op-Ed, *NYT*, March 1, 1990.

46. Lane; possibly also the author of the unsigned *New Republic* editorial cited in Note 8, to judge by the similarity of wording.

47. *NYT*, February 27; *WP–Manchester Guardian Weekly*, March 11, *WP Weekly*, March 5; *CSM*, February 28, 1990.

48. "Talk of the Town," *New Yorker*, August 27, 1990.

49. Gjelten, *New Republic*, March 19 (written weeks earlier; I am concerned only with the facts he describes, not his personal interpretation of them).

50. Pilarte, AP, June 8, 1990.

51. Rohter, *NYT*, March 13, 1990.

52. Broder, *WP–BG*, August 6, 1990.

53. *WSJ*, March 1, 1990.

54. On the Jamaican model, see Chapter 7, pp. 234 f.

55. See *Turning the Tide*, pp. 145 f.

56. See Chapter 8, section 5.

ELEVEN

Democracy in the Industrial Societies

N O BELIEF concerning US foreign policy is more deeply entrenched than the one expressed by *New York Times* diplomatic correspondent Neil Lewis, quoted earlier: "The yearning to see American-style democracy duplicated throughout the world has been a persistent theme in American foreign policy."[1] The thesis is commonly not even expressed, merely presupposed as the basis for reasonable discourse on the US role in the world.

The faith in this doctrine may seem surprising. Even a cursory inspection of the historical record reveals that a persistent theme in American foreign policy has been the subversion and overthrow of parliamentary regimes, and the resort to violence to destroy popular organizations that might offer the majority of the population an opportunity to enter the political arena. Nevertheless, there is a sense in which the conventional doctrine is tenable. If by "American-style democracy" we mean a political system with regular elections but no serious challenge to business rule, then US policymakers doubtless yearn to see it established throughout the world. The doctrine is therefore not undermined by the fact that it is consistently violated under a different interpretation of the concept of democracy: as a system in which citizens may play some meaningful part in the management of public affairs.

This framework of analysis of policy and its ideological image is well confirmed as a good first approximation. Adopting the basic outline, we do not expect that the United States will consistently oppose parliamentary forms. On the contrary, these will be accepted, even preferred, if the fundamental conditions are met.

1. The Preference for Democracy

In the client states of the Third World, the preference for democratic forms is often largely a matter of public relations. But where the society is stable and privilege is secure, other factors enter. Business interests have an ambiguous attitude towards the state. They want it to subsidize research and development, production and export (the Pentagon system, much of the foreign aid program, and so on), regulate markets, ensure a favorable climate for business operations abroad, and in many other ways to serve as a welfare state for the wealthy. But they do not want the state to have the power to interfere with the prerogatives of owners and managers. The latter concern leads to support for democratic forms, as long as business dominance of the political system is secure.

If a country satisfies certain basic conditions, then, the US is tolerant of democratic forms, though in the Third World, where a proper outcome is hard to guarantee, often just barely. But relations with the industrial world show clearly that the US government is not opposed to democratic forms as such. In the stable business-dominated Western democracies, we would not expect the US to carry out programs of subversion, terror, or military assault as has been common in the Third World.

There may be some exceptions. Thus, there is evidence of CIA involvement in a virtual coup that overturned the Whitlam Labor government in Australia in 1975, when it was feared that Whitlam might interfere with Washington's military and intelligence bases in Australia. Large-scale CIA interference in Italian politics has been public knowledge since the congressional Pike Report was leaked in 1976, citing a subsidy of over $65 million to approved political parties and affiliates from 1948 through the early 1970s. In 1976, the Aldo Moro government fell in Italy after revelations that the CIA had spent $6 million to support anti-Communist candidates. At the time, the European Communist parties were moving towards independence of action with pluralistic and democratic tendencies (Eurocommunism), a development that pleased neither Washington nor Moscow, Raymond Garthoff observes, neither of which may "have wanted to see an independent pan-Europe based on local nationalism arise between them." For such reasons, both superpowers opposed the legalization of the Communist Party of Spain and the rising influence of the Communist Party in Italy, and both preferred center-right governments in France. Secretary of State Henry Kissinger described the "major problem" in the Western alliance as "the domestic evolution in many European countries," which might make Western Communist parties more attractive to the public, nurturing moves towards independence and threatening the NATO alliance. "The United States gave a higher priority to the defensive purpose of protecting the Western alliance and American influence in it than to offensive interests in weakening Soviet influence in the East" in those years, Garthoff concludes in his comprehensive study of the period; the phrase "defensive purpose of protecting the Western alliance" refers to the defense of existing privilege from an internal challenge. This was the context for renewed CIA interference with Italian elections, and possibly a good deal more.[2]

In July 1990, President Cossiga of Italy called for an investigation of charges aired over state television that the CIA had paid Licio Gelli to foment terrorist activities in Italy in the late 1960s and 1970s. Gelli was grandmaster of the secret Propaganda Due (P2) Masonic lodge and had long been suspected of a leading role in terrorism and other criminal activities. In those years, according to a 1984 report of the Italian Parliament, P2 and other neo-fascist groups, working closely with elements of the Italian military and secret services, were preparing a virtual coup to impose an ultra-right regime and to block the rising forces of the left. One aspect of these plans was a "strategy of tension" involving major terrorist actions in Europe. The new charges were made by Richard Brenneke, who claims to have served as a CIA contract officer and alleged that the CIA–P2 connections extended over more than twenty years and involved a $10 million payoff. Close links between Washington and the Italian ultra-right can be traced to the strong support for Mussolini's Fascist takeover in 1922.[3]

Nevertheless, the pattern has been one of general support for the industrial democracies.

The historical evidence, to be sure, must be evaluated with some care. It is one thing to overthrow the democratic government of Guatemala and to maintain the rule of an array of murderous gangsters for over three decades, or to help lay the groundwork for a coup and successful mass slaughter in Indonesia. It would be quite a different matter to duplicate these successes in relatively well-established societies; US power does not reach that far. Still, it would be a mistake to suppose that only lack of means prevents the United States from overturning democratic governments in the industrial societies in favor of military dictatorships or death squad democracies on the Latin American model.

The aftermath of World War II is revealing in these respects. With unprecedented economic and military advantages, the US was preparing to become the first truly global power. There are extensive records of the careful thinking of corporate and state managers as they designed a world order that would conform to the interests they represent. While subject to varying interpretations, the evidence none the less provides interesting insight into the complex attitudes of US elites towards democracy at a time when the US was in a position to influence the internal order of the industrial societies.

2. The General Outlines

Taking as general background the sketch in Chapter 1, section 5, let us turn to the central concern of global planners as they confronted the problem of reconstructing a world ravaged by war: the industrial societies that were to be at the core of the world system. What can we learn from this experience about the concept of democracy as understood by the architects of the new global order and their inheritors?

One problem that arose as areas were liberated from Fascism was that traditional elites had been discredited, while prestige and influence had been gained by the resistance movement, based largely on groups responsive to the working class and the poor, and often committed to some version of radical democracy. The basic quandary was articulated by Churchill's trusted adviser, South African Prime Minister Jan Christiaan Smuts, in 1943, with regard to southern Europe: "With politics let loose among those peoples," he said, "we might have a wave of disorder and wholesale Communism."[4] Here the term "disorder" is understood as threat to the interests of the privileged, and "Communism," in accordance with usual convention, refers to failure to interpret "democracy" as elite dominance, whatever the other commitments of the "Communists" may be. With politics let loose, we face a "crisis of democracy," as privileged sectors have always understood.

Quite apart from the superpower confrontation, the United States was committed to restoring the traditional conservative order. To achieve this aim, it was necessary to destroy the anti-Fascist resistance, often in favor of Nazi and Fascist collaborators, to weaken unions and other popular organizations, and to block the threat of radical democracy and social reform, which were live options under the conditions of the time. These policies were pursued worldwide: in Asia, including South Korea, the Philippines, Thailand, Indochina, and crucially Japan; in Europe, including Greece, Italy,

France, and crucially Germany; in Latin America, including what the CIA took to be the most severe threats at the time, "radical nationalism" in Guatemala and Bolivia.[5] Sometimes the task required considerable brutality. In South Korea, about 100,000 people were killed in the late 1940s by security forces installed and directed by the United States. This was before the Korean War, which Jon Halliday and Bruce Cumings describe as "in essence" a phase—marked by massive outside intervention—in "a civil war fought between two domestic forces: a revolutionary nationalist movement, which had its roots in tough anti-colonial struggle, and a conservative movement tied to the *status quo*, especially to an unequal land system," restored to power under the US occupation.[6] In Greece in the same years, hundreds of thousands were killed, tortured, imprisoned or expelled in the course of a counterinsurgency operation, organized and directed by the United States, which restored traditional elites to power, including Nazi collaborators, and suppressed the peasant- and worker-based Communist-led forces that had fought the Nazis. In the industrial societies, the same essential goals were realized, but by less violent means.

In brief, at that moment in history the United States faced the classic dilemma of Third World intervention in large parts of the industrial world as well. The US position was "politically weak" though militarily and economically strong. Tactical choices are determined by an assessment of strengths and weaknesses. The preference has, quite naturally, been for the arena of force and for measures of economic warfare and strangulation, where the US has ruled supreme. In the early postwar period, this was a global problem. Tactical choices largely observed these general conditions, adapted to particular circumstances.

These topics are central to a serious understanding of the contemporary world. The actual history can be discovered in specialized studies devoted to particular instances of what was, in fact, a highly systematic pattern.[7] But it is not readily available to the general public, which is offered a very different version of the general picture and particular cases within it. Take the case of Greece, the first major postwar intervention and a model for much that followed. The US and world market are flooded with such material as the best-selling novel and film *Eleni* by Nicholas Gage, reporting the horrors of the Communist-led resistance. But Greek or even American scholarship that gives a radically different picture, and seriously questions the authenticity even of Gage's special case, is unknown. In Britain, an independent television channel attempted in 1986 to allow the voices of the Communist-led anti-Nazi Greek resistance, defeated by the postwar

British and American campaigns, to be heard for the first time, to present their perception of these events. This effort evoked a hysterical establishment response, calling for suppression of this "one-sided" picture inconsistent with the official doctrine that had hitherto reigned unchallenged. The former head of British political intelligence in Athens, Tom McKitterick, supported the broadcast, observing that "for years we have been treated to a one-sided picture, and the series was a brave attempt to restore the balance." But the establishment counterattack prevailed in an impressive display of the totalitarian mentality and its power in the liberal West. The documentary was barred from rebroadcast or overseas marketing, particularly in Greece— only one example of a long history of suppression.[8]

In the international system envisioned by US planners, the industrial powers were to reconstruct, essentially restoring the traditional order and barring any challenge to business dominance, but now taking their places within a world system regulated by the United States. This world system was to take the form of state-guided liberal internationalism, secured by US power to bar interfering forces and managed through military expenditures, which proved to be a critical factor stimulating industrial recovery. The global system was designed to guarantee the needs of US investors, who were expected to flourish under the prevailing circumstances. This was a plausible expectation at the time, and one that was amply fulfilled. It was not until the late 1950s that Europe, primarily the Federal Republic of Germany, became a significant factor in world production and trade.[9] And until the Vietnam War shifted the structure of the world economy to the benefit of its industrial rivals, the problem faced by the US government with regard to Japan was how to ensure the viability of its economy. Highly profitable foreign investment rapidly grew and transnational corporations, primarily US-based in the earlier period, expanded and flourished.

3. The "Great Workshops": Japan

Within the industrial world, the "natural leaders" were understood to be Germany and Japan, which had demonstrated their prowess during the war years. They were the "greatest workshops of Europe and Asia" (Dean Acheson). It was, therefore, critically important to guarantee that their reconstruction followed a proper course, and that they remained dependent on the United States. Accordingly, East–West trade and moves towards European détente have always been viewed with some concern. Great efforts were also expended to prevent a renewal of traditional commercial relations between Japan and China particularly in the 1950s, well before China too became integrated into the US-dominated global system. A major goal of American diplomatic strategy, outlined by John Foster Dulles at a closed regional meeting of American ambassadors in Asia in March 1955, was "to develop markets for Japan in Southeast Asia in order to counteract Communist trade efforts and to promote trade between Japan and Southeast Asian countries," Chitoshi Yanaga wrote in the 1960s. The general conclusion is amplified by documentation subsequently released in the Pentagon Papers and elsewhere. US intervention in Vietnam was initially motivated, in large measure, by such concerns.[10]

At the time, Japan was not regarded as a serious competitor; we may dismiss self-serving illusions about how Japanese recovery and competition prove that the US was selfless in its postwar planning. It was taken for granted that Japan would, one way or another, regain its status as "the workshop of Asia" and would be at the center of something like the "co-prosperity sphere" that Japanese Fascism had attempted to create. The realistic alternatives, it was assumed, were that this system would be incorporated within the US global order, or that it would be independent, possibly blocking US entry, perhaps even linked to the Soviet Union. As for Japan itself, the prospect generally anticipated was that it might produce "knick-knacks" and other products for the underdeveloped world, as a US survey mission concluded in 1950.[11]

In part, the dismissive assessment of Japan's prospects was based on the failure of Japanese industrial recovery prior to the economic stimulus of military procurements for the Korean War. In part, there was doubtless an element of racism—illustrated, for example, in the reaction of the business community to the democratic labor laws introduced by the US military occupation. These laws were opposed by business generally. They were bitterly denounced by James Lee Kauffman, one of the influential members of the business lobby that worked to impede the democratization of Japan. Representing industrialists with an interest in cheap and docile labor, he wrote indignantly in 1947 that Japanese workers had to be treated as juveniles. "You can imagine what would happen in a family of children of ten years or less if they were suddenly told ... that they could run the house and their own lives as they pleased." Japanese labor had gone "hog wild," he wrote. "If you have ever seen an American Indian spending his money shortly after oil has been discovered on his property you will have some idea of how the Japanese worker is using the Labor Law." The racist attitudes of General MacArthur, American proconsul for Japan after World War II, were notorious. Thus, in congressional testimony in 1951, he said that "Measured by the standards of modern civilization, they would be like a boy of twelve as compared with our development of forty-five years," a fact that allowed us to "implant basic concepts there": "They were still close enough to origin to be elastic and acceptable to new concepts." In more recent years the compliment has been returned by right-wing Japanese commentators on US culture and society.[12]

Nevertheless, some foresaw problems down the road, notably the influential planner George Kennan, who recommended that the US control Japanese oil imports so as to maintain "veto power" over Japan, advice that was followed.[13] This is one of many reasons why the United States has been so concerned to control the oil reserves of the Middle East throughout the postwar period, and presumably also a reason for Japanese reluctance to follow the US lead on Middle East problems.

In Japan the United States was able to act unilaterally, having excluded its allies from any role in the occupation.[14] General MacArthur encouraged steps towards democratization, though within limits. Militant labor action was barred, including some attempts to establish workers' control over production. Even these partial steps towards democracy scandalized the State Department, US corporations and labor leadership, and the US media. George Kennan and others warned against a premature end to the occupation before the economy was reconstructed under stable conservative rule. These pressures led to the "reverse course" of 1947, which ensured that there would be no serious challenge to government–corporate domination over labor, the media and the political system.

Under the reverse course, worker-controlled companies, which were operating with considerable success, were eliminated. Support was given to right-wing socialists who had been Fascist collaborators and were committed to US-style business unionism under corporate control, while leftists who had been jailed under Fascist rule were excluded, the normal pattern worldwide. Labor was suppressed with considerable police violence, and elimination of the right to strike and collective bargaining. The goal was to ensure business control over labor through conservative unions. Industrial unions were undermined by the late 1940s, as the industrial-financial conglomerates [*Zaibatsu*], which were at the heart of Japan's Fascist order, regained their power with the assistance of an elaborate police and surveillance network and rightist patriotic organizations. The Japanese business classes were reconstituted much as under the Fascist regime, placed in power in close collaboration with the authorities of the centralized state. George Kennan, who was one of the leading architects of the reverse course, regarded the early plans to dissolve the *Zaibatsu* as bearing "so close a resemblance to Soviet views about the evils of 'capitalist monopolies' that the measures themselves could only have been eminently agreeable to anyone interested in the further communization of Japan."[15] By 1952 Japan's industrial and financial elites had not only established themselves as the dominant element in Japan, but were exercising "control over a more concentrated and interconnected system of corporations than before the war" (Schonberger). The burden of reconstruction was placed upon the working class and the poor, within a system described as "totalitarian state capitalism" by Sherwood Fine, who served as Director of Economics and Planning in the Economic and Scientific Section throughout the US military occupation. These policies "allowed Japanese corporate elites to avoid the social rationalization that would have provided a thriving domestic market to sustain industry" (Borden)—by now, posing a problem for Japan's Western rivals.

Borden observes that Britain, with its powerful labor unions and welfare system, was concerned over "ultracompetitive export pricing made possible by exploiting labor and enfeebling unions" in Japan under US pressure. "The British response was to defend the rights of Japanese workers and to promote China as the logical outlet for Japan's exports." But those ideas conflicted with US global planning, which sought to prevent Japan from accommodating to Communist China, and with the development model preferred by the US and its Japanese corporate allies. While Japanese corporate conglomerates were reinforced, labor was weakened and splintered, with the collaboration of US labor leaders, as elsewhere in the world. Britain itself was to face a similar attack on unions and the welfare system, as did the United States itself, beginning with the assault on labor in the early postwar period, renewed by the bipartisan consensus of the post-Vietnam period in support of business interests.

The United States essentially reconstructed the co-prosperity sphere of Japanese Fascism, though now as a component of the US-dominated global order. Within it, Japanese state capitalism was granted a relatively free hand. The US undertook the major military burden of crushing indigenous threats to this system, renewing a traditional perception of Japan as a junior partner in the exploitation of Asia.

By now, Japan has perhaps the weakest labor movement in the industrial capitalist world, with the possible exception of the United States itself. It is a disciplined society, under the firm control of the traditional state capitalist management. The Korean War sparked Japanese economic recovery. US military procurement through the 1950s "played a critical role in supplying the dollars, demand, technology, and market for the modernization of the industrial base in Japan," and the rapid increase from 1965 accelerated the process.[16] By the 1970s, these developments were raising serious and unanticipated problems for the US government and corporations—problems that are likely to intensify as it becomes necessary to face the consequences of Reaganite economic mismanagement.

4. The "Great Workshops": Germany

Germany posed many of the same problems, compounded by four-power control. After the consolidation of the three Western zones in 1947, the US began to move towards the partition of Germany. These steps were undertaken at the same time as the reverse course in Japan, and for similar reasons. One reason was the fear of democracy, understood in the sense of popular participation. Eugene Rostow argued in 1947 that "the Russians are much better equipped than we are to play the game in Germany," referring to the "political game"; therefore we must prevent the game from being played. Kennan had noted a year earlier that a unified Germany would be vulnerable to Soviet *political* penetration, so we must "endeavor to rescue Western zones of Germany by walling them off against Eastern penetration"—a nice image—"and integrating them into an international pattern of Western Europe rather than into a united Germany," in violation of wartime agreements. Like George Marshall and Dean Acheson, and knowledgeable analysts generally, Kennan did not expect a Soviet military attack, but rather "described the imbalance in Russian 'political power' rather than 'military power' as the immediate risk faced by the United States" (Schaller).[17]

The main problem, again, was the labor movement and other popular organizations that threatened conservative business dominance. Surveying the declassified record, Carolyn Eisenberg concludes that the fear—indeed "horror"—was "a unified, centralized, politicized labor movement committed to a far-reaching program of social change." After the war, German workers began to form works councils and trade unions, and to develop co-determination in industry and democratic grass-roots control of unions. The State Department and its US labor associates were appalled by these moves towards democracy in the unions and the larger society, with all the problems these developments would pose for the plan to restore the corporate-controlled economic order ("democracy"). The problem was heightened by the fact that in the Soviet zone, semi-autonomous works councils had been established which exercised a degree of managerial authority in de-Nazified enterprises. The British Foreign Office also feared "economic and ideological infiltration" from the East, which it perceived as "something very like aggression." It preferred a divided Germany, incorporating the wealthy Ruhr/Rhine industrial complex within the Western alliance, to a united Germany in which "the balance of advantage seems to lie with the Russians," who could exercise "the stronger pull." In interdepartmental meetings of the British government in April 1946, the respected official Sir Orme Sargent described moves towards establishing a separate Western Germany within a Western bloc as necessary, though it was agreed that they might lead to war: "the only alternative to [partition] was Communism on the Rhine," with the likely eventuality of "a German Government that would be under Communist influence." In the major scholarly monograph on the British role, Anne Deighton describes his intervention as of "critical" significance.[18]

The United States was determined to prevent expropriation of Nazi industrialists and firmly opposed to allowing worker-based organizations to exercise managerial authority. Such developments would pose a serious threat of democracy in one sense of the term, while violating it in the approved sense. The US authorities therefore turned to sympathetic right-wing socialists, as in Japan, while using such means as control of CARE packages, food and other supplies to overcome the opposition of rank-and-file workers. It was finally necessary to "wall off" the Western zone by partition, to veto the major union constitutions, forcefully to terminate social experiments, vetoing state [Laender] legislation, co-determination efforts, and so on. Major Nazi war criminals were recruited for US intelligence and antiresistance activities, Klaus Barbie being perhaps the best known. A still worse Nazi gangster, Franz Six, was pressed into service after his sentence as a war criminal was commuted by US High Commissioner John J. McCloy. He was put to work for Reinhard Gehlen, with special responsibility for developing a "secret army" under US auspices, along with former Waffen-SS and Wehrmacht specialists, to assist military forces established by Hitler in Eastern Europe and the Soviet Union in operations that continued into the 1950s. Gehlen himself had headed Nazi military intelligence on the Eastern front, and was reinstated as head of the espionage and counterespionage service of the new West German state, under close CIA supervision.[19]

Meanwhile, as in Japan, the burden of reconstruction was placed upon German workers, in part by fiscal measures that wiped out the savings of the poor and union treasuries. "So thoroughgoing was the U.S. assault on German labor that even the AFL complained," Eisenberg comments, though the AFL had helped to lay the basis for these consequences by its anti-union activities. Union activists were purged and strikes were blocked by force. By 1949, the State Department expressed its pleasure that "industrial peace had been attained," with a now docile and tractable labor force and an end to the vision of a unified popular movement that might challenge the authority of owners and managers. As Tom Bower describes the outcome in a study of the rehabilitation of Nazi war criminals, "Four years after the war, those responsible for the day-to-day management of post-war Germany were remarkably similar to the management during the days of Hitler," including bankers and industrialists convicted of war crimes who were released and restored to their former roles, renewing their collaboration with US corporations.[20]

In short, the treatment of the two "great workshops" was basically similar.

In later years, as we have seen, the US was distinctly wary of apparent Soviet initiatives for a unified demilitarized Germany and steps towards dismantling the pact system. Western European elites have been no less concerned, for the decline of East–West confrontation might "let politics loose among those people," with all of the attendant dire effects. That has been one of the undercurrents beneath the debate of the 1980s over arms control, security issues, and the political prospects for a united Europe.

5. The Smaller Workshops

In France and Italy, US authorities pursued similar tasks. In both countries, Marshall Plan aid was strictly contingent on exclusion of Communists— including major elements of the anti-Fascist resistance and labor—from the government; "democracy," in the usual sense. US aid was critically important in early years for suffering people in Europe and was therefore a powerful lever of control, a matter of much significance for US business interests and longer-term planning. "If Europe did not receive massive financial assistance and adopt a coherent recovery program, American officials were fearful that the Communist left would triumph, perhaps even through free elections," Melvyn Leffler observes. On the eve of the announcement of the Marshall Plan, Ambassador to France Jefferson Caffery warned Secretary of State Marshall of grim consequences if the Communists won the elections in France: "Soviet penetration of Western Europe, Africa, the Mediterranean, and the Middle East would be greatly facilitated" (May 12, 1947). The dominoes were ready to fall. During May, the US pressured political leaders in France and Italy to form coalition governments excluding the Communists. It was made clear and explicit that aid was contingent on preventing an open political competition, in which left and labor might dominate. Through 1948, Secretary of State Marshall and others publicly emphasized that if Communists were voted into power, US aid would be terminated; no small threat, given the state of Europe at the time.

In France, the postwar destitution was exploited to undermine the French labor movement, along with direct violence. Desperately needed food supplies were withheld to coerce obedience, and gangsters were organized to provide goon squads and strike-breakers, a matter that is described with some pride in semi-official US labor histories, which praise the AFL for its achievements in helping to save Europe by splitting and weakening the labor movement (thus frustrating alleged Soviet designs) and safeguarding the flow of arms to Indochina for the French war of reconquest, another prime goal of the US labor bureaucracy.[21] The CIA reconstituted the Mafia for these purposes, in one of its early operations. The quid pro quo was restoration of the heroin trade. The US government connection to the drug boom continues until today.[22]

US policies towards Italy basically picked up where they had been broken off by World War II. The United States had supported Mussolini's Fascism from the 1922 takeover through the 1930s. Mussolini's wartime alliance with Hitler terminated these friendly relations, but they were reconstituted as US forces liberated southern Italy in 1943, establishing the rule of Field-Marshal Badoglio and the royal family that had collaborated with the Fascist government. As Allied forces drove towards the north, they dispersed the anti-Fascist resistance along with local governing bodies it had formed in its attempt "to create the foundations for a new, democratic, and republican state in the various zones it succeeded in liberating from the Germans" (Gianfranco Pasquino).[23] A center-right government was established with neo-Fascist participation, and the left soon excluded.

Here too, the plan was for the working classes and the poor to bear the burden of reconstruction, with lowered wages and extensive firing. Aid was contingent on removing Communists and left socialists from office, because they defended workers' interests and thus posed a barrier to the intended style of recovery, in the view of the State Department. The

Communist Party was collaborationist; its position "fundamentally meant the subordination of all reforms to the liberation of Italy and effectively discouraged any attempt in northern areas to introduce irreversible political changes as well as changes in the ownership of the industrial companies, . . . disavowing and discouraging those workers' groups that wanted to expropriate some factories" (Pasquino). But the Party did try to defend jobs, wages, and living standards for the poor and thus "constituted a political and psychological barrier to a potential European recovery program," historian John Harper comments, reviewing the insistence of Kennan and others that Communists be excluded from government though agreeing that it would be "desirable" to include representatives of what Harper calls "the democratic working class." The recovery, it was understood, was to be at the expense of the working class and the poor.

Because of its responsiveness to the needs of these social sectors, the Communist Party was labelled "extremist" and "undemocratic" by US propaganda, which also skillfully manipulated the alleged Soviet threat. Under US pressure, the Christian Democrats abandoned wartime promises about workplace democracy and the police, sometimes under the control of ex-Fascists, were encouraged to suppress labor activities. The Vatican announced that anyone who voted for the Communists in the 1948 election would be denied sacraments, and backed the conservative Christian Democrats under the slogan "*O con Cristo o contro Cristo*" ("Either with Christ or against Christ"). A year later, Pope Pius excommunicated all Italian Communists.[24]

A combination of violence, manipulation of aid and other threats, and a huge propaganda campaign sufficed to determine the outcome of the critical 1948 election, essentially bought by US intervention and pressures.

US policies in preparation for the election were designed so that "even the dumbest wop would sense the drift," as the Italian desk officer at the State Department put it with characteristic ruling-class elegance. As thirty years earlier, "the Italians are like children [who] must be led and assisted" (see p. 38). The policies included police violence and threats to withhold food, to bar entry to the US to anyone who voted the wrong way, to deport Italian-Americans who supported the Communists, to bar Italy from Marshall Plan aid, and so on. State Department historian James Miller observes that subsequent economic development was carried out "at the expense of the working class" as the left and the labor movement were "fragmented with U.S. support," and that US efforts undercut a "democratic alternative" to the preferred center-right rule, which proved corrupt and inept. The basic policy premiss was that "as a key strategic entity, Italy's fate remained too important for Italians alone to decide" (Harper)—particularly, the wrong Italians, with their misunderstanding of democracy.

Meanwhile, the US planned military intervention in the event of a legal Communist political victory in 1948, and this was broadly hinted in public propaganda. Kennan secretly suggested that the Communist Party be outlawed to forestall its electoral victory, recognizing that this would probably lead to civil war, US military intervention, and "a military division of Italy." But he was overruled, on the assumption that other means of coercion would suffice. The National Security Council, however, secretly called for military support for underground operations in Italy along with national mobilization in the United States, "in the event the Communists obtain domination of the Italian government by legal means."[25] The subversion of effective democracy in Italy was taken very seriously.

Washington's intention to resort to violence if free elections come out the wrong way is not very easy to deal with, so it has been generally suppressed, even in the scholarly literature. One of the two major scholarly monographs on this period discusses the NSC memoranda, but with no mention of the actual content of the crucial section; the second passes it by in a phrase.[26] In the general literature, the whole matter is unknown.

The CIA operations to control the Italian elections, authorized by the National Security Council in December 1947, were the first major clandestine operation of the newly formed Agency. As noted earlier, CIA operations to subvert Italian democracy continued into the 1970s on a substantial scale.

In Italy too, US labor leaders, primarily from the AFL, played an active role in splitting and weakening the labor movement, and inducing workers to accept austerity measures while employers reaped rich profits. In France, the AFL had broken dock strikes by importing Italian scab labor paid by US businesses. The State Department called on the Federation's leadership to exercise their talents in union-busting in Italy as well, and they were happy to oblige. The business sector, formerly discredited by its association with Italian Fascism, undertook a vigorous class war with renewed confidence. The end result was the subordination of the working class and the poor to the traditional rulers. In the major academic study of US labor in Italy, Ronald Filippelli observes that American aid "had largely been used to rebuild Italy on the old basis of a conservative society" in a "rampant capitalist restoration" on the backs of the poor, "with low consumption and low wages," "enormous profits," and no interference with the prerogatives of management. Meanwhile AFL President George Meany angrily rejected criticism of his anti-labor programs on the grounds that freedom in Italy was not the exclusive concern of its own people; the AFL would therefore pursue its higher goal of "strengthening the forces of liberty and social progress all over the world"—by ensuring that US business interests remained in the ascendant, class collaboration with a vengeance. The result was "a restoration to power of the same ruling class that had been responsible for, and benefited from, fascism," with the working class removed from politics, subordinated to the needs of investors, and forced to bear the burden of the "*Miracolo italiano*," Filippelli concludes.

The policies of the late 1940s "hit the poorer regions and politically impotent social strata hardest," Harper observes, but they did succeed in breaking "rigid labor markets" and facilitating the export-led growth of the 1950s, which relied on "the continuing weakness and remarkable mobility of the Italian working class." These "happy circumstances," he continues, brought further economic development of a certain kind, while the CIA mounted new multimillion-dollar covert funding and propaganda campaigns to ensure that the "felicitous arrangements" would persist.[27]

Later commentators tend to see the US subversion of democracy in France and Italy as a defense of democracy. In a highly regarded study of the CIA and American democracy, Rhodri Jeffreys-Jones describes "the CIA's Italian venture," along with its similar efforts in France, as "a democracy-propping operation," though he concedes that "the selection of Italy for special atten- tion ... was by no means a matter of democratic principle alone"; our passion for democracy was reinforced by the strategic importance of the country. But it was a commitment to "democratic principle" that inspired the US government to impose the social and political regimes of its choice, using the enormous power at its command and exploiting the privation and distress of the victims of the war, who must be taught not to raise their heads if we are to have true democracy.[28]

A more nuanced position is taken by James Miller in his monograph on US policies towards Italy. Summarizing the record, he concludes:

> In retrospect, American involvement in the stabilization of Italy was a significant, if troubling, achievement. American power assured Italians the right to choose their future form of government and also was employed to ensure that they chose democracy. In defense of that democracy against real but probably overesti- mated foreign and domestic threats, the United States used undemocratic tactics that tended to undermine the legitimacy of the Italian state.[29]

The "foreign threats," as he had already discussed, were hardly real; the

Soviet Union watched from a distance as the US subverted the 1948 election and restored the traditional conservative order, keeping to its wartime agreement with Churchill that left Italy in the Western zone. The "domestic threat" was the threat of democracy.

The idea that US intervention provided Italians with freedom of choice while ensuring that they chose "democracy" (in our special sense of the term) is reminiscent of the attitude of the extreme doves towards Latin America: that its people should choose freely and independently, "*except* when doing so would affect U.S. interests adversely*," and that the US had no interest in controlling them, unless developments "get out of control" (see Chapter 8, p. 261).

The democratic ideal, at home and abroad, is simple and straightforward: You are free to do what you want, as long as it is what we want you to do.

6. Some Broader Effects

Apart from the rearmament of Germany within a Western military alliance—which no Russian government could easily accept, for obvious reasons—Stalin observed all of this with relative calm, apparently regarding it as a counterpart to his own harsh repression in Eastern Europe. Nevertheless, these parallel developments were bound to lead to conflict.

In his review of the reverse course in Japan, John Roberts argues that "the American rehabilitation of the monopolistic economies of Western Germany and Japan (largely under prewar leadership) was a *cause*, not a result, of the cold war. Their rehabilitation was, undoubtedly, a vital part of American capitalism's strategy in its all-out vendetta against communism"—meaning, primarily, an attack against the participation of the "popular classes" in some significant range of decision-making. Focusing on Europe, Melvyn Leffler comments that the approach to European recovery led American officials to act

> to safeguard markets, raw materials, and investment earnings in the Third World. Revolutionary nationalism had to be thwarted outside Europe, just as the fight against indigenous communism had to be sustained inside Europe. In this interconnected attempt to grapple with the forces of the left and the potential power of the Kremlin resides much of the international history, strategy, and geopolitics of the Cold War era.[30]

These are critical undercurrents through the modern era, and remain so.

Throughout the reconstruction of the industrial societies, the prime concern was to establish a state capitalist order under the traditional conservative elites, within the global framework of US power, which would guarantee the ability to exploit the various regions that were to fulfill their functions as markets and sources of raw materials. If these goals could be achieved, then the system would be stable and resistant to feared social change, which would naturally be disruptive once the system is operating in a relatively orderly fashion. In the wealthy industrial centers, large segments of the population would be accommodated, and would be led to abandon any more radical vision under a rational cost-benefit analysis.

Once its institutional structure is in place, capitalist democracy will function only if all subordinate their interests to the needs of those who control investment decisions, from the country club to the soup kitchen. It is only a matter of time before an independent working-class culture erodes, along with the institutions and organizations that sustain it, given the distribution of resources and power. And with popular organizations weakened or eliminated, isolated individuals are unable to participate in the political system in a meaningful way. It will, over time, become largely a symbolic pageant or, at most, a device whereby the public can select among competing elite groups and ratify their decisions, playing the role assigned them by progressive democratic theorists of the Walter Lippmann variety.[31] That was a plausible assumption in the early postwar period and has proven largely accurate so far, despite many rifts, tensions and conflicts.

European elites have a stake in the preservation of this system, and fear their domestic populations no less than the US authorities did. Hence their commitment to Cold War confrontation, which came to serve as an effective technique of domestic social management, and their willingness, with occasional mutterings of discontent, to line up in US global crusades. The system is oppressive, and often brutal, but that is no problem as long as others are the victims. It also raises constant threats of large-scale catastrophe, but these too do not enter into planning decisions shaped by the goal of maximization of short-term advantage, which remains the operative principle.

Notes

1. Chapter 8, section 7.

2. John Pilger, *A Secret Country* (Jonathan Cape, 1989); see also his documentary series "The Last Dream," 1988, produced for the Australian Bicentenary with the cooperation of the Australian Broadcasting Company. Jonathan Kwitny, *The Crimes of Patriots* (Norton, 1987). *CIA: the Pike Report* (Spokesman Books, Nottingham 1977); the report was leaked to the *Village Voice* (February 16, 23, 1976). Garthoff, *Détente and Confrontation*, pp. 487 f.

3. Brenneke, TG 1 (Italian TV), July 2; *Il Manifesto*, July 3, 1990. AP, *BG*, July 23, 1990. On US–Italian covert relations in the 1970s and the P2–security services plans, see Edward S. Herman and Frank Brodhead, *The Rise and Fall of the Bulgarian Connection* (Sheridan Square, 1986), ch. 4. As they observe, extensive right-wing terrorism in Europe has been largely ignored in the general literature of terrorology, much of it a transparent propaganda exercise. Also William Blum, *The CIA* (Zed, 1986). On the early postwar years, see also John Ranelagh, *The Agency: the Rise and Decline of the CIA* (Simon & Schuster, 1986). On the US and Mussolini, and the quick return by the Allies to a pro-Fascist stance during the War, see Chapter 1, section 4, above. Brenneke had achieved some notoriety out of the mainstream when he claimed that while working for the CIA, he had taken part in an October 1980 meeting in Paris in which representatives of the Reagan–Bush campaign, including later CIA chief William Casey, Bush aide Donald Gregg, and possibly Bush himself, had bribed Iran to hold the US hostages until after the election, to ensure Reagan's victory. The government brought him to court (directly from a cardiac intensive-care ward) to try him on charges of having falsely made these claims. He was acquitted in Federal Court of these and other charges by a jury "that made no secret of its disbelief in the truthfulness of government witnesses, particularly Gregg," ex-CIA agent David MacMichael observes—noting also that the whole matter was virtually suppressed in the national media; *Lies of Our Times*, August 1990. In the independent press, the story was covered (*Houston Post, Nation, In These Times*, and others).

4. Smuts, cited by Basil Davidson, *Scenes from the Anti-Nazi War* (Monthly Review, 1980), p. 17.

5. On these cases, see Chapter 12, pp. 395 f.

6. Halliday and Cumings, *Korea: the Unknown War* (Viking, Pantheon, 1988).

7. The first major scholarly effort to lay out this pattern is Gabriel Kolko's *Politics of War* (Random House, 1968), which remains extremely valuable, and unique in its scope and depth, despite the flood of new documents and scholarship since.

8. See *Covert Action Information Bulletin*, Winter 1986. Richard Gott, "A Greek tragedy to haunt the old guard," *Guardian* (London), July 5, 1986.

9. Alfred Grosser, *The Western Alliance* (Continuum, 1980), p. 178.

10. Yanaga, *Big Business in Japanese Politics* (Yale, 1968), pp. 265 f. See my *At War with Asia*, Introduction, and *For Reasons of State*, ch. 1 (published in England as *The Backroom Boys* [Fontana]), sec. V; Chomsky and Howard Zinn, eds, *Critical Essays*, vol. 5 of the *Pentagon Papers*. Also a good deal of recent scholarship, including Michael Schaller, "Securing the Great Crescent," *Journal of American History*, September 1982, and his *American Occupation of Japan*; Andrew J. Rotter, *The Path to Vietnam* (Cornell, 1987). Acheson, cited by Schaller, *American Occupation*, p. 97.

11. Ibid., 222. See Chapter 1, pp. 46 f.

12. John Roberts, "The 'Japan Crowd' and the Zaibatsu Restoration," *The Japan Interpreter*, 12, Summer 1979. MacArthur, Howard B. Schonberger, *Aftermath of War* (Kent State, 1989), pp. 52–3. Japanese attitudes, Akio Morita and Shintaro Ishihara, *The Japan That Can Say No*. On the racist attitudes on both sides during the War, which reached shocking proportions, see John Dower, *War without Mercy: Race and Power in the Pacific War* (Pantheon, 1986).

13. See Chapter 1, p. 53.

14. For background on what follows, see Joe Moore, *Japanese Workers and the Struggle for Power, 1945–1947* (University of Wisconsin, 1983); Schaller, *American Occupation*; William Borden, *Pacific Alliance*; Howard Schonberger, "The Japan Lobby in American Diplomacy, 1947–1952," *Pacific Historical Review*, August 1977, and his *Aftermath of War*; Roberts, "The 'Japan Crowd' "; Cumings, "Power and Plenty in Northeast Asia," *World Policy Journal*, Winter 1987–8.

15. Kennan, cited by Schonberger, *Aftermath*, p. 77.

16. Schaller, *American Occupation*, p. 296.

17. Rostow, Kennan, cited by John H. Backer, *The Decision to Divide Germany* (Duke, 1978), pp. 155–6; Schaller, *American Occupation*. See Anne Deighton, *International Affairs*, Summer 1987, on British initiatives in violation of the Potsdam Agreements.

18. Carolyn Eisenberg, "Working-Class Politics and the Cold War: American Intervention in the German Labor Movement, 1945–49," *Diplomatic History*, 7.4, Fall 1983; Deighton; Sargent, quoted from minutes in Anne Deighton, *The Impossible Peace: Britain, the Division of Germany, and the Origins of the Cold War* (Oxford, 1990), p. 73. See also Backer, p. 171; Melvyn Leffler, "The United States and the Strategic Dimensions of the Marshall Plan," *Diplomatic History*, Summer 1988.

19. For more on these matters, see *Turning the Tide*, pp. 197 ff., and sources cited; Christopher Simpson, *Blowback* (Weidenfeld & Nicolson, 1988). On the recruitment of Nazi scientists, see Tom Bower, *The Paperclip Conspiracy* (Michael Joseph, 1987), p. 310; John Gimbel, *Science, Technology, and Reparations* (Stanford, 1990). A review of the latter in *Science* notes that Gimbel's research "demonstrates the dubiousness of subsequent U.S. claims of commercial disinterestedness in the occupation of Germany; just like the Russians, and to a lesser degree the British and the French, the Americans seized enormous quantities of reparations from the defeated country," giving "some credence to the Russian claim that Anglo-American seizures amounted to about $10 billion," the amount demanded (but not received) by the Russians as reparations for the Nazi devastation of the USSR. Raymond Stokes, *Science*, June 8, 1990.

20. Eisenberg; Bower, *The Paperclip Conspiracy*.

21. See Roy Godson, *American Labor and European Politics* (Crane, Russak, 1976).

22. See McCoy, *Politics of Heroin*, and other references of Chapter 4, Note 21.

23. See Chapter 1, section 4. Pasquino, "The Demise of the First Fascist Regime and Italy's Transition to Democracy: 1943–1948," in Guillermo O'Donnell, Philippe C. Schmitter and Laurence Whitehead, *Transitions from Authoritarian Rule: Prospects for Democracy* (Johns Hopkins, 1986). On what follows, see John L. Harper, *America and the Reconstruction of Italy, 1945–1948* (Cambridge University Press, 1986); James E. Miller, "Taking Off the Gloves: The United States and the Italian Elections of 1948," *Diplomatic History*, 7.1, Winter 1983; and his *The United States and Italy, 1940–1950* (University of North Carolina, 1986); Ronald Filippelli, *American Labor and Postwar Italy* (see Chapter 1, section 4).

24. Vatican, Craig Kelly, *The Anti-Fascist Resistance and the Shift in Political-Cultural Strategy of the Italian Communist Party 1936–1948*, PhD Dissertation, UCLA, 1984, p. 10.

25. Harper; Kennan to Secretary of State, *FRUS* 1948, III, pp. 848–9; NSC 1/3, March 8, 1948, *FRUS*, 1948, III, pp. 775 f.

26. Miller, *United States and Italy*, p. 247; Harper, *America and the Reconstruction of Italy*, p. 155, noting the NSC recommendation that "In the case of communist victory, there should be military and economic assistance to the pro-Western forces."

27. Harper, pp. 164–5.

28. Jeffreys-Jones, *The CIA and American Democracy* (Yale, 1989), pp. 50–51.

29. Miller, *United States and Italy*, p. 274.

30. Roberts, Leffler.

31. See next chapter, pp. 367 f.

TWELVE

Force and Opinion

IN HIS study of the Scottish intellectual tradition, George Davie identifies its central theme as a recognition of the fundamental role of "*natural beliefs* or principles of common sense, such as the belief in an independent external world, the belief in causality, the belief in ideal standards, and the belief in the self of conscience as separate from the rest of one." These principles are sometimes considered to have a regulative character; though never fully justified, they provide the foundations for thought and conception. Some held that they contain "an irreducible element of mystery," Davie points out, while others hoped to provide a rational foundation for them. On that issue, the jury is still out.[1]

We can trace such ideas to seventeenth-century thinkers who reacted to the skeptical crisis of the times by recognizing that there are no absolutely certain grounds for knowledge, but that we do, nevertheless, have ways to gain a reliable understanding of the world and to improve that understanding and apply it—essentially the standpoint of the working scientist today. Similarly, in normal life a reasonable person relies on the natural beliefs of common sense while recognizing that they may be parochial or misguided, and hoping to refine or alter them as understanding progresses.

Davie credits David Hume with providing this particular cast to Scottish philosophy, and more generally, with having taught philosophy the proper questions to ask. One puzzle that Hume posed is particularly pertinent to the concerns of these essays. In considering the First Principles of

Government, Hume found "nothing more surprising" than

> to see the easiness with which the many are governed by the few; and to observe the implicit submission with which men resign their own sentiments and passions to those of their rulers. When we enquire by what means this wonder is brought about, we shall find, that as Force is always on the side of the governed, the governors have nothing to support them but opinion. 'Tis therefore, on opinion only that government is founded; and this maxim extends to the most despotic and most military governments, as well as to the most free and most popular.

Hume was an astute observer, and his paradox of government is much to the point. His insight explains why elites are so dedicated to indoctrination and thought control, a major and largely neglected theme of modern history. "The public must be put in its place," Walter Lippmann wrote, so that we may "live free of the trampling and the roar of a bewildered herd," whose "function" is to be "interested spectators of action," not participants. And if the state lacks the force to coerce and the voice of the people can be heard, it is necessary to ensure that that voice says the right thing, as respected intellectuals have been advising for many years.[2]

Hume's observation raises a number of questions. One dubious feature is the idea that force is on the side of the governed. Reality is more grim. A good part of human history supports the contrary thesis put forth a century earlier by advocates of the rule of Parliament against the King, but more significantly against the people: that "the power of the Sword is, and ever hath been, the Foundation of all Titles to Government."[3] Force also has more subtle modes, including an array of costs well short of overt violence that attach to refusal to submit. Nevertheless, Hume's paradox is real. Even despotic rule is commonly founded on a measure of consent, and the abdication of rights is the hallmark of more free societies—a fact that calls for analysis.

1. The Harsher Side

The harsher side of the truth is highlighted by the fate of the popular movements of the past decade. In the Soviet satellites, the governors had ruled by force, not opinion. When force was withdrawn, the fragile tyrannies quickly collapsed, for the most part with little bloodshed. These remarkable successes have elicited some euphoria about the power of "love, tolerance, nonviolence, the human spirit and forgiveness," Václav Havel's explanation for the failure of the police and military to crush the Czech uprising.[4] The thought is comforting but illusory, as even the most cursory look at history reveals. The crucial factor was not some novel form of love and nonviolence; no new ground was broken here. Rather, it was the withdrawal of Soviet force, and the collapse of the structures of coercion based upon it. Those who believe otherwise may turn for guidance to the ghost of Archbishop Romero and countless others who have tried to confront unyielding terror with the human spirit.

The recent events in Eastern and Central Europe are a sharp departure from the historical norm. Throughout modern history, popular forces motivated by radical democratic ideals have sought to combat autocratic rule. Sometimes they have been able to expand the realms of freedom and justice before being brought to heel. Often they are simply crushed. But it is hard to think of another case when established power simply withdrew in the face of a popular challenge. No less remarkable is the behavior of the reigning superpower, which not only did not bar these developments by force as in the past, but even encouraged them, alongside of significant internal changes.

The historical norm is illustrated by the dramatically contrasting case of Central America, where any popular effort to overthrow the brutal tyrannies of the oligarchy and the military is met with murderous force, supported or directly organized by the ruler of the hemisphere. Ten years ago, there were signs of hope for an end to the dark ages of terror and misery, with the rise of self-help groups, unions, peasant associations, Christian base communities, and other popular organizations that might have led the way to democracy and social reform. This prospect elicited a stern response by the United States and its clients, generally supported by its European allies, with a campaign of slaughter, torture, and general barbarism that left societies "affected by terror and panic," "collective intimidation and generalized fear" and "internalized acceptance of the terror," in the words of a Church-based Salvadoran human rights organization (see p. 387). Early efforts in Nicaragua to direct resources to the poor majority impelled Washington to economic and ideological warfare, and outright terror, to punish these transgressions by destroying the economy and social life.

Enlightened Western opinion regards such consequences as a success in so far as the challenge to power and privilege is rebuffed and the targets are properly chosen: killing prominent priests in public view is not clever, but rural activists and union leaders are fair game—and of course peasants, Indians, students, and other low-life generally. Shortly after the murder of the Jesuit priests in El Salvador in November 1989, the wires carried a story by AP correspondent Douglas Grant Mine entitled "Second Salvador Massacre, but of Common Folk," reporting how soldiers entered a working-class neighborhood, captured six men, lined them up against a wall and murdered them, adding a fourteen-year-old boy for good measure. They "were not priests or human rights campaigners," Mine wrote, "so their deaths have gone largely unnoticed"—as did his story, which was buried. This was, after all, just one more episode in the savage outburst of torture, destruction, and murder that Secretary of State James Baker praised as "absolutely appropriate" at a press conference the next day—eliciting no comment, another demonstration of our values.

Mine's report is mistaken in supposing that the murder of priests and human rights campaigners receives notice; that is far from true, as has been amply documented, though too brazen an assault is frowned upon as unwise.[5]

"The same week the Jesuits were killed," Central America correspondent Alan Nairn writes, "at least 28 other civilians were murdered in similar fashion. Among them were the head of the water works union, the leader of the organization of university women, nine members of an Indian farming cooperative, 10 university students, ... Moreover, serious investigation of the Salvadoran murders leads directly to Washington's doorstep."[6] All "absolutely appropriate," hence unworthy of mention or concern. So the story continues, week after grisly week.

The comparison between the Soviet and US satellites is so striking and obvious that it takes real dedication not to perceive it, and outside of Western intellectual circles, it is a commonplace. A writer in the Mexican daily Excelsior, describing how US relations with Latin America deteriorated through the 1980s, comments on the "striking contrast" between Soviet behavior towards its satellites and "U.S. policy in the Western Hemisphere, where intransigence, interventionism and the application of typical police state instruments have traditionally marked Washington's actions": "In Europe, the USSR and Gorbachev are associated with the struggle for freedom of travel, political rights, and respect for public opinion. In the Americas, the U.S. and Bush are associated with indiscriminate bombings of civilians, the organization, training and financing of death squads, and programs of mass murder"—not quite the story in New York and Washington, where the United States is hailed as an "inspiration for the triumph of democracy in our time" (The New Republic).[7] In El Salvador, the journal Proceso of the Jesuit University observed:

The so-called Salvadoran "democratic process" could learn a lot from the capacity for self-criticism that the socialist nations are demonstrating. If Lech Walesa had been doing his organizing work in El Salvador, he would have already entered into the ranks of the disappeared—at the hands of "heavily armed men dressed in civilian clothes"; or have been blown to pieces in a dynamite attack on his union headquarters. If Alexander Dubček were a politician in our country, he would have been assassinated like Héctor Oquelí [the social democratic leader assassinated in Guatemala, by Salvadoran death squads, according to the Guatemalan government]. If Andrei Sakharov had worked here in favor of human rights, he would have met the same fate as Herbert Anaya [one of the many murdered leaders of the independent Salvadoran Human Rights Commission CDHES]. If Ota-Sik or Václav Havel had been carrying out their intellectual work in El Salvador, they would have woken up one sinister morning, lying on the patio of a university campus with their heads destroyed by the bullets of an elite army battalion.[8]

The comparison was broadened in a seminar on Christian opportunity and mission called by the Latin American Council of Churches in San José, Costa Rica, reported in Mexico's leading daily. Participants contrasted positive developments in the Soviet Union and its domains with the circumstances of Central America, "marked by United States intervention and the rightward turn of control of government power." The pastoral letter "Hope against Hope" announced at the end of the meeting went on to say that in this context, "military, institutional, financial, political and cultural powers, means of communication, as well as the power of some churches 'indifferent to social problems' will be deployed with greater force in Central America, 'with serious consequences for the impoverished majority'"; the reference is presumably to the fundamentalist churches backed by the US in an effort to divert the poor population from any struggle for amelioration of the conditions of this meaningless life on earth. The decade of the 1980s "was notable in the region for the growth of the gap between rich and poor, a political rightward turn and a conservative offensive on the economic front." The goal of the Central American peace plan was to "put the Nicaraguan revolution on neoliberal-democracy tracks and to defend governments such as the Salvadoran." With these results achieved, the US-backed regimes and their sponsor will "bury the demands" about human rights and social justice.[9]

The same comparison was drawn by the Guatemalan journalist Julio Godoy after a brief visit to Guatemala. He had fled a year earlier when his newspaper, *La Epoca*, was blown up by state terrorists—an operation that aroused no interest in the United States; it was not reported, though well known. At the time, the media were much exercised over the fact that the US-funded journal *La Prensa*, which was openly aligned with the US-run forces attacking Nicaragua, had missed an issue because of a shortage of newsprint, an atrocity that led to passionate diatribes about Sandinista totalitarianism. In the face of this crime, Western commentators could hardly be expected to notice that the US-backed security forces had silenced the one small independent voice in Guatemala in their usual fashion. This is simply another illustration of the total contempt for freedom of the press in Western circles, revealed as well by the silence that accompanies the violent destruction of the independent Salvadoran press by state terror, the routine closure of newspapers under absurd pretexts and the arrest and torture of journalists in the Israeli-occupied territories and sometimes in Israel proper, the storming of the headquarters of a major South Korean broadcasting network by riot police to arrest the leader of the union on the charge that he had organized labor protests, and other such contributions to order and good form.[10]

Eastern Europeans are, "in a way, luckier than Central Americans," Godoy wrote: "while the Moscow-imposed government in Prague would degrade and humiliate reformers, the Washington-made government in Guatemala would kill them. It still does, in a virtual genocide that has taken more than 150,000 victims . . . [in what Amnesty International calls] a 'government program of political murder'." That, he suggested, is "the main explanation for the fearless character of the students' recent uprising in Prague: the Czechoslovak Army doesn't shoot to kill. . . . In Guatemala, not to mention El Salvador, random terror is used to keep unions and peasant associations from seeking their own way"—and to ensure that the press conforms or disappears, so that Western liberals need not fret over censorship in the "fledgling democracies" they applaud. There is an "important difference in the nature of the armies and of their foreign tutors." In the Soviet satellites, the armies are "apolitical and obedient to their national government," while in the US satellites, "the army *is* the power," doing what they have been trained to do for many decades by their foreign tutor. "One is tempted to believe that some people in the White House worship Aztec gods—with the offering of Central American blood." They backed forces in El Salvador, Guatemala, and Nicaragua that "can easily compete against Nicolae Ceausescu's Securitate for the World Cruelty Prize."

Godoy quotes a European diplomat who says, "as long as the Americans don't change their attitude towards the region, there's no space here for the truth or for hope." Surely no space for nonviolence and love.

One will search far to find such truisms in US commentary, or the West in general, which much prefers largely meaningless (though self-flattering) comparisons between Eastern and Western Europe. Nor is the hideous catastrophe of capitalism in the past years a major theme of contemporary discourse—a catastrophe that is dramatic in Latin America and other domains of the industrial West, in the "internal Third World" of the United States, and the "exported slums" of Europe. Nor are we likely to find much attention to the fact, hard to ignore, that the economic success stories typically involve coordination of the state and financial-industrial conglomerates, another sign of the collapse of capitalism in the past sixty years. It is only the Third World that is to be subjected to the destructive forces of free-market capitalism, so that it can be more efficiently robbed and exploited by the powerful.

Central America represents the historical norm, not Eastern Europe. Hume's observation requires this correction. Recognizing that, it remains true, and important, that government is typically founded on modes of submission short of force, even where force is available as a last resort.

2. The Bewildered Herd and its Shepherds

In the contemporary period, Hume's insight has been revived and elaborated, but with a crucial innovation: control of thought is *more* important for governments that are free and popular than for despotic and military states. The logic is straightforward. A despotic state can control its domestic enemy by force, but as the state loses this weapon, other devices are required to prevent the ignorant masses from interfering with public affairs, which are none of their business. These prominent features of modern political and intellectual culture merit a closer look.

The problem of "putting the public in its place" came to the fore with what one historian calls "the first great outburst of democratic thought in history," the English revolution in the seventeenth century.[11] This awakening of the general populace raised the problem of how to contain the threat.

The libertarian ideas of the radical democrats were considered outrageous by respectable people. They favored universal education, guaranteed health care, and democratization of the law, which one described as a fox, with poor men the geese: "he pulls off their feathers and feeds upon them." They developed a kind of "liberation theology" which, as one critic ominously observed, preached "seditious doctrine to the people" and aimed "to raise the rascal multitude . . . against all men of best quality in the kingdom, to draw them into associations and combinations with one another . . . against all lords, gentry, ministers, lawyers, rich and peaceable men" (historian Clement Walker). Particularly frightening were the itinerant workers and preachers calling for freedom and democracy, the agitators stirring up the rascal multitude, and the printers putting out pamphlets questioning authority and its mysteries. "There can be no form of government without its proper mysteries," Walker warned—mysteries that must be "concealed" from the common folk: "Ignorance, and admiration arising from ignorance, are the parents of civil devotion and obedience," a thought echoed by Dostoevsky's Grand Inquisitor. The radical democrats had "cast all the mysteries and secrets of government . . . before the vulgar (like pearls before swine)," he continued, and had "made the people thereby so curious and so arrogant that they will never find humility enough to submit to a civil rule." It is dangerous, another commentator ominously observed, to "have a people know their own strength." The rabble did not want to be ruled by King or Parliament, but "by countrymen like ourselves, that know our wants." Their pamphlets explained further that "It will never be a good world while knights and gentlemen make us laws, that are chosen for fear and do but oppress us, and do not know the people's sores."

These ideas naturally appalled the men of best quality. They were willing to grant the people rights, but within reason, and on the principle that "when we mention the people, we do not mean the confused promiscuous body of the people." After the democrats had been defeated, John Locke commented that "day-labourers and tradesmen, the spinsters and dairymaids" must be told what to believe; "The greatest part cannot know and therefore they must believe."[12]

Like John Milton and other civil libertarians of the period, Locke held a sharply limited conception of freedom of expression. His Fundamental Constitution of Carolina barred those who "speak anything in their religious assembly irreverently or seditiously of the government or governors, or of state matters." The Constitution guaranteed freedom for "speculative opinions in religion," but not for political opinions. "Locke would not even have permitted people to discuss public affairs," Leonard Levy observes. The Constitution provided further that "all manner of comments and expositions on any part of these constitutions, or on any part of the common or statute laws of Carolines, are absolutely prohibited." In drafting reasons for Parliament to terminate censorship in 1694, Locke offered no defense of freedom of expression or thought, but only considerations of expediency and harm to commercial interests.[13] With the threat of democracy overcome and the libertarian rabble dispersed, censorship was permitted to lapse in England, because the "opinion-formers ... censored themselves. Nothing got into print which frightened the men of property," Christopher Hill comments. In a well-functioning state capitalist democracy like the United States, what might frighten the men of property is generally kept far from the public eye—sometimes with quite astonishing success.

Such ideas have ample resonance until today, including Locke's stern doctrine that the common people should be denied the right even to discuss public affairs. This doctrine remains a basic principle of modern democratic states, now implemented by a variety of means to protect the operations of the state from public scrutiny: classification of documents on the largely fraudulent pretext of national security, clandestine operations, and other measures to bar the rascal multitude from the political arena. Such devices typically gain new force under the regime of statist reactionaries of the Reagan–Thatcher variety. The same ideas frame the essential professional task and responsibility of the intellectual community: to shape the perceived historical record and the picture of the contemporary world in the interests of the powerful, thus ensuring that the public, properly bewildered, keeps to its place and function.

In the 1650s, supporters of Parliament and the army against the people easily proved that the rabble could not be trusted. This was shown by their lingering monarchist sentiments and their reluctance to place their affairs in the hands of the gentry and the army, who were "truly the people"— though the people, in their foolishness, did not agree. The mass of the people are a "giddy multitude," "beasts in men's shapes." It is proper to suppress them, just as it is proper "to save the life of a lunatique or distracted person even against his will." If the people are so "depraved and corrupt" as to "confer places of power and trust upon wicked and undeserving men, they forfeit their power in this behalf unto those that are good, though but a few."[14]

The good and few may be the gentry or industrialists, or the vanguard Party and the Central Committee, or the intellectuals who qualify as "experts" because they articulate the consensus of the powerful (to paraphrase one of Henry Kissinger's insights).[15] They manage the business empires, ideological institutions, and political structures, or serve them at various levels. Their task is to shepherd the bewildered herd and keep the giddy multitude in a state of implicit submission, and thus to bar the dread prospect of freedom and self-determination.

Similar ideas had been forged as the Spanish explorers set about what Tzvetan Todorov calls "the greatest genocide in human history" after they "discovered America" five hundred years ago. They justified their acts of terror and oppression on the grounds that the natives are not "capable of governing themselves any more than madmen or even wild beasts and animals, seeing that their food is not any more agreeable and scarcely better than that of wild beasts" and their stupidity "is much greater than that of children and madmen in other countries" (professor and theologian Francisco de Vitoria, "one of the pinnacles of Spanish humanism in the sixteenth century"). Therefore, intervention is legitimate "in order to exercise the rights of guardianship," Todorov comments, summarizing de Vitoria's basic thought.[16]

When English savages took over the task a few years later, they naturally adopted the same pose while taming the wolves in the guise of men, as George Washington described the objects that stood in the way of the advance of civilization and had to be eliminated for their own good. The English colonists had already handled the Celtic "wild men" the same way, for example, when Lord Cumberland, known as "the butcher," laid waste to the Scottish Highlands before moving on to pursue his craft in North America.[17]

One hundred and fifty years later, their descendants had purged North America of this native blight, reducing the lunatics from ten million to 200,000 according to some recent estimates, and they turned their eyes elsewhere, to civilize the wild beasts in the Philippines. The Indian fighters to whom President McKinley assigned the task of "Christianizing" and "uplifting" these unfortunate creatures rid the liberated islands of hundreds of thousands of them, accelerating their ascent to heaven. They too were rescuing "misguided creatures" from their depravity by "slaughtering the natives in English fashion," as the New York press described their painful responsibility, adding that we must take "what muddy glory lies in the wholesale killing til they have learned to respect our arms," then moving on to "the more difficult task of getting them to respect our intentions."[18]

This is pretty much the course of history, as the plague of European civilization devastated much of the world.

On the home front, the continuing problem was formulated plainly by the seventeenth-century political thinker Marchamont Nedham. The proposals of the radical democrats, he wrote, would result in "ignorant Persons, neither of Learning nor Fortune, being put in Authority." Given their freedom, the "self-opinionated multitude" would elect "the *lowest of the People*" who would occupy themselves with "Milking and Gelding the Purses of the Rich," taking "the ready Road to all licentiousness, mischief, mere Anarchy and Confusion."[19] These sentiments are the common coin of modern political and intellectual discourse; increasingly so as popular struggles did succeed, over the centuries, in realizing the proposals of the radical democrats, so that ever more sophisticated means had to be devised to reduce their substantive content.

Such problems regularly arise in periods of turmoil and social conflict. After the American revolution, rebellious and independent farmers had to be taught by force that the ideals expressed in the pamphlets of 1776 were not to be taken seriously. The common people were not to be represented by countrymen like themselves, that know the people's sores, but by gentry, merchants, lawyers, and others who hold or serve private power. Jefferson and Madison believed that power should be in the hands of the "natural aristocracy," Edmund Morgan comments, "men like themselves" who would defend property rights against Hamilton's "paper aristocracy" and from the poor; they "regarded slaves, paupers, and destitute laborers as an ever-present danger to liberty as well as property."[20] The reigning doctrine, expressed by the Founding Fathers, is that "the people who own the country ought to govern it" (John Jay). The rise of corporations in the nineteenth century, and the legal structures devised to grant them dominance over private and public life, established the victory of the Federalist opponents of popular democracy in a new and powerful form.

Not infrequently, revolutionary struggles pit aspirants to power against one another though united in opposition to radical democratic tendencies among the common people. Lenin and Trotsky, shortly after seizing state power in 1917, moved to dismantle organs of popular control, including factory councils and Soviets, thus proceeding to deter and overcome socialist tendencies. An orthodox Marxist, Lenin did not regard Socialism as a viable option in this backward and underdeveloped country; until his last days, it remained for him an "elementary truth of Marxism, that the victory of socialism requires the joint efforts of workers in a number of advanced countries," Germany in particular.[21] In what has always seemed to me his greatest work, *Homage to Catalonia*, George Orwell described a similar process in Spain, where the Fascists, Communists, and liberal democracies were united in opposition to the libertarian revolution that swept over much of the country, turning to the conflict over the spoils only when popular forces were safely suppressed. There are many examples, often influenced by great-power violence.

This is particularly true in the Third World. A persistent concern of Western elites is that popular organizations might lay the basis for meaningful democracy and social reform, threatening the prerogatives of the privileged. Those who seek "to raise the rascal multitude" and "draw them into associations and combinations with one another" against "the men of best quality" must, therefore, be repressed or eliminated. It comes as no surprise that Archbishop Romero should be assassinated shortly after urging President Carter to withhold military aid from the governing junta, which, he warned, would use it to "sharpen injustice and repression against the people's organizations" struggling "for respect for their most basic human rights."

The Archbishop had put his finger on the very problem that must be overcome, whatever euphemisms and tortured argument are used to conceal that fundamental fact. Accordingly, his request for a "guarantee" that the US government "will not intervene directly or indirectly, with military, economic, diplomatic or other pressure, in determining the destiny of the Salvadoran people" was denied with the promise that aid to the military junta would be reassessed should evidence of "misuse develop." The Archbishop was assassinated, and the security forces turned to the task of demolishing the people's organizations by savage atrocities, beginning with the Rio Sumpul massacre, concealed by the loyal media.

It also comes as no surprise that the Human Rights Administration should see no "misuse developing" as the atrocities mounted, except briefly, when American churchwomen were raped, tortured, and murdered, so that a cover-up had to be arranged. Or that the media and intellectual opinion should largely disregard the assassination of the Archbishop (which did not even merit an editorial in the *New York Times*), conceal the complicity of the armed forces and the civilian government established by the US as a cover for their necessary work, suppress reports on the growing state terror by Church and human rights groups and a congressional delegation, and even pretend that "There is no real argument that most of the estimated 10,000 political fatalities in 1980 were victims of government forces or irregulars associated with them" (*Washington Post*).[22]

When a job is to be done, we must set to it without sentimentality. Human rights concerns are fine when they can be used as an ideological weapon to undermine enemies or to restore popular faith in the nobility of the state. But they are not to interfere with serious matters, such as dispersing and crushing the rascal multitude forming associations against the interests of the men of best quality.

The same dedicated commitment to necessary terror was revealed a decade later, in March 1990, when the Archbishop's assassination was commemorated in El Salvador in an impressive three-day ceremony. "The poor, the humble and the devout flocked by the thousands" to honor his memory at a Mass in the cathedral where he was murdered, the wire services reported, filling the plaza and the streets outside after a march led by sixteen bishops, three from the United States. Archbishop Romero was formally proposed for sainthood by the Salvadoran Church—the first such case since Thomas à Becket was assassinated at the altar over eight hundred years ago. Americas Watch published a report on the shameful decade, symbolically bounded by "these two events—the murder of Archbishop Romero in 1980 and the slaying of the Jesuits in 1989"—which offer "harsh testimony about who really rules El Salvador and how little they have changed," people for whom "priest-killing is still a preferred option" because they "simply will not hear the cries for change and justice in a society that has had too little of either." In his homily, Romero's successor, Archbishop Arturo Rivera y Damas, said: "For being the voice of those without voice, he was violently silenced."[23]

The victims remain without voice, and the Archbishop remains silenced as well. No high-ranking official of the Cristiani government or his ARENA Party attended the Mass, not even their leader Roberto d'Aubuisson, assumed to be responsible for the assassination in coordination with the US-backed security forces. The US government was also notable for its absence. The ceremony in El Salvador passed with scarcely a notice in the country that funds and trains the assassins; commemorations at home also escaped the attention of the national press.[24]

There should be no further embarrassment, however—assuming that there is any now. This will be the last public religious homage to Romero for decades, because Church doctrine prohibits homage to candidates for sainthood. Revulsion at the assassination of Thomas à Becket compelled King Henry II, who was held to be indirectly responsible, to do penance at the shrine. One will wait a long time for a proper reenactment, another sign of the progress of civilization.

The threat of popular organization to privilege is real enough in itself. Worse still, "the rot may spread," in the terminology of political elites; there may be a demonstration effect of independent development in a form that attends to the people's sores. As noted earlier, internal documents and even the public record reveal that a driving concern of US planners has been the fear that the "virus" might spread, "infecting" regions beyond.

This concern breaks no new ground. European statesmen had feared that the American revolution might "lend new strength to the apostles of sedition" (Metternich) and might spread "the contagion and the invasion of vicious principles" such as "the pernicious doctrines of republicanism and popular self-rule," one of the Czar's diplomats warned. A century later, the cast of characters was reversed. Woodrow Wilson's Secretary of State Robert Lansing feared that if the Bolshevik disease were to spread, it would leave the "ignorant and incapable mass of humanity dominant in the earth"; the Bolsheviks, he continued, were appealing "to the proletariat of all countries, to the ignorant and mentally deficient, who by their numbers are urged to become masters, ... a very real danger in view of the process of social unrest throughout the world." Again it is democracy that is the awesome threat. When soldiers and workers' councils made a brief appearance in Germany, Wilson feared that they would inspire dangerous thoughts among "the American negro [soldiers] returning from abroad." Already, he had heard, Negro laundresses were demanding more than the going wage, saying that "money is as much mine as it is yours." Businessmen might have to adjust to having workers on their boards of directors, he feared, among other disasters, if the Bolshevik virus were not exterminated.

With these dire consequences in mind, the Western invasion of the Soviet Union was justified on defensive grounds, against "the Revolution's challenge ... to the very survival of the capitalist order" (John Lewis Gaddis). And it was only natural that the defense of the United States should extend from invasion of the Soviet Union to Wilson's Red Scare at home. As Lansing explained, force must be used to prevent "the leaders of Bolshevism and anarchy" from proceeding to "organize or preach against government in the United States"; the government must not permit "these fanatics to enjoy the liberty which they now seek to destroy." The repression launched by the Wilson Administration successfully undermined democratic politics, unions, freedom of the press, and independent thought, in the interests of corporate power and the state authorities who represented its interests, all with the approval of the media and elites generally, all in self-defense against the "ignorant and mentally deficient" majority. Much the same story was re-enacted after World War II, again under the pretext of a Soviet threat, in reality to restore submission to the rulers.[25]

It is often not appreciated how profound and deeply rooted is the contempt for democracy in the elite culture, and the fear it arouses.

When political life and independent thought revived in the 1960s, the problem arose again, and the reaction was the same. The Trilateral Commission, bringing together liberal elites from Europe, Japan, and the United States, warned of an impending "crisis of democracy" as segments of the public sought to enter the political arena. This "excess of democracy" was posing a threat to the unhampered rule of privileged elites—what is called "democracy" in political theology. The problem was the usual one: the rabble were trying to arrange their own affairs, gaining control over their communities and pressing their political demands. There were organizing efforts among young people, ethnic minorities, women, social activists, and others, encouraged by the struggles of benighted masses elsewhere for freedom and independence. More "moderation in democracy" would be required, the Commission concluded, perhaps a return to the days when "Truman had been able to govern the country with the cooperation of a relatively small number of Wall Street lawyers and bankers," as the American rapporteur commented.[26]

Irving Kristol adds that "insignificant nations, like insignificant people, can quickly experience delusions of significance." But as a leading neoconservative, he has no time for the softer means of manufacture of consent, which are, in any event, not warranted for insignificant people outside the domains of Western civilization. Hence the delusions of significance must be driven from their tiny minds by force: "In truth, the days of 'gunboat diplomacy' are never over. . . . Gunboats are as necessary for international order as police cars are for domestic order."[27]

These ideas bring us to the Reagan Administration, which established a state propaganda agency (the Office of Public Diplomacy) that was by far the most elaborate in American history, much to the delight of the advocates of a powerful and interventionist state who are called "conservatives" in one of the current corruptions of political discourse. When the program was exposed, a high official described it as the kind of operation carried out in "enemy territory"—an apt phrase, expressing standard elite attitudes towards the public. In this case, the enemy was not completely subdued. Popular movements deepened their roots and spread into new sectors of the population, and were able to drive the state underground to clandestine terror instead of the more efficient forms of overt violence that Presidents Kennedy and Johnson could undertake before the public had been aroused.

The fears expressed by the men of best quality in the seventeenth century have become a major theme of intellectual discourse, corporate practice, and the academic social sciences. They were expressed by the influential moralist and foreign affairs adviser Reinhold Niebuhr, who was revered by George Kennan, the Kennedy intellectuals, and many others. He wrote that "rationality belongs to the cool observers" while the common person follows not reason but faith. The cool observers, he explained, must recognize "the stupidity of the average man," and must provide the "necessary illusion" and the "emotionally potent oversimplifications" that will keep the naive simpletons on course. As in 1650, it remains necessary to protect the "lunatic or distracted person," the ignorant rabble, from their own "depraved and corrupt" judgements, just as one does not allow a child to cross the street without supervision.[28]

In accordance with the prevailing conceptions, there is no infringement of democracy if a few corporations control the information system: in fact, that is the essence of democracy. The leading figure of the public relations industry, Edward Bernays, explained that "the very essence of the democratic process" is "the freedom to persuade and suggest," what he calls "the engineering of consent." If the freedom to persuade happens to be concentrated in a few hands, we must recognize that such is the nature of a free society. Since the early twentieth century, the public relations industry has devoted huge resources to "educating the American people about the economic facts of life" to ensure a favorable climate for business. Its task is to control "the public mind," which is "the only serious danger confronting the company," an AT&T executive observed eighty years ago. And today, the *Wall Street Journal* describes with enthusiasm the "concerted efforts" of corporate America "to change the attitudes and values of workers" on a vast scale with "New Age workshops" and other contemporary devices of indoctrination and stupefaction designed to convert "worker apathy into corporate allegiance."[29] The agents of Reverend Moon and Christian evangelicals employ similar devices to bar the threat of peasant organizing and to undermine a Church that serves the poor in Latin America, aided by intelligence agencies and the closely linked international organizations of the ultra-right.

Bernays expressed the basic point in a 1928 public relations manual: "The conscious and intelligent manipulation of the organized habits and opinions of the masses is an important element in democratic society.... It is the intelligent minorities which need to make use of propaganda continuously and systematically." Given its enormous and decisive power, the highly class-conscious business community of the United States has been able to put these lessons to effective use. Bernays's advocacy of propaganda is cited by Thomas McCann, head of public relations for the United Fruit Company, for which Bernays provided signal service in preparing the ground for the overthrow of Guatemalan democracy in 1954, a major triumph of business propaganda with the willing compliance of the media.[30]

The intelligent minorities have long understood this to be their function. Walter Lippmann described a "revolution" in "the practice of democracy" as "the manufacture of consent" has become "a self-conscious art and a regular organ of popular government." This is a natural development when public opinion cannot be trusted:

> In the absence of institutions and education by which the environment is so successfully reported that the realities of public life stand out very sharply against self-centered opinion, the common interests very largely elude public opinion entirely, and can be managed only by a specialized class whose personal interests reach beyond the locality,

and are thus able to perceive "the realities." These are the men of best quality, who alone are capable of social and economic management.

It follows that two political roles must be clearly distinguished, Lippmann goes on to explain. First, there is the role assigned to the specialized class, the "insiders," the "responsible men," who have access to information and understanding. Ideally, they should have a special education for public office, and should master the criteria for solving the problems of society: "In the degree to which these criteria can be made exact and objective, political decision," which is their domain, "is actually brought into relation with the interests of men." The "public men" are, furthermore, to "lead opinion" and take the responsibility for "the formation of a sound public opinion. ... They initiate, they administer, they settle," and should be protected from "ignorant and meddlesome outsiders," the general public, who are incapable of dealing "with the substance of the problem." The criteria we apply to government are success in satisfying material and cultural wants, not whether "it vibrates to the self-centered opinions that happen to be floating in men's minds." Having mastered the criteria for political decision, the specialized class, protected from pubic meddling, will serve the public interest—what is called "the national interest" in the webs of mystification spun by the academic social sciences and political commentary.

The second role is "the task of the public," which is much more limited. It is not for the public, Lippmann observes, to "pass judgment on the intrinsic merits" of an issue or to offer analysis or solutions, but merely, on occasion, to place "its force at the disposal" of one or another group of "responsible men." The public "does not reason, investigate, invent, persuade, bargain or settle." Rather, "the public acts only by aligning itself as the partisan of someone in a position to act executively," once he has given the matter at hand sober and disinterested thought. It is for this reason that "the public must be put in its place." The bewildered herd, trampling and roaring, "has its function": to be "the interested spectators of action," not participants. Participation is the duty of "the responsible man."[31]

These ideas, described by Lippmann's editors as a progressive "political philosophy for liberal democracy," have an unmistakable resemblance to the Leninist concept of a vanguard party that leads the masses to a better life that they cannot conceive or construct on their own. In fact, the transition from one position to the other—from Leninist enthusiasm to "celebration of America"—has proven quite an easy one over the years. This is not surprising, since the doctrines are similar at their root. The critical difference lies in an assessment of the prospects for power: through exploitation of mass popular struggle, or service to the current masters.

There is, clearly enough, an unspoken assumption behind the proposals of Lippmann and others: the specialized class are offered the opportunity to manage public affairs by virtue of their subordination to those with real power—in our societies, dominant business interests, a crucial fact that is ignored in the self-praise of the elect.

Lippmann's thinking on these matters dates from shortly after World War I, when the liberal intellectual community was much impressed with its success in serving as "the faithful and helpful interpreters of what seems to be one of the greatest enterprises ever undertaken by an American president" (*The New Republic*). The enterprise was Woodrow Wilson's interpretation of his electoral mandate for "peace without victory" as the occasion for pursuing victory without peace, with the assistance of the liberal intellectuals, who later praised themselves for having "impose[d] their will upon a reluctant or indifferent majority," with the aid of propaganda fabrications about Hun atrocities and other such devices. They were serving, often unwittingly, as instruments of the British Ministry of Information, which secretly defined its task as "to direct the thought of most of the world."[32]

Fifteen years later, the influential political scientist Harold Lasswell explained in the *Encyclopaedia of the Social Sciences* that when elites lack the requisite force to compel obedience, social managers must turn to "a whole new technique of control, largely through propaganda." He added the conventional justification: we must recognize the "ignorance and stupidity [of] ... the masses" and not succumb to "democratic dogmatisms about men being the best judges of their own interests." They are not, and we must control them, for their own good. The same principle guides the business community. Others have developed similar ideas, and put them into practice in the ideological institutions: the schools, the universities, the popular media, the elite journals, and so on. A challenge to these ideas arouses trepidation, sometimes fury, as in the 1960s when students, instead of simply bowing to authority, began to ask too many questions and to explore beyond the bounds established for them. The pretense of manning the ramparts against the onslaught of the barbarians, now a popular pose, is scarcely more than comical fraud.

The doctrines of Lippmann, Lasswell, and others are entirely natural in any society in which power is narrowly concentrated but formal mechanisms exist by which ordinary people may, in theory, play some role in shaping their own affairs—a threat that plainly must be barred.

The techniques of manufacture of consent are most finely honed in the United States, a more advanced business-run society than its allies and one that is in important ways more free than elsewhere, so that the ignorant and stupid masses are more dangerous. But the same concerns arise in Europe, as in the past, heightened by the fact that the European varieties of state capitalism have not yet progressed as far as the United States in eliminating labor unions and other impediments to rule by men (and occasionally women) of best quality, thus restricting politics to factions of the business party. The basic problem, recognized throughout, is that as the state loses the capacity to control the population by force, privileged sectors must find other methods to ensure that the rascal multitude is removed from the public arena. And the insignificant nations must be subjected to the same practices as the insignificant people. Liberal doves hold that others should be free and independent, but not free to choose in ways that we regard as unwise or contrary to our interests,[33] a close counterpart to the prevailing conception of democracy at home as a form of population control. At the other extreme of the spectrum, we find the "conservatives" with their preference for quick resort to Kristol's methods: gunboats and police cars.

A properly functioning system of indoctrination has a variety of tasks, some rather delicate. One of its targets is the stupid and ignorant masses. They must be kept that way, diverted with emotionally potent oversimplifications, marginalized, and isolated. Ideally, each person should be alone in front of the television screen watching sports, soap operas, or comedies, deprived of organizational structures that permit individuals lacking resources to discover what they think and believe in interaction with others, to formulate their own concerns and programs, and to act to realize them. They can then be permitted, even encouraged, to ratify the decisions of their betters in periodic elections. The rascal multitude are the proper targets of the mass media and a public education system geared to obedience and training in needed skills, including the skill of repeating patriotic slogans on timely occasions.

For submissiveness to become a reliable trait, it must be entrenched in every realm. The public are to be observers, not participants, consumers of ideology as well as products. Eduardo Galeano writes that "the majority must resign itself to the consumption of fantasy. Illusions of wealth are sold to the poor, illusions of freedom to the oppressed, dreams of victory to the defeated and of power to the weak."[34] Nothing less will do.

The problem of indoctrination is a bit different for those expected to take part in serious decision-making and control: the business, state, and cultural managers, and articulate sectors generally. They must internalize the values of the system and share the necessary illusions that permit it to function in the interests of concentrated power and privilege—or at least be cynical enough to pretend that they do, an art that not many can master. But they must also have a certain grasp of the realities of the world, or they will be unable to perform their tasks effectively. The elite media and educational systems must steer a course through these dilemmas—not an easy task, one plagued by internal contradictions. It is intriguing to see how it is faced, but that is beyond the scope of these remarks.

For the home front, a variety of techniques of manufacture of consent are required, geared to the intended audience and its ranking on the scale of significance. For those at the lowest rank, and for the insignificant peoples abroad, another device is available: what a leading turn-of-the-century American sociologist, Franklin Henry Giddings, called "consent without consent": "if in later years, [the colonized] see and admit that the disputed relation was for the highest interest, it may be reasonably held that authority has been imposed with the consent of the governed," as when a parent disciplines an uncomprehending child. Giddings was referring to the "misguided creatures" whom we were reluctantly slaughtering in the Philippines, for their own good.[35] But the lesson holds more generally.

As noted, the Bolshevik overtones are apparent throughout. The systems have crucial differences, but also striking similarities. Lippmann's "specialized class" and Bernays's "intelligent minority," which are to manage the public and their affairs according to liberal democratic theory, correspond to the Leninist vanguard of revolutionary intellectuals. The "manufacture of consent" advocated by Lippmann, Bernays, Niebuhr, Lasswell and others is the Agitprop of their Leninist counterparts. Following a script outlined by Bakunin over a century ago, the secular priesthood in both of the major systems of hierarchy and coercion regard the masses as stupid and incompetent, a bewildered herd who must be driven to a better world—one that we, the intelligent minority, will construct for them, either taking state power ourselves in the Leninist model, or serving the owners and managers of the state capitalist systems if it is impossible to exploit popular revolution to capture the commanding heights.

Much as Bakunin had predicted long before, the Leninist "Red bureaucracy" moved at once to dismantle organs of popular control, particularly, any institutional structures that might provide working people with some influence over their affairs as producers or citizens. Studying Bolshevik development programs from a comparative and historical perspective, Alexander Gerschenkron comments that "Marxian ideology, or any socialist ideology for that matter, has had a very remote, if any, relation to the great industrial transformation engineered by the Soviet government," including the "approximate sixfold increase in the volume of industrial output" by the mid 1950s, "the greatest and the longest [spurt of industrialization] in the history of the country's industrial development," at an extraordinary human cost, primarily to the peasantry.[36] That the same was true of the organization of production and of social and political life generally is too obvious to require comment.

Not surprisingly, the immediate destruction of the incipient socialist tendencies that arose during the ferment of popular struggle in 1917 has been depicted by the world's two great propaganda systems as a victory for Socialism. For the Bolsheviks, the goal of the farce was to extract what advantage they could from the moral prestige of Socialism; for the West, the purpose was to defame Socialism and entrench the system of ownership and management control over all aspects of economic, political, and social life. The collapse of the Leninist system cannot properly be called a victory for Socialism, any more than the collapse of Hitler and Mussolini could be described in these terms; but as in those earlier cases, it does eliminate a barrier to the realization of the libertarian socialist ideals of the popular movements that were crushed in Russia in 1917, Germany shortly after, Spain in 1936, and elsewhere, often with the Leninist vanguard leading the way in taming the rascal multitude with their libertarian socialist and radical democratic aspirations.

3. Short of Force

Hume posed his paradox for both despotic and more free societies. The latter case is by far the more important. As the social world becomes more free and diverse, the task of inducing submission becomes more complex and the problem of unraveling the mechanisms of indoctrination more challenging. But intellectual interest aside, the case of free societies has greater human significance, because here we are talking about ourselves and can act upon what we learn. It is for just this reason that the dominant culture will always seek to externalize human concerns, directing them to the inadequacies and abuses of others. When US plans go awry in some corner of the Third World, we devote our attention to the defects and special problems of these cultures and their social disorders—not our own. Fame, fortune, and respect await those who reveal the crimes of official enemies; those who undertake the vastly more important task of raising a mirror to their own societies can expect quite different treatment. George Orwell is famous for *Animal Farm* and *1984*, which focus on the official enemy. Had he addressed the more interesting and significant question of thought control in relatively free and democratic societies, it would not have been appreciated, and instead of wide acclaim, he would have faced silent dismissal or obloquy. Let us nevertheless turn to the more important and unacceptable questions.

Keeping to governments that are more free and popular, why do the governed submit when force is on their side? First, we have to look at a prior question: to what extent *is* force on the side of the governed? Here some care is necessary. Societies are considered free and democratic in so far as the state's power to coerce is limited. The United States is unusual in this respect: perhaps more than anywhere else in the world, the citizen is free from state coercion—at least, the citizen who is relatively privileged and of the right color, a substantial part of the population.

But it is a mere truism that the state represents only one segment of the nexus of power. Control over investment, production, commerce, finance, conditions of work, and other crucial aspects of social policy lies in private hands. Unwillingness to adapt to this structure of authority and domination carries costs, ranging from state force to the costs of privation and struggle; even an individual of independent mind can hardly fail to compare these to the benefits, however meager, that accrue to submission. Meaningful choices are thus narrowly limited. Similar factors limit the range of ideas and opinion in obvious ways. Articulate expression is shaped by the same private powers that control the economy. It is largely dominated by major corporations that sell audiences to advertisers and naturally reflect the interests of the owners and their market. The ability to articulate and communicate one's views, concerns, and interests—or even to discover them—is thus narrowly constrained as well.

Denial of these truisms about effective power is at the heart of the structure of necessary illusion. Thus, a media critic, reviewing a book on the press in the *New York Times*, refers without argument to the "traditional Jeffersonian role" of the press "as counterbalance to government power." The phrase encapsulates three crucial assumptions, one historical, one descriptive, one ideological. The historical claim is that Jefferson was a committed advocate of freedom of the press, which is false. The second is that the press in fact functions as a counterbalance to government rather than as a faithful servant, presented here as doctrine, thus evading any need to face the massive array of detailed documentation that refutes this dogma. The ideological principle is that Jeffersonian libertarianism (considered abstractly, apart from its realization in practice) would demand that the press be a counterbalance to *government* power. That is incorrect. The libertarian conception is that the press should be independent, hence a counterbalance to centralized power of *any* form. In Jefferson's day, the powers that loomed large were the state, the Church, and feudal structures. Shortly after, new forms of centralized power emerged in the world of corporate capitalism. A Jeffersonian would hold, then, that the press should be a counterbalance to state or corporate power, and critically, to the state–corporate nexus. But to raise this point carries us into forbidden ground.[37]

Apart from the general constraints on choice and articulate opinion inherent in the concentration of private power, it also sets narrow limits on the actions of government. The United States has again been unusual in this respect among the industrial democracies, though convergence towards the US pattern is evident elsewhere. The United States is near the limit in its safeguards for freedom from state coercion, and also in the poverty of its political life. There is essentially one political party, the business party, with two factions. Shifting coalitions of investors account for a large part of political history. Unions, or other popular organizations that might offer a way for the general public to play some role in influencing programs and policy choices, scarcely function apart from the narrowest realm. The ideological system is bounded by the consensus of the privileged. Elections are largely a ritual form. In congressional elections, virtually all incumbents are returned to office, a reflection of the vacuity of the political system and the choices it offers. There is scarcely a pretense that substantive issues are at stake in the presidential campaigns. Articulated programs are hardly more than a device to garner votes, and candidates adjust their messages to their audiences as public relations tacticians advise. Political commentators ponder such questions as whether Reagan will remember his lines, or whether Mondale looks too gloomy, or whether Dukakis can duck the slime flung at him by George Bush's speechwriters. In the 1984 elections, the two political factions virtually exchanged traditional policies, the Republicans presenting themselves as the party of Keynesian growth and state intervention in the economy, the Democrats as the advocates of fiscal conservatism; few even noticed. Half the population does not bother to mark the ballots, and those who take the trouble often consciously vote against their own interest.

The public is granted an opportunity to ratify decisions made elsewhere, in accord with the prescriptions of Lippmann and other democratic theorists. It may select among personalities put forth in a game of symbolic politics that only the most naive take very seriously. When they do, they are mocked by sophisticates. Criticism of President Bush's call for "revenue enhancement" after winning the election by the firm and eloquent promise not to raise taxes is a "political cheap shot," Harvard political scientist and media specialist Marty Linsky comments under the heading "Campaign pledges—made to be broken." When Bush won the election by leading the public in the "read my lips—no new taxes" chant, he was merely expressing his "world view," making "a statement of his hopes." Those who thought he was promising no new taxes do not understand that "elections and governing are different ball games, played with different objectives and rules. ... The purpose of elections is to win," Linsky correctly observes, expressing the cynicism of the sophisticated; and "the purpose of governing is to do the best for the country," he adds, parroting the necessary illusions that respectability demands.[38]

These tendencies were accelerated during the Reagan years. The population overwhelmingly opposed the policies of his Administration, and even the Reagan voters in 1984, by about three to two, hoped that his legislative program would not be enacted. In the 1980 elections, 4 percent of the electorate voted for Reagan because they regarded him as a "real conservative." In 1984, this dropped to 1 percent. That is what is called "a landslide victory for conservatism" in political rhetoric. Furthermore, contrary to much pretense, Reagan's popularity was never particularly high, and much of the population seemed to understand that he was a media creation, who had only the foggiest idea of what government policy might be.[39]

It is noteworthy that the fact is now tacitly conceded; the instant that the "great communicator" was no longer of any use as a symbol, he was quietly tucked away. After eight years of pretense about the "revolution" that Reagan wrought, no one would dream of asking its standard-bearer for his thoughts about any topic, because it is understood, as it always was, that he has none. When Reagan was invited to Japan as an elder statesman, his hosts were surprised—and, given the fat fee, a bit annoyed—to discover that he could not hold press conferences or talk on any subject. Their discomfiture aroused some amusement in the American press: the Japanese believed what they had read about this remarkable figure, failing to comprehend the workings of the mysterious occidental mind.

The hoax perpetrated by the media and the intellectual community is of some interest for Hume's paradox about submission to authority. State capitalist democracy has a certain tension with regard to the locus of power: in principle, the people rule, but effective power resides largely in private hands, with large-scale effects throughout the social order. One way to reduce the tension is to remove the public from the scene, except in form. The Reagan phenomenon offered a new way to achieve this fundamental goal of capitalist democracy. The office of chief executive was, in effect, eliminated in favor of a symbolic figure constructed by the public relations industry to perform certain ritual tasks: to appear on ceremonial occasions, to greet visitors, read government pronouncements, and so on. This is a major advance in the marginalization of the public. As the most sophisticated of the state capitalist democracies, the United States has often led the way in devising means to control the domestic enemy, and the latest inspiration will doubtless be mimicked elsewhere, with the usual time lag.

Even when issues arise in the political system, the concentration of effective power limits the threat. The question is largely academic in the United States because of the subordination of the political and ideological system to business interests, but in democracies to the south, where conflicting ideas and approaches reach the political arena, the situation is different. As is again familiar, government policies that private power finds unwelcome will lead to capital flight, disinvestment, and social decline until business confidence is restored with the abandonment of the threat to privilege; these facts of life exert a decisive influence on the political system (with military force in reserve if matters get out of hand, supported or applied by the North American enforcer). To put the basic point crassly: unless the rich and powerful are satisfied, everyone will suffer, because they control the basic social levers, determining what will be produced and consumed, and what crumbs will filter down to their subjects. For the homeless in the streets, then, the primary objective is to ensure that the rich live happily in their mansions. This crucial factor, along with simple control over resources, severely limits the force on the side of the governed and diminishes Hume's paradox in a well-functioning capitalist democracy in which the general public is scattered and isolated.

Understanding of these basic conditions—tacit or explicit—has long served as a guide for policy. Once popular organizations are dispersed or crushed and decision-making power is firmly in the hands of owners and managers, democratic forms are quite acceptable, even preferable as a device of legitimation of elite rule in a business-run "democracy." The pattern was followed by US planners in reconstructing the industrial societies after World War II, and is standard in the Third World, though assuring stability of the desired kind is far more difficult there, except by state terror. Once a functioning social order is firmly established, an individual who must find a (relatively isolated) place within it in order to survive will tend to think its thoughts, adopt its assumptions about the inevitability of certain forms of authority, and in general, adapt to its ends. The costs of an alternative path or a challenge to power are high, the resources are lacking, and the prospects limited. These factors operate in slave and feudal societies—where their efficacy has duly impressed counterinsurgency theorists (see below, p. 385). In free societies, they manifest themselves in other ways. If their power to shape behavior begins to erode, other means must be sought to tame the rascal multitude.

When force is on the side of the masters, they may rely on relatively crude means of manufacture of consent and need not overly concern themselves with the minds of the herd. Nevertheless, even a violent terror state faces Hume's problem. The modalities of state terrorism that the United States has devised for its clients have commonly included at least a gesture towards "winning hearts and minds," though experts warn against undue sentimentality, arguing that "all the dilemmas are practical and as neutral in an ethical sense as the laws of physics."[40] Nazi Germany shared these concerns, as Albert Speer discusses in his autobiography, and the same is true of Stalinist Russia. Discussing this case, Alexander Gerschenkron observes:

Whatever the strength of the army and the ubiquitousness of the secret police which such a government may have at its disposal, it would be naive to believe that those instruments of physical oppression can suffice. Such a government can maintain itself in power only if it succeeds in making people believe that it performs an important social function which could not be discharged in its absence. Industrialization provided such a function for the Soviet government . . ., [which] did what no government relying on the consent of the governed could have done. . . . But, paradoxical as it may sound, these policies at the same time have secured some broad acquiescence on the part of the people. If all the forces of the population can be kept engaged in the processes of industrialization and if this industrialization can be justified by the promise of happiness and abundance for future generations and—much more importantly—by the menace of military aggression from beyond the borders, the dictatorial government will find its power broadly unchallenged.[41]

The thesis gains support from the rapid collapse of the Soviet system when its incapacity to move to a more advanced stage of industrial and technological development became evident.

4. The Pragmatic Criterion

It is important to be aware of the profound commitment of Western opinion to the repression of freedom and democracy, by violence if necessary. To understand our own cultural world, we must recognize that advocacy of terror is clear, explicit, and principled, across the political spectrum. It is superfluous to invoke the thoughts of Jeane Kirkpatrick, George Will, and the like. But little changes as we move to "the establishment left," to borrow the term used by *Foreign Policy* editor Charles William Maynes in an ode to the American crusade "to spread the cause of democracy."[42]

Consider political commentator Michael Kinsley, who represents "the left" in mainstream commentary and television debate. When the State Department publicly confirmed US support for terrorist attacks on agricultural cooperatives in Nicaragua, Kinsley wrote that we should not be too quick to condemn this official policy. Such international terrorist operations doubtless cause "vast civilian suffering," he conceded. But if they manage "to undermine morale and confidence in the government," then they may be "perfectly legitimate." The policy is "sensible" if "cost-benefit analysis" shows that "the amount of blood and misery that will be poured in" yields "democracy," in the conventional sense already discussed.[43]

As a spokesman for the establishment left, Kinsley insists that terror must meet the pragmatic criterion; violence should not be employed for its own sake, merely because we find it amusing. This more humane conception would readily be accepted by Saddam Hussein, Abu Nidal, and the Hizbollah kidnappers, who, presumably, also consider terror pointless unless it is of value for their ends. These facts help us situate enlightened Western opinion on the international spectrum.

Such reasoned discussion of the justification for terror is not at all unusual, which is why it elicits no reaction in respectable circles just as there is no word of comment among its left-liberal contributors and readers when the *New Republic*, long considered the beacon of American liberalism, advocates military aid to "Latin-style fascists ... regardless of how many are murdered" because "there are higher American priorities than Salvadoran human rights" (see Chapter 10, p. 308).

Appreciation of the "salutary efficacy" of terror—to borrow John Quincy Adams's phrase—has been a standard feature of enlightened Western thought. It provides the basic framework for the propaganda campaign concerning international terrorism in the 1980s. Naturally, terrorism directed against us and our friends is bitterly denounced as a reversion to barbarism. But far more extreme terrorism that we and our agents conduct is considered constructive, or at worst insignificant, if it meets the pragmatic criterion. Even the vast campaign of international terrorism launched against Cuba by the Kennedy Administration, far exceeding anything attributed to official enemies, does not exist in respected academic discourse or the mainstream media. In his standard and much-respected scholarly study of international terrorism, Walter Laqueur depicts Cuba as a sponsor of the crime with innuendos but scarcely a pretense of evidence, while the campaign of international terrorism *against* Cuba merits literally not a word; in fact, Cuba is classed among those societies "free from terror." Latin Americanist Robert Wesson of the Hoover Institute writes that after the Bay of Pigs, when the terror mounted to its peak, "only nonviolent ... measures were taken against Cuban communism"—namely, diplomatic and commercial isolation.[44]

The guiding principle is clear and straightforward: *their* terror is terror, and the flimsiest evidence suffices to denounce it and to exact retribution upon civilian bystanders who happen to be in the way; *our* terror, even if far more extreme, is merely statecraft, and therefore does not enter into the discussion of the plague of the modern age. The practice is understandable on the principles already discussed.[45]

Sometimes, the adaptability of the system might surprise even the most hardened observer. Nothing outraged US opinion more than the shooting down of KAL 007 in September 1983 by the Soviet air force; the densely printed *New York Times* index devoted seven full pages to the atrocity in that month alone. It did not go entirely unnoticed that the reaction was rather different when the US warship *Vincennes* shot down an Iranian civilian airliner in a commercial corridor off the coast of Iran—out of "a need to prove the viability of Aegis," its high-tech missile system, in the judgement of US Navy commander David Carlson, who "wondered aloud in disbelief" as he monitored the events from a nearby naval vessel. This was dismissed as an unfortunate error in difficult circumstances, for which the Iranians were ultimately at fault. The latest act in this instructive drama took place in April 1990, when the commander of the *Vincennes*, along with the officer in charge of anti-air warfare, was given the Legion of Merit award for "exceptionally meritorious conduct in the performance of outstanding service" and for the "calm and professional atmosphere" under his command during the period of the destruction of the Iranian airbus, with 290 people killed. "The tragedy isn't mentioned in the texts of the citations," AP reported. The media apparently found nothing worthy of comment in any of this—though Iranian condemnations of the destruction of the airliner are occasionally noted and dismissed with derision as "boilerplate attacks on the United States."[46]

One may imagine the reaction were Iran to go on from "boilerplate attacks on the United States" to threats to retaliate with military strikes against US targets—perhaps taking its cue from a lead story in the *Boston Globe* by Yossi Melman and Dan Raviv on how to deal with Saddam Hussein: "A strategic strike at their oil fields or an air base might be in order—especially after US intelligence picked up signs that the Iraqi president rewarded the air force pilot who 'mistakenly' attacked the USS *Stark* during the Gulf War."[47]

Western readers would be hard put to learn of the Legion of Merit award to the commander of the *Vincennes*, but it did not go unnoticed in the Third World, where commentators also readily draw the conclusions barred within Western intellectual culture. Commenting on "U.S. imperial policy," *Third World Resurgence* (Malaysia) lists the shooting down of the Iranian airbus among acts of U.S. terrorism in the Middle East, quoting the words of the award and adding that "the Western public, fed on the media, sees the situation in black-and-white one-dimensional terms," unable to perceive what is obvious to those who escape the grip of the Western propaganda system.[48]

Huge massacres are treated by much the same criteria: *their* terror and violence are crimes, *ours* are statecraft or understandable error. In a study of US power and ideology a decade ago, Edward Herman and I reviewed numerous examples of two kinds of atrocities, "benign and constructive bloodbaths" that are acceptable or even advantageous to dominant interests, and "nefarious bloodbaths" perpetrated by official enemies. The reaction follows the same pattern as the treatment of terrorism. The former are ignored, denied, or sometimes even welcomed; the latter elicit great outrage and often large-scale deceit and fabrication, if the available evidence is felt to be inadequate for doctrinal requirements.[49]

One comparison that we presented in great detail was particularly illuminating: the "benign bloodbath" conducted by Indonesia after its invasion of East Timor in 1975, and the "nefarious bloodbath" of the Khmer Rouge when they took over Cambodia in the same year. Reviewing virtually all available material (at that time, covering primarily 1975–77), we showed that the evidence concerning these two horrendous bloodbaths—in the same part of the world, in the same years—was comparable, and indicated that the two slaughters were comparable in scale and character. There were also differences. One was that the Indonesian aggression and bloodbath received critical material and diplomatic support from the United States and its allies, and could have readily been terminated by exposure and withdrawal of this support, while no one offered a serious proposal as to how to mitigate the Pol Pot atrocities; for that reason, the Timor bloodbath was far more significant for the West, at least if elementary moral standards are applicable. A second difference lay in the reaction to the two bloodbaths. Following the pattern illustrated throughout the record that we surveyed, the Timor atrocities, and the crucial contribution of the US and its allies, were suppressed or denied; the media even avoided refugee testimony, exactly as in the case of the US terror bombing of Cambodia a few years earlier. In the parallel case of the Khmer Rouge, in contrast, we documented a record of deceit that would have impressed Stalin, including massive fabrication of evidence, suppression of useless evidence (for example, the conclusions of State Department Cambodia-watchers, the most knowledgeable source, but considered too restrained to serve the purposes at hand), and so forth.

The reaction to the exposure is also instructive: on the Timor half of the comparison, further silence, denial, and apologetics; on the Cambodia half, a great chorus of protest claiming that we were denying or downplaying Pol Pot atrocities. This was a transparent falsehood, though admittedly the distinction between advocating that one try to keep to the truth and downplaying the atrocities of the official enemy is a difficult one for the mind of the commissar, who, furthermore, is naturally infuriated by any challenge to the right to lie in the service of the state, particularly when it is accompanied by a demonstration of the services rendered to ongoing atrocities.[50]

Quite generally, wholesale slaughter is regarded benignly, and the revelation of direct US government participation in it arouses no particular interest, when the means are well suited to our ends.[51] And it is reasonable enough to regard the dilemmas of counterinsurgency as merely "practical" and "ethically neutral." It is simply a matter of finding the proper mix among the various techniques of population control, ranging in practice from B-52 bombing and napalm, to torture and mutilation and disappearance, and to kinder, gentler means such as starvation and totalitarian control in concentration camps called "strategic hamlets" or "model villages." Leading theorists of this form of international terrorism calmly explain that while it is a "desirable goal" to win "popular allegiance" to the government we back or impose, that is a distinctly secondary consideration, and does not provide an appropriate "conceptual framework for counterinsurgency programs." The "unifying theme" should be "influencing *behavior*, rather than attitudes" (Charles Wolf, senior economist of the RAND Corporation). Hume's problem then does not arise; there need be no concern that force is on the side of the governed. For influencing behavior, such techniques as "confiscation of chickens, razing of houses, or destruction of villages" are quite proper as long as "harshness meted out by government forces [is] unambiguously recognizable as deliberately imposed because of behavior by the population that contributes to the insurgent movement." If it is not, terror will be a meaningless exercise. "The crucial point," this respected scholar continues, is to connect all programs "with the kind of population behavior the government wants to promote." Wolf notes a further advantage of this more scientific approach, emphasizing control of behavior rather than attitudes: it should improve the image of counterinsurgency in the United States; we are, after all, an enlightened society that respects science and technology and has little use for mystical rumination on minds and attitudes. Note that when we turn to the United States, where coercive force is not readily available, we must concern ourselves with control of attitudes and opinions.

Even imposing mass starvation is entirely legitimate if it meets the pragmatic criterion, as explained by Professor David Rowe, director of graduate studies in international relations at Yale University. Testifying in Congress before China became a valued ally, Rowe advised that the US should purchase all surplus Canadian and Australian wheat so as to impose "general starvation" on a billion people in China—a cost-effective method, he observed, to undermine the "internal stability of that country." As an expert on the Asian mind, he assured Congress that this policy would be particularly welcomed by the Japanese, because they have had a demonstration "of the tremendous power in action of the United States ... [and] ... have felt our power directly" in the firebombing of Tokyo and at Hiroshima and Nagasaki; it would therefore "alarm the Japanese people very intensely and shake the degree of their friendly relations with us" if we seemed "unwilling to use the power they know we have" in Vietnam and China.[52]

Apart from the scale of his vision, Rowe was following a well-trodden path. As director of the humanitarian program providing food to starving Europeans after World War I, Herbert Hoover advised President Wilson that he was "maintaining a thin line of food" to guarantee the rule of anti-Bolshevik elements. In response to rumors of "a serious outbreak on May Day" in Austria, Hoover issued a public warning that any such action would jeopardize the city's sparse food supply. Food was withheld from Hungary under the Communist Béla Kun government, with a promise that it would be supplied if he were removed in favor of a government acceptable to the US. The economic blockade, along with Romanian military pressure, forced Kun to relinquish power and flee to Moscow. Backed by French and British forces, the Romanian military joined with Hungarian counter-revolutionaries to administer a dose of White terror and install a right-wing dictatorship under Admiral Horthy, who collaborated with Hitler in the next stage of slaying the Bolshevik beast. The threat of starvation was also used to buy the critical Italian elections of 1948 and to help impose the rule of US clients in Nicaragua in 1990, among other noteworthy examples. Dikes were bombed in South Vietnam to eliminate the supply of food for South Vietnamese peasants resisting US aggression and crop destruction was carried out throughout Indochina, as in Central America in recent years. The practice can be traced to the earliest Indian wars, and, of course, was no innovation of the British colonists.[53]

A review of the debate over Central America during the past decade reveals the decisive role of the pragmatic criterion. Guatemala was never an issue, because mass slaughter and repression appeared to be effective. Early on, the Church was something of a problem, but, as Kenneth Freed comments in the *Los Angeles Times*, when "14 priests and hundreds of church workers were killed in a military campaign to destroy church support for social gains such as higher wages and an end to the exploitation of Indians," the church was intimidated and "virtually fell silent." "The physical intimidation eased," the pragmatic criterion having been satisfied. Terror increased again as the US nurtured what it likes to call "democracy." "The victims," a European diplomat observes, "are almost always people whose views or activities are aimed at helping others to free themselves of restraints placed by those who hold political or economic power," such as "a doctor who tries to improve the health of babies" and is therefore "seen as attacking the established order."[54] The security forces of the "fledgling democracy," and the death squads associated with them, appeared to have the situation reasonably well in hand, so there was no reason for undue concern in the United States, and there has been virtually none.

There was some media notice of the atrocious human rights record in Guatemala as Washington moved to discredit President Cerezo and his Christian Democrats, in a policy shift towards more right-wing elements. The proper lessons still have to be taught, however. Thus, Freed stresses Washington's "repugnance" at the extraordinary human rights violations of the security forces that it supports. And in the *New York Times*, Lindsey Gruson reports that Washington is increasing its dependence on the Guatemalan army, which is the source of the abuses, including Guatemalan Military Intelligence, G-2, notorious for its leading role in state terror. But he assures the reader that human rights issues rank high among "American policy goals" for Guatemala, a doctrinal truth resistant to mere fact.[55]

Freed adds that General Hector Gramajo "was a senior commander in the early 1980s, when the Guatemalan military was blamed for the deaths of tens of thousands of people, largely civilians." But, he continues, Gramajo "is seen as a moderate by the U.S. Embassy"—the familiar pattern. Freed quotes a Western diplomat who doubts that Gramajo himself "is promoting all these killings" by death squads linked to the security forces, though "whenever he senses that the left is trying to organize, he permits, if not orders, hard action against them" and "certainly doesn't root out any offenders."

El Salvador and Nicaragua also illustrate the pragmatic criterion. The media pretended not to know that the government of El Salvador was conducting mass slaughter from 1979, and concealed the worst atrocities. By the early 1980s, it appeared that the US might be drawn into an intervention harmful to its interests; accordingly, concern increased, and there were even a few months of fairly honest reporting. But as the terror appeared to be achieving its goals thanks to US guidance and support, qualms dissipated in favor of the celebration of "democracy," while the government continued its programs of terror and intimidation.

Nicaragua was an object of contention, because terror and economic warfare were achieving only limited success. But these were the only concerns, as was made crystal clear when the population finally followed US orders after a decade of terror and destruction in a country already ravaged by Somoza's murderous assault and robbery, leaving all right-thinking people "United in Joy."

Throughout this grim decade of savagery and oppression, liberal humanists have presented themselves as critical of the terror states maintained by US violence in Central America. But that is only a façade, as we see from the demand, virtually unanimous in respectable circles, that Nicaragua must be restored to "the Central American mode" of the death squad regimes, and that the US and its murderous clients must impose the "regional standards" of El Salvador and Guatemala on the errant Sandinistas.[56]

A closer look establishes more firmly the prevailing norms. The record reveals near-unanimous opposition to the Sandinistas, with only tactical disagreement as to how they should be overthrown—in sharp distinction to the gangster states that already meet the "regional standards." Unmentioned in hundreds of columns sampled in the national press is the fact that unlike the regimes favored by the liberal doves, the Sandinistas, whatever their sins, did not engage in mass slaughter, terror and torture; such matters are of near-zero significance to enlightened Western opinion, as this record reveals. Correspondingly, there is agreement that the one military force that must be dismantled is the one that does *not* regularly engage in mass terror against the civilian population. As Edward Herman observed, just as there are "worthy and unworthy victims" (the worthy being those persecuted by official enemies, who arouse great anguish; the unworthy being our victims, whose fate is a matter of indifference)—so there are "worthy and unworthy armies." Worthy armies, such as those of Somoza, El Salvador, Guatemala, Indonesia, and others like them, need no interference, because they are doing their job: they kill and torture for us. The unworthy armies do not meet these high standards, even daring to protect their populations from the killers we dispatch. They must therefore be replaced by a force more congenial to our needs and moral values. All of this is so commonplace as to pass without notice.

Also virtually unmentioned in hundreds of opinion columns on Nicaragua are the programs of social welfare and reform, considered remarkably successful by international agencies until the US was able to reverse the unwelcome progress by the mid 1980s. Strikingly, after the US victory in the 1990 elections in Nicaragua, it was suddenly permitted to take note of these facts, now that the threat to wealth and power had been removed. Throughout, the priorities of enlightened opinion shine through bright and clear.

Returning to Hume's principles of government, it is clear that they must be refined. True, when force is lacking and the standard penalties do not suffice, it is necessary to resort to the manufacture of consent. The populations of the Western democracies—or at least, those in a position to defend themselves—are off limits. Others are legitimate objects of repression, and in the Third World, large-scale terror is appropriate, though the liberal conscience adds the qualification that it must be efficacious. The statesman, as distinct from the ideological fanatic, will understand that the means of violence should be employed in a measured and considered way, just sufficient to achieve the desired ends.

5. The Range of Means

The pragmatic criterion dictates that violence is in order only when the rascal multitude cannot be controlled in other ways. Often, there are other ways. Another RAND corporation counterinsurgency specialist was impressed by "the relative docility of poorer peasants and the firm authority of landlords in the more 'feudal' areas ... [where] the landlord can exercise considerable influence over his tenant's behavior and readily discourage conduct inconsistent with his own interests."[57] It is only when the docility is shaken, perhaps by meddlesome priests, that firmer measures are required.

One option short of outright violence is legal repression. In Costa Rica, the United States was willing to tolerate social democracy. The primary reason for the benign neglect was that labor was suppressed and the rights of investors were offered every protection. The founder of Costa Rican democracy, José Figueres, was an avid partisan of US corporations and the CIA, and was regarded by the State Department as "the best advertising agency that the United Fruit Company could find in Latin America." But the leading figure of Central American democracy fell out of favor in the 1980s, and had to be censored completely out of the Free Press, because of his critical attitude towards the US war against Nicaragua and Washington's moves to restore Costa Rica as well to the preferred "Central American mode." Even the effusive editorial and lengthy obituary in the *New York Times* lauding this "fighter for democracy" when he died in June 1990 were careful to avoid these inconvenient deviations.

In earlier years, when he was better behaved, Figueres recognized that the Costa Rican Communist Party, particularly strong among plantation workers, was posing an unacceptable challenge. He therefore arrested its leaders, declared the Party illegal, and repressed its members. The policy was maintained through the 1960s, while efforts to establish any working-class party were banned by the state authorities. Figueres explained these actions with candor: it was "a sign of weakness. I admit it, when one is relatively weak before the force of the enemy, it is necessary to have the valor to recognise it." These moves were accepted in the West as consistent with the liberal concept of democracy, and indeed, were virtually a precondition for US toleration of "the Costa Rican exception."[58]

Sometimes, however, legal repression is not enough; the popular enemy is too powerful. The alarm bells are sure to ring if they threaten the control of the political system by the business–landowner elite and military elements properly respectful of US interests. Signs of such deviation call for stronger measures. Such was the case in El Salvador. After the harsh repression of nonviolent activities, "the masses were with the guerrillas" by early 1980 in the judgement of José Napoleón Duarte, the US-imposed figurehead. To bar the threat of nationalism responsive to popular demands and pressures, it was therefore necessary to resort to a "war of extermination and genocide against a defenseless civilian population," to borrow the terms of Archbishop Romero's successor a few months after the assassination. Meanwhile Duarte praised the army for its "valiant service alongside the people against subversion" as he was sworn in as civilian president of the military junta to provide a cover for active US engagement in the slaughter, and thus to become a respected figure in Western circles.[59]

The broader framework was sketched by Father Ignacio Martín-Baró, one of the Jesuit priests assassinated in November 1989 and a noted Salvadoran social psychologist, in a talk he delivered in California on "The Psychological Consequences of Political Terrorism," a few months before he was murdered.[60] He stressed several relevant points. First, the most significant form of terrorism, by a large measure, is state terrorism—that is, "terrorizing the whole population through systematic actions carried out by the forces of the state." Second, such terrorism is an essential part of a "government-imposed sociopolitical project" designed for the needs of the privileged. To implement it, the whole population must be "terrorized by an internalized fear."

Martín-Baró only alludes to a third point, which is the most important one for a Western audience: the sociopolitical project and the state terrorism that helps to implement it are not specific to El Salvador, but are common features of the Third World domains of the United States, for reasons deeply rooted in Western culture, institutions, and policy planning, and fully in accord with the values of enlightened opinion. These crucial factors explain much more than the fate of El Salvador.

In the same talk, Martín-Baró referred to the "massive campaign of political terrorism" in El Salvador a decade ago, conducted with US backing and initiative. He noted further that "since 1984, with the coming of so-called democratic government in El Salvador under Duarte, things seemed to change a bit," but in reality "things did not change. What changed was that the terrorized population was reduced to only two options: to go to the mountains and join the ranks of the rebels, or to comply—at least openly—with the programs imposed by the government." The killings then reduced in scale, a development that occasioned much self-praise here for our benign influence. The reason for the decline, he observes, is that "there was less need for extraordinary events, because people were so terrorized, so paralyzed."

The objective remained the same: "eliminating all significant opposition and protest." The "dirty war has at no time stopped being an essential ingredient in the sociopolitical project that the United States is trying to achieve in El Salvador," even after "formal democracy" was introduced "to legitimize the war" in Western eyes. These methods succeeded in "the dismantling of the popular mass organizations," as "the very existence of organizations unsympathetic to the government became impossible, and those militants who were not exterminated had to flee to the countryside or to go underground, or, choked with terror, abandon the struggle." By "weakening the support bases of the revolutionary movement in all sectors of the population, . . . there is no doubt that the dirty war was successful—a macabre success to be sure, but successful none the less."[61]

Throughout the decade, and well after "democracy" was established, the Salvadoran Church and human rights groups continued to describe how the security forces of the "fledgling democracy," with the full knowledge and cooperation of their US sponsors, imposed upon Salvadoran society a regime of "terror and panic, a result of the persistent violation of basic human rights," marked by "collective intimidation and generalized fear, on the one hand, and on the other the internalized acceptance of the terror because of the daily and frequent use of violent means. . . . In general, society accepts the frequent appearance of tortured bodies, because basic rights, the right to life, has absolutely no overriding value for society" (Socorro Juridico, December 1985). This last comment also applies to the supervisors, as underscored by Secretary of State George Shultz a few months later in one of his lamentations on terrorism, a talk delivered just as the US was carrying out the terror bombing of Libya, killing many civilians to much applause at home. In El Salvador, he declared, "the results are something all Americans can be proud of"—at least, all Americans who enjoy the sight of tortured bodies, starving children, terror and panic, and generalized fear.[62]

In a paper on mass media and public opinion in El Salvador which he was to have delivered at an International Congress in December 1989, the month after he was assassinated, Martín-Baró wrote that the US counterinsurgency project "emphasized merely the formal dimensions of democracy," and that the mass media must be understood as a mechanism of "psychological warfare." The small independent journals in El Salvador, mainstream and pro-business but still too undisciplined for the rulers, had been taken care of by the security forces a decade earlier in the usual efficacious manner—kidnapping, assassination, and physical destruction, events considered here too insignificant even to report. As for public opinion, Martín-Baró's unread paper reports a study showing that among workers, the lower middle class, and the poor, less than 20 percent feel free to express their opinions in public, a figure that rose to 40 percent for the rich—another tribute to the salutary efficacy of terror, and another result that "all Americans can be proud of."[63]

The continuity of US policy is well illustrated by the record of the Atlacatl Battalion, "whose soldiers professionally obeyed orders from their officers to kill the Jesuits in cold blood," Americas Watch observed on the tenth anniversary of the assassination of Archbishop Romero, proceeding to review some of the achievements of this elite unit, "created, trained and equipped by the United States." It was formed in March 1981, when fifteen specialists in counterinsurgency were sent to El Salvador from the US Army School of Special Forces. From the start, the Battalion "was engaged in the murder of large numbers of civilians." A professor at the US Army School of the Americas in Fort Benning, Georgia, described its soldiers as "particularly ferocious": "We've always had a hard time getting [them] to take prisoners instead of ears." In December 1981, the Battalion took part in an operation in which hundreds of civilians were killed in an orgy of murder, rape, and burning—over 1000, according to the Church legal aid office. Later it was involved in the bombing of villages and the murder of hundreds of civilians by shooting, drowning, and other methods, the vast majority being women, children, and the elderly. This has been the systematic pattern of special warfare in El Salvador since the first major military operation in May 1980, when six hundred civilians were murdered and mutilated at the Rio Sumpul in a joint operation of the Salvadoran and Honduran armies, a slaughter revealed by Church sources, human rights investigators, and the foreign press, but not the US media, which also have their psychological warfare function.[64]

The Lawyers Committee for Human Rights alleged in a letter to Defense Secretary Cheney that the killers of the Jesuits were trained by US Special Forces up to three days before the assassinations. Father Jon de Cortina, Dean of Engineering at the Jesuit University in El Salvador where the priests were murdered, alleged further that the US military instructors were the same US soldiers who were trapped in a San Salvador hotel a few days later, in a highly publicized incident. In earlier years, some of the Atlacatl Battalion's worst massacres occurred when it was fresh from US training.[65]

The nature of Salvadoran army training was described by a deserter who received political asylum in Texas in July 1990 after the immigration judge rejected a State Department request that he be denied asylum and sent back to El Salvador. In this "fledgling democracy" the wealthy are immune from conscription; rather, teenagers are rounded up in sweeps in slums and refugee camps. According to this deserter—whose name was withheld by the court, for obvious reasons—conscripts were made to kill dogs and vultures by biting their throats and twisting off their heads, and had to watch as soldiers tortured and killed suspected dissidents, tearing out their fingernails, cutting off their heads, cutting a body to pieces "as though it was a toy and they played with the arms for entertainment," or starving and torturing them to death. Recruits were told that they would be assigned the same tasks, and that torturing people and animals "makes you more of a man and gives you more courage."[66]

In another recent case, an admitted member of a Salvadoran death squad associated with the Atlacatl Battalion, César Vielman Joya Martínez, testified on his first-hand experience in state terror, providing detailed information about the murder operations with the complicity of US intelligence advisers and the government to the highest level, including evidence extremely relevant to the murder of the Jesuit priests. His testimony is corroborated by an associate who also defected, in allegations to a Mexican rights commission. After an initial pretense that it would investigate Martínez's story, the Bush Administration proceeded to make every effort to silence him and ship him back to probable death in El Salvador, despite the pleas of human rights organizations and Congress that he be protected and that his testimony be heard. The treatment of the main witness to the assassination of the Jesuits was similar.[67]

It might be noted that the treatment of the murdered Jesuit intellectuals themselves is not really different. Their murder and the judicial inquiry (such as it is) received attention, but not what they had to say. About this one will find very little, even when it would take no initiative to discover it. For example, the August 1990 conference of the American Psychological Association in Boston had a series of panels and symposia dealing with the work of Father Martín-Baró, including one in which the videotape of his California talk shortly before his assassination was played. The conference was covered by the *Boston Globe*, but not these sessions. On the day they were held, the *Globe* preferred a paper on male facial expressions that are attractive to women.[68] First things first, after all.

When Antonio Gramsci was imprisoned after the Fascist takeover of Italy, the government summed up its case by saying: "We must stop this brain from functioning for twenty years."[69] Our current favorites leave less to chance: the brains must be stopped from functioning for ever, and we agree that their thoughts about such matters as state terrorism had best not be heard.

The results of US military training are evident in abundance in the documentation by human rights groups and the Salvadoran Church. They are graphically described by Reverend Daniel Santiago, a Catholic priest working in El Salvador, in the Jesuit journal *America*. He reports the story of a peasant woman, who returned home one day to find her mother, sister, and three children sitting around a table, the decapitated head of each person placed carefully on the table in front of the body, the hands arranged on top "as if each body was stroking its own head." The assassins, from the Salvadoran National Guard, had found it hard to keep the head of an eighteen-month-old baby in place, so they nailed the hands onto it. A large plastic bowl filled with blood was tastefully displayed in the center of the table.[70]

To take just one further example, striking because of the circumstances, we may turn back to January 1988, when the US completed its demolition of the Central America peace accords, exempting its murderous clients from the provisions calling for "justice, freedom and democracy," "respect for human rights," and guarantees for "the inviolability of all forms of life and liberty." Just as this cynical success was being recorded, the bodies of two men and a teenage boy were found at a well-known death squad dumping ground, blindfolded with hands tied behind their backs and signs of torture. The nongovernmental Human Rights Commission, which continues to function despite the assassination of its founders and directors, reported that thirteen bodies had been found in the preceding two weeks, most showing signs of torture, including two women who had been hanged from a tree by their hair, their breasts cut off and their faces painted red. The reports were given anonymously, in fear of state terror. No one failed to recognize the traditional marks of the death squads. The information was reported by the wire services and prominently published in Canada, but not by the US national press.[71]

Reverend Santiago writes that macabre scenes of the kind he recounts are designed by the armed forces for the purpose of intimidation.

> People are not just killed by death squads in El Salvador—they are decapitated and then their heads are placed on pikes and used to dot the landscape. Men are not just disemboweled by the Salvadoran Treasury Police; their severed genitalia are stuffed into their mouths. Salvadoran women are not just raped by the National Guard; their wombs are cut from their bodies and used to cover their faces. It is not enough to kill children; they are dragged over barbed wire until the flesh falls from their bones while parents are forced to watch. . . . The aesthetics of terror in El Salvador is religious.

The intention is to ensure that the individual is totally subordinated to the interests of the Fatherland, which is why the death squads are sometimes called the "Army of National Salvation" by the governing ARENA Party, whose members (including President Cristiani) take a blood oath to the "leader-for-life," Roberto d'Aubuisson.

The armed forces "scoop up recruits" from the age of thirteen, and indoctrinate them with rituals adopted from the Nazi SS, including brutalization and rape, so that they are prepared for killing with sexual overtones, as a religious rite. The stories of training "are not fairy tales"; they are "punctuated with the hard evidence of corpses, mutilated flesh, splattered brains and eyewitnesses." This "sadomasochistic killing creates terror," and "terror creates passivity in the face of oppression. A passive population is easy to control," so that there will be plenty of docile workers, and no complaints, and the sociopolitical project can be pursued with equanimity.

Reverend Santiago reminds us that the current wave of violence is a reaction to attempts by the Church to organize the poor in the 1970s. State terror mounted as the Church began forming peasant associations and self-help groups, which, along with other popular organizations, "spread like wildfire through Latin American communities," Lars Schoultz writes. That the United States should turn at once to massive repression, with the cooperation of local elites, will surprise only those who are willfully ignorant of history and the planning record.[72]

Father Ignacio Ellacuría, rector of the Jesuit University before he was assassinated along with Father Martín-Baró, described El Salvador as "a lacerated reality, almost mortally wounded." He was a close associate of Archbishop Romero and was with him when the Archbishop wrote to President Carter, pleading in vain for the withdrawal of aid from the junta. The Archbishop informed Father Ellacuría that his letter was prompted "by the new concept of special warfare, which consists in murderously eliminating every endeavor of the popular organizations under the allegation of Communism or terrorism . . ."[73] Special warfare—whether called counterinsurgency, or low-intensity conflict, or some other euphemism—is simply international terrorism—and it has long been official US policy, a weapon in the arsenal used for the larger sociopolitical project.

The same has been true in neighboring Guatemala. Latin America scholar Piero Gleijeses writes that in the traditional "culture of fear," ferocious repression sufficed to impose peace and order; "Just as the Indian was branded a savage beast to justify his exploitation, so those who sought social reform were branded communists to justify their persecution." The decade 1944–54 was a unique departure, marked by "political democracy, the strong communist influence in the administration of President Jacobo Arbenz (1951–54), and Arbenz's agrarian reform"—"years of spring in the country of eternal tyranny," in the words of a Guatemalan poet. Half a million people received desperately needed land, the first time in the country's history that "the Indians were offered land, rather than being robbed of it":

> A new wind was stirring the Guatemalan countryside. The culture of fear was loosening its grip over the great masses of the Guatemalan population. In a not unreachable future, it might have faded away, a distant nightmare.

The Communist Party leaders were regarded by the US Embassy as the sole exception to venality and ambition. They "were very honest, very committed," "the only people who were committed to hard work," one Embassy official commented. "This was the tragedy," he added: they were "our worst enemies," and had to be removed along with the reforms they helped to implement.

The nightmare was restored in a coup organized by the CIA, with the cooperation of Guatemalan officers who betrayed their country in fear of the regional superpower, Gleijeses concludes. With regular US support, the regime of terror and torture and disappearance has been maintained, peaking in the late 1960s with direct US government participation. As the terror somewhat abated, there was "a wave of *concientización* (heightening of political awareness)," largely under Church auspices. It inspired the usual reaction: the army "intensified the terror, murdering cooperative leaders, bilingual teachers, community leaders, and grassroots organizers"—in fact, following the same script as in El Salvador and Nicaragua. By the early 1980s, the terror reached the level of wholesale massacre in the Indian highlands. The Reagan Administration was not merely supportive but enthusiastic about the achievements of their friends.

Recall that the Guatemalan generals are moderates who observe the pragmatic criterion. When Indians who had fled to the mountains to survive drifted back, unable to cope with the harsh conditions and begging forgiveness, "the army was generous," Gleijeses observes: "It no longer murdered the supplicants, except now and then, as a reminder."

When order was once again restored, the generals accepted US advice and instituted a democratic façade, behind which they and their allies in the oligarchy would continue to rule. The same terror that controlled the Church also silenced the call for reform; "rare is the Guatemalan who expresses his political beliefs," Gleijeses comments. Peasants say that they will not support advocates of agrarian reform because they "don't want any trouble" from the army. "Arbenz taught us how to build a house," one told an anthropologist, "but not how to make it strong, and at the first wind the house fell on top of us." Democracy in the preferred mode is unlikely to face any popular threat, under these conditions.[74]

The basic problem of the "years of spring" was the excess of freedom and democracy. The CIA warned in 1952 that the "radical and nationalist policies" of the government had gained "the support or acquiescence of almost all Guatemalans," a sign of what the CIA was later to call their "low level of intellectualism" (see p. 51). Worse yet, the government was proceeding "to mobilize the hitherto politically inert peasantry" and to create "mass support for the present regime." It was advancing these goals by labor organization, agrarian and other social reform, and nationalist policies "identified with the Guatemalan revolution of 1944." The revolution had aroused "a strong national movement to free Guatemala from the military dictatorship, social backwardness, and 'economic colonialism' which had been the pattern of the past," and "inspired the loyalty and conformed to the self-interest of most politically conscious Guatemalans." The government's democratic programs offered the public a means to participate in achieving these goals, which ran directly counter to the interests of the oligarchy and US agribusiness. After affairs had been restored to normal by the CIA coup, a secret State Department intelligence report commented that the democratic leadership that had thankfully been overthrown had "insisted upon the maintenance of an open political system," thus allowing the Communists to "expand their operations and appeal effectively to various sectors of the population." Neither the military "nor self-seeking politicians" were able to overcome this deficiency, finally cured by the coup.[75]

Once again, the US found itself in the familiar stance: politically weak, but militarily and economically strong. Policy choices follow naturally.

It has been a constant lament of US government officials that the Latin American countries are insufficiently repressive—too open, too committed to civil liberties, unwilling to impose sufficient constraints on travel and dissemination of information, and in general reluctant to adhere to US social and political standards, thus tolerating conditions in which dissidence can flourish and reach a popular audience.[76]

At home, even tiny groups may be subject to severe repression if their potential outreach is perceived to be too great. During the campaign waged by the national political police against the Black Panthers—including assassination, instigation of ghetto riots, and a variety of other means—the FBI estimated the "hard core members" of the targeted organization at only eight hundred, but added ominously that "a recent poll indicates that approximately 25 per cent of the black population has a great respect for the [Black Panther Party], including 43 per cent of blacks under 21 years of age." The repressive agencies of the state proceeded with a campaign of violence and disruption to ensure that the Panthers did not succeed in organizing as a substantial social or political force—with great success, as the organization was decimated and the remnants proceeded to self-destruct. FBI operations in the same years targeting the entire New Left were motivated by similar concerns. The same internal intelligence document warns that "the movement of rebellious youth known as the 'New Left,' involving and influencing a substantial number of college students, is having a serious impact on contemporary society with a potential for serious domestic strife." The New Left has "revolutionary aims" and an "identification with Marxism–Leninism." It has attempted "to infiltrate and radicalize labor," and after failing "to subvert and control the mass media" has established "a large network of underground publications which serve the dual purpose of an internal communication network and an external propaganda organ." It thus poses a threat to "the civilian sector of our society," which must be contained by the state security apparatus.[77]

Freedom is fine, but within limits.

In the international arena, tactical choices are bounded narrowly by the fundamental institutional imperatives. Positions along this spectrum are by no means fixed. Thus Henry Kissinger was a dove with regard to China, where he agreed with Richard Nixon that the hardline policy was unproductive and that other measures could draw China into the US-dominated global system. At the same time he was a hawk with regard to the Middle East, supporting Israel's refusal to accept a full-scale peace treaty offered by Egypt and Jordan in early 1971 and blocking State Department moves towards a diplomatic resolution of the Arab–Israeli conflict, establishing a policy that still prevails and explains much of what is happening in that region today.[78] His successor, Zbigniew Brzezinski, has a record as an extreme hawk, but in the 1990 crisis in the Gulf he strongly opposed the strategic conception of the Administration, joining those who urged reliance on sanctions rather than seeking a victory through the threat or use of military force, with its probable consequences for US interests in the Middle East and beyond. There are many other examples.

We can learn a good deal by attention to the range of choices. Keeping just to Latin America, consider the efforts to eliminate the Allende regime in Chile. There were two parallel operations. Track II, the hard line, aimed at a military coup. This was concealed from Ambassador Edward Korry, a Kennedy liberal, whose task was to implement Track I, the soft line; in Korry's words, to "do all within our power to condemn Chile and the Chileans to utmost deprivation and poverty, a policy designed for a long time to come to accelerate the hard features of a Communist society in Chile." The soft line was an extension of the long-term CIA effort to control Chilean democracy. One indication of its level is that in the 1964 election the CIA spent twice as much per Chilean voter to block Allende as the total spent per voter by both parties in the US elections of the same year.[79] Similarly in the case of Cuba, the Eisenhower Administration planned a direct attack while Vice-President Nixon, keeping to the soft line in a secret discussion of June 1960, expressed his concern that according to a CIA briefing, "Cuba's economic situation had not deteriorated significantly since the overthrow of Batista," then urging specific measures to place "greater economic pressure on Cuba."[80]

To take another informative case: in 1949 the CIA identified "two areas of instability" in Latin America—Bolivia and Guatemala.[81] The Eisenhower Administration pursued the hard line to overthrow capitalist democracy in Guatemala but chose the soft line with regard to a Bolivian revolution that had the support of the Communist Party and radical tin miners, had led to expropriation, and had even moved towards "criminal agitation of the Indians of the farms and mines" and a pro-peace conference, a right-wing archbishop warned. The White House concluded that the best plan was to support the least radical elements, expecting that US pressures, including domination of the tin market, would serve to control unwanted developments. Secretary of State John Foster Dulles urged that this would be the best way to contain the "Communist infection in South America." Following standard policy guidelines, the US took control over the Bolivian military, equipping it with modern armaments and sending hundreds of officers to the "school of coups" in Panama and elsewhere. Bolivia was soon subject to US influence and control. By 1953, the National Security Council noted improvement in "the climate for private investment," including "an agreement permitting a private American firm to exploit two petroleum areas."[82]

A military coup took place in 1964. A 1980 coup was carried out with the assistance of Klaus Barbie, who had been sent to Bolivia when he could no longer be protected in France, where he had been working under US control to repress the anti-Fascist resistance, as he had done under the Nazis. According to a recent UNICEF study, one in three Bolivian infants dies in the first year of life, so that Bolivia has the slowest rate of population growth in Latin America along with the highest birth rate. The FAO estimates that the average Bolivian consumes 78 percent of daily minimum calorie and protein requirements, and that more than half of Bolivian children suffer from malnutrition. Of the economically active population, 25 percent are unemployed and another 40 percent work in the "informal sector" (for example, smuggling and drugs). The situation in Guatemala we have already reviewed.[83]

Several points merit attention. First, the consequences of the hard line in Guatemala and the soft line in Bolivia were similar. Second, both policy decisions were successful in their major aim: containing the "Communist virus," the threat of "ultranationalism." Third, both policies are evidently regarded as quite proper, as we can see in the case of Bolivia by the complete lack of interest in what has happened since (apart from possible costs to the US through the drug racket); and with regard to Guatemala, by the successful intervention under Kennedy to block a democratic election, the direct US participation in murderous counterinsurgency campaigns under Lyndon Johnson, the continuing supply of arms to Guatemala through the late 1970s (contrary to illusory claims) and the reliance on our Israeli mercenary state to fill any gaps when congressional restrictions finally took effect, the enthusiastic US support for atrocities that go well beyond even the astonishing Guatemalan norm in the 1980s, and the applause for the "fledgling democracy" that the ruling military now tolerates as a means to extort money from Congress. We may say that these are "messy episodes" and "blundering" (which in fact succeeded in its major aims), but nothing more (Stephen Kinzer).[84] Fourth, the soft line and the hard line were adopted by the same people, at the same time, revealing that the issues are tactical, involving no departure from shared principle. All of this provides insight into the nature of policy, and the political culture in which it is formed.

The same methods apply generally, as in cases already discussed, and many others like them. The cover story throughout is that the subversion of democracy is undertaken in self-defense against the Soviet threat; we had no choice, as the editor of *Foreign Affairs* explains (see p. 13). John Lewis Gaddis comes closer to the mark when he observes that "the increasing success of communist parties in Western Europe, the Eastern Mediterranean, and China" justifiably aroused "suspicion about the Soviet Union's behavior," even though their popularity "grew primarily out of their effectiveness as resistance fighters against the Axis."[85] The rascal multitude are the problem, and they have to be brought to heel by other means if democratic processes cannot be properly channeled.

6. The Untamed Rabble

Hume's paradox of government arises only if we suppose that a crucial element of essential human nature is what Bakunin called "an instinct for freedom." It is the failure to act upon this instinct that Hume found surprising. The same failure inspired Rousseau's classic lament that people are born free but are everywhere in chains, seduced by the illusions of the civil society that is created by the rich to guarantee their plunder. Some may adopt this assumption as one of the "natural beliefs" that guide their conduct and their thought. There have been efforts to ground the instinct for freedom in a substantive theory of human nature. They are not without interest, but they surely come nowhere near establishing the case. Like other tenets of common sense, this belief remains a regulative principle that we adopt, or reject, on faith. Which choice we make can have large-scale consequences for ourselves and others.

Those who adopt the common-sense principle that freedom is our natural right and essential need will agree with Bertrand Russell that anarchism is "the ultimate ideal to which society should approximate." Structures of hierarchy and domination are fundamentally illegitimate. They can be defended only on grounds of contingent need, an argument that rarely stands up to analysis. As Russell went on to observe seventy years ago, "the old bonds of authority" have little intrinsic merit. Reasons are needed for people to abandon their rights, "and the reasons offered are counterfeit reasons, convincing only to those who have a selfish interest in being convinced. . . . The condition of revolt," he went on, "exists in women towards men, in oppressed nations towards their oppressors, and above all in labour towards capital. It is a state full of danger, as all past history shows, yet also full of hope."[86]

Russell traced the habit of submission in part to coercive educational practices. His views are reminiscent of seventeenth- and eighteenth-century thinkers who held that the mind is not to be filled with knowledge "from without, like a vessel," but "to be kindled and awaked. . . . The growth of knowledge [resembles] the growth of Fruit; however external causes may in some degree cooperate, it is the internal vigour, and virtue of the tree, that must ripen the juices to their just maturity." Similar conceptions underlie Enlightenment thought on political and intellectual freedom, and on alienated labor, which turns the worker into an instrument for other ends instead of a human being fulfilling inner needs—a fundamental principle of classical liberal thought, though long forgotten, because of its revolutionary implications. These ideas and values retain their power and their pertinence, though they are very remote from realization, anywhere. As long as this is so, the libertarian revolutions of the eighteenth century remain far from consummated, a vision for the future.[87]

One might take this natural belief to be confirmed by the fact that despite all efforts to contain them, the rabble continue to fight for their fundamental human rights. And over time, some libertarian ideals have been partially realized or have even become common coin. Many of the outrageous ideas of the seventeenth-century radical democrats, for example, seem tame enough today, though other early insights remain beyond our current moral and intellectual reach.

The struggle for freedom of speech is an interesting case—and a crucial one, since it lies at the heart of a whole array of freedoms and rights. A central question of the modern era is when, if ever, the state may act to interdict the content of communications. As noted earlier, even those regarded as leading libertarians have adopted restrictive and qualified views on this matter.[88] One critical element is seditious libel, the idea that the state can be criminally assaulted by speech, "the hallmark of closed societies throughout the world," legal historian Harry Kalven observes. A society that tolerates laws against seditious libel is not free, whatever its other virtues. In late-seventeenth-century England, men were castrated, disemboweled, quartered and beheaded for the crime. Throughout the eighteenth century, there was a general consensus that established authority could be maintained only by silencing subversive discussion, and "any threat, whether real or imagined, to the good reputation of the government" must be barred by force (Leonard Levy). "Private men are not judges of their superiors ... [for] This wou'd confound all government," one editor wrote. Truth was no defense: true charges are even more criminal than false ones, because they tend even more to bring authority into disrepute.[89]

Treatment of dissident opinion, incidentally, follows a similar model in our more libertarian era. False and ridiculous charges are no real problem; it is the unconscionable critics who reveal unwanted truths from whom society must be protected.

The doctrine of seditious libel was also upheld in the American colonies. The intolerance of dissent during the revolutionary period is notorious. The leading American libertarian, Thomas Jefferson, agreed that punishment was proper for "a traitor in thought, but not in deed," and authorized internment of political suspects. He and the other Founders agreed that "traitorous or disrespectful words" against the authority of the national state or any of its component states was criminal. "During the Revolution," Leonard Levy observes,

> Jefferson, like Washington, the Adamses, and Paine, believed that there could be no toleration for serious differences of political opinion on the issue of independence, no acceptable alternative to complete submission to the patriot cause. Everywhere there was unlimited liberty to praise it, none to criticize it.

At the outset of the Revolution, the Continental Congress urged the states to enact legislation to prevent the people from being "deceived and drawn into erroneous opinion." It was not until the Jeffersonians were themselves subjected to repressive measures in the late 1790s that they developed a body of more libertarian thought for self-protection—reversing course, however, when they gained power themselves.[90]

Until World War I, there was only a slender basis for freedom of speech in the United States, and it was not until 1964 that the law of seditious libel was struck down by the Supreme Court. In 1969, the Court finally protected speech apart from "incitement to imminent lawless action." Two centuries after the Revolution, the Court at last adopted the position that had been advocated in 1776 by Jeremy Bentham, who argued that a free government must permit "malcontents" to "communicate their sentiments, concert their plans, and practice every mode of opposition short of actual revolt, before the executive power can be legally justified in disturbing them." The 1969 Supreme Court decision formulated a libertarian standard which, I believe, is unique in the world. In Canada, for example, people are still imprisoned for promulgating "false news," recognized as a crime in 1275 to protect the King.[91]

In Europe, the situation is still more primitive. France is a striking case, because of the dramatic contrast between the self-congratulatory rhetoric and repressive practice so common as to pass unnoticed. England has only limited protection for freedom of speech, and even tolerates such a disgrace as a law of blasphemy. The reaction to the Salman Rushdie affair, most dramatically on the part of self-styled "conservatives," was particularly noteworthy. Rushdie was charged with seditious libel and blasphemy in the courts, but the High Court ruled that the law of blasphemy extended only to Christianity, not to Islam, and that only verbal attack "against Her Majesty or Her Majesty's Government or some other institution of the state" counts as seditious libel. Thus the Court upheld a fundamental doctrine of the Ayatollah Khomeini, Stalin, Goebbels, and other opponents of freedom, while recognizing that English law protects only domestic power from criticism. Doubtless many would agree with Conor Cruise O'Brien, who, when Minister for Posts and Telegraphs in Ireland, amended the Broadcasting Authority Act to permit the Authority to refuse to broadcast any matter that, in the judgement of the Minister, "would tend to undermine the authority of the state."[92]

We should also bear in mind that the right to freedom of speech in the United States was not established by the First Amendment to the Constitution, but only through dedicated efforts over a long period by the labor movement, the civil rights and anti-war movements of the 1960s, and other popular forces. James Madison pointed out that a "parchment barrier" will never suffice to prevent tyranny. Rights are not established by words, but won and sustained by struggle.

It is also worth recalling that victories for freedom of speech are often won in defense of the most depraved and horrendous views. The 1969 Supreme Court decision was in defense of the Ku Klux Klan from prosecution after a meeting with hooded figures, guns, and a burning cross, calling for "burying the nigger" and "sending the Jews back to Israel." With regard to freedom of expression there are basically two positions: you defend it vigorously for views you hate, or you reject it in favor of Stalinist/Fascist standards.[93]

Whether the instinct for freedom is real or not, we do not know. If it is, history teaches that it can be dulled, but has yet to be killed. The courage and dedication of people struggling for freedom, their willingness to confront extreme state terror and violence, are often remarkable. There has been a slow growth of consciousness over many years, and goals have been achieved that were considered utopian or scarcely contemplated in earlier eras. An inveterate optimist can point to this record and express the hope that with a new decade, and soon a new century, humanity may be able to overcome some of its social maladies; others might draw a different lesson from recent history. It is hard to see rational grounds for affirming one or the other perspective. As in the case of many of the natural beliefs that guide our lives, we can do no better than to choose according to our intuition and hopes.

The consequences of such a choice are not obscure. By denying the instinct for freedom we will only prove that humans are a lethal mutation, an evolutionary dead end; by nurturing it, if it is real, we may find ways to deal with dreadful human tragedies and problems that are awesome in scale.

Notes

1. Davie, *The Democratic Intellect* (University of Edinburgh, 1961), pp. 274 f.

2. See my "Intellectuals and the state," 1977, reprinted in *Towards a New Cold War, Necessary Illusions*. Clinton Rossiter and James Lare, eds, *The Essential Lippmann: a Political Philosophy for Liberal Democracy* (Harvard, 1982), pp. 91–2.

3. Marchamont Nedham, 1650, cited by Edmund S. Morgan, *Inventing the People* (Norton, 1988), p. 79; Hume, p. 1, cited with the qualification just noted.

4. Cited with approval by Timothy Garton Ash, *New York Review of Books*, January 18, 1990, and William Luers, *Foreign Affairs*, Spring 1990.

5. Mine, AP, November 28; Rita Beamish, AP, November 29, 1989. On the reaction to the murder and torture of priests and human rights campaigners, see *Manufacturing Consent*, ch. 2; *Necessary Illusions*, pp. 138 f. On failed efforts to explain the facts away and escape the obvious consequences, see ibid., pp. 145–8.

6. Nairn, "Murder bargain," *Cleveland Plain Dealer*, February 16, 1990.

7. John Saxe-Fernandez, *Excelsior*, November 21, 1989, in *Latin America News Update*, January 1990; *TNR*, March 19, 1990.

8. Quoted by Jon Reed, *Guardian* (New York), May 23, 1990.

9. Guillermo Melendez, *Excelsior*, April 7, 1990; *Central America NewsPak*, April 9, 1990. On the efficient demolition of the peace plan by the US government and its media, and the role

of Oscar Arias in the operation, see *Culture of Terrorism*, ch. 7; *Necessary Illusions*, pp. 89 ff. and Appendix IV, sec. 5. Also Chapter 2, pp. 77 f.; Chapter 8, section 6; Chapter 9, pp. 297 f.

10. See *Necessary Illusions*, pp. 41–2, 123–30; Appendix V, secs 6, 7. Godoy, *Nation*, March 5. Korea, AP, May 5, 1990.

11. Margaret Judson, cited by Leonard W. Levy, *Emergence of a Free Press* (Oxford University Press, 1985), p. 91.

12. Christopher Hill, *The World Turned Upside Down* (Penguin, 1975). With regard to Locke, Hill adds, "at least Locke did not intend that priests should do the telling; that was for God himself."

13. Levy, *Emergence*, pp. 98–100. On the "massive intolerance" of Milton's *Areopagitica*, commonly regarded as a groundbreaking libertarian appeal, see John Illo, *Prose Studies* (May 1988). Milton himself explained that the purpose of the tract was "so that the determination of true and false, of what should be published and what should be suppressed, might not be under control of . . . unlearned men of mediocre judgment," but only "an appointed officer" of the right persuasion, who will have the authority to ban work he finds to be "mischievous or libellous," "erroneous and scandalous," "impious or evil absolutely against faith or manners," as well as "popery" and "open superstition."

14. Morgan, *Inventing the People*, pp. 75–6.

15. See Chapter 8, p. 253.

16. Todorov, *The Conquest of America* (Harper & Row, 1983), pp. 5, 150.

17. Francis Jennings, *Empire of Fortune* (Norton, 1988), ch. 1. Indians have "nothing human except the shape," Washington wrote: ". . . the gradual extension of our settlements will as certainly cause the savage, as the wolf, to retire; both being beasts of prey, tho' they differ in shape." Ibid., p. 62; Richard Drinnon, *Facing West*, p. 65, citing a Washington letter of 1783.

18. See *Turning the Tide*, pp. 162–3.

19. Morgan, p. 79 (emphasis in original).

20. Ibid., pp. 168 f.

21. Lenin, 1922, cited by Moshe Lewin, *Lenin's Last Struggle* (Pantheon, 1968). Lewin's interpretation of Lenin's goals and efforts is far from what I have indicated here, however.

22. James R. Brockman, *America*, March 24, 1990. On the atrocities of 1980 and the media suppression, see *Towards a New Cold War*, Introduction; *Turning the Tide*. On the Romero assassination and the US reaction, ibid., pp. 102 ff.; *Manufacturing Consent*, pp. 48 ff.

23. Douglas Grant Mine, AP, March 23, 24; Americas Watch, *A Year of Reckoning*, March 1990.

24. I saw one notice of the anniversary, in the religion pages of the *Boston Globe*, by Richard Higgins, who is writing a book about Romero: "Religion Notebook," *BG*, March 24, 1990, p. 27.

25. For references here and below, where not otherwise cited, see *Turning the Tide; Necessary Illusions*. For Lansing and Wilson, Lloyd Gardner, *Safe for Democracy* (Oxford University Press), pp. 157, 161, 261, 242. Gaddis, pp. 14 f., above.

26. Samuel Huntington, in Crozier, Huntington and Watanuki, *Crisis of Democracy* (see Introduction Note 1).

27. *WSJ*, December 13, 1973.

28. See my review/ article in *Grand Street*, Winter 1987.

29. Cited by Herbert Schiller, *The Corporate Takeover of Public Expression* (Oxford University Press, 1989).

30. McCann, *An American Company* (Crown, 1976), p. 45. On the ludicrous performance of the media, see also *Turning the Tide*, pp. 164 f. Also William Preston and Ellen Ray, "Disinformation and mass deception: democracy as a cover story," in Richard O. Curry, ed., *Freedom at Risk* (Temple, 1988).

31. Rossiter and Lare, *The Essential Lippmann*.

32. Cited from secret documents by R.R.A. Marlin, "Propaganda and the Ethics of Persuasion," *International Journal of Moral and Social Studies*, Spring 1989. For more on these matters, see "Intellectuals and the State."

33. See Chapter 8, p. 261; Chapter 11, pp. 346 f.

34. Galeano, *Days and Nights of Love and War* (Monthly Review, 1983).

35. See *Turning the Tide*, pp. 162 f.

36. Gerschenkron, *Economic Backwardness in Historical Perspective*, pp. 146, 150.

37. Ron Rosenbaum, review of Ellis Cose, *The Press, NYT Book Review*, April 9, 1989. The full statement, even more misleading, is that the author spotlights "the relationship between the corporate structure of the press and its traditional Jeffersonian role. ..." On the extraordinary extent to which critique of the descriptive dogma is evaded, even in an academic setting, see *Necessary Illusions*, Appendix I, section 2. On Jefferson and the press, see Leonard Levy, *Jefferson and Civil Liberties: the Darker Side* (Harvard, 1963; Ivan Dee, 1989); Levy, *Emergence*.

38. Linsky, *BG*, July 7, 1990.

39. See *Turning the Tide*, ch. 5; Thomas Ferguson and Joel Rogers, *Right Turn* (Hill & Wang, 1986); Michael Benhoff, *Z Magazine*, March 1989 (letters); Ferguson, *Socialist Review* 19.4, 1989.

40. George Tanham and Dennis Duncanson, "Some dilemmas of counterinsurgency," *Foreign Affairs*, 48.1, 1969.

41. Gerschenkron, *Economic Backwardness in Historical Perspective*, pp. 28–9.

42. Maynes, *Foreign Policy*, Spring 1990. See Chapter 10, p. 309.

43. For further details, see *Culture of Terrorism*, pp. 77–8; and on the concept of democracy held by Kinsley and his colleagues, Chapter 10.

44. For details on Laqueur's remarkable apologetics for terror in what is regarded as serious scholarship, see *Necessary Illusions*, pp. 113, 277 f. Wesson, "Historical Overview and Analysis," in Jan Triska, ed., *Dominant Powers and Subordinate States*, pp. 58–9. On US terrorist operations against Cuba, see *Necessary Illusions*, pp. 274 f., and sources cited. On these and other measures, including global economic blockade, and the background, see Morris Morley, *Imperial State: The United States and Revolution and Cuba, 1952–1986* (Cambridge University Press, 1987).

45. For some more recent discussion, see *Pirates and Emperors*; *Necessary Illusions*, pp. 269 f.; Edward Herman and Gerry O'Sullivan, *The "Terrorism" Industry* (Pantheon, 1990); Alexander George, ed., *Western State Terrorism* (Polity Press, 1991).

46. Carlson, *U.S. Naval Institute Proceedings*, September 1989; *LAT*, September 3, 1989; AP, April 23, 1990; Philip Shenon, *NYT*, July 6, 1990.

47. Melman and Raviv, *BG*, August 5, 1990.

48. *Third World Resurgence* (Malaysia), October 1990.

49. Chomsky and Herman, *Political Economy of Human Rights*.

50. For review and further discussion, see *Manufacturing Consent*, ch. 6, sec. 2; *Necessary Illusions*, pp. 154 ff.

51. A striking example was the reaction to the 1965 slaughter in Indonesia, and to new evidence of US participation in it revealed in 1990. For discussion, see my article in *Z Magazine*, September 1990. See also Ellen Ray and William Schaap, and Ralph McGehee, in *Lies of Our Times* (August 1990), on the *New York Times* coverup.

52. See my "Responsibility of Intellectuals," reprinted in *American Power and the New Mandarins* and *Chomsky Reader* (Rowe); and "Objectivity and liberal scholarship," in *American Power* (Wolf).

53. Gardner, *Safe for Democracy*, pp. 244 f., 255.

54. Freed, *LAT*, April 14, 1990.

55. Freed, *LAT*, May 7, 1990; Lindsey Gruson, *NYT*, July 5, 1990. For an analysis of Gruson's observations on flaws in Guatemalan "democracy" in earlier articles, while absolving the US of any responsibility and not questioning its commitment to democracy, see Edward Herman, "Gruson on Guatemala," *Lies of Our Times*, August 1990.

56. For extensive documentation on the matters discussed here, see *Necessary Illusions*.

57. Edward Mitchell, *Asian Survey*, August 1967.

58. See *Necessary Illusions*, pp. 62 f., 111 f., 263 ff.; my "Letter from Lexington" in *Lies of Our Times* (July 1989); Winson, *Coffee & Modern Costa Rican Democracy*, pp. 54–5.

59. See *Turning the Tide*, pp. 106 f., 109 ff.; *Necessary Illusions*, pp. 78–9.

60. Martín-Baró, Symposium, Berkeley, California, January 17, 1989, sponsored by the Mental Health Committee of the Committee for Health Rights in Central America (CHRICA, San Francisco), which made the transcript available.

61. Martín-Baró, "From Dirty War to Psychological War," paper presented at the 21st Congress of the Interamerican Psychological Society, Havana, 1987; reprinted in Adrianne Aron, ed., *Flight, Exile, and Return*, CHRICA, 1988.

62. Socorro Juridico, which operated under the jurisdiction of the San Salvador Archdiocese,

paper presented at an International Seminar on Torture in Latin America in Buenos Aires. Shultz, address of April 14, 1986. See *Necessary Illusions*, pp. 69 f., for further details.

63. Martín-Baró, "Mass Media and Public Opinion in El Salvador," excerpts in *Interamerican Public Opinion Report*, January 1990. On the destruction of the Salvadoran media, and the reaction here, see *Necessary Illusions*, pp. 41–2.

64. Americas Watch, *A Year of Reckoning*. On the Rio Sumpul massacre, see *Towards a New Cold War, Turning the Tide*.

65. Lawyers Committee, letter of April 20 to Defense Secretary Richard Cheney; *El Salvador on Line* (Washington), April 30; Alexander Cockburn, *Nation*, May 14, 1990. Father de Cortina, *Cape Codder* (Orleans, MA), May 1, 1990.

66. Robert Kahn, Pacific News Service, July 9–13; Mary Cabezas, *Guardian* (London), August 1, 1990.

67. COHA *News and Analysis*, June 21; Andrew Blake, *BG*, July 12, March 16; Lawrence Ross, *San Francisco Chronicle*, July 12; Alexander Cockburn and Richard McKerrow, *In These Times*, August 1, 1990. Martínez's testimony of August 18, 1989, detailing the workings of the death squads in which he participated, is available from the Marin Interfaith Task Force on Central America, 25 Buena Vista, Mill Valley CA 94941. On the initial reaction to Martínez's revelations, before the assassination of the Jesuits, see Chapter 9, pp. 292 f. His case is pending at the time of writing.

68. *BG*, August 14, 1990.

69. Giorgio Amendola, *Storia del PCI* (Riuniti, Rome 1979), p. 142, cited by Kelly, *The Anti-Fascist Resistance*, p. 10.

70. Daniel Santiago, "The Aesthetics of Terror, the Hermeneutics of Death," *America*, March 24, 1990.

71. *Toronto Globe & Mail*, February 3; AP, February 2, 3, 1988. See my article in *Z Magazine*, March 1988, for many further details on these and other cases.

72. Schoultz, *National Security and United States Policy*, pp. 88 f.

73. Ellacuría, "The UCA Regarding the Doctorate given to Monsignor Romero," March 1985; reprinted in the Nicaraguan Jesuit journal *Envío*, January 1990; Brockman.

74. Gleijeses, *Politics and Culture in Guatemala* (Michigan, 1988), sponsored by the State Department.

75. See *Necessary Illusions*, pp. 263 f.; *Culture of Terrorism*, p. 127.

76. Ibid. For additional examples, see *On Power and Ideology*, pp. 22 f.; *Necessary Illusions*, pp. 67–8, Appendix V, sec. 1.

77. *Special Report of Interagency Committee on Intelligence* (Ad Hoc), Chairman J. Edgar Hoover, along with the directors of the CIA, DIA, and NSA, prepared for the President, June 25, 1970, marked "Top Secret." A censored version was later released. Quotes below are from Book 7, Part 1: *Summary of Internal Security Threat*. For more extensive discussion, see my introduction to N. Blackstock, ed., *COINTELPRO* (Vintage, 1976); Kenneth O'Reilly, *Racial Matters* (Free Press, 1989).

78. See references of Chapter 1, Note 85.

79. Gregory Treverton, *Covert Action* (Basic Books, 1987), p. 18.

80. Memorandum for Assistant to the President for National Security Affairs, 25 June 1960, Secret.

81. CIA, *Review of the World Situation*, 17 August 1949.

82. Bryce Wood, *The Dismantling of the Good Neighbor Policy* (University of Texas, 1985). NSC 141/1, "Progress Report," July 23, 1953.

83. *Turning the Tide*, pp. 198 f.; *Latinamerica Press* (Lima), December 24, 1987.

84. Kinzer, *NYT*, January 10, 1988. Kinzer is quite familiar with the facts, having co-authored an important book on the topic: Stephen Schlesinger and Stephen Kinzer, *Bitter Fruit* (Doubleday, 1982).

85. Gaddis, *Long Peace*, p. 37.

86. For fuller discussion, see my *Problems of Knowledge and Freedom*, memorial lectures for Russell delivered at Trinity College, Cambridge (Pantheon, 1971).

87. James Harris, Ralph Cudworth. See my *Cartesian Linguistics* (Harper & Row, 1966), and for further discussion, "Language and Freedom," reprinted in *For Reasons of State* and *Chomsky Reader*.

88. For further discussion and references, see *Necessary Illusions*, Appendix V, sec. 8.

89. Levy, *Emergence of a Free Press*, pp. xvii, 9, 102, 41, 130.

90. Ibid., pp. 178–9, 297, 337 ff.; Levy, *Jefferson and Civil Liberties*, pp. 25 f.

91. Levy, *Emergence*, pp. 6, 167.

92. For a few of the many examples that might be cited in the case of France, see *Necessary Illusions*, p. 344. On the Rushdie affair, see Christopher Frew, "Craven evasion on the threat to freedom," *Scotsman*, August 3, 1989, referring to the shameful behavior of Paul Johnson and Hugh Trevor-Roper—who were not alone. High Court, *NYT*, April 10, 1990. O'Brien quoted in *British Journalism Review*, vol. 1, no. 2, Winter 1990.

93. Levy, *Emergence*, pp. 226–7; Harry Kalven, *A Worthy Tradition* (Harper & Row, 1988), pp. 63, 227 f., 121 f. No such brief commentary on freedom of speech can pretend to be adequate. As noted, more complex questions arise when we pass from expression of views to expression that borders on incitement to action (say, ordering a killer with a gun to shoot), and when we consider the right to a private space and other matters.

AFTERWORD

THIS book went to press just as the US and Britain were about to launch their bombing of Iraq in mid January 1991. Events since well illustrate its major theses.

Given the US role as global enforcer, elites face the task of maintaining obedience not only at home, where the "ignorant and meddling outsiders" must be reduced to their spectator status, but also in the former colonial domains ("the South"). As discussed in the text, these themes have long been common coin among the educated classes.

In the South, violence remains a feasible option. Few in the South would contest the judgement of the *Times of India* that in the Gulf crisis the traditional warrior states—the US and UK—sought a "regional Yalta where the powerful nations agree among themselves to a share of Arab spoils . . . [Their] conduct throughout this one month [January–February 1991] has revealed the seamiest sides of Western civilisation: its unrestricted appetite for dominance, its morbid fascination for hi-tech military might, its insensitivity to 'alien' cultures, its appalling jingoism. . . ." The general mood was captured by Cardinal Paulo Evaristo Arns of São Paulo, Brazil, who wrote that in the Arab countries "the rich sided with the US government while the *millions* of poor condemned this military aggression." Throughout the Third World, "there is hatred and fear: When will they decide to invade us," and on what pretext?[1]

Within the US, the major issue remains the unraveling of the society under the impact of the Reagan–Bush social and economic programs. These reflected a broad elite consensus in favor of a welfare state for the rich even beyond the norm. Policy was designed to transfer resources to privileged sectors, with the costs to be borne by the general population and future generations. Given the narrow interests of its constituency, the Administration has no serious proposals to deal with the consequences of these policies.

It is therefore necessary to divert the public. Two classic devices are to inspire fear of terrible enemies and worship of our grand leaders, who rescue us just in the nick of time. The enemies may be domestic (criminal Blacks, uppity women, subversives undermining the tradition, etc.), but foreign demons have natural advantages. The Russians served the purpose for many years; their collapse has called for innovative and audacious tactics. As the standard pretext vanished, the domestic population has been frightened—with some success—by images of Qaddafi's hordes of international terrorists, Sandinistas marching on Texas, Grenada interdicting sea lanes and threatening the homeland itself, Hispanic narco-traffickers directed by the arch-maniac Noriega, and crazed Arabs generally, most recently, the Beast of Baghdad, after he underwent the usual conversion from favored friend to Attila the Hun after committing the one unforgivable crime, the crime of disobedience, on August 2, 1990.

The scenario requires Awe as well as Fear. There must, then, be foreign triumphs, domestic ones being beyond even the imagination of the cultural managers. Our noble leaders must courageously confront and miraculously defeat the barbarians at the gate, so that we can once again "stand tall" (the President's boast, after overcoming Grenada's threat to our existence) and march forward towards a New World Order of peace and justice. Since each foreign triumph is in fact a fiasco, the aftermath must be obscured as the government–media alliance turns to some new crusade.

The barbarians must be defenseless: it would be foolish to confront anyone who might fight back. Moreover, the notable rise in the moral and cultural level of the general population since the 1960s, including the unwillingness to tolerate atrocities and aggression, a grave disease called "the Vietnam syndrome," has further limited the options. The problem was addressed in a National Security Policy Review from the first months of the Bush presidency, dealing with "third world threats."

It reads: "In cases where the U.S. confronts much weaker enemies, our challenge will be not simply to defeat them, but to defeat them decisively and rapidly." Any other outcome would be "embarrassing" and might "undercut political support," understood to be thin.[2] The intervention options are therefore restricted to clandestine terror (called "low-intensity conflict," etc., often assisted by mercenary states), or quick demolition of a "much weaker enemy." Disappearance of the Soviet deterrent enhances this second option: the US need no longer fight with "one hand tied," that is, with concern for the consequences to itself.

1. The "Gulf War" in Retrospect

Two crucial events of 1991 were the final break-up of the Soviet empire and the Gulf conflict. With regard to the former, the US was largely an observer, with little idea what to do as the system lurched from one crisis to another. The media ritually laud George Bush's consummate skill as a statesman and crisis manager, but the exercise lacks spirit. The response to Saddam Hussein's aggression, in contrast, was a Washington operation throughout, with Britain loyally in tow.

Holding all the cards, the US naturally achieved its major aims, demonstrating that "what we say goes," as the President put it. The proclamation was directed to dictators and tyrants, but it is beyond dispute that the US has no problem with murderous thugs who serve US interests, and will attack and destroy committed democrats if they depart from their service function. It suffices to recall Bush's esteem for Marcos, Mobutu, Ceauşescu, Suharto, Saddam Hussein, and other favored friends, his actions in Central America, and the rest of the shabby record.[3] The correct reading of his words, clearly enough, is: "What we say goes, whoever you may be." The lesson is understood by the traditional victims, as noted.

Now that the US victory in the Gulf has been secured, jingoist rhetoric has subsided, and it is possible to survey just what happened in the misnamed "Gulf War"—misnamed, because there never was a war, at least, if the concept involves two sides in combat. That didn't happen in the Gulf.

The crisis began with the Iraqi invasion of Kuwait, which left hundreds killed, according to human rights groups. That hardly qualifies as war.

Rather, in terms of crimes against peace and against humanity, it falls roughly into the category of the Turkish invasion of northern Cyprus, Israel's invasion of Lebanon in 1978, or the US invasion of Panama. In these terms it falls well short of Israel's 1982 invasion of Lebanon, and cannot remotely be compared with the near-genocidal Indonesian conquest of East Timor, to mention only two cases of aggression and atrocities that continue with the decisive support of those who most passionately professed their outrage over Iraq's invasion.

In subsequent months, Iraq was responsible for terrible crimes in Kuwait, with several thousand killed and many tortured. But that is not war either; rather, state terrorism, of the kind familiar among US clients.

The next phase of the conflict began with the US-led attack of January 16. Its first component targeted the civilian infrastructure, including power, sewage, and water systems; that is, a form of biological warfare, having little relation to driving Iraq from Kuwait—rather, designed for long-term US political ends. This too is not war, but state terrorism, on a colossal scale.

The second component of the attack was the slaughter of Iraqi soldiers in the desert, largely unwilling Shi'ite and Kurdish conscripts, it appears, hiding in holes in the sand or fleeing for their lives—a picture remote from the disinformation relayed by the press about colossal fortifications, artillery powerful beyond our imagining, vast stocks of chemical and biological weapons at the ready, and so on. Pentagon and other sources give estimates in the range of 100,000 defenseless victims killed. Again this exercise does not qualify as war; it is "simply massacre and murderous butchery," to use the words of a British observer of the US conquest of the Philippines at the turn of the century. The desert slaughter was a "turkey shoot," as some US forces described it, borrowing the term used by their forebears as they were butchering Filipinos[4]—one of those deeply rooted themes of the culture that surface at appropriate moments, as if by reflex.

Months later, US Army officials revealed what the Pentagon expected: not war, but slaughter. The ground attack began with plows mounted on tanks and earthmovers to bulldoze live Iraqi soldiers into trenches in the desert, an "unprecedented tactic" that was "hidden from public view," Patrick Sloyan reported. The commander of one of the three brigades involved said that thousands of Iraqis may have been killed; the other commanders refused estimates. "Not a single American was killed during the attack that made an Iraqi body count impossible," Sloyan continues. The report elicited little interest or comment. Nor did the "murderous butchery" generally.[5]

The goal of the attack on the civilian society was no secret: the population was to be held hostage to induce the military to overthrow Saddam and wield the "iron fist" as he himself had done with US support before stepping out of line. Administration reasoning was outlined by *New York Times* chief diplomatic correspondent Thomas Friedman. If Iraqis suffered sufficient pain, some general might topple Mr. Hussein, "and then Washington would have the best of all worlds: an iron-fisted Iraqi junta without Saddam Hussein," a return to the happy days when Saddam's "iron fist . . . held Iraq together, much to the satisfaction of the American allies Turkey and Saudi Arabia," not to speak of the boss in Washington.[6]

The operation of holding a civilian population hostage while tens of thousands die from starvation and disease raises only one problem: unreasonable softhearted folk may feel some discomfort at having "sat by and watched a country starve for political reasons," precisely what would happen, UNICEF Director of Public Affairs Richard Reid predicted, unless Iraq were permitted to purchase "massive quantities of food"—though it was already far too late, he reported, for the children under two, who had stopped growing since late 1990 because of severe malnutrition. But Bush's ex-pal helped the President out of this dilemma. The *Wall Street Journal* observed that Saddam's "clumsy attempt to hide nuclear-bomb-making equipment from the U.N. may be a blessing in disguise, U.S. officials say. It assures that the allies [read: US and UK] can keep economic sanctions in place to squeeze Saddam Hussein without mounting calls to end the penalties for humanitarian reasons."[7] The operation could thus proceed unhampered by the bleeding hearts.

In keeping with its fabled dedication to international law and morality, the US demanded that compensation to the victims of Iraq's crimes must have higher priority than any purchase of food that might be allowed— under UN (meaning US) control, of course; a country that commits the crime of disobeying Washington has plainly lost any claim to sovereignty. While proclaiming this stern doctrine with suitable majesty, the Bush Administration kept pressure on Nicaragua to force those other miscreants, who had committed the same crime, to abandon their claims to reparations for a decade of US terror and illegal economic warfare as mandated by the International Court of Justice. Nicaragua finally succumbed, a capitulation scarcely noticed by the media, mesmerized by Washington's lofty rhetoric about Iraq's responsibilities to its victims. A few days later, the US cancelled Nicaragua's $260 million debt; the *Times* published the information in a Reuters dispatch, omitting the paragraph on Nicaragua's abandonment of its $17 billion claim, which had not been reported. The front pages, the same day, quoted a US official: "If you're going to build any kind of credibility for a new world order, you've got to make people accountable to legal procedures, and Saddam's flaunted every one."[8] Unlike us.

The final phase of the conflict began immediately after the cease-fire, as Iraqi elite units slaughtered first the Shi'ites of the south and then the Kurds of the north, with the tacit support of the Commander-in-Chief, who had called upon Iraqis to rebel when that suited his purposes, then went fishing when the "iron fist" struck.

Returning from a March 1991 fact-finding mission, Senate Foreign Relations Committee staff member Peter Galbraith reported that the Administration did not even respond to Saudi proposals to assist Shi'ite and Kurdish rebels, and that the Iraqi military did not attack until it had "a clear indication that the United States did not want the popular rebellion to succeed." A BBC investigation found that "several Iraqi generals made contact with the United States to sound out the likely response if they moved against Saddam," but received no support, concluding that "Washington had no interest in supporting revolution; that it would prefer Saddam Hussein to continue in office, rather than see groups of unknown insurgents take power." An Iraqi general who escaped to Saudi Arabia told the BBC that "he and his men had repeatedly asked the American forces for weapons, ammunition and food to help them carry on the fight against Saddam's forces," only to be refused each time. As his men fell back towards US–UK positions, the Americans blew up an Iraqi arms dump to prevent them from obtaining arms, and then "disarmed the rebels." Reporting from northern Iraq, ABC correspondent Charles Glass described how "Republican Guards, supported by regular army brigades, mercilessly shelled Kurdish-held areas with Katyusha multiple rocket launchers, helicopter gunships and heavy artillery," while journalists observing the slaughter listened to General Schwarzkopf boasting to his radio audience that "we had destroyed the Republican Guard as a militarily effective force" and eliminated the military use of helicopters.[9]

Such truths are not quite the stuff of which heroes are fashioned, so the story was finessed at home, though it could not be totally ignored, particularly the attack on the Kurds, with their Aryan features and origins; the Shi'ites, who appear to have suffered even worse atrocities right under the gaze of Stormin' Norman, raised fewer problems, being mere Arabs.

In brief, from August 1990 there was little that could qualify as "war." Rather, there was a brutal Iraqi takeover of Kuwait, followed by various forms of slaughter and state terrorism, the scale corresponding roughly to the means of violence in the hands of the perpetrators, and their impunity. Furthermore, Saddam's indiscretion offered an opportunity to provide useful instruction to anyone who might have odd ideas about disobeying US orders. This is another standard policy; thus, in October 1991, Washington once again blocked European and Japanese efforts to call off the embargo that the US imposed on Vietnam sixteen years ago after direct conquest failed.[10] The decision to renew the embargo was accompanied with much indignation about Vietnam's failure to meet its moral responsibility to Americans with regard to MIAs, the sole humanitarian issue that remains from US aggression that killed millions of people and destroyed three countries. The decision to extend the punishment of Vietnam was the only action commemorating the thirtieth anniversary of John F. Kennedy's escalation of the US war in South Vietnam from murderous terror to outright aggression, as he sent US Air Force units to bombard the countryside and authorized US advisers to take part in combat operations. It coincided with a vast display of outrage over Japan's failure to apologize for its attack on a military base in a US colony fifty years ago. This macabre spectacle passed virtually without awareness or comment, an achievement that could hardly be duplicated in a well-run totalitarian state.

Those who do not follow the rules must be severely punished, and others must learn these lessons—but not the American public, who are to be regaled with tales about the nobility of our aspirations, the grand achievements of our leaders, and the moral depravity of others.

2. Deterring Iraqi Democracy

Iraqi opposition forces have always been given short shrift in Washington, hence ignored in the media. They were rebuffed by the Bush Administration in February 1990, when they sought support for a call for parliamentary democracy. The same was true in Britain. In mid August, Kurdish leader Jalal Talabani flew to Washington to seek support for guerrilla operations against Saddam's regime. Neither Pentagon nor State Department officials would speak to him; he was rebuffed again in March 1991. The likely reason was concern over the sensibilities of the Turkish "defender of civilized values," who looked askance at Kurdish resistance.[11]

The Iraqi democratic opposition was scrupulously excluded from the mainsteam media throughout the Gulf crisis, a fact readily explained when we hear what they had to say.

On the eve of the air war, the German press published a statement of the Iraqi Democratic Group reiterating its call for the overthrow of Saddam Hussein but also opposing "any foreign intervention in the Near East," criticizing US "policies of aggression" in the Third World and its intention to control Middle East oil, and rejecting UN resolutions "that had as their goal the starvation of our people." The statement called for the withdrawal of US–UK troops, withdrawal of Iraqi troops from Kuwait, self-determination for the Kuwaiti people, "a peaceful settlement of the Kuwait problem, democracy for Iraq, and autonomy for Iraq–Kurdistan." A similar stand was taken by the Teheran-based Supreme Assembly of the Islamic Revolution in Iraq (in a communiqué from Beirut); the Iraqi Communist Party; Mas'ud Barzani, the leader of the Kurdistan Democratic Party; and other prominent opponents of the Iraqi regime, many of whom had suffered bitterly from Saddam's atrocities. Falih 'Abd al-Jabbar, an Iraqi journalist in exile in London, commented: "Although the Iraqi opposition parties have neither given up their demand for an Iraqi withdrawal from Kuwait nor their hope of displacing Saddam some time in the future, they believe that they will lose the moral right to oppose the present regime if they do not side with Iraq against the war." "All the opposition parties are agreed in calling for an immediate withdrawal of Iraqi forces from Kuwait," British journalist Edward Mortimer reported, "but most are very unhappy about the military onslaught by the US-led coalition" and preferred economic and political sanctions.

A delegation of the Kuwaiti democratic opposition in Amman in December 1990 had taken the same position. On British television in February 1991, anti-Saddam Arab intellectuals, including the prominent Kuwaiti opposition leader Dr. Ahmed al-Khatib—who had already, in October 1990, strenuously opposed military action—were unanimous in calling for a cease-fire and for serious consideration of Saddam's February 15 withdrawal offer.

The silence here was deafening, and instructive. Unlike Bush and his associates, the international peace movement and Iraqi democratic opposition had always opposed Saddam Hussein. But they also opposed the quick resort to violence to undercut the possibility of a peaceful resolution of the conflict. Such an outcome would have avoided the slaughter of tens of thousands of people, the destruction of two countries, harsh reprisals, an environmental catastrophe, further slaughter by the Iraqi government, and the likely emergence of another murderous US-backed tyranny in Iraq. But it would not have taught the crucial lesson that "what we say goes."

With the mission accomplished, the disdain for Iraqi democrats continued unchanged. A European diplomat observed that "the Americans would prefer to have another Assad, or better yet, another Mubarak in Baghdad," referring to their "military-backed regimes," Assad's being particularly odious. A diplomat from the US-run coalition said that "we will accept Saddam in Baghdad in order to have Iraq as one state." A State Department official told a European envoy that the US would be satisfied with "an Iraqi Assad," "a reliable and predictable enemy."

In mid-March, Leith Kubba, head of the London-based Iraqi Democratic Reform Movement, alleged that the US insistence that "changes in the regime must come from within, from people already in power," amounted to a call for military dictatorship. Another leading activist, banker Ahmad Chalabi, observed that the US was "waiting for Saddam to butcher the insurgents in the hope that he can be overthrown later by a suitable officer," an attitude rooted in the US policy of "supporting dictatorships to maintain stability." Official US spokesmen confirmed that the Bush Administration would have no dealings with Iraqi opposition leaders: "We felt that political meetings with them . . . would not be appropriate for our policy at this time," State Department spokesman Richard Boucher stated on March 14, as Saddam's "iron fist" was decimating the opposition.

Kuwaiti democrats too discovered that Bush would lend them no support. The reason offered was the President's commitment to the principle of noninterference in internal affairs, so profound, officials explained, that he could not mention the word "democracy" even in private communications to the Emir. "You can't pick out one country to lean on over another," one official said. Surely we will never find the US "leaning on" Nicaragua or Cuba, for example, or moving beyond the narrowest interpretation of international law. As human rights abuses mounted in postwar Kuwait, Bush became "the foremost apologist for the perpetrators," observed Aryeh Neier, director of Human Rights Watch, noting that Bush's apologetics for repression were featured on the front page of the Kuwait government daily.

American democracy also took the usual licking. Polls a few days before the mid January bombing showed about 2–1 support for a peaceful settlement based on Iraqi withdrawal along with an international conference on the Arab–Israeli conflict. Few if any of those who expressed this position had heard any public advocacy of it; the media had been virtually uniform in following the President's lead, dismissing "linkage" as an unspeakable crime—in this unique case. It is unlikely that any knew that their views were shared by Iraqi democratic forces; or that an Iraqi proposal in the terms they advocated had been released a week earlier by US officials, who found it reasonable, and had been flatly rejected by Washington; or that an Iraqi withdrawal offer had been considered by the National Security Council as early as mid August, but was dismissed, and effectively suppressed, apparently because it was feared that it might "defuse the crisis," as the *Times* diplomatic correspondent reported Administration concerns.[12] Suppose that the crucial facts had reached the public and the issues had been honestly addressed. Then support for a diplomatic settlement would have been far higher, and it might have been possible to avoid the huge slaughter preferred by the Administration for its particular purposes: to establish the efficacy of violence and teach lessons in obedience, to secure the dominant role of the US in the Gulf, and to keep domestic problems in the shadow.

3. "The Best of All Worlds"

Despite its victory, Washington did not quite achieve "the best of all worlds," because no suitable clone of the Beast of Baghdad was found. Needless to say, not everyone shared the Washington–media conception of "the best of all worlds." Well after hostilities ended, the *Wall Street Journal* broke ranks and offered space to an authentic representative of the Iraqi democratic opposition, Ahmad Chalabi. He described the outcome as "the worst of all possible worlds" for the Iraqi people, whose tragedy is "awesome."[13]

The doctrinal system did face a problem as the Bush Administration lent its support to Saddam's crushing of the internal opposition. The task was the usual one: to portray Washington's stance in a favorable light, not easy after the months of tributes to our leader's magnificent show of principle and courage in confronting the rampaging Beast. But the transition was smooth and impressive. True, few can approach our devotion to the most august principles. But our moral purity is tempered with an understanding of the need for "pragmatism" and "stability," useful concepts that translate as "doing what we choose."

In a typical example of the genre, *Times* Middle East correspondent Alan Cowell attributed the failure of the rebels to the fact that "very few people outside Iraq wanted them to win"; here the concept "people" is used in the conventional doctrinal sense, meaning people who count, not "meddling outsiders," quite a few of whom wanted the rebels to win. The "allied campaign against President Hussein brought the United States and its Arab coalition partners to a strikingly unanimous view," Cowell continued: "Whatever the sins of the Iraqi leader, he offered the West and the region a better hope for his country's stability than did those who have suffered his repression."[14]

This version of the facts, the standard one, merits a few questions. To begin with, who are these "Arab coalition partners"? Answer: six are family dictatorships, established by the Anglo–American settlement to manage Gulf oil riches in the interests of the foreign masters, what British imperial managers called an "Arab façade" for the real rulers. The seventh is Syria's Hafez el-Assad, a minority-based tyrant indistinguishable from Saddam Hussein. That these partners should share Washington's preference for Saddam Hussein's variety of "stability" is hardly a surprise.

The last of the "coalition partners," Egypt, is the only one that could be called "a country." Though a tyranny, it has a degree of internal freedom. We therefore turn to its semi-official press to assess the "strikingly unanimous view." The *Times* article is datelined Damascus, April 10. The day before, Deputy Editor Salaheddin Hafez of Egypt's leading daily, *Al-Ahram*, commented on Saddam's demolition of the rebels "under the umbrella of the Western alliance's forces." US support for Saddam Hussein proved what Egypt had been saying all along, Hafez wrote. American rhetoric about "the savage beast" was merely a cover for the true goals: to cut Iraq down to size and establish US hegemony in the region. The West turned out to be in total agreement with the beast on the need to "block any progress and abort all hopes, however dim, for freedom or equality and for progress towards democracy," working in "collusion with Saddam himself" if necessary.

Egypt's reaction hardly came as a surprise. The "victory celebration" in Egypt had been "muted and totally official," correspondent Hani Shukrallah reported from Cairo. "Cairenes are identifying more with the vanquished 'enemy' than the triumphant 'allies'," particularly the poor and students, three of whom were killed by police in an anti-government demonstration. Post-cease-fire developments seemed "to have intensified the [popular] feelings of anger against the leading members of the anti-Iraq coalition," feelings exacerbated by Kuwait's atrocities against Egyptians. The Egyptian press also bitterly condemned the US conditions imposed on Iraq, a transparent effort to ensure US–Israeli military dominance, *Al-Ahram* charged. "Not in over a decade have Egyptians felt and expressed so intently their hostility to the US, Israel and the West," political scientist Ahmad Abdallah observed.

It is true that there was some regional support for the US stance apart from the friendly club of Arab tyrants. Turkish President Turgut Ozal doubtless nodded his head in approval. He had made use of the opportunity offered by the Gulf crisis to step up attacks on his own Kurdish population, confident that the US media would judiciously refrain from reporting the bombings of Kurdish villages and the plight of hundreds of thousands of refugees trying to survive the cold winter in the mountains without aid or provisions. The reader of the European press, human rights reports, or exotic US sources (see Note 1) could learn something of the winter 1990–91 exploits of the man whom George Bush hailed as "a protector of peace," who joined all of us who "stand up for civilized values around the world." But those who depended on the mass and prestige media were shielded from such improper thoughts.

The US stance also received support in Israel, where many commentators agreed with retiring Chief-of-Staff Dan Shomron that it was preferable for Saddam Hussein to remain in power. "We are all with Saddam," one headline read, reporting the view of Labor dove Avraham Burg that "in the present circumstances Saddam Hussein is better than any alternative" and that "a Shi'ite empire" from Iran to the territories would be harmful to Israel. Another leading dove, Ran Cohen of Ratz, also wanted "Saddam to continue to rule, so that perhaps the hope for any internal order will be buried" and the Americans will stay in the region and impose a "compromise." Suppression of the Kurds was a welcome development, an influential commentator explained in the *Je-*

rusalem Post, because of "the latent ambition of Iran and Syria to exploit the Kurds and create a territorial, military, contiguity between Teheran and Damascus—a contiguity which embodies danger for Israel."[15] None of this makes particularly good copy. Best to leave it in oblivion.

The "strikingly unanimous view" supporting US "pragmatism," then, included offices in Washington and New York, and US clients in the region, but left out a few others—notably, Iraqi democrats in exile and the Arab population of the region. Respectable opinion in the United States could not care less.

The *Times* version kept to convention in approving US support for Hussein's terror in the name of "stability." One must, however, bear in mind the technical meaning of the term, explained in the internal record. Thus when Guatemala tried a brief experiment with capitalist democracy forty years ago, the US was at first willing to stand back because President Arbenz seemed to have "no real sympathy for the lower classes." But when he carried out successful reforms, US policy changed, and he was overthrown in favor of a murderous military regime that has been kept in power by regular US intervention ever since. The usual reasons were explained by a State Department official:

Guatemala has become an increasing threat to the stability of Honduras and El Salvador. Its agrarian reform is a powerful propaganda weapon; its broad social program of aiding the workers and peasants in a victorious struggle against the upper classes and large foreign enterprises has a strong appeal to the populations of Central American neighbors where similar conditions prevail.

In short, "stability" means security for "the upper classes and large foreign enterprises." It is therefore possible to destabilize in the name of stability, as explained by the editor of *Foreign Affairs*, James Chace: Nixon–Kissinger "efforts to destabilize a freely elected Marxist government in Chile" were undertaken because "we were determined to seek stability." Only the naive will sense a contradiction here.[16]

Returning to the Gulf . . . By the summer of 1991, state priorities had shifted, but it would have been too much to allow the August 2 anniversary to pass without notice. A last-ditch effort was therefore necessary to portray the outcome as a Grand Victory. Even with the journalistic achievements of the preceding year, such as the suppression of the possibilities for a negotiated settlement and the rigorous exclusion of Iraqi democrats, it was no simple matter to chant the praises of the Bush–

Baker–Schwarzkopf team in the light of the "awesome tragedy" they left in their wake. But even this task was not too onerous. On the anniversary, the *New York Times* editors dismissed the qualms of "the doubters," concluding that Mr. Bush had acted wisely: he "avoided the quagmire and preserved his two triumphs: the extraordinary cooperation among coalition members and the revived self-confidence of Americans," who felt "relief and pride—relief at miraculously few US casualties and pride in the brilliant performance of the allied forces."[17]

These are chilling words. One can readily understand the reaction of the non-people of the world.

4. Marching Forward

Despite the "two triumphs," the images of the Gulf were too sordid to be left in the public memory: hundreds of thousands killed and the toll mounting as a long-term consequence of the terrorist attack on the civilian society; the Gulf tyrannies safeguarded from any democratic pressures; Saddam Hussein firmly in power, having demolished popular rebellions with tacit US support. We therefore turn to a new triumph: James Baker's brilliant pursuit of the "peace process," as he exploited the "historic window of opportunity" with the "rejectionists" in disarray to advance the US goals of "territorial compromise," "land for peace," and "autonomy" for the Palestinians.

As Baker's conference opened in Madrid, its utility in obscuring Gulf realities was indicated obliquely by *Times* diplomatic correspondent R.W. Apple: "Critics have suggested that the United States achieved far too little in the war, because Saddam Hussein was not overthrown, Iran remained as hostile and Kuwait as undemocratic as ever, and Saudi Arabia shed neither its isolation nor its archaic ways." But the "remarkable tableau" in Madrid revealed "that a very great deal had changed," as "George Bush and the United States today plucked the fruits of victory in the Persian Gulf war," though we do not yet know "how sweet they will be."

To rephrase in more accurate terms, by limiting the options in the Gulf to violence, Washington was able to achieve its basic goals. But the public must not perceive that the outcome revealed the priorities of those who ran the show. The consequences of Washington's decisions must therefore be construed as a failure to achieve our noble goals, now to be compensated with "sweet" diplomatic triumphs.

In another paean to our leader's "vision of the future," Apple explained why Bush could now "dream such great dreams" about Middle East peace: there is no fear that "regional tensions" might lead to superpower confrontation, and "no longer must the United States contend with countries whose cantankerousness was reinforced by Moscow's interest in continuing unrest."[18] Translating again: with the Soviet deterrent gone, the US feels powerful enough to ram through its own traditional policies in defiance of its NATO allies, the non-aligned countries, the major Arab states, in fact, virtually the entire world—unacceptable truths to which we return.

Such commentary was typical across a broad spectrum, including much of Europe, which has largely come to accept the extension of the Monroe Doctrine to the Middle East. The acclaim even extended to sectors of Palestinian opinion. Thus Middle East scholar Walid Khalidi, an adviser to the Jordanian–Palestinian delegation, hailed "the personal commitment of the president of the U.S. . . . to a just and comprehensive settlement."[19]

A different picture was presented by a highly respected Israeli journalist, Danny Rubinstein, one of the most informed and acute observers of policy in the occupied territories. The "autonomy" proposed by the US and Israel, he wrote, is "autonomy as in a POW camp, where the prisoners are 'autonomous' to cook their meals without interference and to organize cultural events." Palestinians are to be granted essentially what they already have: control over local services. He noted further that even advocates of Greater Israel have not called for literal annexation of the territories—which would require Israel to provide the "restricted services" available to Israel's second-class Arab citizens. The governing Likud party calls for extension of Israeli sovereignty, not annexation; "autonomy" under Israeli sovereignty only bolsters the current system: heavy taxation with little offered in return.[20] Rubinstein's interpretation appears quite realistic.

To understand the unfolding events, we must begin, as usual, by translating the rhetoric of political discourse into English. The term "peace process" refers to the process of achieving US goals, not efforts to reach peace. "Rejectionists" are those who reject the right to self-determination of Israeli Jews, or more broadly, those who reject US demands; those who reject the rights of Palestinians are "moderates" or "pragmatists." The terms "land for peace" and "territorial compromise" refer to the traditional position of the Israeli Labor Party (the Allon Plan), which grants Israel control over the desirable land and resources of the occupied territories but leaves the population stateless or under Jordanian administration, so that Israel does not have to face "the demographic problem." The latter is another term of art, referring to the problem of too many Arabs in the state defined by law as "the sovereign State of the Jewish people" in Israel or the diaspora, not the state of its citizens. Many Palestinians regard the Labor Party position as "much worse than the Likud's autonomy plan," Israeli dove Shmuel Toledano observes, agreeing with this judgement.[21] In fact, Likud occupation policies have often been less harsh than those of Labor, contrary to the standard picture of Labor doves versus Likud hawks.

The two major Israeli political groupings (Labor and Likud), with unfailing US support, agree that Palestinians cannot be permitted to control their own land and resources, as they would under meaningful autonomy. Israel relies heavily on West Bank water; control over water has also been a major factor in conflict over the Golan Heights and southern Lebanon. Some of the most favored suburbs are in the West Bank, including the vastly expanded area called "Jerusalem." Israel has also benefited from readily exploitable Palestinian labor and a controlled market for Israeli exports, though these needs will reduce if the Arab boycott becomes more permeable, and if Soviet Jews directed to Israel agree to do the dirty work assigned to Palestinians.

The issue is not security. As David Ben-Gurion observed in December 1948, "An Arab state [west of the Jordan] would be less dangerous than a state linked to Transjordan [now Jordan], and maybe tomorrow to Iraq." Labor government cabinet records (1967–77) also reveal few security concerns linked to the territories. Nothing since has changed that assessment. The problem lies elsewhere: withdrawing from the conquered territories, Israel could not "exist according to the scale, spirit, and quality she now embodies," as General Ezer Weizmann explained in justification of Israel's decision to attack Egypt in 1967, when he was one of the top military planners.[22]

The US has tended to favor Labor Party rejectionism. It is more rational than the Likud variety, which has no long-term provision for the population of the occupied territories except eventual "transfer" (expulsion). The US also objects to the brazen settlement programs of Likud, preferring Labor's technique of quietly "building facts" that will determine the final outcome—for example, "thickening" existing settlements rather than marching out to found a new one the day James Baker lands in Tel Aviv. But the disagreements are narrow, more over method than goal. Labor, Likud, and the US are all committed to "the autonomy of a POW camp."

Tactical disagreements have sometimes led to conflict, including the Bush–Shamir conflict of late 1991 over loan guarantees. These loans are designated for absorption of Soviet immigrants, thus freeing other funds for the accelerating Israeli settlement of the territories. The Bush–Shamir conflict was largely over timing, not principle. US agreement to provide financial support for immigrants/settlements would have made it impossible for the US Arab allies to attend the Madrid conference; a few months down the road, the matter can perhaps be handled without too much fanfare.

These disputes have been taken to signify a shift in US policy towards a neutral ("honest broker") or even pro-Arab position. These judgements reflect the success of the doctrinal system in establishing US rejectionism as the basis for any discussion. Within this sharply skewed framework, the Washington variety of rejectionism can be perceived as "pro-Arab," in that it conflicts with the even more extreme stand of Yitzhak Shamir and Ariel Sharon. In fact, the evidence suggests little departure from traditional policies.

5. The US versus the Peace Process

For many years, the US has stood virtually alone in blocking a diplomatic settlement in the Middle East. The UN record brings out the facts and the issues clearly. The Security Council was eliminated as a forum years ago, thanks to the US veto. The General Assembly regularly passes resolutions calling for a conference on the Arab–Israeli conflict, most recently, in December 1990 (144–2, US and Israel in opposition). In December 1989, the vote was 151–3, Dominica joining the two rejectionist states; a year earlier, 138–2; and so on. The US has also barred other initiatives. Given US power, its opposition amounts to a veto. Accordingly, the peace process has been effectively deterred.

The ideological system naturally presents the picture differently. We read constantly that the Middle East is "littered with American peace plans,"[23] and that US efforts have run aground because of the fanaticism of Middle East extremists. Such descriptions conform to the conventions: the "peace process" is restricted to US government initiatives. It follows as a matter of logic that the US is always advancing the peace process, even as it bars efforts to achieve peace, in splendid isolation. It is all really quite simple, once the norms of political correctness are understood.

Departing from these norms, it is easy to understand the traditional US opposition to the peace process. The UN resolutions call for an *international* conference, and the US brooks no interference in what President Eisenhower described as the most "strategically important area in the world," with its enormous energy reserves. As Henry Kissinger explained in a private communication, one of his major policy goals was "to ensure that the Europeans and Japanese did not get involved in the diplomacy," a goal achieved at Camp David in 1978, and again today in the official "peace process." Furthermore, UN and other initiatives endorse a Palestinian right of self-determination, which would entail Israeli withdrawal from the occupied territories. While there has been elite disagreement over the matter, the prevailing judgement has been that enhancement of Israeli power contributes to US domination of the region. For such reasons, the US has always blocked attempts at diplomatic resolution.[24]

It should be noted that US hostility to diplomacy in the Middle East is nothing unusual. Southeast Asian and Central American conflicts provide examples familiar to people not confined by doctrinal constraints. The same has been true commonly with regard to arms control and other issues. Such hostility is the natural concomitant of the role of global enforcer, committed to policies with little appeal to targeted populations but with ample force at the ready.

The basic terms of the international consensus on the Arab–Israel conflict were expressed in a resolution brought to the Security Council in January 1976, calling for a settlement on the pre-June 1967 borders (the Green Line) with "appropriate arrangements . . . to guarantee . . . the sovereignty, territorial integrity and political independence of all states in the area and their right to live in peace within secure and recognized boundaries," including Israel and a new Palestinian state in the West Bank and Gaza Strip. The resolution was backed by Egypt, Syria, Jordan, and the PLO—in fact "prepared" by the PLO according to Israel's UN Ambassador Haim Herzog, now President. It was strenuously opposed by Israel and vetoed by the United States.

These facts are automatically cut out of history, along with others unacceptable to US power, including repeated PLO initiatives through the 1980s calling for negotiations with Israel leading to mutual recognition. The truth has been distorted beyond recognition, especially by the Newspaper of Record. Its correspondent Thomas Friedman has shown particular dedication to the task. His effective suppression of the facts now permits him to spin wondrous tales about "the birth of a new pragmatism among the Palestinians" from the late 1980s, raised "another important notch" through Baker's benign influence at Madrid. Until Madrid, Friedman continues, "Both sides have hidden behind [the] argument . . . that there is no one on the other side with whom to negotiate"—*Times*speak for the fact that the PLO has for years been calling on Israel to negotiate, but Israel refuses. The Palestinians at Madrid called "explicitly for a two-state solution," Friedman writes admiringly—so different from the despised PLO, which supported (or perhaps "prepared") the 1976 UN resolution calling for a two-state settlement and was proposing negotiations to this end through the 1980s.[25]

Lying behind these gambits is the belief that US-backed Israeli violence has finally brought the Palestinians to heel. It is therefore possible, at last, to concede that the Palestinian leadership advocates a two-state settlement. It remains necessary, however, to conceal the many years of deceit in the service of US rejectionism: hence the pretense that reiteration of the long-held PLO position by the spokespersons at Madrid is a breakthrough, indeed a tribute to the US government and its steadfast refusal to allow the PLO to participate in the "peace process"—though everyone is aware that the "new pragmatists" have longstanding ties with the PLO and consult regularly with it. The next step in advancing the Party Line is to attribute to the "new pragmatists" a willingness to settle for far less, in fact, to accept the demands of US rejectionism, presented as the sage and even-handed proposal of the honest broker. The great achievement of Madrid, we read, was "the Palestinian self-adjustment to the real world," Palestinian acceptance of "a period of autonomy under continued Israeli domination"; meanwhile, Israel can build the facts of its permanent domination with US aid. This willingness to follow US orders—"the real world"—has "tossed the negative stereotypes out the window," *Times* reporter Clyde Haberman concludes, referring to the stereotypes invented and carefully cultivated by the *Times* and its colleagues for many years. With their "new pragmatism," Palestinians are at last willing "to talk to Israel, to set aside all-or-nothing demands, to accept half a loaf in the form of interim self-rule under Israeli domination." Richard C. Hottelet adds that the new leadership was granted the honor of sitting "at the table with the President of the United States" during "James Baker's masterpiece" because "they are not demanding all or nothing, as their predecessors did for 70 years."[26] Others chimed in with similar flights of fancy.

The PLO can be justly condemned for many crimes and stupidities. But it is beyond question that in the *real* real world, it has for years been calling for a two-state settlement in accord with the international consensus, and for negotiations with Israel leading to mutual recognition. But reality has been effectively purged from the doctrinal system.

Over the years, the US has proceeded to implement its unilateral rejectionist program. The current circumstances afford an opportunity to carry the process further. Gorbachev's presence at Madrid was intended to provide a thin disguise for unilateral US control; he was acceptable as the powerless leader of a country fading into oblivion. The "peace process" is structured in accordance with US intentions. Palestinians are not permitted to select their own representatives, and those who pass US–Israeli inspection are part of a Jordanian delegation. The US alone dictates the terms. The peace process that the world has sought for many years can be consigned to the ash heap of history.

6. The Evolution of US Policy

The "peace process" is concerned with the consequences of the June 1967 war, which left Israel in control of Egypt's Sinai peninsula, the Syrian Golan Heights, the Gaza Strip, and the West Bank. Other issues are not under consideration. To mention only one, while Jordan's illegitimate occupation of the West Bank since 1949 figures prominently in US–Israeli propaganda, the fact that the Palestinian state proposed in the 1947 UN resolution was partitioned between Jordan and Israel, with a measure of collusion, and that Egypt fought in the 1948 war in part to counter the ambitions of Britain's Jordanian client, is left to scholarly monographs.[27]

Another settled issue is that negotiations are based on UN resolution 242, adopted by the Security Council in November 1967. This resolution keeps to interstate relations, avoiding the Palestinian issue, and is therefore acceptable to Washington, as distinct from UN resolutions dating back to December 1948 that endorse Palestinian rights that the US does not acknowledge (though in some cases the US voted for the resolutions that it will not allow to be implemented). Crucially *not* settled is what UN 242 means; it was left intentionally vague to assure at least formal acceptance by the states of the region.

UN 242 opens by "emphasizing the inadmissibility of the acquisition of territory by war and the need to work for a just and lasting peace in which every State in the area can live in security." It calls for "withdrawal of Israeli armed forces from territories occupied in the recent conflict," "termination of all claims or states of belligerency and respect for and acknowledgment of the sovereignty, territorial integrity and political independence of every State in the area and their right to live in peace within secure and recognized boundaries . . ."

Two crucial questions of interpretation arise: First, what is the meaning of the phrase "from territories occupied" (all? most? some?). Second, what is to be the fate of the indigenous population of the former Palestine, who are not a State and therefore do not fall under the resolution?

Both questions were addressed by the Security Council in January 1976, in the resolution discussed earlier, which incorporated the basic wording of UN 242. Both were answered by the call for a two-state settlement on the Green Line. The US veto effectively terminated any UN role in the peace process. The two basic questions concerning UN 242 therefore remain unresolved. To be more precise, they will be resolved by force, that is, by the United States, in international isolation.

A different answer had been formulated by UN mediator Gunnar Jarring in a February 1971 proposal, accepted by President Sadat of Egypt, calling for a full peace treaty on the Green Line with nothing for the Palestinians. Israel recognized that Sadat had made a genuine peace offer, but rejected it with no counteroffer; the Labor Party was committed to broader territorial gains. The Israeli rejection clearly showed that the basic problem is not Palestinian rights per se, but rather the fact that recognizing them would end Israeli control over the territories.

The US backed Israel's rejection of the Sadat offer, adopting Kissinger's policy of "stalemate." The Jarring–Sadat peace proposal has thereby been barred from history, at least in the United States. In Israel, in contrast, even conservative Middle East specialists recognize that Israel may have "missed a historic opportunity" in 1971.[28]

The Jarring–Sadat proposal was similar to the interpretation of UN 242 outside of Israel, as well as to official US policy (the Rogers Plan). That the US shared this understanding is also indicated by a secret State

Department study of the negotiations leading to UN 242, leaked to US journalist and Middle East historian Donald Neff.[29] The study has been kept secret "so as not to embarrass Israel," Neff concludes. It quotes the chief American negotiator, Arthur Goldberg, who informed King Hussein of Jordan that the US "could not guarantee that everything would be returned to Jordan; some territorial adjustments would be required," but there must be "a mutuality in adjustments." Secretary of State Dean Rusk confirmed to Hussein that the US "would use its influence to obtain compensation to Jordan for any territory it was required to give up." Goldberg informed other Arab states "that the United States did not conceive of any substantial redrawing of the map." Israel's withdrawal would be "total except for minor adjustments," with compensation to Jordan for any such adjustments. Goldberg's assurances led the Arab states to agree to UN 242. Rusk confirmed to Neff that "we never contemplated any significant grant of territory to Israel as a result of the June 1967 war," but only "minor adjustments in the western frontier of the West Bank," "demilitarization measures in the Sinai and Golan Heights," and "a fresh look" at the status of Jerusalem. "Resolution 242 never contemplated the movement of any significant territories to Israel," Rusk stated.

It is commonly claimed that Goldberg and the US government rejected this interpretation of UN 242. Thus the *New York Times* alleges that the Israeli version, which permits Israel to incorporate unspecified parts of the conquered territories, is "supported" by Goldberg, citing later pro-Israel public statements, hardly relevant.[30]

One of the most respected advocates of Israeli rejectionism, Yale Law professor and former government official Eugene Rostow, claims that he "helped produce" UN 242, and has repeatedly argued that it authorizes continued Israeli control over the territories. David Korn, former State Department office director for Israel and Arab–Israeli affairs, responded that "Professor Rostow may think he 'helped produce' Resolution 242, but in fact he had little if anything to do with it." He was an "onlooker," like "many others who have claimed a hand in it." "It was U.S. policy at the time and for several years afterward," Korn continues, "that [any border] changes would be no more than minor." Korn confirms that "both Mr. Goldberg and Secretary of State Dean Rusk told King Hussein that the United States would use its influence to obtain territorial compensation from Israel for any West Bank lands ceded by Jordan to Israel," and that Jordan's acquiescence was based on these promises. Rostow's evasive response contests none of these statements.[31]

The available evidence indicates that the US kept to the international consensus until February 1971, when it rejected the Jarring–Sadat initiative. US isolation increased in the mid 1970s as the consensus shifted to recognition of a Palestinian right of self-determination. Coincidentally, it was in February 1971 that George Bush became part of the executive apparatus as UN Ambassador. A compliant bureaucrat, Bush has adhered to US rejectionism throughout, and gives no indication of any departure today.

Kissinger's policy of "stalemate" led directly to the 1973 war. Sadat's repeated warnings that he would go to war if the US and Israel blocked his diplomatic initiatives were dismissed during this period of US–Israeli triumphalism, on the assumption that "war is not the Arab's game," as explained by Israeli Arabist and former director of military intelligence General Yehoshaphat Harkabi (now a dove).[32] On the same assumptions, the US rebuffed Sadat's offers to drop Soviet patronage and transform Egypt into a US client state.

The 1973 war shattered these illusions. It turned out to be a near thing, and Kissinger realized that policy must shift. The US then turned to the natural fallback position, accepting Egypt as a US client and moving to exclude it from the conflict. This was the goal of Kissinger's "step-by-step" diplomacy, a process advanced by Sadat's 1977 trip to Jerusalem and consummated with the Camp David Israel–Egypt peace treaty, which returned the Sinai to Egypt and offered the Palestinians "autonomy" under Israeli rule for an interim period.

The import of Camp David was evident at once.[33] With the major Arab deterrent removed and a huge increase in US aid, Israel would be free to accelerate its takeover of the occupied territories and to invade Lebanon, which it had subjected to devastating bombardment and other attacks for years, as part of its terrorist interaction with the PLO. In 1978, Israel invaded Lebanon, killing several thousand people, driving out hundreds of thousands more, and placing the southern zone under the rule of a murderous client force. Israel remains in defiance of UN Security Council resolution 425 (March 1978) ordering it to withdraw from Lebanon immediately and unconditionally. In 1982, Israel invaded again after a year of Israeli terror attacks intended (in vain) to elicit a PLO response that would serve as a pretext for its plan to destroy the

PLO as a political force and place Lebanon under Israeli suzerainty. Integration of the occupied territories meanwhile continued apace, with lavish US funding.

These consequences of US policies are sometimes called "ironic," a technical term that refers to predictable consequences of policy that blatantly contradict professed ideals. In Israel, again, the facts are frankly acknowledged. Strategic analyst Avner Yaniv writes that by removing Egypt from the conflict, the Camp David agreement left Israel "free to sustain military operations against the PLO in Lebanon as well as settlement activity on the West Bank." Expressing a broad consensus, he adds that the 1982 invasion of Lebanon was intended to "undermine the position of the moderates within [the PLO] ranks" and thus to block "the PLO 'peace offensive' " and "to halt [the PLO's] rise to political respectability." It should be called "the war to safeguard the occupation of the West Bank," General Harkabi observed, having been motivated by Begin's "fear of the momentum of the peace process." The US backed Israel's aggression, presumably for the same reasons.[34]

Sadat's 1977 peace proposal was less acceptable from the US–Israeli perspective than his 1971 offer, because it called for Palestinian self-determination. Nevertheless, Sadat is hailed as one of the grand figures of the age for his 1977 efforts, while the 1971 proposal has been excised from history. The reasons are those just reviewed. In 1971, the US backed Israel's rejection of his peace initiative; by 1977, Washington had agreed to accept Egypt as a client state. While dismissing Sadat's proposals, the US could proceed with its own rejectionist project, with Sadat playing his assigned role, thereby achieving heroic stature. As is often the case, history is a tale dictated by the powerful to their servants.

The US mediator at Camp David, Sol Linowitz, commented that Palestinians rejected "autonomy" because it would preclude authentic self-government. Prime Minister Menachem Begin favored the autonomy proposal, according to *Times* correspondent Sabra Chatrand, "because the idea seemed to resolve the Palestinian issue while leaving Israel in fundamental control of West Bank and Gaza." Both Linowitz and the *Times* regard Palestinian discontent with this outcome as entirely unreasonable. It reveals only that Palestinians "never miss an opportunity to miss an opportunity," in the oft-repeated formula of Israeli diplomat Abba Eban.

Chatrand observes that today, "after years of conflict with Israel, uncounted deaths, and even more hardship, Palestinians have abandoned their earlier conditions"—yet another demonstration of the "salutary efficacy" of terror. She also reports that the United States "tried and failed to get Israel to stop building Jewish settlements in the occupied territories," while vastly increasing US aid for their construction.[35] The convention is that the US is a helpless victim, unable to influence the projects it lavishly funds, another "irony."

7. Bush–Baker Diplomacy

Until 1988, the US and Israel were satisfied with the status quo, content merely to rebuff Arab and other peace initiatives while Israel extended its harsh rule over the territories with US aid. Problems arose, however, with the outbreak of the *intifada* and the increased Israeli repression, which created negative images and other unwanted costs. Furthermore, PLO insistence on a political settlement was becoming more difficult to suppress. The problem was getting serious by late 1988, when the US refused to permit Yasser Arafat to address the UN in New York, causing it to convene in Geneva. By then, Secretary of State George Shultz and domestic commentators were becoming an international laughingstock with their frantic cries that Arafat had failed to repeat the "magic words" dictated to him by Washington. The wise decision was made to resort to a familiar diplomatic ploy: to pretend that Arafat had accepted US demands, welcome his invented capitulation, then impose upon him the US terms. It was assumed correctly that the media and intellectual opinion would reflexively adopt Washington's concoctions, ignoring the fact—transparent to any literate person—that Arafat's positions remained as far from Washington's as before, and that no Palestinian spokesperson could possibly accept the US terms. The farce was played perfectly, and entered history.[36]

The PLO's reward for its invented capitulation was a low-level "dialogue" to divert world attention while Israel turned to harsher measures to suppress the *intifada*. Predictably, the PLO leadership played along, contributing to the success of the repression. The transcript of the first meeting was leaked and published prominently in Egypt and Israel. The US stated two conditions for "dialogue." There would be no international conference, and the PLO must call off the "riots, which we view as terrorist acts against Israel" (the *intifada*). Thus Palestinians must accept the previous conditions of brutal repression and steady dispossession.

The working assumptions were explained by Labor's Defense Secretary, Yitzhak Rabin, who informed Peace Now leaders in February 1989 that he welcomed the meaningless dialogue, which would offer Israel time to employ "harsh military and economic pressure"; "In the end they will be broken," and will accept Israel's terms. These plans were implemented, with much success.

In particular, the threat of democracy was overcome. The *intifada* had raised a serious challenge to the quasi-feudal structure of Palestinian society,[37] but the new popular committees and other initiatives of the rascal multitude were weakened and perhaps demolished by US-backed Israeli violence.

Meanwhile, Israel and the US initiated their own diplomatic track, to deflect the risk of an authentic peace process. The Likud–Labor coalition government proposed the "Shamir Plan" in May 1989, more accurately the Shamir–Peres Plan.[38] The plan's "Basic Premises" are: (1) there can be no "additional Palestinian state in the Gaza district and in the area between Israel and Jordan"; (2) "Israel will not conduct negotiations with the PLO"; (3) "there will be no change in the status of Judea, Samaria and Gaza other than in accordance with the basic guidelines of the Government" of Israel, which reject Palestinian self-determination. The phrase "additional Palestinian state" reflects the US–Israeli position that there already is a Palestinian state, namely, Jordan. Hence the issue of self-determination for Palestinians does not arise, contrary to what is believed by those "whose cantankerousness was reinforced by Moscow": Jordanians, Palestinians, Europeans, and others similarly misguided. The Basic Premises incorporate the "Four No's" of the official Labor Party program: no return to the 1967 borders, no removal of settlements, no negotiations with the PLO, no Palestinian state. The plan then calls for "free and democratic elections" under Israeli military occupation with the PLO excluded and the unacceptable leadership interned in Israeli prison camps.

The US endorsed this forthcoming proposal. James Baker explained that "our goal all along has been to try to assist in the implementation of the Shamir initiative. There is no other proposal or initiative that we are working with." In December 1989, the Department of State released the Baker Plan, which stipulated that Israel would attend a "dialogue" in Cairo with Egypt and acceptable Palestinians, who would be permitted to discuss implementation of the Shamir Plan, but nothing else.[39]

All of this took place long before the Gulf War, and while the US–PLO "dialogue" was spinning along in its intentionally pointless way. Standard doctrine is that Arafat lost his place at the table "as a result of his support for Iraq in the gulf war," and that "the principal causes of the PLO's weakness" are PLO support for Saddam Hussein and failure to expel the perpetrators of a thwarted terrorist action in May 1990.[40] This version is without merit, as inspection of dates and documents clearly demonstrates; it merely offers new pretexts for old policies.

The official "peace process" includes Camp David and Madrid, and various fables about forthcoming Israeli offers, but not the essential history, tucked safely away in the memory hole. Since Camp David, mainstream US discussion has ranged between the hawks, who hold that Palestinians deserve nothing, and the doves, like *Times* Middle East specialist Thomas Friedman, who argue that this stand is not in Israel's interest: "Only if you give the Palestinians something to lose is there a hope that they will agree to moderate their demands," Friedman observes, abandoning their hope for mutual recognition in a two-state settlement—a "demand" that he refused to report and regularly denied while producing the "balanced and informed coverage" that won him a Pulitzer Prize. "I believe that as soon as Ahmed has a seat on the bus, he will limit his demands," Friedman added. He advised Israel to run the territories on the model of South Lebanon, which is controlled by Israeli troops and a terrorist surrogate army, with a hideous torture chamber in Khiam where hundreds are held hostage to ensure that the population submits, and with regular bombardment beyond Israeli-occupied Lebanon to prevent resistance—called "terrorism."[41]

One might ask what the reaction would be if some commentator were to advise South African whites that it would be in their interest to give Sambo a seat on the bus, or to advise Syria that they should run what is now Israel as they do the Bekaa valley, though they should give Hymie a seat on the bus so that he will limit his demands. The comparison provides no little insight into Western culture.

8. Israel's Policy Spectrum

As noted, the US has tended to prefer the policies of the Israeli Labor Party. Its current head, Shimon Peres, is portrayed as "moderate" and "pragmatic," as are earlier leaders, and the Founding Fathers, David Ben-Gurion and Chaim Weizmann. To understand US policy and ideology, it is therefore important to recognize just what their positions have been.

Traditional Labor Party doctrine was expressed by Prime Minister Golda Meir in addressing new Soviet immigrants on the Golan Heights in September 1971: "The borders are determined by where Jews live, not where there is a line on a map." Minister of Defense Moshe Dayan emphasized that Israeli rule over the territories is "permanent": "The settlements are forever, and the future borders will include these settlements as part of Israel." Dayan's advice was that Israel should tell the Palestinian refugees in the territories "that we have no solution, that you shall continue to live like dogs, and whoever wants to can leave—and we will see where this process leads. . . . In five years we may have 200,000 less people—and that is a matter of enormous importance." Shimon Peres objected to the advice that Israel become "like Rhodesia," arguing that Israel's international image and prospects for immigration would be harmed. Dayan responded that any "moral aspect" is contrary to Zionist principles. Dayan's 200,000 would be in addition to the 200,000 shepherded across the Allenby Bridge to Jordan by Labor dove Haim Herzog, commander of the conquered West Bank after the 1967 war— "willingly," he adds, as proven by documents with their fingerprints; many "agreeing" after being kicked and clubbed with rifle butts by paratroopers and border guards, then fleeing in panic to Jordan, according to the soldier who spent four months placing their "willing" prints on the documents at the Bridge where Herzog's buses deposited them.[42]

Ben-Gurion's views were similar during the period of his political influence. Israeli journalist Amnon Kapeliouk observed that "every child in Israel knows one of the most famous expressions of the founder of the Jewish state, David Ben-Gurion: 'It is not important what the Gentiles say, what matters is what the Jews do'." Ben-Gurion wrote that "a Jewish state . . . will serve as an important and decisive stage in the realization of Zionism," but only a *stage*: the borders of the state "will not be fixed for eternity," but will expand either by agreement with the Arabs "or by some other way," once "we have force at our disposal" in a Jewish state. His long-term vision included Jordan and beyond, sometimes even "the Land of Israel" from the Nile to the Euphrates. During the 1948 war, he held that "to the Arabs of the Land of Israel only one function remains—to run away." The perspective is traditional. Chaim Weizmann, the first President of Israel and the most revered Zionist figure, remarked that the British had informed him that in Palestine "there are a few hundred thousand Negroes, but that is a matter of no significance." Weizmann had in turn informed Lord Balfour after World War I that "the issue known as the Arab problem in Palestine will be of merely local character and, in effect, anyone cognizant of the situation does not consider it a highly significant factor." Hence displacement of the inhabitants by Jewish settlement raises no moral issue. The current President, Haim Herzog, expressed the basic guidelines in 1972: "I do not deny the Palestinians any place or stand or opinion on every matter. But certainly I am not prepared to consider them as partners in any respect in a land that has been consecrated in the hands of our nation for thousands of years. For the Jews of this land there cannot be any partner."[43]

Labor controlled the political system until 1977. The government's first policy decision after the June 1967 war was taken on June 19, when a divided (11–10) cabinet proposed a settlement with Syria and Egypt on the Green Line (with Israel keeping Gaza), but no mention of Jordan and the West Bank. This proposal is described by Abba Eban as "the most dramatic initiative that the government of Israel ever took before or since." It was kept secret, though transmitted to Washington, to be passed on to Arab states.

In September 1967, Shimon Peres presented a plan based on the principle that "Israel's new map will be determined by its policies of settlement and new land-taking." He therefore called for "urgent efforts" to establish settlements not only in East Jerusalem, but also "to the north, south and east," including Hebron, Gush-Etzion, etc.; the Jordan valley; "the central region of the mountains of Shechem [Nablus]"; the Golan Heights, the El-Arish region in the Sinai, and the Red Sea access.[44] The policies adopted were even more extreme, including the expulsion of thousands of Bedouins into the desert, their homes, mosques, and graveyards destroyed to clear the lands for the all-Jewish city of Yamit in northeastern Sinai, steps that led directly to the 1973 war.

In 1968, the Allon Plan—Israel will take the land and resources it wants, but not responsibility for the Arab population—became official Labor policy, and remains so, varying with contingencies, to this day. Likud's position is that Israel will extend its sovereignty over the territories with "autonomy" for the Palestinians. US discussion is largely limited to the same narrow spectrum.

9. The Prospects

For Washington's purposes, it is not of great moment that the "peace process" succeed. If it does, the US will have imposed its traditional rejectionist program, demonstrating anew our high-minded benevolence and virtue and the grandeur of our leaders. If the "peace process" fails, we will read of "a classic cultural clash between American and Middle Eastern instincts," a conflict between Middle Eastern fanaticism and Baker's "quintessentially American view of the world: that with just a little bit of reasonableness these people should be able to see that they have a shared interest in peace that overrides their historical antipathies."[45] In the short term, it's a win-win situation for US power.

As already discussed, US diplomacy is guided by a strategic conception that has changed little over the years (pp. 53 f., 179–85). The primary concern is the energy resources of the region, to be managed by the "Arab façade" in the interests of the US and its British lieutenant. The family dictatorships must be protected from indigenous nationalism by regional enforcers, with US–British muscle in reserve. There has long been a tacit alliance between the Arab façade and the regional gendarmes.[46] It is coming closer to the surface now that Arab nationalism has been dealt another crushing blow, thanks to the murderous gangster who disobeyed orders, and PLO tactics of more than the usual incompetence. The family dictatorships therefore have less need than before to make pro-Palestinian gestures. Accordingly, the prospects for US rejectionism have improved.

Regional actors are granted rights insofar as they contribute to "stability," in the technical sense. Israel has been considered a barrier to Arab nationalism since the 1960s, and has also served US interests worldwide, carrying out tasks that the US had to delegate to others because of domestic opposition or for other reasons, and cooperating in intelligence matters and weapons production and testing. The Palestinians offer neither wealth nor power. Accordingly, they have no rights, by the most elementary principles of statecraft. The Israeli lobby, with its political clout and its finely honed techniques of slander and intimidation, has helped to contain discussion largely within the framework of US–Israeli rejectionism. No significant domestic force calls for Palestinian rights.

Basic assumptions have hardly changed since 1948 (pp. 55–7). The operative principles were well expressed by *New Republic* editor Martin

Peretz, just as Israel was about to invade Lebanon in 1982. He advised Israel to administer to the PLO a "lasting military defeat" that "will clarify to the Palestinians in the West Bank that their struggle for an independent state has suffered a setback of many years." Then "the Palestinians will be turned into just another crushed nation, like the Kurds or the Afghans," and the Palestinian problem—which "is beginning to be boring"—will be resolved.[47] His timing may have been off, but basic principles are resilient in states with unchallenged power. From Chaim Weizmann to Yitzhak Rabin today, it is assumed that with sufficient force and resolve, the "insignificant Negroes" will be "crushed" and "broken"; they will "die" or "turn into human dust and the waste of society." Peretz's attitude towards the Kurds also captures US policy succinctly, as we have recently seen once again.

Control over Middle East energy provides leverage in world affairs and guarantees a substantial flow of capital to the economies of the United States and Britain. The system of regional management has changed over time, but the operative principles have not. The course of diplomacy is understandable in these terms.

From the US perspective, a preferred outcome of the current diplomatic maneuvers would include an agreement enabling Israel to extend its control over the territories ("autonomy"); extension of commercial and diplomatic relations between Israel and the Gulf rulers; moves towards a Golan Heights settlement that would ensure Israeli control of the water resources while satisfying Syrian nationalism, at least symbolically. If its rejectionist program is not advanced, the US will win a propaganda victory by placing the blame on Middle East fanatics who have again disrupted Washington's noble intentions. Traditional policies can then be pursued in other ways.

If US interests are reassessed and Washington decides to permit a genuine political settlement, Israel does have options, despite its dependency on the United States. In the 1950s, Prime Minister Moshe Sharett privately deplored the "preaching" of high-level Labor Party officials "in favor of acts of madness" and "the diabolical lesson of how to set the Middle East on fire" with "acts of despair and suicide" that will terrify the world as "we go crazy," if crossed—an early expression of the "Samson complex." After the Lebanon invasion, Aryeh (Lova) Eliav, one of Israel's best-known doves, deplored the attitude of "those who brought the 'Samson complex' here, according to which we shall kill and bury all the Gentiles around us while we ourselves shall die with them." Others too have regarded the greatest danger facing Israel as the "collective version" of Samson's revenge against the Philistines. Israel's nuclear armaments, well known to US authorities for many years, render such thinking more than empty threats. Writing in 1982, three Israeli strategic analysts observed that Israel's nuclear-armed missiles were able to reach "many targets in southern USSR," a threat—real or pretended—that may well have been aimed at the United States, putting US planners on notice that pressures on Israel to accept a political settlement could lead to an international conflagration. The reasoning was explained further in the Labor Party journal *Davar*, reporting Israel's reaction to the Saudi peace plan of August 1981, with its "signs of open-mindedness and moderation" that the government of Israel regarded as a serious threat. Israel's response was to send jets over the oilfields, a warning to the West of Israel's capacity to cause immense destruction to the world's major energy reserves if pressed towards an unwanted peace, *Davar* reported.[48] The world has changed since, but Israel's "Samson option," as Seymour Hersh calls it in a recent book, remains alive.

Israeli analysts today express much concern over what may lie ahead. Lieutenant-Colonel Ron Ben-Yishai, a leading military commentator, observed on the eve of the Madrid conference that "this might be the last chance we have to make peace." He expected the current diplomatic efforts to fail, a broad consensus. The result will be a war that will last "a minimum of three to four weeks," a "conventional war" with some surface-to-surface missiles, with uncertain prospects and surely grim consequences.[49] There have been a rash of similar predictions, referring to a war against Syria, perhaps Iran, that Israel might initiate with a preemptive strike, a war which may well include the use of nuclear weapons. The US will surely do what it can to prevent that, but even US power reaches only so far.

If the US keeps to its rejectionist stand, Israel will continue to integrate the territories, the core local conflict will remain unresolved, turbulence and antagonisms will fester and intermittently explode, and a stable regional settlement—let alone a just one—is most unlikely.

Meanwhile, new and more imaginative ways will have to be found to "put the public in its place," and to deter the dread threats of democracy and freedom.

Notes

1. On Third World reactions, see my articles in *Z Magazine*, May, October 1991, and in Cynthia Peters, ed., *Collateral Damage* (South End, 1992).

2. Maureen Dowd, *NYT*, February 23, 1991.

3. See references of Note 1.

4. Luzviminda Francisco and Jonathan Fast, *Conspiracy for Empire* (Quezon City, 1985), pp. 302, 191.

5. *Newsday*, September 12, 1991, p. 1. The *Boston Globe* gave the story a few lines on p. 79, September 13. The *Times* ran a tepid account a few days later; Eric Schmitt, *NYT*, September 15.

6. *NYT*, July 7, 1991.

7. Kathy Blair, *Toronto Globe and Mail*, June 17, 1991; *WSJ*, July 5, 1991.

8. Andrew Rosenthal, *NYT*, September 26; Reuters, *NYT*, September 26; Reuters, *BG*, September 26, 1991. On US pressures, see above, p. 315.

9. John Simpson, *Spectator* (London), August 10; Glass, ibid., April 13, 1991.

10. Mary Kay Magistad, *BG*, October 20, 1991.

11. See references of Note 1 for further details and sources, here and below.

12. See pp. 190 f., 203 f., above; and references of Note 1 for more recent information.

13. *WSJ*, April 8, 1991.

14. *NYT*, April 11, 1991.

15. Ron Ben-Yishai, *Ha'aretz*, March 29; Shalom Yerushalmi, *Kol Ha'ir*, April 4; Moshe Zak, editor of *Ma'ariv*, *JP*, April 4, 1991.

16. Piero Gleijeses, *Shattered Hope* (Princeton, 1991), pp. 125, 365. Chace, *NYT Magazine*, May 22, 1977.

17. Editorial, *NYT*, August 2, 1991.

18. Apple, *NYT*, October 30, September 22, 1991.

19. *Journal of Palestine Studies*, Autumn 1991.

20. Rubinstein, *Ha'aretz*, October 23, 24, 1991.

21. *Ha'aretz*, March 8, 1991.

22. Avi Shlaim, *Collusion across the Jordan*, p. 364. Cabinet records, Yossi Beilin, *Mehiro shel Ihud* (Revivim, 1985). Weizmann, *Ha'aretz*, March 20, 1972. On Israel's decision for war, see Andrew and Leslie Cockburn, *Dangerous Liaison* (HarperCollins, 1991).

23. Editorial, *Boston Globe*, October 20, 1991.

24. For Eisenhower, see Steven Spiegel, *The Other Arab-Israeli Conflict* (Chicago, 1985), p. 51; Kissinger, my *Towards a New Cold War*, p. 457n.

25. Friedman, *NYT*, November 4, 1991. On his remarkable record, see my *Necessary Illusions*, particularly Appendix 5.4.

26. Haberman, *NYT*, November 10, 17; Hottelet, *Christian Science Monitor*, November 25, 1991.

27. See particularly Shlaim, op. cit. Also Itamar Rabinovitch, *The Road Not Taken* (Oxford, 1991), p. 171.

28. Rabinovitch (op. cit., p. 108), asking whether Israel also missed such an opportunity when a Syrian proposal was rejected in 1949.

29. Noring and Smith, *The Withdrawal Clause in UN Security Council Resolution 242 of 1967*, February 1978; Neff, *Middle East International*, September 13, 1991.

30. Sabra Chatrand, *NYT*, October 29, 1991.

31. Rostow, Korn, *New Republic*, October 21, November 18, November 25, 1991.

32. Amnon Kapeliouk, *Israel: la fin des mythes* (Albin Michel, 1975), p. 281. See my *Peace in the Middle East?* (Pantheon, 1974), ch. 4.

33. For an ongoing review, see *Towards a New Cold War* and my articles cited there.

34. *Necessary Illusions*, pp. 174 f., 276. See also my *Fateful Triangle* and *Pirates and Emperors*.

35. Chatrand, *NYT*, November 5, 1991.

36. For specifics, here and below, see my articles in *Z Magazine*, March 1989, January 1990, and *Necessary Illusions*.

37. For discussion from Israeli sources, see my article in *Z Magazine*, July 1988.

38. Israeli Government Election Plan, Jerusalem, May 14, 1989, Embassy of Israel.

39. Thomas Friedman, *NYT*, October 19, 1989; US Department of State press release, December 6, 1989.

40. Friedman, *NYT*, November 4; Editorial, *BG*, October 6, 1991.

41. Friedman, *Yediot Ahronot*, April 7; *Hotam*, April 15, 1988.

42. Kapeliouk, op. cit., pp. 21, 29; Beilin, op. cit., pp. 42–3; "Herzog's transfer," *Kol Ha'ir*, November 8; No'omi Cohen-David, *Kol Ha'ir*, November 15, 1991.

43. Kapeliouk, op cit., p. 220; Shabtai Teveth, *Ben-Gurion and the Palestinian Arabs* (Oxford, 1985), pp. 187 f., and Benny Morris, review of Teveth, *Jerusalem Post*, October 11, 1985; see also *Fateful Triangle*, pp. 161 f. Weizmann, Yosef Heller, *The Struggle for the State: Zionist Diplomacy of the Years 1936–48* (Jerusalem, 1985, Jewish Agency protocols, Hebrew); Yosef Gorny, *Zionism and the Arabs* (Oxford, 1985), p. 110. Beilin, op. cit., p. 47.

44. Beilin, op. cit., pp. 15 f., 43.

45. Thomas Friedman, *NYT*, May 19, 17, 1991.

46. See *Towards a New Cold War*, *Fateful Triangle*; Cockburn and Cockburn, *Dangerous Liaison*.

47. Interview in *Ha'aretz*, June 4, 1982; see *Fateful Triangle*, p. 199. On the racist effusions of Peretz and others, see *Necessary Illusions*, p. 315.

48. See *Fateful Triangle*, pp. 464 ff.

49. "Elazar," *Jerusalem Post Magazine*, October 4; *Yediot Ahronot*, November 15, 1991.

INDEX